EIGHTEENTH CENTURY
# English Drinking Glasses
*An Illustrated Guide*

*To Mary, who shared the effort this volume entailed*

# Eighteenth Century
# English Drinking Glasses
## *An Illustrated Guide*

L.M. Bickerton

*With a Bibliography of English Glass*
*by D. Robert Elleray*

ANTIQUE COLLECTORS' CLUB

© 1971 L.M. Bickerton
© 1986 Second revised edition L.M. Bickerton
World copyright reserved
ISBN 1 85149 351 4


First published in 1971 by Barrie & Jenkins Ltd., London
This edition first published 1986 for the Antique Collectors' Club by the
Antique Collectors' Club Ltd.
Reprinted 1987
Reprinted 1991
Reprinted 2000

British Library Cataloguing-in-Publication Data
A catalogue record for this book is available from the British Library


Printed in England by the Antique Collectors' Club Ltd., Church Street,
Woodbridge, Suffolk

# ANTIQUE COLLECTORS' CLUB

*For Collectors — By Collectors — About Collecting*

THE ANTIQUE COLLECTORS' CLUB was formed in 1966 and quickly grew to a five figure membership spread throughout the world. It publishes the only independently run monthly antiques magazine, *Antique Collecting*, which caters for those collectors who are interested in widening their knowledge of antiques, both by greater awareness of quality and by discussion of the factors which influence the price that is likely to be asked. The Antique Collectors' Club pioneered the provision of information on prices for collectors and the magazine still leads in the provision of detailed articles on a variety of subjects.

It was in response to the enormous demand for information on 'what to pay' that the price guide series was introduced in 1968 with the first edition of *The Price Guide to Antique Furniture* (completely revised 1978 and 1989), a book which broke new ground by illustrating the more common types of antique furniture, the sort that collectors could buy in shops and at auctions rather than the rare museum pieces which had previously been used (and still to a large extent are used) to make up the limited amount of illustrations in books published by commercial publishers. Many other price guides have followed, all copiously illustrated, and greatly appreciated by collectors for the valuable information they contain, quite apart from prices. The Price Guide Series heralded the publication of many standard works of reference on art and antiques. *The Dictionary of British Art* (now in six volumes), *The Pictorial Dictionary of British 19th Century Furniture Design*, *Oak Furniture* and *Early English Clocks* were followed by many deeply researched reference works such as *The Directory of Gold and Silversmiths*, providing new information. Many of these books are now accepted as the standard work of reference on their subject.

The Antique Collectors' Club has widened its list to include books on gardens and architecture. All the Club's publications are available through bookshops world wide and a full catalogue of all these titles is available free of charge from the addresses below.

Club membership, open to all collectors, costs little. Members receive free of charge *Antique Collecting*, the Club's magazine (published ten times a year), which contains well-illustrated articles dealing with the practical aspects of collecting not normally dealt with by magazines. Prices, features of value, investment potential, fakes and forgeries are all given prominence in the magazine.

Among other facilities available to members are private buying and selling facilities and the opportunity to meet other collectors at their local antique collectors' club. There are over eighty in Britain and more than a dozen overseas. Members may also buy the Club's publications at special pre-publication prices.

As its motto implies, the Club is an organisation designed to help collectors get the most out of their hobby: it is informal and friendly and gives enormous enjoyment to all concerned.

ANTIQUE COLLECTORS' CLUB
5 Church Street, Woodbridge, Suffolk IP12 1DS, UK.
Tel: 01394 385501 Fax: 01394 384434
Email: sales@antique-acc.com   Website: www.antique-acc.com

and

Market Street Industrial Park, Wappingers' Falls, NY 12590, USA.
Tel: 914 297 0003 Fax: 914 297 0068
Email: info@antiquecc.com   Website: www.antiquecc.com

# Acknowledgements

My first thanks must be accorded to Laurence Boreham for introducing me to the study and collection of English glass: the enthusiasm which he communicated was the starting-point of this volume. It was increased by the gift of a copy of E. Barrington Haynes's *Glass through the Ages* from the Hon. Mrs. R.J.P. Wyatt from whom also I learned something of Hartshorne's own tireless researches and meticulous scholarship. My library was doubled by Derek Davis's gift of a copy of his book on the subject; from him I also gained, by his wise counsel, an appreciation of the quality, variety and craftsmanship of glass of the eighteenth century.

I am even more indebted to the owners of private collections listed below and to the curators of collections also listed for the opportunity they have given me of handling, photographing and studying thousands of specimens during the past few years. They have shown me kindness, hospitality and friendship; no words of mine can express sufficient thanks, nor can I even mention the names of many who, for obvious reasons, wish to remain anonymous. To one owner especially, Graeme Cranch, I must record my appreciation of his encouragement and belief that I could add something useful to the literature of the subject.

Finally, I have to thank two collaborators who have contributed directly to the production of this volume, my colleague Robert Elleray who has been responsible for the extensive bibliography which will undoubtedly prove to be one of its most important features, and my wife who accompanied me on most of my expeditions, took notes by the hour and was responsible for typing almost the entire manuscript. Additional typing was also undertaken by my secretary, Gillian Dodds, who also conducted for me a questionnaire on glass in public collections.

Mr. and Mrs. K.A. Alexander
Mr. L.C. Boreham
Mrs. Chevallier
Mr. and Mrs. A.G. Cranch
Mr. R. Lymbery
Mr. C. Minns
Mr. J.V. Paterson
The Brierley Hill Glass Collection, Dudley
The Cecil Higgins Museum, Bedford
Harveys of Bristol
The King's Lynn Museum
Pilkington Glass Museum
The Portsmouth City Museums
The Royal Scottish Museum, Edinburgh
The Southampton Art Gallery
The Worthing Museum and Art Gallery

Mr. G.M. Pinker
Mr. W.A.D. Riley-Smith
Sir Ernest Taylor
Mr. C.P.C. de Wesselow
Mr. O. Wyatt
The. Hon. Mrs. R.J.P. Wyatt

# Acknowledgements: Revised Edition

It is very satisfying for an author to find his work accepted as a valuable tool by the public to whom it was addressed. The first edition having been out of print for many years it was therefore pleasing to be approached by John Steel of the Antique Collectors' Club with the suggestion that a revised enlarged edition be prepared.

To assimilate the events of fourteen years in the field of English drinking glasses has been a major undertaking which would have been quite impossible without the help of Perran Wood of Sotheby Parke Bernet and Co. and Rachel Russell of Christie Manson and Woods Ltd: they have given me access to the sale catalogues for the whole period and have supplied me with the excellent photographs included in this volume. I am greatly indebted to them both.

In addition my old friend Derek Davis, now of Asprey and Co. PLC, has allowed me to use photographs of many superb drinking glasses which have passed through his hands in recent years.

I must also acknowledge the access to reserve collections afforded me by many museums and the support of my wife in the typing of the revised sections and in tolerating my many absences from home.

Finally, I must thank most warmly my former colleague, Robert Elleray, who has undertaken the not inconsiderable task of bringing the bibliography up-to-date.

# Preface

Since the publication in 1897 of Albert Hartshorne's monumental *Old English Glasses* there has been, first, a steady trickle, more recently such a flood of books on the subject that any addition to its spate demands explanation and justification. Many aspects of English glassmaking require further study, the whole question of provenance being the most intriguing and the most elusive; dating of glasses is also far from precise and much work needs to be done on the development of wheel-engraving, enamelling and gilding in England. Unfortunately, excavation of factory sites, which has yielded such important evidence in determining the provenance of pottery and porcelain, does not apply to glass since every scrap of waste from breakages or spoilages was used in succeeding batches. Cullet was, indeed, such an important ingredient that, as W.A. Thorpe[1] quotes, poor people earned a livelihood by collecting all kinds of broken glass for sale to makers. The alternative method of determining where glass vessels were made – by chemical analysis – is therefore rendered equally unreliable since the contents varied from pot to pot. Thorpe's conclusion remains unchallenged 'There is no type of eighteenth century metal either in England or Ireland which can be ascribed to any particular glasshouse.'[2]

It is not the author's intention, however, to advance new theories: it is rather to compile a working manual which could be of assistance to collectors, students, antique dealers and museum curators by bringing together a series of illustrations of all types of eighteenth century drinking glasses, providing a uniform system of describing them and adding an extensive bibliography. No single volume can hope to be exhaustive – indeed one of the attractions of the subject is its almost infinite variety – but it has been felt that within the scope of some 1200 illustrations it will be possible to display most stem formations, types of bowl and foot, engraving and enamelling commonly encountered and provide a convenient means of referring to them.

Mr. Elleray's bibliography used in conjunction with the general index, will direct the reader to sources of information on many aspects of English glass which are obviously beyond the scope of this guide. As the reader will quickly perceive, the bibliography is far wider than the subject of the book: indeed it covers the whole field of English glass studies over the last hundred years.

It was, in fact, a strange coincidence which brought this about. In discussing with Mr. Elleray my own plans for a bibliography limited to items on eighteenth century drinking glasses, I discovered that he had already assembled most of the material now published. He generously offered to make his work available to me but it seemed to me and to my publishers that this opportunity of making available the fruits of Mr. Elleray's wider research should not be missed. This decision was reinforced by the knowledge that no comparable, up-to-date bibliography is available elsewhere.

1. Thorpe, W.A. *History of English and Irish glass*, p.35, footnote.

2. Ibid.

# Contents

# 1.

# Historical Introduction

Men have been fascinated by both glass and wine for a very long time though when the two came to be used together is a matter for conjecture. The histories of both date back to at least the third millennium BC but there is as yet no evidence that glass vessels suitable for drinking wine could have been made much earlier than the first century BC when the art of glass-blowing was developed.

Beakers and bowls for liquids soon began to appear, a goblet of the 4th century AD in the Worthing Museum bearing the inscription in Greek 'Use me and good health to you' strongly suggesting that it was indeed intended for wine. Glass, however, would hardly have been the material commonly used for drinking any kind of liquids. Its manufacture required high temperatures, the vessels were fragile, quite unsuitable for regular daily use, and so glass would be the prerogative of the wealthy.

For many centuries the position remained the same, horn, wood, pottery or pewter being preferred for their relative cheapness and undoubted durability. Venice became dominant in glass manufacture in the fifteenth century, a position it was to retain for more than 300 years, its drinking glasses being of a fineness, delicacy and intricacy which caused them to rival gold and silver on the tables of the nobility.

The virtual monopoly held by Venice, whose secrets were divulged on pain of death, was broken in England by the arrival in 1571 of Jacopo Verzelini who produced fine Venetian-type wares for twenty-one years, of which perhaps a dozen are still extant. Most of these are goblets; amazingly enough one was found in the attic of a country house in 1978. On being sold at Christie's it realised £75,000. A glass industry of a kind had existed in England since the early thirteenth century, when Laurens Vitrearius arrived here from Normandy, setting up his furnace near Chiddingfold on the Sussex/Surrey border. That he made window glass for Westminster Abbey is well documented and fragments of glass from the site suggest that he may also have made blown vessels.

Window and bottle glass continued to be made down the centuries, the number of names of glass-makers known to us suggesting that the industry flourished moderately. The evidence for fine table glass, apart from Verzelini's, is so scanty and so doubtful, however, that it must be discounted. The records of the Glass Sellers' Company show that they were having to rely upon imports, mostly still from Venice, until almost the end of the seventeenth century. Two complete specimens, both engraved in diamond-point, have a distinct English association suggesting English manufacture. They are the Royal Oak Goblet engraved with a portrait of Charles II and his wife Catherine, dated 1663, and the Exeter Flute, also engraved with a portrait of Charles II and the inscription 'God bless King Charles the Second'. This is in the Exeter City Museum. Neither of these nor fragments in various collections convincingly prove the existence of English glass-houses capable of producing fine table-ware. Indeed, despite the claims for the Exeter Flute, an almost identical flute but engraved with the portrait of a young boy above the inscription 'Wilhelmus Prince d'Orange...' in the British Museum, is given a Dutch provenance.

But in 1674 the Glass Sellers' Company were rewarded for their persistence in trying to encourage English fine glass-making. They had engaged George Ravenscroft, possibly already operating a glass-house at the Savoy, to experiment further at Henley-on-Thames where, by 1676, he had succeeded in producing what he called 'flint' glass, that is glass with a high lead content. The drinking glasses, decanters and other wares he produced had qualities quite different from the thinly blown soda-glass of European imports. The English glass industry was born! This new metal, lending itself to solid, substantial thicker-walled glasses, appealed both to the ingenuity of the eighteenth century craftsman and to his customers.

Glass-houses sprang up in many parts of the country where coal was readily available for firing the furnaces, in the Midlands and the North-East for example. Styles seem to have been adopted uniformly, no one area being known as the birth-place of a distinct type. Perhaps the one exception to this rule is Newcastle, where a drinking glass with a slightly longer stem, often allied with a beautifully engraved bowl, can be associated with that city with some confidence.

### Heavy Balusters (c.1685-1710)

By 1700 the Venetian influence, previously very apparent, had disappeared altogether from English drinking glasses, giving way to a style which has become known as the 'heavy balusters'. Glasses were normally made in three pieces, bowl, stem and foot, the stem being the part which changed most fundamentally and which characterised the periods into which we divide eighteenth century glasses. Early bowls, however, tended to be either of conical or funnel shape with a solid base; the foot was conical or dome-shaped, invariably with a folded rim. Into the stem were introduced the baluster shapes popular in the architecture of the period to which were added natural and geometric shapes according to the ingenuity of the craftsman or designer. So we find the true and inverted baluster, cylinder, ball, mushroom and acorn knops as well as annular rings in a wide variety of combinations.

Dwarf ale glasses of this period were made with winged or pincered knops as well as a form of decoration of the bowl known as flammiform gadrooning in which the wrythen lines were pulled up towards the rim to give an impression of rising flames.

All these early glasses are, of course, greatly sought after by the collector. Innovations in the conformation of the stem or the introduction of an unusual bowl, which might pass completely unnoticed by the uninitiated, are of vital interest. The addition of such engraving as is found for example on the Royal Oak Goblet makes such a piece of documentary importance of great historic as well as monetary value.

### Light Balusters (c.1710-1760)

Even before the inevitable Excise Tax was applied to the glass industry the early heavy design gradually gave way to a generally lighter glass for which the term 'balustroid' was coined by W.A. Thorpe, indicating a stem still made up of knops, either singly or in groups but very obviously smaller than in the heavy balusters. This is a very large class varying from glasses still close to the heavy balusters, with such well-defined knops as the cylinder, mushroom and acorn mentioned earlier, but degenerating into miniscule swellings hardly deserving recognition as knops.

One form of light baluster, however, is so outstanding that special mention must be made of it – the previously mentioned 'Newcastle light baluster'. Although it would be foolhardy for anyone to ascribe a provenance to a drinking glass without convincing documentary evidence, a strong case can be made for linking these glasses, with a stem an inch or more longer than normal, with Newcastle. What distinguishes them, apart from their height, is the excellent quality of craftsmanship, the delightful combinations of modest knops but above all the frequency of engraving found on the bowls, engraving of such quality that could only have been achieved in Holland. Indeed in many cases a legend in Dutch is incorporated into the engraving. The ease with which Newcastle-made glasses could be shipped to Holland for engraving certainly makes the attribution acceptable even though still not completely verifiable.

## Plain and Hollow Stems (c.1730-1775)

Balustroids continued to be made until or even a little after the middle of the century: the bowls with a heavy base had disappeared but the folded foot was still a normal feature. Almost as early as the balustroid an even lighter form emerged, having a completely plain stem, the folded foot disappearing about 1740. The plainness is occasionally relieved by such small decorative features as a vermiform collar at the centre of the stem or by plain collars at top and bottom: the stem is occasionally found in tapered form. Another decorative effect frequently used in drawn trumpets is the tear, mostly at the top of the stem, occasionally in the centre. The hollow stem, a simple tube, seems to have been made in small quantities and for a limited period around the middle of the century.

Early drinking glasses had been made for ale and wine, an occasional dram glass and mead glass also surviving from around 1700. Larger capacity goblets were made from Ravenscroft's time onwards as well as other table wares such as tazzas, sweetmeats and covered bowls.

From about 1730 cordial glasses begin to appear, with baluster stems, but the ratafia and toasting glass make their appearance during the plain stem period. Except for the mead glass, which seems to have been made during the baluster period only, all the varieties of drinking glass mentioned continued throughout the century.

## Moulded Pedestal Stems (c.1715-1765)

With the accession of George I there was introduced to the glass industry, either by his influence or in his honour, a form of stem completely different from anything produced before or since. There is evidence to support the theory that this moulded pedestal form did in fact originate in the Bohemia/Silesia area, hence the popularly-used alternative 'Silesian stem'.

The earliest form, with four sides, the mould incorporating crowns on the shoulders, certainly dates from very early in the reign of George I, more than one example having been found also bearing the moulded legend GOD SAVE KING GEORGE or the letters GR on the shoulders. Gradually the number of sides increased, first to six, then to eight, eventually degenerating into a debased form which has lost all the crispness of moulding, with shoulders so rounded as almost to have disappeared. In the middle of the century this moulded form was most frequently employed in the manufacture of sweetmeat glasses.

### Air Twists (c.1745-1770)

The gradual reduction of the weight of metal in drinking glasses had reached its fullest extent in the plain and hollow stems but they certainly lacked consumer appeal. Encouraged by the Excise Acts of 1745 and 1777 to continue the policy of weight reduction but determined to make their wares more attractive, the glass-makers developed the tear to achieve one of the most pleasing decorative forms ever devised. Several tears were introduced into a cylinder of glass so that by heating, twisting and drawing out, a pattern of filaments of air could be produced.

Most frequent is the multiple-spiral air twist in which up to twelve filaments are incorporated with an evenness and accuracy which are a high tribute to the skill of the eighteenth century craftsmen. Modern attempts to copy the technique have been markedly unsuccessful. Variants on the theme – two flat filaments only, giving the 'mercury' twist, one twist inside another, swelled knops – all most delightful, held their popularity with the public for some twenty-five years.

### Opaque Twist Stems (c.1755-1780)

Opaque white glass, formed by the addition of oxide of tin to the mix, had been used extensively by the Venetians in their *latticino* and *vetro di trino* techniques. Rods of white glass were now placed vertically round a circular mould into which clear glass was poured. Employing exactly the same method as in making air twists the resulting white filaments, which could be drawn out to be as fine as threads of cotton, were devised in scores of delicate, delightful and ingenious patterns. The names collectors have used to describe them give some idea of their variety – spiral gauzes, lace twist, lace twist outlined, corkscrew, spiral threads outside tapes.

Although the vast majority of opaque twist stems are plain, one or more swelled knops are sometimes found; more rarely still is the use of coloured rods in combination with opaque white. Why so few were made is something of a mystery since the method of producing enamel colours was well known. Davis & Middlemas report in *Coloured glass* 'Glasses and table-ware in colours of green, blue, opaque white and sometimes ruby red started to flow from the glass-houses. Decanters, jugs and bowls were also made…' This quotation refers to the period after 1750 and the same chapter gives a list of the colouring agents used to produce the range of colours made.

Red, blue, green, maroon and yellow rods were used in stems of drinking glasses; collectors today find them irresistible, paying many times the price the same glass would command if opaque white only had been used. Such a price difference inevitably encourages reproductions which are all too common today. Probably of Continental origin, they are not difficult to detect. Light weight makes one immediately suspicious since this indicates absence of lead in the metal, but the threads themselves are weak in colour, lacking the solidity and brilliance of those in genuine English glasses.

A combination of air and opaque twists in the same stem – the mixed twist – is pleasant to find and the idea of combining sections of different stem formations was practised often enough for their recognition as a distinct class – the composite stem. Plain sections, balusters and twists are found combined, the vast majority of specimens comprising an air twist with a plain section or a knop. Use of opaque twists or faceted sections is much rarer and combinations of more than two so rare that the author has come across only one, opaque twist and plain sections separated by a beaded knop in the stem of a goblet.

**Faceted Stems (c.1780-1825)**

Although there is evidence of faceting of a much earlier date than 1780 the number of examples is so small that one is very tempted to find alternative reasons for the apparent date. The examples quoted by E. Barrington Haynes, for instance, include one probably of German origin, another of doubtful date and a third which cannot with any certainty be attributed to an English glass cutter.

Mirror glass was undoubtedly produced, cut and polished by the early 1700s; some faceted stems certainly pre-date 1780 but several factors incline one to consider them as exceptional pieces.

By 1785 the beam engine of Matthew Bolton had already begun to be employed in polishing plate glass but it was both massive and expensive. Michael Wright, of the Science Museum, South Kensington, suggests it is much more likely that the production of faceted stems was still accomplished with the hand or foot-operated wheel or by water-wheel where this source of power was available. Only in a factory operating on a large scale would steam power have been an economic alternative to cheap manual labour. The probability is that during the late eighteenth century cutting and polishing were cottage industries rather than workshops employing fifty men or more which became the pattern fifty years later.

The Excise Act of 1777, doubling the tax on glass, including 'enamel' glass, certainly spelled the end of the opaque-twist and encouraged the smaller glass with faceted stem. With a strange absence of logic, almost simultaneously Ireland was granted free trade, permitting tax-free Irish glass to compete with the heavily taxed English product. The result was a boom in the Irish glass industry and the establishment of factories in Ireland by English glass makers. The product, in whichever country it was made, was exactly the same. Because the Irish specialised in cut glass all such good quality table-ware is commonly attributed to that country without any justification whatever unless pieces are marked (as some were) or a pattern was used which was peculiar to a known factory.

Faceting on wine glasses was almost invariably diamond or hexagonal with cutting frequently extending to the base of the bowl or even to the foot, but there are also examples of vertical fluting on the stem, a style which became more prevalent as the century ended and during the early 1900s. A central or shoulder knop is by no means uncommon. One can readily imagine the scintillating effect of a table laid with faceted stem drinking glasses, cut bowls and dishes illuminated by a bright chandelier!

**Rudimentary Stems**

Glasses with very short stems or with the bowl set directly on the foot are to be found throughout the century, from the dwarf ales referred to in the section on heavy balusters to the goblets of about 1800 with the typical 'lemon squeezer' square moulded foot.

Many of these glasses were for such sweets as jelly, custard or syllabub, sometimes with handles, very often pan-topped to facilitate the use of a spoon. Into the group must be brought the strange series called 'Monteiths'. The shorter *OED* in its definition includes the note 'Named, according to Anthony Wood, after a certain Monsieur Monteigh'. It is suggested by some that the scalloped rim of these small vessels, usually some three or four inches high, bore some resemblance to the flounced hem of the Monsieur's gown. Whatever the source of the word it is used now to describe these bowls, frequently of double ogee shape, usually but not always with scalloped rim which presumably held nuts, salt or some form of confectionary. Few can be dated to earlier than 1750, the majority to the end of the century. An alternative term for them is 'bonnet glasses'.

Dram glasses, rummers and tankards must be included; dram glasses are found from as early as 1730; rummers (a corruption of the German 'roemer' – a popular sixteenth to seventeenth century drinking glass) in the last quarter of the eighteenth century; tankards throughout the century, being included, indeed, in Ravenscroft's price-lists.

# 2.
# Classification

Any consideration of English drinking glasses produced throughout the whole of the eighteenth century involves some attempt at classification for the dual purpose of ensuring that the author covers the subject systematically and that the reader is led through it in an orderly and intelligible progression, having a recognised skeleton upon which to append the information gleaned from this and other sources.

During the seventy years or so since Hartshorne[1] first attempted an appreciation of this hitherto unexplored subject, a classification has slowly evolved, that produced by Haynes[2] being one of his most valuable contributions to the study of glass. Although many years have elapsed since *Glass through the Ages* was revised, they have proved the soundness of the principle he adopted – classification by stem formation. Hartshorne, understandably, was groping in the dark: most of his sixteen groups were based on stem formation, but by no means all and certainly not in chronological order, 'Air-twisted stems and bell-shaped bowls' preceding 'Baluster stems', whereas champagnes, sweetmeats and tavern glasses formed other groups irrespective of type of stem.

In 1927 Thorpe[3] published the fruits of much research and scholarship and divided his subject into three divisions for the period prior to 1675, 'The age of adoption', 'The age of assimilation' and 'The Ravenscroft revolution', understandable enough for this historical section. For the period 1675 to 1850, however, he adopted three more divisions, partly stylistic, partly chronological, 'The age of design', 'The age of ornament' and 'The Anglo-Irish revival: cut glass', which summarise the main developments but give little help towards the presentation of a workable classification.

Ten years later Arthur Churchill Ltd. produced a catalogue[4] which achieved a considerable advance, the arrangement being by stem formation in chronological order with the exception of subjects such as Lynn bowls, champagnes and sweetmeats, inserted illogically. However, as the following summary of its main division shows, an order was emerging and a chronology had been attempted:

1 Heavy balusters (1685-1710)
2 Silesian stemmed glasses (1710-20)
3 Light balusters (1720-40)
4 Plain and simply knopped glasses (1700-1800)
5 Air twists (1740-60)
6 Opaque twists (1760-80)
7 Colour twists (1770-80)
8 Facet-cut stems (1770-90)

Another eleven years elapsed before E. Barrington Haynes produced *Glass*

1. Hartshorne, A. *Old English glasses*, 1897

2. Haynes, E.B. *Glass through the Ages*, 2nd ed. 1959.

3. Thorpe, W.A. *History of English and Irish glass*, 1927.

4. Arthur Churchill Ltd. *Catalogue of old English glass*, 2nd. ed. 1937.

*through the Ages,* notable for the absence of cross-classification and reassessment of the dates suggested by Arthur Churchill Ltd. in 1937. The term 'balustroid' was introduced as an alternative to 'simply knopped glasses' and a useful section was included to embrace the heterogenous and numerous glasses with very short stems or no stems at all which defied inclusion in the other categories. It is a system which has so fully proved its soundness that only minor amendments are suggested to make it of even greater convenience and assistance to collectors.

Heavy balusters, for example, are again restored to the dignity of a separate class on the grounds that they are of distinctive form and are regarded by collectors as of much greater importance than the lighter glasses which followed. The balustroid section is retained but, as seems logical, now includes the Newcastle balusters. There seems little justification, either, for the provision of a separate class for hollow stems, a type comparatively few in number and satisfactorily accommodated as a subdivision of balusters and plain straight stems.

In suggesting the subdivisions enumerated below, the principle has been followed of proceeding from the simple to the more complex: thus, under 'Balustroids', arrangement has been from one to three or more knops; moulded pedestals have been arranged by number of sides from four to eight (equally tenable on chronological grounds) and air twists and opaque twists have been divided into the two main sections, first single, then double series, with subsections within them of increasing complexity. Whether or not it is possible to argue that development of air and opaque twists follows a chronological order, no proof is forthcoming and the probability is that the simple form preceded the complex.

For the sake of collectors fortunate enough to possess English glasses earlier than the heavy baluster a simple classification is suggested which provides for an arrangement according to the most prominent decorative feature.

Schedules have also been provided for those who wish to arrange engraved and enamelled glasses together, and are prepared to depart from the strict principle of classification by stem type for this purpose. The arrangement of glasses with rudimentary stems is another exception to the rule for reasons which are obvious. In some cases it would be possible to guess at a chronological order but guesswork is an unsatisfactory principle: the one employed, classification first by purpose and then by distinguishing feature may be empirical but will suffice until a chronology can be established.

**VENETIAN DECORATIVE FEATURES**
Façon de Venise sixteenth and
seventeenth centuries
*Hollow-blown knops*
*Lions' mask knops*
*Filigree-work*
*Latticino*
*Vetro de trina (lace-glass)*
*Painting and gilding*
*Other features*
English glass of lead 1670-1700

*Hollow-blown knops*
*Rope twists*
*Prunts*
*Gadrooning*
*Pincered wings*
*Flammiform decoration*
*Other features*

**HEAVY BALUSTERS (c.1685-1710)**
Inverted baluster
Angular knop

Annulated knop
Drop knop
Ball knop
Mushroom knop
Acorn knop
Cylinder knop
Egg knop
Other knops

## BALUSTERS (c.1710-35)
Inverted baluster
True baluster
Angular knop
Annulated knop
Drop knop
Ball knop
Mushroom knop
Acorn knop
Cylinder knop
Egg knop
Other knops
Hollow knops

## BALUSTROIDS (c.1725-60)
Inverted baluster
True baluster
Other knops – single knop
Other knops – two knops
Other knops – three knops
Other knops – more than three
   knops (including bobbin knops)
Newcastle balusters

## MOULDED PEDESTAL STEMS (c.1715-65)
Four-sided
Six-sided
Eight-sided
Debased

## PLAIN STEMS (c.1730-75)
Two-piece stems
   *Drawn trumpet bowls*
   *Drawn trumpet bowls with tears*
   *Other bowls*
Three-piece stems
   *Bell bowl*
   *Round-funnel bowl*
   *Ogee bowl*

*Bucket bowl*
*Cup bowl*
*Ovoid bowl*
*Other bowls*
Collared stems
Hollow stems

## AIR-TWIST STEMS (c.1745-70)
Single series; two piece, unknopped
   *MSAT without collars*
   *MSAT with collar*
   *Pair of corkscrews*
   *Other twists*
Single series; two piece, knopped
   *Single-knop MSAT*
   *Two or more knops MSAT*
Single series; three piece, unknopped
   *MSAT without collar*
   *MSAT with collar*
   *Pair of corkscrews*
   *Four corkscrews*
   *Spiral cable (single or pair)*
   *Other twists*
Single series; three piece, knopped
   *Single-knop*
   *Single knop, other twists*
   *Two or more knops*
Double series; two piece, unknopped
Double series; three piece, unknopped
   *Pair spiral threads outside cable*
   *Four spiral threads outside cable*
   *Six- to twelve-ply spiral band outside cable*
   *Other twists*
Double series; three piece, knopped
Triple series

## INCISED-TWIST STEMS (c.1745-65)
Coarse twist, unknopped
Coarse twist, knopped
Fine twist, unknopped
Fine twist, knopped

## COMPOSITE STEMS (c.1745-75)
Plain section over air twist
Air twist over plain section
Plain section over opaque twist
Opaque twist over plain section
Plain section with air and opaque twists

Plain section with mixed twist
Knop over air twist
Air twist over or divided by knop
Knop over opaque twist
Opaque twist over knop
Any other two stem formations
Three or more stem formations
(other than plain section with air
and opaque twists)

## OPAQUE-TWIST STEMS (c.1755-80)
Single series; unknopped
*MSOT(multiple-spiral opaque twist)*
*Corkscrew*
*Lace twist outlined*
*Spiral gauzes or cables*
*Alternating twists*
*Other twists*
Single series; knopped
*MSOT*
*Other twists*
Double series; unknopped
*Ten- to twenty-ply spiral band outside*
*pair spiral tapes or threads*
*Solid spiral band outside pair spiral*
*tapes or threads*
*Four- to twelve-ply spiral band outside*
*gauze*
*Pair spiral threads outside gauze*
*Three or four spiral threads outside*
*gauze*
*Four- to twelve-ply spiral band (or pair)*
*outside lace twist or corkscrew*
*Spiral threads outside lace twist or*
*corkscrew*
*Pair corkscrews outside spiral threads,*
*cable or gauze*
*Pair spiral threads outside cable*
*Other twists*
Double series; knopped
*Single knop; two to four spiral threads*
*outside gauze*
*Single knop; other twists*
*Two knops*
*Three knops*
*Four or more knops*
Triple series

## MIXED AND COLOUR TWIST STEMS (c.1755-75)
Single series; air alternating with
opaque white
Double series; air outside opaque
white
Double series; opaque white outside
air
Single series; colour only
Single series; colour with air or
opaque white
*Colour and air, unknopped*
*Colour and opaque white, unknopped*
*Colour and opaque white, knopped*
Double series; colour and opaque
white, unknopped
*Inner twist of opaque white*
*Inner twist of opaque white and colour*
*Inner twist of colour only*
Double series; colour and opaque
white, knopped
Single series; air, opaque white and
colour
Double series; air, opaque white and
colour

## FACETED STEMS (c.1760-1810)
Unknopped stems
*With diamond faceting*
*Hexagonal faceting*
*Vertical fluting*
Knop at top of stem
*With diamond faceting*
*Other facets*
Centre-knopped stem
*With diamond faceting*
*Other facets*
Two or more knops

## RUDIMENTARY STEMS
Ale glasses
*Wrythen bowl and/or plain stem*
*Wrythen bowl, winged stem*
*Wrythen bowl, knopped stem*
*Moulded bowl*
*Plain bowl, no stem*
*Plain bowl, knopped stem*
*Fluted bowl*

Jelly glasses without handles
  *Hexagonal bowl*
  *Plain round bowl*
  *Moulded round bowl*
  *Pan-topped bowl*
Jelly glasses – C-handles
Jelly glasses – B-handles
Monteiths or Bonnet glasses
  *Plain*
  *Moulded*
  *Cut*
Posset glasses
Dram glasses
  *Plain stem*
  *Knopped stem*
  *Knop as stem*
  *No stem*
Rummers
  *Cup bowl*
  *Double-ogee bowl*
  *Bucket bowl*
  *Other bowls*
Wine flutes
Tankards
Tumblers

**DECORATION: DIAMOND-POINT ENGRAVING**
Ownership
Public events
Private affairs
Persons (including Jacobites)
Places
Myths and legends
Other subjects

**DECORATION: WHEEL-ENGRAVING AND STIPPLING**
Persons
  *Royalty*
  *Williamites*
  *Jacobites*
  *Titled families*
  *Commoners*
  *Corporate bodies*
Public events
  *Historical events: military*
  *Historical events: naval (including*

  *Privateers)*
  *Historical events: civil*
  *Politics and elections*
  *Other subjects*
Private affairs
  *Family occasions and events*
  *Friendship and conviviality*
  *Business*
  *Sports and recreations*
  *Other subjects (including Masonics)*
Places
  *Countries and states*
  *Towns and villages: England*
  *Towns and villages: Holland*
  *Other towns and villages*
  *Imaginary scenes, e.g. Chinese gardens*
  *Individual buildings*
Natural and geometric forms
  *'Flowered' borders*
  *Hops and barley*
  *Fruiting vine*
  *Fruiting apple*
  *Other decorative forms*
Myths and legends
Stippled decoration

**DECORATION: ENAMELLING**
Ownership (including armorials)
Portraits
Sports and pastimes
Pastoral scenes
Classical landscapes and ruins
Birds and insects
Fruit and trees
Hops and barley
Floral borders
Other subjects (including Masonics)

**DECORATION: GILDING**

# 3.
# Stem Formations

### Venetian Influences

The term 'façon de Venise', adopted in so many countries of Europe to describe glasses made in Venetian style, is testimony in itself to the influence of that great glassmaking centre on design and decoration during the fifteenth, sixteenth and seventeenth centuries. Delicacy, ingenuity, richness, fragility, are all terms which could be used of the wares exported by Venice and so highly prized by their eventual owners. Nevertheless, it is interesting to see from John Greene's drawings of the glasses which he ordered from Murano about 1670 that English taste was already in favour of the less flamboyant, more conservative shapes – a conical foot, simple hollow-knopped stem and conical bowl.

English glassmakers during the last quarter of the seventeenth century could not wholly escape from Venetian influence, however, and there were many Italian glassworkers employed in this country. Consequently, Venetian decorative effects persisted until about 1700 – rope twists, used in handles and stems; wings forming the stem or incorporated in a collar below the bowl; prunts with characteristic raspberry moulding applied as buttons on the stem; trailing seen as looped threads round body or base of a bowl; flammiform gadrooning seen in spikes leaping outwards from the bowl; 'nipt diamond waies', frequently adopted by Ravenscroft himself and seen as diamond-shaped compartments made by pinching together the metal of a bowl whilst still soft enough to be worked.

### Heavy Balusters

By the turn of the century, Venetian effects had been abandoned in favour of the simple, solid, pure shapes of conical bowls, well-proportioned knops and workmanlike feet with folded rims to guard against accidental chipping. It cannot be said that such glasses were never decorated but the addition of diamond-point or wheel-engraving was so rare that it is safe to assume that their makers and purchasers alike were as completely satisfied with them then as collectors are today.

This short period, from 1685 to about 1710, produced the finest drinking glasses this country has seen, pleasing to eye, comfortable to grasp, sturdy, strong, splendidly epitomising the qualities admired by an Englishman.

### Light Balusters

Before the end of the first quarter of the eighteenth century experimentation or perhaps the eternal search for novelty had resulted in a diversification of bowl shapes (the conical bowl with solid base being replaced by the bell, thistle and trumpet), and a more complex stem with lighter knops which gradually replaced those, such as cylinder, mushroom, acorn and egg, which demanded ample material for their execution.

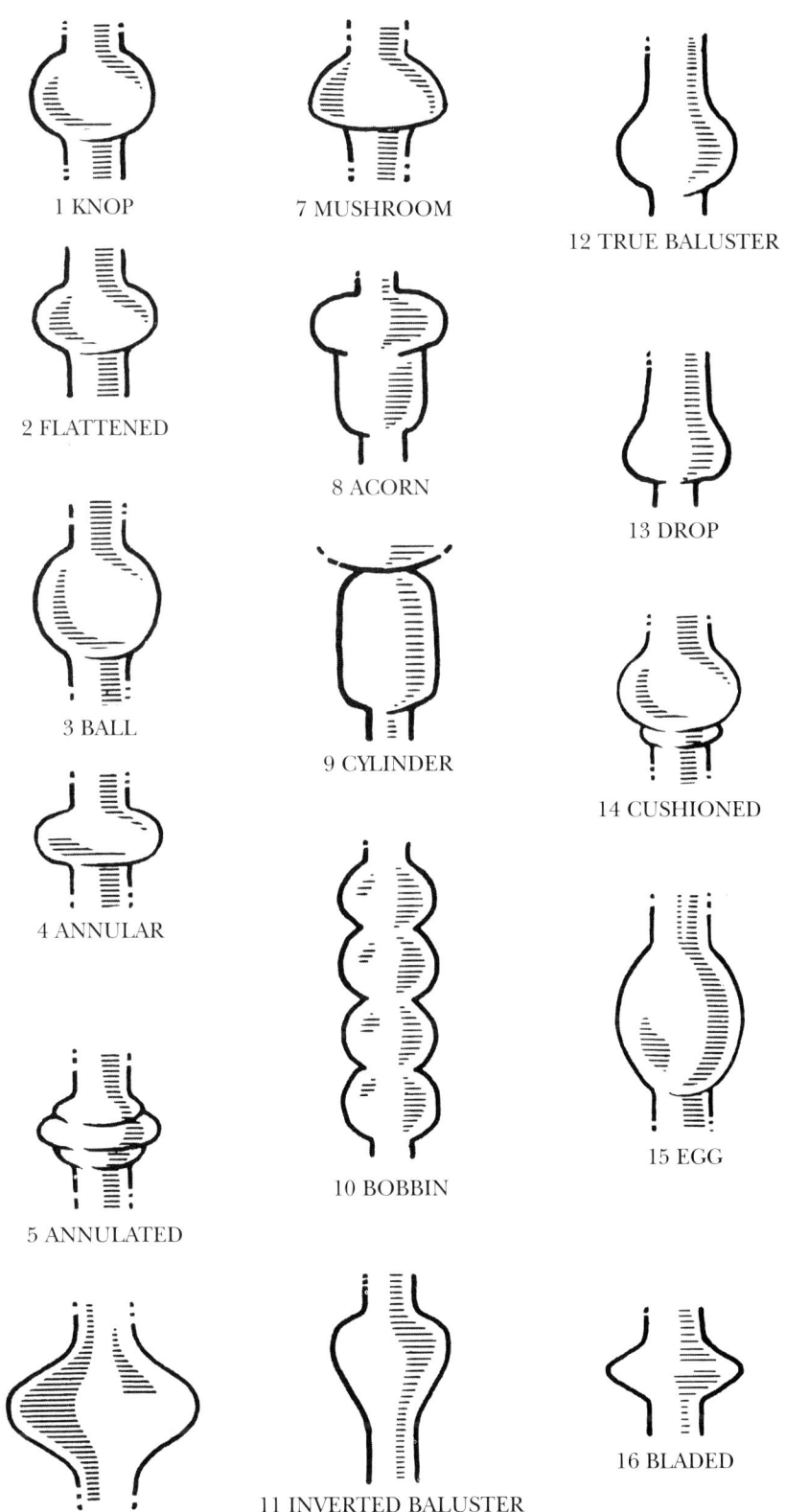

1 KNOP

7 MUSHROOM

12 TRUE BALUSTER

2 FLATTENED

8 ACORN

13 DROP

3 BALL

9 CYLINDER

14 CUSHIONED

4 ANNULAR

10 BOBBIN

15 EGG

5 ANNULATED

16 BLADED

6 ANGULAR

11 INVERTED BALUSTER

## Balustroids

The trend continued from 1725 until soon after the middle of the century when the baluster stem disappeared completely, knops being separated by lengths of plain stem giving an attenuated look which reached its climax in the type known as the 'Newcastle' baluster, that favourite vehicle for wheel-engraving, in which the stem was made thinner and longer than ever, broken by delicate knops, frequently beaded but, strangely enough, producing a glass which had its own distinctive charm and elegant appeal.

Balustroids abounded and are still among the most commonly encountered glasses to be found in the dealers' hands; suffering as they do in painful comparison with their stronger predecessors they are rather despised. The types of knop found in baluster and balustroid stems are illustrated.

## Moulded Pedestal Stems

It seems rather pedantic to retain the description 'moulded pedestal stems' for glasses now commonly referred to as 'Silesian' but the doubtful origin of the latter term and its lack of reference to a distinctive method of manufacture make it unacceptable for every reason save brevity. No doubt its introduction was more or less contemporary with the accession of George I in 1714; a small number survive in the earliest, four-sided, form bearing the legend moulded round the top of the pedestal LONG LIVE KING GEORGE. Nevertheless, the distinguishing feature is the use of a mould in making the stem, first four-sided, then six- and eight-sided and finally becoming so debased, with rounded shoulders, that the distinctive moulded characteristic almost disappears. In its four- or six-sided form this type of stem applied almost exclusively to wines but after the introduction of eight-sided moulds, especially with the addition of collars above and below, it was most frequently used in the manufacture of sweetmeats (often erroneously referred to as 'champagnes'. Champagne was in fact drunk from a flute).

## Plain Stems

Though plain-stemmed glasses, many of them of simple, heavy manufacture for tavern use, persist throughout the middle fifty years of the century and form the least avidly collected group, they display surprising variety. The majority have trumpet bowls, the stem often enlivened by a long tear and occasionally by the addition of collars. No problems of description are encountered save that of distinguishing between two- and three-piece glasses. In the two-piece form the bowl and stem are clearly made from the same gathering of metal, no weld or joint between bowl and stem being either visible or possible.

## Air-Twist Stems

It would be logical to assume that the air twist developed from the tear and this may well have been the method of evolution, since air twists are also formed from air trapped in the metal during stem manufacture. Two methods seem to have been used, (i) an indentation of a squat cylinder of metal by tool or mould, covering the indentations by another coating of glass and creating the twist by drawing out and twisting until the requisite pattern and thickness were achieved, or (ii) by pricking the top of a squat cylinder with pins set into a bobbin-shaped tool and thus forming regular patterns of air bubbles which become an air twist by drawing and twisting. The latter method was employed especially in the manufacture of multiple-spiral air twists, a term occurring so frequently that the abbreviation MSAT is used.

Since it is possible to create an air twist and then, after adding metal which increases the diameter, to repeat the process, the terms 'single series' (SSAT) and 'double series' (DSAT) are used to differentiate between them.

Strangely enough, although double-series air twists were much more complicated to make, single-series twists other than the MSAT are scarcer and of more interest to the collector, the most attractive of all being the so-called 'mercury twist'. This was produced by using two flat pins in the pricking tool so that when the stem was drawn out a series of wide corkscrews was created, reflecting the light so brilliantly that they appeared to be filled with quick silver. There are, however, so many gradations between corkscrews with almost round section and the true 'mercury twist' that no attempt is usually made to differentiate between them. Readers should be aware that 'mercury twist' is often loosely used to describe any corkscrew and should note the difference between Plates 406 and 417. When the stem contains knops – and these can be from one to five – only two types of twist occur, the MSAT and a pair of corkscrews.

### Incised-Twist Stems

Closely related to the air twist, indeed sometimes spoken of as the 'poor man's air twist', is the incised-twist or wrythened stem. The twist can be coarse or fine and coarse twists are found in soda glass also, when they are almost always associated with a waisted bell bowl and folded foot.

### Composite Stems

This most attractive section contains many interesting combinations of plain stem with air or opaque twists and occasionally a mixture of all three. Haynes's[1] definition of a plain section as one which exceeds half an inch in length avoids confusion with a normal trumpet bowl above a shoulder-knopped MSAT stem. Glasses in this section are particularly and consistently well made, almost as though the extra complexity of construction demanded extra care and craftsmanship.

### Opaque-Twist Stems

The opaque twist, introduced in 1755-60 (though Francis Buckley[2] records a dated specimen of 1747) owes much to the Venetian *latticino* technique of the early seventeenth century. In English stems it was formed by the introduction of opaque-white glass rods in the stem mould, the delicate patterns being produced by drawing and twisting and repeating the process for double-series twists. The results were ingenious and charming and evidently extremely popular, thousands having survived the vicissitudes of two centuries. As with air

1. Op. cit., p.241.

2. Quoted in Thorpe, op. cit., p.213.

twists the single series (SSOT) are rarer and in greater demand than the double series (DSOT).

**Mixed and Colour-Twist Stems**

Instead of opaque-white rods, opaque rods in such enamel colours as red, blue, brown, green and pink and, rarely, yellow, were introduced, usually in combination with opaque white but occasionally alone. At the time of manufacture this was seen, no doubt, as a pretty but unimportant variation; those who adopted it could never have imagined the competition for their glasses today!

Another pretty combination was achieved by mixing air and opaque twists, an air twist within an opaque in a double-series stem or vice versa; less frequently an air twist alternating with opaque white in a single series. Rarest of all is the combination of air, opaque white and colour in the same stem.

**Faceted Stems**

Cutting of bowls and stems of drinking glasses, as well as of larger vessels, was practised many years before the date given for the commencement of this period but the early examples quoted by various writers represented occasional demonstrations of the art rather than a widespread fashion. It was the development of grinding techniques in Ireland and England which facilitated the production of faceted glasses and changed many of the features which had remained constant for so long. The conical foot tended to disappear, being replaced by the flat foot, the pontil-mark being ground out; many types of bowl, the trumpet and the bell bowl especially, were abandoned because they were unsuitable for faceting; a new attraction was added to the dinner-table – drinking glasses with stems brilliantly reflecting the light and matching the cut bowls, jugs and salts and candelabra which were already popular. The stem section is normally hexagonal, containing six to eight bands of diamond or hexagonal facets. A shoulder or central knop is often seen. A less frequently encountered feature is the alternation of vertical flutes and facets or notched flutes; after 1800, however, stems comprised of vertical flutes only supersede facets. Both facets and flutes can continue over the base of bowl (very rarely over the whole surface) and appear as bridge-flutes on the foot.

By the beginning of the last quarter of the century the faceted stem had almost completely captured the market: it reigned until the early years of the nineteenth century and was the last distinctive stem form in the history of English drinking glasses: since then we have seen many styles resurrected, attenuated and debased but the Victorians, for all their inventiveness, failed to find an equally popular successor.

**Rudimentary Stems**

Throughout the eighteenth century a wide variety of small glasses was being produced with many purposes in mind – glasses for jellies, custard, sweetmeats of all kinds, glasses for short drinks, gins and drams, small footed bowls for salt or nuts or confectionery. In many of them can be seen characteristics which allow a reasonably accurate dating; others are extremely difficult to place in a chronological sequence. One characteristic they share, however; the stem is either almost or entirely lacking, automatically excepting them from a classification based on stem formation. They have their own fascination, however, and most collectors include a selection of interesting types in their cabinets: the simple classification suggested attempts little more than an obvious and simple order and certainly does not succeed in proving an evolutionary progression.

### Engraved, Enamelled and Gilded Glasses

Any attempt at chronology has been similarly abandoned in the case of engraved and enamelled glasses, in the belief that the subject of the decoration is of most importance.

# 4.
# The Bowl

## Shapes

Within each stem group a further subdivision is possible according to type of bowl, this being the most distinctive feature after the stem. Its importance in the description of a glass is obvious, making necessary a key to bowl nomenclature. The twelve shapes most commonly encountered are illustrated.

During the heavy baluster period the pointed round-funnel and conical bowls with solid base predominated, bell and thistle shapes making up the remainder. The bell bowl persisted throughout all periods until the introduction of the faceted stem when the ovoid bowl became popular, no doubt because its shape was more suitable for bridge cutting.

The drawn trumpet bowl is particularly associated with plain stem glasses and the ogee and round funnel with opaque twists; similarly incised twists are mostly found in combination with a waisted bell bowl or trumpet bowl. Otherwise there is a fascinating diversity of combinations of bowl and stem.

Many bowl shapes will be seen in elongated or waisted form, with everted or folded rim and with solid base. The commoner variations are: waisted bell or bucket bowls; solid base to conical, bell and thistle bowls; variations in depth and shape of the pan in pan-topped bowls, giving rise to such terms as 'saucer-topped' or 'cup-topped'.

Faceting often disguises the original shape making recognition difficult and there are other drinking glasses of the late eighteenth and early nineteenth centuries, especially rummers, found in many tantalising shapes. Although they are derived from the earlier styles exact terminology has not been developed to describe their precise shapes.

## Decoration

Five forms of applied decoration are found on the bowl – diamond-point, or 'scratch', engraving, wheel-engraving, stipple engraving, enamelling, gilding and cutting – in addition to forms of moulding and tooling which are part of the initial process of manufacture. Engraving and painting on glass have been used from ancient times and both are found on eighteenth century English drinking glasses, though painting with enamel colours and gilding were introduced only in the second half of the century.

## Diamond Point

Engraving scratched on the bowl by means of a diamond point is a technique particularly suited to the hard metal of soda-glass. It is found on the English goblets of the late sixteenth century made by Jacopo Verzelini and on such seventeenth century specimens as the Exeter flute and the Royal Oak goblet if these can be given an English provenance, which is by no means certain. There

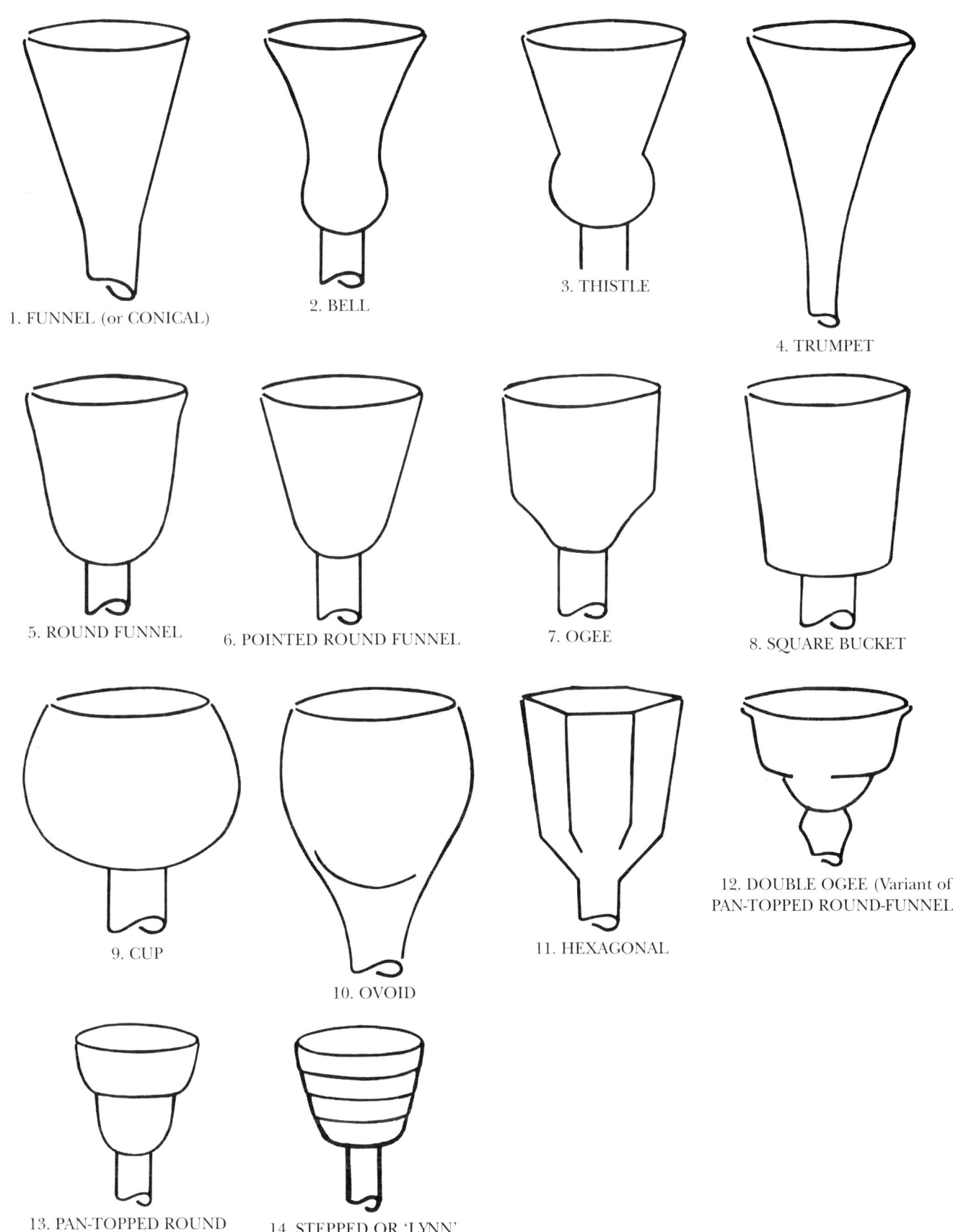

1. FUNNEL (or CONICAL)

2. BELL

3. THISTLE

4. TRUMPET

5. ROUND FUNNEL

6. POINTED ROUND FUNNEL

7. OGEE

8. SQUARE BUCKET

9. CUP

10. OVOID

11. HEXAGONAL

12. DOUBLE OGEE (Variant of PAN-TOPPED ROUND-FUNNEL)

13. PAN-TOPPED ROUND FUNNEL

14. STEPPED OR 'LYNN'

are good grounds for believing that the engraving was done in Holland, the Prince of Orange flute in the British Museum being of exactly the same type as the Exeter flute, with the engraving tentatively ascribed to Cristoffel Jansz Meyer: one could cite also the 'Master of Yerst' as the engraver of a wine glass of similar date in the Pilkington Glass Museum.

It was a technique less well suited to lead glass, its exponents during the eighteenth century mostly being amateurs who wished to inscribe their own simple marks of ownership. Notable exceptions are the few 'Amen' glasses and a small group of Jacobites.

### Wheel Engraving

The equally ancient technique of wheel engraving, however, found its ideal medium in lead glass and was applied to many thousands of English glasses after about 1725. In many cases the decoration is nothing more than a simple floral border – advertised by sellers as 'flowered' glass – but in other cases the craftsmanship is of great delicacy and highest quality, low relief sculpture being exploited to produce light and shade. From the frequency with which these superlative engravings are accompanied by legends in Dutch and from our knowledge of individual Dutch engravers, it has been concluded that most, if not all, of the work of this quality was done in Holland, certainly the home of the renowned Jacob Sang whose signature appears on the foot or pontil-mark of some of the finest work of this period.

Flowered glasses, Jacobites, Williamites, Frigate glasses and those with simple inscriptions were almost certainly engraved in England since most of them demanded only modest skill and hardly justified the cost of transport to Holland. Surprisingly little is known, however, about English engravers or centres where engraving was practised until after 1800; after that date English craftsmanship was able to match the best in the world.

Engraving of any kind adds greatly to the interest of a glass, whether it is a simple fruiting vine border on a wine glass or hops and barley on an ale. Frequently engraving can have documentary importance, recording the names of societies, personalities in the public eye, customs and historical events. An armorial bearing can often provide us with a precise date for the engraving and by inference for that type of glass. The 'Williamites', of course, commemorating an event in 1690 but engraved half a century later, provide the most obvious warning against always assuming that engraving and manufacture are contemporary.

Much of the engraving is of poor quality with little aesthetic appeal but the Dutch engravers already referred to were in a different class. Because it is so often found on the Newcastle light balusters there are convincing grounds for accepting the theory that when high quality was required – coats of arms for example – Newcastle-made glasses were regularly shipped across to Holland for engraving. Some years ago there was a display case in the Boymans Museum, Rotterdam, filled with beautifully engraved drinking glasses and labelled 'Dutch eighteenth century drinking glasses'. On pointing out that all the glasses were English the reply was that the engraving was Dutch! Jacob Sang of Amsterdam is the name synonymous with the most superb wheel engraving of the eighteenth century.

## Stipple Engraving

If in wheel engraving the Dutch could claim no more than having raised the craft to an excellence not previously attained, stipple engraving was surely their undisputed contribution to the art of glass decoration. This most exacting technique, more closely related to diamond point than wheel engraving, was achieved by lightly striking the glass bowl with a diamond or hard metal point to create dots which, by their degree of closeness or separation formed an image, virtually invisible until the glass is held against the light.

Fortunately most stipple engravers signed their work so that their names and the periods during which they exercised their skill are known to us. The earliest artist in the field is thought to be Anna Roemers Visscher to whom a number of specimens are attributed, including a roemer of about 1650 in the British Museum. Signed examples by her are in the collection of the Rijks Museum, Amsterdam, and the Hamburg Museum of Art.

It was in the eighteenth century, however, that stippling flourished, David Wolff of the Hague being probably the best known: he was active from 1784 to 1795. An earlier worker was Frans Greenwood of Dordrecht (1680-1761) signed copies of whose work, as early as 1720, are in the British Museum and the Victoria and Albert Museum. Other known stipple engravers are A. Schouman, 1747, J.G. Smeyseer, c.1780, G.H. Hoolaart and L. Adams. After a century and a half of neglect this most demanding technique has happily been revived in England by Laurence Whistler.

## Enamelling

Although the art of decorating glass in enamel colours, fused to the surface by firing, had been practised in Islamic countries in medieval times and in Venice and Germany in the sixteenth and seventeenth centuries, no attempt to pursue this art in England seems to have been made until after 1750. Dossie,[1] writing in 1758 says 'The practice of enamel-painting is of late introduction amongst us'; by 1760 it seems to have been flourishing in two centres at least, Bristol and Newcastle. Michael Edkins was certainly working in Bristol as a decorator of porcelain from about 1762, also painting glass, Delftware and even coaches in order to maintain his extraordinary family of thirty-three children.[2] Newcastle was the adopted home of the Beilby family, two, or possibly three, of whom were actively engaged in enamel decoration of drinking glasses from about 1760 to 1780. Some of their work is signed and, thanks to Thomas Bewick,[3] we have a detailed account of their activities from 1767 to about 1778 when the brother and sister chiefly concerned, William and Mary Beilby, seem to have left Newcastle for Fifeshire.

It seems reasonable to assume that the glasses decorated by the Beilbys were made locally, especially since the majority are opaque-white twists characterised by a limited range of double-series patterns. The enamelling, too, has a uniformity of style and subject which allows one to attribute glasses to the Beilbys with reasonable certainty. Most work was in white enamel, the designs ranging from simple floral borders through a series of typically eighteenth century scenes – shooting, fishing, Classical ruins, shepherds and shepherdesses – but occasionally more elaborate designs in a full range of

1. Dossie, R. *Handmaid to the arts*, 2 vols. 1758.

2. Owen, H. *Two centuries of ceramic art in Bristol*, 1873, pp 330-2.

3. Bewick, T. *Memoir of Thomas Bewick*, 1862.

enamel colours were undertaken. Their most spectacular, and probably William Beilby's earliest work, is seen in a series of goblets bearing the royal arms and commemorating the birth of the Prince of Wales (later George IV); these have become known as 'Royal Beilbys'.

It is not reasonable to assume, however, that all enamelling in white on clear glass was carried out by them, any more than one can assert that Michael Edkins was responsible for all enamel decoration on coloured glass. There are several glasses, for example, bearing enamelled portraits of the Young Pretender which can hardly be by the same hand as the Royal Beilbys! No doubt future research will reveal evidence of other enamellers of the period even though it is noticeably lacking at present.

### Gilding

Many glasses show traces of oil-gilding, that is, gilding applied by means of an oil adhesive. It was not fixed and was therefore relatively impermanent; however there are many examples extant on which the gilding is still intact, which suggests that some decorators mastered the art of firing. The patterns seen most frequently are fruiting vine decoration on wine glasses and hops and barley on ales. No doubt enamellers did their own gilding; there is little evidence of gilding specialists except Absolon at Great Yarmouth towards the end of the century and James Giles working at Bristol at about the same time. Giles's work reached a very high standard: he decorated decanters and bottles, usually of blue glass but sometimes of green or white, with exotic birds, fruit, landscapes and figures in gold with occasional use of coloured enamels. The Jacobs family worked in the same city, applying geometrical and floral designs to coloured glass. Neither Giles nor Jacobs appears to have decorated wine glasses but Absolon gilded rummers and goblets with such legends as A PRESENT FROM YARMOUTH or SUCCESS TO FARMING. His work is frequently signed under the foot.

### Cutting

Apart from a few dated or engraved examples whose provenance or actual dates of cutting have been questioned, faceted English drinking glasses are not known before 1750 and there are very few which can be attributed with any certainty to a date earlier than 1760. The example quoted by Hartshorne in *Old English glasses*, Plate 47, and discussed by Haynes is reproduced as Plate 839; it could well be of German origin or faceted later than the period 1729-51 when Frederick Louis, eldest son of George II, was Prince of Wales. Stylistically the glass belongs to the first quarter of the century.

Two fiscal measures affected the production of drinking glasses, the Excise Act of 1745 which placed the tax of 1d. per pound on materials used for glassmaking and the 1777 Act which doubled the tax and included a tax on 'enamelled glass' effectively spelling the end of the opaque-twist stem. At the same time – in 1780 to be exact – free trade was permitted between England and Ireland. As a result many English glassmakers moved their works and workers to Ireland, producing there the heavier glass vessels which could be shipped back to England without tax or import duty.

English-made glasses inevitably became smaller but the fashion for faceted stems compelled manufacturers to follow it. Cut glass became the vogue, drinking glasses and sweetmeats with faceted stems replacing the opaque twist. What proportion was made in Ireland is a matter for conjecture.

The faceted stem is often associated with additional engraving and cutting such as scalloping of the rim of the foot, scale-cutting of the bowl and decorating the bowl with stars and polished circles in a band below the rim as well as the engraving and stippling described earlier.

## Moulding

The use of moulds in the manufacture of drinking glasses has already been remarked upon in describing moulded pedestal stems. It was a technique applied most attractively to glasses with other stem formations also, occurring most frequently at the base of wine glasses in the form of ribs or flutes or honeycomb moulding and frequently extending over the whole bowl as honeycomb or panel moulding, the decoration being repeated on the foot. This more extensive moulding is found most often on sweetmeats. Wrythen moulding, that is vertically moulded flutes given a twist by the glassblower, is found in late seventeenth century ales and persists in similar glasses throughout the eighteenth century.

# 5.

# The Foot

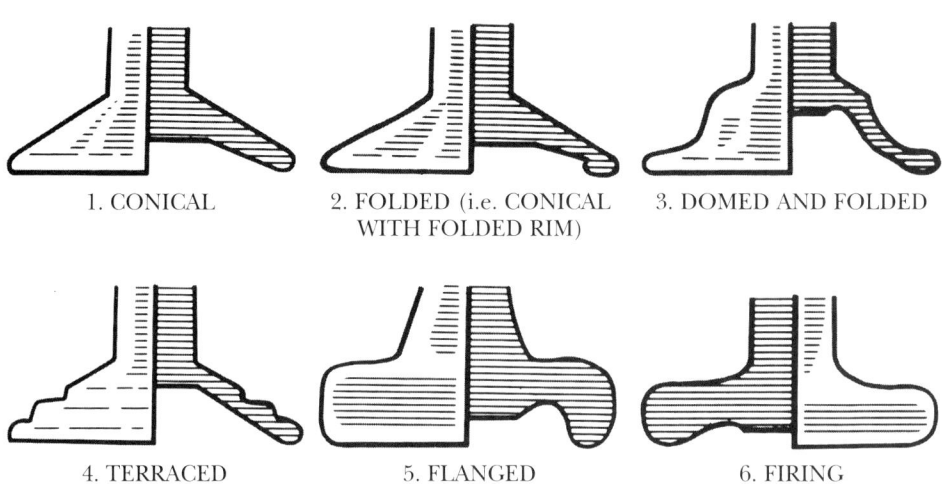

1. CONICAL     2. FOLDED (i.e. CONICAL WITH FOLDED RIM)     3. DOMED AND FOLDED

4. TERRACED     5. FLANGED     6. FIRING

In the formation of the foot there is both variation and evolution. Its function is to give adequate support to the glass, allowing it to stand firmly on the table, a good general rule being that the diameter of the foot should at least equal that of the bowl. To this rule there are exceptions in both directions; massive feet are seen often enough to make one suspect that many glasses have been trimmed to remove chips; occasionally a glass with a large bowl has a considerably smaller foot, but if it is original (the rim folded for example) there can be no argument.

The shape of the foot is dictated by two other factors, the need to protect the table from the pontil-mark and any special function which demands modification. Throughout the first three-quarters of the eighteenth century the pontil-mark was rough and a conical foot necessary to give the required clearance. Until 1730 or 1740 a folded foot was normal, its abandonment being difficult to understand. The double thickness of a foot at the rim gives splendid protection against chipping, is an attractive decorative feature and used so little additional metal that saving weight could hardly be the reason for rejecting it. Perhaps folded feet were too robust and in their disuse we see an early example of built-in obsolescence?

The next significant change came about 1775 with the introduction of faceted stems, themselves the product of improved cutting and polishing techniques. Since stems could be ground so accurately and so cheaply, why not be rid altogether of the troublesome pontil-mark? Once it had been ground out there was no need for the conical foot, the firmer flat foot being preferable. It has become axiomatic that every glass of the eighteenth century will have either a pontil-mark or the evidence of grinding out: it is not equally true that every glass with a pontil-mark belongs to that century for there was a mid-nineteenth century revival and there are many twentieth century forgeries.

'Firing glasses', so called from the custom of rapping the table in concert after drinking a toast, thereby making a noise like the firing of a pistol, demanded sturdy feet, considerably thicker than usual and are normally appended to dram glasses; terracing allowed extra strength to be built into the construction of the foot, occasionally becoming such a decorative feature that it is appropriately described as a 'beehive' foot.

The domed foot is an alternative to the conical form frequently occurring in the first half of the century and usually with a folded rim; the helmet shape is a rare, more pronounced form of domed foot but is not to be confused with the exceptionally high dome characteristic of some baluster stems of German origin. Dram glasses are seen with flanged as well as firing feet; bonnet glasses are found with a variety of moulded, scalloped and square feet.

The square foot which became popular in the early years of the nineteenth century marked the first significant innovation after the ground-out pontil made the flat foot possible. It is found especially on rummers in combination with a moulded dome giving the characteristic 'lemon-squeezer' effect but is also seen on dwarf ales, salts and the bonnet glasses or Monteiths already mentioned.

# 6.

# Dating

Haynes's chronology has not been seriously challenged since the second edition of *Glass through the Ages* appeared in 1959 and it has been adopted here with very slight modifications. The periods quoted are simply those during which the styles were current since it would be manifestly impossible to say exactly when the first and last specimens were made. Dating is, indeed, an extremely difficult exercise and it will be useful to examine the evidence upon which a system can be based.

Few glasses bear a manufacturer's mark but some are found, notably the raven's head seal of Ravenscroft (accurately placing such glasses within the period May 1677 to May 1681) and the engraved marks on Waterford, Cork, Belfast and other Irish glass. Especially when the period of a factory's activities is brief, the dates of its products can be placed within those limits; when it survived for many decades and constantly repeated the same patterns, as was the case in the nineteenth century, such evidence is not very helpful.

Documentary evidence is of great importance. John Greene's designs[1] for glasses ordered from the firm Allesio Morelli in Venice between 1667 and 1672 are preserved in the Sloane MSS in the British Museum and give us a clear indication of the styles current at that time. Francis Buckley's research[2] into advertisements appearing in eighteenth century newspapers provides further information about the types of glass being sold, but unfortunately such general terms are employed that few inferences can be drawn. Thomas Bett's accounts, published by Buckley in *Glass*[3] are typical of another useful source. From the entry 'Wormed Egg Bowl Wine', for example, we learn that Thomas Bett was selling air-twist ('wormed') wine glasses at seven shillings per dozen; from another entry in 1757 we find that 'Enamelled Shank Flutes', that is ale glasses with opaque-twist stems, were already being made.

Engravings on glasses can give an approximate date if it is borne in mind that events and personalities continued to be of public interest for many years and that engravings of them could be applied to earlier glasses. Some engravings include a date and these are particularly valuable; the series of glasses, diamond-scratch engraved with descriptive scenes, mottoes and dates within the period of Verzelini's monopoly (1575-91) have been accepted as the products of his factory and as bearing contemporary dates; there are also glasses signed and dated by the engraver, providing a reliable indication of the date when the glasses were made; similarly Jacob Sang's signature can be linked with the dates between which he is known to have been working.

Such considerations do not apply, however, to all dated glasses; Williamites bearing the date 1690 are simply commemorating the Battle of the Boyne fought in that year, but the glasses were made half a century later; Jacobite engravings give no indication of date and continued to be made during the whole period from 1730 to 1800. Inferences can be drawn though, from the

1. Reproduced in Hartshorne, op. cit., Plate 30, and in Thorpe, op. cit., Fig.16.

2. Buckley, F. *Old English glass*, 1925.

3. Vol.5, p.300 (July 1928).

Frigate glasses, for the dates when the ships were operating are known and also those of their captains, so that we can safely date to 1757, for example, the opaque twists which were invariably used below bowls invoking success to the Eagle Frigate.

Similarly, we can link together the opaque twists which characterise the vast majority of the glasses decorated in enamel colours by the Beilbys at Newcastle-on-Tyne with the dates (c.1760-78) during which they are known to have been engaged in this art. It is extremely likely that these glasses were manufactured locally and if so would be made in the Dagnia Glasshouse under the direction of John Williams or by Airey Cookson and Co. – thereby approaching an exact provenance for one group of glasses with more probability than any other group except the sealed glasses of Ravenscroft. Beilby decoration is found on other types of glasses – Silesian stems, air twists and, very rarely, incised twists – so that the possibility of earlier glasses being decorated to special order must not be overlooked.

Glasses and goblets are frequently encountered which contain coins sealed in the base. Rarely do these provide any evidence of date, the only fact proved being the date *after* which the glass must have been made. Sometimes the coins may be regarded as newly minted; Thorpe accepts the 1678[1] coin in a goblet in the British Museum as an accurate date but another glass, then in Wilfred Buckley's collection, he dates five years later than the 1680[2] coin it contains, whilst a third, in the Victoria and Albert Museum (Rees Price Collection), he evidently feels is considerably later than the 1664[3] coin it contains since he simply describes it as 'late 17th century'. Examples of Jacobite glasses of the eighteenth century which contain Stuart coins are well known and this use of coins a century earlier than the glasses themselves can be easily understood.

An interesting dating technique which has been exploited by Chambon[4] derives from the almost photographic attention to detail observed by Dutch painters of the seventeenth century. He has examined paintings of interiors and of still-life and has been able to show the forms of many glasses in use (not necessarily manufactured then but of no later date) at the time of the painting's execution. It is a line of inquiry which might possibly yield useful results if applied to English paintings and drawings; the well-known painting by Kneller, now in the National Portrait Gallery, of two members of the Kit-Kat Club taking wine from glasses which have derived their name from the Club, is an obvious example of material which might well merit further investigation along the lines already pursued by Frank Davis[5].

To conclude, then, it must be accepted that dating of eighteenth century glasses on stylistic grounds will be vague: few thoroughly documented specimens are known and styles overlapped for many years. Nevertheless, the periods are sufficiently well defined to enable one to provide a workable chronology even though it is doubtful whether many writers would have the temerity to agree with Thorpe's statement that 'It is, I think, possible to date most glasses within ten years, and a good many as near as five.'

1. Thorpe, op. cit., p.128.

2. Ibid., Plate xxix.

3. Ibid., Plate lxxvii.

4. Chambon, R. *History of Belgian glass from the 2nd century to the present*, 1955.

5. Davis, Frank. 'Kneller portrait illustrates fashions in 18th century glass', *Illustrated London News*, Jan 8th 1966, p.27.

# 7.
# Values (i) in 1970

Such are the fluctuations of market prices that any attempt to suggest, other than in the broadest terms, what one might expect to pay for drinking glasses would be confusing and misleading. During the past fifteen years prices have risen with a rapidity which collectors of the 1940s and 1950s find quite extraordinary and necessitate considerable caution in predicting the limits which will be reached in future decades.

Museum directors as well as private collectors, interested in acquiring representative examples of eighteenth century craftsmanship, have begun to realise the once plentiful and rather despised drinking glasses of the period are rapidly disappearing from the dealers' cabinets and that the rarer types are increasingly difficult to find. Nevertheless, their prices are still (1971) considerably lower than those of any other craft product of the century – silver, porcelain, furniture and even fine earthenware – which are now beyond the reach of most purses. Plain-stemmed drinking glasses and the commoner opaque twists can still be acquired for less than twenty pounds and jelly glasses may well be picked up for less than five.

At the other extreme it is possible to pay four figures for a superbly engraved or enamelled goblet and hundreds of pounds for a simple wine glass with a colour-twist stem: it is clear that the collector needs some guide to comparative values. Perhaps the most satisfactory indication of prices can be found by reference to a single sale since this indicates the date on which a glass had a definite market value though it must be borne in mind that if bought by a dealer it would retail at 20 or 30 per cent more.

The sale at Sotheby's of the Walter F. Smith collection was by far the most extensive and important of recent years, extending over four days in 1967 and 1968. Formed by the late Walter F. Smith Junior, of Trenton, New Jersey, acting upon expert advice, it contained superb examples in every category.

Among the early glasses there were numerous wrythen ale and wine glasses with flammiform and pincered decoration of the bowl and winged or baluster stems (Plates 45 and 775) which brought between £100 and £400, though £520 was paid for one with more pronounced Venetian character. A bobbin-knopped sweetmeat glass of about 1685 sold for £190 but a patch-stand or small tazza of the same period with a stem composed of eight graduated knops brought only £85. Another glass of this type but with a gadrooned bowl of goblet or mead-glass proportions (Plate 264) brought £470, however, and others of similar character realised from £85 to £300.

Heavy balusters dating to about 1700 hardly failed to exceed £100 for any perfect specimens and the rarer knops realised much higher prices. Examples of the commoner inverted baluster stems (Plate 52) realised £220 or £250; an angular knop (Plate 73) made £150, a drop knop (Plate 84) £135, another with a heavier knop £290; an annulated knop (Plate 77) with a slight chip on the rim made £150. The rarer knops referred to are the acorn, mushroom, cylinder and egg knops; acorn knops realised £400 and £550 (Plate 105); mushroom knops £180, £130, £200, £260 (Plates 100, 101 and 102) whilst for one magnificent glass with an acorn above a mushroom knop £520 was paid; earlier cylinder knops were generally more expensive still, £300, £460, £620 and, for a slightly heavier specimen than Plate 109, £310. Egg knops (Plate 111) are the rarest category of all, this great collection containing only one and that a modest six inches in height: it brought £460.

Silesian stems were made from about 1710, when they were four-sided and supported a funnel bowl, until well into the second half of the century when six or eight sides were the fashion and the sharp moulding had become rounded and debased. Of them all the rarest and most expensive is the four-sided stem which bears in moulded relief, a word on each side, the legend GOD SAVE KING GEORGE (Plate 286); the only other example in the Smith sale realised £620. In striking contrast was the cut-glass sweetmeat with an eight-sided Silesian stem which brought only £22: a feature of the sale was the relatively low price realised by most sweetmeats, even the finest scarcely exceeding £100.

Not many balustroids were included unless they had the additional attraction of engraving and these will be referred to later. A few examples, however, will give some idea of prices obtained for a class of considerable interest to those forming less ambitious collections. The inverted baluster was a popular eighteenth century feature and one typical glass with bell bowl, IB knop, basal knop and folded foot (Plate 125) realised £35; another similar glass but with an annulated knop above the IB (Plate 159) made £42.

Plain-stemmed glasses, unengraved, realised the lowest prices of all, as one would expect, two drawn trumpets (Plate 335) making only £28 for the pair. A cordial, being rarer, (Plate 365) made £45 and had the added feature of a domed foot; a ratafia, perfectly plain but even rarer still sold for £145! A toasting glass (Plates 332 and 333) realised £30 and the unusual feature of a double collar below a trumpet bowl (Plate 375) attracted a final bid of only £22. Ale glasses, if plain, made £18 for one and £30 for a pair but another specimen with tall round-funnel bowl engraved with hops and barley and a domed and folded foot, made £42.

Glasses with air-twist stems normally command relatively modest prices unless the twist is exceptionally rare or the number of knops more than three. A cordial with the rare combination of an eleven-ply spiral band outside a single mercurial corkscrew reached £95 and another cordial with deceptive trumpet bowl and a double-series twist made £130. A glass with five knops and a bucket bowl (Plate 494) has similar stem but a bell bowl with Jacobite engraving sold for £290 and one with four knops (Plate 493) and a domed foot made £300. A more common type of multiple-spiral air twist – an ale glass engraved with hops and barley on a two-knopped stem (Plate 473) – sold for £75 and this price was about average for air twists with some particularly attractive feature.

Next to plain stems the opaque twist with an ordinary ogee or round-funnel bowl is the commonest and least expensive. Features which made them more attractive were cordial bowls, one with a round funnel (Plate 632) bringing £65; another with a double-ogee bowl and a mixture of an air spiral cable and spiral opaque thread made £150 and a ratafia (Plate 677) with normal double twist but a deceptive bowl sold for the even higher price of £175. At the lower end of the scale was £34 for a simple round-funnel bowl with a double-series twist, the bowl being engraved with fruiting vine and a moth; £50 and £55 were paid for sweetmeats with double-ogee bowls and single and double opaque twists respectively.

Closely allied with opaque twists and almost always in association with them are colour twists, one of the most desirable classes of eighteenth century drinking glasses and one of the classes most fraught with danger, for high prices have encouraged late copies and many genuine glasses of the period are in soda metal and of Continental origin. Red, green and blue are found most often and are very desirable in good strong colours; yellow (canary) is the most sought after and any good specimens bring very high prices. One with a pair of opaque-white corkscrews enclosing a yellow spiral centre (Plate 734) realised £300 and was the only canary twist in the sale; a firing glass (Plate 723) with alternate white and green threads outside a spiral gauze reached £270 and a glass with engraved bell bowl and the rare combination of spiral air cable and single pale green spiral thread (Plate 716) brought £240. An unusual glass with slender trumpet bowl and a stem comprising an opaque-white spiral thread outside an opaque-white lace twist edged with red and green (Plate 731 but this edged with red and turquoise) made £400, the highest price in this category except for a fine goblet with a white corkscrew edged with orange and green which exceeded it by £20 and a candlestick with an opaque-white lace twist encircled by a blue and white spiral thread which realised £1,350. None failed to exceed £100, a typical and more frequently encountered combination of bell bowl, opaque-white corkscrew spiral edged with brown and green (Plate 728 but this also has a pair of white spiral threads) bringing £120.

Faceted stems, dating to the last quarter of the century and for that reason in less demand realised comparatively modest prices, unless enhanced by engraving or rare bowl formation. A set of three, cut all over the bowls with diamond facets which continued down the stems (Plate 751) made only £50 and a cordial with double-ogee bowl (Plate 741 but this is a wine) brought £45. Among the sweetmeats the faceted examples brought the lowest prices, one with scalloped rim and knopped stem (Plate 768 but this has an ogee bowl) realising £28.

Finally, there is the large class of engraved and enamelled glasses which, if of good quality, bring uniformly high prices, whatever the stem formation. Although this sale did not contain a parallel the addition of a stipple-engraved portrait by David Wolff to a single-faceted stem (Plate 1,051), for example, would increase its value at least tenfold and probably twentyfold. The most superb eighteenth century engraving was done in Holland, many consignments of Newcastle glasses being shipped there for engraving before sale either on the Continent or in England. It would appear that most of them were to satisfy specific commissions – especially for family coats of arms – rather than as speculative risks by the glass-dealer. Large quantities of English glasses, however, especially those with tall, slender knopped stems associated with Newcastle, remained in Holland and were engraved for Dutch customers with a wide variety of scenes and mottoes of their own country – canals, gardens, ships, drinking scenes, portaits, emblems of friendship, arms of the House of Orange, Dutch cities and private families, executed with incomparable skill and not infrequently signed. So many specimens were included in the Smith sale that it is impracticable to review them here and a few typical examples must suffice. Generally prices ranged from just below £100 to £1,100 for a portrait glass of Prince Charles Edward beneath the motto AUDIENTOR IBO (Plate 892) and £1,800 for the rarest engraving of all, an 'Amen' glass (Plate 834), so called because they were characterised by the royal cypher JR and, in diamond point, either two or four verses of the Jacobite version of the National Anthem:

*God Save the King I pray,*        *God Bless the Prince of Wales*
*God bless the King I pray,*       *The true-born Prince of Wales*
*God Save the King;*                 *Sent us by Thee*
*Send Him Victorious*           *Grant us one favour more*
*Happy and Glorious*             *The King for to restore*
*Soon to Reign Over us*        *As Thou has done before*
*God Save the King.*                *The Familie.*

*God Bless the subjects all*      *God Save the Church I pray*
*And save both great and small*  *And Bless the Church I pray*
*in every station*                  *Pure to remain*
*That will bring home the King*  *Against all Heresie*
*Who has best right to reign*    *And Whigs Hypocrisie*
*It is the only thing*           *Who strive maliciously*
*Can save the Nation.*         *Her to defame.*

Less exotic Jacobites also commanded good prices, a typical example having a trumpet bowl engraved with a rose and two buds, an oak leaf and the motto FIAT (Plate 882) on a multiple-spiral air-twist stem which sold for £240. A very attractive and rarely seen example of the 'Boscobel oak' Jacobite on what is erroneously known as a Kit-Kat stem (Plate 872) made £440. (The true Kit-Kat has a plain stem ending with a true baluster, not like 117 which has an inverted baluster.) Of the two Williamites in the sale one was extraordinary in that the engraving (on a bell bowl above a true baluster stem) showed a continuous scene of William III with cavalry and infantry crossing the River Boyne in the middle of which was a riderless horse. Above the scene was, in script, IN GLORIOUS MEMORY OF THE CROSSING and below it the date (of the battle, not the glass), 1690. It compares with Plates 846 and 848 which are the more usual representations of the subject. The Smith glass made £420 despite a small chip in the foot.

Among the portrait glasses was one with an engraving in profile of the Duke of Cumberland with his full title engraved round it to form a circular medallion (Plate 918). The Duke's career as a military commander was erratic but when he defeated the Jacobites at Culloden he was a popular hero and these glasses would have been used to drink many a toast in his name. This example sold for £170 and the same price was obtained for a portrait glass of Sarah Siddons (Plate 938).

Many Newcastle light balusters are found engraved with the arms of Dutch cities, this sale including specimens with the arms of Amsterdam (£220), of Holland (stipple-engraved) (£300), Rotterdam (£240), Delft (£170) and

Overyssel (£170). As will be seen, stipple-engraved glasses bring particularly high prices, whatever the stem formation, authentic specimens by such artists as David Wolff (Plate 1,051) or Frans Greenwood always arousing great interest; a glass attributed to another stipple-engraver, J. Van den Blyk, sold for £300.

Privateer glasses were engraved to commemorate the success of privately owned frigates which, in the mid-1700s, harassed the French to great effect. Most privateers sailed from Bristol and the most famous of all was the Eagle Frigate commanded by Captain Dibden (*London Chronicle*, Apr. 11th 1757) and later by Captain Knill. The fact that they are associated with an opaque-white twist comprising a pair of spiral gauzes (Plates 940, 942 and 943) suggests that they were made by a glasshouse in Bristol. This sale yielded one of the rarest engravings SUCCESS TO THE LYON PRIVATEER of which only one other example is known and was bought for £500.

Enamelled glasses form another attractive and expensive section and enamelled glass, in the absence of indications to the contrary, is synonymous with the work of the Beilby family. The art of enamelling, usually in white but, exceptionally, in a full range of colours for the armorial and signed royal goblets which are probably the most highly prized of all eighteenth century glasses, was perfected by William and Mary, two of the seven children of William Beilby Senior who was a jeweller and silversmith in Durham. The family moved to Newcastle shortly before William Senior died in 1765. Another brother, Ralph, a skilled engraver of heraldic subjects, no doubt supervised the accuracy of the armorial designs.

The bulk of their work, however, consisted in the decoration of small wines (most frequently ogee or round-funnel bowls on double-series opaque-white twist stems, supporting the theory that these were stock lines of the glasshouses in the Newcastle area) with simple floral designs or charming country scenes with shepherds and shepherdesses tending their flocks; another series depicted such sports as skating and wildfowling, representations of Classical ruins forming a further large group. Although opaque twist stems are most frequently found in association with enamelling, it is found occasionally on air twists, Newcastle light balusters, plain stems, incised twists and even Silesian stems. No important specimens were included in this sale but consistently high prices were realised for even the simplest decoration; a band of fruiting vine on a very ordinary opaque-twist wine glass made £95 (Plate 1,127, but this has a bell bowl instead of a round funnel) and £250 was paid for a goblet with plain stem and an ogee bowl decorated in white enamel with a growing vine (Plate 1,113 shows the identical design on a dram glass).

As a rough guide to 1969 prices the following table might be useful but should be regarded only as an indication of price levels. Rarity of bowl formation, addition of engraving or enamelling or an unusual stem feature can considerably increase their value; conversely, defects such as chips on rim or foot will inevitably reduce their value.

| | |
|---|---|
| Under £10 | Jelly glasses, wines after 1800, rummers. |
| £10-£20 | Plain-stemmed glasses with drawn trumpet or bell bowl. |
| £20-£30 | Opaque twists, faceted stems, balustroids with simple knops; unknopped multiple-spiral air twists. |

| £30-£40 | Air twists with more interesting twists and single-knopped multiple-spiral air twists; balustroids with a series of simple knops; Silesian stemmed and faceted sweetmeats; opaque twists with knops. |
| £40-£60 | Air twists with two knops; incised twists, engraved rummers and goblets, sweetmeats with knopped stems. |
| £60-£100 | Ratafias and cordials; sweetmeats with attractive features; 'Newcastle' light balusters and air twists with some engraving; glasses with very simple enamel decoration; light balusters with good knops – Kit-Kat, annulated, etc.; wine glasses with Silesian stem; mead glasses, early wrythen ales. |
| £100-£200 | Heavy balusters; colour twists; attractively engraved 'Newcastle' balusters and air twists; Jacobites; Beilby enamelled glasses; good ratafias; Lynn glasses; sweetmeats with heavy knops. |
| £200-£400 | Rare heavy balusters – cylinder, acorn, mushroom; bobbin knops; important Jacobite and Williamite engravings; stipple engraving; armorial engravings; rare colour twists; air twists with more than three knops. |
| £400 and over | Superb cylinder, acorn and egg knops; signed Dutch engravings; superb enamelled glasses; rare colour twists; rare Jacobites; Anglo-Venetian glasses; perry or cider glasses; 'Amen' glasses; Privateers. |

# Values: (ii) in 1985

The effects of inflation and increasing interest in collecting English eighteenth century drinking glasses have greatly influenced prices. In some cases the changes have been surprisingly modest, in others very considerable indeed. All but the rarer forms of baluster or balustroid have hardly kept pace with inflation whilst enamel decoration or finely engraved glasses have risen dramatically. The following table summarises the present position as reflected in prices reached at auction. No major sale such as the Walter F. Smith sale in 1968 can be used as a single point of reference so the prices quoted are those realised during the past few years and, at best, can only be a rough guide to present day values.

| Below £50 | Bonnet glasses, plain stems. |
| £50-£100 | Sweetmeats, air and opaque twists. |
| £100-£250 | Good balusters, balustroids, incised twists, some Jacobites, engraved glasses, cordials, ratafias. |
| £250-£500 | Colour twists, Jacobites, Williamites, mead glasses, heavy balusters with good knops, unusual engravings. |
| £500-£1,000 | Engraved glasses of finest quality, the best heavy balusters, engraved cider glasses. |
| £1,000-£5,000 | Beilbys, engraved portrait Jacobites, stipple engravings, seventeenth century English glasses. |
| Over £5,000 | Armorial Beilbys, Amen glasses (£8,000 in 1980), Royal Armorial Beilbys (£19,500 in 1975). |

# 8.

# Reproductions, Soda Glasses and Forgeries

**B**ooks cannot be infallible guides: they serve as a valuable introduction to a subject and can impart a great deal of useful information. In most subjects connoted by 'Applied arts', however, they should lead to handling of the specimens themselves, a maxim certainly true of glass. No amount of reading can completely equip one to distinguish between the genuine and the spurious, between the original and its copy. Nevertheless, photography does help to bridge the gap between verbal description and specimen: to find an illustration which closely parallels a glass which is offered for sale encourages the prospective purchaser to treat the offer seriously and to make further inquiries. Even from photographs one can learn to look suspiciously upon glasses with a very high domed foot or upon specimens purporting to date to about 1700 which do not have a folded rim.

Such facts will soon be apparent to the collector with only modest experience: it is by no means so easy to recognise the glasses of the mid-nineteenth century, made after the patterns of the eighteenth century, complete with pontil-mark, folded foot and decorative twists and intended to demonstrate the glassmaker's mastery of his craft. The first differentiating characteristic is design, for the glassmaker of 1851 has unconsciously absorbed the feeling of his period and his trumpet bowl will tend to flare out in sympathy with its flamboyance; the second lies in construction, the 1851 glass being markedly freer from the slight imperfections, the stresses and striations and tool marks to be seen in glasses of a century earlier.

**Fakes and Forgeries**

Photography will not completely protect the collector from the forgeries, many of them imported from the Continent, which are the inevitable consequence of rising prices. Hundreds of these have appeared in this country of recent years and many dealers and collectors have been deceived. Passing them on to the antique trade has become a highly developed sales technique, usually following a familiar pattern. A country gentleman in well-worn tweeds enters an antique shop and asks whether there would be any interest in a few old glasses which he has in a shopping-basket. He is clearing up the estate of an aunt and has found half a dozen in a cupboard. They looked rather old and might be worth a few pounds. The dealer releases them from the amateurish packing and to his delight finds that they are a set of mixed twists - cotton and air - very desirable and selling at upwards of forty pounds each. The country gentleman wonders whether they might be worth five pounds apiece, the glasses have pontil-mark, folded foot and striated bowls and the dealer is only too ready to conclude the purchase at the suggested price.

It is not long before he discovers that the glasses are virtually worthless but before then he may well have sold some to unsuspecting collectors – a friend of mine keeps a row of his 'mistakes' in the cloakroom – and either his purse or his reputation will have suffered. Where has he made his mistake? He certainly could not have learned to detect such fakes from photographs, but even a slight experience of handling genuine glasses would have taught him that these were much too light in weight and that they lacked the ring, colour and quality of lead glass. Photographs might have warned him that these were too good to be true, for folded feet are only infrequently found with air twists, very rarely indeed with opaque twists and not at all with mixed twists. Finally, he ought to have been very suspicious about any set of glasses of that date. Fortunately forgers frequently overreach themselves!

## Soda glasses

Mention of weight and ring leads to a brief consideration of another type of glass which comprises neither copies nor fakes but which sometimes confuses the inexperienced collector. This is soda glass, light in weight, the metal containing seeds and blemishes and usually associated with small, poor quality versions of lead glasses. Most stem formations can be found in soda glass except mixed twists and faceted stems, the Silesian and coarse incised-twist stems being most frequently encountered; it is thought that these glasses were made for export: they were certainly intended for a cheaper market. There should be little difficulty in recognising soda metal but in case of doubt physical and chemical tests are possible. Since glass fluoresces under ultra-violet light according to the elements of its composition, a distinction is easily seen between lead and soda glass, the former emitting a barely discernible blue light, the latter having a yellow content clearly seen on the rim. The chemical test demands extremely careful application. If a minute spot of hydrofluoric acid is applied to an unimportant part of the glass such as the pontil-mark and a second spot of sulphide of ammonia is superimposed the reaction will produce either a black or a white mark; black indicates the presence of lead, white the presence of soda. The chemicals should be washed off immediately after the test, and the hydrofluoric acid which is corrosive and highly dangerous should be handled and stored with great care.

Such tests are not normally required but there are cases such as colour twists, for example, where differentiation between a genuine lead glass and its contemporary Continental counterpart or modern reproduction is all important in determining its value. Fakes and forgeries do not always involve the metal of the glass but are usually related to value; whenever prices become exceptionally high the forger is quick to take advantage of demand; heavy balusters, mixed and colour twists, Jacobite, Williamite and 'Amen' glasses all need to be examined expertly before purchase. Engraving is all too easily applied to genuine glasses of the correct type but recent engraving is raw and white and the skill of the forger is rarely equal to the exact reproduction of the work of the eighteenth century craftsman.

### Repaired Glasses

A number of firms specialise in the repair of broken glasses and are so skilful that it is extremely difficult to detect the replacement of a broken bowl with another of the same period or to be sure that stem, foot and bowl are parts of the original glass. The important test is that of balance and grace; ugly glasses were rare in the eighteenth century. Many glasses have been slightly altered to disguise a chip on the rim of either bowl or foot and until recently such repairs have reduced the value to less than half. Even today imperfect specimens are shunned by many collectors but they find a much readier market than ten years ago, presumably among collectors who can no longer afford the very high prices of the rarer types in perfect condition. Most repairs fall into two categories – trimming or flattening. The only remedy for a chip on the rim of the bowl is to remove a sufficient depth by grinding down. This can alter the balance of the glass and can also be detected by the elimination of the rounded contour of the original rim caused by reheating the sheared-off bowl in the mouth of the furnace. This was necessary for pleasant drinking and will be found in all eighteenth century glasses in original condition. A sharp, ground-off edge is evidence either of repair or later date. Chips on the foot can be treated in the same way and if the chip is large enough the reduction in diameter of the foot can make the glass look top-heavy; if only one side of the foot is ground down the stem will no longer be in the centre. The normal rule that the radius of the foot should not vary and that its diameter should at least equal that of the bowl is a good guide. Alternatively, if the chip is on the underside of the foot only it can can be removed by flattening, that is by polishing it out. Such flats are readily seen by examination in a good light – indeed the difference in thickness will be felt simply by passing the rim of the foot through thumb and finger.

# Notes on the Plates

## Descriptions

Descriptions of the glasses follow a regular pattern, each entry being divided into eight parts which are always enumerated in the same order.

- (a) Purpose of glass (wine, cordial, ale, etc.)
- (b) The bowl (shape, moulding, decoration, engraving)
- (c) The stem (knops in order from the top, the outer twist followed by the inner in the case of double-series twists)
- (d) The foot (shape, if other than conical, moulding, decoration)
- (e) Height in inches
- (f) Approximate date
- (g) Provenance (if other than English) and Collections (where known)
- (h) Present owner (public collections only)

The figure and plate numbers given in the captions to photographs of glasses from the Hartshorne Collection refer to those of Hartshorne's own book, *Old English Glasses*, details of which appear in the Bibliography.

## Abbreviations

Some abbreviations are already well established in glass literature, MSAT for multiple-spiral air twist, for example; several others listed below have been devised to avoid wearisome repetition in the captions. General acceptance of them would provide writers with a useful series of shorthand descriptions of particular value in cataloguing.

| | |
|---|---|
| DF | Domed foot |
| D & FF | Domed and folded foot |
| DSAT | Double-series air twist |
| DSOT | Double-series opaque twist |
| FF | Folded foot |
| IB | Inverted baluster |
| MSAT | Multiple-spiral air twist |
| MSOT | Multiple-spiral opaque twist |
| OW | Opaque white |
| RF | Round funnel |
| SSAT | Single-series air twist |
| SSOT | Single-series opaque twist |

## Terminology

Most of the terms used in the captions and in the classification will be self-evident or readily understood by reference to the appropriate plates or line-drawings. A few require definition, however, if readers are to be saved the trouble of constant reference to other works: if fuller information is required reference to the Index will direct the reader to relevant entries in the Bibliography.

**ALE**: a glass of 3-5oz capacity on stems of varying lengths; the bowl is in most cases the elongation of an ogee or round-funnel wine.

**BALUSTER**: strictly a form of knop illustrated in Plates 131-42, but loosely employed to describe a stem with any of the knops in sections 2 and 3.

**BALUSTROID**: a stem containing knops of small and relatively insignificant character.

**CHAMPAGNE**: a glass of 4-6oz capacity, the bowl being wide and relatively shallow, most frequently of double-ogee form. It must be suitable as a drinking glass. The term is of doubtful authenticity as there is no proof that this shape of bowl was used for champagne in the eighteenth century.

**COLLAR**: a sharp-edged flange frequently occurring between bowl and stem and between stem and foot. The decorative bands encircling stems, especially of air twists, e.g. vermiform (if wavy) or coiled, are also referred to as 'collars'.

**CORDIAL**: a glass of 1oz capacity on a tall, stout stem.

**DEBASED PEDESTAL STEM**: a stem in which the moulding has become indefinite, the shoulders rounded.

**DRAM GLASS**: capacity up to 3oz; short or rudimentary stem.

**FLAMMIFORM**: a decorative effect achieved by forming spikes of glass protruding from the bowl and usually at the termination of wyrthen moulding.

**FLUTE CORDIAL**: *see* Ratafia.

**GADROONING**: a decorative effect obtained by pinching the glass into ribs, at the base of a bowl for example.

**GIN GLASS**: a miniature wine glass.

**GOBLET**: a glass with large bowl.

**JELLY GLASS**: short glasses with rudimentary stem or set directly on the foot, intended for jellies or ices; often with single or double handles.

**KNOP**: a protuberance in the stem of a glass.

**MEAD GLASS**: an early glass with cup-shaped bowl which is gadrooned at the base: a term of doubtful authenticity.

**MONTEITH**: small glass with double-ogee or cup-shaped bowl, rather wider than a jelly glass and intended for salt or, possibly, for sweetmeats.

**'NIPT DIAMOND WAIES'**: a decorative effect formed by pinching the glass, at the base of a bowl for example, into diamond-shaped compartments: the phrase is taken from Ravenscroft's usage in 1675.

**POSSET GLASS**: a low cylindrical vessel equipped with handles and a spout.

**PRUNT**: a circular or oval blob of glass added for decorative purposes and impressed to give dimpled (raspberry) effect.

**RATAFIA**: (also known as a 'flute cordial'): capacity 1-1½oz; characterised by very narrow bowl.

**RUMMER**: capacity more than 4oz: a term applied to small goblets after c.1780.

**SWEETMEAT**: similar in form to champagne but unsuited for drinking by reason of dentated, cut or otherwise irregular rim. Possibly all so-called 'champagnes' were for sweetmeats.

**TOASTING GLASS**: having an exceedingly slender stem, easily snapped between the fingers.

**TOASTMASTER'S GLASS**: a cordial or dram glass with deceptive bowl.

# Venetian Decorative Features
## *Soda Glass*

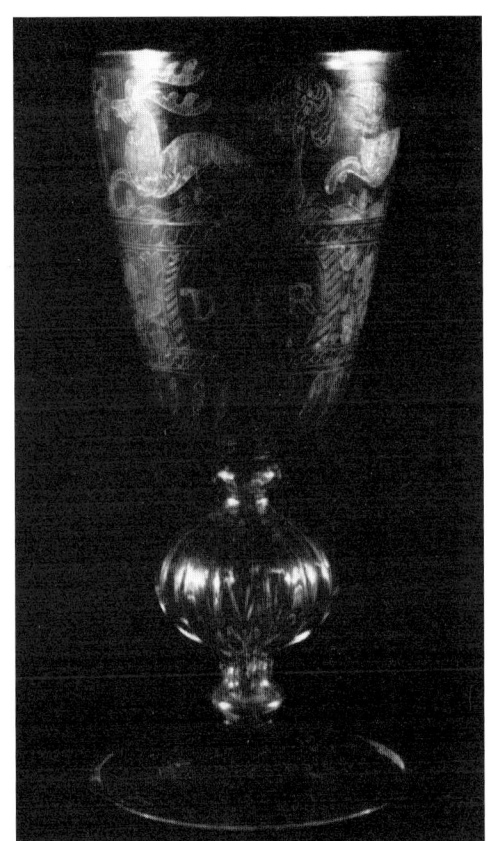

**1 and 2.** Goblet in soda glass; RF bowl engraved in diamond-point (attributed to Anthony de Lysle) JOHN JONE, DIER 1581 and the Royal Elizabethan Arms. Ht. 8½ins. c.1581. A Verzelini goblet.          *Victoria and Albert Museum.*

**3 and 4.** Goblet in soda glass; ovate bowl with engraving in diamond-point (attr. to Anthony de Lysle), the inscription TO HIS BROTHER RICHARD GREENHAL and a panel enclosing the date 1584; gadrooned hollow IB knop between collars; FF, damaged and repaired. Ht. 6⅛ins. c.1584. A Verzelini goblet.          *Christie's.*

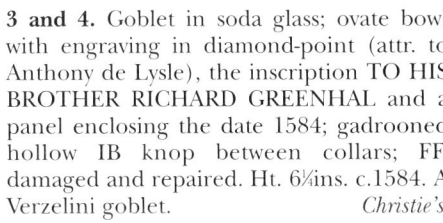

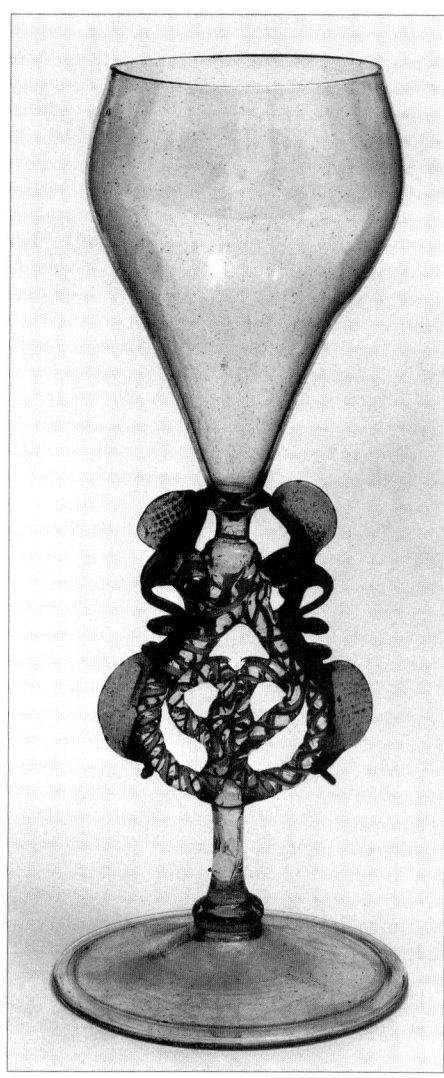

**5.** Goblet; 'Façon de Venise'; cup-shaped bowl with tapering base; serpentine stem with pincered wings; FF. Ht. 8ins. c.1675. Netherlands. *Sotheby's.*

**6.** Wine glass; 'Façon de Venise'; funnel bowl inscribed below rim in diamond-point A MONSIEUR GERRARD BERNSAW...; serpentine stem with blue pincered fringes; flat foot inscribed in diamond-point MONSIEUR GLAÜBERG AT FAIT...LE 12 XBRE 84. Ht. 6½ins. 1684. German or Low Countries. *Sotheby's.*

**7.** Goblet (lead glass); 'Façon de Venise' conical bowl decorated round base with 'nipt diamond waies'; wrythen serpentine stem with pincered fringes; FF. Ht. 9⅜ins. c.1680. *Ex Beves Collection. Sotheby's.*

Venetian Decorative Features – Soda Glass

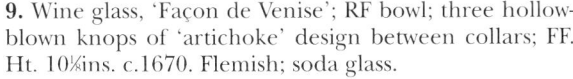

**8.** Goblet; bucket bowl, gadrooned base; wrythen serpentine stem, pincered fringes; (replacement silver and wood foot). Anglo-Venetian. Ht. 11⅛ins. c.1685.

*Sotheby's.*

**9.** Wine glass, 'Façon de Venise'; RF bowl; three hollow-blown knops of 'artichoke' design between collars; FF. Ht. 10¼ins. c.1670. Flemish; soda glass.

*Harvey's Wine Museum, Bristol.*

**10.** Wine glass, 'Façon de Venise'; conical bowl; two hollow-blown knops between collars; FF. Ht. 6⅞ins. c.1680. Netherlands; soda glass.

*[Walter F.] Smith Collection. Harvey's Wine Museum, Bristol.*

Venetian Decorative Features – Soda Glass

**11.** Wine glass, 'Façon de Venise';
conical bowl with 'nipt diamond waies';
hollow-blown quatrefoil knop between
collars; radially moulded FF. Ht. 5¼ins.
c.1680. Netherlands; soda glass.
*Smith Collection.*
*Harvey's Wine Museum, Bristol.*

**13.** Wine glass, 'Façon de Venise'; flared
funnel bowl over double collar and
quatrefoil knop, basal knop; FF. Ht.
6ins. c.1665. Netherlands.      *Christie's.*

**12.** Wine glass, 'Façon de Venise';
funnel bowl; double collar above
hollow-blown quatrefoil knop; FF. Ht.
5¼ins. c.1665. Soda glass.
*Pilkington Glass Museum, St. Helens.*

Venetian Decorative Features – Soda Glass

**14.** Goblet; bucket bowl, 'nipt diamond waies' on the underside; two hollow-blown quatrefoil knops; FF. Ht. 7¼ins. c.1685. Despite the crizzled glass and traces of lead this goblet is considered to be of Netherlandish manufacture.
*Ex Horridge and W.F. Smith Collections.*
*Sotheby's.*

**15.** Wine glass, 'Façon de Venise'; pointed RF bowl with trailed threads and spiked gadrooning; two hollow-blown knops between collars flanked by scroll handles; FF. Ht. 7⅜ins. c.1670. Netherlands; soda glass.
*Harvey's Wine Museum, Bristol.*

**16.** Wine glass; pointed RF bowl; latticino stem and foot, stem comprising two hollow-blown knops between collars. Ht. 5ins. c.1680. Anglo-Venetian; soda glass.
*Harvey's Wine Museum, Bristol.*

Venetian Decorative Features – Soda Glass

**17.** Wine glass, 'vitro di trina'; RF bowl; hollow-blown flattened and IB knops between collars; FF. Ht. 6⅛ins. 16th/17th century. Venetian; soda glass.
*Harvey's Wine Museum, Bristol.*

**18.** Wine glass, 'vitro di trina'; RF bowl; hollow-blown flattened and IB knops between collars; FF. Ht. 6⅛ins. 16th/17th century. Venetian; soda glass.
*Harvey's Wine Museum, Bristol.*

**19.** Bottle decanter; lipped pan; spherical body decorated with 'nipt diamond waies'; swan-neck handle; FF. Ht. 7⅜ins. c.1665. English; brownish soda glass.
*Pilkington Glass Museum, St. Helens.*

**20.** Goblet; funnel bowl with gadrooned and trailed ornament; collar above hollow IB knop with five applied raspberry prunts and containing a pair of William and Mary 3d coins dated 1689, collar; FF. Ht. 8ins. c.1690. *Christie's.*

# English Glass of Lead

**21.** Decanter jug; crizzled body decorated with 'nipt diamond waies' and pincered vertical bands with a wrythen handle; contemporary silver cover. Ht. 9½ins. c.1775. Attributed to Ravenscroft. *Sotheby's.*

**22.** Decanter of crizzled glass decorated with 'nipt diamond waies' and seven vertical winged ribs; plain loop handle; later gilt-metal foot. Ht. 7⅞ins. c.1674. Attributed to Ravenscroft.
*Ex Mrs. Richards Collection. Sotheby's.*

**23.** Goblet; cup bowl with vertical moulding continuing into stem which has the raven's head seal used by George Ravenscroft and raspberry prunts; moulded, high D & FF. Ht. 6½ins. c.1678.
*Wm. Buckley Collection.*
*Victoria and Albert Museum.*

**24.** Wine glass; RF bowl with spiked gadrooning and engraved in diamond-point with deer-hunt below inscription DEGESONT HEYT VAN DE HEER VAN YERST (To the health of the Master of Yerst); hollow-blown quatrefoil knop between collars; basal knop; engraved FF. Ht. 6ins. c.1681. Probably from the Savoy Glasshouse; engraved in Holland.
*Pilkington Glass Museum, St. Helens.*

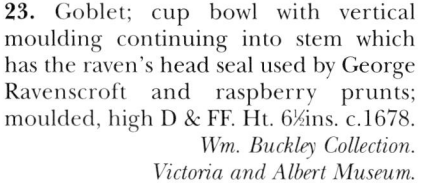

**25.** Wine glass; funnel bowl; hollow IB knop; FF. Ht. 6½ins. c.1670. Of light metal; perhaps a Greene's pattern glass.
*Sotheby's.*

Venetian Decorative Features – English Glass of Lead

**26.** Wine glass after Greene pattern; pointed RF bowl; hollow-blown knop between collars; FF. Ht. 7ins. c.1680. Thin, slightly opaque-white metal. *Hartshorne Collection.*

**28.** Wine glass; RF bowl with spiked gadrooning; hollow-blown quatrefoil knop; FF. Ht. 7ins. c.1675. Hawley-Bishopp period.

**27.** Wine glass; conical bowl, solid base; hollow-blown quatrefoil knop between collars. FF. Ht. 5⅜ins. c.1680.
*Smith Collection. Harvey's Wine Museum, Bristol.*

Venetian Decorative Features – English Glass of Lead

**29.** Goblet; slightly waisted RF bowl; hollow knop containing 6d. piece of William III dated 1690, between collars; small basal knop; FF. Ht. 9ins. c.1690.
*Victoria and Albert Museum.*

**30.** Goblet; pointed RF bowl; hollow-blown knop (containing silver 6d. dated 1703) decorated with five raspberry prunts, above a hollow IB knop; FF. Ht. 8⅝ins. c.1705. *Cecil Higgins Museum, Bedford.*

**31.** Wine glass; bucket bowl; rope twist round a raspberry prunt between two small knops; basal knop; FF. Ht. 7ins. c.1700.
*Hartshorne Collection.*

**32.** Bowl and cover; pear-shaped body with band of trailed loops and 'nipt diamond waies'; pair of ribbed handles; cover similarly decorated and terminating in rope-twist handle above a frilled collar. Ht. 9ins. c.1690. *Cecil Higgins Museum, Bedford.*

Venetian Decorative Features – English Glass of Lead

**33.** Flask; ovoid body with pinched strapwork and raspberry prunts; trailed monogram A H (*Aqua Hierosolymurum* = Jerusalem water?). Ht. 4⅜ins. c.1700.

*Hartshorne Collection.*

**34.** Reverse of 33 showing trailed letter H.

**35.** Decanter-jug; vermicular collar at base of conical neck; onion-shaped body with wrythen gadrooning; pinched swan-neck handle; stopper tooled to match gadrooning. Ht. 5⅛ins. c.1685. This specimen appears to be the only one to survive.

*Pilkington Glass Museum, St. Helens.*

Venetian Decorative Features – English Glass of Lead

**36.** Bowl and cover, both gadrooned; the bowl has threaded decoration below rim; the cover terminates in a beaded knop. Ht. 6¼ins. c.1700. Compare with posset pot in Thorpe, *English and Irish Glass*, Plate lxxvi.

**37.** Mead glass; cup bowl with gadrooned base; double knop above plain stem; basal knop; FF. Ht. 5⅛ins. c.1700.

*Smith Collection.*
*Harvey's Wine Museum, Bristol.*

**38.** Goblet; cup bowl, gadrooned lower half; hollow stem, round knop over IB; FF. Ht. 8½ins. c.1700.

*Christie's.*

**39.** Mead glass; cup-shaped bowl, gadrooned lower half; flattened knop, basal knop; FF. Ht. 5¾ins. c.1710.

*Sotheby's.*

Venetian Decorative Features – English Glass of Lead

**40.** Sweetmeat; wide shallow bowl; collar, annulated knop, basal knop; FF. Ht. 4ins. c.1720.
*Sotheby's.*

**41.** Goblet; cup-shaped bowl, gadrooned lower part; stem comprising large hollow knop containing William III sixpence dated 1696 above a plain section and collars; FF. Ht. 8½ins. c. 1700.
*Christie's.*

**42.** Sweetmeat; shallow bucket bowl with everted rim and gadrooned lower half; straight stem between collars; FF. Ht. 4ins. c.1730. *Christie's.*

**43.** Sweetmeat; 'mortar'-shaped bowl, gadrooned lower part, folded rim; indented straight stem; FF. Ht. 3⅜ins. c.1730.
*Ex Sir Percival David Collection. Christie's.*

**44.** Bowl and cover; cup-shaped body with band of trailed loops and 'nipt diamond waies' which extend to D & FF; cover decorated to match terminating in crown knop with four pinched strapwork loops and trefoil pincered finial. Ht. 15ins. c.1675. Ravenscroft period.

*Hartshorne Collection.*

**45.** Dwarf ale glass; part wrythen bowl; collar, pincered winged knop and basal knop; FF. Ht. 5½ins. c.1700.

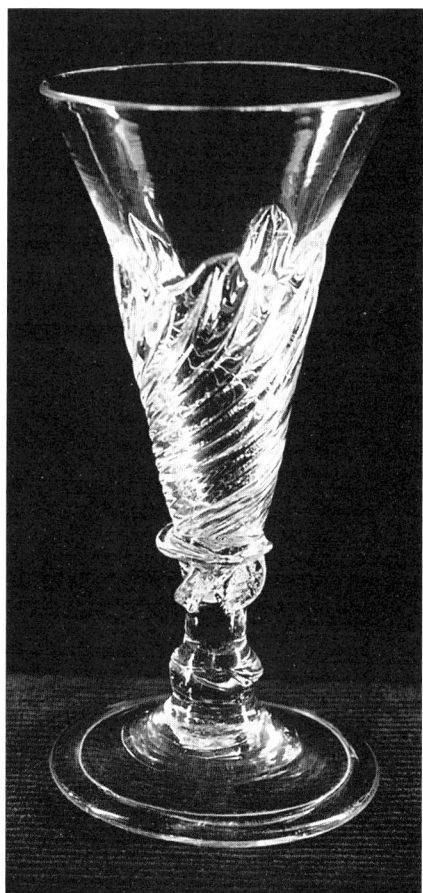

**46.** Dwarf ale glass; wrythen bowl with flammiform fringe; collar, winged knop, basal knop; FF. Ht. 5⅛ins. c.1700.      *Asprey.*

**47.** Dwarf ale glass; part wrythen bowl with flammiform fringe; collar, five-winged pincered knop and basal knop; FF. Ht. 5⅜ins. c.1700.

*Cecil Higgins Museum, Bedford.*

Venetian Decorative Features – English Glass of Lead

**48.** Dwarf ale glass; part wrythen bowl with flammiform fringe; wrythen knop; FF. Ht. 6ins. c.1700. *Smith Collection; S.G. Hewlett Collection. Harvey's Wine Museum, Bristol.*

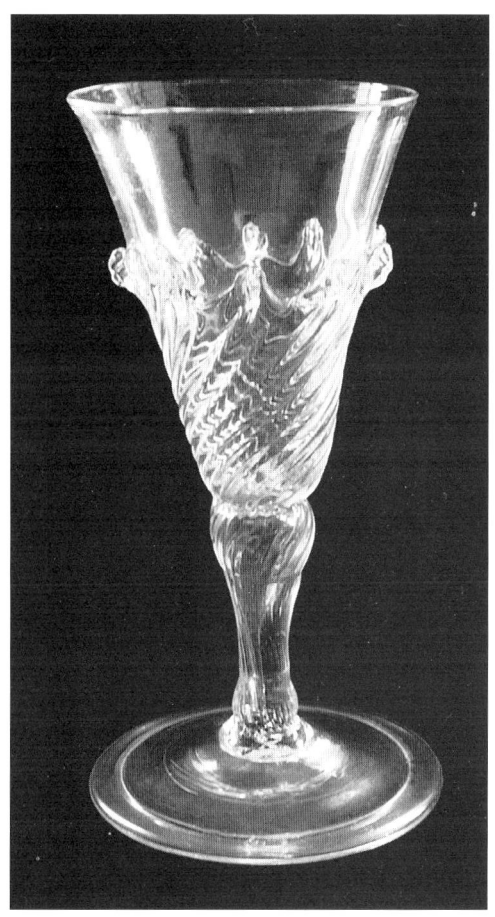

**49.** Ale glass; fluted bowl with flammiform fringe; short stem with teared shoulder and basal knops; FF. Ht. 5¼ins. c.1710. *Asprey.*

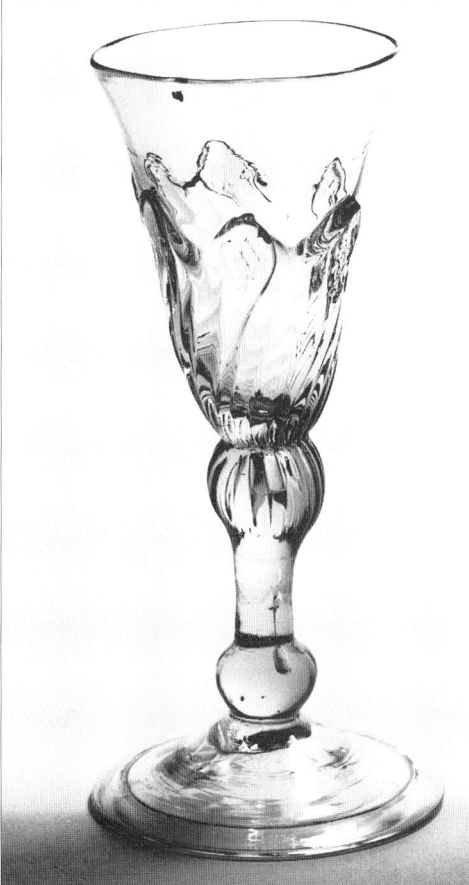

**50.** Ale glass; wrythen gadrooning lower part of bowl; short plain stem between knops; FF. c.1700. *Asprey.*

**51.** Ale glass; funnel bowl with wrythen moulding and flammiform gadrooning; shoulder and basal knops. FF. Ht. 6ins. c.1700.

*Sotheby's.*

# II
# Heavy Balusters

**52.** Goblet; conical bowl, solid base; IB with tear; FF. Ht. 6⅜ins. c.1700.

*Hartshorne Collection.*

**53.** Goblet; funnel bowl, solid base with tear; IB with tear; D & FF. Ht. 8ins. c.1700.

**54.** Wine glass; funnel bowl, solid base with tear; IB with tear; basal knop; FF. Ht. 5⅜ins. c.1710.

**56.** Goblet; RF bowl scratch-engraved WILLIAM RAMPSHAW OF SAHAM EX DONO THOS SHINN ESQR 1762; teared IB stem; FF. Ht. 11¼ins. c.1762 but glass c.1700. *Christie's.*

**55.** Goblet; RF bowl engraved with fruiting vine; IB with large tear, basal knop; DF. Ht. 13¼ins. c.1730. *Christie's.*

**57.** Wine glass; cup-topped bowl; IB knop with tear; FF. Ht. 5¼ins. c.1700.

58. Goblet; RF bowl; round knop, IB and basal knop, all teared; FF. Ht. 11¼ins. c.1700.
 *Pilkington Glass Museum, St. Helens.*

59. Wine glass; bell bowl, solid base; IB with tear and basal knop; FF. Ht. 5½ins. c.1710.

60. Wine glass; conical bowl, solid base with tear; IB knop with tear; FF. Ht. 5¼ins. c.1700.
 *Tibbenham Collection, Ipswich Museum.*

61. Wine glass; RF bowl, solid base; IB with tear, basal knop; D & FF. Ht. 6⅛ins. c.1700. *Christie's.*

Heavy Balusters

**62.** Goblet; pointed RF bowl, solid base; heavy teared knop, basal knop; FF. Ht. 7ins. c.1700.

*Tibbenham Collection, Ipswich Museum.*

**63.** Toastmaster's glass; deceptive funnel bowl; heavy ball knop above straight stem with tear; FF. Ht. 5ins. c.1720.

*Tibbenham Collection, Ipswich Museum.*

**64.** Wine glass; funnel bowl, solid base with tear; elongated teared IB; FF. Ht. 5⅜ins. c.1700.

*Cecil Higgins Museum, Bedford.*

**65.** Wine glass; pointed RF bowl, solid base; teared ovoid knop, teared basal knop; FF. Ht. 7ins. c.1700.

*Tibbenham Collection,*
*Ipswich Museum.*

**66.** Wine glass; bell bowl, solid base; teared angular knop; FF. Ht. 4⅜ins. c.1720.

*Tibbenham Collection,*
*Ipswich Museum.*

**67.** Wine glass; bell bowl; squat IB over plain section; FF. Ht. 6½ins. c.1720.

*Tibbenham Collection,*
*Ipswich Museum.*

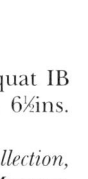

**68.** Wine glass; bell bowl, solid base with tear; 3-ringed annulated knop; FF. Ht. 6ins. c.1720.

*Tibbenham Collection,*
*Ipswich Museum.*

Heavy Balusters

**69.** Goblet; conical bowl, solid base; wide angular and basal knops; D & FF. Ht. 8ins. c.1710.

*Tibbenham Collection, Ipswich Museum.*

**70.** Goblet; RF bowl; IB and basal knops with tears; FF. Ht. 8½ins. c.1720.

**71.** Wine glass; RF bowl, solid base; wide angular and basal knops, both teared; D & FF. Ht. 5¾ins. c.1700.

**72.** Goblet; RF bowl, solid base; wide angular and basal knops, both teared; FF. Ht. 8¼ins. c.1710.

**73.** Wine glass; conical bowl, solid base; wide angular and basal knops, both teared; FF. Ht. 7¼ins. c.1700.

**74.** Wine glass; bell bowl, solid base; flattened knop above teared wide angular and basal knops; FF. Ht. 6¼ins. c.1715.

**75.** Wine glass; funnel bowl, solid base with tear; collar above wide angular knop and teared swelled knop; FF. Ht. 5⅜ins. c.1700.

**76.** Wine glass; funnel bowl, solid base, cushioned; angular knop above teared swelled knop; terraced foot. Ht. 5¼ins. c.1725.

**77.** Wine glass; bell bowl, solid base; 7-ringed annulated knop over small baluster; FF. Ht. 6ins. c.1725.

**78.** Sweetmeat; panel-moulded bowl; 5-ringed annulated knop over ball and basal knops; domed and terraced foot. Ht. 5½ins. c.1725.

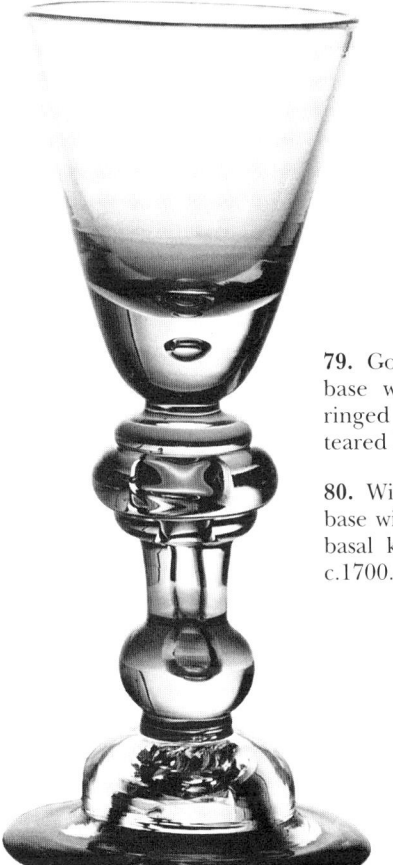

**79.** Goblet; funnel bowl, solid base with tear, cushioned; 3-ringed annulated knop above teared IB; FF. Ht. 9ins. c.1715.

**80.** Wine glass; RF bowl, solid base with tear; annulated knop, basal knop; D & FF. Ht. 6ins. c.1700.  *Christie's.*

**81.** Wine glass; bell bowl, solid base; 5-ringed annulated knop over true baluster. Ht. 7ins. c.1715.

**82.** Wine glass; bell bowl, solid base; 5-ringed annulated knop over true baluster. Ht. 6½ins. c.1725.
*Tibbenham Collection, Ipswich Museum.*

**83.** Dram glass; funnel bowl, solid base with tear; 3-ringed annulated knop; basal knop; DF. Ht. 5¼ins. c.1715.

**84.** Wine glass; tulip bowl, solid base; drop knop; D & FF. Ht. 6½ins. c.1710.

**85.** Goblet; tulip bowl, solid base; drop knop; D & FF. Ht. 8¾ins. c.1710.
*Tibbenham Collection, Ipswich Museum.*

**86.** Wine glass; tulip bowl, solid base; teared drop knop; D & FF. Ht. 6¾ins. c.1700.
*Smith Collection. Harvey's Wine Museum, Bristol.*

Heavy Balusters

**87.** Wine glass; lipped bucket bowl; flattened knop above teared drop knop and basal knop; D & FF. Ht. 5⅞ins. c.1710.

**88.** Wine glass; bell bowl, solid base; drop knop above squat true baluster; D & FF. Ht. 7ins. c.1710.

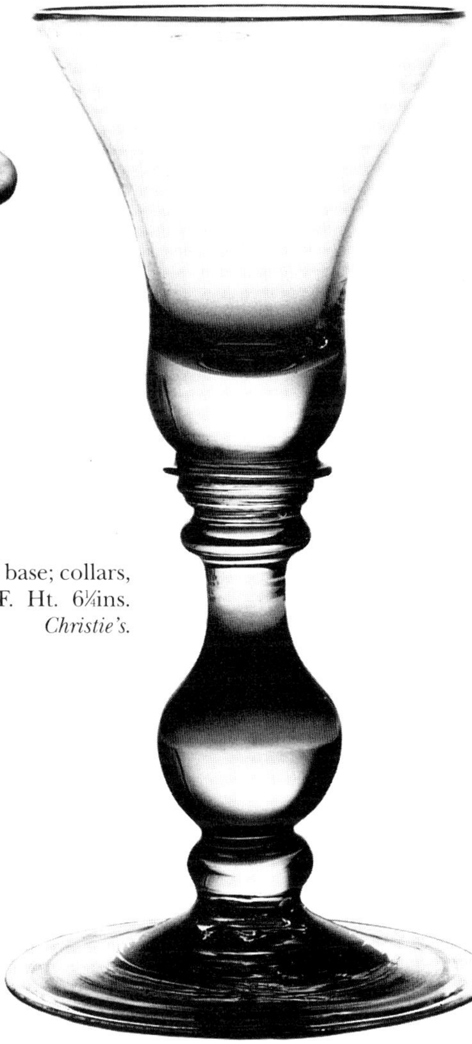

**89.** Wine glass; bell bowl, solid base; flattened knop over drop knop, true baluster and basal knops; DF. c.1710.
*Christie's.*

**90.** Wine glass; bell bowl, solid base; collars, true baluster, basal knop; FF. Ht. 6¼ins. c.1700.
*Christie's.*

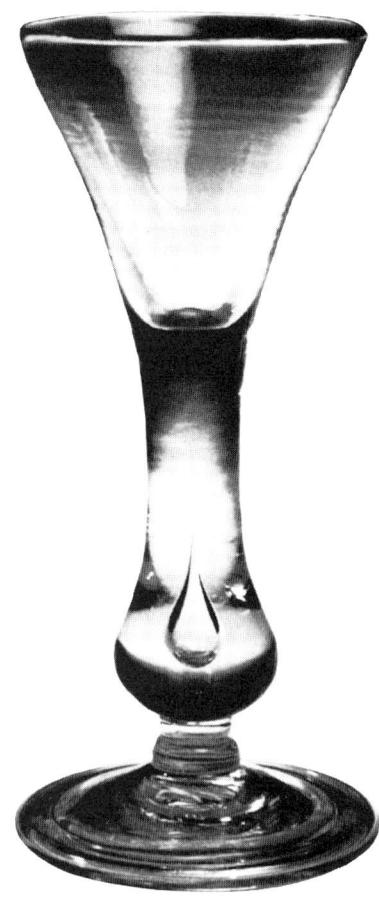

**91.** Wine glass; bell bowl, solid base; drop knop; DF. Ht. 5⅜ins. c.1710.

**92.** Wine glass; drawn trumpet bowl; teared drop knop; FF. Ht. 6⅛ins. c.1710.
*Asprey.*

**93.** Wine glass; drawn trumpet bowl extending into a drop knop; FF. Ht. 6ins. c.1725.

*Tibbenham Collection,
Ipswich Museum.*

**94.** Wine glass; bell bowl, solid teared base; large true baluster with large tear, between cushion knops; D & FF. Ht. 6ins. c.1710.    *Sotheby's.*

Heavy Balusters

**95.** Wine glass; funnel bowl, solid base with tear; teared ball knop; FF. Ht. 6¾ins. c.1700.

**96.** Wine glass; RF bowl, solid base; ball knop with tear; flat foot. Ht. 4⅜ins. c.1700.

*Tibbenham Collection, Ipswich Museum.*

**97.** Wine glass; bell bowl, solid base; annular knop, round knop and basal knop with tears; terraced foot. Ht. 5½ins. c.1710. *Asprey.*

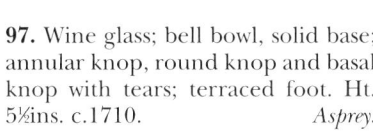

**98.** Dram glass; RF bowl, solid base; ball knop and basal knop; FF. Ht. 4¼ins. c.1700.
*Hartshorne Collection. (Fig. 305).*

**99.** Wine glass; funnel bowl; two ball knops and basal knop; FF. Ht. 5¾ins. c.1715.

**100.** Goblet; round funnel bowl; teared mushroom knop over teared basal knop; FF. Ht. 9½ins. c.1710.

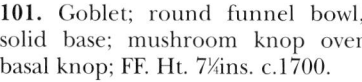

**101.** Goblet; round funnel bowl, solid base; mushroom knop over basal knop; FF. Ht. 7¼ins. c.1700.

**102.** Wine glass; thistle bowl, solid base; teared mushroom knop over basal knop; FF. Ht. 7½ins. c.1710.

103. Wine glass; round funnel bowl, solid base; teared acorn knop over basal knop; FF. Ht. 5½ins. c.1700.

104. Wine glass; pan-topped bowl, solid base; teared acorn knop over basal knop; FF. Ht. 5⅝ins. c.1710.

105. Goblet; thistle bowl, solid base; acorn knop over basal knop; FF. Ht. 8½ins. c.1710.

106. Wine glass; funnel bowl, everted rim; acorn knop over basal knop; FF. Ht. 8ins. c.1720. *Christie's.*

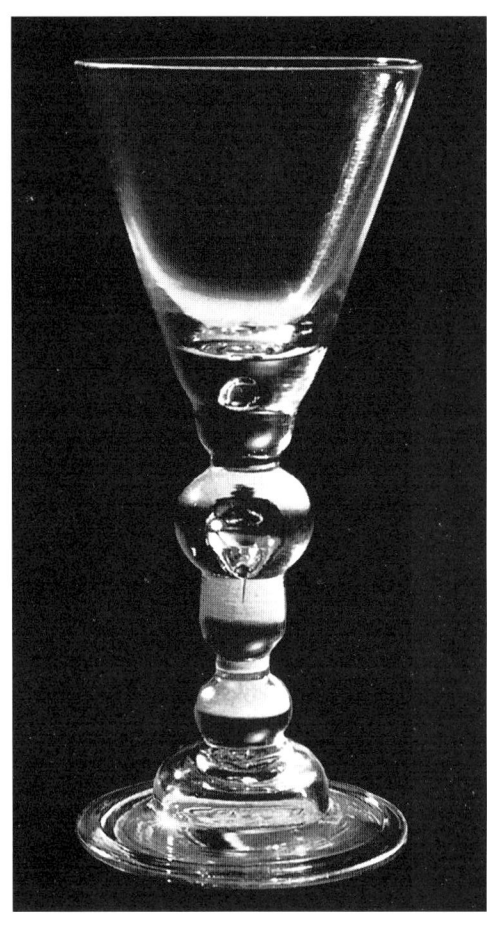

**107.** Wine glass; conical bowl, solid base with tear; acorn knop with tear, ball knop; D & FF. c.1710. *Asprey.*

**108.** Wine glass; funnel bowl, solid base with tear; cylinder knop with large tear, basal knop; FF. Ht. 5½ins. c.1700. *Christies.*

**109.** Wine glass; bell bowl, teared solid base; flattened knop and collar above teared cylinder knop with cushion knop and basal knop; D & FF. Ht. 6⅜ins. c.1710. *Cecil Higgins Museum, Bedford.*

**110.** Wine glass; bell bowl, teared solid base; flattened knop and collar above teared cylinder knop; basal knop; FF. Ht. 7ins. c.1710. *Smith Collection. Harvey's Wine Museum, Bristol.*

**111.** Wine glass; funnel bowl, solid base; teared egg knop; FF. Ht. 5⅞ins. c.1700.

**112.** Wine glass; pointed RF bowl, solid base, everted rim; four knops; DF. Ht. 6ins. c.1715.
*Tibbenham Collection, Ipswich Museum.*

**113.** Wine glass; RF bowl, solid base with tear; egg-knop with large tear; FF. Ht. 7ins. c.1710. *Sotheby's.*

**114.** Ale glass; funnel bowl, solid base; cushioned knop over ball knop; DF. Ht. 6¾ins. c.1700.

**115.** Goblet; conical bowl; teared cushioned knop and basal knop; FF. Ht. 9¾ins. c.1710.
*Smith Collection. Harvey's Wine Museum, Bristol.*

**116.** Wine glass; conical bowl, solid base; stem with swelled knop containing tear; FF inscribed in diamond-point J.A. SLADE. Ht. 8½ins. c.1710.                *Christie's.*

Heavy Balusters

# III
# Balusters

**117.** Wine glass; drawn trumpet bowl; IB in centre of plain stem; DF. Ht. 6⅛ins. c.1720. These glasses are commonly referred to as of 'Kit-Kat' type but see article by Treglown and Mortimer, *Country Life* 2/7/81 pp. 46-8. *Sotheby's.*

**118.** Wine glass; bell bowl, solid base; IB knop with large tear; basal knop; FF. Ht. 7ins. c.1730.

**119.** Wine glass; waisted bell bowl, solid base; flattened, IB and basal knops; FF. Ht. 6ins. c.1730.
*Hartshorne Collection.*

**120.** Wine glass; bell bowl, solid base; IB knop with tear; DF. Ht. 7ins. c.1730.
*Hartshorne Collection. (Fig.195).*

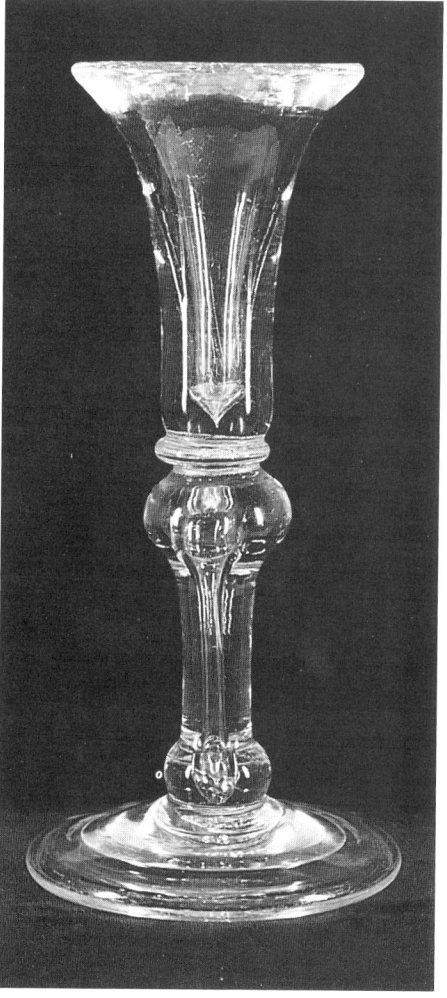

**122.** Toastmaster's glass; deceptive waisted bell bowl; collar above teared IB and basal knops; FF. Ht. 6ins. c.1730.

**121.** Wine glass; waisted bell bowl, solid base; annular knop over teared IB; basal knop; D & FF. Ht. 6¾ins. c.1730.

Balusters

**123.** Wine glass; bucket bowl; teared IB and basal knops; FF. Ht. 7ins. c.1720.
*Cecil Higgins Museum, Bedford.*

**124.** Champagne glass; cup bowl with everted rim and engraved border; IB knop; D & FF. Ht. 4¼ins. c.1730.

**125.** Wine glass; waisted bell bowl, solid base; teared IB and basal knops; FF. Ht. 6½ins. c.1730.

**126.** Wine glass; RF bowl; angular knop above cushioned IB. Ht. 7ins. c.1730.

Balusters

**127.** Champagne glass; pan-topped RF bowl, everted rim; collar above beaded ball knop, teared IB and basal knops; DF. Ht. 6½ins. c.1730.

**128.** Ale glass; elongated bell bowl, solid base; IB. Ht. 8¼ins. c.1740.

*Tibbenham Collection, Ipswich Museum.*

**129.** Wine glass; bell bowl, solid base; teared knop over IB and basal knop. Ht. 6½ins. c.1740.

*Tibbenham Collection, Ipswich Museum.*

**130.** Wine glass; bell bowl, solid base; teared knop above IB; FF. Ht. 6¼ins. c.1740.

*Tibbenham Collection, Ipswich Museum.*

Balusters

**131.** Wine glass; waisted bell bowl, solid base with tear; 4-ringed annulated knop over true baluster and basal knops. Ht. 6⅜ins. c.1730.

**132.** Wine glass; waisted bell bowl; collar and flattened knop over true baluster and basal knop; FF. Ht. 5⅜ins. c.1730. *Worthing Museum.*

**133.** Wine glass; trumpet bowl, solid base; collar, shoulder knop, true baluster, basal knop (Kit-Kat stem). Ht. 6⅜ins. c.1720.
*Christie's.*

**134.** Wine glass; trumpet bowl, solid base; collar and flattened knop over true baluster; DF. Ht. 7ins. c.1720.

**135.** Wine glass; trumpet bowl, solid base with tear; collar, flattened knop, true baluster and basal knop; FF. Ht. 7½ins. c.1720.
*Smith Collection. Harvey's Wine Museum, Bristol.*

**136.** Wine glass; waisted bell bowl, solid base; collar, small round knop, true baluster and basal knop; FF. Ht. 7ins. c.1730.

**137.** Cordial; trumpet bowl, solid base; collars, flattened knop, true baluster and basal knop. Ht. 6½ins. c.1720.

**138.** Wine glass; trumpet bowl, solid base; cushioned (or double) knop with tear, squat, semi-hollow true baluster; DF. Ht. 6½ins. c.1725.
*Tibbenham Collection, Ipswich Museum.*

**139.** Wine glass; bell bowl, engraved border of fruiting vine; three knops over true baluster; DF. Ht. 7⅛ins. c.1730.     *Christie's.*

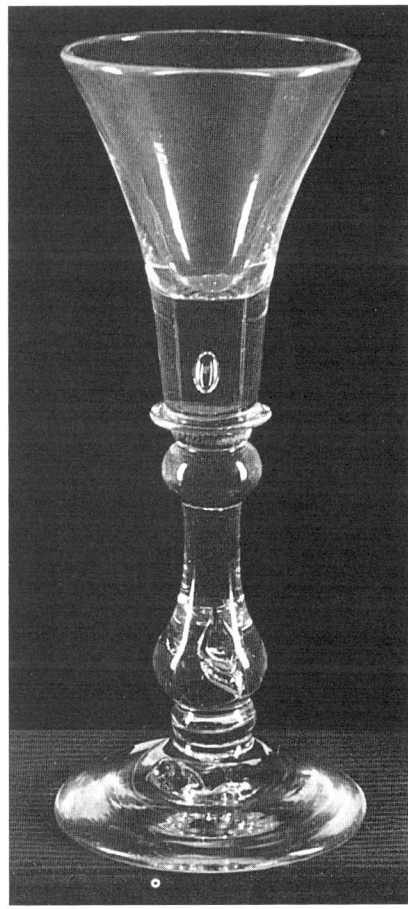

**140.** Wine glass; pointed RF bowl, solid base; angular knop over true baluster. Ht. 6ins. c.1730.

**141.** Cordial; trumpet bowl, solid base with tear; collar over round knop, true baluster and basal knop. Ht. 6½ins. c.1720.

**142.** Wine glass; waisted bell bowl, engraved floral border below rim, solid base; two true balusters in tandem; basal knop. Ht. 6¾ins. c.1730.

**143.** Wine glass; lipped RF bowl; ball knop over angular knop, teared true baluster and basal knop; D & FF. Ht. 7⅜ins. c.1730.

**144.** Wine glass; thistle bowl engraved with Baroque border below rim and birds in flight, solid base; angular knop between two ball knops, all teared; FF. Ht. 6⅞ins. c.1730.

*Smith Collection. Harvey's Wine Museum, Bristol.*

**145.** Wine glass; pointed RF bowl; ball knop over teared angular and basal knops; D & FF. Ht. 7¼ins. c.1730.

*Hartshorne Collection. (Fig.175).*

Balusters

**146.** Wine glass; bell bowl, solid base; angular knop over semi-hollow ovoid knop; D & FF. Ht. 6ins. c.1715.

**147.** Wine glass; waisted bell bowl, solid base; 5-ringed annulated knop, teared angular knop and basal knop. Ht. 6⅜ins. c.1730.

**148.** Wine glass; moulded trumpet bowl; triple collar above 3-ringed annulated knop, smaller annulated knop and basal knop; similarly moulded D & FF. Ht. 7ins. c.1730.
*Pilkington Glass Museum, St. Helens.*

**149.** Ale glass; waisted bell bowl, solid base; 5-ringed annulated knop; basal knop; FF. Ht. 7⅛ins. c.1730.
*Cecil Higgins Museum, Bedford.*

Balusters

**150.** Wine glass; conical bowl 'nipt diamond waies' type decoration; triple collar over two 3-ringed annulated knops and basal knop; D & FF, moulded to match bowl. Ht. 6½ins. c.1730. *Hartshorne Collection. (Fig. 171).*

**151.** Wine glass; bell bowl, solid base; 5-ringed annulated knop over true baluster. c.1730.

**152.** Wine glass; bell bowl, solid base; 3-ringed annulated knop over teared IB and basal knop; FF. Ht. 5¾ins. c.1740.
*Tibbenham Collection, Ipswich Museum.*

**153.** Wine glass; bell bowl, solid base; 3-ringed annulated knop with tear, basal knop; FF. Ht. 6¼ins. c.1725.
*Tibbenham Collection, Ipswich Museum.*

**154.** Gin glass; bell bowl, solid base; flattened knop, 3-ringed annulated knop, basal knop; FF. Ht. 4¾ins. c.1720.
*Hartshorne Collection. (Fig. 294).*

Balusters

**155.** Wine glass; waisted bell bowl, teared solid base; 3-ringed annulated knop, teared stem and basal knop; FF. Ht. 6½ins. c.1720.
*Hartshorne Collection. (Fig. 196).*

**156.** Wine glass; lipped square bucket bowl; 3-ringed annulated knop with tear; basal knop; D & FF. Ht. 6ins. c.1720.

**157.** Wine glass; bell bowl, solid base; 3-ringed annulated knop over teared IB; basal knop; DF. Ht. 6½ins. c.1730.

**158.** Sweetmeat; pan-topped moulded RF bowl; 3-ringed annulated knop over teared IB; basal knop; radially moulded D & FF. Ht. 5ins. c.1730.

Balusters

**159.** Wine glass; waisted bell bowl, solid base; 3-ringed annulated knop over teared IB and basal knops; FF. Ht. 6¾ins. c.1730.

**160.** Wine glass; bell bowl, solid base; 3-ringed annulated knop over teared IB; basal knop. Ht. 6½ins. c. 1730.

*Smith Collection. Harvey's Wine Museum, Bristol.*

**161.** Wine glass; bell bowl; 3-ringed annulated knop, basal knop; D & FF. Ht. 6½ins. c.1730.                    *Christie's.*

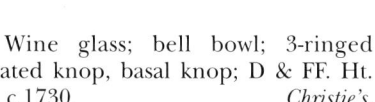

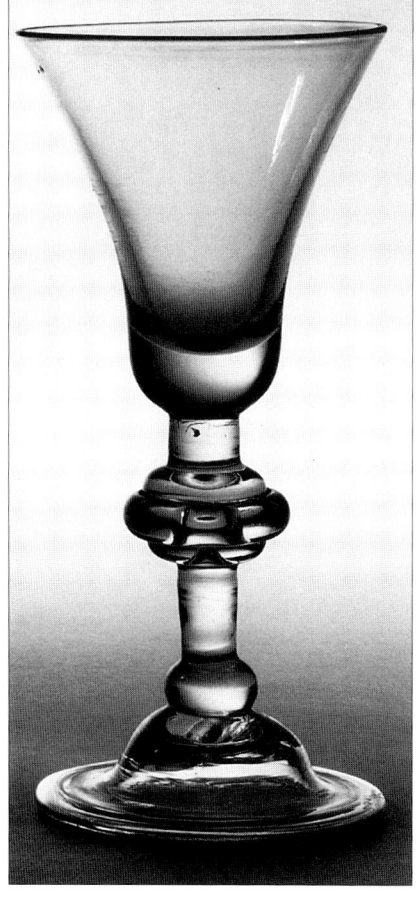

**162.** Wine glass; waisted bell bowl, solid base; flattened and annular knops above ball knop; basal knop. Ht. 6½ins. c.1730.

Balusters

**163.** Wine glass; bell bowl; two ball knops; DF. Ht. 7⅜ins. c.1730.

**164.** Goblet; bell bowl, solid base; teared heavy knop bisecting straight stem. Ht. 9ins. c.1720.

*Tibbenham Collection,*
*Ipswich Museum.*

**165.** Sweetmeat; cup bowl, folded rim; double ball knop; FF. Ht. 4⅛ins. c.1730.

**166.** Goblet; RF bowl, everted rim; two ball knops over IB and basal knop. Ht. 8½ins. c.1710.

*Tibbenham Collection,*
*Ipswich Museum.*

**167.** Wine glass; doubly cushioned teared knop; basal knop; DF. Ht. 6½ins. c.1730.
*Tibbenham Collection, Ipswich Museum.*

**168.** Sweetmeat; panel-moulded pan-topped RF bowl; beaded ball knop over IB; panel-moulded D & FF. Ht. 5½ins. c.1730.
*Hartshorne Collection.*

**169.** Champagne glass; ogee bowl, everted rim; double collar above teared ball knop, 3-ringed annulated knop and teared IB; domed and terraced foot. Ht. 5½ins. c.1730.

**170.** Champagne glass; pan-topped RF bowl, everted rim; collars above teared ball knop and small plain knop; domed and terraced foot. Ht. 6ins. c.1730.
*Hartshorne Collection.*

**171.** Sweetmeat (?); flared bowl engraved with pattern of fruiting vine; composite stem – central beaded knop between two annulated knops; domed and terraced foot. Ht. 6¼ins. c.1740. *Christie's.*

**172.** Wine glass; bell bowl, solid base; knop, cushioned teared IB, basal knop; DF. Ht. 7ins. c.1730.
*Tibbenham Collection, Ipswich Museum.*

**173.** Wine glass; trumpet bowl; flattened knop, ball knop; FF. Ht. 6¾ins. c.1725.

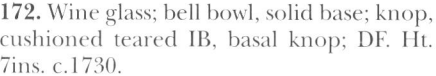

Balusters

**174.** Wine glass; panel-moulded cup bowl; beaded ball knop; radially moulded foot. Ht. 6½ins. c.1735.

**175.** Sweetmeat; pan-topped RF bowl; beaded ball knop; DF. Ht. 4¾ins. c.1735.

**176.** Sweetmeat; honeycomb-moulded cup-topped RF bowl; ball knop; D & FF moulded to match. Ht. 7ins. c.1735.

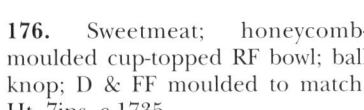

**177.** Wine glass; conical bowl; mushroom knop and basal knop, both teared; FF. Ht. 5½ins. c.1715.

Balusters

**178.** Goblet; RF bowl; hollow acorn and basal knops; FF. Ht. 7ins. c.1715.

**179.** Wine glass; oval pan-topped RF bowl, engraved floral border; solid base; acorn knop between small ball knops; DF. Ht. 6⅜ins. c.1730.

**180.** Wine glass; bell bowl, solid base; flattened knop and collar over cylinder knop; basal knop; FF. Ht. 6½ins. c.1720.
*Smith Collection. Harvey's Wine Museum, Bristol.*

Balusters

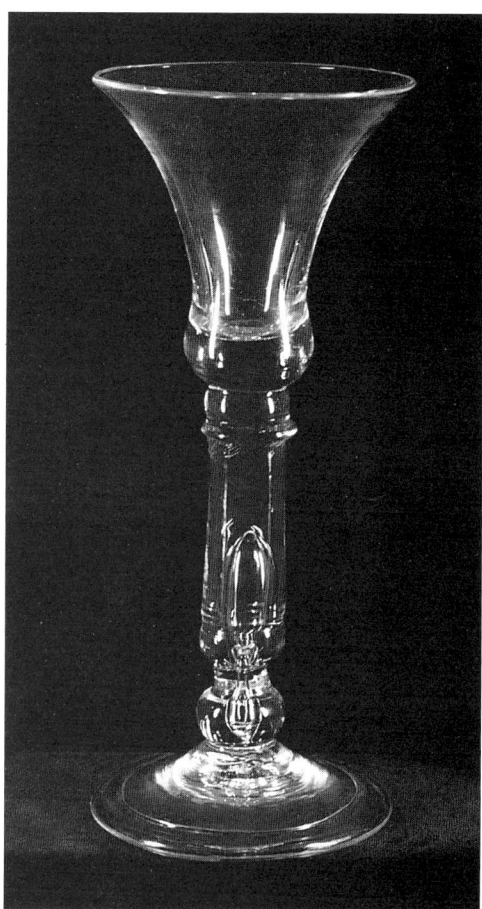

**181.** Wine glass; bell bowl; flattened knop over teared cylinder knop; basal knop; FF. Ht. 5½ins. c.1730.
*Worthing Museum.*

**182.** Wine glass; waisted bell bowl, solid base; flattened knop; collar, teared cylinder and basal knops; FF. Ht. 7ins. c.1730.

**183.** Wine glass; bell bowl, solid base; flattened knop, cylinder and basal knops, all teared; FF. Ht. 6¾ins. c.1715.
*Cecil Higgins Museum, Bedford.*

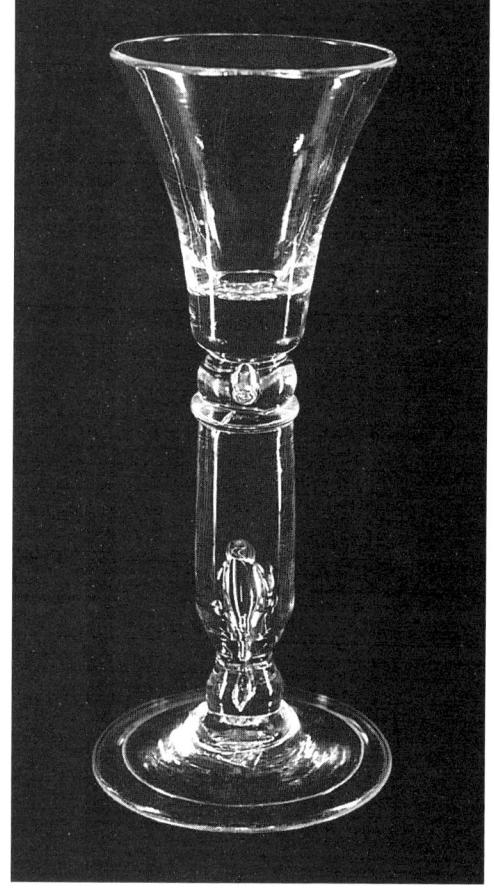

**184.** Wine glass; bell bowl, solid base; teared dumb-bell knop; basal knop; FF. Ht. 8⅜ins. c.1720.

Balusters

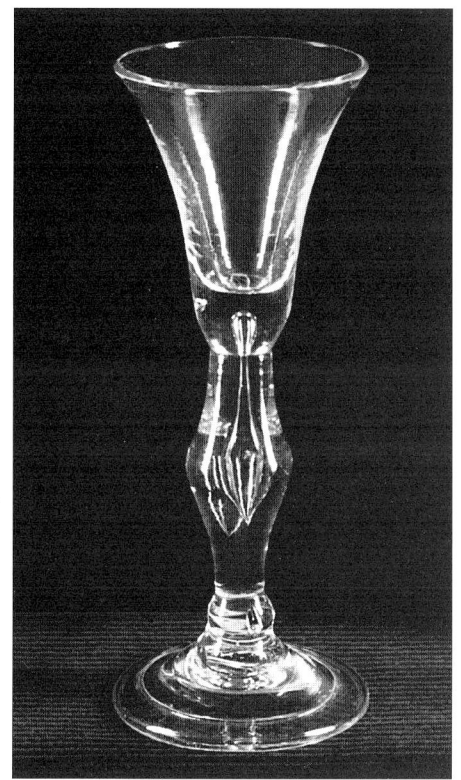

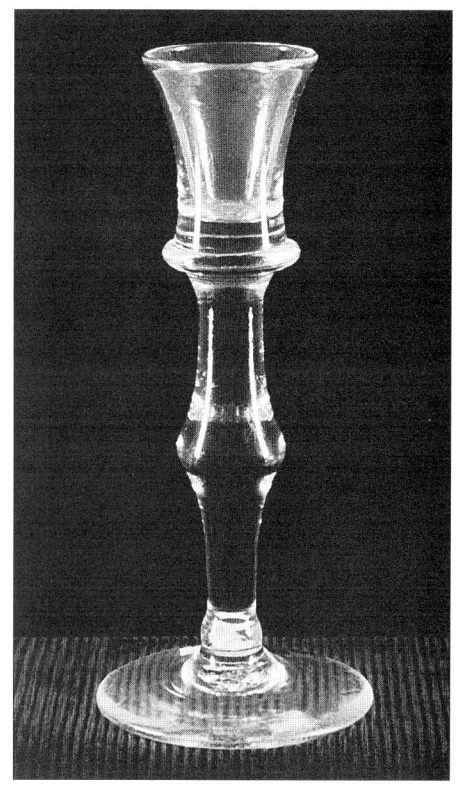

**185.** Wine glass; bell bowl, teared solid base; teared swelled knop; basal knop; FF. Ht. 5¼ins. c.1720.

**186.** Cordial; trumpet bowl, solid base with tear; collar, teared swelled knop; FF. Ht. 6¾ins. c.1715.

**187.** Toastmaster's glass; deceptive waisted bucket bowl; collar above swelling knop; basal knop. Ht. 6¼ins. c.1715.

**188.** Toastmaster's glass; deceptive ovoid bowl; swelled knop. Ht. 5¼ins. c.1740.
*Tibbenham Collection, Ipswich Museum.*

**189.** Sweetmeat; saucer-topped cup bowl; centre swelled knop; flat foot. Ht. 6¾ins. c.1730.
*Tibbenham Collection, Ipswich Museum.*

**190.** Wine glass; conical bowl, solid base; inverted cone stem with tear. Ht. 6¼ins. c.1710.
*Tibbenham Collection, Ipswich Museum.*

# IV
# Balustroids

**191.** Wine glass; bell bowl, solid base; IB. Ht. 7ins. c.1740.

**192.** Wine glass; tulip bowl; IB. Ht. 6⅜ins. c.1740.
*Tibbenham Collection, Ipswich Museum.*

**193.** Wine glass; trumpet bowl; collars above semi-hollow IB, basal collar. Ht. 5⅜ins. c.1740.
*Tibbenham Collection, Ipswich Museum.*

**194.** Wine glass; trumpet bowl; teared IB at centre. Ht. 7ins. c.1750.
*Hartshorne Collection. (Fig. 190).*

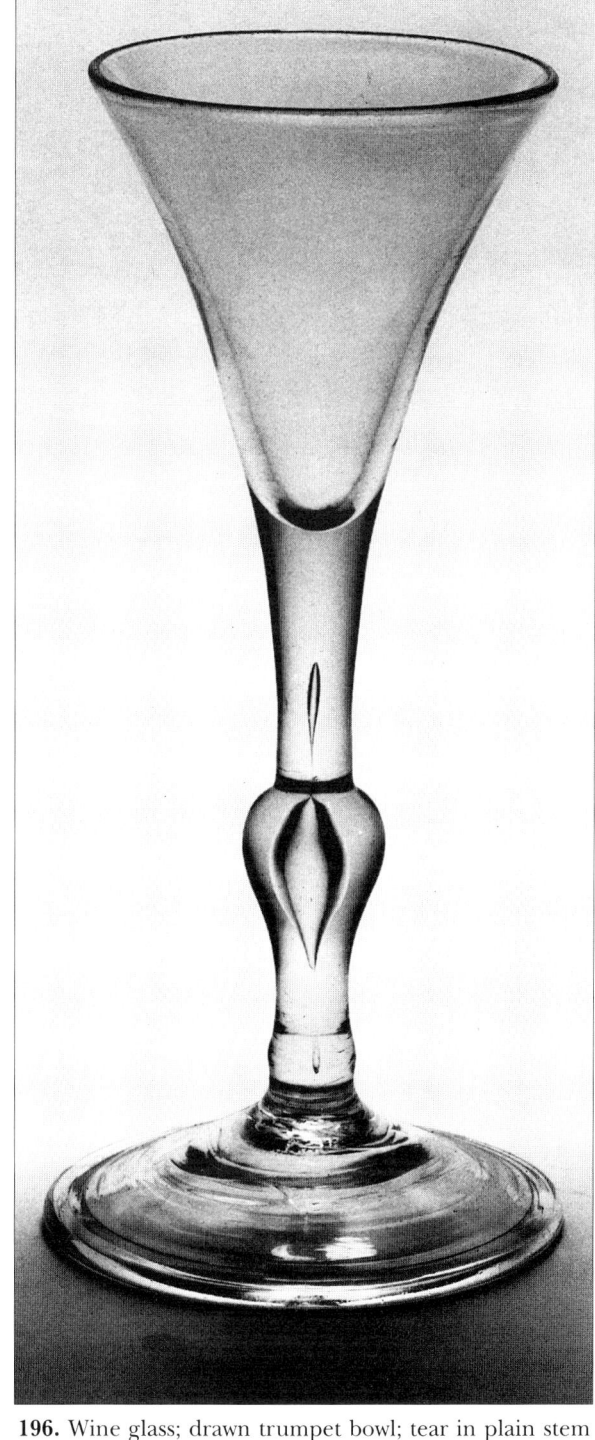

**196.** Wine glass; drawn trumpet bowl; tear in plain stem above IB with large tear. FF. Ht. 6¾ins. c.1720. See note to 117.
*Sotheby's.*

**195.** Wine glass; bell bowl; ball knop in straight stem; FF. Ht. 6¾ins. c.1740.
*Tibbenham Collection, Ipswich Museum.*

**197.** Wine glass; funnel bowl; semi-hollow stem above knop and basal knop; DF. Ht. 7ins. c.1740.
*Tibbenham Collection,*
*Ipswich Museum.*

**198.** Wine glass; bell bowl; flattened knop; teared IB, basal knop; FF. Ht. 6¼ins. c.1740.
*Tibbenham Collection,*
*Ipswich Museum.*

**199.** Wine glass; bell bowl, solid base; teared IB; FF. Ht. 6½ins. c.1740.
*Tibbenham Collection,*
*Ipswich Museum.*

**200.** Wine glass; trumpet bowl; knop, collar, semi-hollow IB; FF. Ht. 6¾ins. c.1725.

*Tibbenham Collection,*
*Ipswich Museum.*

Balustroids

**201.** Wine glass; trumpet bowl; teared IB at centre; FF. Ht. 6ins. c.1750.

**202.** Wine glass; trumpet bowl; teared IB at base; FF. Ht. 7ins. c.1750. *Hartshorne Collection.*

**203.** Wine glass; waisted bell bowl; thin teared stem above teared IB; basal knop; FF. Ht. 6¾ins. c.1750.

**204.** Wine glass; bell bowl, engraved fruiting vine below rim, solid base; IB at base. Ht. 7¼ins. c.1740. *Portsmouth City Museums.*

Balustroids

**205.** Wine glass; trumpet bowl; IB at base; basal knop; DF. Ht. 7¼ins. c.1750. *Hartshorne Collection. (Fig. 189).*

**207.** Sweetmeat glass; pan-topped RF bowl, dentated rim; IB shoulder knop; radially moulded foot. Ht. 3⅝ins. c.1740.

**206.** Ale glass; bell bowl, solid base; IB at base; DF. Ht. 8ins. c.1750.

Balustroids

**209.** Wine glass; bell bowl, engraved fruiting vine border below rim; knop at shoulder, true baluster at base; basal knop; FF. Ht. 6½ins. c.1750.

*Hartshorne Collection.*

**208.** Wine glass; trumpet bowl; collar, true baluster, basal knop. Ht. 6¾ins. c.1740.
*Tibbenham Collection, Ipswich Museum.*

**210.** Wine glass; RF bowl; knop at shoulder; FF. Ht. 6ins. c.1750.

Balustroids

**211.** Gin glass; bell bowl; knop at shoulder; FF. Ht. 4¼ins. c.1740. Soda glass.

**212.** Ale glass; bell bowl; wide annular knop over teared swelled knop; FF. Ht. 5⅜ins. c.1740.

**213.** Wine glass; funnel bowl; acorn-type knop at shoulder. Ht. 6ins. c.1730.

**214.** Wine glass; trumpet bowl, solid base; collar between pair of flattened knops; FF. Ht. 7ins. c.1730.

Balustroids

**215.** Wine glass; trumpet bowl; ball knop resting on a cushioned collar, basal knop; FF. Ht. 6ins. c.1740.
*Tibbenham Collection, Ipswich Museum.*

**217.** Wine glass; ogee bowl; centre knop. FF. Ht. 5½ins. c.1750.
*Worthing Museum.*

**218.** Wine glass; drawn trumpet bowl; plain stem bisected by knop; FF. Ht. 5¾ins. c.1740.
*Tibbenham Collection, Ipswich Museum.*

Balustroids

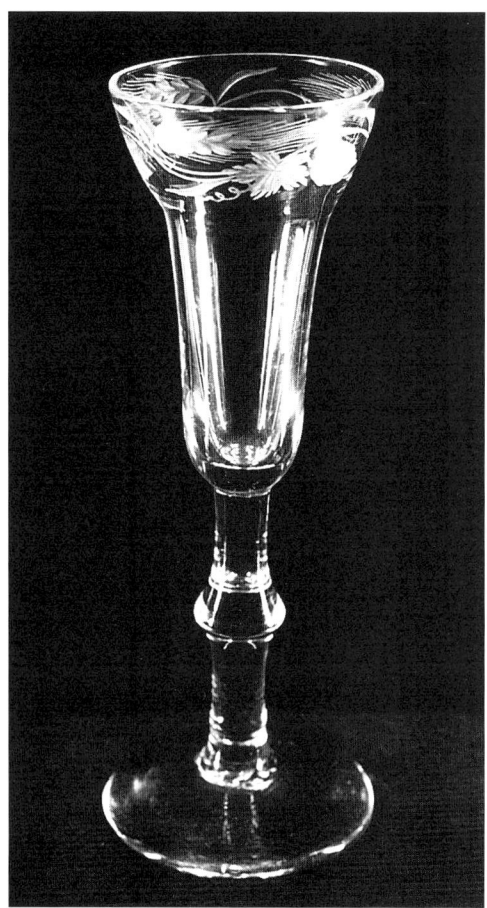

**219.** Wine glass; trumpet bowl; stem bisected by teared ball knop; DF. Ht. 6½ins. c.1740.
*Tibbenham Collection, Ipswich Museum.*

**220.** Ale glass; pan-topped RF bowl, engraved border of hops and barley below rim; centre knop. Ht. 7⅞ins. c.1740.
*Cecil Higgins Museum, Bedford.*

**221.** Cider glass; waisted bell bowl, solid base, engraved decoration of fruiting apple branch; centre knop; DF. Ht. 8ins. c.1740.

**222.** Wine glass; ribbed cup bowl, everted rim, swelled centre knop. Ht. 7¼ins. c.1740.

Balustroids

**223.** Wine glass; drawn trumpet bowl, engraved flower and moth; centre knop. Ht. 6¾ins. c.1750.

**224.** Goblet; double-ogee bowl; centre knop and basal knop; radially moulded foot. Ht. 7½ins. c.1740.   *Worthing Museum.*

**225.** Wine glass; RF bowl, everted rim; teared swelled knop, basal knop; D & FF. Ht. 5½ins. c.1740.

*Tibbenham Collection, Ipswich Museum.*

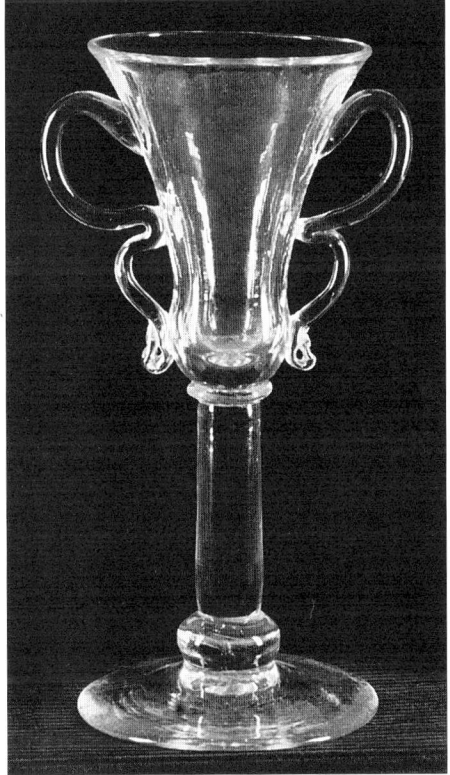

**226.** Cordial; bell bowl, solid base with tear; teared swelled centre knop; basal knop. Ht. 6¾ins. c.1735.

**227.** Wine glass (?); bell bowl with pair of applied B-handles; collar; basal knop. Ht. 6½ins. c.1735.

**228.** Wine glass; tulip bowl, solid base; basal knop. Ht. 7½ins. c.1740.

*Portsmouth City Museums.*

Balustroids

**229.** Wine glass; trumpet bowl; thinning stem; ball knop above basal knop; DF. Ht. 6⅜ins. c.1740.
*Hartshorne Collection. (Fig. 198).*

**230.** Wine glass; cup-topped pointed RF bowl; hollow drop-knop, basal knop; D & FF. Ht. 6¼ins. c.1740.
*Tibbenham Collection, Ipswich Museum.*

**231.** Wine glass; drawn trumpet bowl; cushioned knop over basal knop; DF. Ht. 6½ins. c.1735.

**232.** Wine glass; bell bowl, solid base; flattened knop; cushioned knop at base. Ht. 6ins. c.1730.

Balustroids

**233.** Wine glass; bell bowl, solid-base; cushioned knop at base; FF. Ht. 7¼ins. c.1740.

**234.** Wine glass; pointed RF bowl; knops at shoulder and centre; FF. Ht. 6¼ins. c.1750.

**235.** Ale glass; pointed RF bowl engraved with hops and barley; IB and angular knops. Ht. 7½ins. c.1740.

*Tibbenham Collection,*
*Ipswich Museum.*

**236.** Wine glass; ogee bowl; annular knops at shoulder and centre; small basal knop; FF. Ht. 5¼ins. c.1750.
*Hartshorne Collection.*

Balustroids

**237.** Wine glass; RF bowl; flattened knop, teared stem and annular knop; FF. Ht. 6ins. c.1750.

**238.** Wine glass; RF bowl; flattened knop, teared stem and bladed knop; FF. Ht. 5⅜ins. c.1750.

**239.** Wine glass; pan-topped RF bowl, engraved floral border below rim; flattened knop, teared stem with bladed knop; small basal knop; FF. Ht. 6ins. c.1750.

**240.** Wine glass; RF bowl, moulded base; annular shoulder knop, wrythen ball knop at centre; FF. Ht. 5⅜ins. c.1750.

Balustroids

**242.** Goblet; bell bowl; double-cushioned teared knop, teared IB, basal knop. Ht. 7½ins. c.1740.
*Tibbenham Collection, Ipswich Museum.*

**241.** Goblet; ogee bowl, engraved border of flowering foliage; tapering stem, basal knop; DF. Ht. 7ins. c.1740. Set of four. *Christie's.*

**243.** Wine glass; RF bowl; knops at shoulder and base; teared stem between; FF. Ht. 6⅜ins. c.1750.

Balustroids

**244.** Gin glass; bell bowl; annular and basal knops; FF. Ht. 4⅛ins. c.1740.

**245.** Wine glass; bell bowl, solid base; annular knop over beaded IB; FF. Ht. 7ins. c.1730.

**246.** Wine glass; bell bowl, solid base; beaded ball knop over teared IB. Ht. 6¾ins. c.1750.

**247.** Wine glass; bell bowl; large teared knop, semi-hollow IB, teared basal knop. Ht. 7½ins. c.1740.
*Tibbenham Collection, Ipswich Museum.*

Balustroids

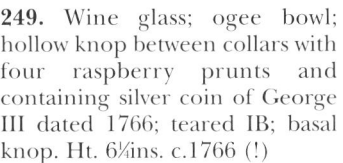

**249.** Wine glass; ogee bowl; hollow knop between collars with four raspberry prunts and containing silver coin of George III dated 1766; teared IB; basal knop. Ht. 6¼ins. c.1766 (!)

**248.** Wine glass; bell bowl, solid base; hollow knop containing coin over teared IB; FF. c.1730. *Asprey.*

**250.** Detail of 249 showing hollow knop and coin.

**251.** Wine glass; cup-topped RF bowl, solid base; bladed knop, teared stem and basal knop; FF. Ht. 6ins. c.1750.

**252.** Wine glass; bell bowl, solid base; drop knop over IB. Ht. 7ins. c.1730.

**253.** Mead glass; cup bowl with gadrooned base; cushioned knop, teared stem and basal knop; FF. Ht. 4½ins. c.1720.

Balustroids

**254.** Wine glass; RF bowl, slightly everted rim; flattened knop between two angular knops; DF. Ht. 7ins. c.1740.

**255.** Wine glass; bell bowl; three knops; FF. Ht. 6ins. c.1750.

**256.** Wine glass; moulded cup bowl, everted rim; double knop over IB and basal knop; panel-moulded DF. Ht. 7ins. c.1740.

**257.** Wine glass; RF bowl; annular knop, teared swelled and basal knops; FF. Ht. 6ins. c.1750.

**258.** Ale glass; trumpet bowl; two 3-ringed annulated knops over a true baluster; terraced foot. Ht. 7⅜ins. c.1730.

**259.** Mead glass; cup bowl, gadrooned base; flattened knop, teared knop and slight basal knop; FF. Ht. 4⅜ins. c.1730.

Balustroids

**260.** Wine glass; bell bowl; flattened, 3-ringed annulated IB and basal knops; FF. Ht. 7ins. c.1730.
*Hartshorne Collection.*

**261.** Wine glass; bell bowl, solid base; collars over swelled and cushion knops; DF. Ht. 6½ins. c.1730.

**262.** Wine glass; bell bowl; collars, 3-ringed, teared, annulated knop. Ht. 6ins. c.1740.
*Tibbenham Collection, Ipswich Museum.*

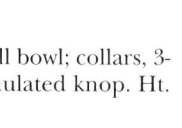

**263.** Wine glass; bell bowl; pair of true balusters in tandem, both teared, over basal knop; FF. Ht. 5ins. c.1730.

Balustroids

**264.** Mead glass; cup bowl, gadrooned base; semi-hollow bobbin-knopped stem (four diminishing knops); basal knop; FF. Ht. 5ins. c.1720.

*Hartshorne Collection.*

**265.** Sweetmeat; triple-ogee bowl; bobbin-knopped stem (six knops); DF. Ht. 4½ins. c.1720.

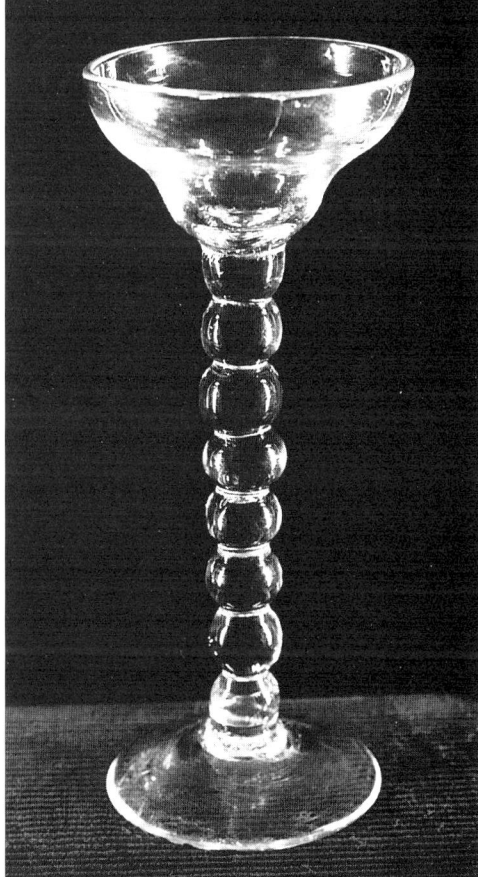

**266.** Wine glass; tulip bowl; bobbin knopped stem (eight knops); D & FF. c.1735.

*Tibbenham Collection, Ipswich Museum.*

**267.** Sweetmeat; double-ogee bowl; bobbin-knopped stem (eight knops). Ht. 6⅝ins. c.1720.

*Cecil Higgins Museum, Bedford.*

Balustroids

119

**268.** Wine glass; bell bowl; knop above cushioned teared knop, basal knop. Ht. 7¼ins. c.1740.
*Tibbenham Collection, Ipswich Museum.*

**269.** Wine glass; RF bowl; angular knop, knop, large teared knop, IB, basal knop. Ht. 7½ins. c.1740.
*Tibbenham Collection, Ipswich Museum.*

**270.** Wine glass; bell bowl, solid base; angular knop, 5-ringed annulated knop, basal knop. Ht. 7½ins. c.1725.
*Tibbenham Collection, Ipswich Museum.*

**271.** Wine glass; bell bowl, solid base; double-cushioned teared ball knop; basal knop; DF. Ht. 7ins. c.1740.
*Tibbenham Collection, Ipswich Museum.*

**272.** Wine glass; bell bowl, solid base; 'Newcastle' light baluster, swelled knop, knop above large teared knop; DF. Ht. 7ins. c.1740.
*Tibbenham Collection, Ipswich Museum.*

Balustroids

**273.** Wine glass; bell bowl, solid base; 'Newcastle' light baluster, acorn knop, knop, basal knop, DF. Ht. 7ins. c.1740.

*Tibbenham Collection,*
*Ipswich Museum.*

**274.** Wine glass; RF bowl engraved with band of fruiting vine with polished fruits below rim; 'Newcastle' light baluster, angular knop, teared IB, basal knop. Ht. 7ins. c.1740.

*Tibbenham Collection,*
*Ipswich Museum.*

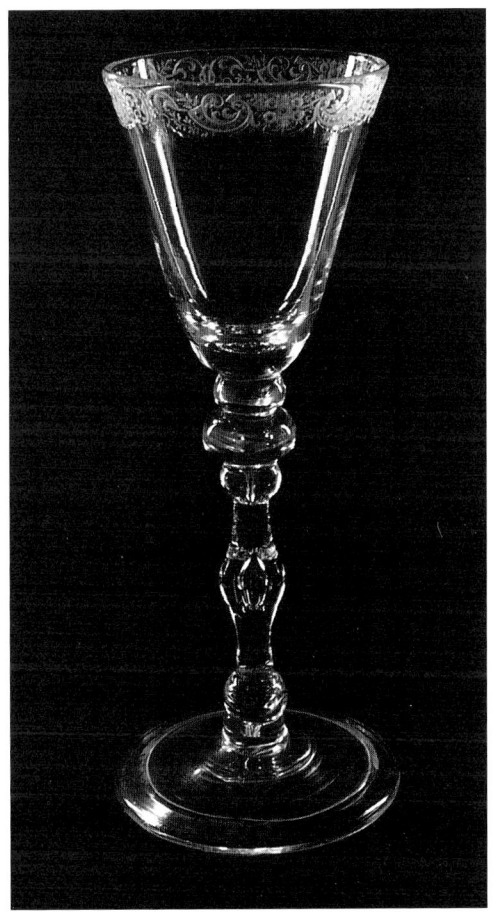

**275.** Wine glass; pointed RF bowl with Baroque engraved border below rim; 'Newcastle' light baluster stem including teared swelled knop; FF. Ht. 6⅝ins. c.1750.

*Smith Collection. Harvey's Wine*
*Museum, Bristol.*

**276.** Wine glass; trumpet bowl with engraved border of fruiting vine below rim; 'Newcastle' light baluster stem including beaded acorn knop and IB. Ht. 7ins. c.1750.

*Hartshorne Collection. (Fig. 192).*

Balustroids

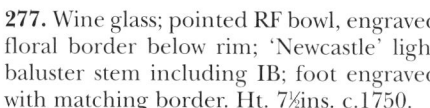

**277.** Wine glass; pointed RF bowl, engraved floral border below rim; 'Newcastle' light baluster stem including IB; foot engraved with matching border. Ht. 7½ins. c.1750.

*Smith Collection. Harvey's Wine Museum, Bristol.*

**278.** Wine glass; trumpet bowl with engraved border of fruiting vine; 'Newcastle' light baluster stem including beaded acorn and IB knops. Ht. 6⅝ins. c.1750.

*Smith Collection. Harvey's Wine Museum, Bristol.*

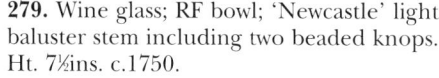

**279.** Wine glass; RF bowl; 'Newcastle' light baluster stem including two beaded knops. Ht. 7½ins. c.1750.

**280.** Wine glass; pointed RF bowl, engraved border of foliate branches below the rim; 'Newcastle' light baluster stem including 3-ringed annulated knop. Ht. 8¼ins. c.1750.

*Worthing Museum.*

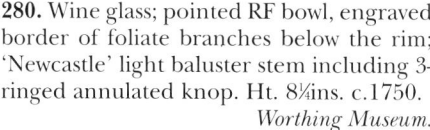

**281.** Wine glass; trumpet bowl; 'Newcastle' light baluster stem including beaded acorn knop and swelled knop. Ht. 7¼ins. c.1750.

Balustroids

**282.** Wine glass; bell bowl; 'Newcastle' light baluster stem including angular and IB knops; FF. Ht. 8½ins. c.1750.

**283.** Wine glass; RF bowl, engraved key pattern band below rim; 'Newcastle' light baluster stem including annular knop between opposing balusters; DF. Ht. 7ins. c.1750.

**284.** Wine glass; pointed RF bowl; 'Newcastle' light baluster stem including teared annular and angular knops; FF. Ht. 8¼ins. c.1750. *Worthing Museum.*

**285.** Wine glass; RF bowl; 'Newcastle' light baluster stem including beaded shoulder knop and IB. Ht. 7ins. c.1750.

# V
# Moulded Pedestal Stems

**286.** Wine glass; conical bowl, solid base; four-sided teared pedestal stem ('Silesian'), moulded crowns on shoulders and moulded legend GOD SAVE KING GEORGE; FF. Ht. 6¼ins. c.1715. *Hartshorne Collection.*

**287.** Wine glass; conical bowl, solid teared base; four-sided moulded pedestal stem, moulded in relief on shoulders GOD SAVE YE KING G R, the initials separated by a portrait bust of George I; FF. Ht. 6¼ins. c.1715.
*Ex Littledale Collection. Sotheby's.*

**288.** Wine glass; conical bowl, solid base with tear; four-sided pedestal stem with moulded legend GOD SAVE YE KING; FF. Ht. 6½ins. c.1715. *Asprey.*

**290.** Wine glass; conical bowl, solid base; four-sided teared pedestal stem with diamonds on shoulders; FF. Ht. 7¼ins. c.1720.

**289.** Wine glass; conical bowl, solid base; four-sided teared pedestal stem with rounded shoulders; FF. Ht. 5⅜ins. c.1720. Soda glass.

**291.** Wine glass; thistle bowl, solid base; four-sided pedestal stem with crowns on shoulders; FF. Ht. 6¼ins. c.1720.

**292.** Wine glass; RF bowl, solid base with tear; four-sided pedestal stem with lobed ribs on each side and diamonds on shoulders; FF. Ht. 6¼ins. c.1705.
*Smith Collection. Harvey's Wine Museum, Bristol.*

Moulded Pedestal Stems

**293.** Wine glass; bell bowl, solid base; ball knop over four-sided pedestal stem with rounded shoulders and long tear. Ht. 6⅜ins. c.1720.

**294.** Wine glass; thistle bowl, solid base; collar over four-sided pedestal stem with rounded shoulders and tear; collar; FF. Ht. 6½ins. c.1710.

**295.** Toastmaster's glass; deceptive trumpet bowl engraved with rose and butterfly (Jacobite); four-sided pedestal stem with rounded shoulders; FF. Ht. 5⅛ins. c.1715.
*Hartshorne Collection. (Fig. 306).*

**296.** Wine glass; conical bowl, solid base; six-sided pedestal stem with stars on shoulders; FF. Ht. 6⅝ins. c.1715. *Smith Collection.*
*Harvey's Wine Museum, Bristol.*

Moulded Pedestal Stems

**297.** Wine glass; pointed RF bowl, solid base; six-sided teared pedestal stem, diamonds on shoulders; FF. Ht. 7½ins. c.1720.

**298.** Wine glass; pointed RF bowl, solid base; flattened knop above six-sided teared pedestal stem; FF. Ht. 5⅜ins. c.1730. Soda glass.

**299.** Sweetmeat; saucer-topped honeycomb-moulded cup bowl; six-sided pedestal stem between collars; D & FF, moulded to match. Ht. 5⅜ins. c.1740.

**300.** Sweetmeat; double-ogee lattice-moulded bowl; beaded knop over eight-sided pedestal stem, diamonds on shoulders, collars; D & FF to match. Ht. 6⅜ins. c.1745.
*Sotheby's.*

**302.** Wine glass; pointed RF bowl, solid base, on cushion knop; eight-sided pedestal stem, diamonds on shoulders; FF. Ht. 5⅜ins. c.1725.

**301.** Sweetmeat; vertically-ribbed flared bowl, scalloped rim; beaded knop over eight-sided pedestal stem, diamonds on shoulders, collars at base; moulded DF. Ht. 7ins. c.1745.                                    *Sotheby's.*

**303.** Wine glass; conical bowl, solid base with tear; eight-sided moulded pedestal stem, diamonds on shoulders; FF. Ht. 6½ins. c.1750.

*Tibbenham Collection, Ipswich Museum.*

Moulded Pedestal Stems

**304.** Sweetmeat; double-ogee panel-moulded bowl, everted rim; eight-sided moulded pedestal stem between collars; domed, panel-moulded foot. Ht. 6½ins. c.1750.
*Tibbenham Collection,*
*Ipswich Museum.*

**305.** Sweetmeat; double ogee bowl, everted rim and panel-moulded; eight-sided moulded pedestal stem with winged shoulders, between collars; panel-moulded domed foot. Ht. 6ins. c.1750.
*Tibbenham Collection,*
*Ipswich Museum.*

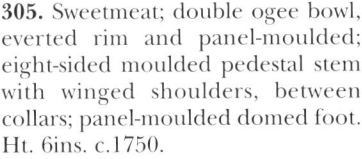

**306.** Sweetmeat; ogee bowl with dentated rim; six-sided moulded pedestal stem, diamonds on shoulders, between collars. D & FF. Ht. 6ins. c.1730. *Sotheby's.*

**307.** Wine glass; bucket bowl; eight-sided pedestal stem, diamonds on shoulders; collars. Ht. 7⅛ins. c.1745.
*Harvey's Wine Museum, Bristol.*

Moulded Pedestal Stems

**308.** Champagne glass; ogee bowl, everted rim; eight-sided pedestal stem, diamonds on shoulders, between collars; FF. Ht. 6¼ins. c.1745.

**309.** Champagne glass; panel-moulded ogee bowl, everted rim; eight-sided pedestal stem between collars; panel-moulded D & FF. Ht. 6⅜ins. c.1745.

**310.** Champagne glass; double-ogee bowl, everted rim; eight-sided pedestal stem, diamonds on shoulders, between collars; D & FF. Ht. 6½ins. c.1745.

**311.** Sweetmeat; honeycomb-moulded double-ogee bowl, everted rim; eight-sided pedestal stem between collars; D & FF to match. Ht. 6½ins. c.1745.

Moulded Pedestal Stems

**312.** Sweetmeat; honeycomb-moulded double-ogee bowl, everted rim; eight-sided pedestal stem between collars; D & FF to match. Ht. 7⅛ins. c.1745.

*Worthing Museum.*

**313.** Sweetmeat; honeycomb-moulded double-ogee bowl, everted rim; eight-sided pedestal stem between collars; DF to match. Ht. 6ins. c.1745.

**314.** Sweetmeat; panel-moulded double-ogee bowl with everted rim and diamond-studded base; eight-sided pedestal stem with diamond shoulders between collars; DF to match. Ht. 6¾ins. c.1745.

**315.** Champagne glass; panel-moulded double-ogee bowl with diamond-studded base; slightly twisted eight-sided pedestal stem between collars; DF to match. Ht. 5½ins. c.1750.

Moulded Pedestal Stems

**316.** Sweetmeat; panel-moulded double-ogee bowl with everted rim; eight-sided pedestal stem between collars; D & FF to match. Ht. 6½ins. c.1750.

**317.** Champagne glass; double-ogee bowl, slightly everted rim; eight-sided pedestal stem, diamonds on shoulders, collared base; DF. Ht. 7ins. c.1750.

**318.** Champagne glass; cup-topped RF bowl; angular knop above eight-sided pedestal stem, diamonds on shoulders; basal knop; D & FF. Ht. 6⅜ins. c.1745.

**319.** Champagne glass; double-ogee bowl, slightly everted rim; eight-sided pedestal stem, diamonds on shoulders, between collars; D & FF. Ht. 6½ins. c.1745.

Moulded Pedestal Stems

**320.** Champagne glass; panel-moulded double-ogee bowl; eight-sided pedestal stem, diamonds on shoulders; basal knop; DF to match. Ht. 7ins. c.1745.

**321.** Champagne glass; panel-moulded cup bowl; eight-sided pedestal stem between collars; DF to match. Ht. 6ins. c.1755.
*Smith Collection. Harvey's Wine Museum, Bristol.*

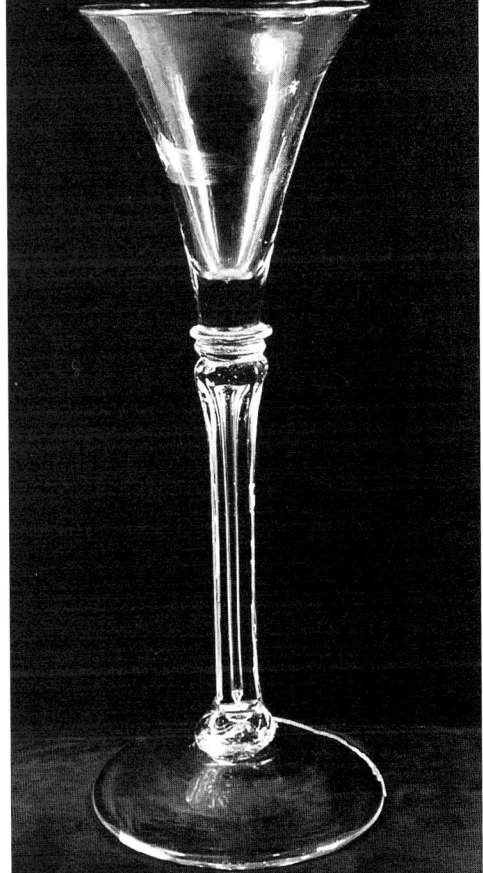

**322.** Wine glass; pointed RF bowl; collar over four-sided debased moulded pedestal stem with long tear. Ht. 6½ins. c.1750.
*Tibbenham Collection, Ipswich Museum.*

**323.** Wine glass; trumpet bowl, solid base; collars above attenuated four-sided pedestal stem with long tear; basal knop. Ht. 7½ins. c.1760.
*Hartshorne Collection. (Fig. 90).*

Moulded Pedestal Stems

**324.** Wine glass; hammered RF bowl; debased eight-sided pedestal stem, rounded shoulders, collared base; FF. Ht. 6¾ins. c.1760.

**325.** Sweetmeat; panel-moulded cup bowl, everted rim; debased eight-sided pedestal stem, rounded shoulders; FF to match. Ht. 4⅛ins. c.1760.

**326.** Wine glass; bucket bowl; eight-sided moulded pedestal stem, rounded shoulders, between single and triple collars, D & FF. Ht. 7ins. c.1750.

*Tibbenham Collection,*
*Ipswich Museum.*

**327.** Sweetmeat; cup bowl with everted rim and vertical panel-moulding; eight-sided moulded pedestal stem, between collars; FF. Ht. 7¼ins. c.1750.

*Tibbenham Collection,*
*Ipswich Museum.*

**Moulded Pedestal Stems**

**328.** Sweetmeat; large RF bowl, everted rim, twelve-sided debased moulded pedestal stem between collars; D & FF. Ht. 6⅜ins. c.1750.
*Tibbenham Collection, Ipswich Museum.*

**329.** Goblet; cup bowl, band of finely cut vertical flutes; debased eight-sided pedestal stem between collars; DF. Ht. 7ins. c.1765.

**330.** Wine glass; thistle bowl; diamond-studded, spirally-moulded six-sided pedestal stem; FF. Ht. 5ins. c.1725. *Sotheby's.*

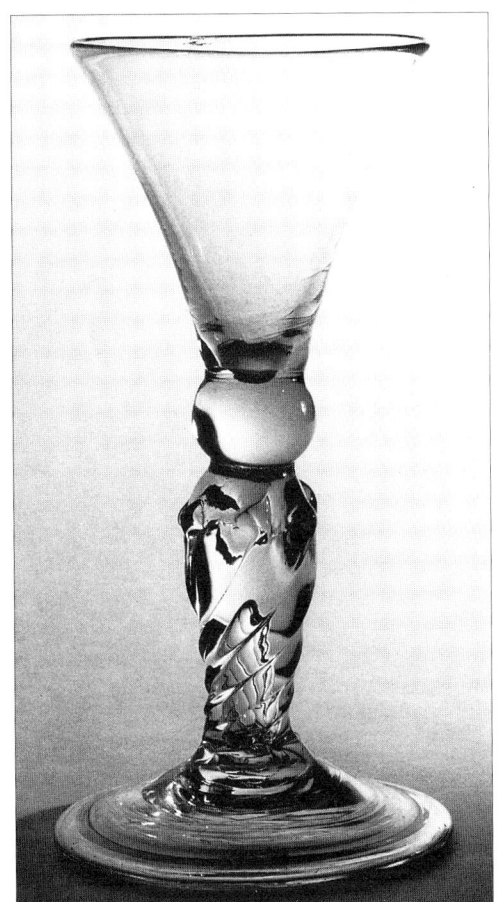

**331.** Sweetmeat; double-ogee bowl, everted rim; debased eight-sided pedestal stem between collars; FF. Ht. 6⅜ins. c.1760.

# VI
# Plain Straight Stems

**332.** Toasting glass; drawn trumpet bowl, flared. Ht. 7ins. c.1750.

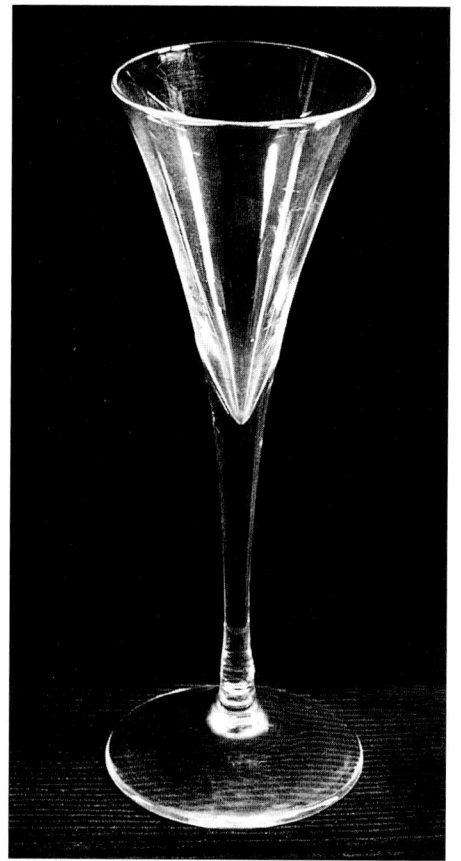

**333.** Toasting glass; drawn trumpet bowl. Ht. 7⅜ins. c.1750.
*Hartshorne Collection. (Fig. 89).*

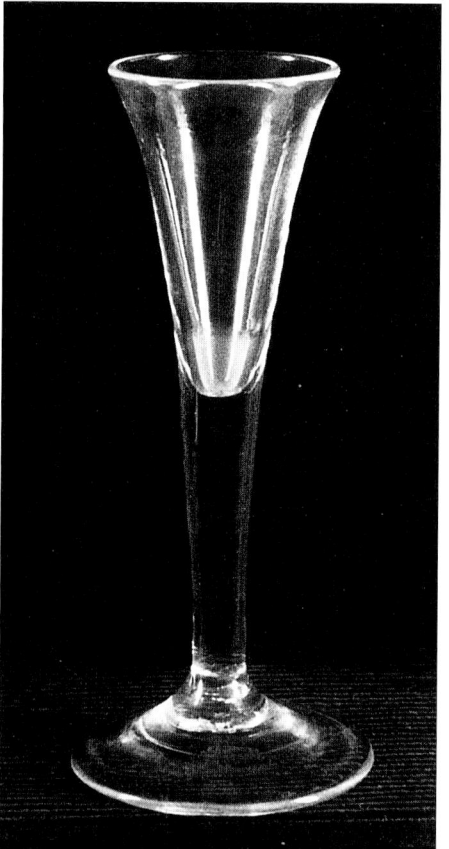

**334.** Wine glass; drawn trumpet bowl. Ht. 5ins. c.1750.
*Hartshorne Collection.*

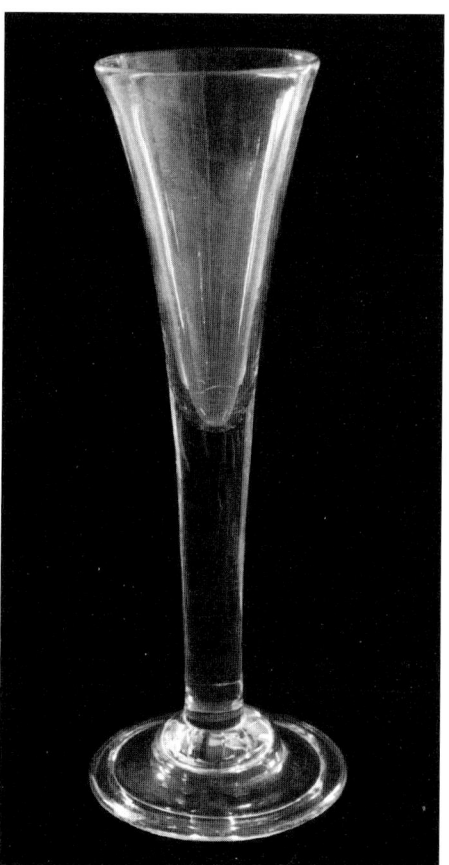

**335.** Wine glass; drawn trumpet bowl; D & FF. Ht. 8¼ins. c.1740.
*Smith Collection. Harvey's Wine Museum, Bristol.*

136

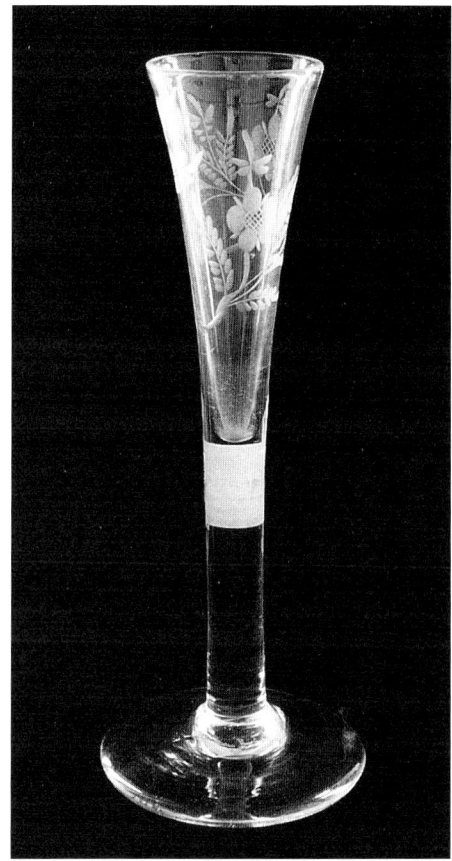

**336.** Ratafia; drawn trumpet bowl, engraved with floral spray. Ht. 7⅛ins. c.1750.

*Smith Collection. Harvey's Wine Museum, Bristol.*

**337.** Ale glass; waisted bell bowl engraved with hops and barley; plain stem. Ht. 7¼ins. c.1740. *Christie's.*

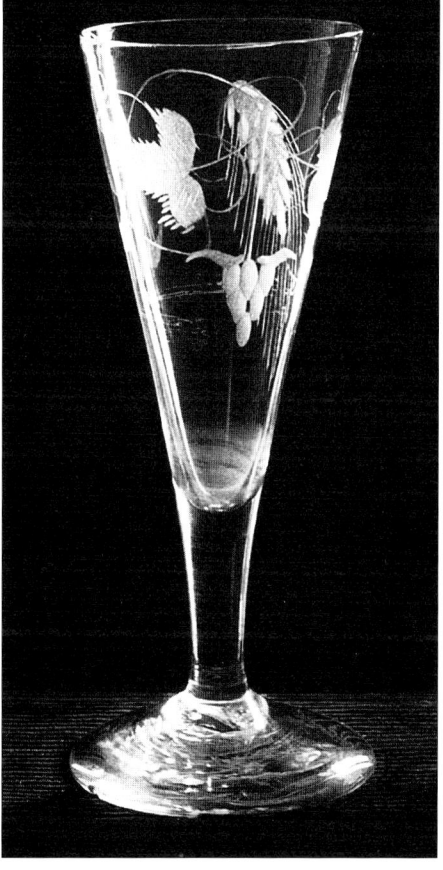

**338.** Short ale glass; drawn trumpet bowl, engraved with hops and barley. Ht. 6ins. c.1750. *Hartshorne Collection.*

Plain Straight Stems

**339.** Short ale glass; funnel bowl, engraved with hops and barley; FF. Ht. 6ins. c.1740.
*Worthing Museum.*

**340.** Gin glass; fluted ovoid bowl; FF. Ht. 3¾ins. c.1740. *Hartshorne Collection.*

**341.** Gin glass; vertically moulded drawn trumpet bowl; FF. Ht. 3¾ins. c.1740.

**342.** Wine glass; drawn trumpet bowl engraved with deep floral band; plain stem with tear; FF. Ht. 5½ins. c.1740.
*Tibbenham Collection, Ipswich Museum.*

**343.** Wine glass; trumpet bowl engraved with fruiting vine and bird in flight; hollow straight stem. Ht. 6ins. c.1750.
*Tibbenham Collection, Ipswich Museum.*

**344.** Gin glass; drawn trumpet bowl, engraved festoons below rim; FF. Ht. 4¾ins. c.1740. *Hartshorne Collection. (Fig. 20a).*

Plain Straight Stems

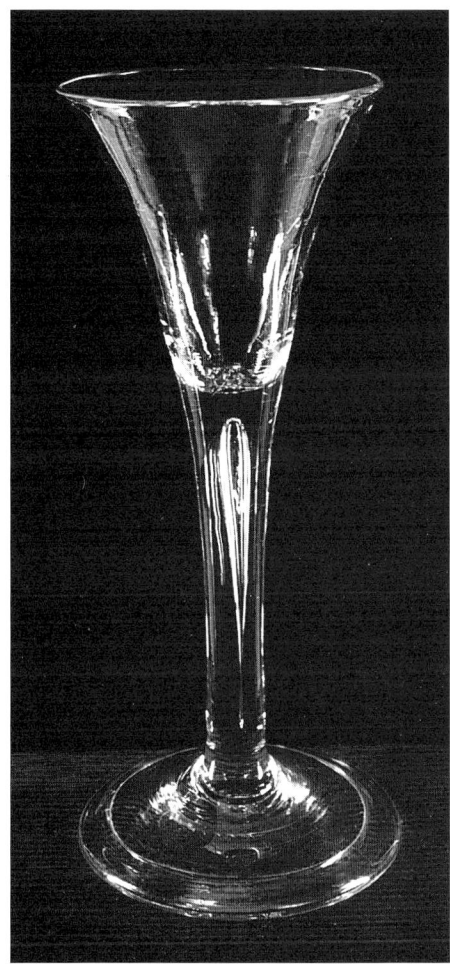

**345.** Wine glass; drawn trumpet bowl, teared stem; FF. Ht. 7¼ins. c.1740.

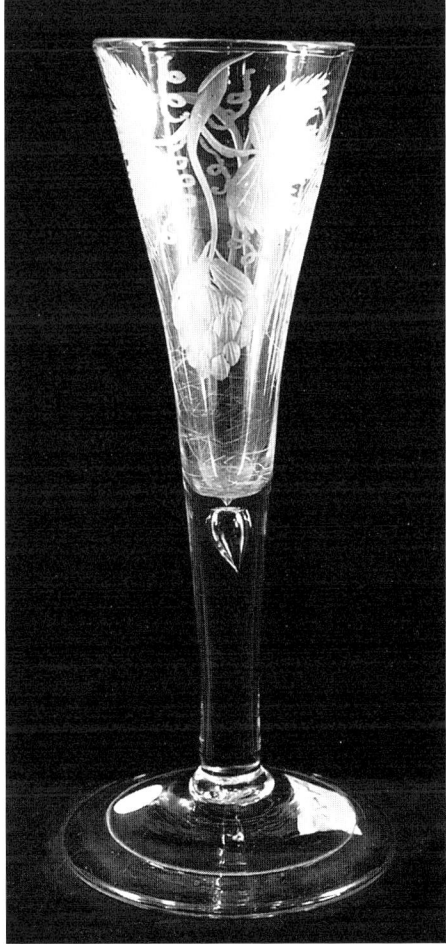

**347.** Wine glass; drawn trumpet bowl; teared stem; FF. Ht. 6ins. c.1740. Soda glass.

**346.** Ale glass; drawn trumpet bowl, engraved with hops and barley; teared stem; FF. Ht. 7½ins. c.1740.
*Hartshorne Collection. (Fig. 273).*

Plain Straight Stems

**348.** Firing glass (?); drawn trumpet bowl; teared stem. Ht. 5ins. c.1750.

**349.** Wine glass; drawn trumpet bowl; teared stem; FF. Ht. 6½ins. c.1740. *Hartshorne Collection.*

**350.** Wine glass; waisted bell bowl with tear in solid base; FF. Ht. 8ins. c.1740.

**351.** Wine glass; waisted bell bowl with tear in solid base; FF. Ht. 5½ins. c.1740. *Hartshorne Collection.*

Plain Straight Stems

**352.** Dram glass; fluted ovoid bowl. Ht. 3½ins. c.1750.
*Hartshorne Collection.*

**353.** Dram glass; ogee bowl, engraved fruiting vine and bird in flight; terraced foot. Ht. 5½ins. c.1740. *Hartshorne Collection.*

**354.** Wine glass; RF bowl. Ht. 5⅜ins. c.1750.

**355.** Wine glass; pan-topped square bucket bowl; straight stem; 'helmet' DF. Ht. 6ins. c.1740. *Christie's.*

Plain Straight Stems

141

**356.** Wine glass; panel-moulded bell bowl; plain stem; D & FF. Ht. 7ins. c.1740.
*Tibbenham Collection, Ipswich Museum.*

**357.** Wine glass; ogee bowl, engraved in Jacobite manner; FF. Ht. 5⅛ins. c.1740.

**358.** Wine glass; ovoid bowl; FF. Ht. 6ins. c.1740.

Plain Straight Stems

**359.** Wine glass, waisted bell bowl, solid base; teared stem; FF. Ht. 6ins. c.1740.
*Hartshorne Collection. (Fig. 201).*

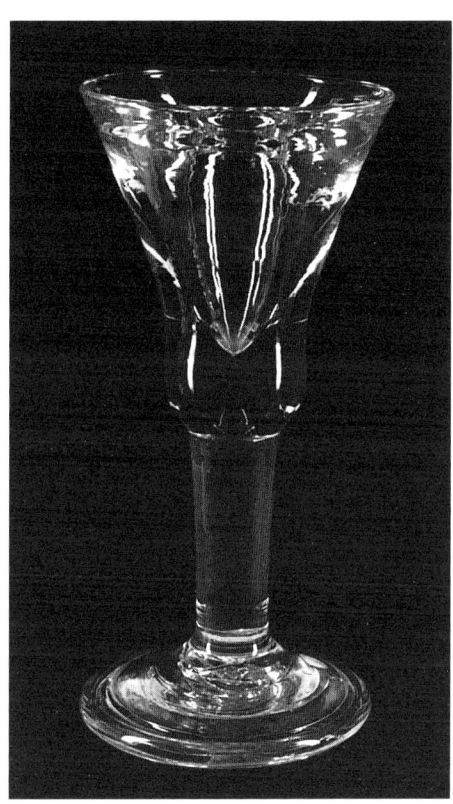

**360.** Toastmaster's glass; deceptive bell bowl; FF. Ht. 7ins. c.1740.

**361.** Ale glass; waisted bell bowl, engraved hops and barley; FF. Ht. 7½ins. c.1740.
*Hartshorne Collection. (Fig. 272).*

**362.** Ale glass; vertically moulded bell bowl; D & FF. Ht. 6¾ins. c.1740.
*Hartshorne Collection.*

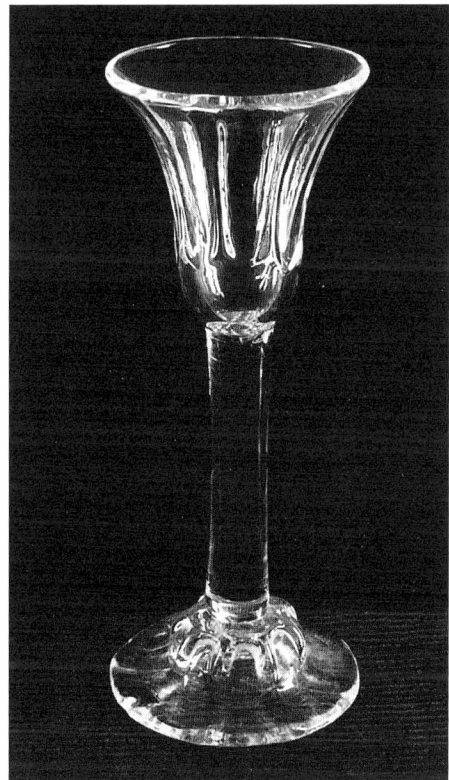

**363.** Wine glass; vertically moulded bell bowl; moulded domed foot. Ht. 5⅞ins. c.1750.

**364.** Wine glass; hammered bell bowl. Ht. 7½ins. c.1750.

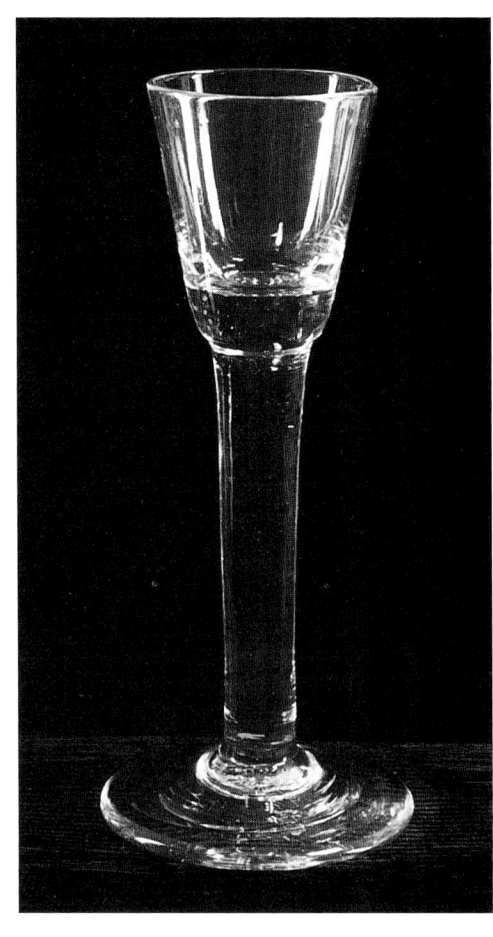

**365.** Cordial; RF bowl, solid base. Ht. 6½ins. c.1750.

**366.** Wine glass; RF bowl, fluted base; FF. Ht. 6ins. c.1740.

**367.** Ale glass; RF bowl; FF. Ht. 6ins. c.1740.

**368.** Wine glass; ogee bowl; fluted base. Ht. 6½ins. c.1750.

Plain Straight Stems

**369.** Goblet; bucket bowl; FF. Ht. 6⅜ins. c.1740.
*Hartshorne Collection.*

**370.** Wine glass; bucket bowl. Ht. 6ins. c.1750.

**371.** Wine glass; cup bowl; FF. Ht. 7⅛ins. c.1740.

**372.** Wine glass; ovoid bowl, moulded base and engraved floral border below rim; FF. Ht. 5⅝ins. c.1740.

Plain Straight Stems

**373.** Champagne glass (?); slightly waisted pan bowl; D & FF. Ht. 6½ins. c.1740.

**374.** Wine glass; stepped RF ('Lynn') bowl; plain stem. Ht. 6ins. c.1760.           *Sotheby's.*

**375.** Wine glass; trumpet bowl; collar. Ht. 7ins. c.1750.

**376.** Wine glass; drawn trumpet bowl; plain stem commencing with triple-ringed collar. Ht. 6⅜ins. c.1740.

*Tibbenham Collection, Ipswich Museum.*

Plain Straight Stems

**377.** Wine glass; bell bowl; thin stem between triple and quadruple collars; FF. Ht. 6¾ins. c.1740.

**378.** Wine glass; ogee bowl, engraved sprays of flowers; collar; FF. Ht. 5½ins. c.1740.

**379.** Cordial; RF bowl, solid base with tear, basal knop; FF. Ht. 6½ins. c.1740.

*Tibbenham Collection, Ipswich Museum.*

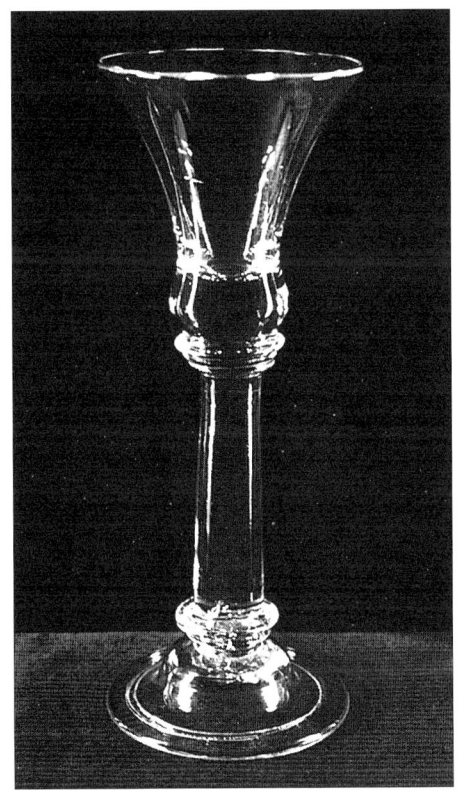

**380.** Wine glass; bell bowl, solid base; tapering stem between collars; D & FF. Ht. 7ins. c.1740.

*Cecil Higgins Museum, Bedford.*

**381.** Dram glass; vertically moulded conical bowl; collar. Ht. 4ins. c.1750.

**382.** Wine glass; ogee bowl; hollow stem. Ht. 4¾ins. c.1760.

**383.** Wine glass; trumpet bowl; hollow stem; FF. Ht.6⅜ins. c.1750.
*Smith Collection. Harvey's Wine Museum, Bristol.*

**384.** Wine glass; RF bowl, engraved fruiting vine and butterfly; hollow stem; D & FF. Ht. 6½ins. c.1745.
*Pilkington Glass Museum, St. Helens.*

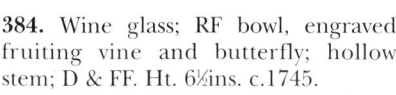

**385.** Wine glass; trumpet bowl; hollow stem; FF. Ht. 6¼ins. c.1745.

Plain Straight Stems

**386.** Sweetmeat; lipped RF bowl; semi-hollow swelling stem between collars; high conical foot. Ht. 7ins. c.1750 (unfinished glass?).

**387.** Goblet; saucer-topped, vertically moulded RF bowl; hollow stem with swelled centre knop. Ht. 6¼ins. c.1750.
*Tibbenham Collection, Ipswich Museum.*

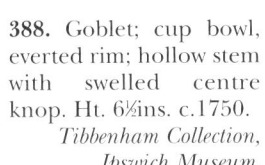

**388.** Goblet; cup bowl, everted rim; hollow stem with swelled centre knop. Ht. 6½ins. c.1750.
*Tibbenham Collection, Ipswich Museum.*

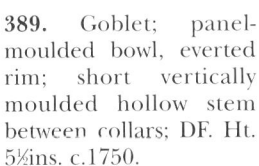

**389.** Goblet; panel-moulded bowl, everted rim; short vertically moulded hollow stem between collars; DF. Ht. 5½ins. c.1750.
*Tibbenham Collection, Ipswich Museum.*

Plain Straight Stems

# VII
# Air-Twist Stems

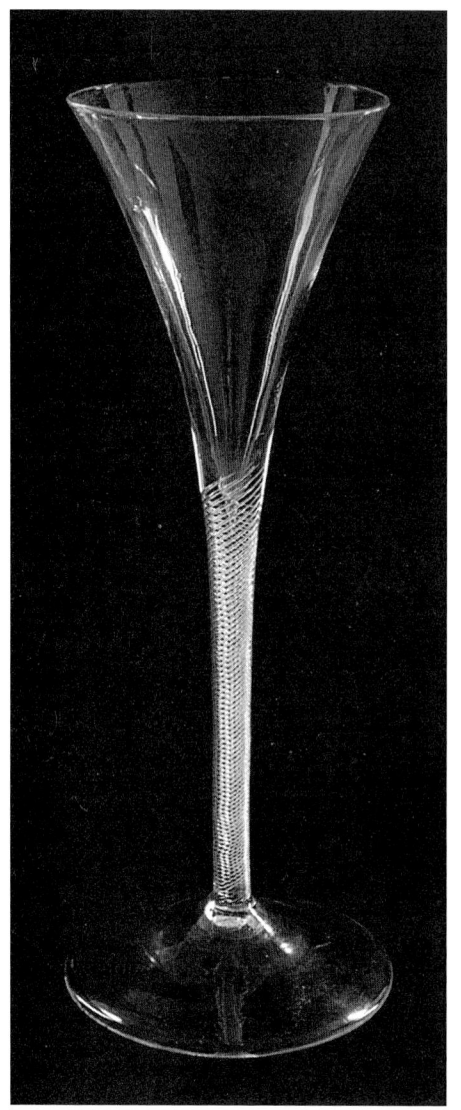

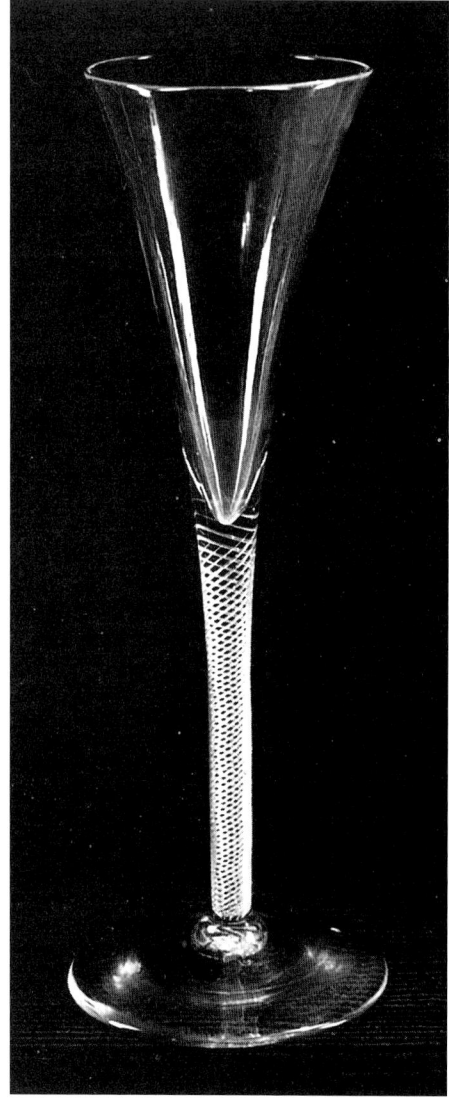

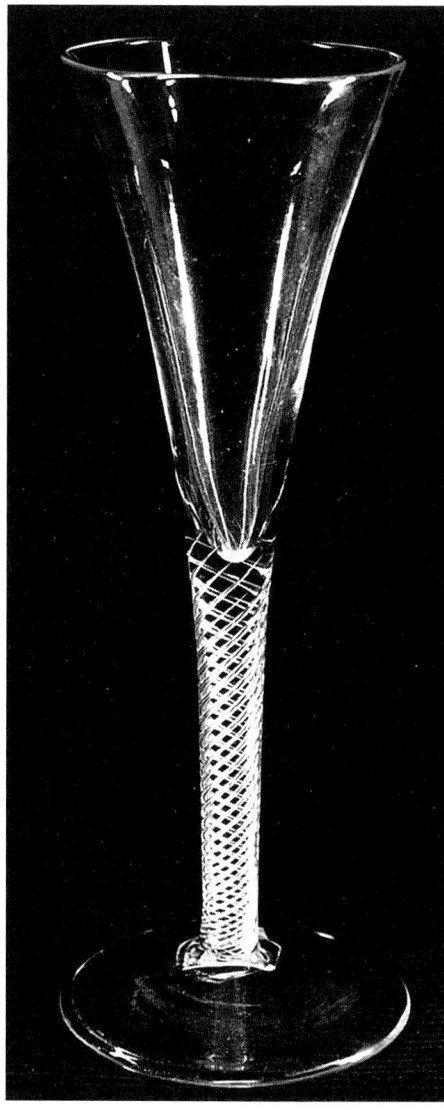

**390.** Toasting glass; drawn trumpet bowl; MSAT. Ht. 7⅞ins. c.1750.
*Smith Collection. Harvey's Wine Museum, Bristol.*

**391.** Wine flute; drawn trumpet bowl; MSAT. Ht. 7¾ins. c.1750.

**392.** Wine flute; drawn trumpet bowl; MSAT; FF. Ht. 7¼ins. c.1750.

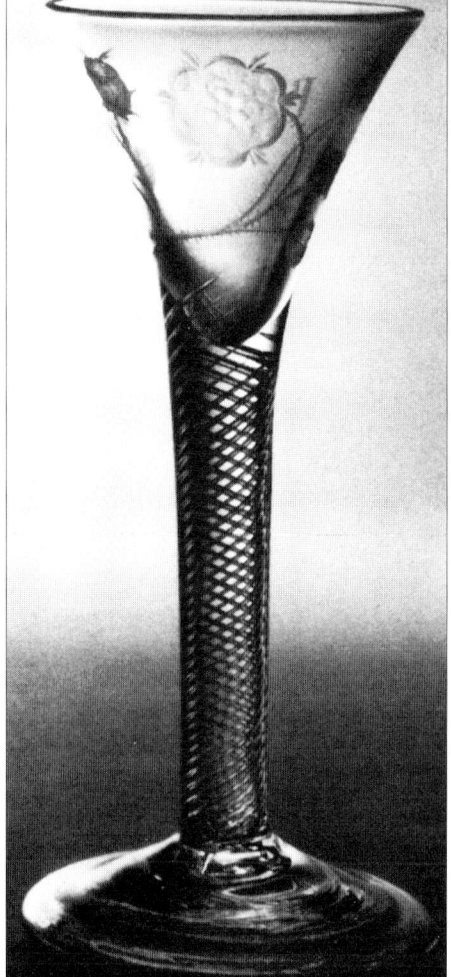

**393.** Wine glass; drawn trumpet bowl with Jacobite engraving; MSAT. c.1750.

*Christie's.*

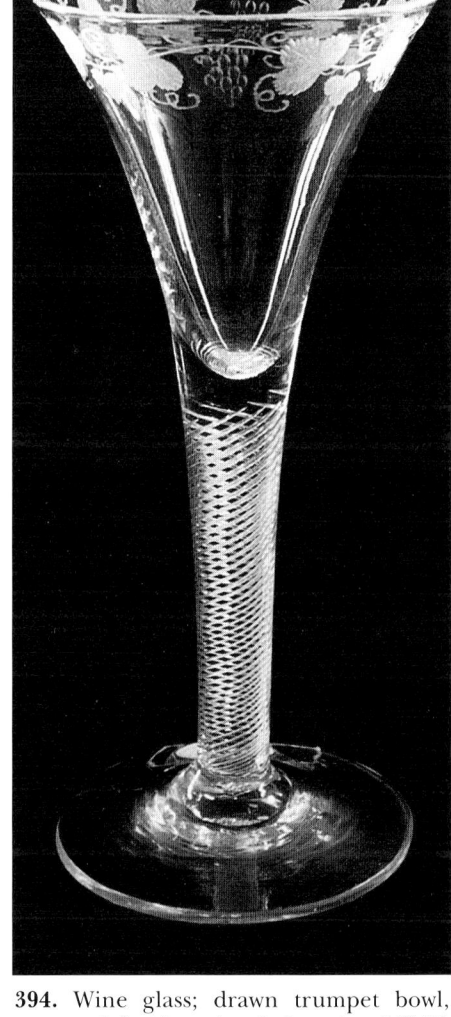

**394.** Wine glass; drawn trumpet bowl, engraved fruiting vine below rim; MSAT. Ht. 7ins. c.1750.

*Harvey's Wine Museum, Bristol.*

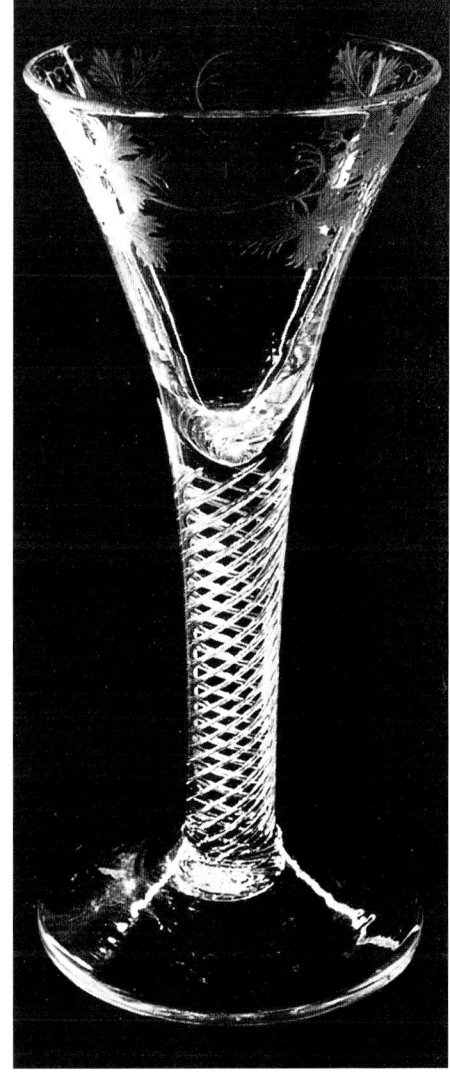

**395.** Wine glass; drawn trumpet bowl, engraved fruiting vine; MSAT. Ht. 6½ins. c.1750.

**Air-Twist Stems**

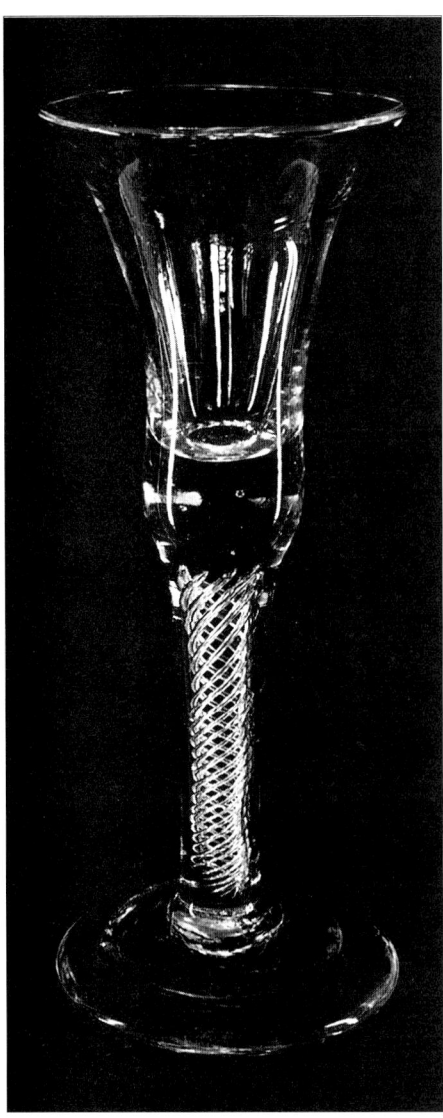

**396.** Wine glass; waisted bell bowl, solid base; MSAT. Ht. 6¾ins. c.1750.

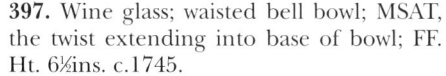

**397.** Wine glass; waisted bell bowl; MSAT, the twist extending into base of bowl; FF. Ht. 6½ins. c.1745.

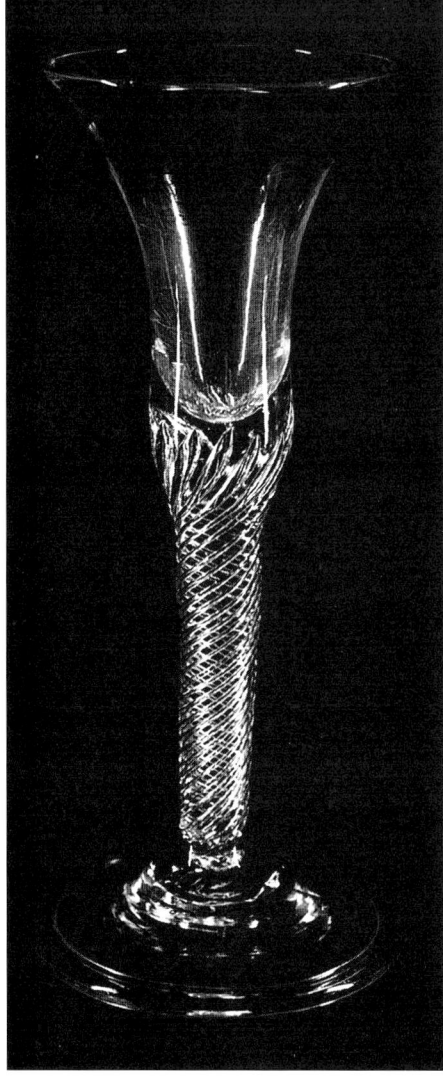

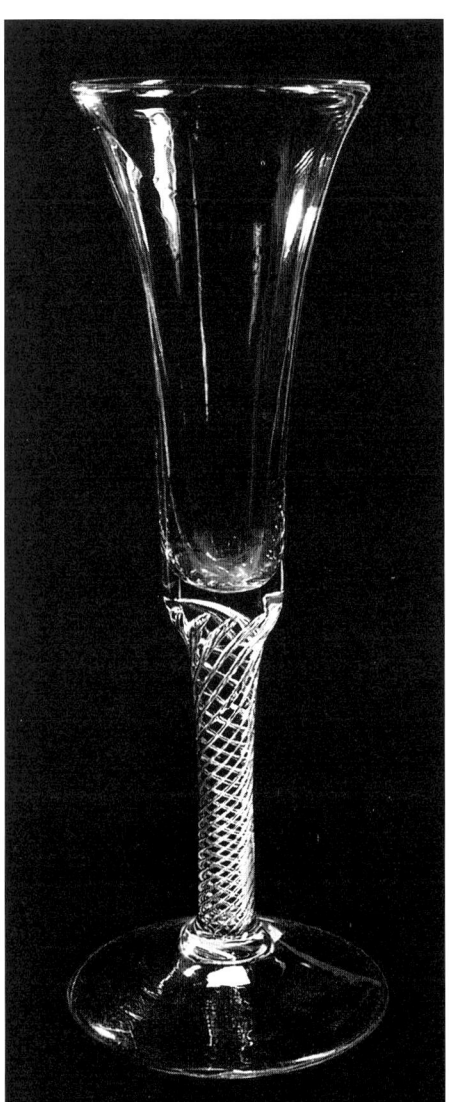

**398.** Ale glass; bell bowl, solid base; MSAT continuing into base of bowl. Ht. 9ins. c.1750.

*Tibbenham Collection, Ipswich Museum.*

Air-Twist Stems

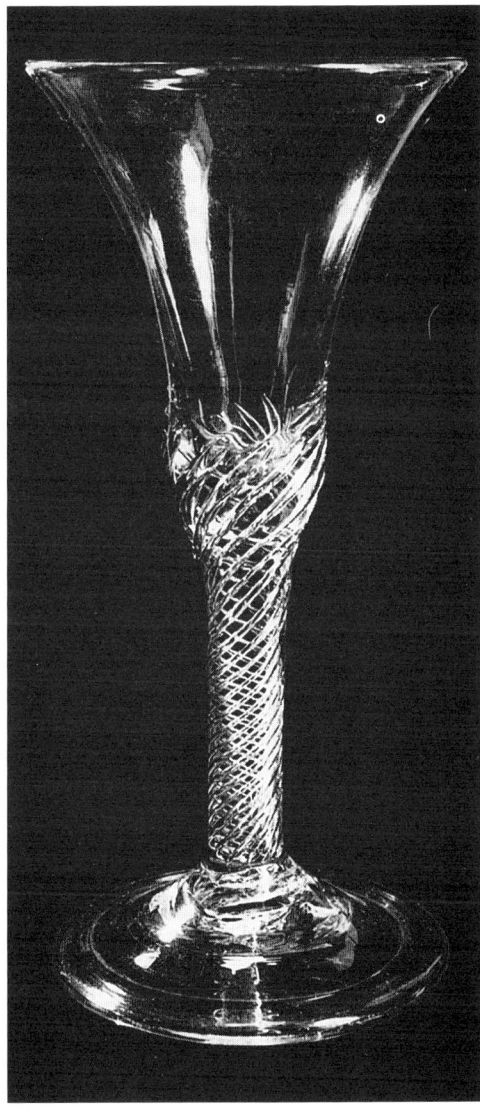

**399.** Wine glass; bell bowl, solid base; MSAT continuing into base of bowl; FF. Ht. 6⅞ins. c.1750. *Tibbenham Collection, Ipswich Museum.*

**400.** Wine glass; bell bowl, solid base; MSAT, continuing into base of bowl; DF. Ht. 7ins. c.1750.
*Tibbenham Collection, Ipswich Museum.*

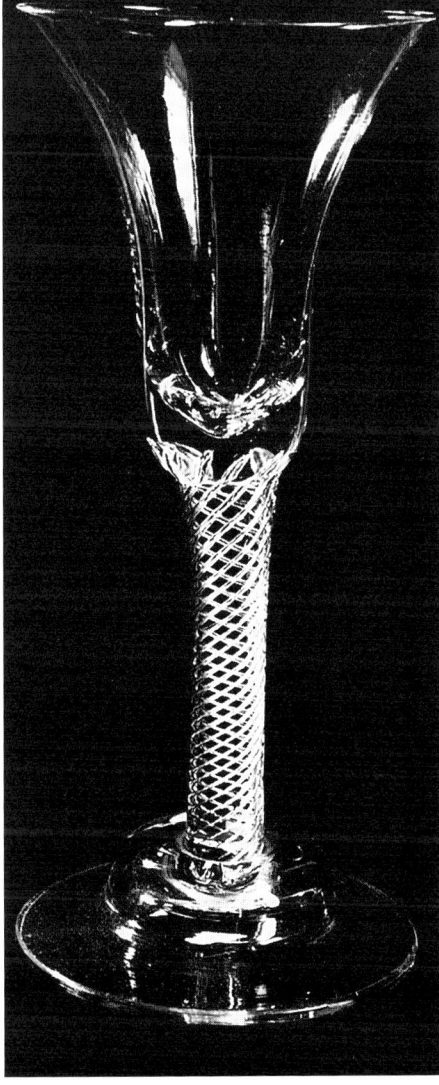

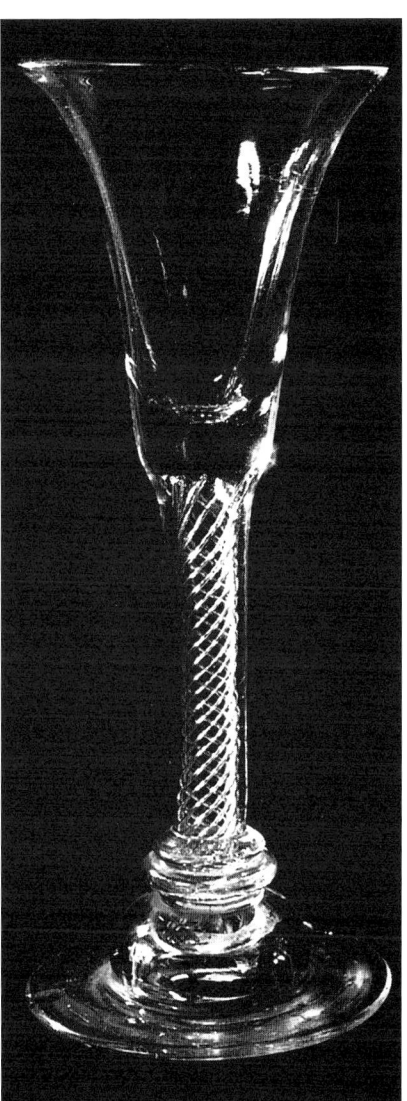

**401.** Wine glass; bell bowl, solid base; MSAT terminating in 3-ringed collar; DF. Ht. 7ins. c.1750.
*Tibbenham Collection, Ipswich Museum.*

**402.** Firing glass; bell bowl, solid base; MSAT, the twist extending into base of bowl. Ht. 4ins. c.1750.

**403.** Wine glass; RF bowl, hammered base; MSAT; DF. Ht. 6ins. c.1750.     *Ipswich Museum.*

**404.** Wine glass; bucket bowl; MSAT. Ht. 7¼ins. c.1750.

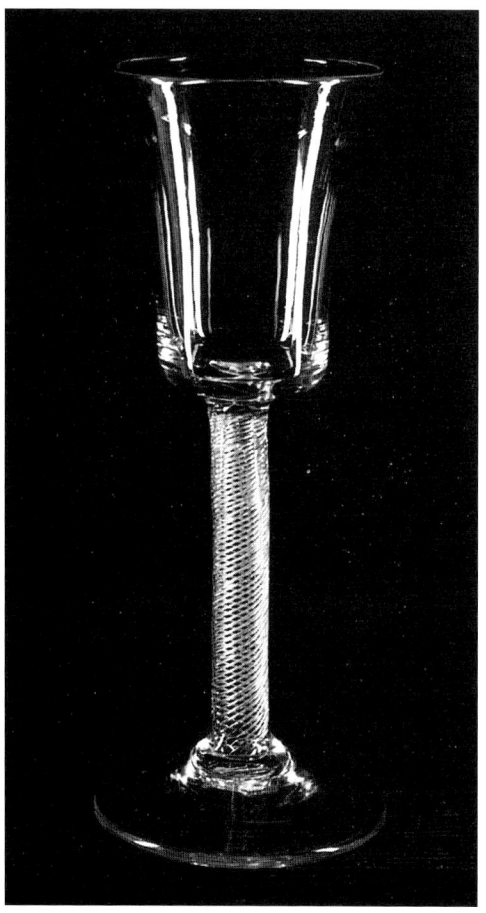

**405.** Toastmaster's glass; deceptive funnel bowl, engraved with band of hatched crescents below rim; MSAT. Ht. 5¼ins. c.1750.
*Tibbenham Collection,*
*Ipswich Museum.*

Air-Twist Stems

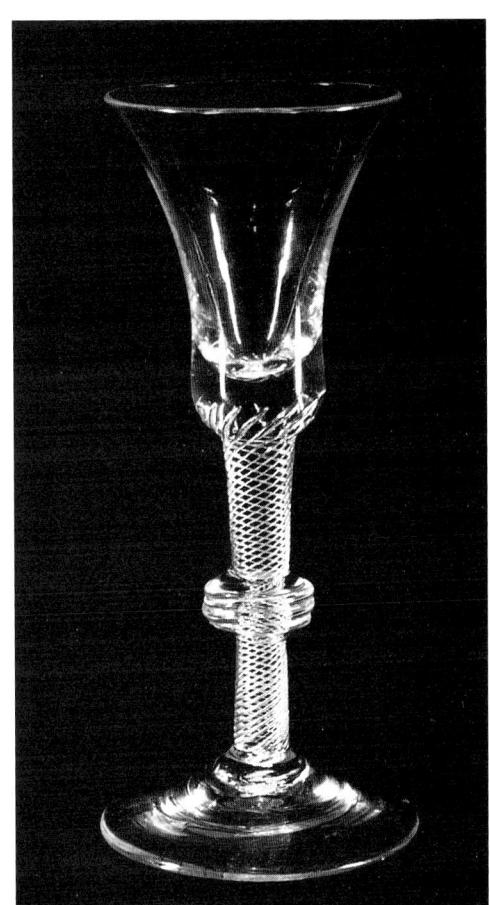

**406.** Ale glass; RF bowl, engraved hops and barley; MSAT. Ht. 7⅜ins. c.1750.

**407.** Wine glass; bell bowl, solid base; MSAT with central coil collar. Ht. 6⅞ins. c.1750.

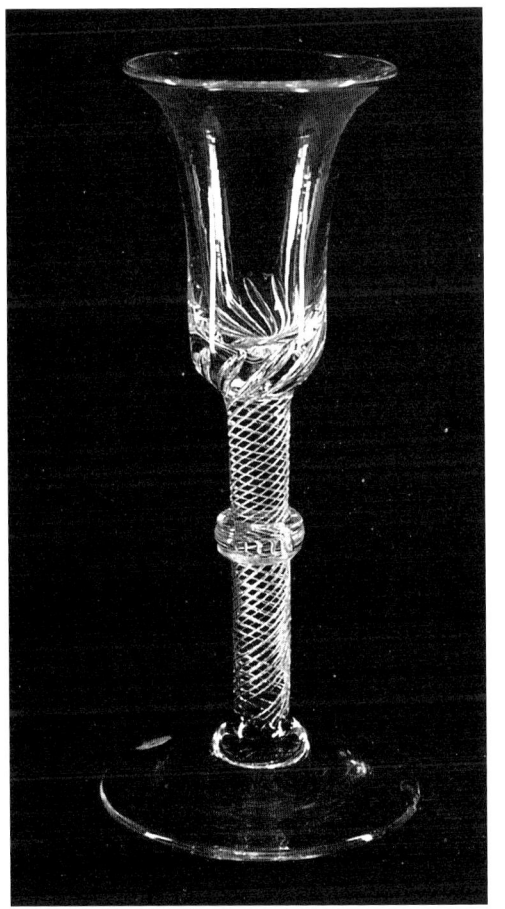

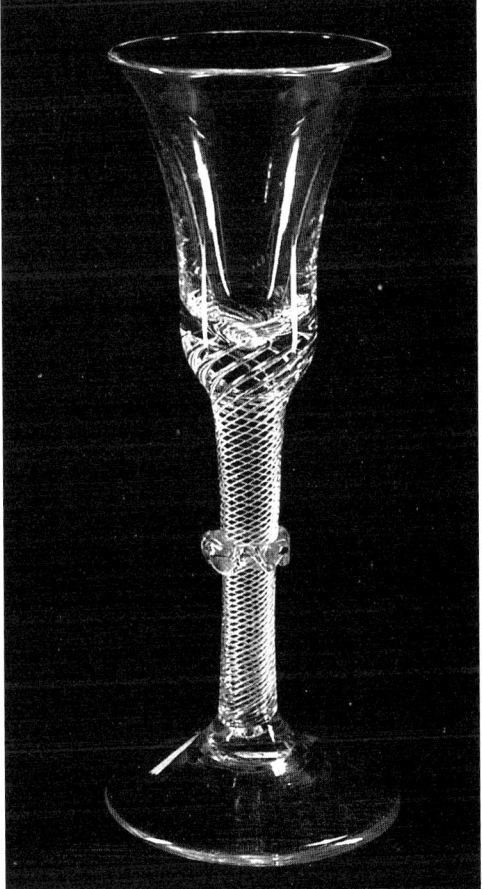

**408.** Wine glass; bell bowl, solid base; MSAT, the twist extending into base of bowl; central collar. Ht. 6¾ins. c.1750.

**409.** Wine glass; bell bowl, solid base; MSAT, the twist extending into base of bowl; central vermiform collar. Ht. 6⅜ins. c.1750. *Hartshorne Collection. (Fig. 188).*

Air-Twist Stems

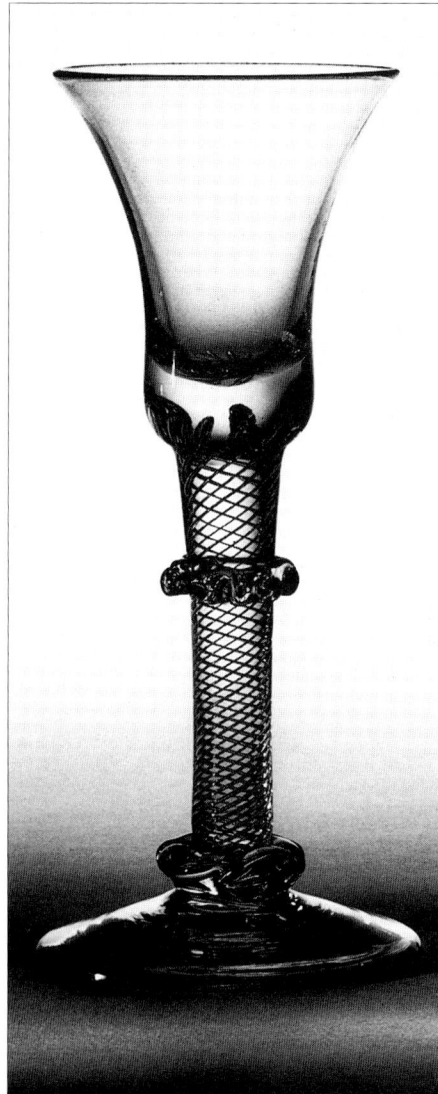

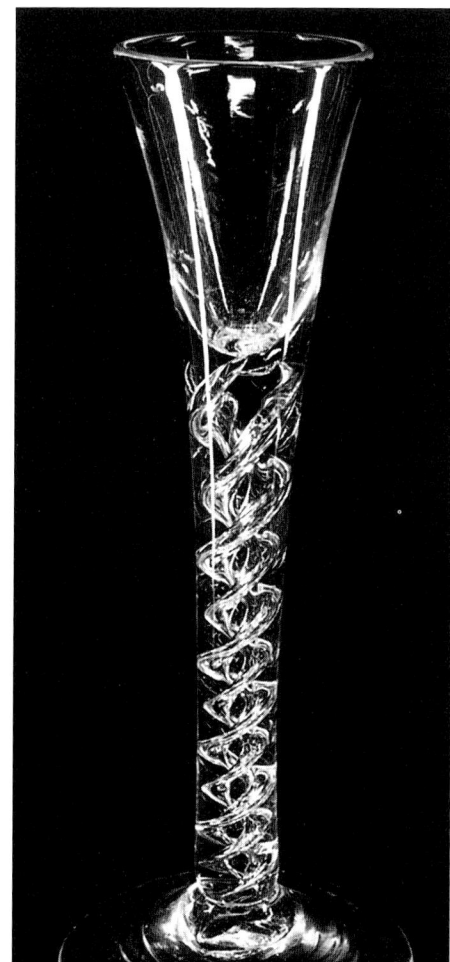

**410.** Wine glass; bell bowl; MSAT with central and basal vermiform collars. c.1750.                                 *Christie's.*

**411.** Cordial glass; drawn trumpet bowl; SSAT stem – pair of corkscrews ('mercury twist'). Ht. 7ins. c.1750.

**412.** Wine glass; drawn trumpet bowl; SSAT – pair of corkscrews 'mercury twist'. Ht. 6¼ins. c.1750.

*Tibbenham Collection, Ipswich Museum.*

Air-Twist Stems

**413.** Champagne glass; double ogee bowl; collar; MSAT with central double-ringed collar; moulded domed foot. Ht. 5⅞ins. c.1750.

**414.** Cider glass; bucket bowl, engraved border of apple branch below rim; SSAT – pair of corkscrews ('mercury twist'). Ht. 6⅝ins. c.1750.
*Hartshorne Collection. (Plate 51).*

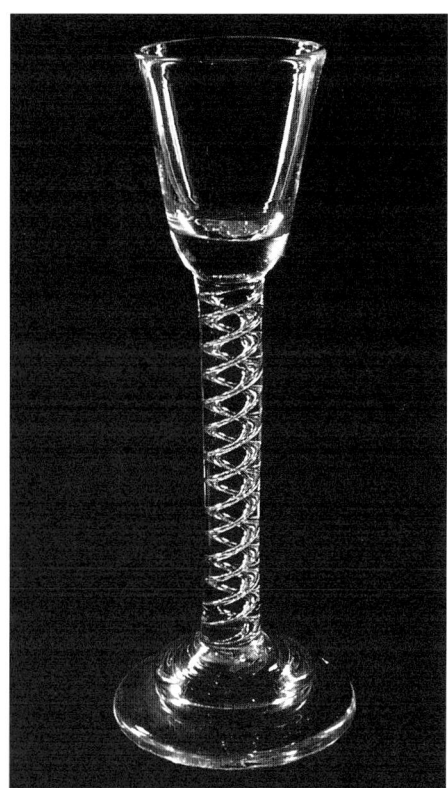

**415.** Cordial; RF bowl, SSAT – pair of corkscrews; DF. Ht. 6⅞ins. c.1750.
*Smith Collection. Harvey's Wine Museum, Bristol.*

**416.** Wine glass; ogee bowl; SSAT – pair of corkscrews. Ht. 6ins. c.1750.

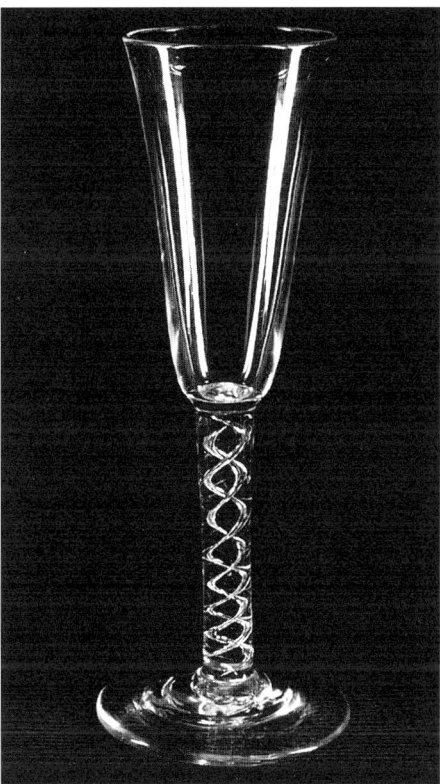

**417.** Ale glass; RF bowl; SSAT – pair of corkscrews. Ht. 7¾ins. c.1750.

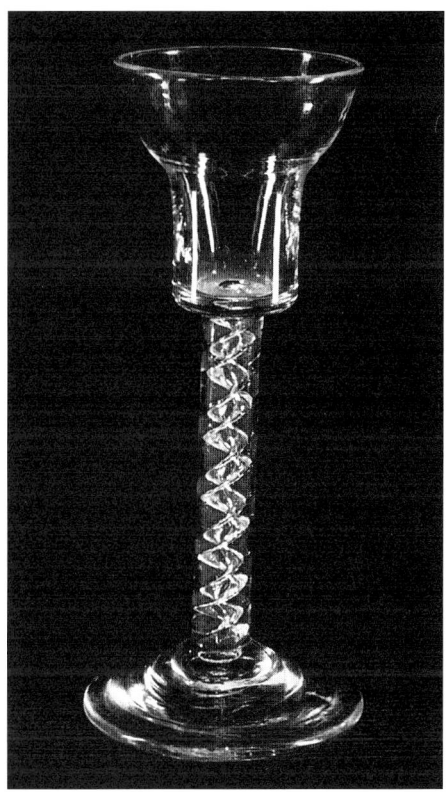

**418.** Wine glass; pan-topped bucket bowl; SSAT – pair of corkscrews. Ht. 6ins. c.1750.
*Hartshorne Collection.*

**419.** Wine glass; RF bowl, slightly wrythen vertical moulding; SSAT – pair of spiral cables; foot moulded to match bowl. Ht. 6ins. c.1750.
*Tibbenham Collection, Ipswich Museum.*

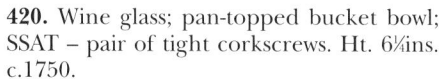

**420.** Wine glass; pan-topped bucket bowl; SSAT – pair of tight corkscrews. Ht. 6¼ins. c.1750.

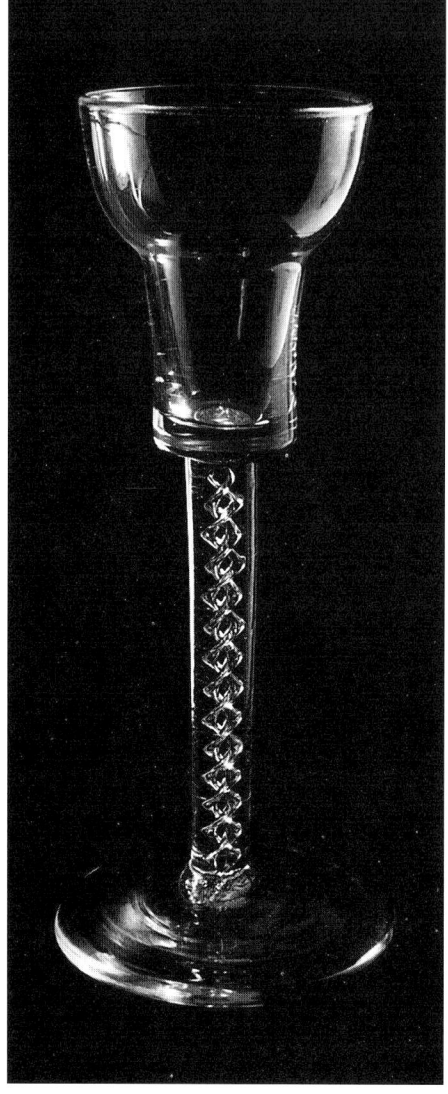

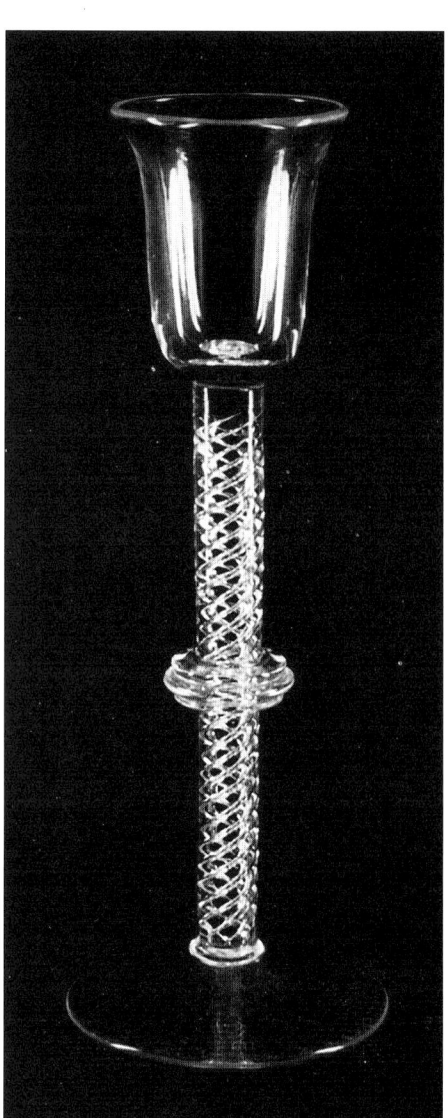

**421.** Cordial; lipped RF bowl; SSAT – four corkscrews; annulated collar. Ht. 7ins. c.1755.

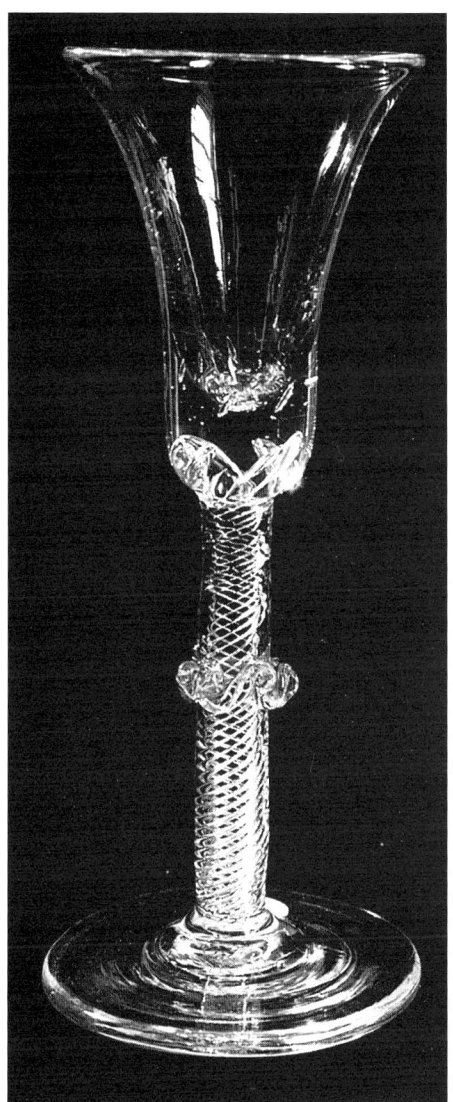

**422.** Wine glass; bell bowl; MSAT, vermiform collar. c.1750.
*Tibbenham Collection, Ipswich Museum.*

**423.** Wine glass; funnel bowl; MSAT with two vermicular collars. Ht. 6¼ins. c.1760.
*Christie's.*

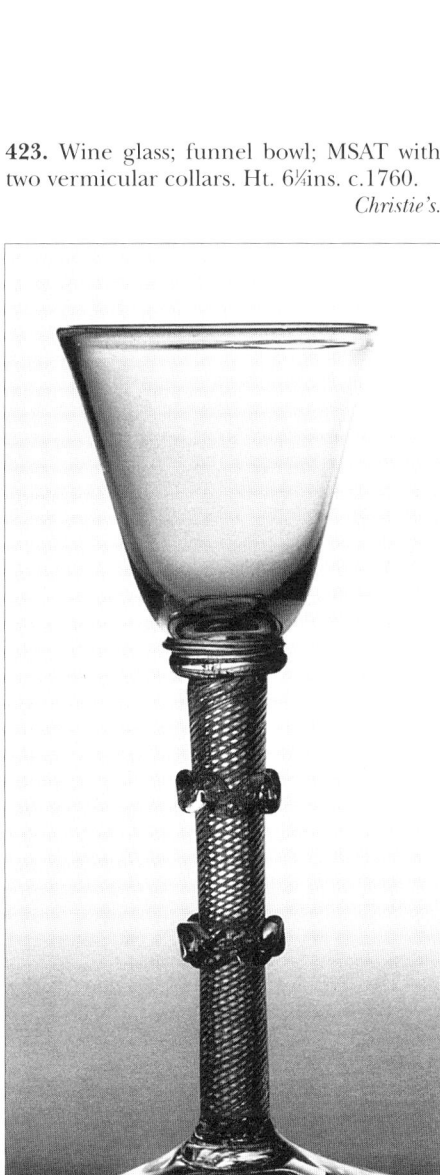

**424.** Ale glass; ogee bowl engraved with hops and barley; SSAT – four spiral twists. Ht. 7ins. c.1750.
*Tibbenham Collection, Ipswich Museum.*

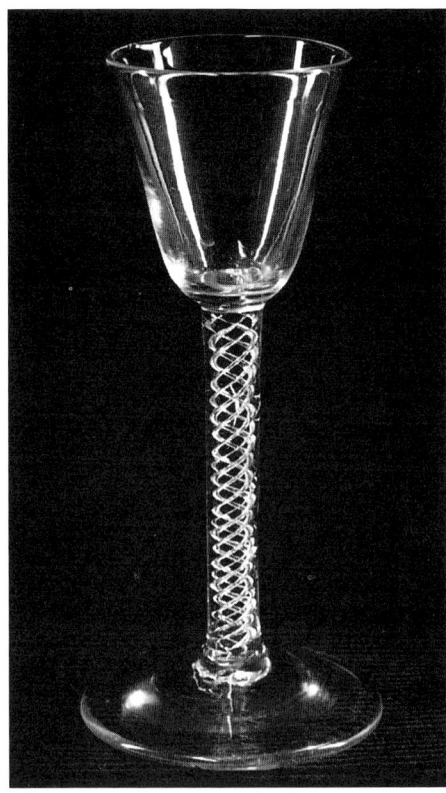

**425.** Wine glass; pointed RF bowl; SSAT – four corkscrews. Ht. 5⅝ins. c.1750.
*Hartshorne Collection.*

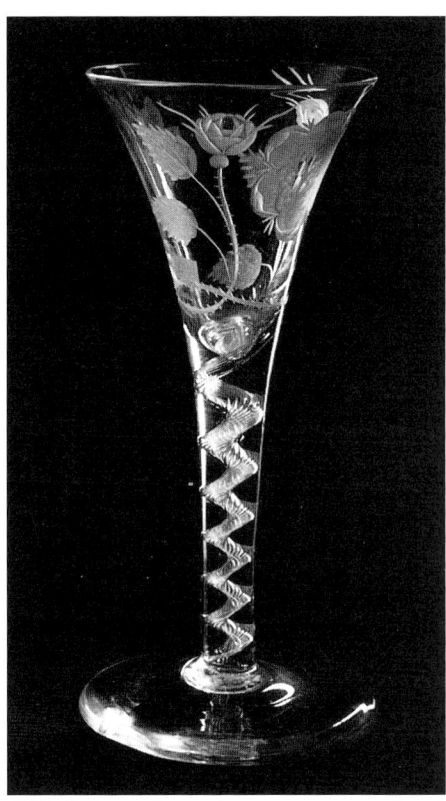

**426.** Wine glass; drawn trumpet bowl engraved with rose and two buds; SSAT – spiral cable (Jacobite). c.1750.
*Hartshorne Collection.*

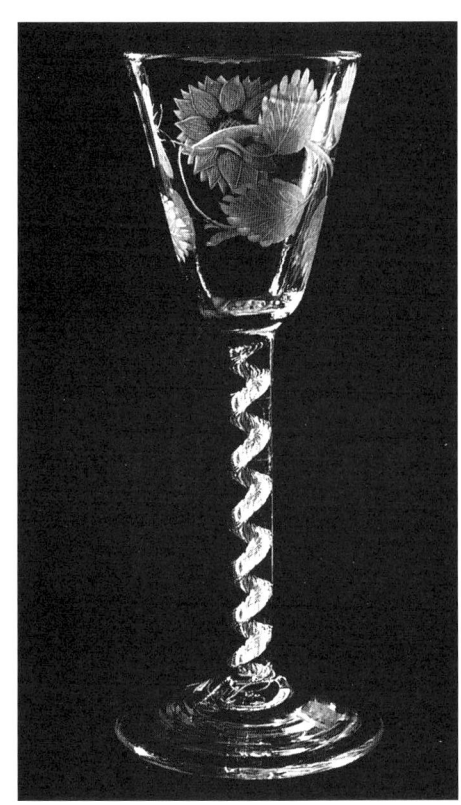

**427.** Wine glass; pointed RF bowl engraved with rose and moth (Jacobite); SSAT stem – single spiral cable. Ht. 6ins. c.1750.
*Tibbenham Collection, Ipswich Museum.*

**428.** Wine glass; RF bowl, engraved floral design; SSAT – spiral cable. Ht. 6¼ins. c.1750.

**429.** Wine glass; pointed RF bowl, engraved fruiting vine; SSAT – spiral cable. Ht. 6ins. c.1750.

**430.** Wine glass; pointed RF bowl, honeycomb-moulded base; SSAT – spiral cable. Ht. 6⅛ins. c.1750.

**431.** Wine glass; pan-topped RF bowl; SSAT – spiral cable. Ht. 6¼ins. c.1750.        *Hartshorne Collection.*

**432.** Goblet; bucket bowl; SSAT – single spiral cable. Ht. 7½ins. c.1750.

*Tibbenham Collection, Ipswich Museum.*

**433.** Ale glass; pan-topped funnel bowl engraved below the rim with a band of honeysuckle (? Jacobite): DSAT – spiral cable outside vertical thread. Ht. 7¼ins. c.1750.        *Asprey.*

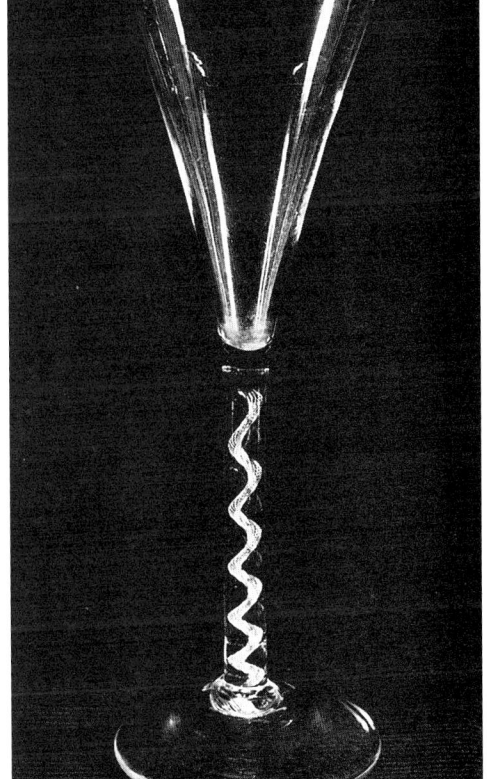

**434.** Wine flute; trumpet bowl; SSAT – spiral cable. Ht. 7½ins. c.1750.        *Portsmouth City Museums.*

Air-Twist Stems

**435.** Wine glass; pointed RF bowl; SSAT stem — vertical cable. Ht. 6½ins. c.1750.
*Tibbenham Collection, Ipswich Museum.*

**436.** Wine glass; moulded RF bowl; SSAT – pair spiral cables. Ht. 6ins. c.1750.

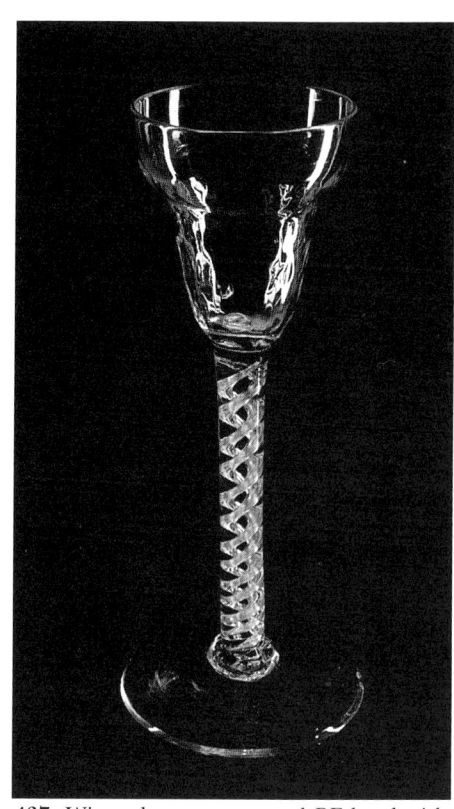

**437.** Wine glass; pan-topped RF bowl with moulded base; SSAT – pair spiral cables. Ht. 6⅓ins. c.1750.

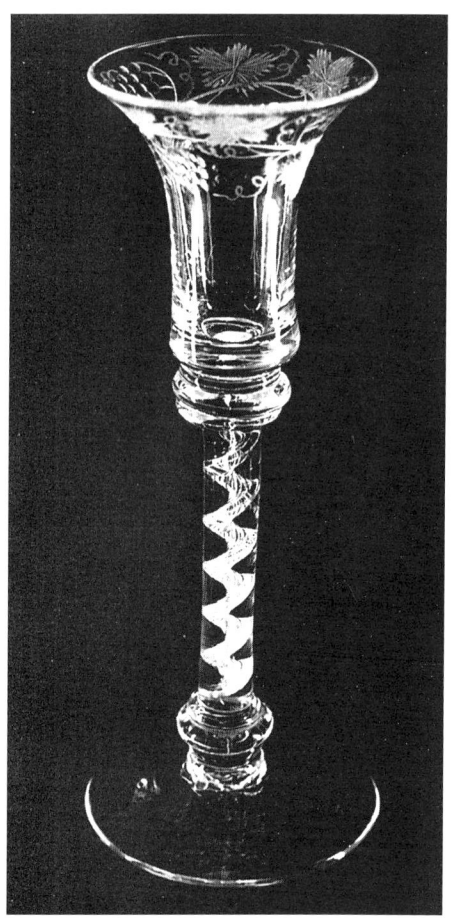

**438.** Cordial; waisted bucket bowl, engraved border of fruiting vine below rim; double collar; SSAT – spiral gauze; basal knop. Ht. 6⅜ins. c.1750.
*Cecil Higgins Museum, Bedford.*

**439.** Ale glass; RF bowl; SSAT – spiral gauze. Ht. 7⅛ins. c.1750.

Air-Twist Stems

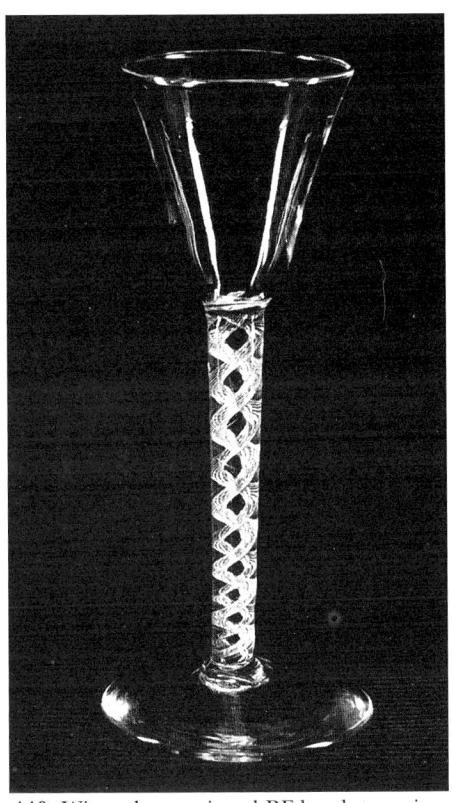

**440.** Wine glass; pointed RF bowl; tapering stem with SSAT – pair spiral gauzes. Ht. 6ins. c.1750.

**441.** Wine glass; ogee bowl, moulded base; shoulder-knopped MSAT. Ht. 6¼ins c.1750.
*Smith Collection.*

**442.** Wine glass; RF bowl, moulded base; shoulder-knopped MSAT. Ht. 6ins. c.1750.
*Hartshorne Collection.*

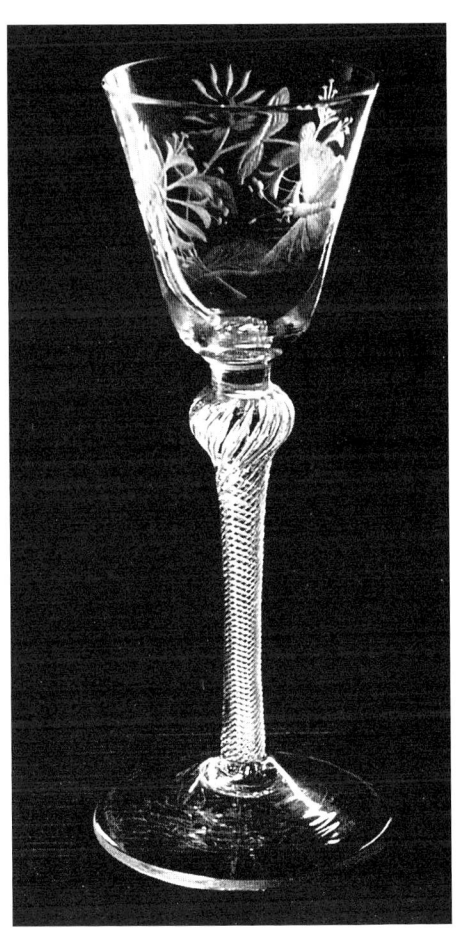

**443.** Wine glass; RF bowl, engraved moth and honeysuckle (? Jacobite); shoulder-knopped MSAT. Ht. 5¾ins. c.1750.

**444.** Wine glass; RF bowl, moulded base; shoulder-knopped MSAT. Ht. 6ins. c.1750.

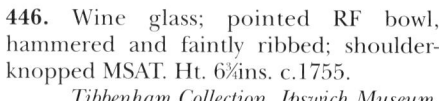

**446.** Wine glass; pointed RF bowl, hammered and faintly ribbed; shoulder-knopped MSAT. Ht. 6¾ins. c.1755.
*Tibbenham Collection, Ipswich Museum.*

**445.** Wine glass; pointed RF bowl, moulded base; shoulder-knopped MSAT. Ht. 7ins. c.1750.

**447.** Wine glass; pointed RF bowl, moulded base; shoulder-knopped MSAT. Ht. 6½ins. c.1750.

Air-Twist Stems

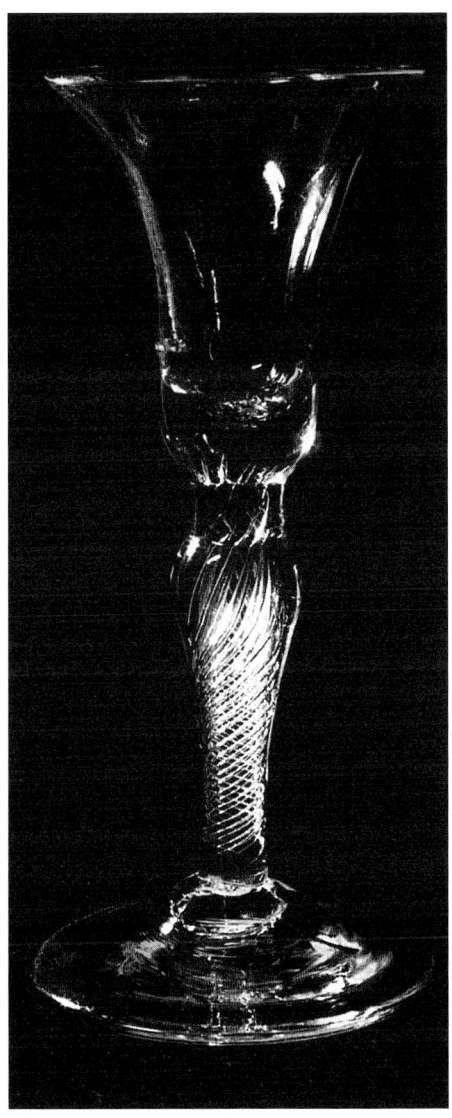

**448.** Wine glass; bell bowl, solid base; shoulder-knopped MSAT. Ht. 6⅜ins. c.1755.

*Tibbenham Collection, Ipswich Museum.*

**449.** Wine glass; pointed RF bowl, moulded base; shoulder-knopped MSAT. Ht. 5½ins. c.1750.

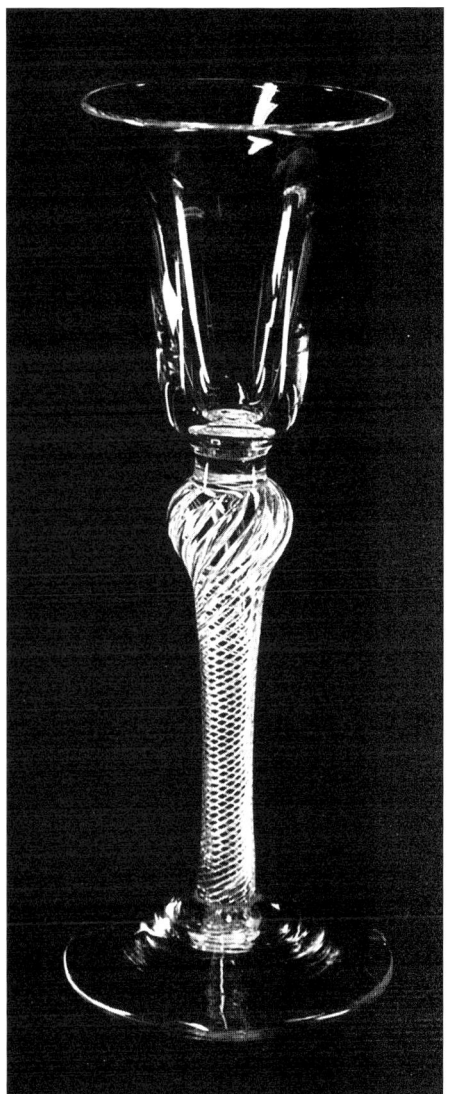

**450.** Wine glass; bell bowl; shoulder-knopped MSAT. Ht. 6½ins. c.1750.

*Hartshorne Collection.*

**451.** Wine glass; bell bowl, solid base; shoulder-knopped MSAT. Ht. 6¾ins. c.1750.

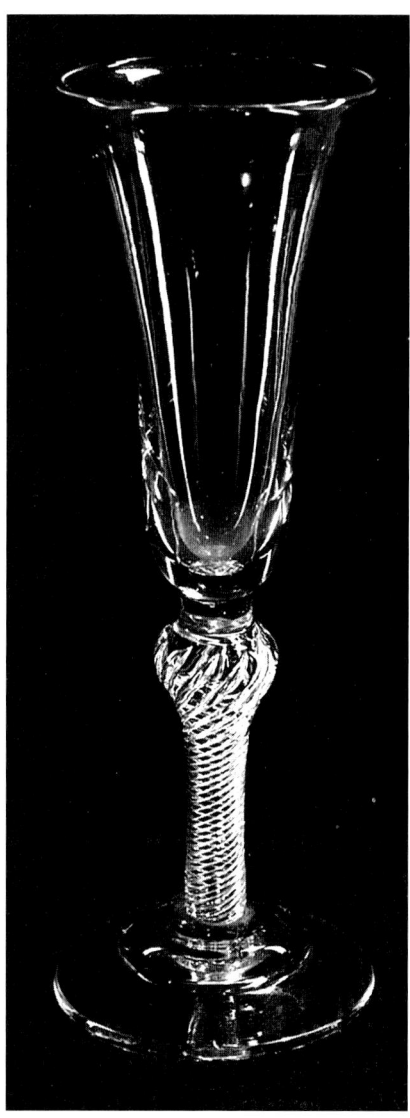

**453.** Wine glass; vertical rib-moulded waisted bell bowl; shoulder-knopped MSAT; DF to match. Ht. 5¾ins. c.1750.

**452.** Ale glass; bell bowl; shoulder-knopped MSAT; DF. Ht. 8¾ins. c.1750.

*Hartshorne Collection.*

Air-Twist Stems

**454.** Wine glass; RF bowl, engraved fruiting vine; MSAT with central swelling knop. Ht. 6⅛ins. c.1750.

**455.** Wine glass; RF bowl; centre-swelled knop MSAT. Ht. 6¼ins. c.1755.
*Tibbenham Collection, Ipswich Museum.*

**456.** Wine glass; pan-topped RF bowl; centre-swelled-knop MSAT; FF. Ht. 6¼ins. c.1755.
*Tibbenham Collection, Ipswich Museum.*

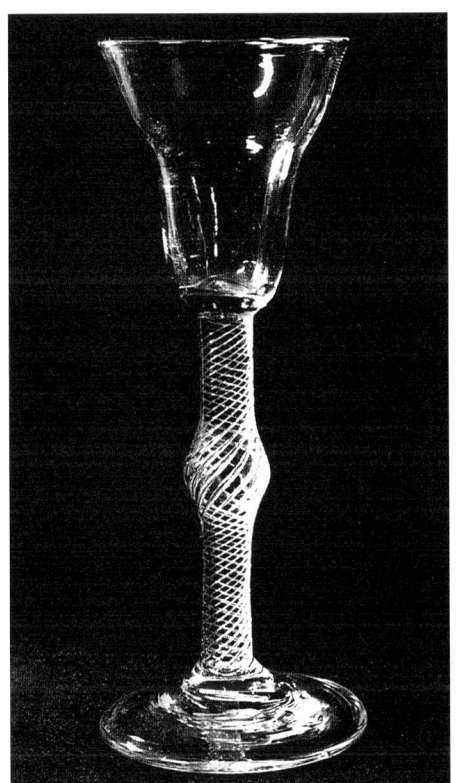

**457.** Wine glass; pan-topped RF bowl; centre-knopped MSAT. Ht. 6¼ins. c.1755.
*Tibbenham Collection, Ipswich Museum.*

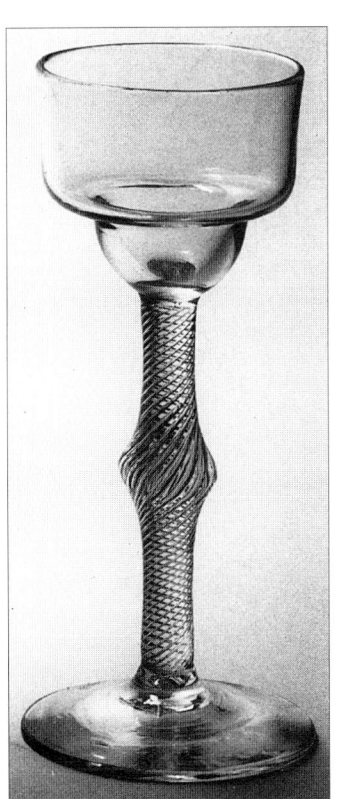

**458.** Wine glass; deep pan-topped RF bowl; MSAT with swelled knop. Ht. 5¾ins. c.1750.
*Sotheby's.*

**459.** Wine glass; pan-topped RF bowl; MSAT with central swelling knop. Ht. 6ins. c.1750.

**460.** Wine glass; pan-topped, vertically moulded RF bowl, engraved floral band below rim; MSAT with central swelled knop. Ht. 5⅝ins. c.1750.

**461.** Ale glass; pan-topped RF bowl; MSAT with central swelled knop. Ht. 8¼ins. c.1750.

**462.** Sweetmeat; double-ogee bowl; collar; DSAT – four spirals outside vertical thread with IB shoulder knop and basal knop; D & FF. Ht. 6¼ins. c.1750. *Asprey.*

**463.** Ale glass; pan-topped RF bowl; centre-knopped MSAT. Ht. 7⅜ins. c.1755. *Tibbenham Collection, Ipswich Museum.*

Air-Twist Stems

**464.** Wine glass; ogee bowl; centre-knopped MSAT. Ht. 6¾ins. c.1755.
*Tibbenham Collection, Ipswich Museum.*

**465.** Toastmaster's glass; deceptive funnel bowl; 3-ringed collar; MSAT with central swelled knop; D & FF. Ht. 7ins. c.1750.
*Cecil Higgins Museum, Bedford.*

**466.** Wine glass; bell bowl; MSAT with central ball knop. Ht. 6½ins. c.1750.

**467.** Sweetmeat; double-ogee bowl; 3-ringed collar; shoulder-knopped SSAT with pair of corkscrews ('mercury twist'); D & FF. Ht. 7¼ins. c.1745.

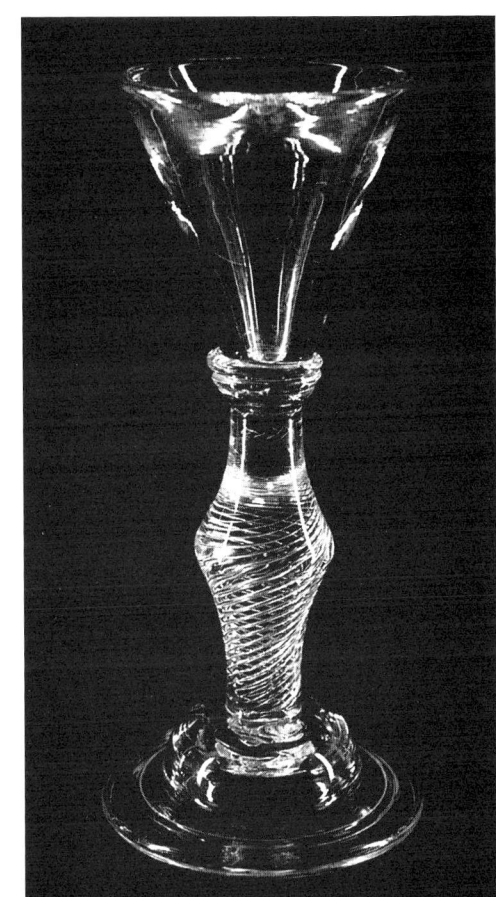
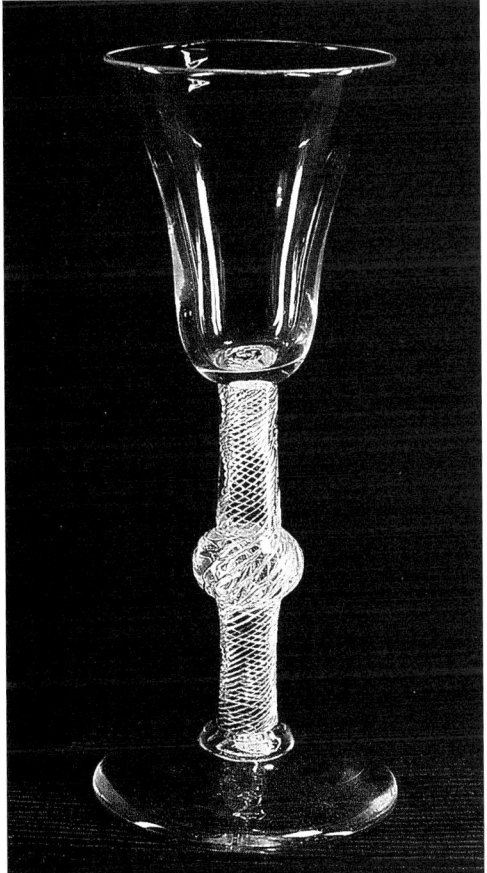

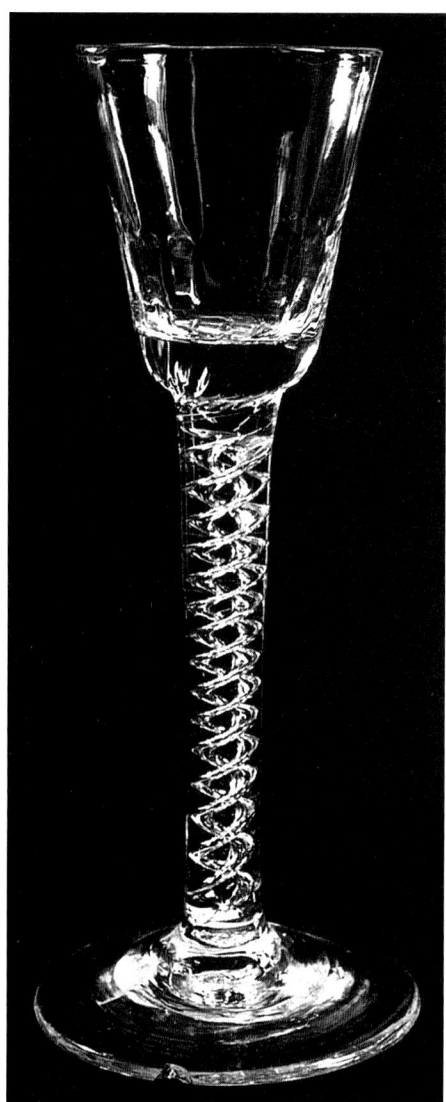

**468.** Cordial or small wine glass; RF bowl with vertical moulding round the base; SSAT – a pair of corkscrews ('mercury twist'). Ht. 6⅜ins. c.1750.

*Tibbenham Collection, Ipswich Museum.*

**469.** Cordial; drawn trumpet bowl engraved with rose-bud and insect; SSAT ('mercury twist'). Ht. 6⅜ins. c.1750.

*Sotheby's.*

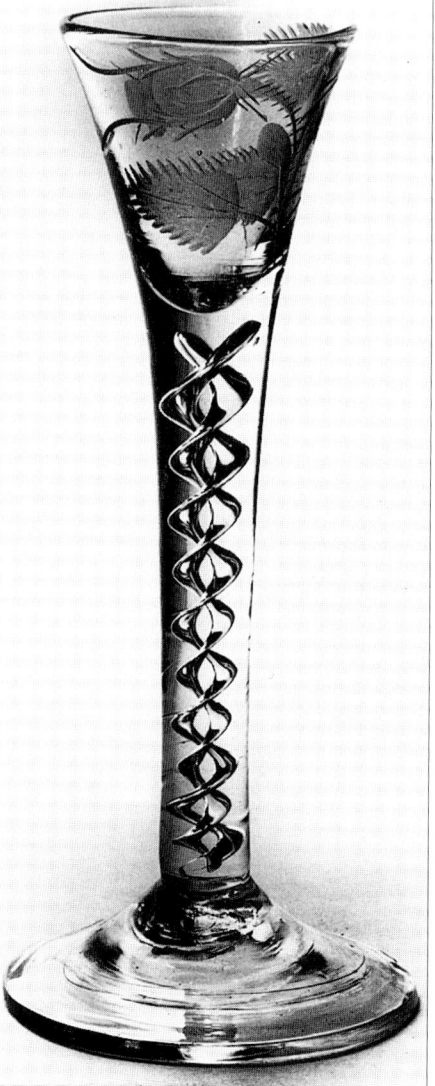

**470.** Wine glass; RF bowl, engraved moth and lilies-of-the-valley; shoulder-and-centre-knopped MSAT. Ht. 6ins. c.1750.

Air-Twist Stems

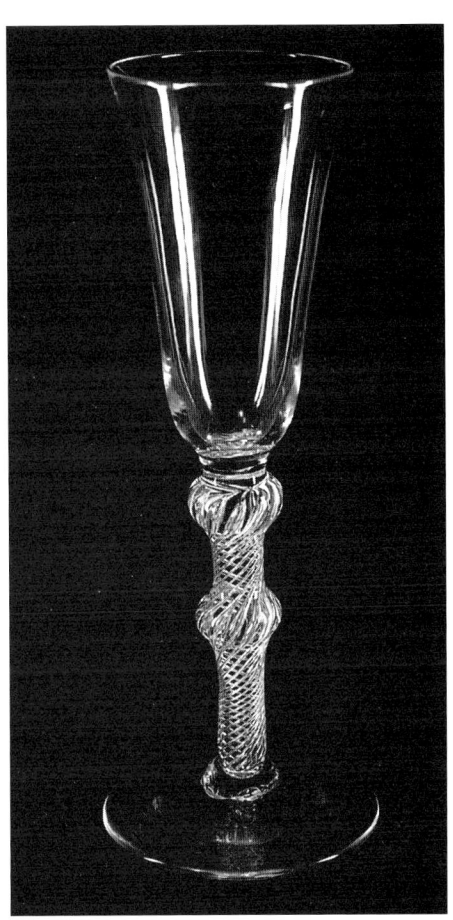

**471.** Wine glass; cup bowl, moulded base; shoulder- and centre-knopped MSAT. Ht. 6½ins. c.1750. *Worthing Museum.*

**472.** Ale glass; RF bowl; shoulder- and centre-knopped MSAT. Ht. 7¾ins. c.1750.

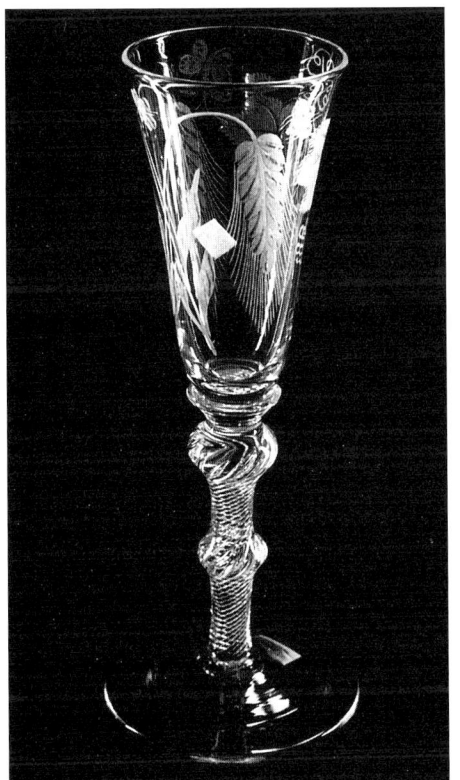

**473.** Ale glass; RF bowl, engraved hops and barley; shoulder- and centre-knopped MSAT. Ht. 7¾ins. c.1750.
*Hartshorne Collection. (Plate 50).*

**474.** Wine glass; pan-topped RF bowl; shoulder- and centre-knopped MSAT. Ht. 6¼ins. c.1750.

**475.** Wine glass; waisted bucket bowl; shoulder- and centre-knopped MSAT. Ht. 6ins. c.1750.

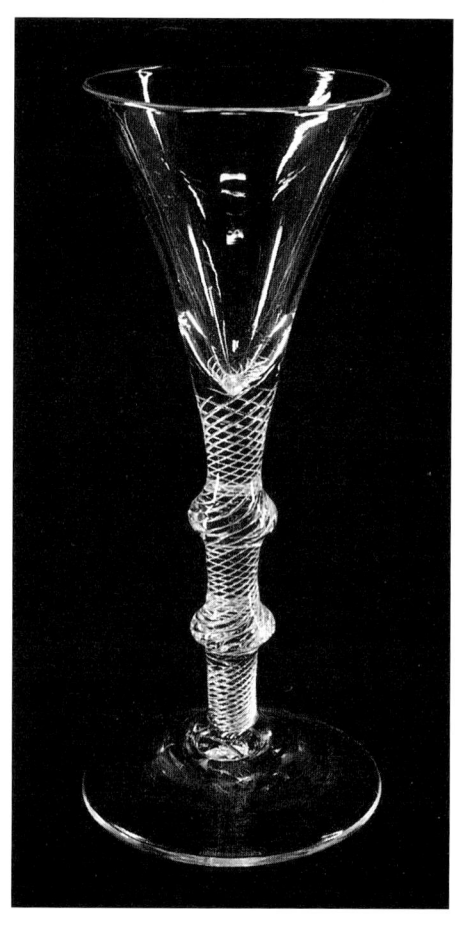

**476.** Wine glass; trumpet bowl; double-knopped MSAT. Ht. 7ins. c.1750.
*Dr. Reed Collection.*

**477.** Wine glass; pointed RF bowl engraved with border of fruiting vine; double-knopped MSAT. Ht. 6ins. c.1755.
*Tibbenham Collection, Ipswich Museum.*

**478.** Wine glass; pan-topped pointed RF bowl; double-knopped MSAT. Ht. 6¼ins. c.1750. *Sotheby's.*

**479.** Wine glass; bell bowl, solid base; MSAT with shoulder knop and swelled knop. Ht. 6⅜ins. c.1755.
*Tibbenham Collection, Ipswich Museum.*

**480.** Wine glass; pointed RF bowl; two-ringed collar over double-knopped MSAT. Ht. 6¼ins. c.1755.
*Tibbenham Collection, Ipswich Museum.*

Air-Twist Stems

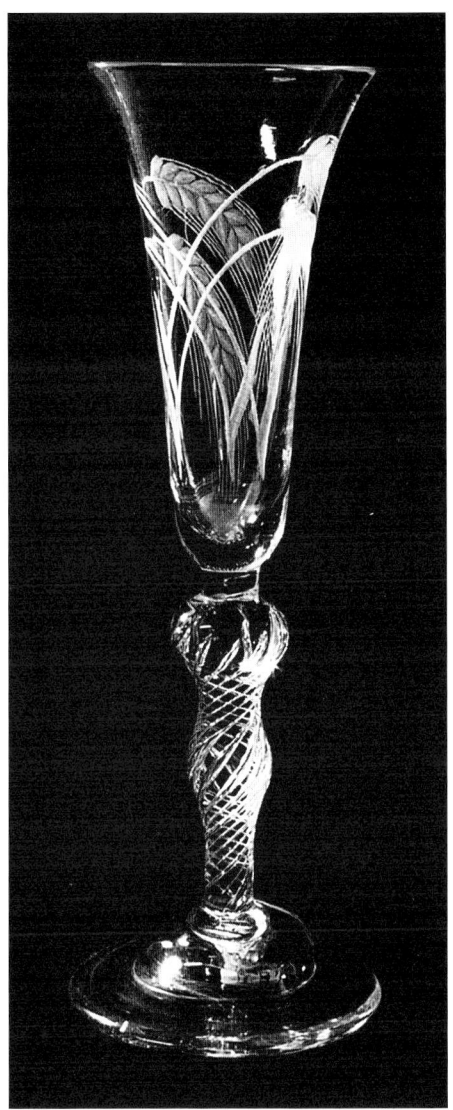

**482.** Ale glass; fluted RF bowl, solid base; double-knopped MSAT. Ht. 8⅜ins. c.1755.
*Tibbenham Collection, Ipswich Museum.*

**481.** Ale glass; waisted pointed RF bowl engraved with hops and barley; double-knopped MSAT stem; DF. c.1750.
*Tibbenham Collection, Ipswich Museum.*

**483.** Ale glass; RF bowl, double-knopped MSAT. Ht. 8ins. c.1755.
*Tibbenham Collection, Ipswich Museum.*

**484.** Wine glass; waisted bucket bowl; double-knopped MSAT. Ht. 6⅜ins. c.1755.
*Tibbenham Collection, Ipswich Museum.*

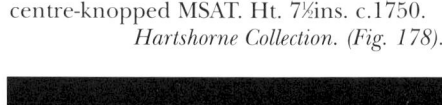

**486.** Wine glass; bell bowl, engraved Baroque border below rim; shoulder- and centre-knopped MSAT. Ht. 7½ins. c.1750.
*Hartshorne Collection. (Fig. 178).*

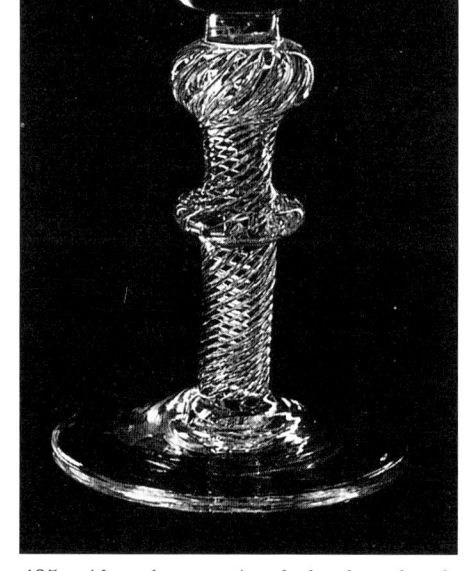

**485.** Ale glass; waisted bucket bowl, engraved hops and barley; shoulder- and centre-knopped MSAT. Ht. 8ins. c.1750.

Air-Twist stems

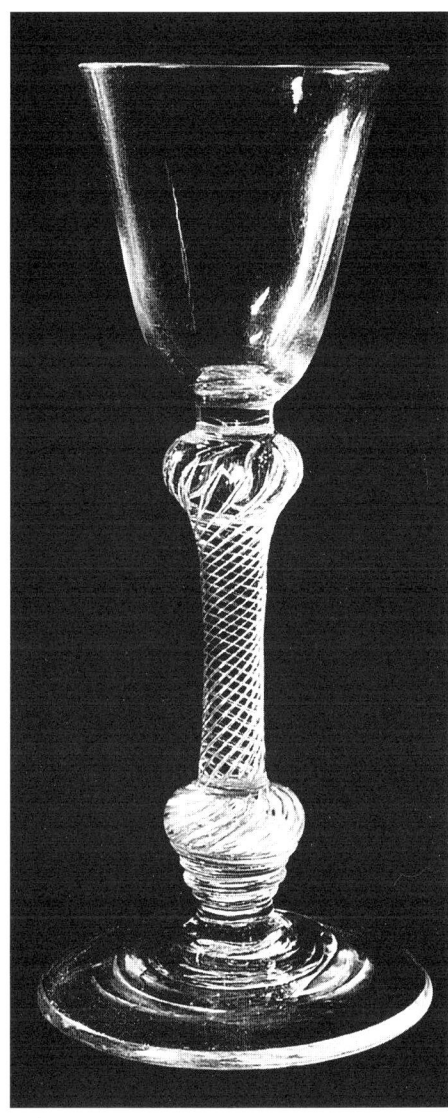

**487.** Wine glass; RF bowl; MSAT with shoulder and basal knops over a 3-ringed collar. Ht. 6½ins. c.1755.

*Tibbenham Collection, Ipswich Museum.*

**488.** Wine glass; pan-topped RF bowl; MSAT with shoulder and basal knops. Ht. 6ins. c.1755.

*Tibbenham Collection, Ipswich Museum.*

**489.** Wine glass; pointed RF bowl; MSAT with shoulder and basal knops. Ht. 6ins. c.1750.

**490.** Wine glass; bucket bowl, engraved floral design; MSAT with shoulder and basal knops. Ht. 6½ins. c.1750.

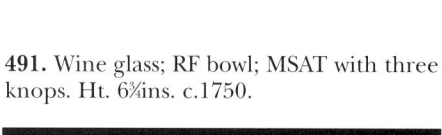

**491.** Wine glass; RF bowl; MSAT with three knops. Ht. 6¾ins. c.1750.

**492.** Wine glass; waisted bucket bowl; MSAT with four knops; DF. Ht. 6½ins. c.1750.

*Smith Collection. Harvey's Wine Museum, Bristol.*

Air-Twist Stems

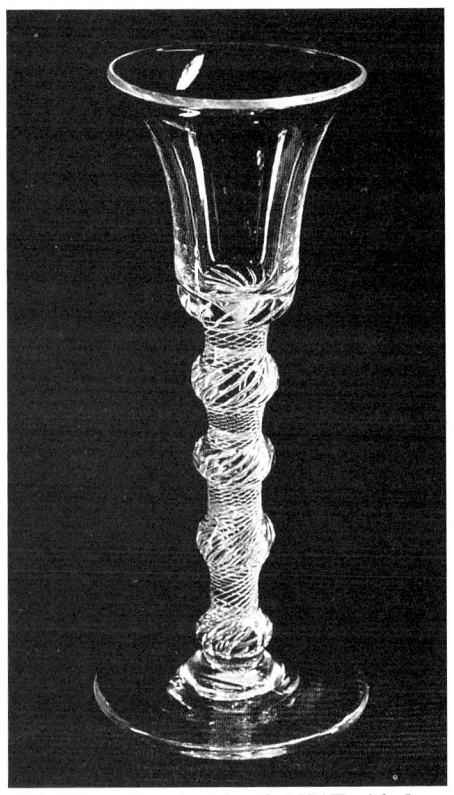

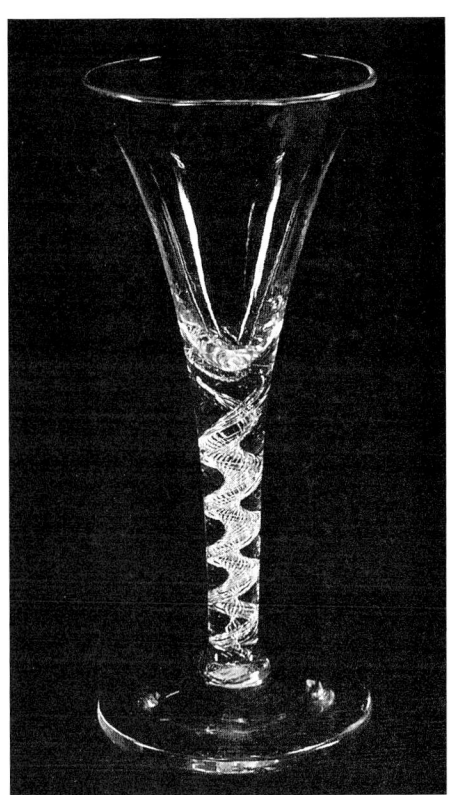

**493.** Wine glass; bell bowl; MSAT with four knops. Ht. 6¼ins. c.1750.

**494.** Wine glass; bell bowl with Jacobite engraving; MSAT with five knops. Ht. 6ins. c.1750.

**495.** Wine glass; trumpet bowl; DSAT – multi-ply spiral band outside cable. Ht. 7ins. c.1750.

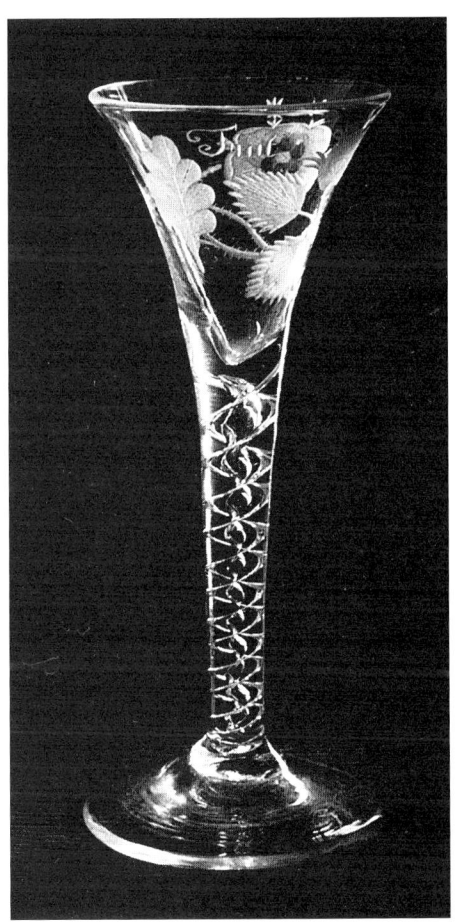

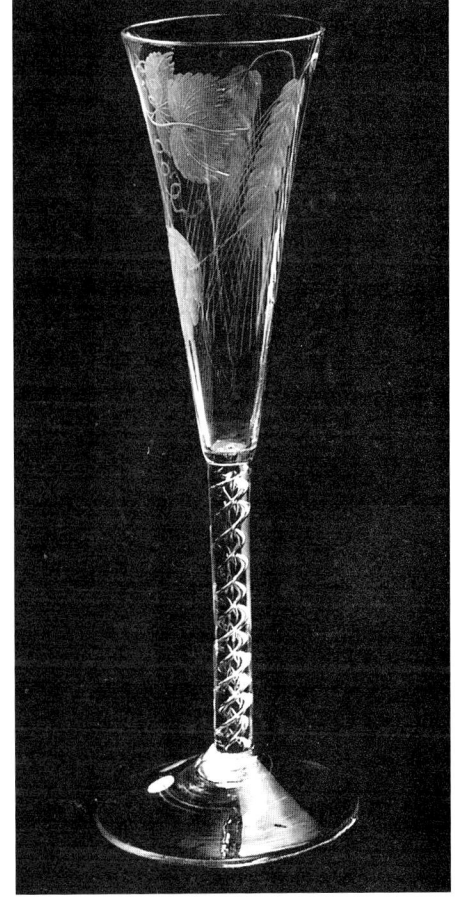

**496.** Wine glass; trumpet bowl with Jacobite engraving and inscribed FIAT; DSAT – pair of corkscrews outside pair of spiral threads. Ht. 7½ins. c.1750.

**497.** Ale flute; slightly flared funnel bowl engraved with hops and barley; DSAT – two spiral tapes outside loose vertical threads. Ht. 8½ins. c.1750. *Sotheby's.*

Air-Twist Stems

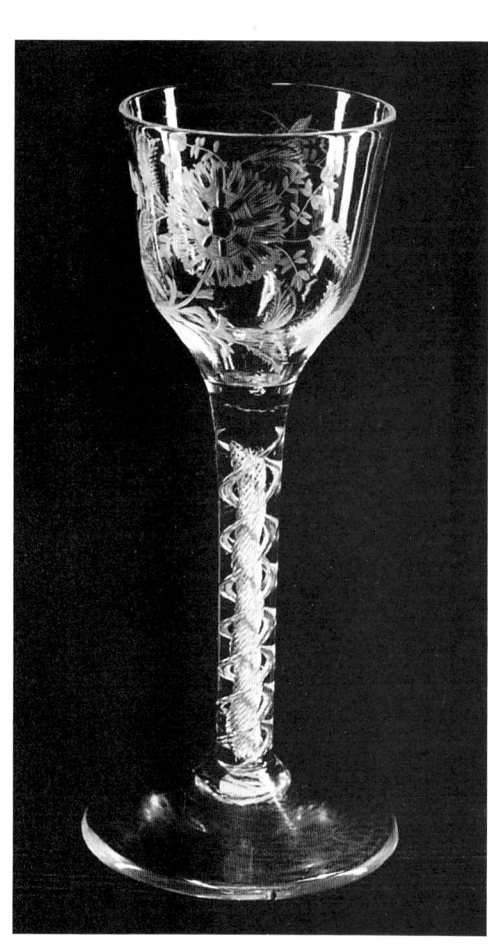

**498.** Wine glass; ogee bowl engraved in Jacobite style; DSAT – pair of corkscrews outside cable. Ht. 5½ins. c.1750.

**499.** Wine glass; rib-moulded RF bowl; DSAT – pair of corkscrews outside cable. Ht. 6ins. c.1750.
*Worthing Museum.*

**500.** Wine glass; pan-topped RF bowl; DSAT – pair of corkscrews outside cable. Ht. 6ins. c.1750.
*Hartshorne Collection.*

**501.** Wine glass; flared bucket bowl; mixed twist – pair of opaque white spiral threads outside vertical air cable. Ht. 6¼ins. c.1755. *Sotheby's.*

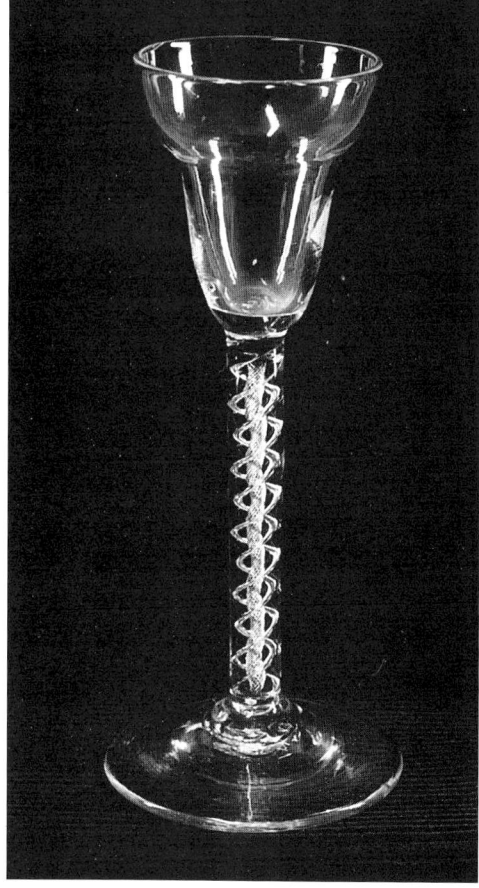

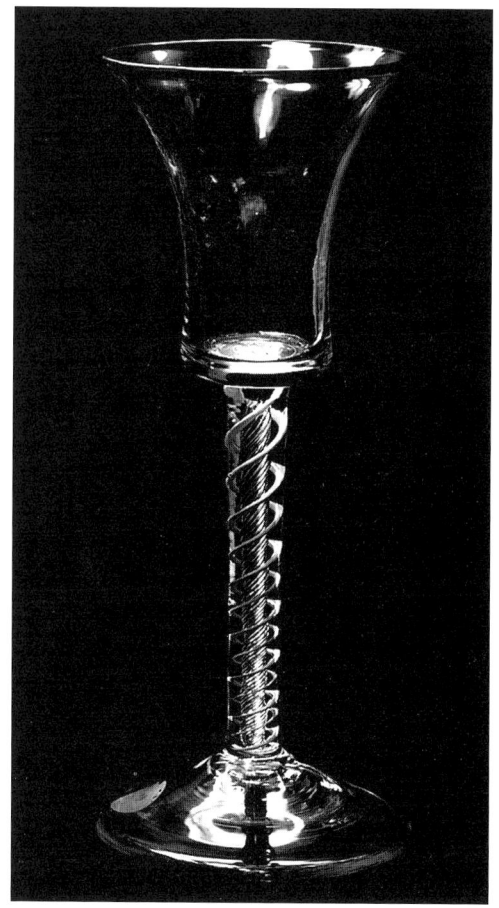

Air-Twist Stems

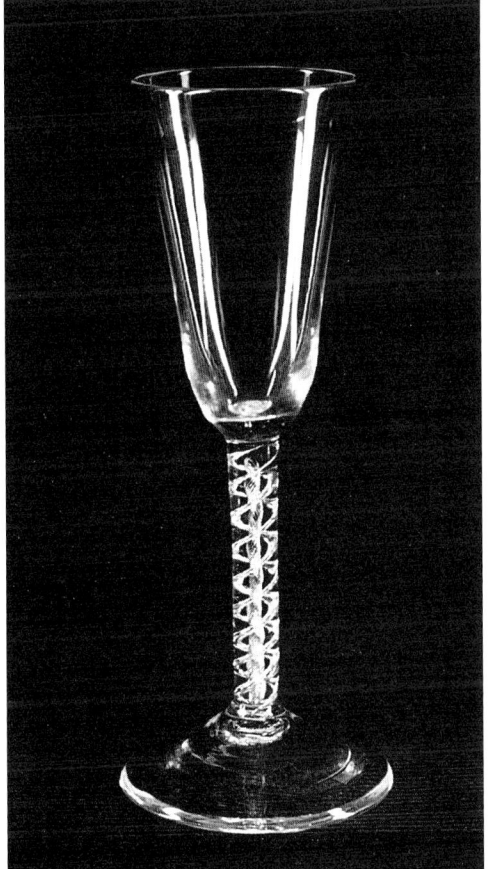

**502.** Ale glass; pointed RF bowl; DSAT – pair of spiral threads outside vertical cable. Ht. 8⅛ins. c.1755.
*Tibbenham Collection, Ipswich Museum.*

**503.** Goblet; ogee bowl with faintly moulded flutes; DSAT – pair of corkscrews outside cable. Ht. 7ins. c.1750.

**504.** Ale glass; RF bowl; DSAT – pair of corkscrews outside cable. Ht. 7½ins. c.1750.

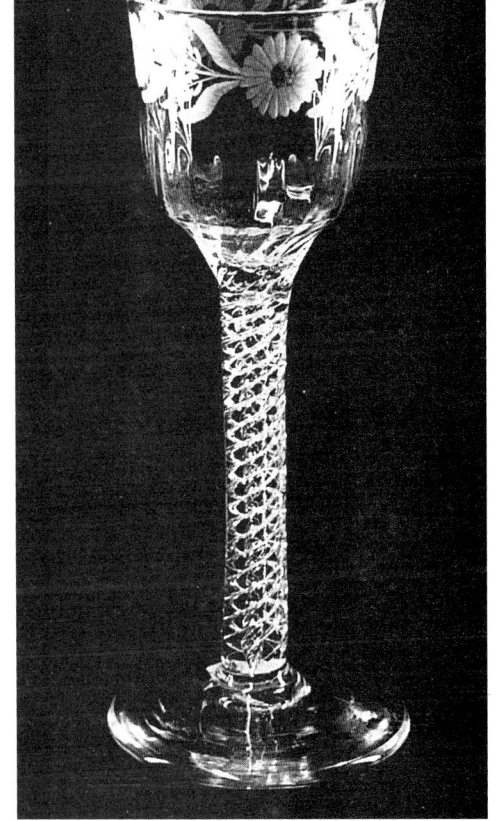

**505.** Wine glass; ogee bowl with basal flutes and engraved floral band below rim; DSAT – four spirals outside cable. Ht. 6ins. c.1750.

**507.** Wine glass; ogee bowl, engraved with border of fruiting vine; DSAT – four spiral threads outside pair of spiral threads. Ht. 5¾ins. c.1755.

*Tibbenham Collection, Ipswich Museum.*

**506.** Wine glass; ogee bowl with basal flutes and engraved formal band below rim; DSAT – four spirals outside cable. Ht. 5⅞ins. c.1750.

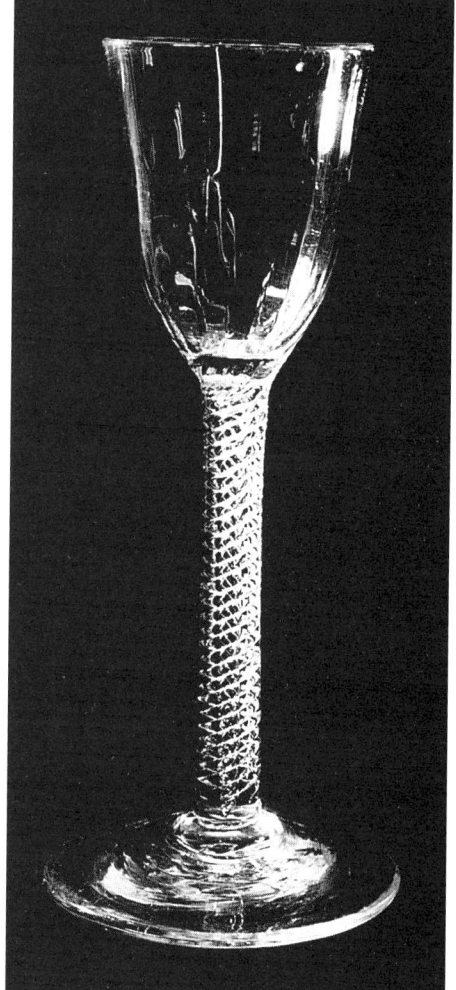

**508.** Wine glass; pointed RF bowl with faint vertical ribs; DSAT – four spiral threads outside pair of spiral threads. Ht. 6⅛ins. c.1755.

*Tibbenham Collection, Ipswich Museum.*

Air-Twist Stems

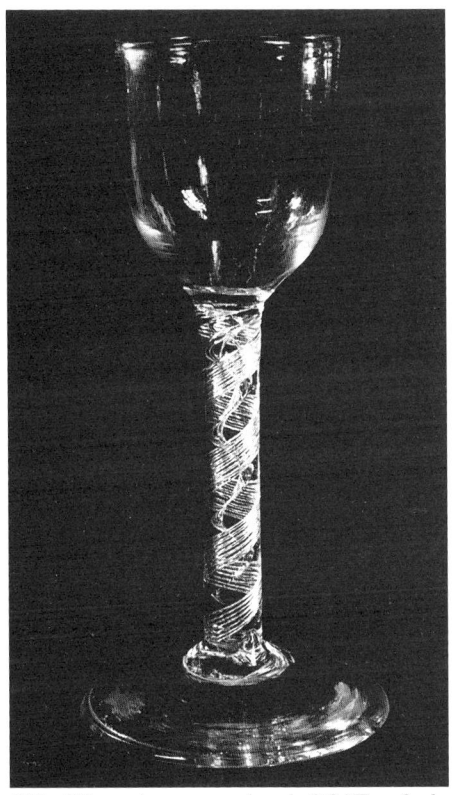

**509.** Wine glass; ogee bowl; DSAT – 6-ply band outside single corkscrew. Ht. 5⅝ins. c.1755.

*Tibbenham Collection, Ipswich Museum.*

**510.** Ale glass; pointed RF bowl; DSAT – 7-ply spiral bands outside slightly twisted vertical column. Ht. 8ins. c.1755.

*Tibbenham Collection, Ipswich Museum.*

**511.** Cordial; square bucket bowl; DSOT – 7-ply spiral band outside pair of loose vertical threads; DF. Ht. 6⅜ins. c.1765.

*Ex Francis L. Dickson Collection. Sotheby's.*

**512.** Cordial; RF bowl engraved with floral border; DSAT – spiral cable outside vertical thread. Ht. 6⅜ins. c.1750. *Sotheby's.*

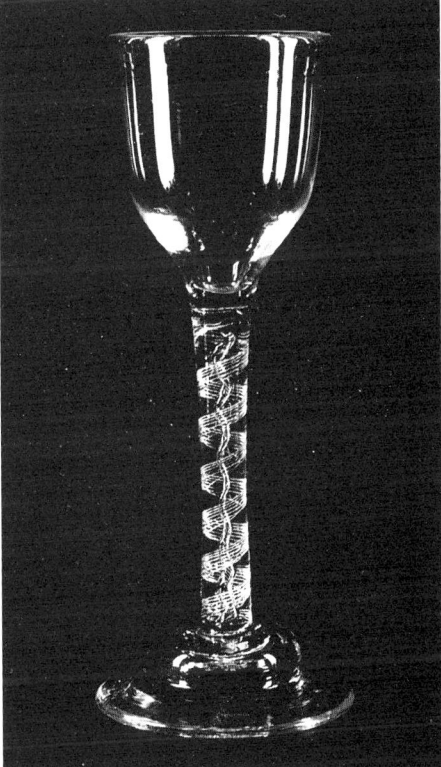

**513.** Wine glass; ogee bowl, DSAT – 7-ply spiral band outside thin spiral cable; DF. Ht. 6¼ins. c.1750. *Worthing Museum.*

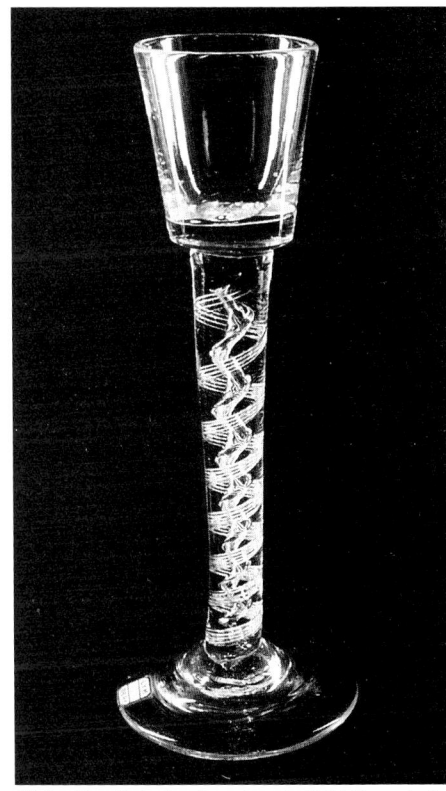

**514.** Cordial; bucket bowl; DSAT – 4-ply spiral band outside spiral cable. Ht. 6⅜ins. c.1750.

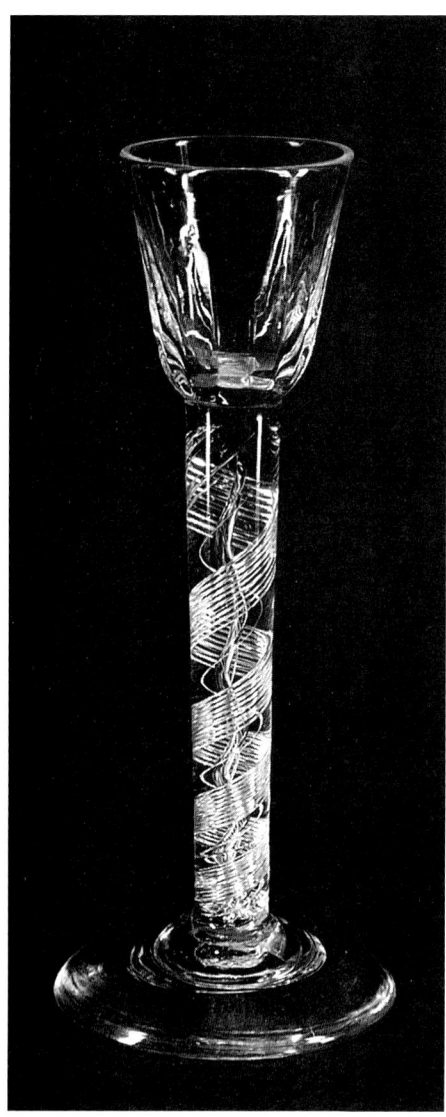

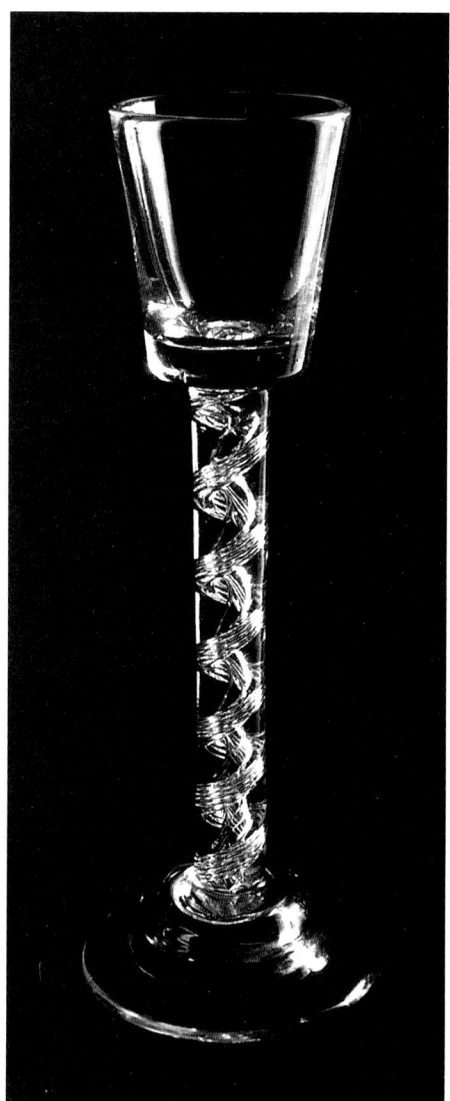

**515.** Cordial; fluted RF bowl; DSAT – 9-ply spiral band outside thin spiral cable. Ht. 6½ins. c.1750.

**516.** Cordial; bucket bowl; DSAT – 4-ply spiral band outside loose spiral cable; DF. Ht. 6½ins. c.1750.

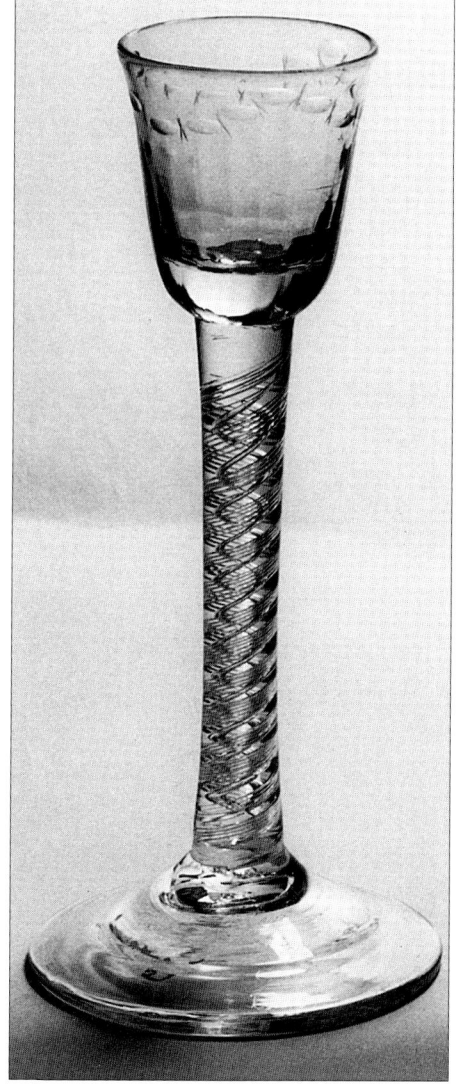

**517.** Cordial; fluted RF bowl; DSAT – 6-ply spiral band outside pair of spiral threads. c.1750. *Sotheby's.*

Air-Twist Stems

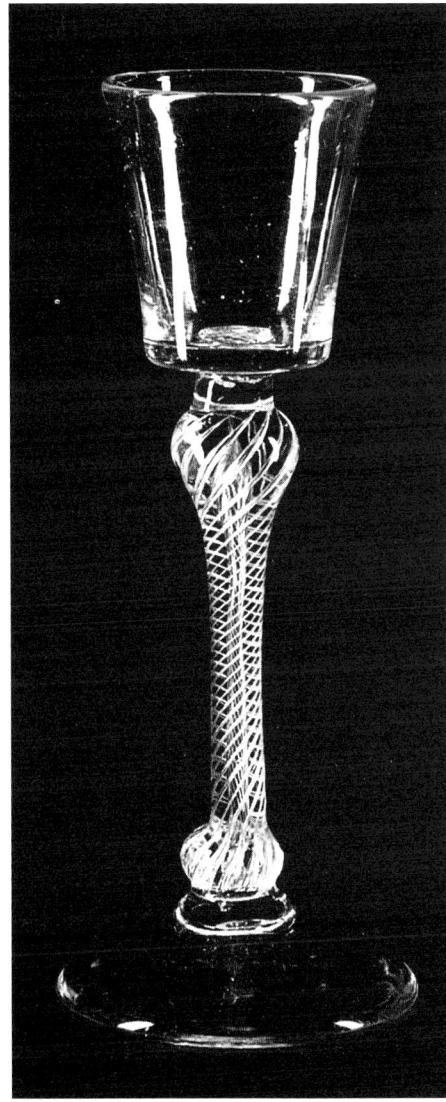

**518.** Cordial; bucket bowl; DSAT with shoulder and basal knops – MSAT outside thin cable. Ht. 6¼ins. c.1750.

*Worthing Museum.*

**520.** Sweetmeat; pan-topped RF bowl with dentated rim; collar, SSAT – spiral gauze; D & FF. Ht. 7⅜ins. c.1745.

*Ex W.F. Smith Collection. Sotheby's.*

**519.** Wine glass; RF bowl engraved with rose and two buds; DSAT stem – single spiral thread inside MSAT; DF. c.1745.

*Asprey.*

# VIII
# Incised-Twist Stems

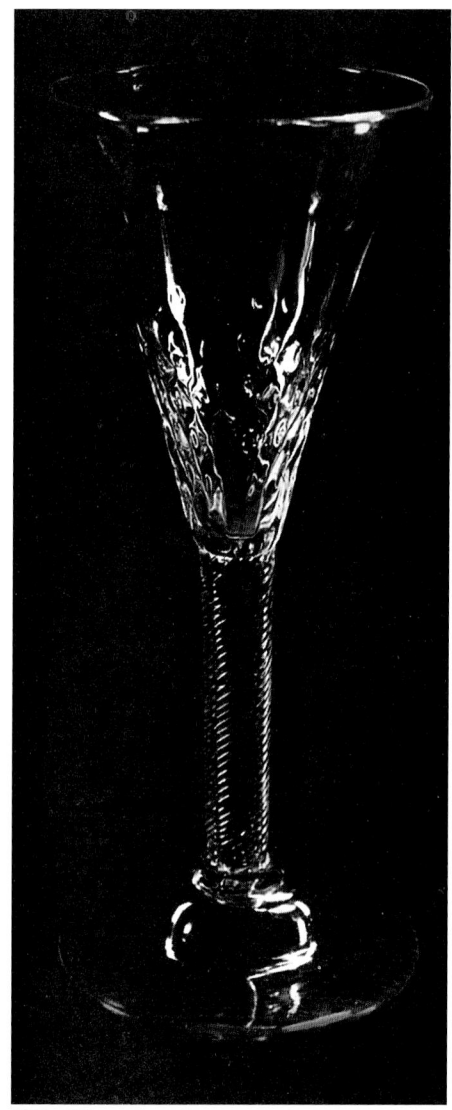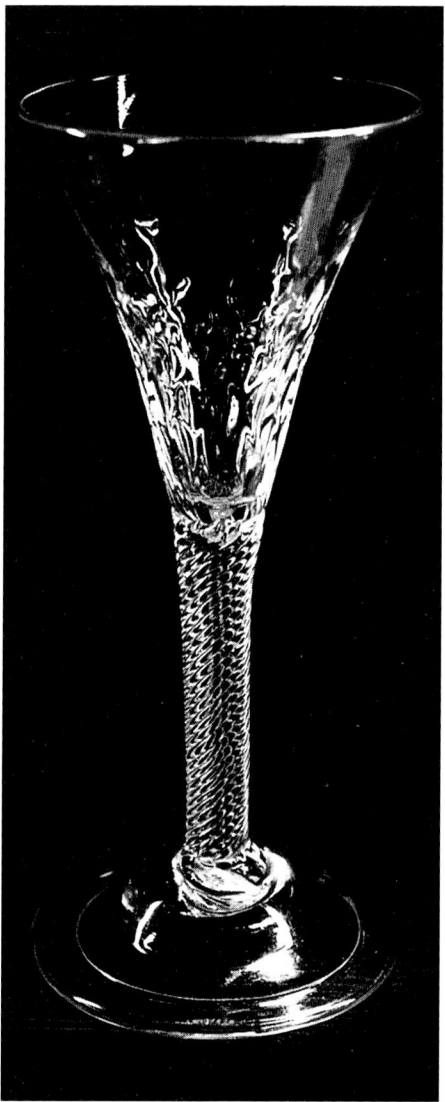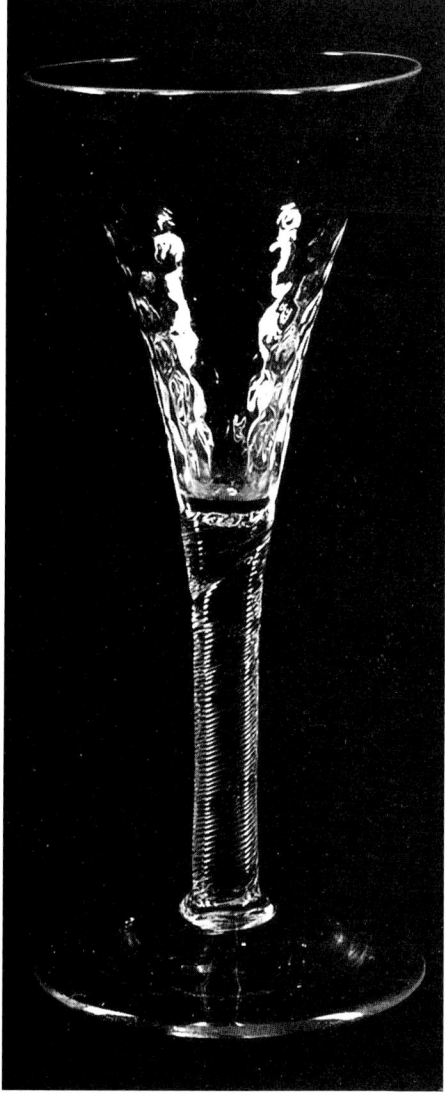

**521.** Wine glass; hammered trumpet bowl; coarse incised twist; DF. Ht. 7ins. c.1755.

**522.** Wine glass; hammered trumpet bowl; coarse incised twist; D & FF. Ht. 6½ins. c.1755.

**523.** Wine glass; hammered trumpet bowl; coarse incised twist. Ht. 6¾ins. c.1755.

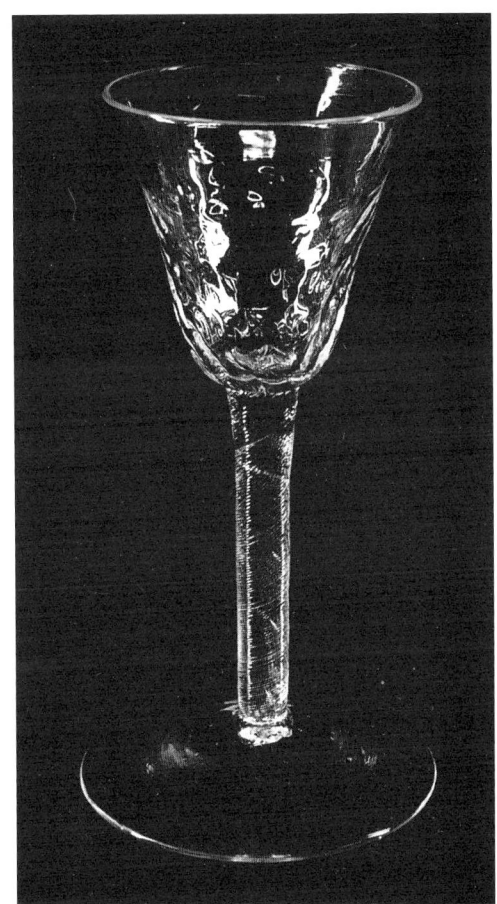

**524.** Wine glass; hammered RF bowl; coarse incised twist. Ht. 5½ins. c.1755.

**525.** Goblet; RF bowl; coarse incised twist. Ht. 8⅔ins. c.1760.
*Smith Collection.*
*Harvey's Wine Museum, Bristol.*

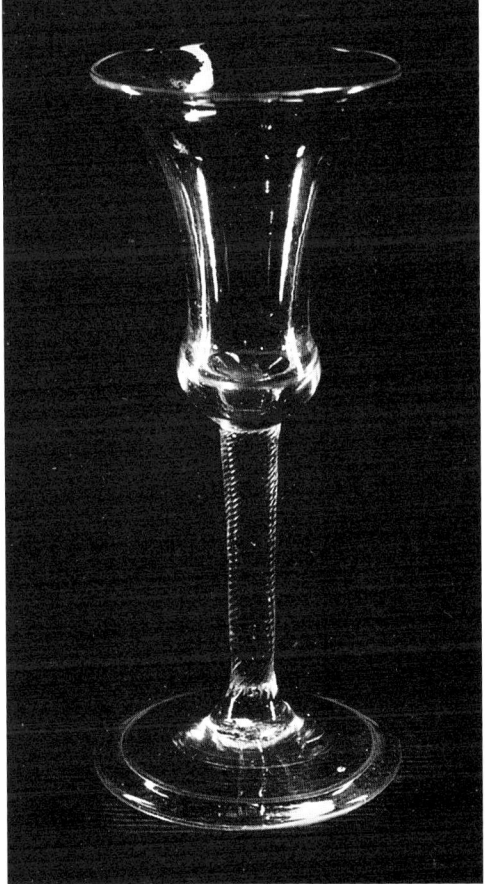

**526.** Wine glass; RF bowl; coarse incised twist; DF. Ht. 5⅜ins. c.1760.

**527.** Wine glass; waisted bell bowl, solid base; coarse incised twist; FF. Ht. 6½ins. c.1755. Soda glass.
*Hartshorne Collection.*

Incised-Twist Stems

**528.** Wine glass; hammered RF bowl; shoulder-knopped coarse incised twist. Ht. 6½ins. c.1760.

**529.** Wine glass; large RF bowl with basal flutes; fine incised twist. Ht. 5½ins. c.1760.

**530.** Wine glass; pointed RF bowl, hammered base; fine incised twist stem. Ht. 6½ins. c.1755.
*Tibbenham Collection, Ipswich Museum.*

**531.** Wine glass; wide-mouthed bell bowl; centre-swelled knop, coarse incised twist stem with basal knop; narrow FF. Ht. 6½ins. c.1755.
*Tibbenham Collection, Ipswich Museum.*

Incised-Twist Stems

**532.** Sweetmeat; ribbed bowl with scalloped rim; centre-knopped incised twist stem; DF ribbed to match. Ht. 6⅜ins. c.1760.     *Sotheby's.*

**533.** Wine glass; RF bowl; fine incised twist. Ht. 6ins. c.1760.

**534.** Ale glass; hammered bell bowl; fine incised twist. Ht. 7ins. c.1760.

Incised-Twist Stems

# IX
# Composite Stems

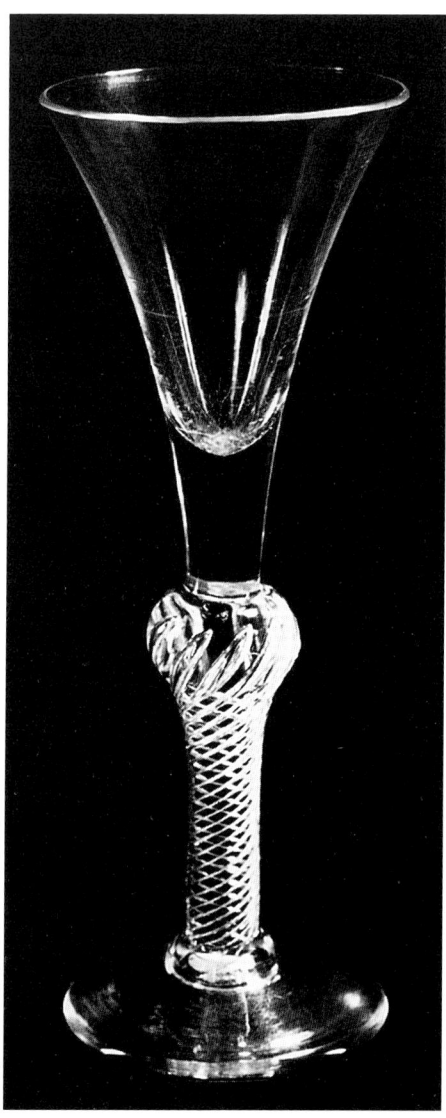

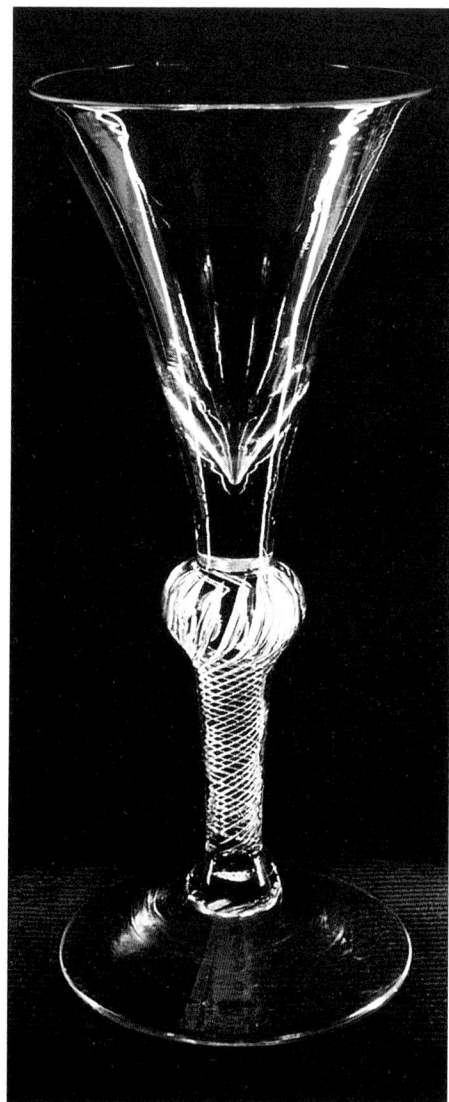

**535.** Wine glass; drawn trumpet bowl; composite stem, plain section over shoulder-knopped MSAT. Ht. 7¼ins. c.1750.
*Tibbenham Collection, Ipswich Museum.*

**536.** Wine glass; trumpet bowl; plain section over shoulder-knopped MSAT. Ht. 6¾ins. c.1750.

**537.** Ale glass; trumpet bowl; plain section over shoulder-knopped MSAT. Ht. 9ins. c.1750.

**538.** Wine glass; trumpet bowl; composite stem, short plain section over IB from which develops MSAT. Ht. 6⅜ins. c.1750.
*Tibbenham Collection, Ipswich Museum.*

**539.** Wine glass; trumpet bowl; plain section over MSAT with shoulder and swelled centre knops. Ht. 6½ins. c.1750.

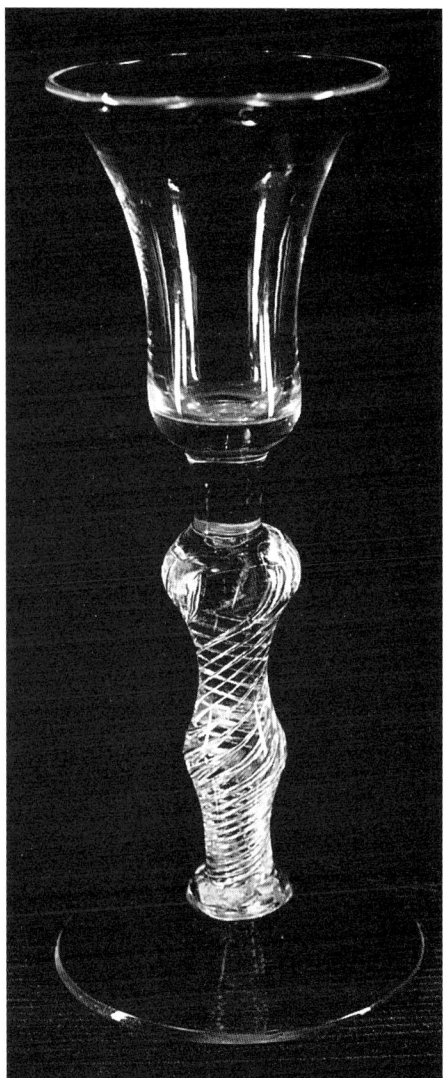

**540.** Wine glass; bell bowl; plain section over MSAT with shoulder and swelled centre knops. Ht. 6⅞ins. c.1750.
*Portsmouth City Museums.*

**541.** Wine glass; bell bowl; hollow knop (containing Charles II 6d. dated 1687) between collars, over double-knopped MSAT. Ht. 6¾ins. c.1750.          *Hartshorne Collection. (Plate 37).*

**542.** Wine glass; bell bowl, solid base; swelled knop, knop, large teared knop, DF. Ht. 7¼ins. c.1740.
          *Tibbenham Collection, Ipswich Museum.*

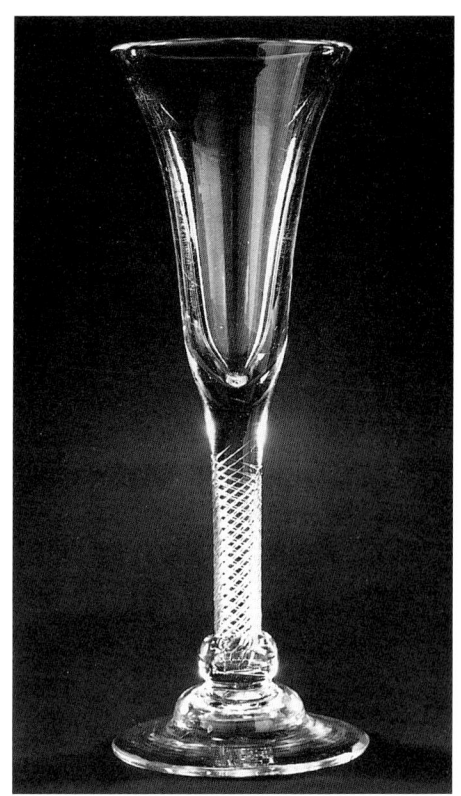

**543.** Ale glass; bell bowl; composite stem comprising MSAT over a flattened knop. DF. Ht. 9ins. c.1750.
          *Pilkington Glass Museum, St. Helens.*

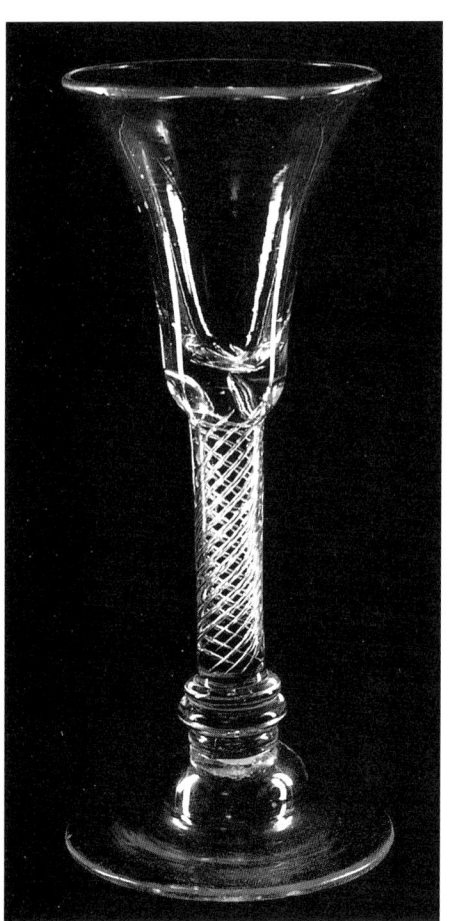

**544.** Wine glass; bell bowl, solid base; MSAT over annulated knop; DF. Ht. 6¾ins. c.1750.

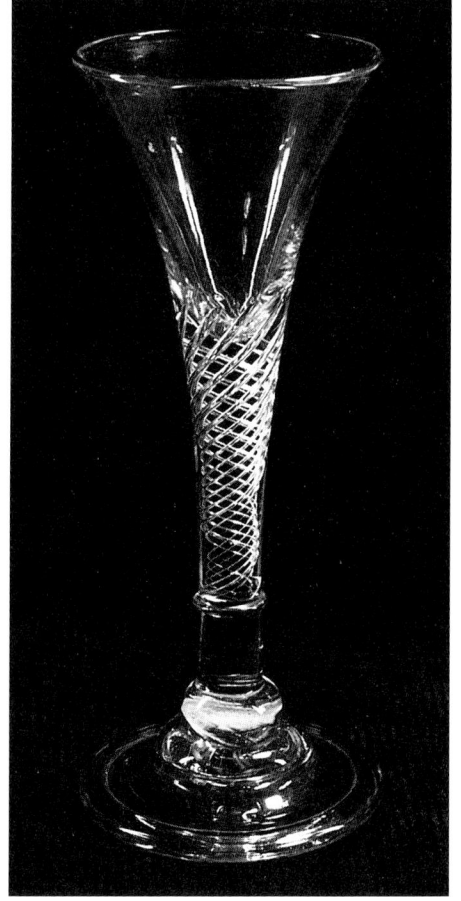

**545.** Wine glass; trumpet bowl; MSAT over collar and basal knop; D & FF. Ht. 7¼ins. c.1750.

190                                                             Composite Stems

**546.** Ale glass; drawn trumpet bowl; composite stem, MSAT over teared IB. Ht. 8¾ins. c.1750.

*Tibbenham Collection, Ipswich Museum.*

**547.** Wine glass; drawn trumpet bowl; composite stem, MSAT over teared IB and basal knop. Ht. 6½ins. c.1750.

*Tibbenham Collection, Ipswich Museum.*

**548.** Wine glass; bucket bowl, everted rim; composite stem, MSAT over teared squat IB; DF. Ht. 6⅛ins. c.1750.

*Tibbenham Collection, Ipswich Museum.*

**549.** Wine glass; tulip bowl; MSAT over IB knop; DF. Ht. 6ins. c.1750.

**550.** Goblet; RF bowl, composite stem, centre knopped MSAT over teared IB and basal knop. Ht. 8ins. c.1750.

*Tibbenham Collection, Ipswich Museum.*

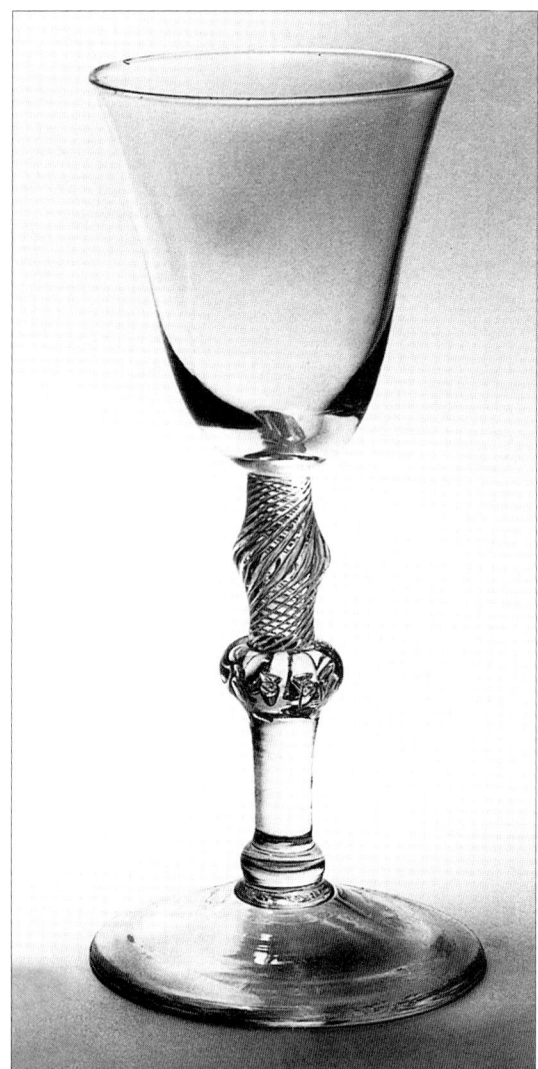

**551.** Wine glass; RF bowl; composite stem – MSAT with swelled knop, teared IB, plain section, basal knop. Ht. 7½ins. c.1750. *Sotheby's.*

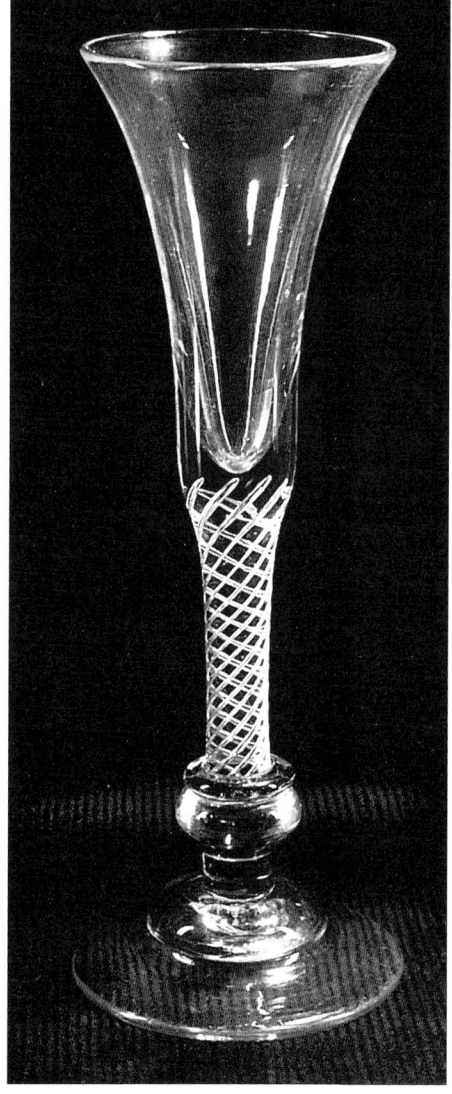

**552.** Ale glass; waisted bell bowl; MSAT over cushioned knop; DF. Ht. 9⅜ins. c.1750.

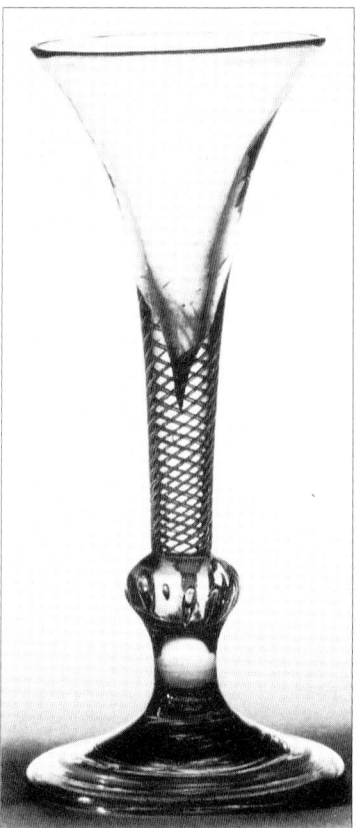

**553.** Wine glass; drawn trumpet bowl; composite stem – MSAT over teared IB. Ht. 7⅛ins. c.1750. *Christie's.*

Composite Stems

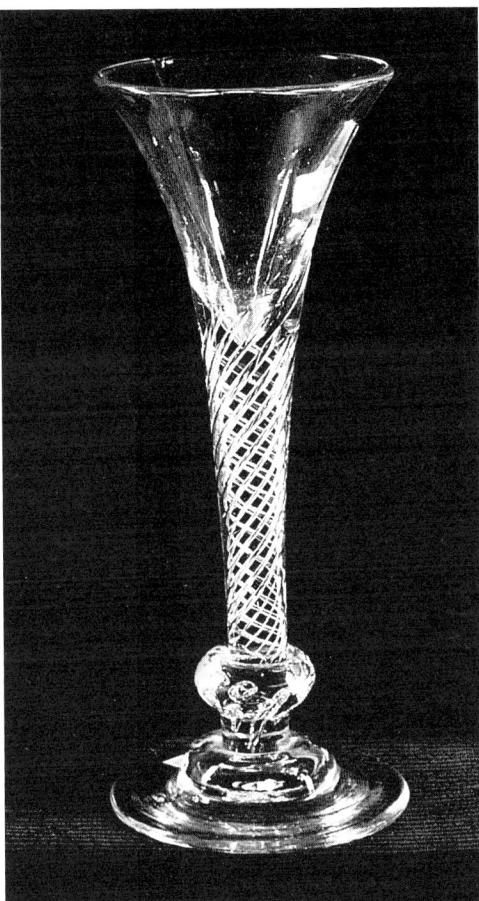

**554.** Wine glass; trumpet bowl; MSAT over beaded knop; DF. Ht. 7ins. c.1750.   *Hartshorne Collection.*

**555.** Wine glass; wide pointed RF bowl; MSAT over beaded IB knop; DF. Ht. 6½ins. c.1750.

*Hartshorne Collection.*

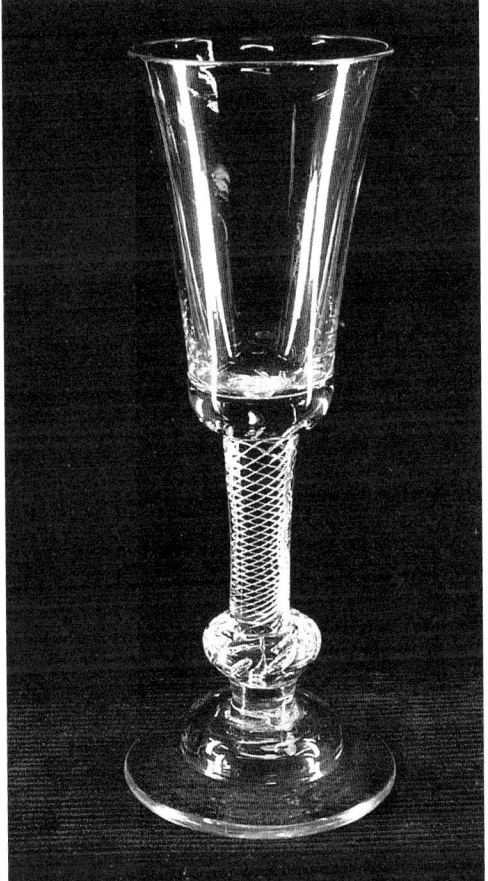

**556.** Ale glass; long bucket bowl; MSAT over beaded knop; DF. Ht. 7½ins. c.1750.

**557.** Wine glass; trumpet bowl; MSAT over collars and beaded knop; DF. Ht. 6⅝ins. c.1750.

Composite Stems

**558.** Wine glass; bell bowl; annulated knop between two opposing MSAT balusters. Ht. 6¼ins. c.1750.

**559.** Wine glass; RF bowl; beaded knop between two opposing MSAT balusters. Ht. 6⅜ins. c.1750.

**560.** Wine glass; bell bowl, engraved foliate scrolls below rim; plain stem with central beaded knop; DF. Ht. 6⅞ins. c.1735.

*Sotheby's.*

Composite Stems

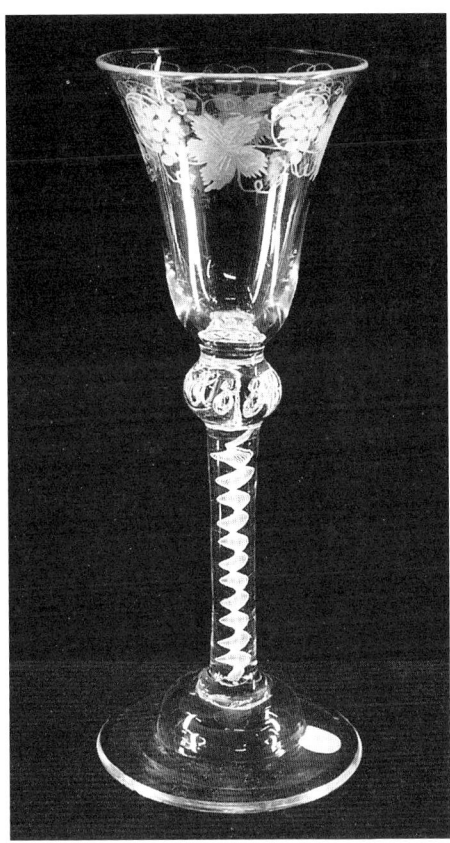

**561.** Wine glass; RF bowl; composite stem – beaded knop over DSOT – pair of spiral threads outside pair of loose corkscrews. Ht. 6¾ins. c.1765. *Christie's.*

**562.** Wine glass; bell bowl, engraved with band of fruiting vine below rim; beaded knop over SSOT – multi-ply corkscrew; DF. Ht. 7ins. c.1765.

**563.** Wine glass; RF bowl; faceted knop over DSOT – four spiral threads outside gauze. Ht. 6ins. c.1770.

**564.** Goblet; RF bowl with applied band near base; composite stem comprising SSOT – a multi-ply spiral band – between collars, a beaded knop and a short plain section; DF. Ht. 10½ins. c.1765. *Sotheby's.*

# X
# Opaque-Twist Stems

**565.** Wine glass; stepped RF ('Lynn') bowl; MSOT; FF. Ht. 5½ins. c.1760.
*Hartshorne Collection. (Fig. 218).*

**566.** Wine glass; RF bowl; MSOT; FF. Ht. 6⅜ins. c.1765.
*Tibbenham Collection, Ipswich Museum.*

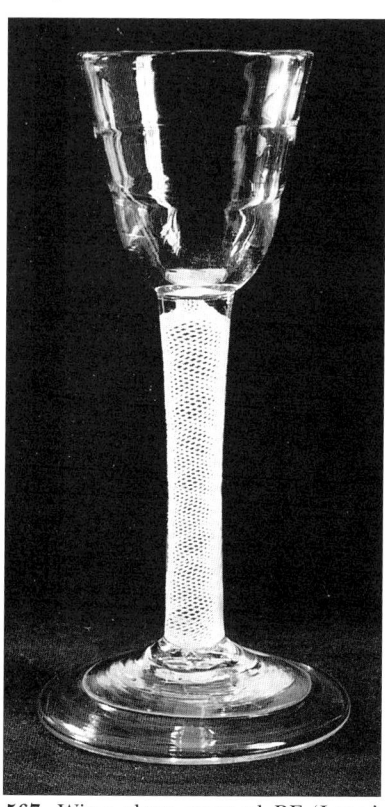

**567.** Wine glass; stepped RF 'Lynn' bowl; MSOT; FF. c.1765.
*Tibbenham Collection, Ipswich Museum.*

**568.** Stepped 'Lynn' bowl – detail of 567.
*Tibbenham Collection, Ipswich Museum.*

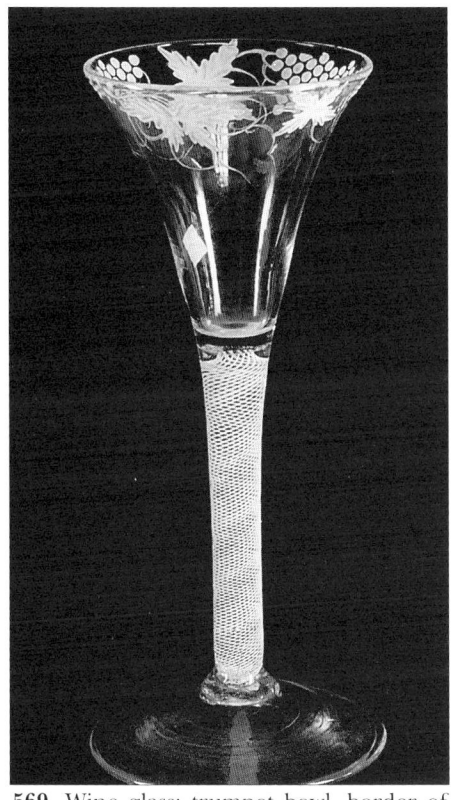

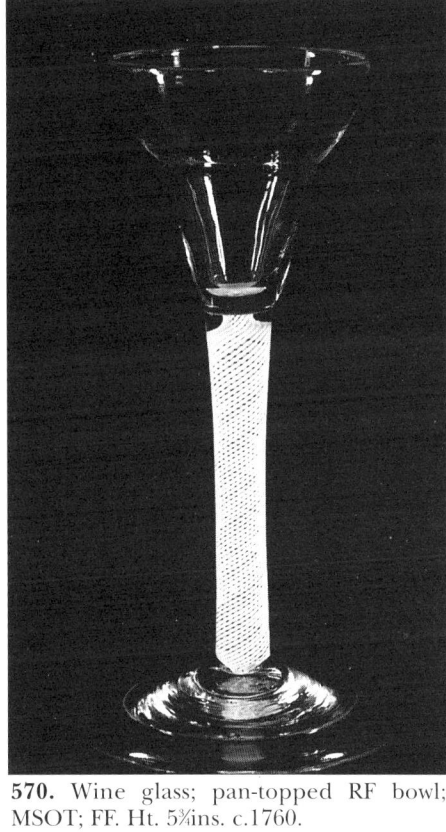

**569.** Wine glass; trumpet bowl, border of fruiting vine in white enamel ('Beilby'); MSOT. Ht. 7ins. c.1765.

*Hartshorne Collection.*

**570.** Wine glass; pan-topped RF bowl; MSOT; FF. Ht. 5⅜ins. c.1760.

**571.** Wine glass; RF bowl; MSOT. Ht. 6ins. c.1765.

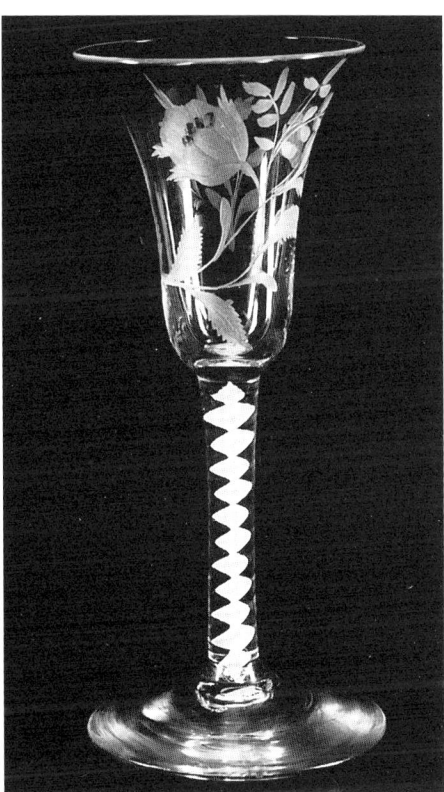

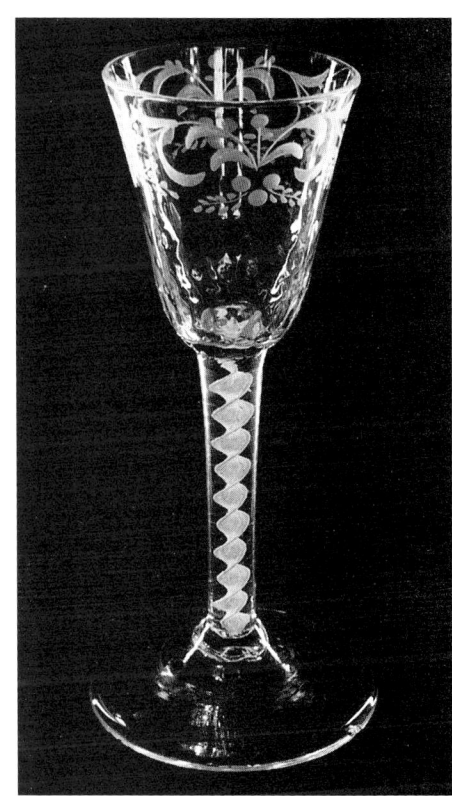

**572.** Sweetmeat; vertically ribbed, lipped, ogee bowl; triple collar, MSOT stem; DF to match bowl. Ht. 5⅜ins. c.1770. *Sotheby's.*

**573.** Wine glass; bell bowl with floral engraving; SSOT – single corkscrew. Ht. 6½ins. c.1765.

**574.** Wine glass; pointed RF bowl with hammered base and 'flowered' engraved border; SSOT – single corkscrew. Ht. 6ins. c.1765.

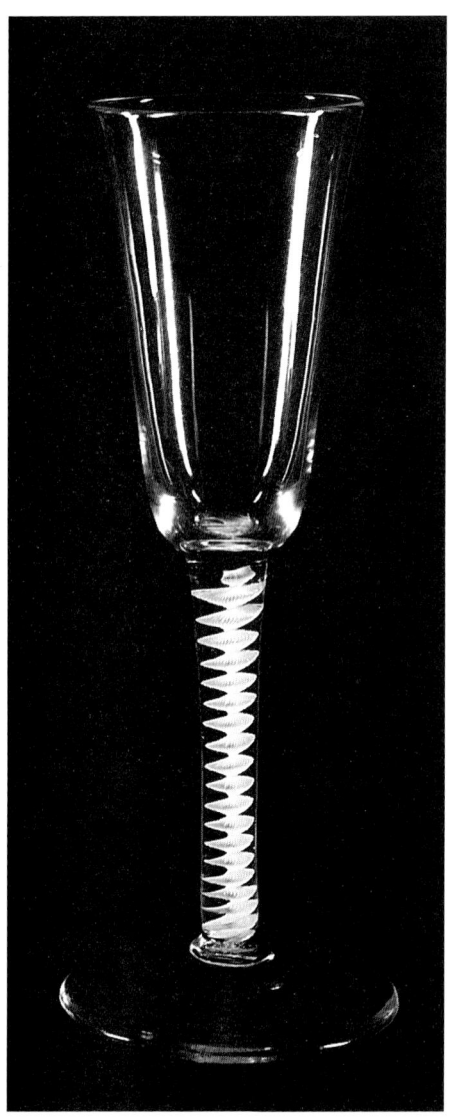

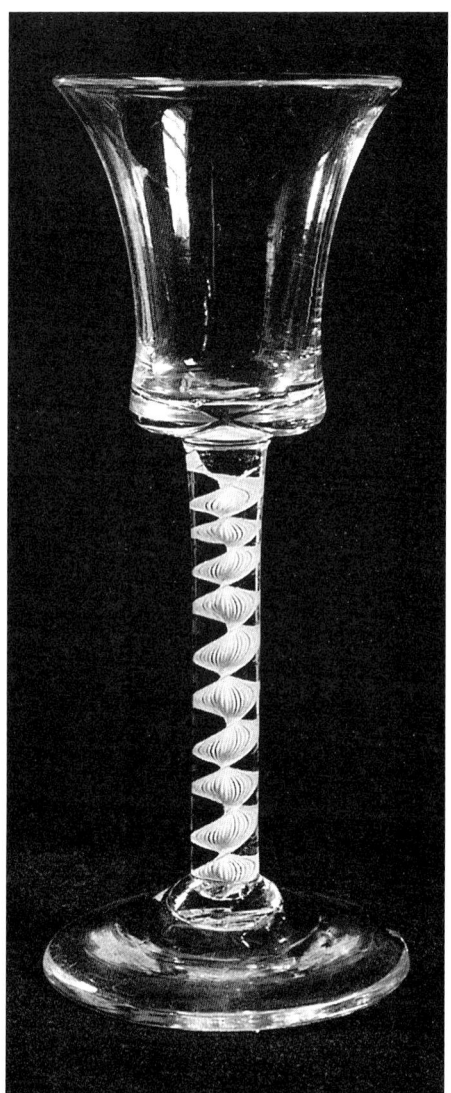

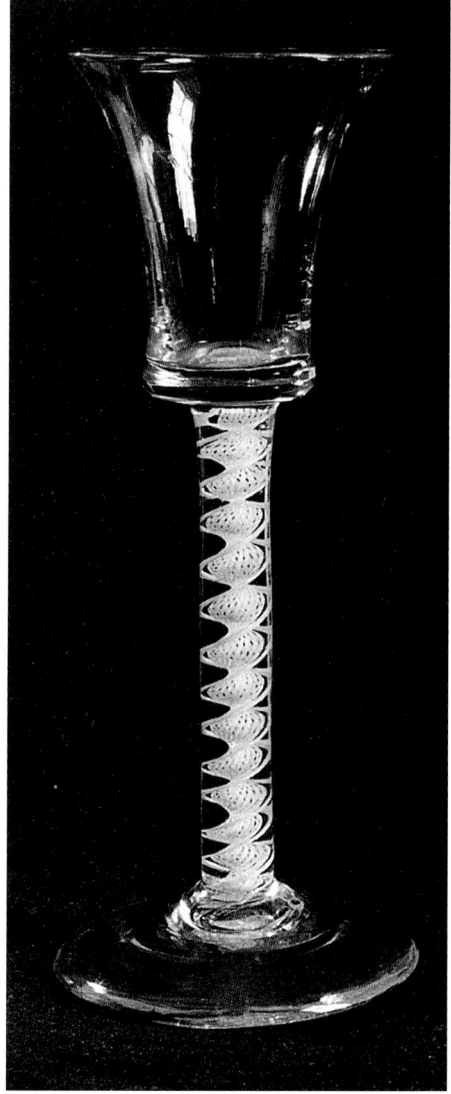

**575.** Ale glass; RF bowl; SSOT – single corkscrew. Ht. 8¼ins. c.1765.

**576.** Wine glass; waisted bucket bowl; SSOT – corkscrew. Ht. 6ins. c.1765.
*Tibbenham Collection, Ipswich Museum.*

**577.** Wine glass; waisted bucket bowl; SSOT – lace twist outlined. Ht. 6ins. c.1765.
*Tibbenham Collection, Ipswich Museum.*

Opaque-Twist Stems

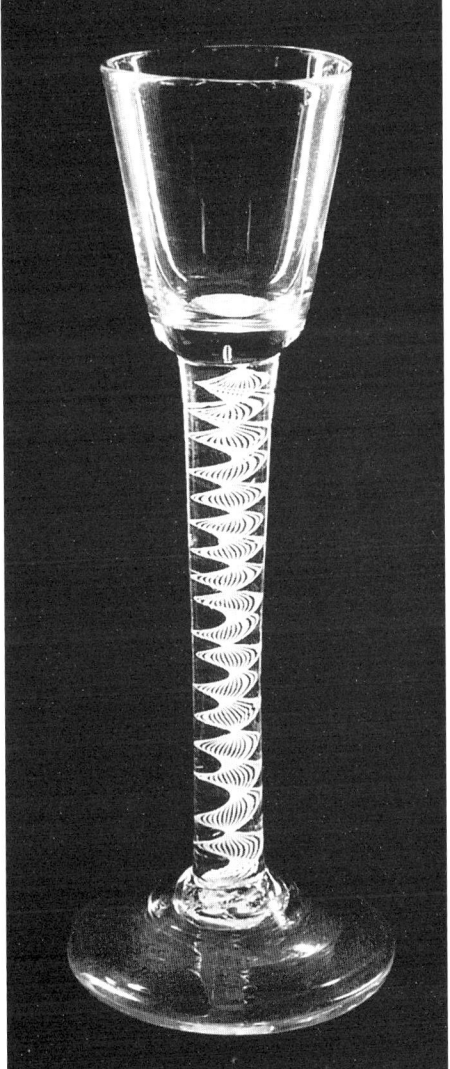

**579.** Cordial; RF bowl; SSOT – single loose corkscrew. Ht. 7⅛ins. c.1765.

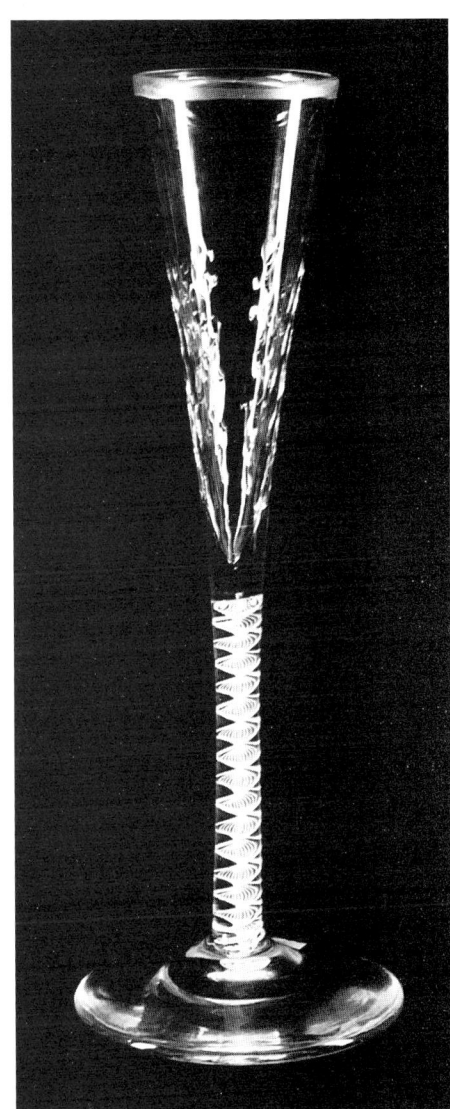

**580.** Ratafia; trumpet bowl, hammered base, gilded rim; SSOT – single loose corkscrew. Ht. 7½ins. c.1765.

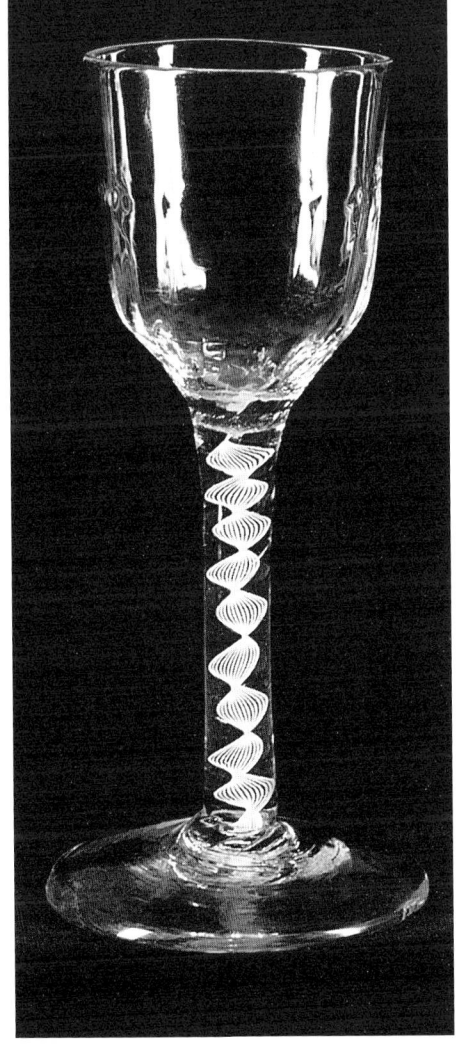

**578.** Wine glass; fluted ogee bowl; SSOT – single loose corkscrew. Ht. 6ins. c.1765.

**581.** Sweetmeat; double-ogee bowl with looped arcading terminating in eight prunts on the rim; SSOT – single corkscrew, between collars; D & FF. Ht. 6ins. c.1760. *Cecil Higgins Museum, Bedford.*

**582.** Ale glass; pointed RF bowl, engraved hops and barley; SSOT – four corkscrews. Ht. 7½ins. c.1765. *Hartshorne Collection.*

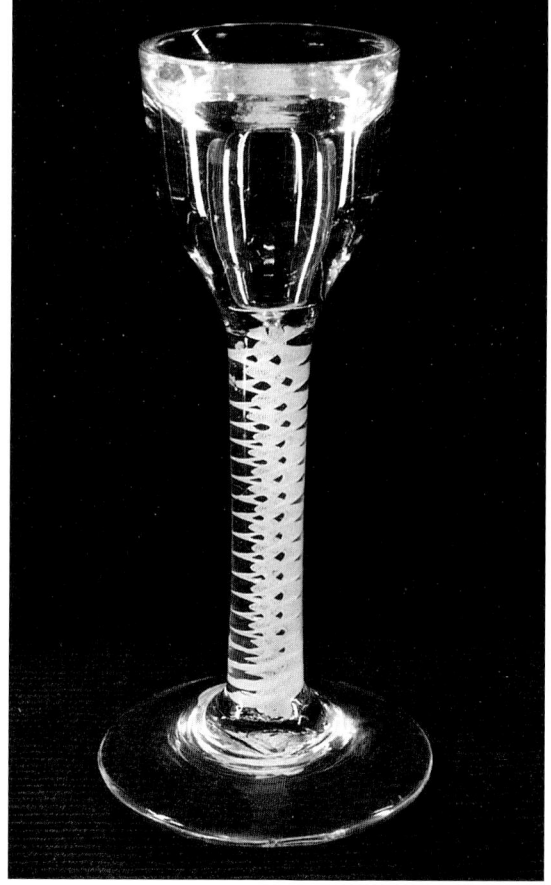

**583.** Toastmaster's glass; deceptive ogee bowl; SSOT – four corkscrews. Ht. 5¾ins. c.1765.

Opaque-Twist Stems

**584.** Wine glass; ogee bowl, spirally moulded base; SSOT – lace twist outlined. Ht. 6ins. c.1760.

**585.** Wine glass; ogee bowl with vertical fluting; SSOT – lace twist outlined. Ht. 6¼ins. c.1765.
*Tibbenham Collection, Ipswich Museum.*

**586.** Wine glass; RF bowl; SSOT – lace twist outlined. Ht. 5⅜ins. c.1765.
*Tibbenham Collection, Ipswich Museum.*

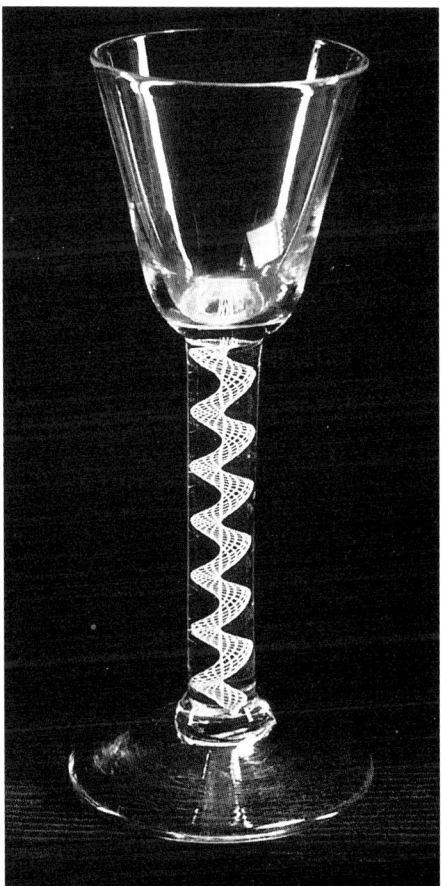

**587.** Wine glass; RF bowl; SSOT – single spiral gauze. Ht. 5¾ins. c.1760.
*Hartshorne Collection.*

Opaque-Twist Stems

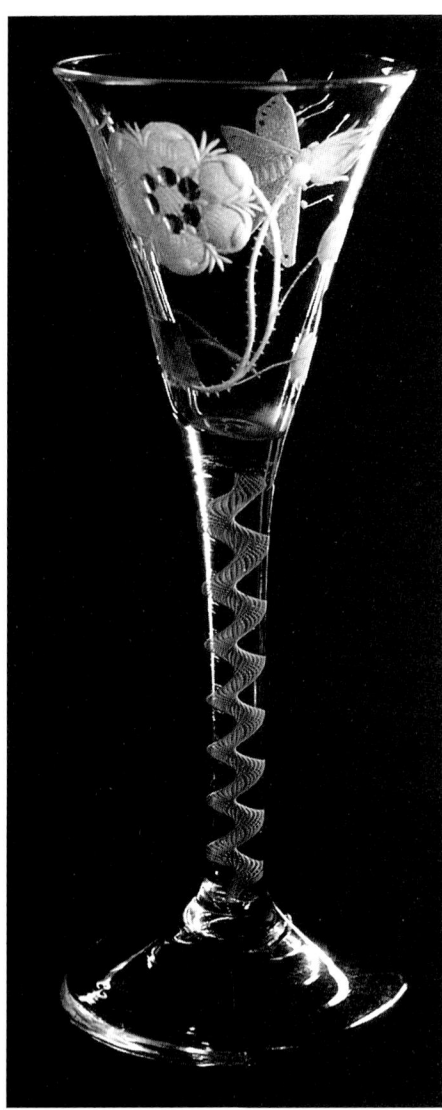

**588.** Wine glass; trumpet bowl, engraved rose, two buds and moth (Jacobite); SSOT – single spiral cable. Ht. 6¾ins. c.1760.
*Hartshorne Collection.*

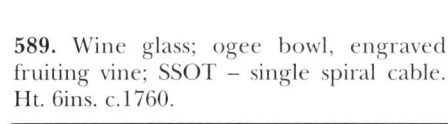

**589.** Wine glass; ogee bowl, engraved fruiting vine; SSOT – single spiral cable. Ht. 6ins. c.1760.

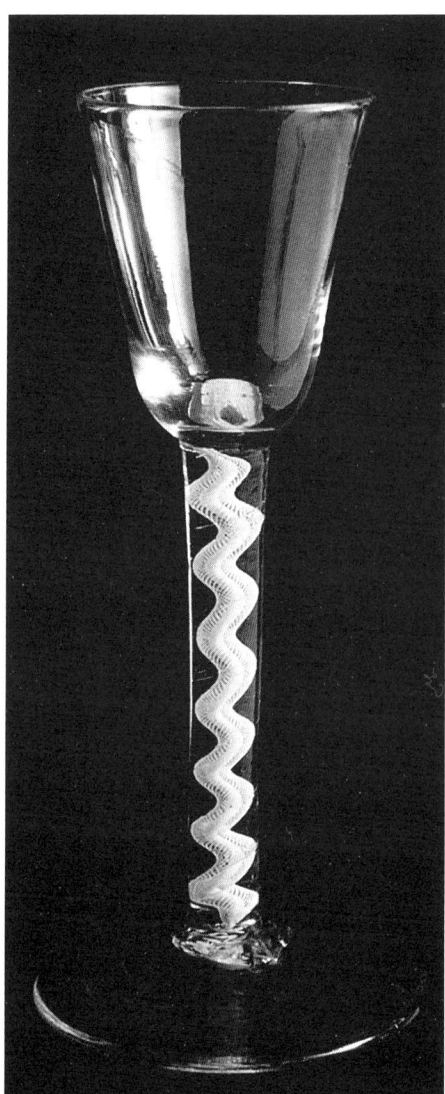

**590.** Wine glass; RF bowl; SSOT – single spiral gauze with core. Ht. 6ins. c.1760.

Opaque-Twist Stems

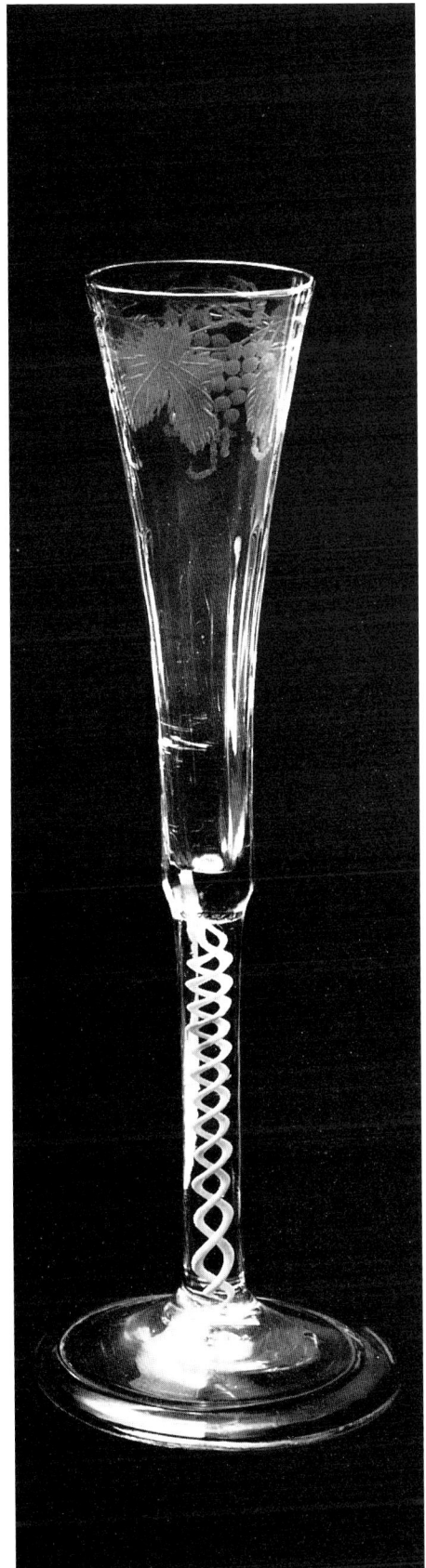

**592.** Wine glass; RF bowl; SSOT – spiral gauze alternating with pair of heavy spiral threads. Ht. 5⅞ins. c.1765.
*Tibbenham Collection, Ipswich Museum.*

**593.** Wine glass; waisted bucket bowl, engraved fruiting vine; SSOT – pair of spiral gauzes. Ht. 6½ins. c.1760.

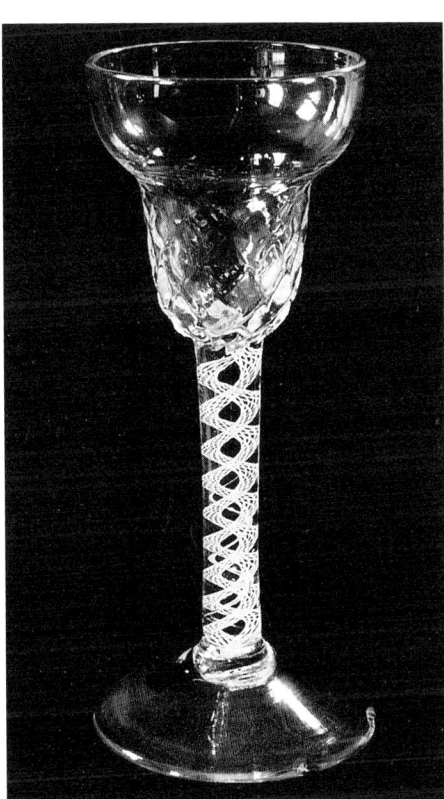

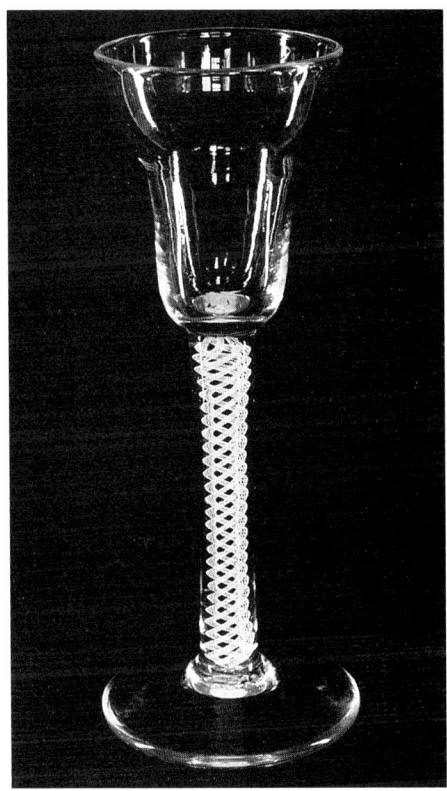

**591.** Ratafia; waisted funnel bowl engraved with fruiting vine round rim, moulded fluting to lower half; SSOT – pair of heavy spiral threads; FF. Ht. 8½ins. c.1770. *Sotheby's.*

**594.** Wine glass; pan-topped RF bowl, moulded lower half; SSOT – pair of spiral gauzes. c.1760.

**595.** Wine glass; pan-topped RF bowl; SSOT – four spiral gauzes. Ht. 6ins. c.1765.

Opaque-Twist Stems

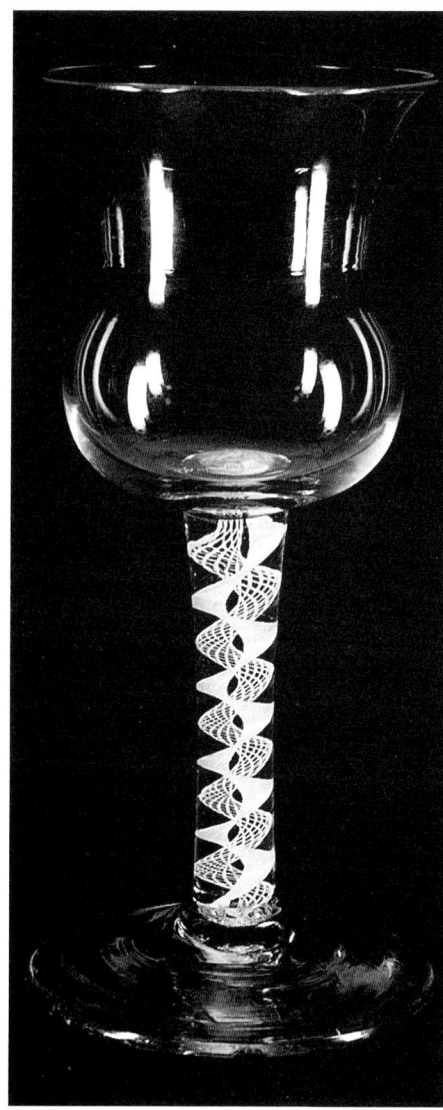

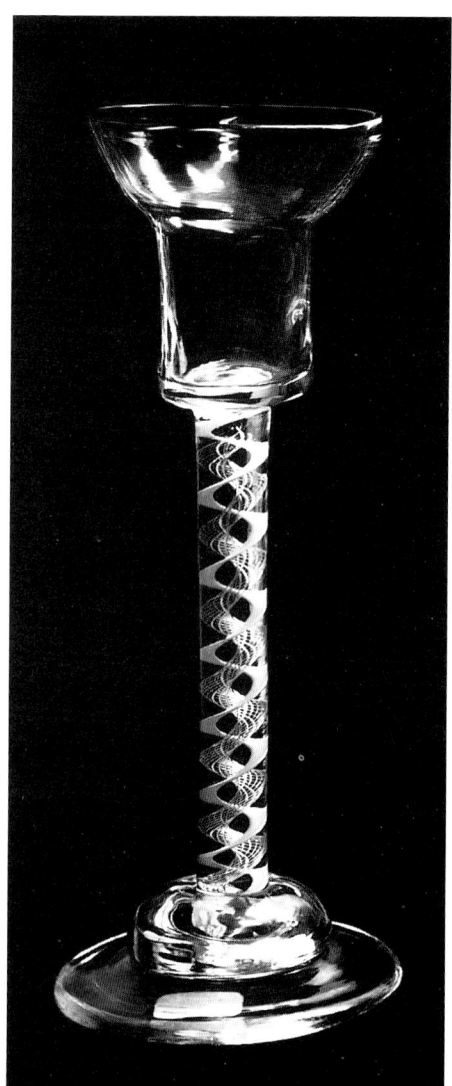

**596.** Wine glass; large tulip bowl; SSOT – corkscrew alternating with spiral gauze. Ht. 7¾ins. c.1765.

**597.** Wine glass; pan-topped bucket bowl; double-series mixed twist – single opaque corkscrew alternating with spiral air gauze; DF. Ht. 6⅛ins. c.1760. *Sotheby's.*

**598.** Wine glass; waisted ogee bowl engraved with border of fruiting vine; SSOT – spiral tape alternating with spiral gauze. Ht. 5⅞ins. c.1765.
*Tibbenham Collection, Ipswich Museum.*

Opaque-Twist Stems

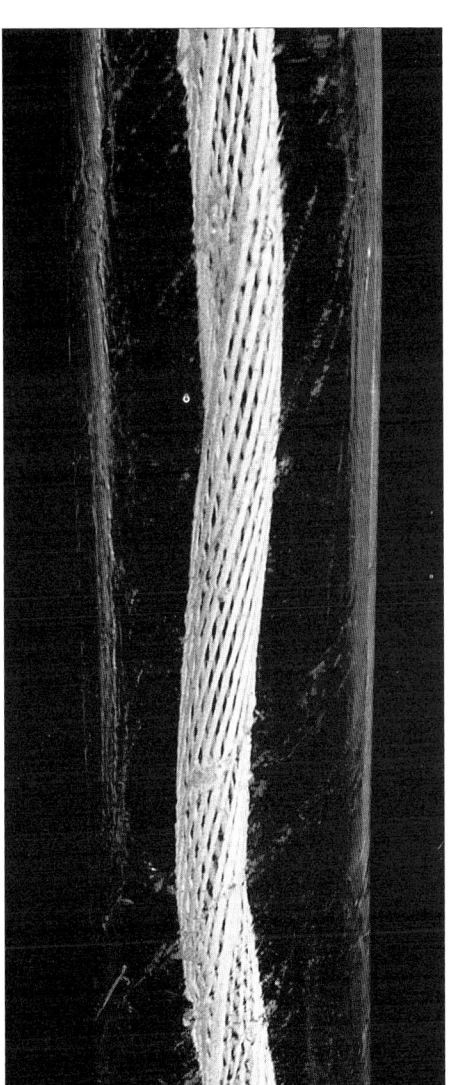
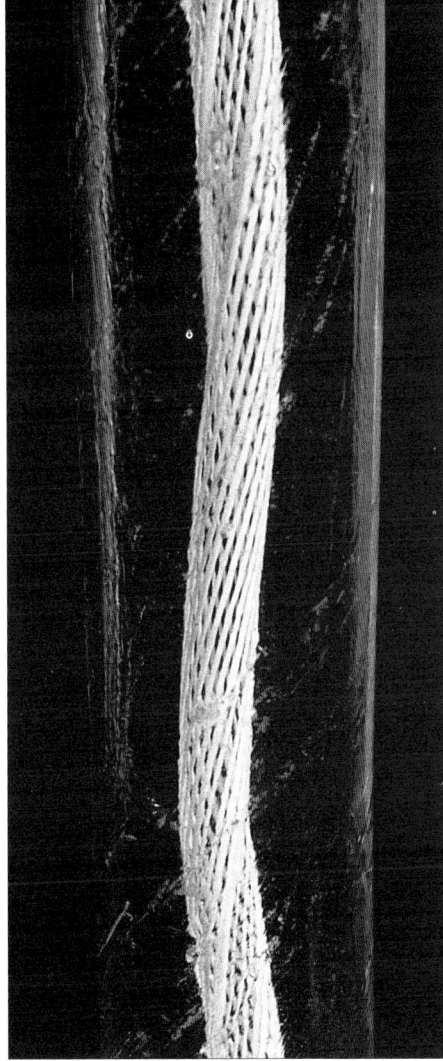

**599.** Wine glass; pointed RF bowl; SSOT –
single vertical gauze. Ht. 6¼ins. c.1765.
*Tibbenham Collection, Ipswich Museum.*

**600.** Single vertical gauze – close-up of 599.
*Tibbenham Collection, Ipswich Museum.*

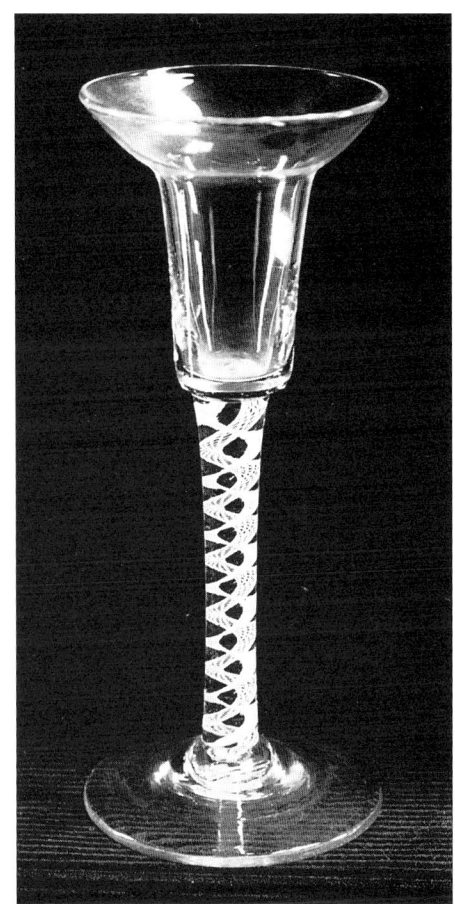

**601.** Wine glass; saucer-topped bucket
bowl; SSOT – corkscrew alternating with
spiral gauze. Ht. 6ins. c.1765.

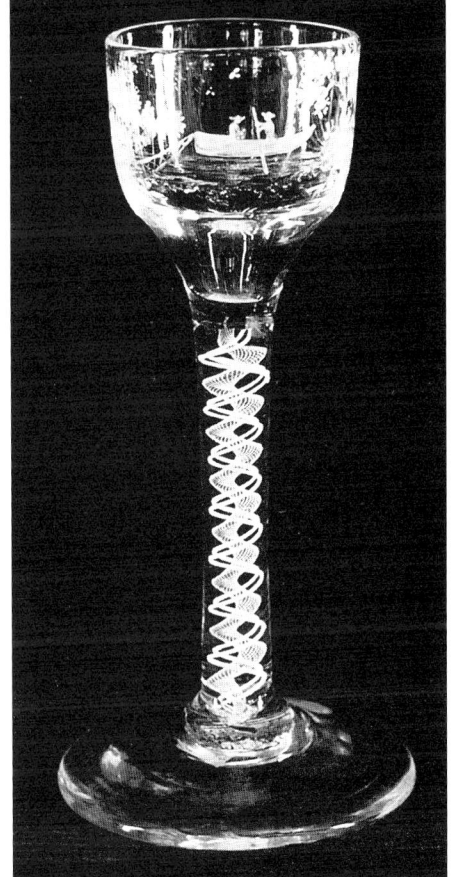

**602.** Wine glass; ogee bowl decorated in
white enamel with fishing scene; SSOT –
pair of heavy spiral threads alternating with
spiral gauze. Ht. 5⅜ins. c.1770. Attributed
to Beilby.

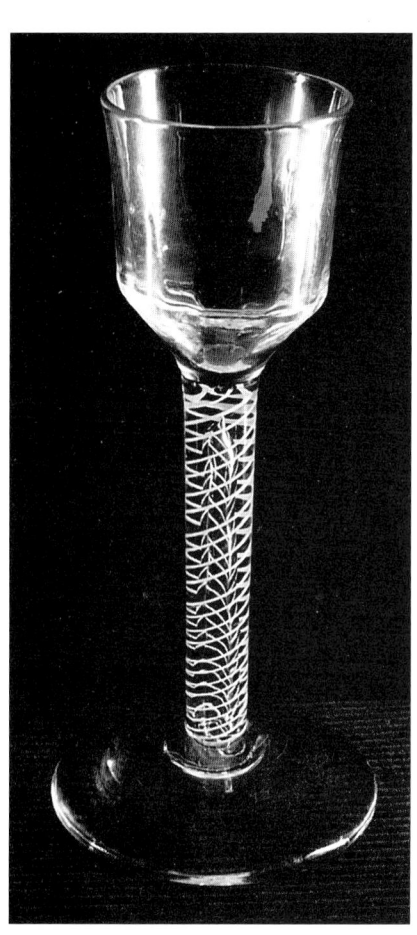

**603.** Wine glass; ogee bowl; SSOT – four heavy spiral threads outside long tear. Ht. 5⅜ins. c.1765.

**604.** Sweetmeat; cup bowl with dentated (or 'cogwheel' or 'pincered') rim and OW vertical stripes; MSOT stem with shoulder and basal knops; panel-moulded foot. Ht. 4ins. c.1760.

**605.** Sweetmeat; double-ogee bowl with dentated rim; shoulder-knopped MSOT; radially moulded foot. Ht. 3⅜ins. c.1760.

**606.** Sweetmeat; panel-moulded double-ogee bowl with dentated rim; MSOT stem with shoulder and basal knops; radially moulded foot. Ht. 4ins. c.1760.

Opaque-Twist Stems

**607.** Wine glass; trumpet bowl; shoulder-knopped MSOT. Ht. 6ins. c.1760.

**608.** Wine glass; waisted bell bowl, solid base, engraved fruiting vine; MSOT with shoulder and basal knops. Ht. 6¾ins. c.1760.

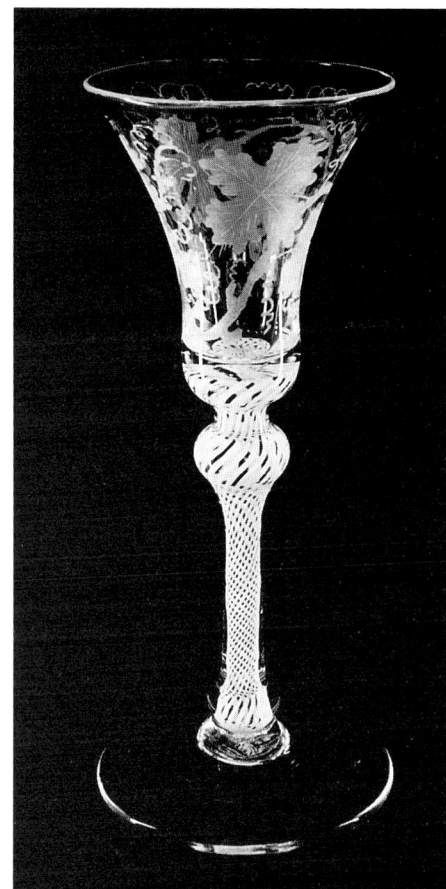

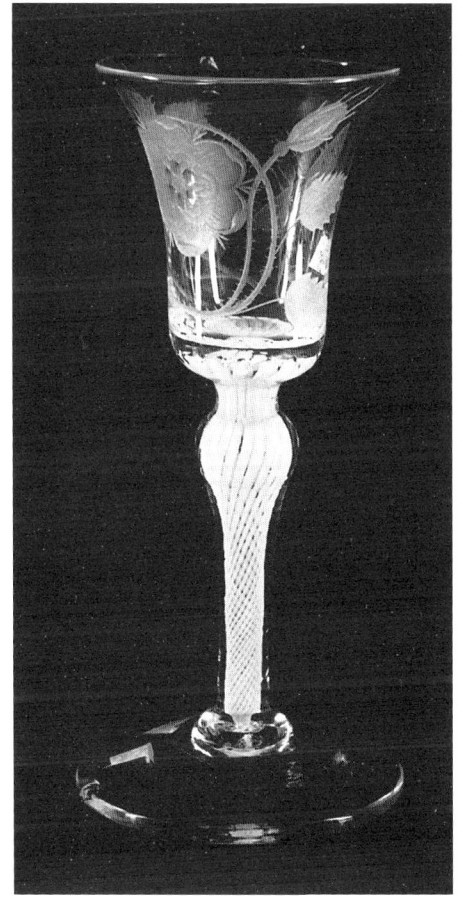

**609.** Wine glass; bell bowl, engraved rose, two buds and moth (Jacobite); shoulder-knopped MSOT. Ht. 6½ins. c.1760.
*Hartshorne Collection. (Plate 44).*

**610.** Wine glass; bell bowl; SSOT – multiple spiral commencing at base of bowl and continuing through a shoulder knop. Ht. 6½ins. c.1770. *Asprey.*

**611.** Wine glass; ogee bowl; centre-knopped MSOT. Ht. 6½ins. c.1760.

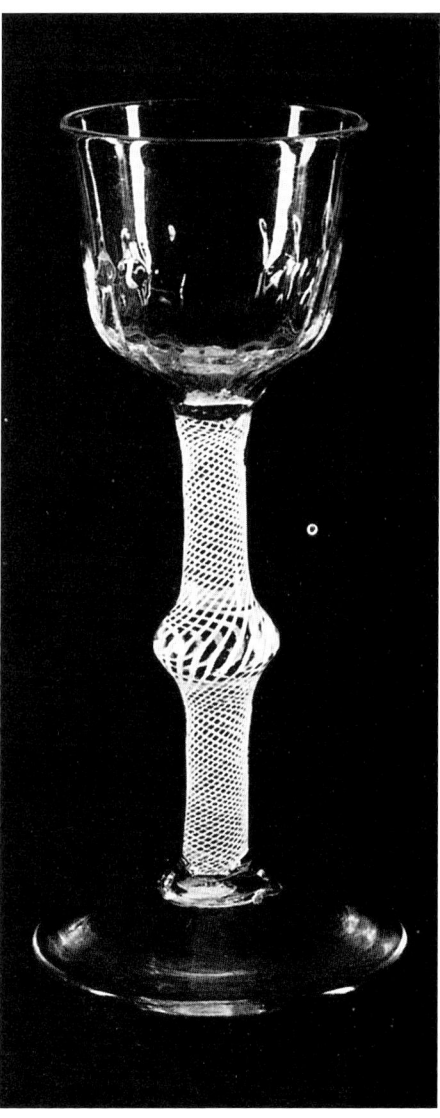

**612.** Wine glass; ogee bowl with basal flutes; centre-knopped MSOT. Ht. 5½ins. c.1760.

**613.** Wine glass; RF bowl; centre-knopped MSOT. Ht. 6ins. c.1760.

*Portsmouth City Museums.*

Opaque-Twist Stems

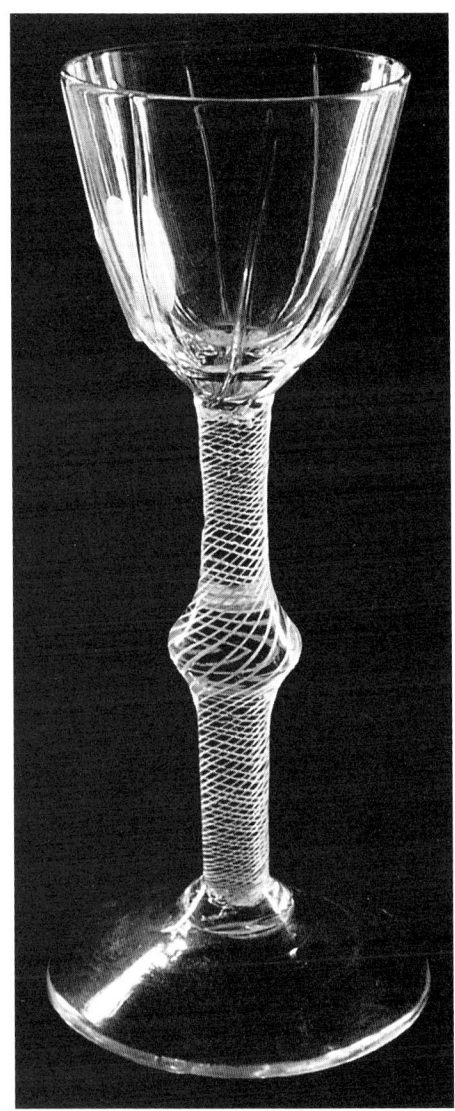

**614.** Wine glass; RF bowl with vertical ribs; centre-knopped MSOT. Ht. 6ins. c.1760.
*Smith Collection.*
*Harvey's Wine Museum, Bristol.*

**615.** Wine glass; tulip bowl; MSOT with central swelled knop; FF. Ht. 7ins. c.1765.
*Tibbenham Collection, Ipswich Museum.*

**616.** Ale glass; hammered ogee bowl; centre-knopped MSOT. Ht. 7½ins. c.1760.

Opaque-Twist Stems

**617.** Wine glass; large RF bowl; MSOT with shoulder and basal knops. Ht. 6½ins. c.1760.

**618.** Cordial glass; RF bowl, basal flutes; MSOT with shoulder and central knops. Ht. 6⅜ins. c.1760.

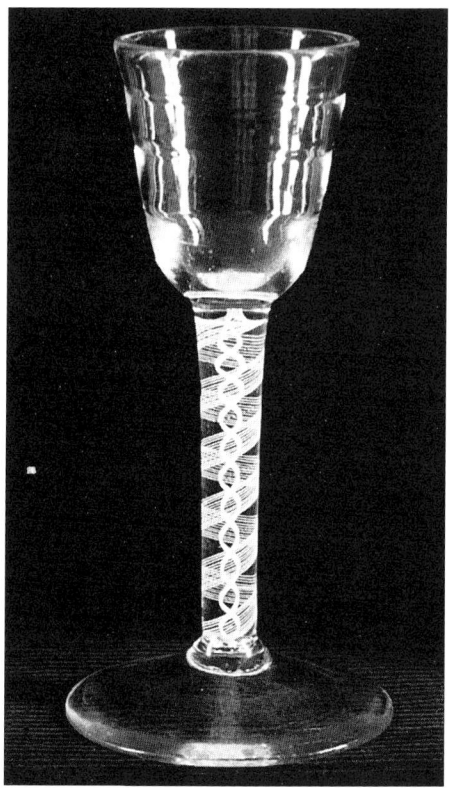

**619.** Sweetmeat; lipped double-ogee bowl with honeycomb moulding; shoulder-knopped SSOT – 20-ply spiral band, between collars; D & FF to match. Ht. 6¾ins. c.1760.

**620.** Wine glass; stepped RF ('Lynn') bowl; DSOT – 17-ply spiral band outside pair of spiral tapes. Ht. 5⅜ins. c.1765.
*Tibbenham Collection, Ipswich Museum.*

**621.** Wine glass; stepped RF ('Lynn') bowl; DSOT – 12-ply spiral band outside pair of spiral tapes. Ht. 5½ins. c.1765.
*Hartshorne Collection.*

Opaque-Twist Stems

**622.** Wine glass; stepped RF ('Lynn') bowl; DSOT – 12-ply spiral band outside pair of spiral tapes. Ht. 6¼ins. c.1765.

**623.** Wine glass; stepped RF ('Lynn') bowl; DSOT – 12-ply spiral band outside pair of spiral tapes. Ht. 6ins. c.1765.

**624.** Wine glass; octagonal ogee bowl; DSOT – 12-ply spiral band outside pair of spiral tapes. Ht. 6ins. c.1765.

**625.** Ale glass; RF bowl engraved with hops and barley; DSOT – 12-ply spiral band outside pair of spiral tapes. c.1765.

Opaque-Twist Stems

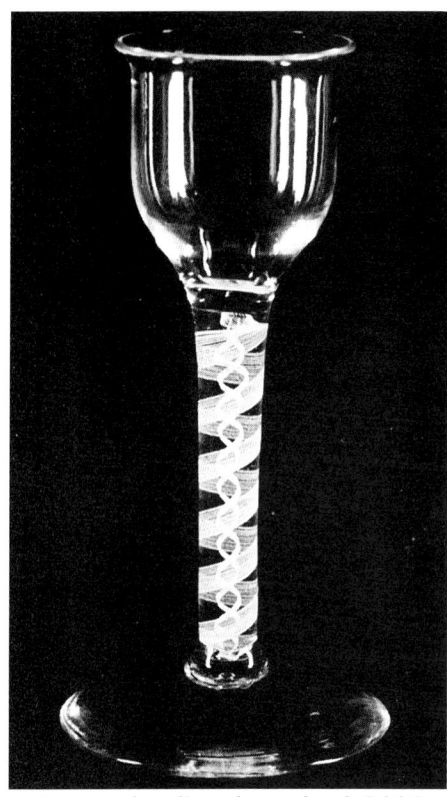

**626.** Wine glass; lipped ogee bowl; DSOT – 12-ply spiral band outside pair of spiral tapes. Ht. 5½ins. c.1765. *Worthing Museum.*

**627.** Wine glass; ogee bowl, hammered base; DSOT – 12-ply spiral band outside pair of spiral tapes. Ht. 6ins. c.1765.

**628.** Ratafia; trumpet bowl engraved with floral border round rim; DSOT – multi-ply spiral band round pair of spiral tapes. Ht. 6¾ins. c.1770. *Sotheby's.*

**629.** Ratafia; trumpet bowl with moulded fluting; DSOT – multi-ply spiral band outside pair of heavy spiral tapes. c.1770. *Asprey.*

**630.** Wine glass; large ogee bowl, engraved fruiting vine and bird in flight; DSOT – 11-ply spiral band outside pair of spiral tapes. Ht. 7ins. c.1765. *Hartshorne Collection.*

Opaque-Twist Stems

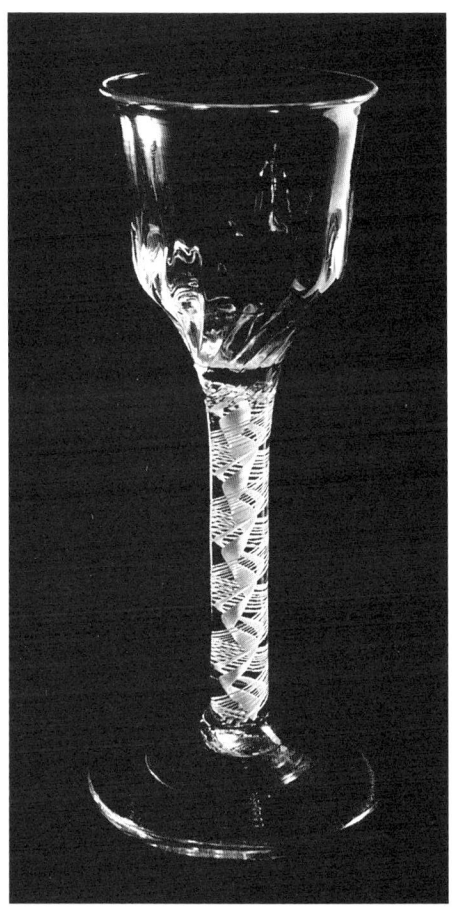

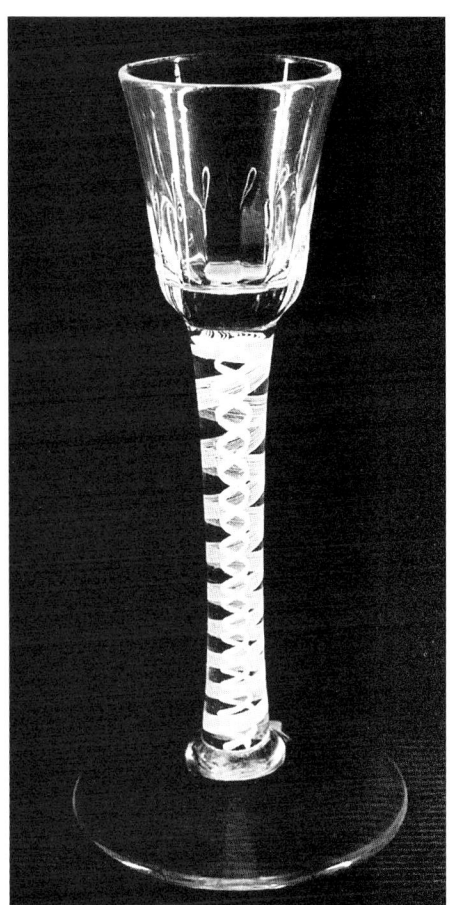

**631.** Wine glass; ogee bowl with wrythen-moulded base and everted rim; DSOT – 8-ply spiral band outside wide and narrow spiral tapes. Ht. 6ins. c.1765.

**632.** Cordial; RF bowl with basal flutes; DSOT – 18-ply spiral band outside pair of spiral tapes. Ht. 6½ins. c.1765.
*Worthing Museum.*

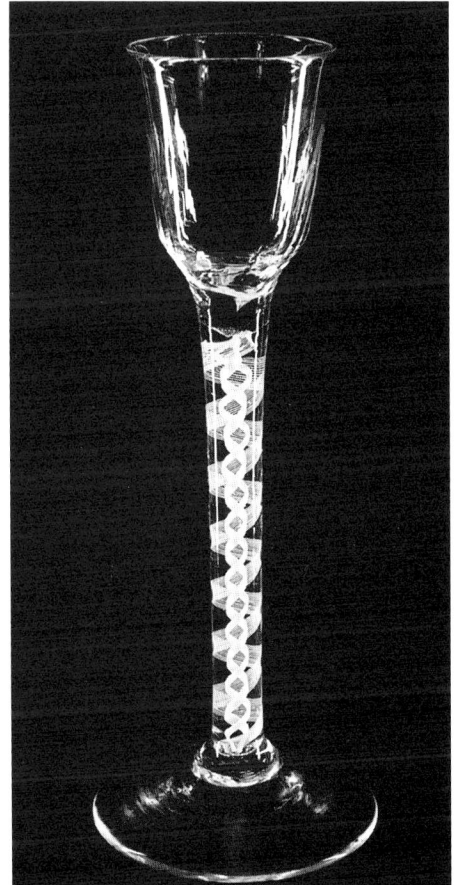

**633.** Cordial; ogee bowl with faint vertical fluting; DSOT – 12-ply spiral band outside pair of spiral tapes. Ht. 7ins. c.1765.

**634.** Cordial; slightly hammered RF bowl, engraved fruiting vine; DSOT – 12-ply spiral band outside pair of spiral tapes. Ht. 6⅜ins. c.1765.

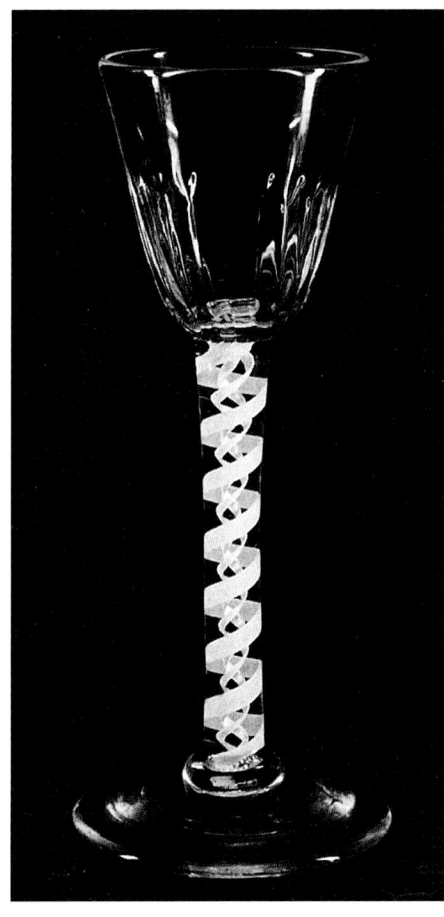

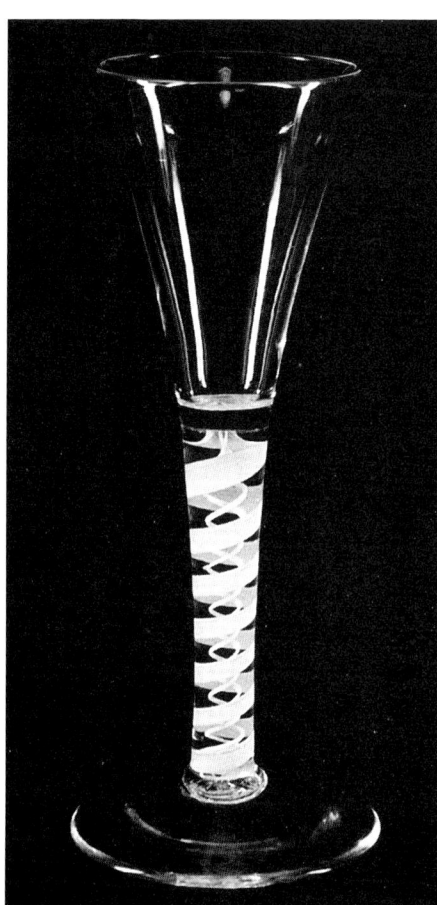

**635.** Wine glass; RF bowl with basal flutes; DSOT – solid spiral band outside pair of spiral tapes. Ht. 6ins. c.1765.

**636.** Wine glass; trumpet bowl; DSOT – solid spiral band outside pair of spiral tapes. Ht. 7ins. c.1765.

**637.** Wine glass; pan-topped trumpet bowl; DSOT – solid spiral band outside pair of spiral tapes. Ht. 6ins. c.1765.

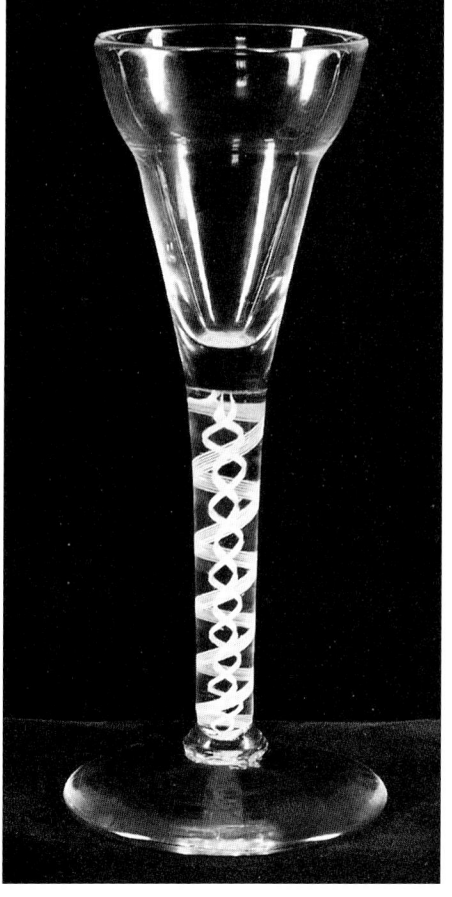

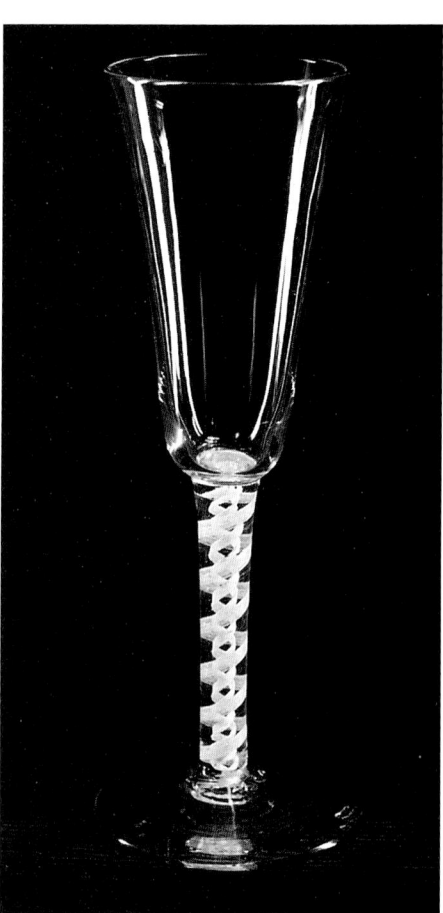

**638.** Ale glass; RF bowl; DSOT – solid spiral band outside pair of spiral tapes. Ht. 7½ins. c.1765. *Worthing Museum.*

Opaque-Twist Stems

**639.** Ale glass; RF bowl, hammered base; DSOT – solid spiral band outside pair of spiral tapes. Ht. 7½ins. c.1765.

**640.** Ratafia; RF bowl with basal flutes; DSOT – solid spiral band outside pair of spiral tapes. Ht. 7ins. c.1765.

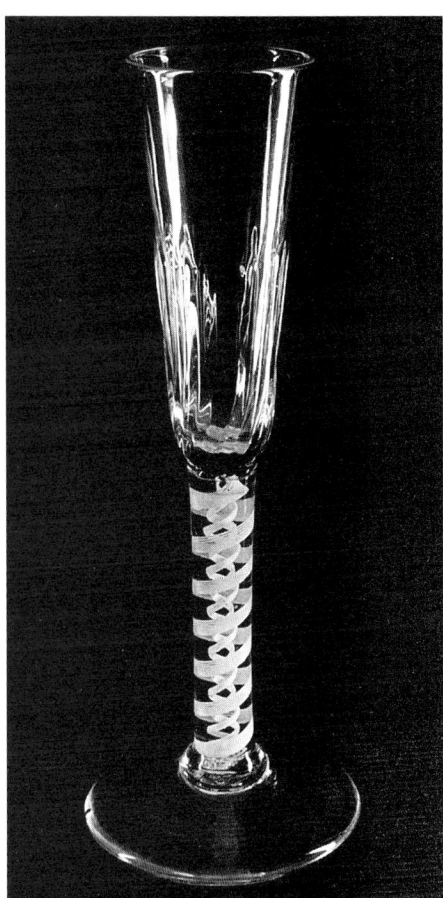

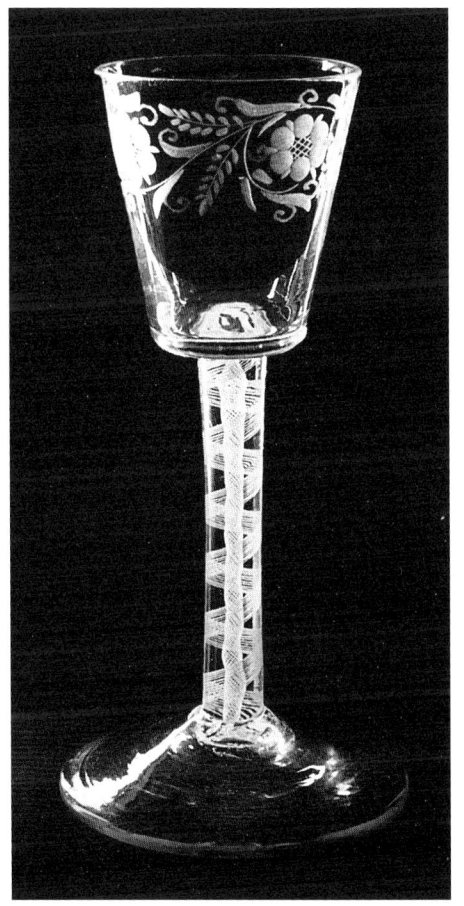

**641.** Wine glass; bucket bowl with engraved 'flowered' border below rim; DSOT – 12-ply spiral band outside gauze. Ht. 6ins. c.1765.

**642.** Wine glass; hexagonal, panel-moulded bowl; DSOT – 8-ply spiral band outside gauze. Ht. 6ins. c.1765.

Opaque-Twist Stems

215

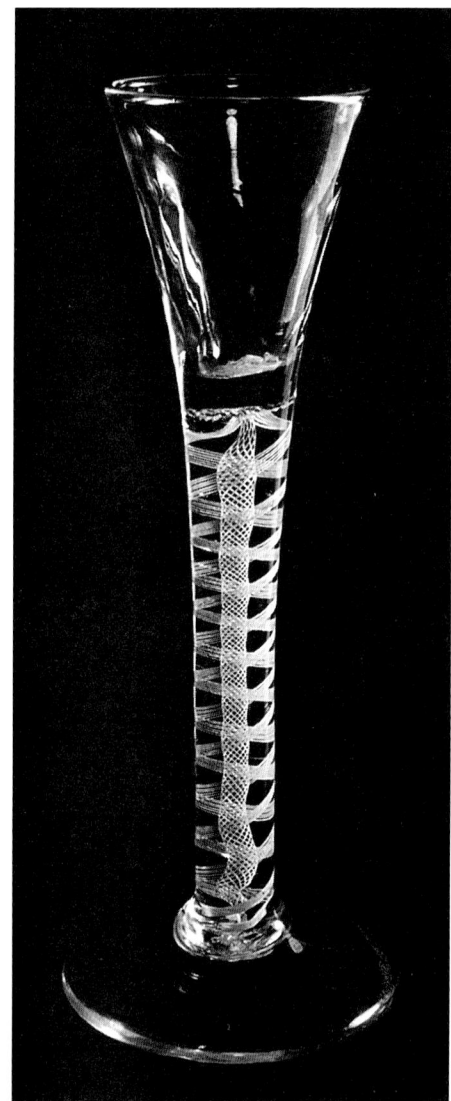

**643.** Cordial; trumpet bowl with faint basal fluting; DSOT – pair of 7-ply spiral bands outside gauze. Ht. 7ins. c.1765.

**644.** Wine glass; RF bowl with a seal on each side embodying the arms 'a fesse between three garbs, in an arabesque border'; DSOT – pair of spiral tapes outside gauze; FF. Ht. 6ins. c.1765. The seals are an extremely rare feature on a wine glass. *Hartshorne Collection. (Fig. 219).*

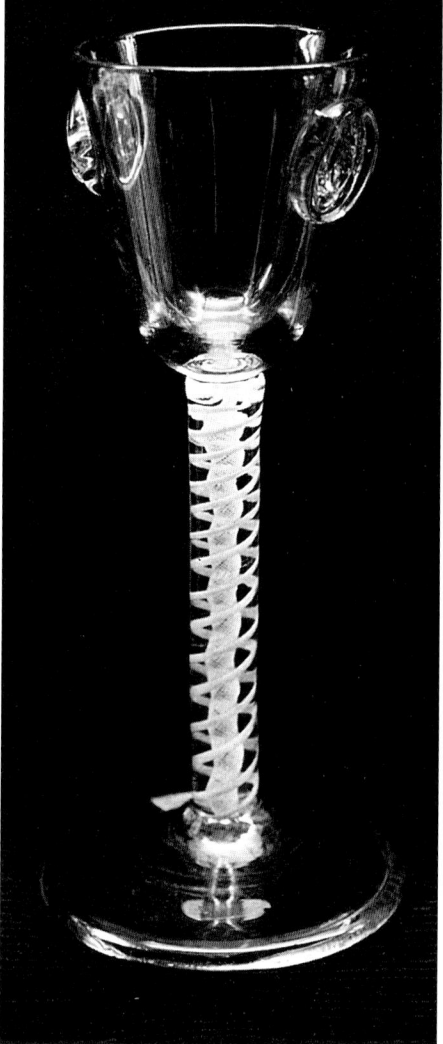

**645.** Wine glass; RF bowl; DSOT – pair of spiral tapes outside gauze. Ht. 6ins. c.1765. *Worthing Museum.*

Opaque-Twist Stems

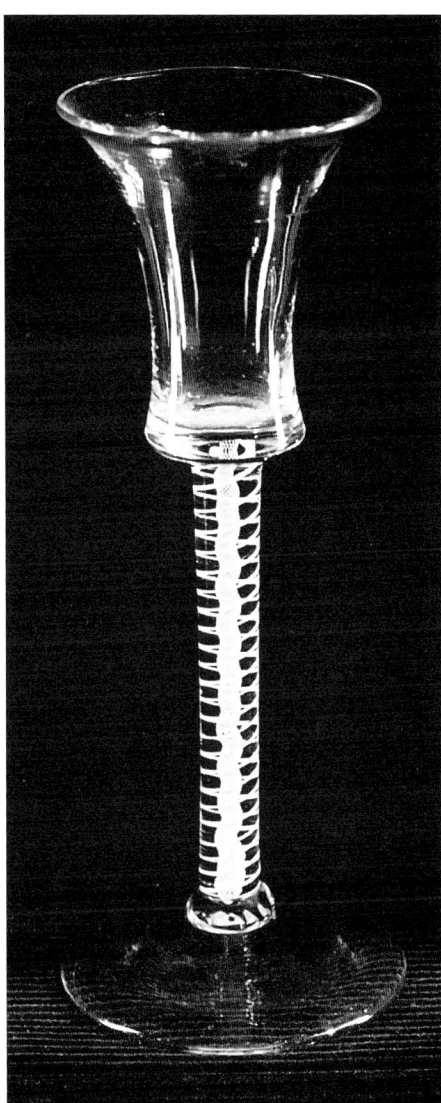

**648.** Wine glass; waisted bucket bowl; DSOT – pair of spiral threads outside gauze. Ht. 6¼ins. c.1765.
*Hartshorne Collection.*

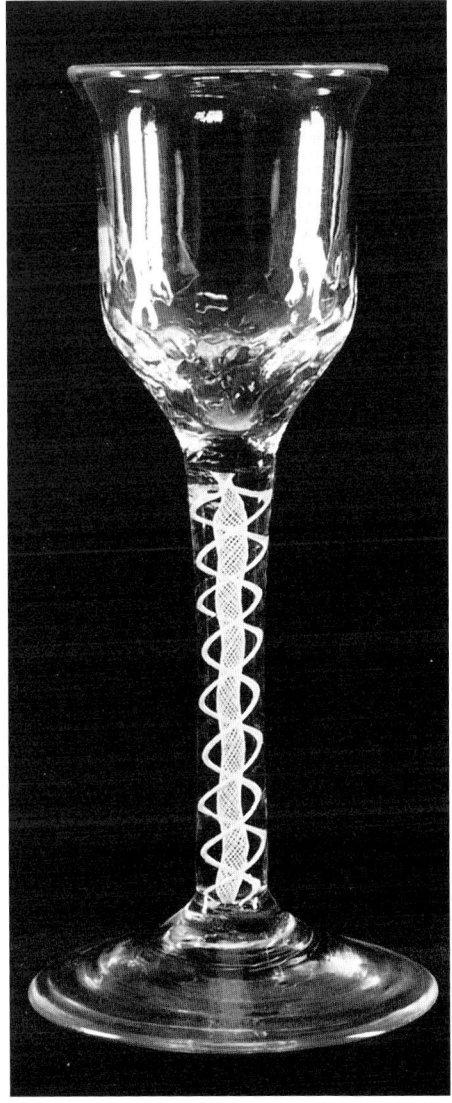

**647.** Wine glass; lipped ogee bowl; DSOT – pair of heavy spiral threads outside gauze. Ht. 5¾ins. c.1765.  *Hartshorne Collection.*

**646.** Ratafia; trumpet bowl; DSOT – pair of tapes outside vertical gauze. Ht. 6⅜ins. c.1770. *Pilkington Glass Museum, St. Helens.*

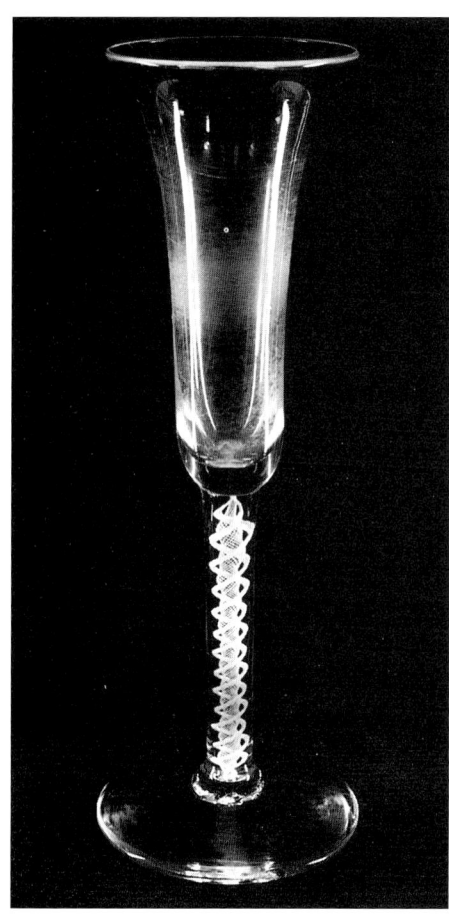

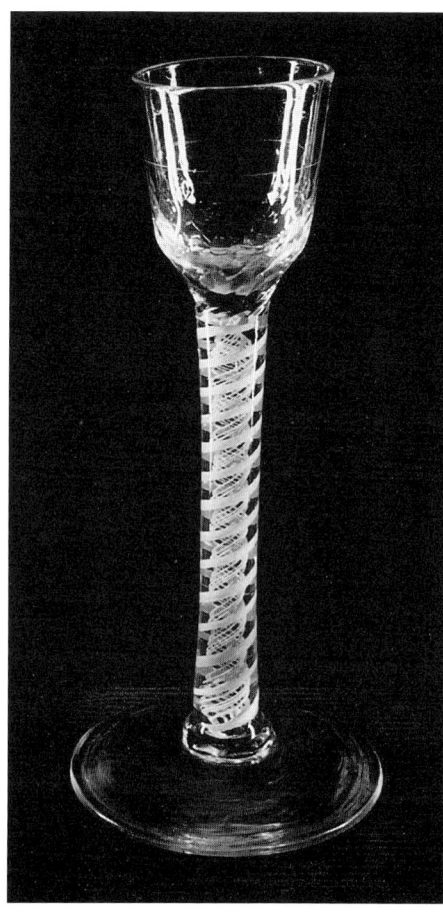

**649.** Ale glass; long bell bowl; DSOT – pair of spiral tapes outside gauze. Ht. 7¾ins. c.1765.

**650.** Cordial; ogee bowl, hammered base; DSOT – pair of spiral tapes outside gauze. Ht. 6½ins. c.1765.

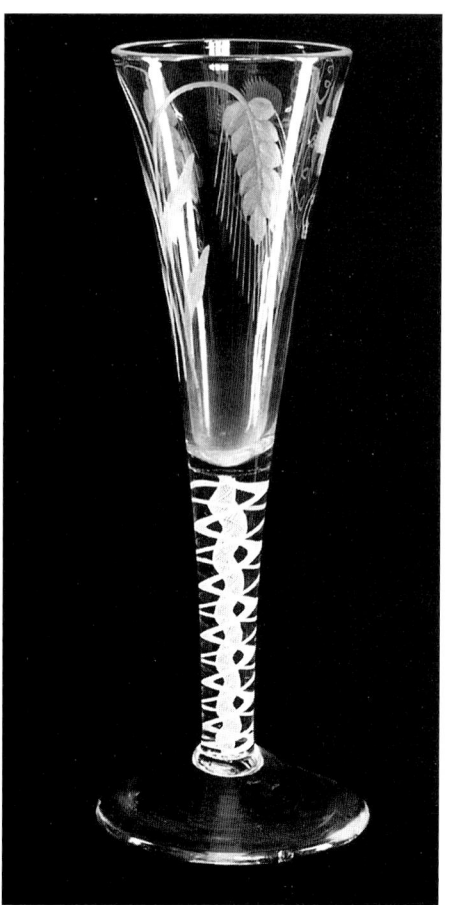

**651.** Ale glass; trumpet bowl, engraved hops and barley; DSOT – corkscrew and spiral thread alternating outside spiral gauze. Ht. 7⅜ins. c.1765.

*Hartshorne Collection.*

**652.** Wine glass; ogee bowl with vertically moulded base; DSOT – three spiral threads outside spiral gauze. Ht. 7ins. c.1765.

Opaque-Twist Stems

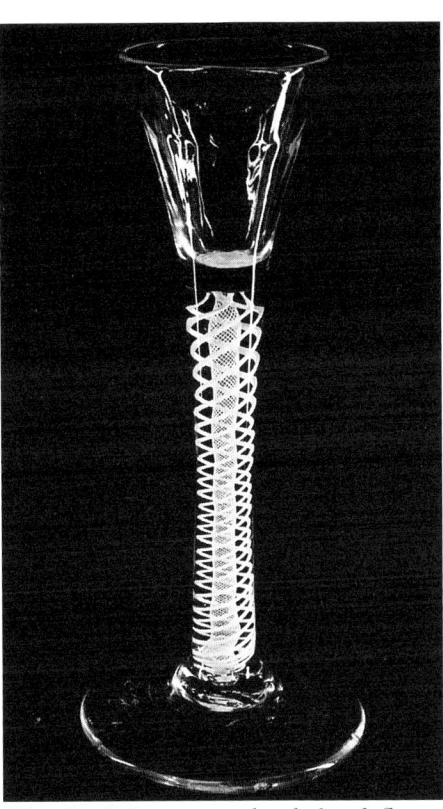

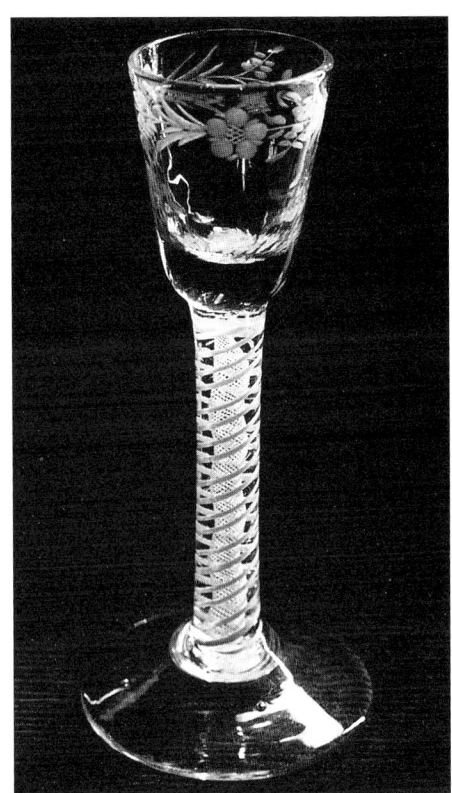

**653.** Wine glass; ogee bowl, gilt rim; DSOT – four heavy spiral threads outside gauze. Ht. 5¾ins. c.1770.

**654.** Cordial; trumpet bowl, basal flutes; DSOT – four spiral threads outside gauze. Ht. 6½ins. c.1770.

**655.** Cordial; RF bowl, basal flutes, engraved floral band below rim; DSOT – four heavy spiral threads outside gauze. Ht. 6¼ins. c.1770.

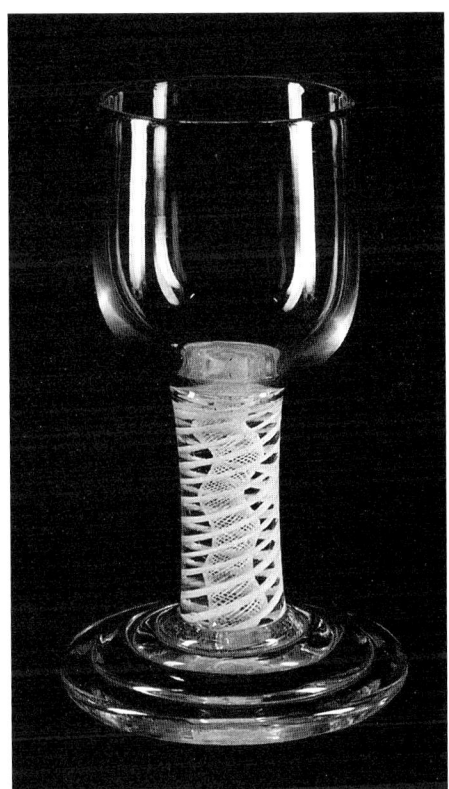

**656.** Mead glass; cup bowl, gadrooned base; DSOT – four heavy spiral threads outside gauze; FF. Ht. 6¼ins. c.1770.

**657.** Dram glass; trumpet bowl; DSOT – four heavy spiral threads outside spiral gauze; firing foot. Ht. 4½ins. c.1770.

**658.** Firing glass; cup bowl; DSOT – four heavy spiral threads outside spiral gauze; terraced foot. Ht. 4¾ins. c.1770.

Opaque-Twist Stems

219

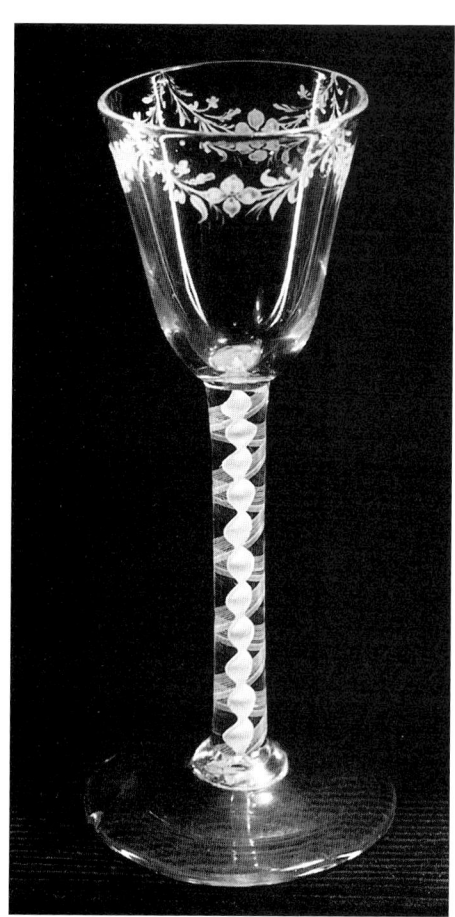

**659.** Wine glass; cup bowl, engraved flowers and bird in flight; DSOT – 4-ply spiral band outside corkscrew. Ht. 5½ins. c.1770.

**660.** Wine glass; pointed RF bowl decorated with festoons in white enamel; DSOT – 12-ply spiral band outside corkscrew. Ht. 6ins. c.1770. Attributed to Beilby.

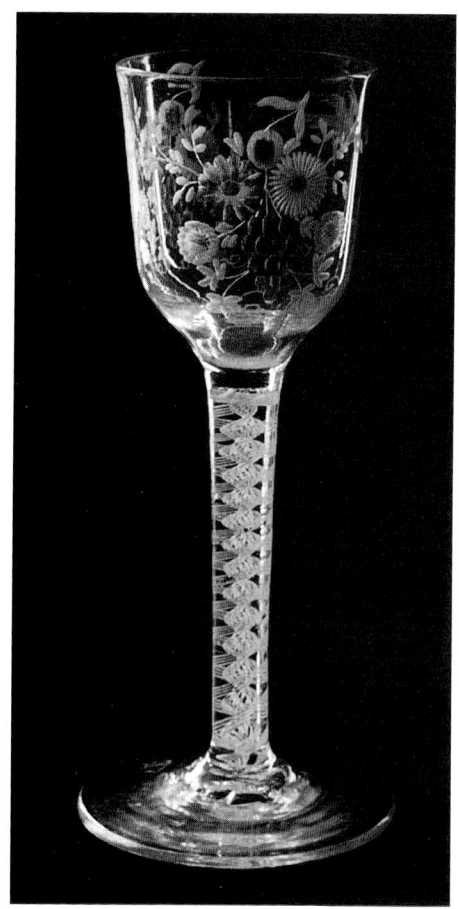

**661.** Wine glass; ogee bowl; DSOT – 5-ply spiral band outside multi-ply corkscrew. Ht. 5¾ins. c.1770.

**662.** Wine glass; ogee bowl, engraved fruiting vine and bird in flight; DSOT – 4-ply spiral band outside lace twist. Ht. 6ins. c.1770.

**663.** Wine glass; ogee bowl with basal flutes; DSOT – pair of 6-ply spiral bands outside lace twist. Ht. 5½ins. c.1770.
*Hartshorne Collection. (Fig. 240).*

**664.** Wine glass; ogee bowl with engraved border of fruiting vine and basal flutes; DSOT – pair of 6-ply spiral bands outside lace twist. Ht. 6ins. c.1770.

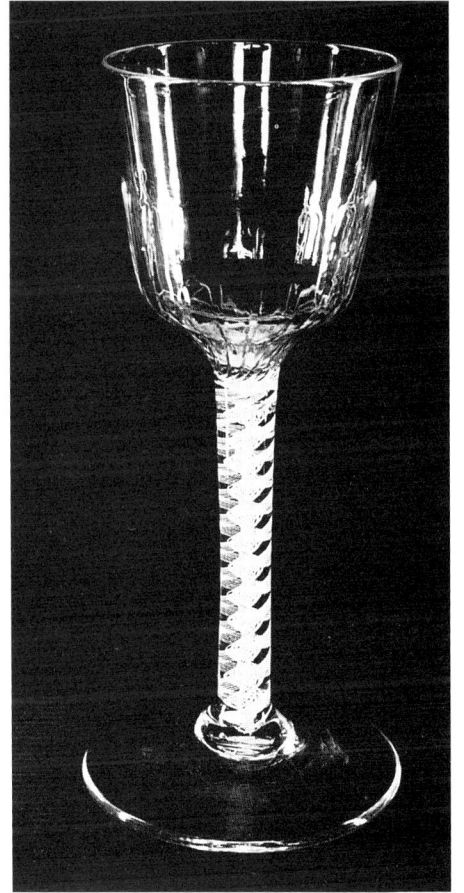

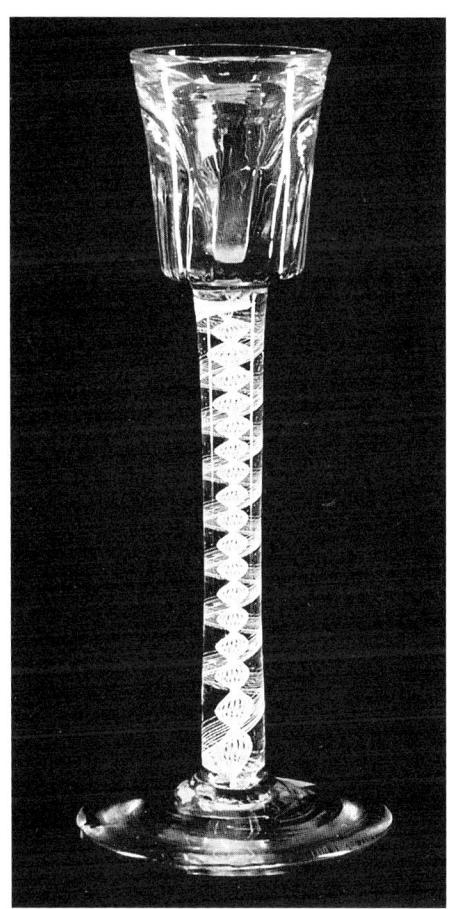

**665.** Wine glass; ogee bowl with basal flutes; DSOT – 8-ply spiral band outside lace twist. Ht. 6½ins. c.1770.

**666.** Toastmaster's glass; deceptive bucket bowl with basal flutes; DSOT – 11-ply spiral band outside lace twist. Ht. 7ins. c.1770.
*Hartshorne Collection. (Plate 52/2).*

Opaque-Twist Stems

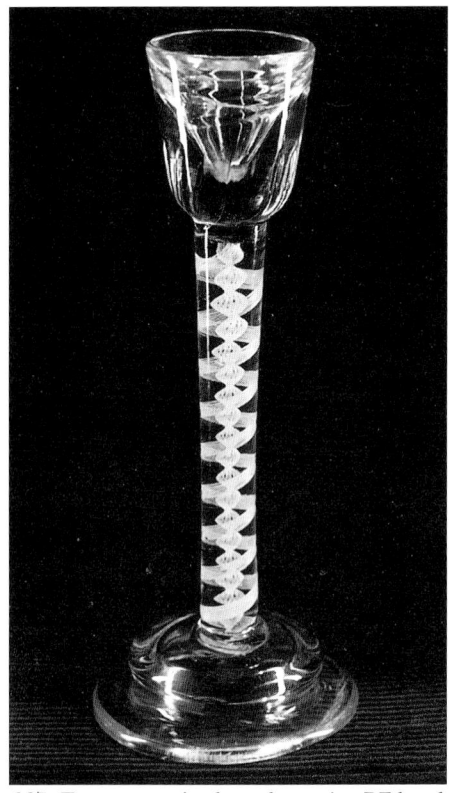

**667.** Toastmaster's glass; deceptive RF bowl with basal flutes; DSOT – 12-ply spiral band outside lace twist; 'helmet' domed foot. Ht. 6½ins. c.1770.

**668.** Firing glass; ogee bowl; DSOT – pair of 6-ply spiral bands outside lace twist; terraced foot. Ht. 3¾ins. c.1770.
*Worthing Museum.*

**669.** Firing glass; ovoid bowl with basal flutes; DSOT – pair of 9-ply spiral bands outside lace twist; terraced foot. Ht. 4ins. c.1770.
*Hartshorne Collection.*

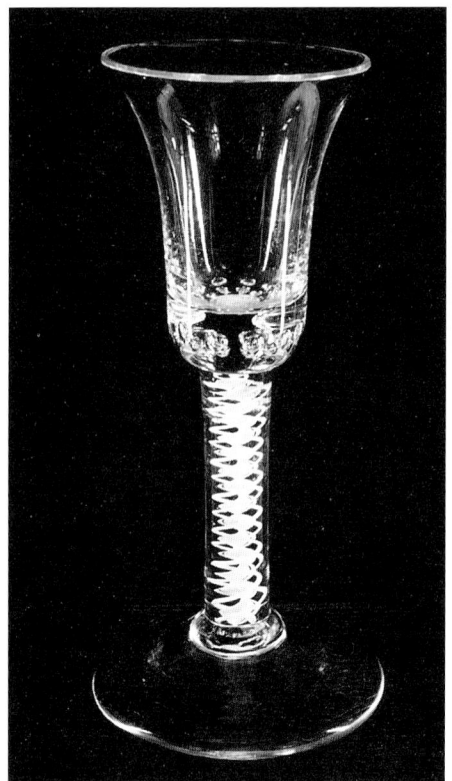

**670.** Wine glass; bell bowl with solid teared base; DSOT – pair of heavy spiral threads outside corkscrew. Ht. 6¼ins. c.1770.

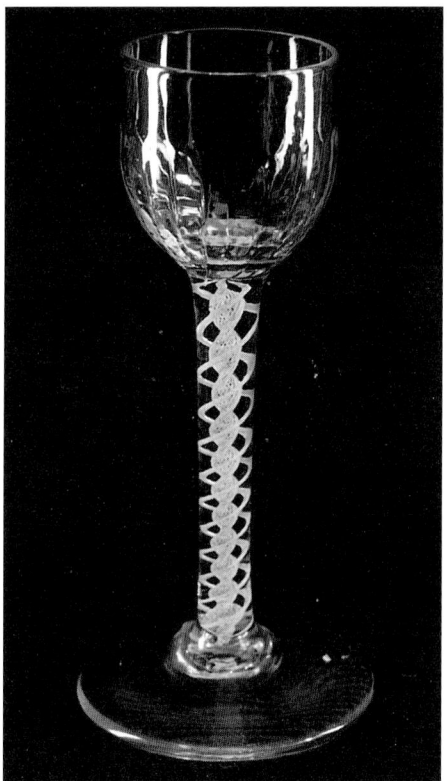

**671.** Wine glass; ovoid bowl with basal flutes; DSOT – pair of spiral tapes outside a multi-ply corkscrew. Ht. 5¾ins. c.1770.

**672.** Wine glass; ogee bowl decorated with pastoral scene in white enamel ('Beilby'); DSOT – pair of heavy spiral threads outside lace twist. Ht. 5¾ins. c.1770.

Opaque-Twist Stems

**673.** Sweetmeat; honeycomb-moulded double-ogee bowl with everted rim; collar; DSOT – pair of spiral tapes outside lace twist; D & FF to match. Ht. 6½ins. c.1770.

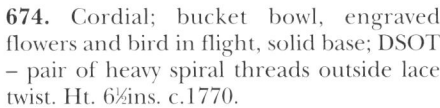

**674.** Cordial; bucket bowl, engraved flowers and bird in flight, solid base; DSOT – pair of heavy spiral threads outside lace twist. Ht. 6½ins. c.1770.
*Hartshorne Collection. (Fig. 299).*

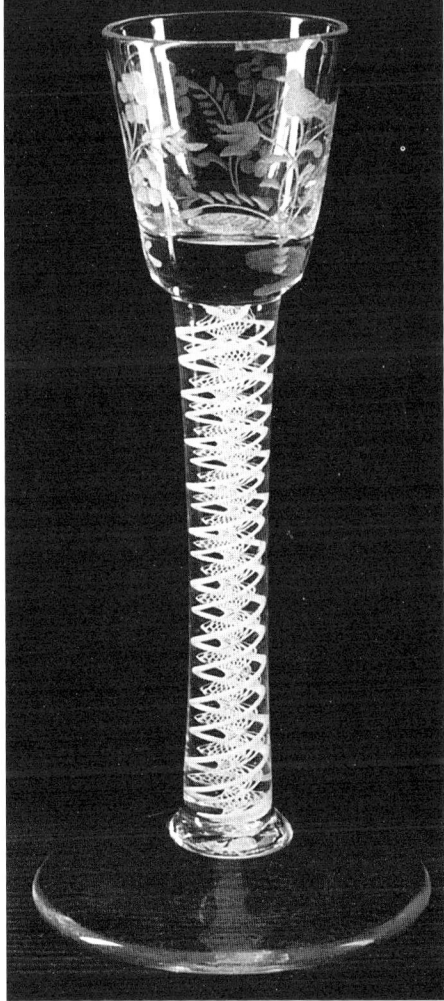

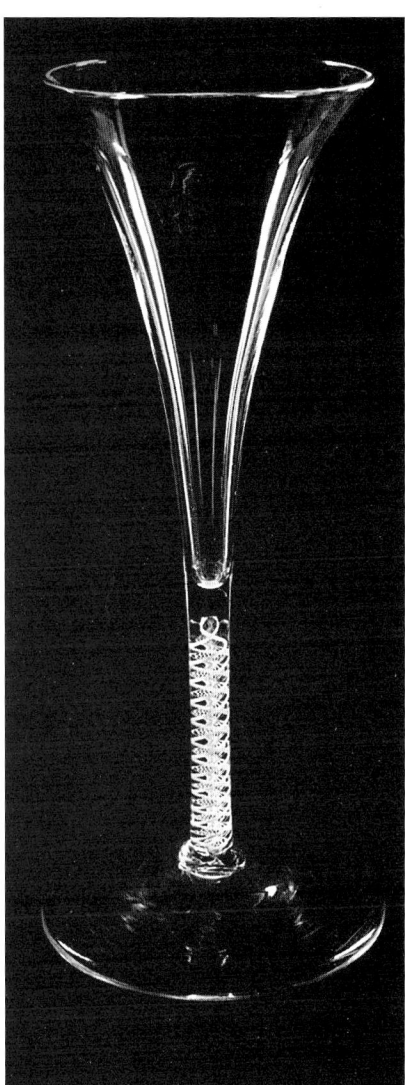

**675.** Wine flute; trumpet bowl; DSOT – pair of heavy spiral threads outside lace twist. Ht. 7½ins. c.1770.

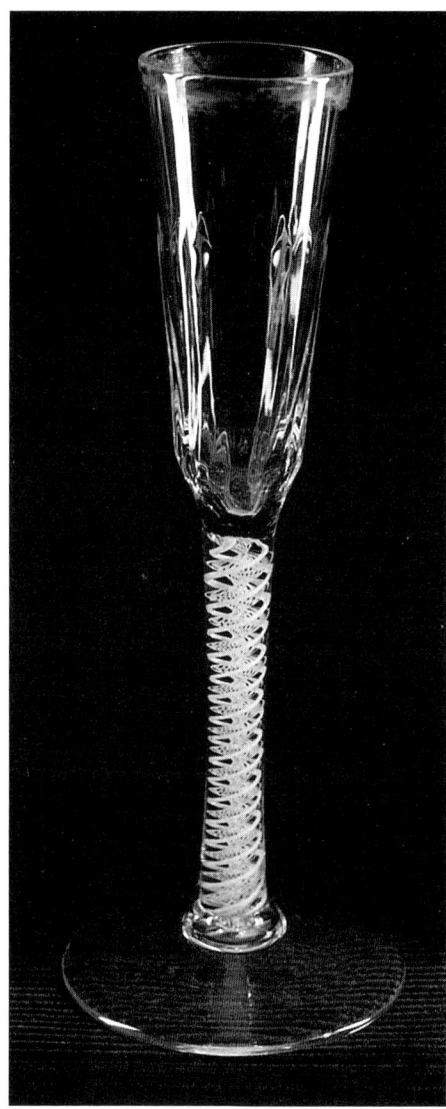

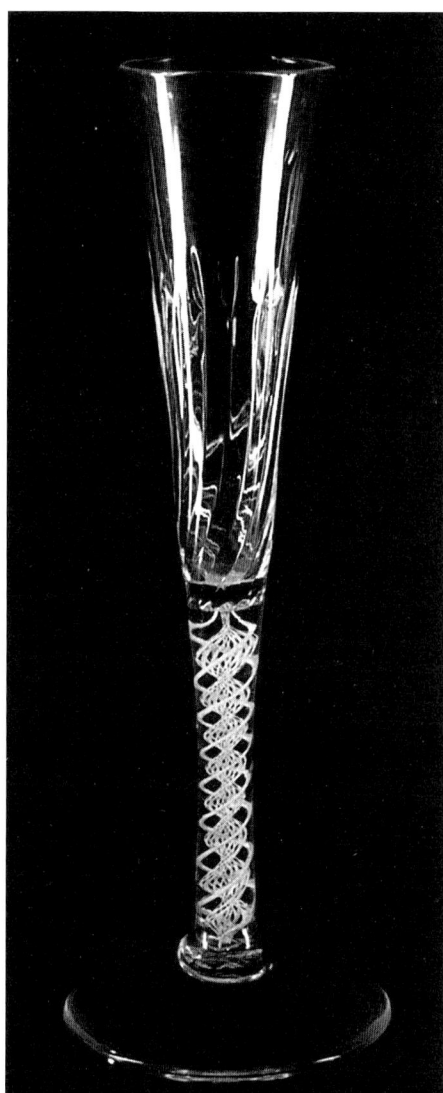

**676.** Ratafia; ogee bowl with basal flutes; DSOT – pair of heavy spiral threads outside lace twist. Ht. 7⅛ins. c.1770.

**677.** Ratafia; trumpet bowl with basal flutes; DSOT – pair of heavy spiral threads outside lace twist. Ht. 8ins. c.1770.

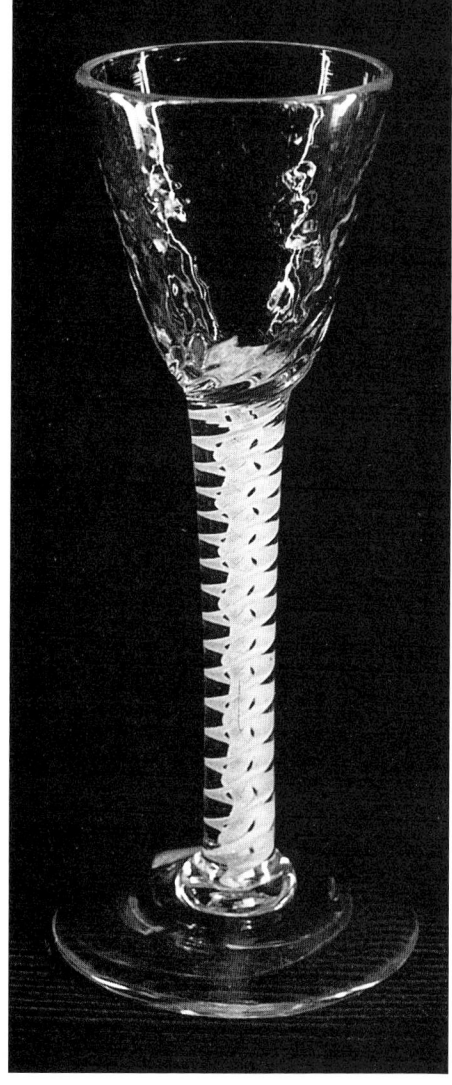

**678.** Wine glass; pointed RF bowl, hammered; DSOT – pair of corkscrews outside spiral cable. Ht. 6ins. c.1770.

Opaque-Twist Stems

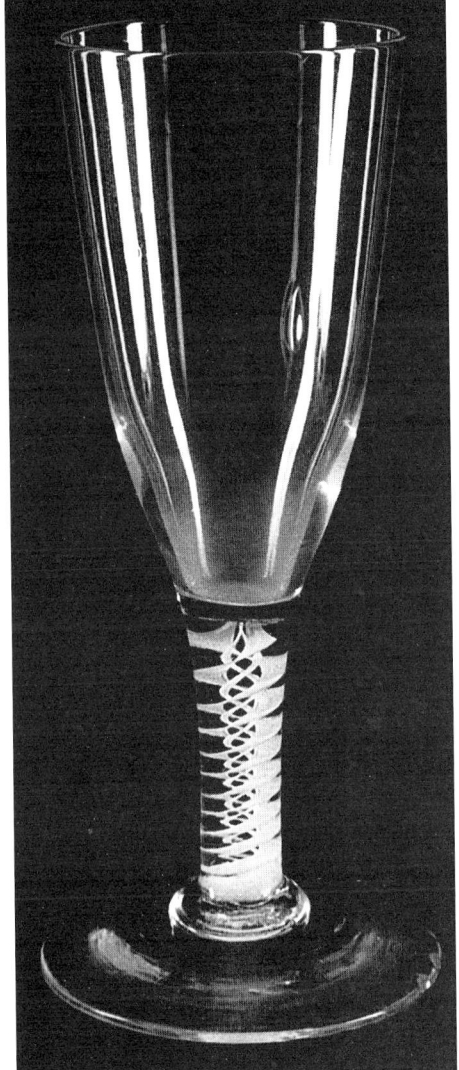

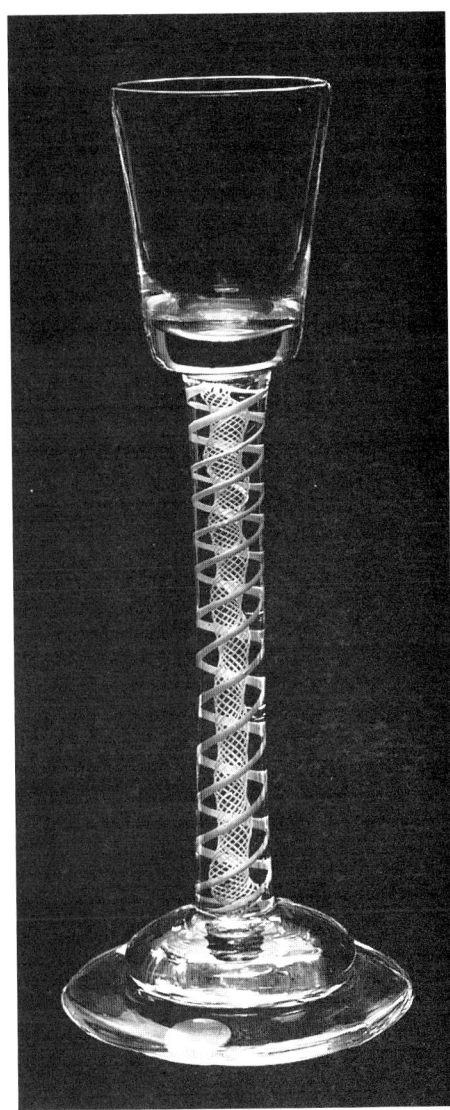

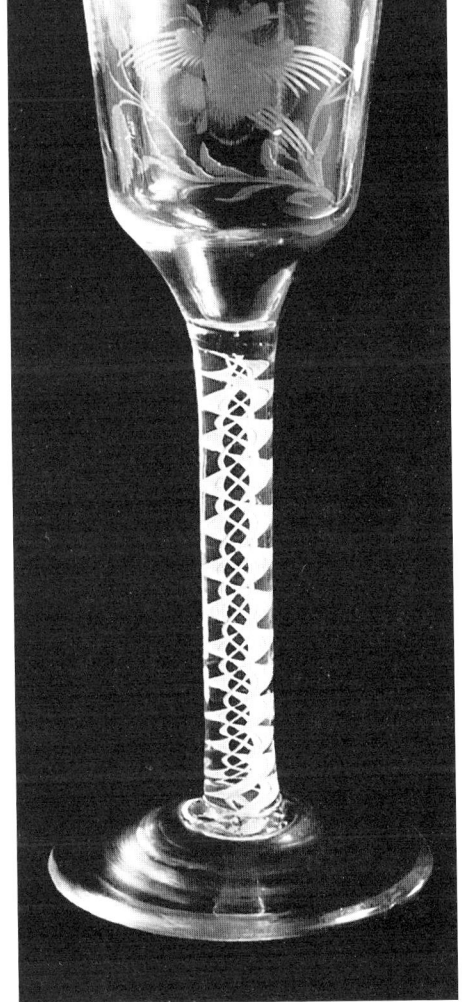

**680.** Short ale glass; ogee bowl; DSOT – pair of corkscrews outside pair of heavy spiral threads. Ht. 6½ins. c.1770.

*Hartshorne Collection. (Fig. 278).*

**681.** Cordial; bucket bowl; DSOT – pair of tapes outside gauze; DF. Ht. 6⅝ins. c.1765.

*Sotheby's.*

**679.** Wine glass; ogee bowl engraved in Jacobite manner; DSOT – pair of multi-ply corkscrews outside pair of spiral threads. Ht. 6ins. c.1770.

Opaque-Twist Stems

**682.** Small goblet; ogee bowl with slightly everted rim; DSOT – pair of heavy spiral threads outside vertical cable. Ht. 7¼ins. c.1770.

**683.** Ale glass; pointed RF bowl, engraved hops and barley; DSOT – pair of spiral threads outside spiral cable. Ht. 8⅛ins. c.1770.

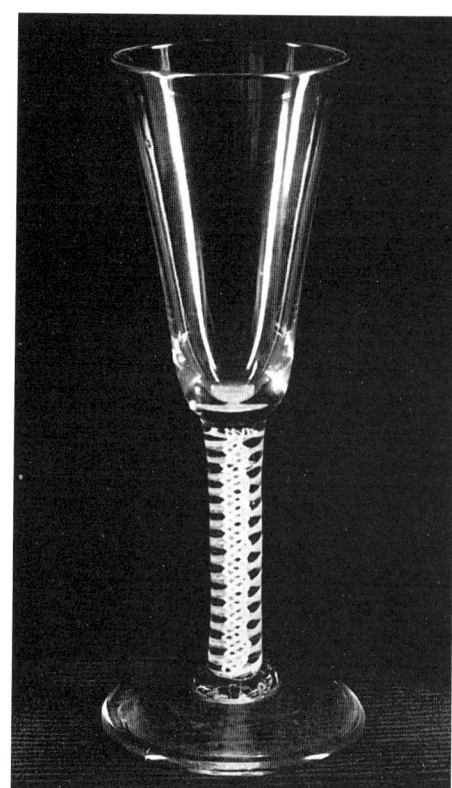

**684.** Ale glass; pointed RF bowl; DSOT – pair of 4-ply spiral bands outside four heavy spiral threads. Ht. 7ins. c.1770.

**685.** Wine glass; lipped ogee bowl, engraved floral band; DSOT – 12-ply spiral band outside four spiral threads. Ht. 5⅜ins. c.1770.

**686.** Wine glass; RF bowl, hammered and fluted; DSOT – pair of heavy spiral threads outside four heavy spiral threads. Ht. 6ins. c.1770.

**687.** Goblet; RF bowl, everted rim, honeycomb moulding at base; DSOT – four spiral threads outside vertical gauze; FF. Ht. 8⅜ins. c.1770. *Sotheby's.*

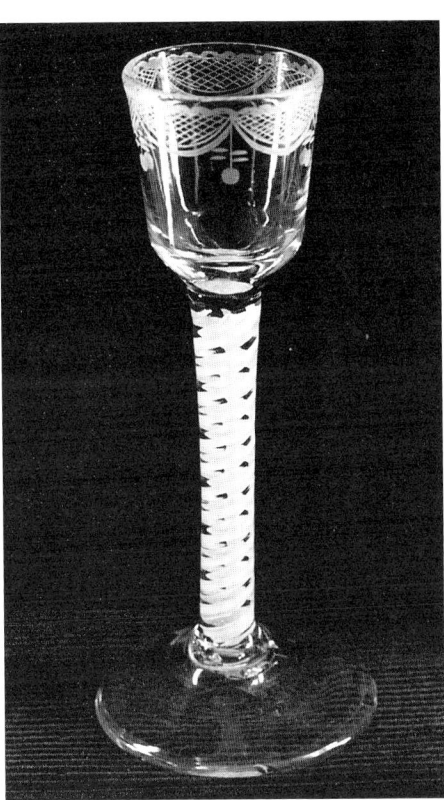

**688.** Cordial; ogee bowl, engraved festoons below rim; DSOT – pair of solid spiral bands outside corkscrew. Ht. 6¼ins. c.1770. *Hartshorne Collection. (Fig. 301).*

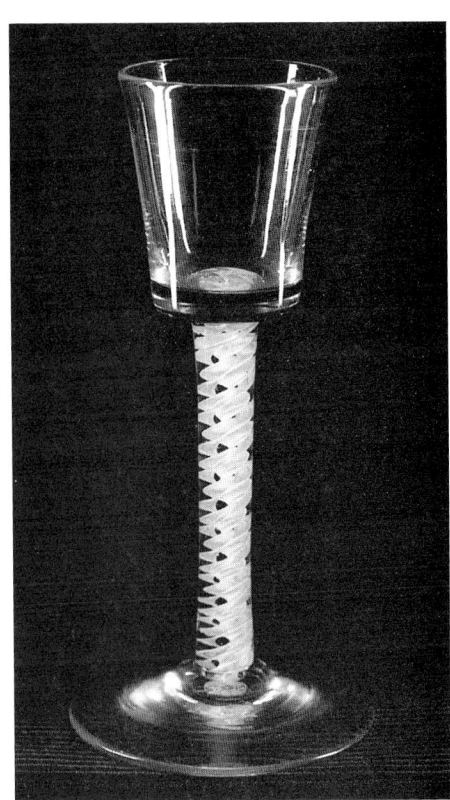

**689.** Wine glass; bucket bowl; DSOT – pair of spiral tapes outside corkscrew. Ht. 6ins. c.1770.

**690.** Deceptive glass; ogee bowl; DSOT – pair of spiral gauzes outside pair of heavy spiral tapes. Ht. 5½ins. c.1770. *Sotheby's.*

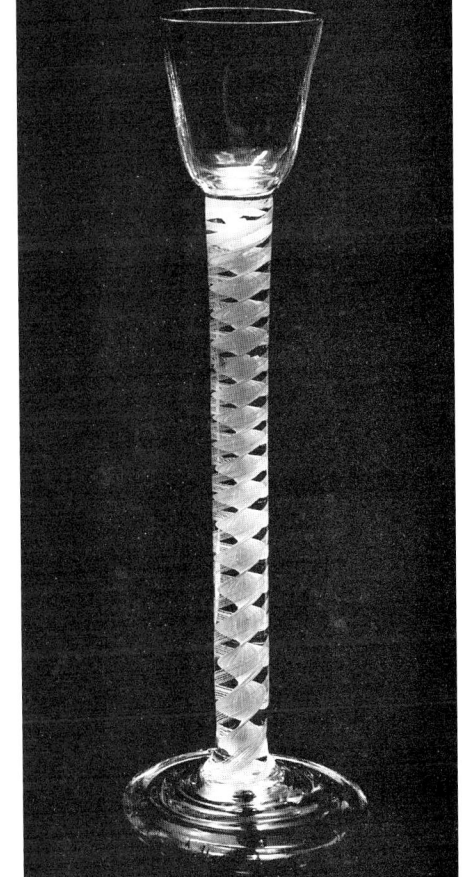

**691** Cordial; RF bowl; tall DSOT – multi-ply spiral band outside a corkscrew; terraced foot. Ht. 10ins. c.1765. Glasses with such exceptionally long stems are sometimes referred to as 'Captain' glasses. *Sotheby's.*

Opaque-Twist Stems

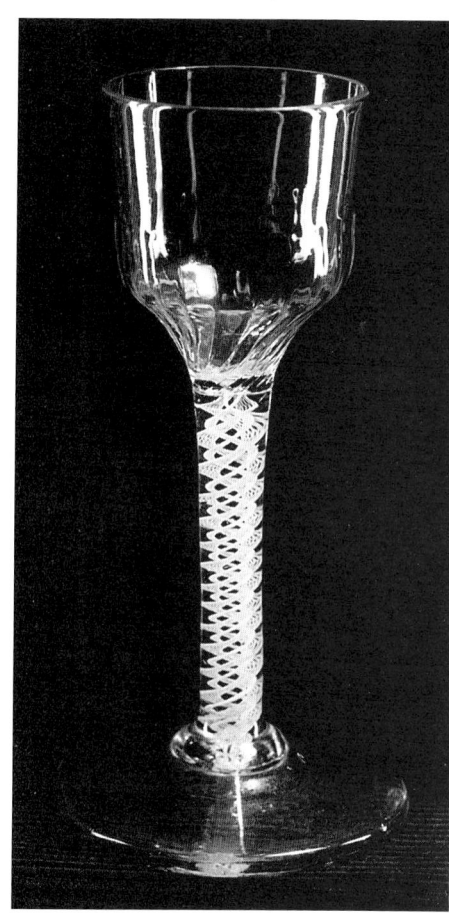

**692.** Wine glass; ogee bowl with basal flutes; DSOT – pair of spiral gauzes outside pair of spiral tapes. Ht. 5⅜ins. c.1770.
*Worthing Museum.*

**693.** Firing glass; stepped RF ('Lynn') bowl; DSOT – pair of 2-ply spiral bands outside pair of multi-ply spiral tapes. Ht. 6ins. c.1770.

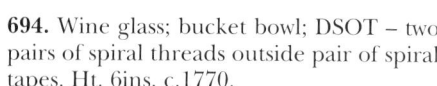

**694.** Wine glass; bucket bowl; DSOT – two pairs of spiral threads outside pair of spiral tapes. Ht. 6ins. c.1770.

**695.** Wine flute; trumpet bowl; DSOT – pair of 5-ply spiral bands outside four spiral threads. Ht. 7ins. c.1770.

Opaque-Twist Stems

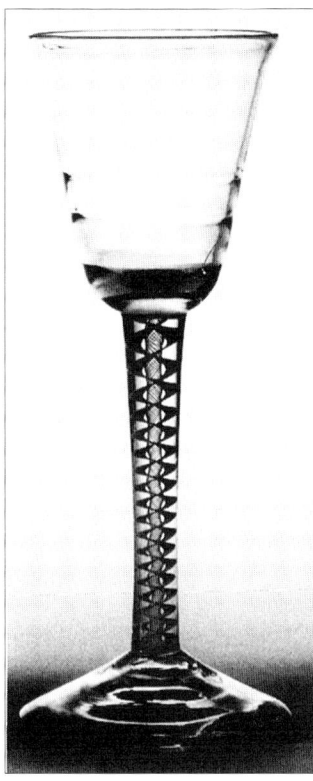

**696.** Wine glass; stepped pointed RF ('Lynn') bowl; DSOT – pair of spiral tapes outside gauze. c.1770.
*Christie's.*

**697.** Wine glass; lipped ogee bowl; central-knopped DSOT – pair of spiral threads outside gauze. Ht. 6ins. c.1770.
*Hartshorne Collection. (Fig. 231).*

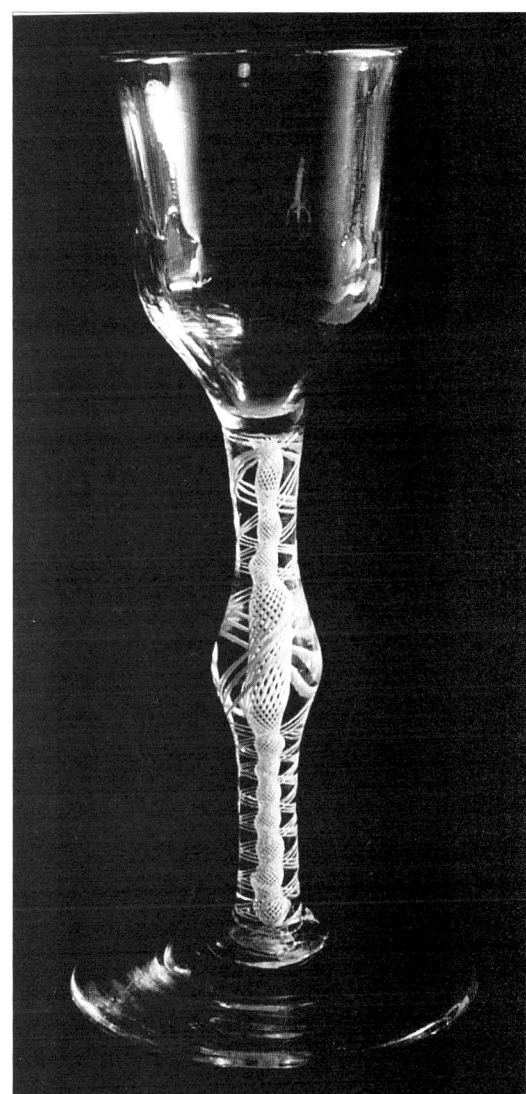

**698.** Wine glass; ogee bowl, moulded base; DSOT – pair of 3-ply spiral bands outside gauze; central swelled knop. Ht. 6ins. c.1770.

Opaque-Twist Stems

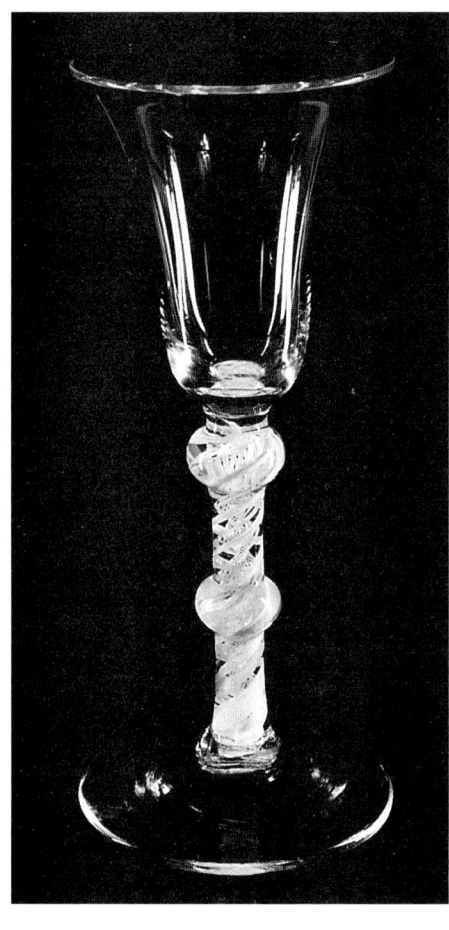

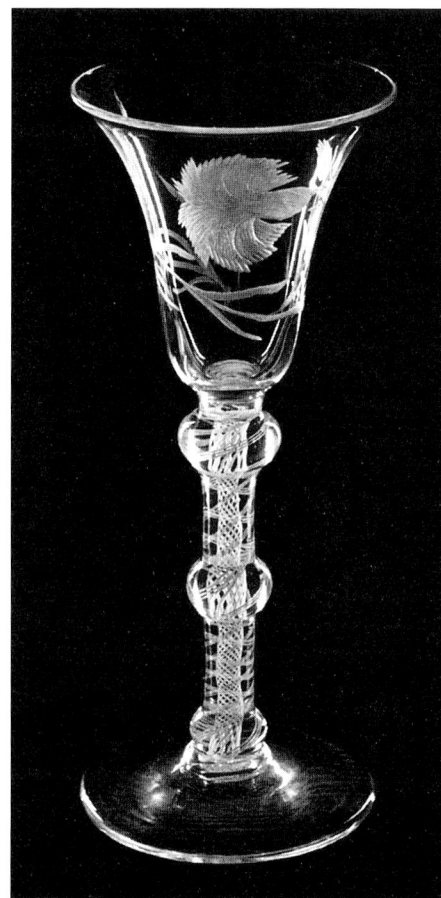

**699.** Wine glass; bell bowl; DSOT with two knops – pair of spiral tapes outside lace twist. Ht. 6¾ins. c.1770.

**700.** Wine glass; bell bowl, engraved carnation (? Jacobite); DSOT with three knops – pair of 3-ply spiral bands outside gauze. Ht. 6½ins. c.1770.

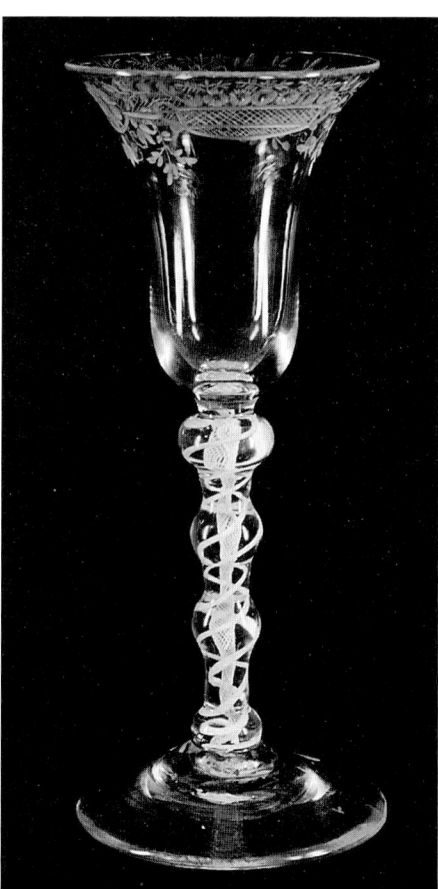

**701.** Wine glass; bell bowl, engraved fruiting vine and bird in flight; DSOT with four knops – pair of spiral tapes outside gauze. Ht. 6¾ins. c.1770.

**702.** Wine glass; bell bowl, engraved floral band below rim; DSOT with four knops – pair of spiral tapes outside gauze. Ht. 6¾ins. c.1770.

Opaque-Twist Stems

# XI
# Mixed and Colour-Twist Stems

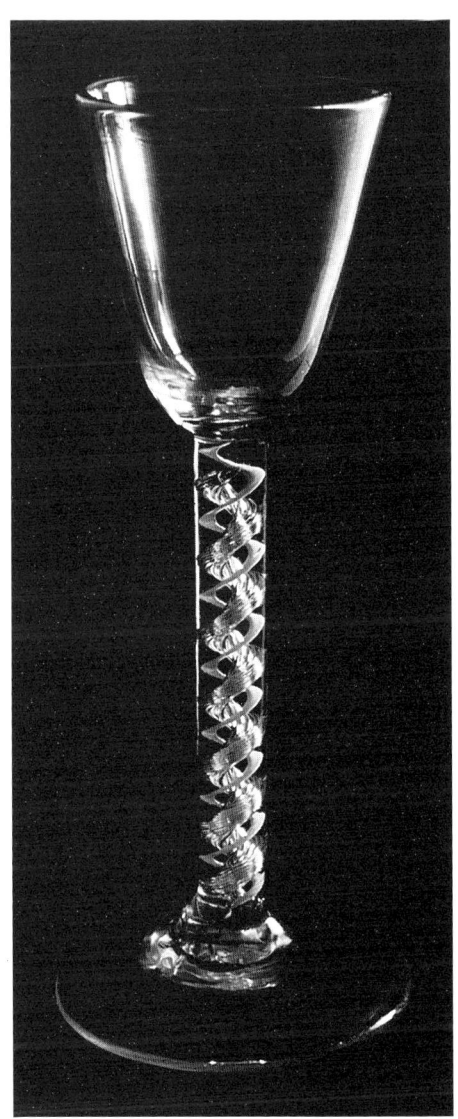

**703.** Wine glass; pointed RF bowl; single-series mixed twist – spiral air cable alternating with opaque corkscrew. Ht. 6¼ins. c.1760.

**704.** Wine glass; pointed RF bowl; single-series mixed twist – spiral air cable alternating with heavy opaque spiral thread. Ht. 6ins. c.1760.
*Hartshorne Collection. (Fig. 183).*

**705.** Wine glass; bell bowl engraved with hibiscus and bud, on reverse a bird in flight; colour twist stem – single spiral turquoise thread alternating with spiral air gauze. Ht. 6⅞ins. c.1765. *Christie's.*

**706.** Wine glass; RF bowl; double-series mixed twist – pair of spiral air threads outside loose multi-ply opaque corkscrew. Ht. 5¾ins. c.1760.

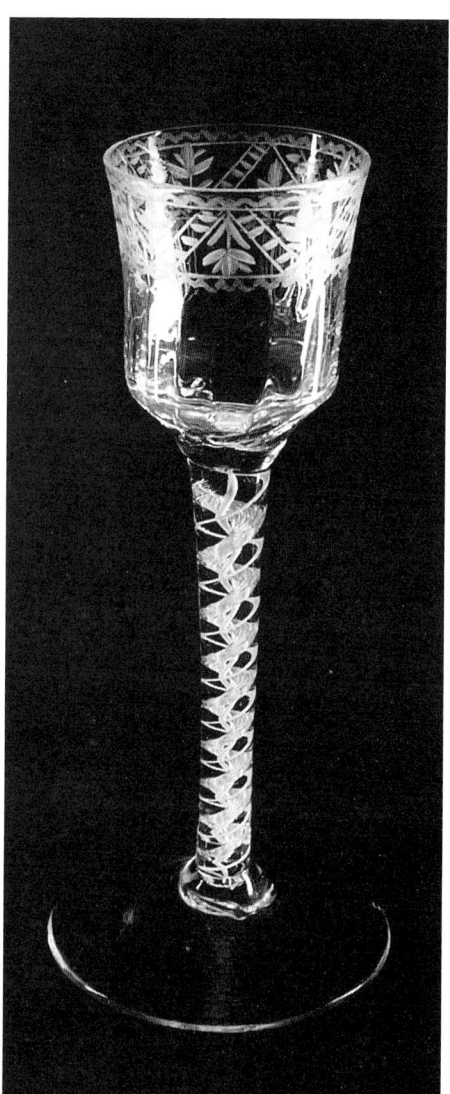

**707.** Wine glass; waisted ogee bowl with basal flutes and engraved formal border below rim; double-series mixed twist – spiral air cable alternating with heavy spiral thread outside slightly spiral opaque rod. Ht. 6¼ins. c.1760.

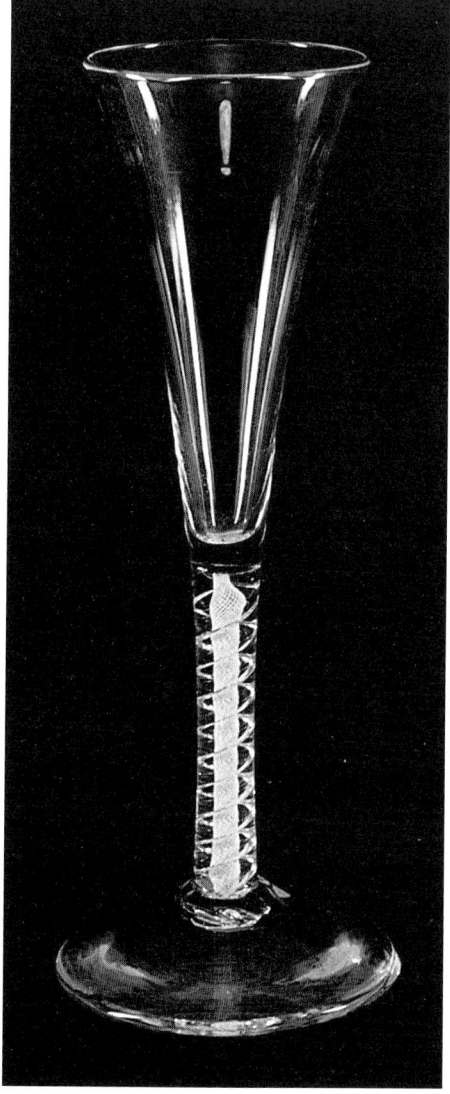

**708.** Wine flute; trumpet bowl; double-series mixed twist – pair of air spirals outside opaque gauze. Ht. 7⅛ins. c.1760.

Mixed and Colour-Twist Stems

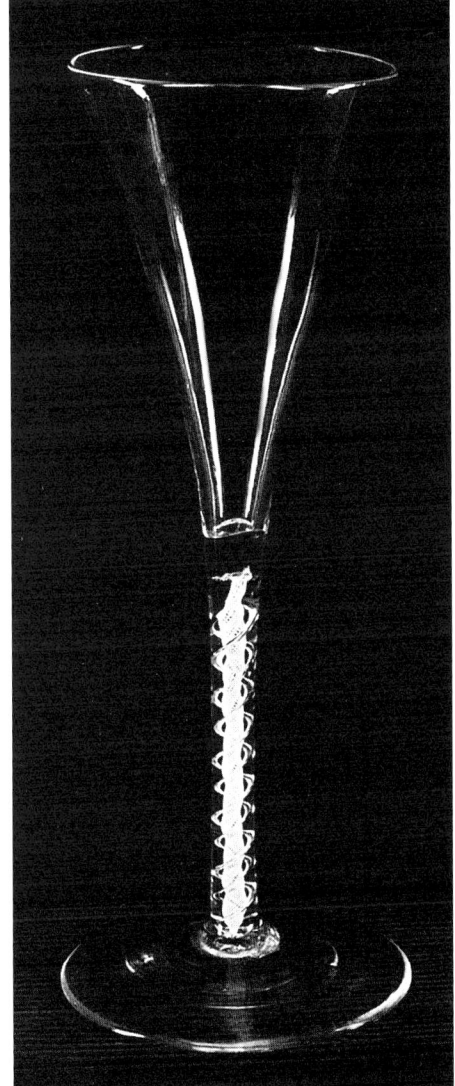

**710.** Wine flute; trumpet bowl; double-series mixed twist – pair of air spirals outside opaque gauze. Ht. 7⅜ins. c.1760.

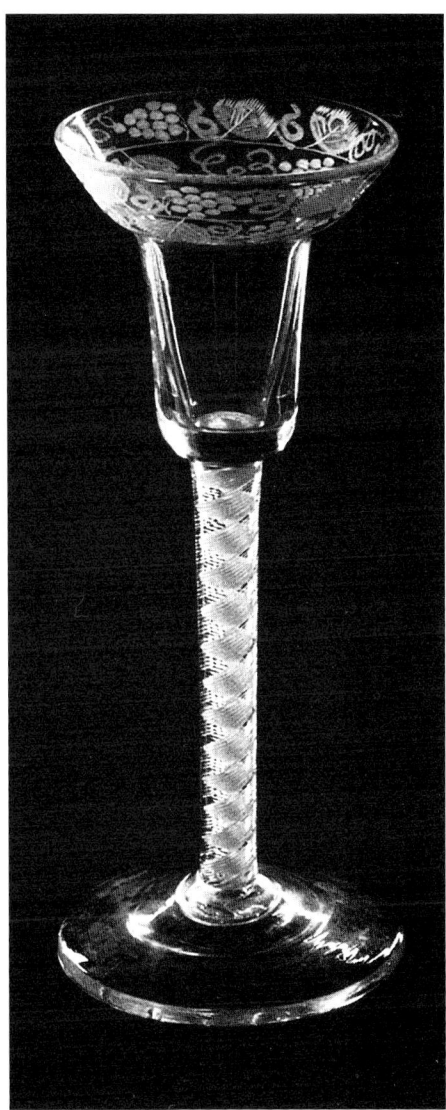

**711.** Wine glass; saucer-topped bucket bowl, engraved fruiting vine below rim; double-series mixed twist – MSAT outside multi-ply opaque corkscrew. Ht. 6½ins. c.1760.

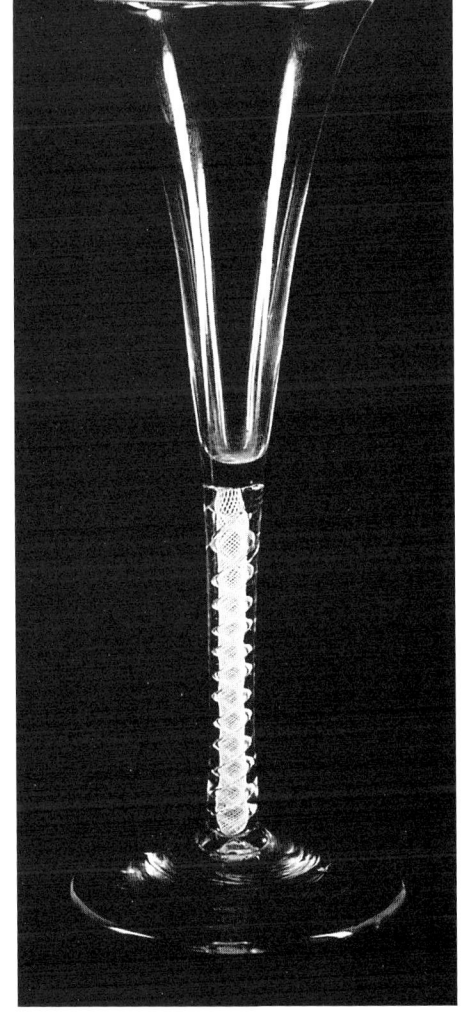

**709.** Wine flute; trumpet bowl; double-series mixed twist – pair of air spirals outside opaque gauze. Ht. 7½ins. c.1760.

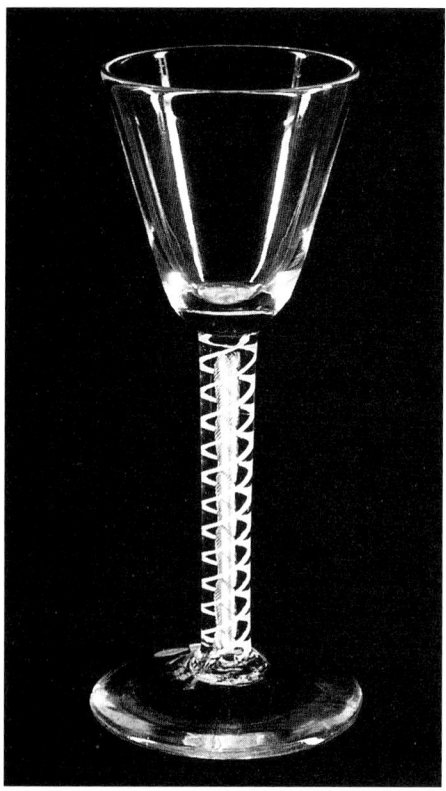

**712.** Wine glass; pointed RF bowl; double-series mixed twist – pair of heavy opaque spiral threads outside air cable. Ht. 6½ins. c.1760.

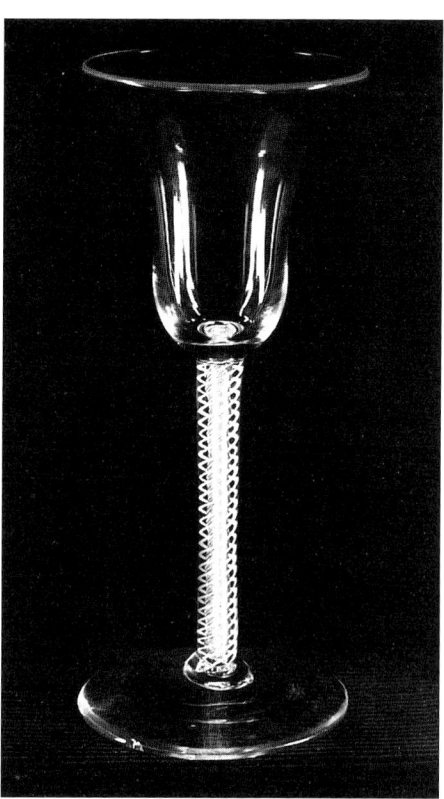

**713.** Wine glass; bell bowl; double-series mixed twist – four opaque spiral threads outside air cable. Ht. 7ins. c.1760.

**714.** Wine glass; tulip bowl; double-series mixed twist – pair of opaque corkscrews outside pair of air corkscrews. Ht. 6ins. c.1760.

**715.** Wine glass; RF bowl; colour-twist stem – pair of brown heavy spiral threads only. Ht. 6ins. c.1770.

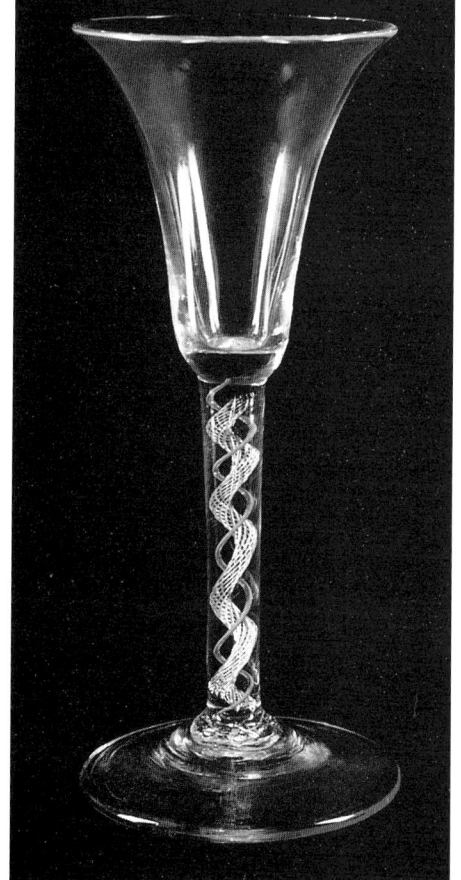

**716.** Wine glass; bell bowl; single-series colour twist – spiral air gauze alternating with spiral red thread. Ht. 7ins. c.1760.

Mixed and Colour-Twist Stems

**717.** Wine glass; RF bowl; single-series colour twist – opaque corkscrew edged red and green alternating with opaque spiral gauze. Ht. 5¾ins. c.1770.

**718.** Wine glass; ogee bowl, fluted lower half; colour twist – spiral gauze alternating with wide spiral tape edged with blue. Ht. 5⅞ins. c.1770. *Sotheby's.*

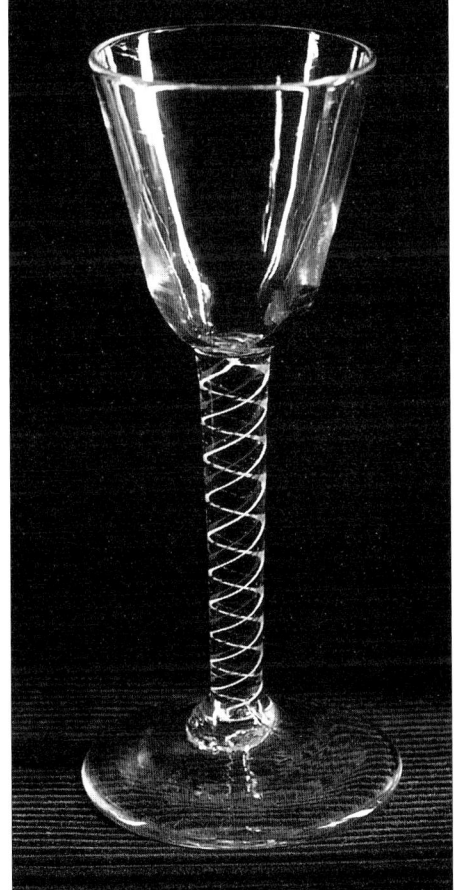

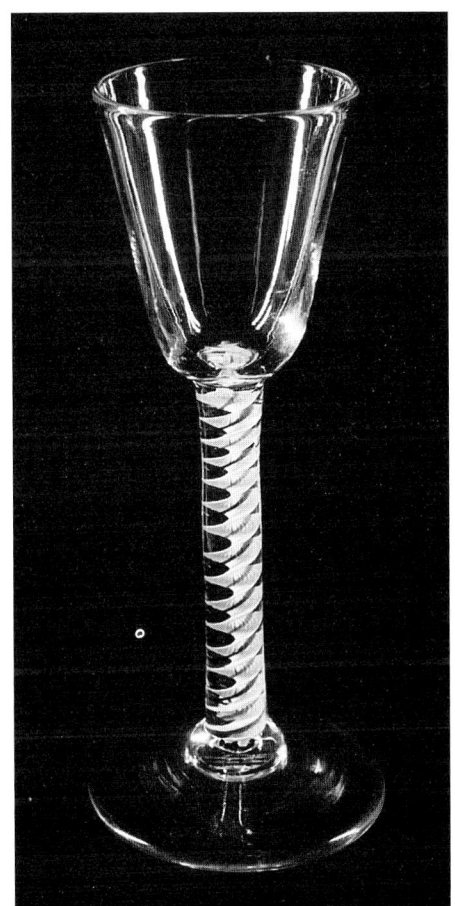

**719.** Wine glass; RF bowl; 'tartan' twist, comprising threads of blue, red, green and opaque white. Ht. 5¾ins. c.1770.

**720.** Wine glass; RF bowl; double-series colour twist – pair of red and blue heavy spiral threads alternating outside OW corkscrew. Ht. 6ins. c.1770.

Mixed and Colour-Twist Stems

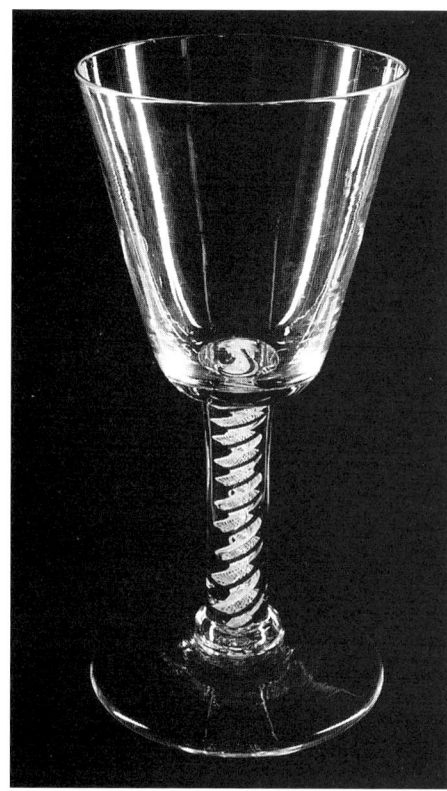

**721.** Goblet; RF bowl; double-series colour twist – pair of blue heavy spiral threads outside OW lace twist. Ht. 7½ins. c.1770.

**722.** Firing glass; trumpet bowl; double-series colour twist – pair of green and white heavy spiral threads outside OW gauze. Ht. 4½ins. c.1770.

**723.** Firing glass; trumpet bowl; double-series colour twist – pair of green and white spiral threads outside OW gauze. Ht. 4⅜ins. c.1770.

**724.** Ale glass; ogee bowl; double-series colour twist – pair of mixed OW and blue corkscrews outside pair of heavy spiral OW threads. Ht. 7⅛ins. c.1770.

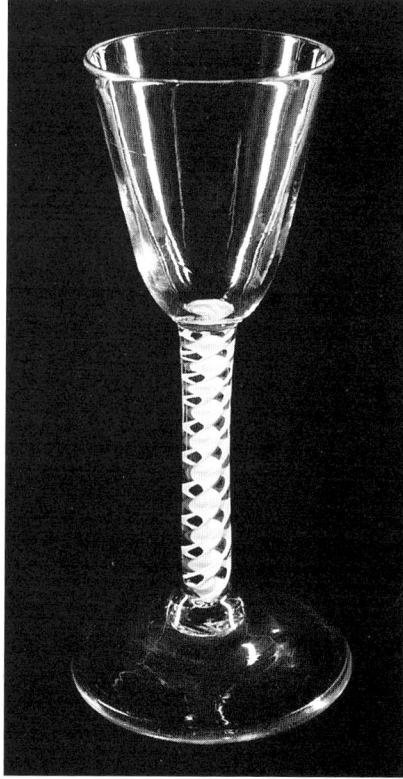

**725.** Wine glass; pointed RF bowl; double-series colour twist – pair of heavy spiral OW threads outside OW corkscrew edged with pink. Ht. 6ins. c.1770.

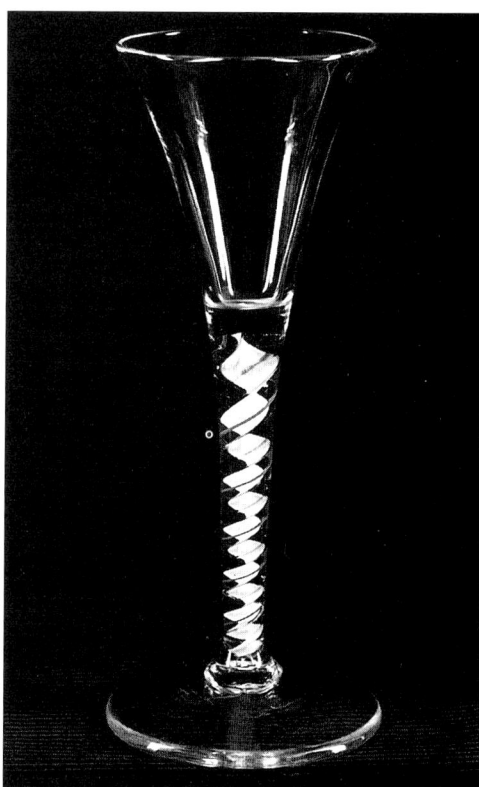

**726.** Wine glass; trumpet bowl; double-series colour twist – pair of alternating red and green spiral threads outside OW corkscrew edged with blue and green. Ht. 6⅛ins. c.1770. *Hartshorne Collection.*

Mixed and Colour-Twist Stems

**727.** Wine glass; bell bowl, solid base; double-series colour twist – pair of heavy OW spiral threads outside OW corkscrew edged alternately with green and maroon. Ht. 6¼ins. c.1770. *Hartshorne Collection.*

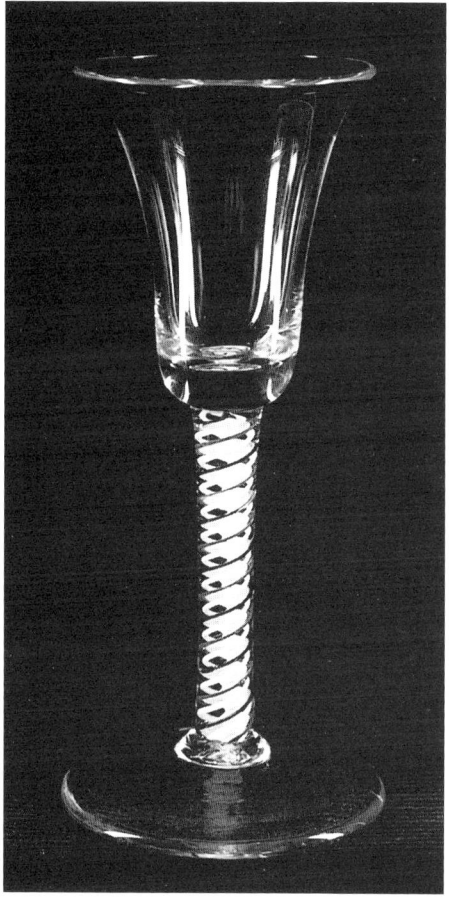

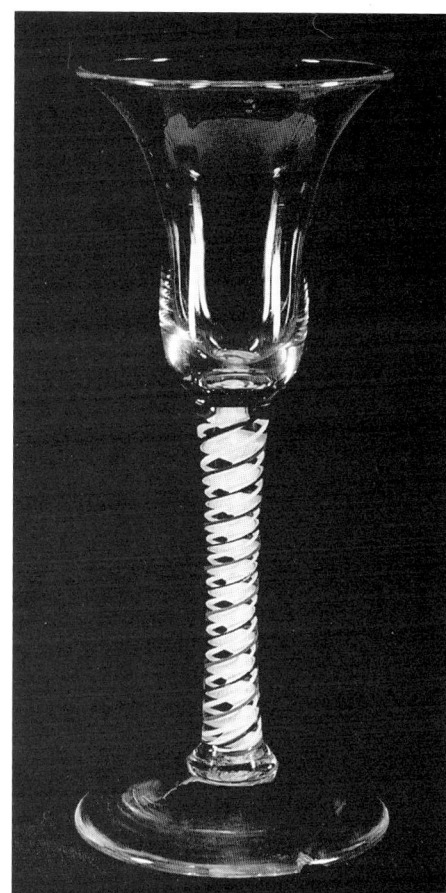

**728.** Wine glass; waisted bell bowl; double-series colour twist – pair of heavy OW spiral threads outside OW corkscrew edged with green and maroon. Ht. 6⅜ins. c.1770.

**729.** Wine glass; bell bowl; double-series colour twist – pair of OW spiral tapes outside OW corkscrew edged with red and green. Ht. 6¼ins. c.1770.

**730.** Wine glass; ogee bowl; double-series colour twist – pair of OW spiral tapes outside OW edged with blue. Ht. 6ins. c.1770.

Mixed and Colour-Twist Stems

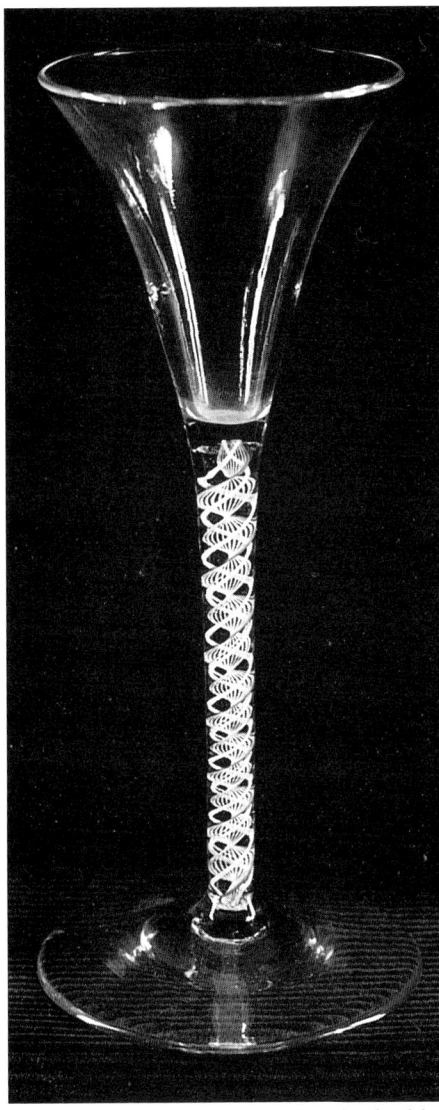

**731.** Wine glass; trumpet bowl; double-series colour twist – pair of OW heavy threads outside OW loose multi-ply corkscrew edged with red and turquoise. Ht. 6¾ins. c.1770.

**732.** Wine glass; bell bowl; double-series colour twist – pair of OW spiral gauzes outside yellow lace twist edged with white. Ht. 5⅞ins. c.1770.

*Cecil Higgins Museum, Bedford.*

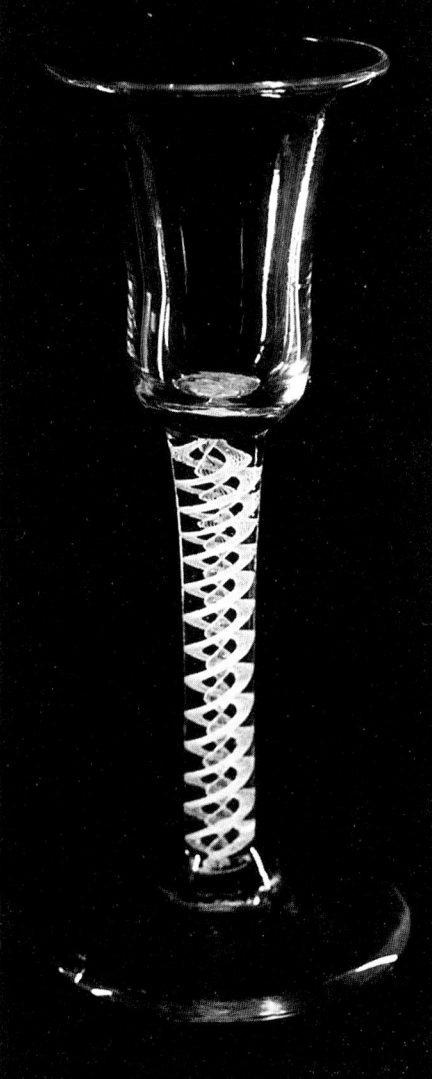

**733.** Wine glass; RF bowl; double-series colour twist – 12-ply OW spiral band outside pair of pale blue heavy spiral threads. Ht. 5⅝ins. c.1770.

Mixed and Colour-Twist Stems

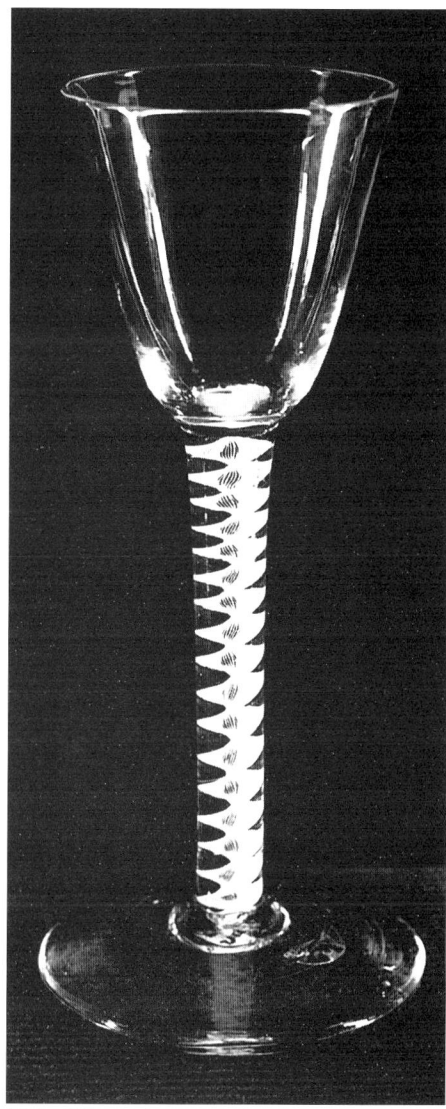

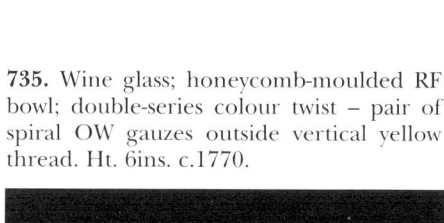

**735.** Wine glass; honeycomb-moulded RF bowl; double-series colour twist – pair of spiral OW gauzes outside vertical yellow thread. Ht. 6ins. c.1770.

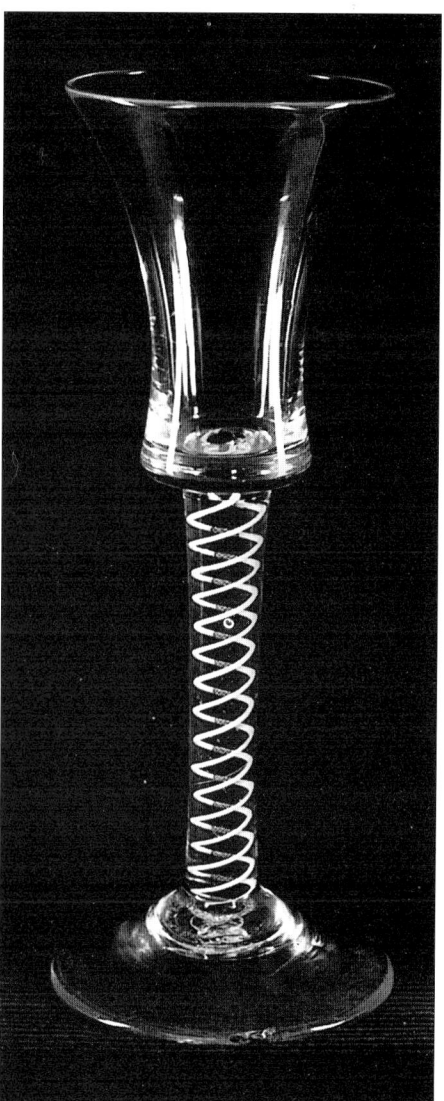

**734.** Wine glass; RF bowl; double-series colour twist – OW corkscrew outside column of six yellow threads. Ht. 5⅞ins. c.1770. *Cecil Higgins Museum, Bedford.*

**736.** Wine glass; waisted bucket bowl; double-series colour twist – pair of pink spiral heavy threads outside mauve gauze. Ht. 7ins. c.1770.

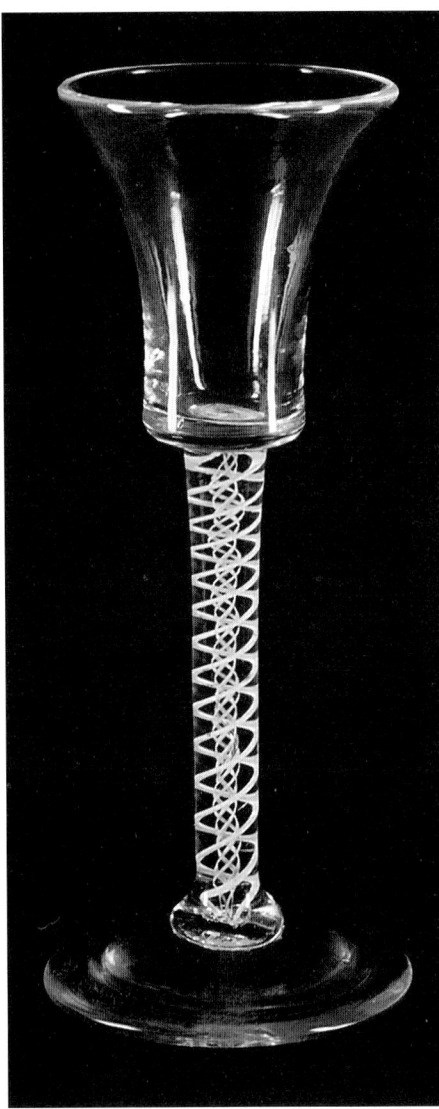

**737.** Wine glass; waisted bucket bowl; double-series colour twist – pair of OW spiral heavy threads outside column of four yellow spiral threads. Ht. 6¼ins. c.1770.

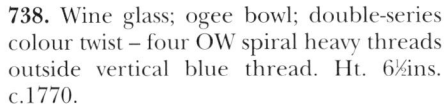

**738.** Wine glass; ogee bowl; double-series colour twist – four OW spiral heavy threads outside vertical blue thread. Ht. 6½ins. c.1770.

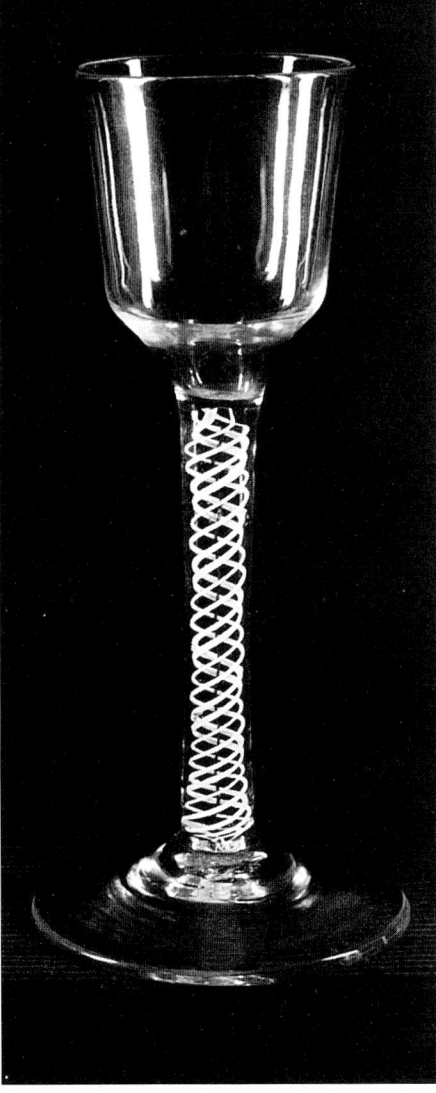

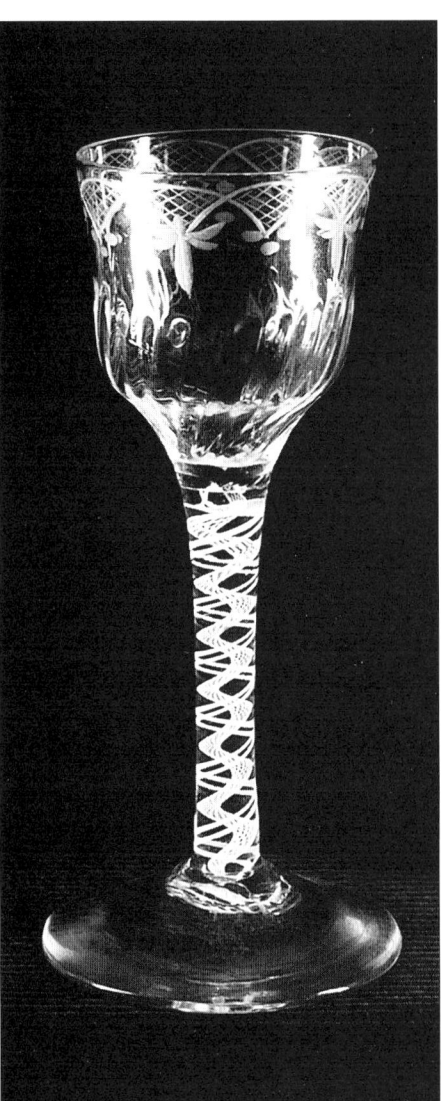

**739.** Wine glass; ogee bowl with engraved festoons below rim and basal flutes; double-series colour twist – 2-ply OW spiral band outside pale blue spiral gauze. Ht. 5⅝ins. c.1770.

Mixed and Colour-Twist Stems

# XII
# Faceted Stems

**740.** Wine glass; bell bowl; diamond-faceted stem. Ht. 6½ins. c.1785.

**741.** Wine glass; pan-topped ogee bowl; diamond-faceted stem. Ht. 6ins. c.1785.
*Hartshorne Collection.*

**742.** Wine glass; pan-topped RF bowl, faceted base; diamond-faceted stem. Ht. 7¼ins. c.1785.

**743.** Wine glass; ogee bowl with basal flutes; scalloped, diamond-faceted stem; scalloped, faceted foot. Ht. 6ins. c.1785.

**744.** Wine glass; RF bowl with engraved border of fruiting vine below rim and basal fluting and cutting; diamond-faceted stem. Ht. 6ins. c.1785.

**745.** Ale glass; RF bowl; diamond-faceted stem. Ht. 8¼ins. c.1785.

**746.** Goblet; RF bowl; border of engraved stars below rim; diamond-faceted stem. Ht. 6¼ins. c.1800.

Faceted Stems

**747.** Wine glass; RF bowl, engraved flowers and birds in flight below formal border; hexagonal-faceted stem; engraved foot. Ht. 5½ins. c.1785.

**748.** Wine glass; RF bowl, engraved rose, two buds and butterfly (Jacobite type); hexagonal-faceted stem. Ht. 5½ins. c.1785.

**749.** Wine glass; pointed RF bowl, engraved and polished formal border below rim, faceted base; hexagonal-faceted stem. Ht. 6ins. c.1785.

**750.** Wine glass; ovoid bowl, engraved bee and flowers with polished petals; hexagonal-faceted stem; ground-out pontil-mark. Ht. 4⅝ins. c.1790.

**751.** Wine glass; honeycomb-moulded ovoid bowl; hexagonal-faceted stem. Ht. 6¾ins. c.1785.

**752.** Wine glass; cup bowl with overall honeycomb-moulded pattern; hexagonal-faceted stem. Ht. 6¾ins. c.1785.
*Honeyborn House Museum, Brierley Hill. Asprey.*

**753.** Wine glass; pan-topped bowl; hexagonal-faceted stem. Ht. 5½ins. c.1785.
*Christie's.*

**754.** Ratafia; RF bowl, engraved and polished festoons; hexagonal-faceted stem. Ht. 6¼ins. c.1785.
*Harvey's Wine Museum, Bristol.*

Faceted Stems

**755.** Goblet; ovoid bowl, engraved rose and bud (Jacobite type); hexagonal-faceted stem. Ht. 7ins. c.1790.

*Hartshorne Collection. (Fig. 250).*

**756.** Wine glass; lipped ogee bowl, engraved floral design; stem comprising alternate flutes and facets. Ht. 6ins. c.1785.

**757.** Wine glass; ovoid bowl, engraved flowers with polished petals and scale-cut base; notched stem. Ht. 5ins. c.1790.

**758.** Wine glass; ovoid bowl; notched stem. Ht. 5½ins. c.1790.

**759.** Sweetmeat; double-ogee cut bowl with scalloped rim; hexagonal columnar stem; domed foot with scalloped edge. Ht. 6⅛ins. c.1760.

Faceted Stems

**760.** Dram glass; RF bowl, engraved hops and barley (!); scale-cut base; hexagonal-fluted stem; faceted foot. Ht. 4¼ins. c.1790. *Hartshorne Collection. (Fig. 281).*

**761.** Goblet; straight-sided bowl, engraved initials J M in a decorative border; fluted, incurved stem. Ht. 7ins. c.1800.

**762.** Christening glass (?); ovoid bowl engraved A T P and, on other side, I H S, within shields flanked by floral engraving; fluted, incurved stem. Ht. 4⅜ins. c.1800.

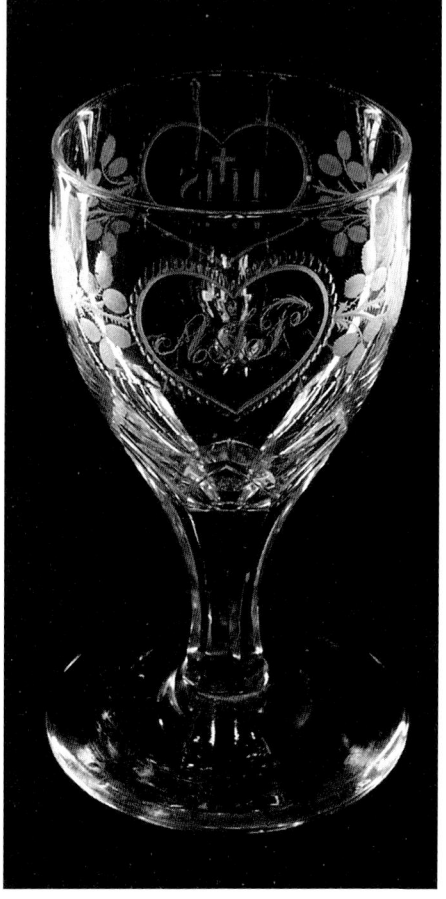

**763.** Wine glass; RF bowl, engraved band of fruiting vine with polished fruits; scale-cut base; diamond-faceted stem with single knop. Ht. 5⅛ins. c.1785.

Faceted Stems

**764.** Sweetmeat; faceted double-ogee bowl with band of engraved stars below the rim; diamond-faceted stem with two knops; faceted DF. Ht. 7ins. c.1790.

**765.** Wine glass; hexagonally cut ogee bowl; diamond-faceted stem with shoulder knop; faceted foot. Ht. 5½ins. c.1785.

**766.** Wine glass; waisted ogee bowl, scale-cut base; diamond-faceted stem with central knop. Ht. 5⅞ins. c.1785.

**767.** Wine glass; ogee bowl with gilt rim and scale-cut base; diamond-faceted stem with central knop. Ht. 5½ins. c.1785.

**768.** Sweetmeat; cup bowl, notched rim, fluted base; central-knopped stem with vertical flutes; DF. Ht. 6¼ins. c.1785.
*Ipswich Museum.*

**769.** Sweetmeat; double-ogee cut bowl with scalloped rim; vertically-fluted stem; octagonal foot. Ht. 6ins. c.1790.
*Ipswich Museum.*

**770.** Ale glass; RF bowl, engraved hops and barley; two faceted knops in a fluted stem. Ht. 8⅜ins. c.1785.

**771.** Wine glass; RF bowl; everted rim engraved with fictitious (?) arms, scale-cut base; faceted bobbin-knopped stem. Ht. 5¾ins. c.1785.

# XIII
# Rudimentary Stems

 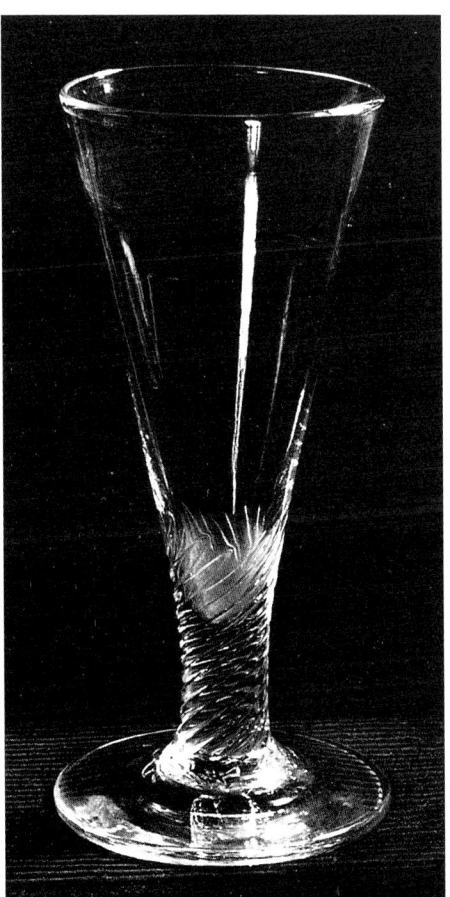 

**772.** Dwarf ale glass; wrythen bowl; no stem. Ht. 4¼ins. 18th century.
*Smith Collection. Harvey's Wine Museum, Bristol.*

**773.** Dwarf ale glass; trumpet bowl; short wrythen stem. Ht. 5¼ins. Late 18th century.
*Hartshorne Collection.*

**774.** Dwarf ale glass; trumpet bowl; wrythen base and short wrythen stem. Ht. 5ins. Late 18th century.

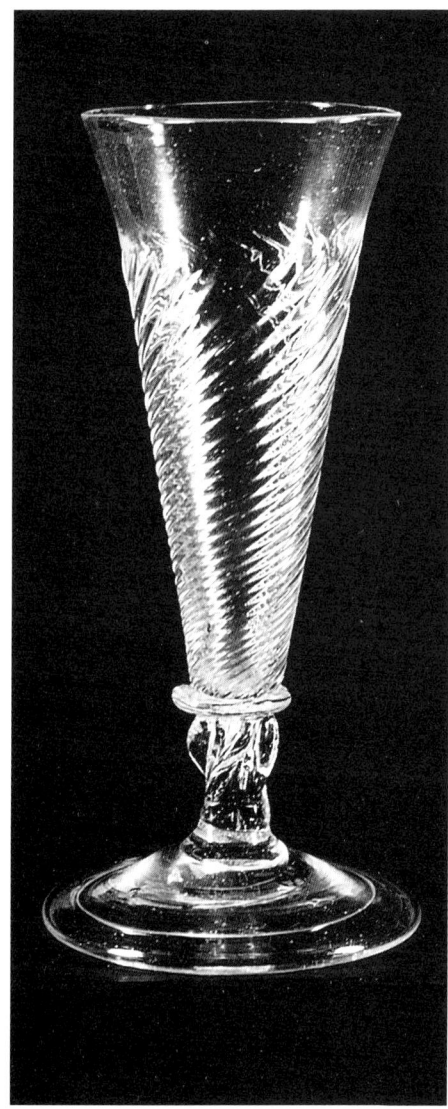

**775.** Dwarf ale glass; wrythen trumpet bowl; collar; winged knop; FF. Ht. 6ins. Early 18th century.

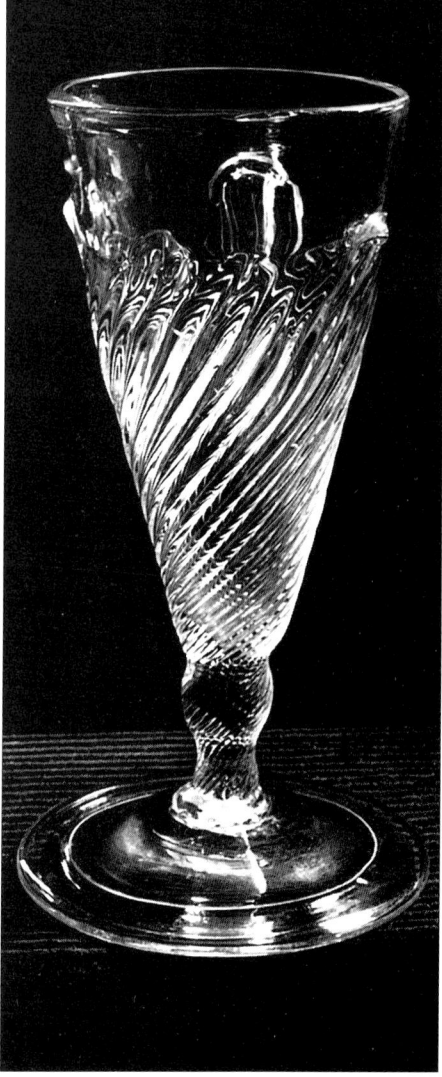

**776.** Dwarf ale glass; wrythen-funnel bowl; wrythen knop; FF. Ht. 4½ins. Early 18th century.

**777.** Dwarf ale glass; wrythen-funnel bowl; two wrythen knops; FF. Ht. 5¼ins. Early 18th century.

Rudimentary Stems

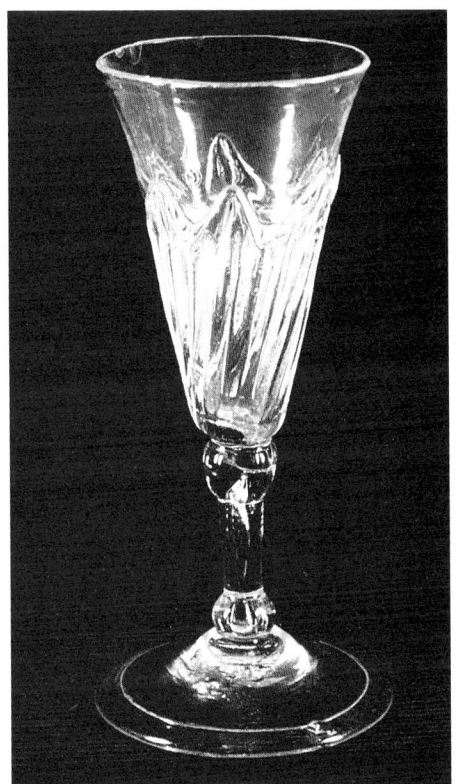

**778.** Short ale glass; wrythen-funnel bowl with flammiform fringe; short plain stem between two knops; FF. Ht. 6ins. Mid 18th century.

**779.** Short ale glass; wrythen-funnel bowl with flammiform fringe; short plain stem between wrythen knop and basal knop; FF. Ht. 6¼ins. Mid 18th century.

**780.** Short ale glass; wrythen-funnel bowl; two flattened knops. Ht. 5¼ins. Mid 18th century.

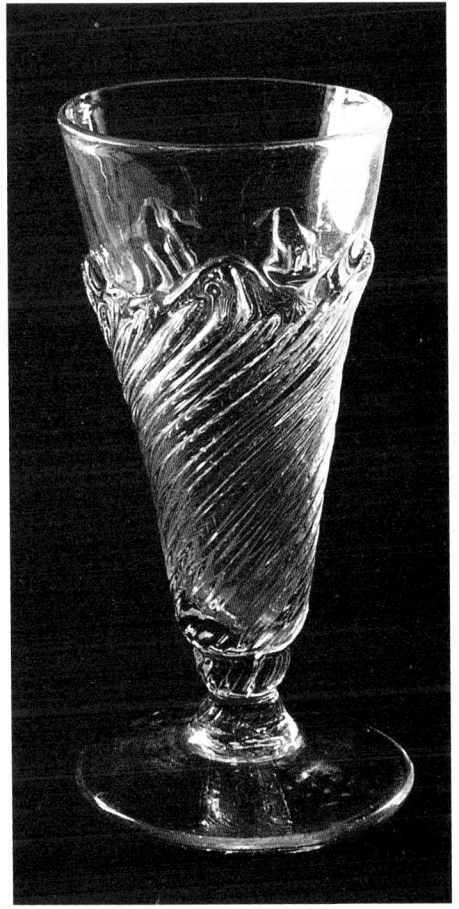

**781.** Dwarf ale glass; wrythen-funnel bowl with flammiform fringe; wrythen knop. Ht. 4½ins. Mid 18th century.

*Smith Collection.*
*Harvey's Wine Museum, Bristol.*

**782.** Short ale glass; panel-moulded funnel bowl, engraved hops and barley; collar above true baluster. Ht. 7ins. c.1800.

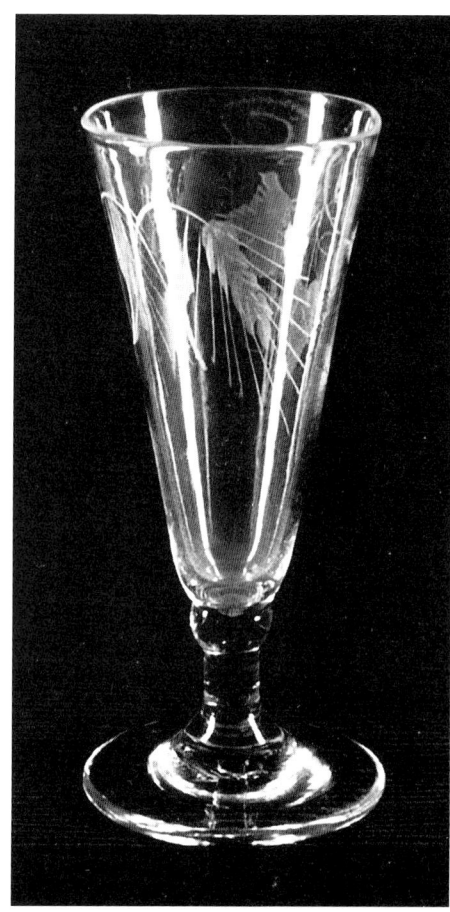

**783.** Short ale glass; lipped RF bowl with gadrooned base; two wrythen knops above short wrythen stem; FF. Ht. 5¾ins. Early 18th century.

**784.** Short ale glass; pointed RF bowl, engraved hops and barley; knop above short plain stem. Ht. 4¾ins. Late 18th century. *Hartshorne Collection.*

**785.** Jelly glass; wrythen-hexagonal bowl; wrythen knop as stem; wrythen DF. Ht. 4ins. Early 18th century.

**786.** Jelly glass; bell bowl; flattened knop as stem. Ht. 3¾ins. Late 18th century.

Rudimentary Stems

**787.** Jelly glass; honeycomb-moulded flared bowl; collar; moulded FF. Ht. 2⅛ins. Mid 18th century.

**788.** Jelly glass; flared bowl with folded rim and gadrooned base; FF with high dome. Ht. 2ins. Mid 18th century.

**789.** Jelly glass; lipped RF bowl with 'nipt diamond waies'; ball knop; moulded DF. Ht. 3½ins. Early 18th century.

**790.** Jelly glass; panel-moulded pan-topped bowl; collar; panel-moulded DF. Ht. 4ins. Early 18th century.

**791.** Jelly glass; pan-topped, honeycomb-moulded bowl; DF moulded to match. Ht. 4½ins. c.1750.

Rudimentary Stems

**792.** Jelly glass; wrythen pan-topped bowl; collar; panel-moulded D & FF. Ht. 3½ins. Early 18th century.

**794.** Jelly glass; pan-topped bowl; collar; flat foot. Ht. 4½ins. c.1780.

**793.** Jelly glass; pan-topped bowl with moulded fluting; bladed collar; D & FF. Ht. 5ins. c.1750.

**795.** Jelly glass; straight-sided bowl; pair of B-handles; DF. Ht. 3⅜ins. c.1750.

**796.** Jelly glass; cup bowl; pair of B-handles; beaded knop; DF. Ht. 4¼ins. c.1750.

**797.** Monteith (or 'bonnet' glass); double-ogee honeycomb-moulded bowl; flattened knop; scalloped foot. Ht. 3ins. c.1750.

**798.** Monteith; double-ogee honeycomb-moulded bowl with blue rim. Ht. 3ins. c.1750.

**799.** Monteith; ogee bowl with notched rim and notched ribs; collar above rudimentary stem; stepped square-moulded 'lemon-squeezer' base. Ht. 3½ins. c.1800.

**800.** Monteith; diamond-cut cup bowl; faceted collar and rudimentary stem; lozenge-shaped foot. Ht. 3¾ins. c.1800.

**801.** Monteith; cut double-ogee bowl with scalloped rim; collar above short plain stem; square solid base. Ht. 3½ins. c.1800.

**802.** Monteith; cut double-ogee bowl with scalloped rim; set directly upon a circular faceted foot. Ht. 3ins. c.1800.

**803.** Posset pot; vertically moulded cylindrical body; pair of single-looped handles; swan-neck spout with raven's head seal; high-kick base. Pale blue, slightly crizzled metal. Ht. 3⁹⁄₁₆ins. c.1677. The seal indicates that this pot was made by George Ravenscroft of the Henley-on-Thames and Savoy Glasshouses. It originated, with two others, also sealed, from Wentworth Woodhouse and was probably made for William Wentworth, Earl of Stafford (1626-95). *Pilkington Glass Museum, St. Helens.*

**804.** Dram glass; funnel bowl; short plain stem; FF. Ht. 3½ins. c.1740.

**805.** Firing glass; funnel bowl engraved THE FRIENDLY SOCIETY; firing foot. Ht. 3¾ins. c.1740.
*Harvey's Wine Museum, Bristol.*

Rudimentary Stems

**806.** Dram glass; deceptive conical bowl; collar; short plain stem bisected by flattened knop. Ht. 4½ins. c.1800.

**807.** Dram glass; bell bowl; beaded knop as stem; DF. Ht. 4ins. c.1750.
*Hartshorne Collection.*

**808.** Firing glass; funnel bowl, engraved rose, two buds, oak leaf and REDEAT (Jacobite); set directly upon a firing foot. Ht. 3½ins. c.1745.

**809.** Firing glass; waisted bell bowl, solid base; set directly upon a firing foot. Ht. 4½ins. c.1740.
*Hartshorne Collection. (Fig. 307).*

Rudimentary Stems

**810.** Dram glass; bell bowl; foot a similar but smaller bowl; (single and double measure). Ht. 4ins. c.1750.

**811.** Rummer; conical bowl; annulated knop over short plain stem; flat foot. Ht. 6ins. c.1790.

**812.** Rummer; ogee bowl with engraved formal border below rim; large flat facets at base of bowl; collar above short plain stem; flat foot. Ht. 5½ins. c.1800.

**813.** Rummer; bucket bowl, fluted base; bladed knop. Ht. 5ins. Early 19th century.
*Portsmouth City Museums.*

**814.** Rummer; square bucket bowl engraved T J G and agricultural arms above SPEED THE PLOUGH (*see also* 990); square-moulded 'lemon-squeezer' base. Ht. 5¼ins. Early 19th century.

**815.** Rummer; incurved bowl, engraved with ballooning scene (*see also* 964); collar above rudimentary stem; square-moulded 'lemon-squeezer' base. Ht. 5¾ins. c.1800.                *King's Lynn Museum.*

**816.** Tankard; band of eight threads below rim; gadrooned base containing Maundy penny (? 1767); single-loop handle. Ht. 6ins. c.1770.

**817.** Tankard; band of three threads below rim; gadrooned base; single-loop handle. Ht. 6ins. c.1770.

**818.** Tankard; band of eight threads below rim; gadrooned base; single-loop handle. Ht. 4⅛ins. c.1770.

**819.** Tankard; band of multiple threads below rim; coin dated 1762 in base; single-loop handle. Ht. 4½ins. c.1765.

**820.** Tumbler; barrel shaped. Ht. 5¼ins. c.1800.

**821.** Tumbler; stepped cylindrical bowl with seven corrugations ('Lynn'); low kick. Ht. 4⅜ins. c.1775. *King's Lynn Museum.*

**822.** Tumbler; stepped cylindrical bowl with six narrow and three broad corrugations ('Lynn'); low kick. Ht. 3⅝ins. c.1775. *King's Lynn Museum.*

**823.** Tumbler; stepped cylindrical bowl with four corrugations ('Lynn'); low kick. Ht. 4⅜ins. c.1775. *King's Lynn Museum.*

Rudimentary Stems

**824.** Finger-bowl; cylindrical form with eight corrugations ('Lynn'). Ht. 3ins., diam. 4⅛ins. c.1800.
*Museum of Social History, King's Lynn.*

**826.** Salt; flat-cut bowl with scalloped rim; collar over short plain stem; hollow moulded foot. Ht. 3¼ins. c.1800.

**825.** Decanter with five corrugations ('Lynn'), spire stopper. Ht. 11ins. Early 19th century. *Museum of Social History, King's Lynn.*

Rudimentary Stems

# XIV
# Decoration: Diamond-point Engraving

**827.** Goblet; pointed RF bowl, solid teared base inscribed in diamond-point ROBERT BUXTON AT THE OXFORD INN EXON, surrounded by scroll-work; cushioned knop, basal knop; FF. Ht. 7⅛ins. c.1720. The Exeter archives record a Robert Buxton as Innkeeper of the Oxford Inn in 1726.
*Sotheby's.*

**828.** Wine glass; funnel bowl, solid base, engraved in diamond-point C.A. JONES 1840; annulated knop, basal knop; D & FF. Ht. 6½ins. c.1710.
*Sotheby's.*

**829.** Wine glass; bell bowl, solid base, engraved in diamond-point E. TRAVELLER; MSAT with beaded collar; DF. Ht. 6¾ins. c.1750. *Ipswich Museum.*

**830.** Rummer; bucket bowl engraved in diamond-point H S within a garland of leaves; moulded base; short plain stem divided by bladed knop; flat foot. Ht. 5⅛ins. c.1800.

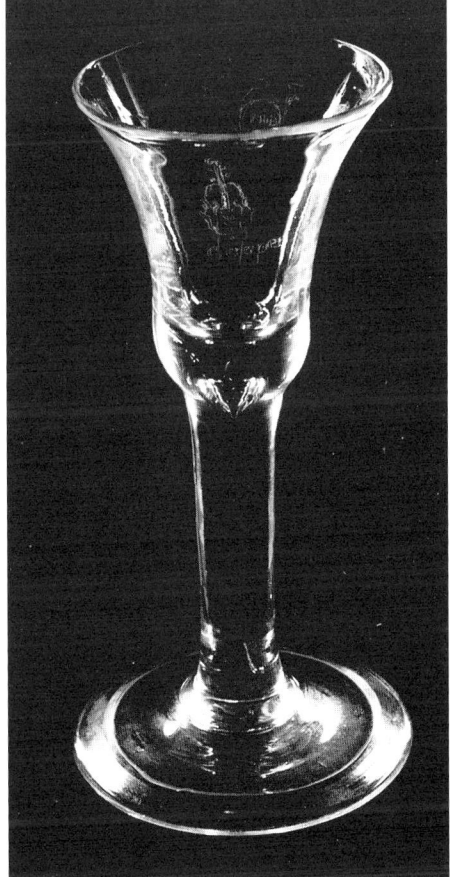

**831.** Wine glass; bell bowl, solid base with tear, engraved in diamond-point COOPER below cello on one side, GILES inside a French horn on the other and dated 1757; plain stem; FF. Ht. 6⅛ins. c.1740 (engraved later?).

**832.** Wine glass; drawn trumpet bowl engraved in diamond-point with the Royal Crown above the cypher J R with two verses of the Jacobite hymn ending with AMEN; plain stem with tear. Ht. 7⅛ins. c.1745. The 'Burn-Murdoch Amen glass'.
*Ex Horridge, Plesch, Burn-Murdoch and Clements Collections. Christie's.*

**833.** Wine glass; drawn trumpet bowl, engraved in diamond-point with cypher of James VIII in monogram below a crown, flanked by verses of Jacobite hymn ending with AMEN; tear in plain stem; FF engraved TO THE PROSPERITY OF THE FAMILY OF LOCHIELL. Ht. 6½ins. c.1750.
*Royal Scottish Museum, Edinburgh.*

**834.** Goblet; drawn trumpet bowl, engraved in diamond-point with a blackbird on a rose bough looking behind at a dragon-fly on a spray of carnation, the inscription THE GLORIOUS MEMORY undulating below the rim; plain stem with tear; FF. (Disguised Jacobite, i.e. pretending to be a Williamite but with the Jacobite emblems.) Ht. 8⅜ins. c.1740.
*Cecil Higgins Museum, Bedford.*

**835.** Reverse of 834 showing engraving of dragon-fly.

**836.** Wine glass; trumpet bowl, engraved in diamond-point with Welsh dragon, scale-cut base; six-sided fluted stem. Ht. 5⅜ins. c.1785.

**837.** Goblet; RF bowl engraved in diamond-point THE NOBLE NAVIGATION ANNE 1771; DSOT – pair of heavy spiral threads outside lace twist. Ht. 8ins. c.1771.

*Pilkington Glass Museum, St. Helens.*

**838.** Goblet; trumpet bowl, engraved in diamond-point with trees in leaf; plain stem; FF. Ht. 9⅜ins. c.1745.

# XV
# Decoration:
# Wheel-Engraving and Stippling

 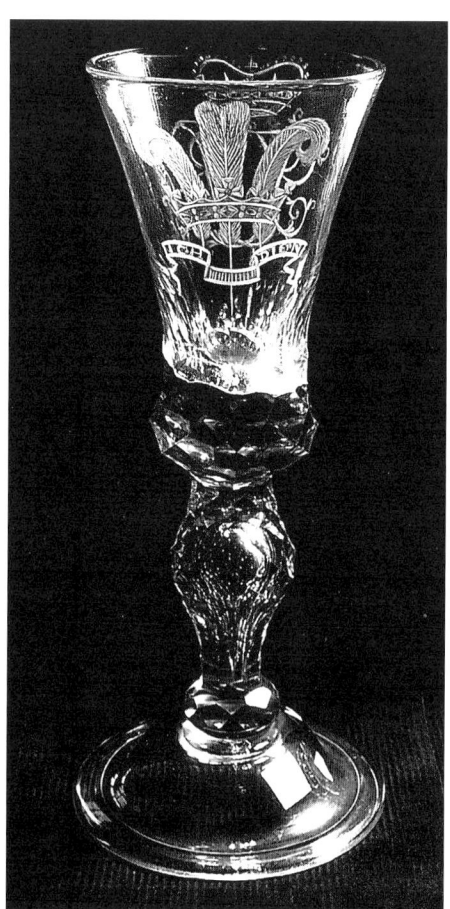 

**839.** Goblet; thistle bowl, solid faceted base, engraved with crown above monogram F P and on the reverse the Prince of Wales's feathers. The monogram refers to Frederick, father of George III and the glass was probably engraved to commemorate his creation as Prince of Wales in 1729; diamond-faceted teared swelled knop and faceted basal knop; D & FF. Ht. 10¼ins. c.1730.
NOTE: F.B. Haynes suggests that this may be a Lauenstein glass (op. cit., p. 284); if English it is either an extraordinarily early example of faceting, or, more probably, was faceted later. *Hartshorne Collection. (Plate 47).*

**840.** Reverse of 839 showing Prince of Wales's feathers.

**841.** Goblet; RF bowl engraved with Royal coat of arms and signed on foot by Jacob Sang; stem comprising two faceted ball knops above faceted IB knop and basal knop; stepped foot with scalloped rim. Ht. 7⅛ins. c.1760. Jacob Sang was working c.1752-62. *Hartshorne Collection.*

**842.** Wine glass; pointed RF bowl engraved with the Royal coat of arms; 'Newcastle' light baluster. c.1750. *Asprey.*

**843.** Goblet; drawn trumpet bowl engraved with a portrait bust of William III surrounded by foliate scrolls and a ribbon inscribed THE GLORIOUS AND IMMORTAL MEMORY OF KING WILLIAM III; over the portrait AND HIS QUEEN MARY; drawn teared stem; FF engraved with a floral border. Ht. 9⅜ins. c.1730. (Williamite). *Sotheby's.*

**844.** Wine glass; thistle bowl engraved THE MEMORY OF KING WILLIAM surmounted by a crown; 6-sided moulded pedestal stem between collars; FF. Ht. 6⅝ins. c.1715 (Williamite). *Sotheby's.*

Wheel-Engraving and Stippling

**845.** Firing glass; drawn trumpet bowl engraved below the rim THE GLORIOUS MEMORY OF KING WILLIAM above a band of stylised flowers; short thick plain stem; firing foot engraved on base with a sunflower. Ht. 4⅛ins. c.1740 (Williamite).

*Sotheby's.*

**846.** Wine glass; trumpet bowl, engraved equestrian portrait of William III within a ribbon lettered THE GLORIOUS MEMORY OF KING WILLIAM and on the reverse BOYNE 1ST JULY 1690; plain stem between collars; FF. (Williamite.) Ht. 6⅛ins. c.1740.

**847.** Reverse of 846.

**848.** Wine glass; RF bowl, engraved band of fruiting vine above THE IMMORTAL MEMORY; centre-knopped MSAT. (Williamite.) Ht. 7½ins. c.1750.

*Hartshorne Collection. (Plate 67).*

**849.** Reverse of 848 showing engraving of rose and single bud.

Wheel-Engraving and Stippling

**850.** Wine glass; RF bowl, engraved with portrait of William III within the inscription GLORIOUS MEMORY; plain stem; FF. (Williamite.) Ht. 6⅛ins. c.1740.

**851.** Reverse of 850 showing engraving of an Irish harp below a crown.

**852.** Cordial; bucket bowl, engraved with portrait of William III within the inscription THE IMMORTAL MEMORY and on the reverse an Irish harp below a crown; plain stem. (Williamite.) Ht. 6½ins. c.1740. *Cecil Higgins Museum, Bedford.*

**853.** Cordial; RF bowl inscribed round rim THE GLORIOUS MEMORY OF KING WILL II above a stylised band; plain stem with tear; D & FF. Ht. 6¾ins. c.1740.
*Christie's.*

Wheel-Engraving and Stippling

**854.** Goblet; bucket bowl engraved with an equestrian figure below a ribbon inscribed THE GLORIOUS MEMORY OF KING WILLIAM and on reverse BOYNE 1ST JULY 1690 and J W MAXWELL, fluted lower part; flattened knop in short stem; flat foot. Ht. 6ins. c.1800. (Late Williamite.) *Christie's.*

**855.** Wine glass; ovoid bowl, engraved THE ROYAL DOZEN. THE KING QUEEN AND : TEN : CHILDREN!; plain stem. Ht. 4⅜ins. c.1774. *Cecil Higgins Museum, Bedford.*

**856.** Wine glass; RF bowl engraved with a portrait of Frederick the Great (attributed to Jacob Sang); 'Newcastle' light baluster stem including two beaded knops and an IB with large tear. c.1745. *Asprey.*

**857.** Wine glass; RF bowl, engraved with portrait of the King of Prussia between floral sprays; composite stem – MSAT over IB. Ht. 7⅛ins. c.1750.

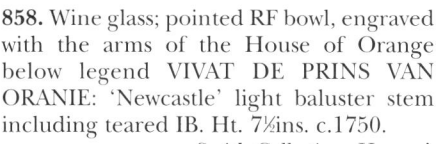

**858.** Wine glass; pointed RF bowl, engraved with the arms of the House of Orange below legend VIVAT DE PRINS VAN ORANIE: 'Newcastle' light baluster stem including teared IB. Ht. 7½ins. c.1750.
*Smith Collection. Harvey's Wine Museum, Bristol.*

Wheel-Engraving and Stippling

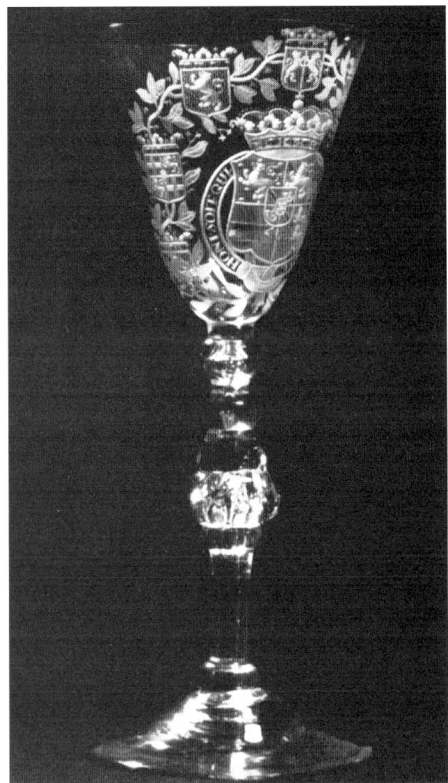

**859.** Wine glass; pointed RF bowl, Dutch engraved with the Royal coat of arms of William IV of Orange and Princess Anne, daughter of George II of England; 'Newcastle' light baluster stem including beaded knop. c.1740. *Asprey*.

**860.** Goblet; funnel bowl engraved with the arms of the United Provinces of the Netherlands flanked by lion supporters; teared IB over teared basal knop; FF engraved with floral design. Ht. 8¼ins. Glass c.1700, engraving c.1750. *Christie's*.

**861.** Goblet; RF bowl engraved with the arms of Anne, daughter of George II encircled by the inscription HONI SOIT QUI MAL Y PENSE and those of the United Provinces of the Netherlands. Ht. 8⅛ins. c.1745. Relates to the marriage of Anne to William, Prince of Orange in 1734. *Christie's*.

**862.** Wine glass; RF bowl engraved with the arms of the United Provinces of the Netherlands with the inscription VIGILATE DEO CONFIDENTE; 'Newcastle' light baluster stem. Ht. 7ins. c.1750. *Sotheby's*.

**863.** Goblet; funnel bowl, solid base Dutch-engraved with the arms of a nobleman; four-sided moulded pedestal stem; FF with an engraved band of foliage. Ht. 8⅓ins. c.1720. *Christie's*.

**864.** Goblet; pointed RF bowl engraved with figure of Peace and Plenty (?) over Continental coat of arms; eight-sided pedestal stem, diamonds on shoulders; FF. c.1745. *Asprey.*

**865.** Wine glass; pointed RF bowl engraved with a Continental coat of arms; eight-sided diamond-studded pedestal stem; FF. c.1745. *Asprey.*

**866.** Wine glass; RF bowl engraved with the arms of six of the Seven Provinces for the Dutch East India Company (VOC); 'Newcastle' light baluster stem with a central teared knop. Ht. 7½ins. c.1750. *Asprey.*

**867.** Wine glass; RF bowl engraved with coat of arms in the manner of Jacob Sang; 'Newcastle' light baluster stem including teared angular knop. c.1750. *Asprey.*

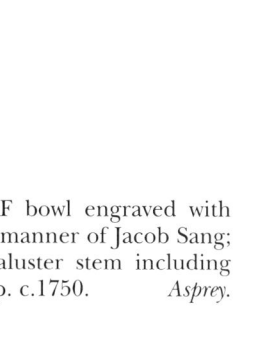

Wheel-Engraving and Stippling

**868.** Wine glass; RF bowl engraved with dove over armorial bearings; 'Newcastle' light baluster stem with beaded knop in centre. c.1745. *Asprey.*

**869.** Wine glass; drawn trumpet bowl engraved with five-petalled flower (? buttercup) and butterfly; plain stem with tear. (Jacobite.) Ht. 6⅛ins. c.1740.

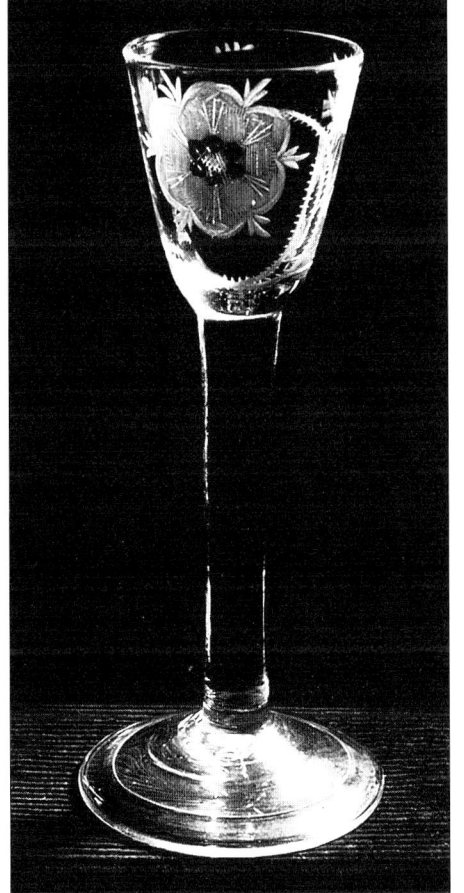

**870.** Wine glass; RF bowl, engraved rose and single bud; plain stem; FF. (Jacobite.) Ht. 6¾ins. c.1740.

**871.** Wine glass; bucket bowl, engraved rose, single bud and butterfly; plain stem; FF. (Jacobite.) Ht. 6½ins. c.1740.

Wheel-Engraving and Stippling

**872.** Wine glass; trumpet bowl, engraved portrait of Charles II in the Boscobel oak beneath three crowns; IB, erroneously termed Kit-Kat stem. (Jacobite.) Ht. 7ins. c.1740.

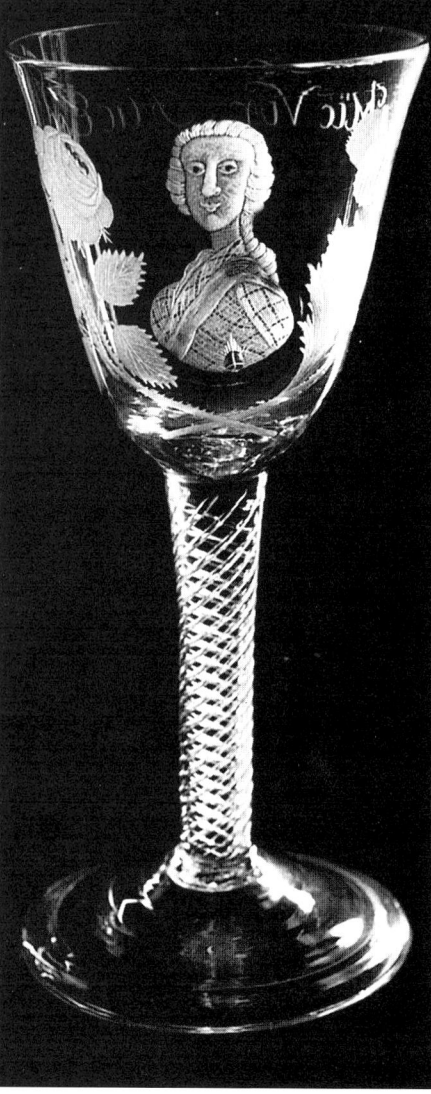

**873.** Wine glass; pointed RF bowl, engraved full-face portrait of Prince Charles Edward in Highland costume between thistle spray on his left and rose with single bud on his right with, on the reverse, the motto HIC VIR HIC EST (the portrait after an engraving by Sir Robert Strange); MSAT; FF. (Jacobite.) Ht. 7⅜ins. c.1760.

*Cecil Higgins Museum, Bedford.*

**874.** Reverse of 873 showing the engraved motto HIC VIR HIC EST.

Wheel-Engraving and Stippling

**875.** Wine glass; pointed RF bowl, engraved on one side with profile portrait of Prince Charles Edward or James Francis Edward below the motto AUDENTIOR IBO and on the reverse a six-petalled rose with two buds; MSAT; foot engraved with thistle leaves. (Jacobite.) Ht. 6ins. c.1750. *Cecil Higgins Museum, Bedford.*

**876.** Wine glass; pan-topped bucket bowl, engraved round the rim with band of rose, oak leaves and other Jacobite symbols; MSAT. (Jacobite.) Ht. 6⅜ins. c.1750.

Wheel-Engraving and Stippling

**877.** Goblet; bucket bowl, engraved rose and two buds below motto TURNO TEMPUS ERIT and on the reverse the motto FIAT; MSAT with vermiform collar; foot engraved with the motto REDEAT. (Jacobite.) Ht. 8½ins. c.1750.

**878.** Reverse of 877 showing engraved motto FIAT.

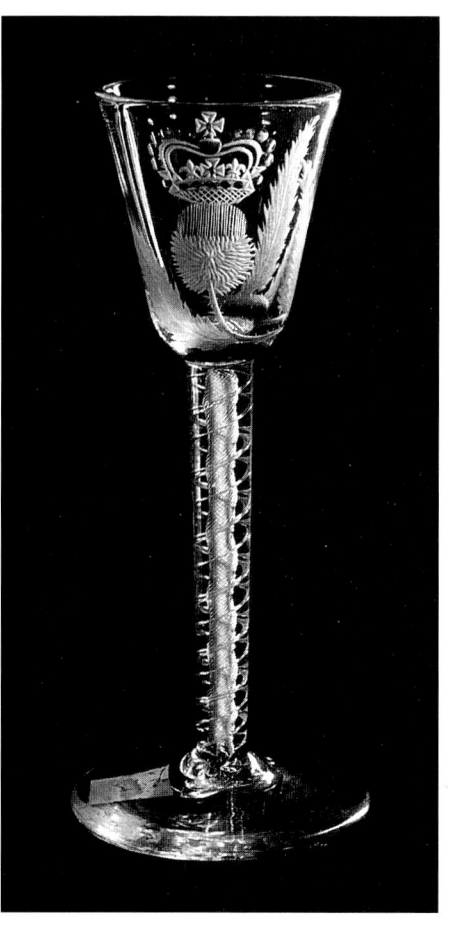

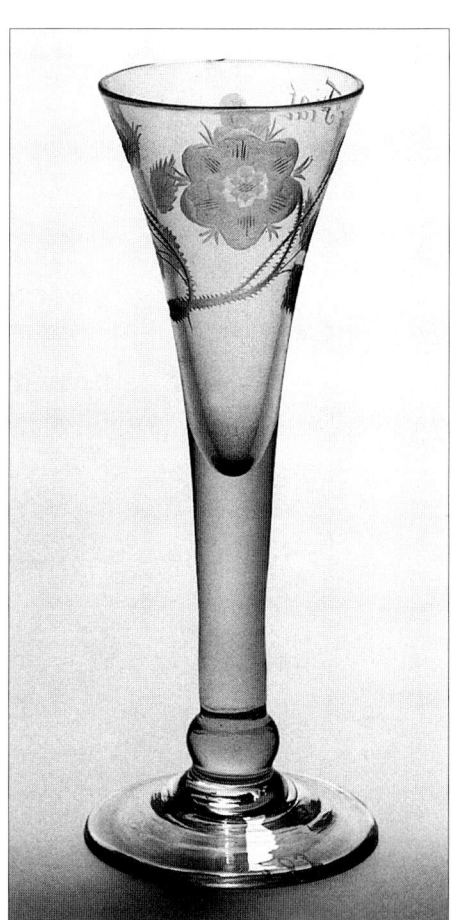

**879.** Wine glass; RF bowl, engraved with crowned thistle; DSAT – pair of spiral threads outside cable. (Jacobite.). Ht. 6¼ins. c.1750.

**880.** Wine glass, drawn trumpet bowl engraved with rose and two buds and the motto FIAT; plain stem with basal knop. (Jacobite.) Ht. 6½ins. c.1745.
*Ex Milsted and W.F. Smith Collections.*
*Sotheby's.*

Wheel-Engraving and Stippling

**881.** Wine glass; RF bowl engraved with a portrait bust of Prince Charles Edward Stuart in Highland dress within a ribbon inscribed AUDENTIOR IBO; on reverse a seven-petalled rose; plain stem; foot engraved with a thistle. (Jacobite.) Ht. 7½ins. c.1745. *Sotheby's.*

**882.** Wine glass; drawn trumpet bowl, engraved rose and two buds, oak leaf and motto FIAT; MSAT. (Jacobite.) Ht. 6ins. c.1750.

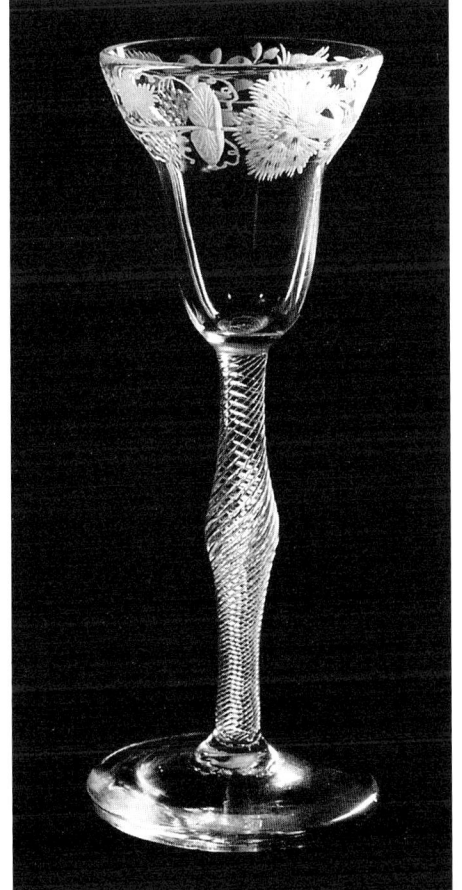

**883.** Wine glass; pan-topped RF bowl, engraved band of apple, pear, rose, carnation, vines and honeysuckle; MSAT with central swelled knop. (Jacobite.) Ht. 6¼ins. c.1750.

**884.** Wine glass; pan-topped RF bowl, engraved band of crowned thistle, rose with two buds and oak leaf; MSAT with central swelled knop. (Jacobite.) Ht. 5⅜ins. c.1750.

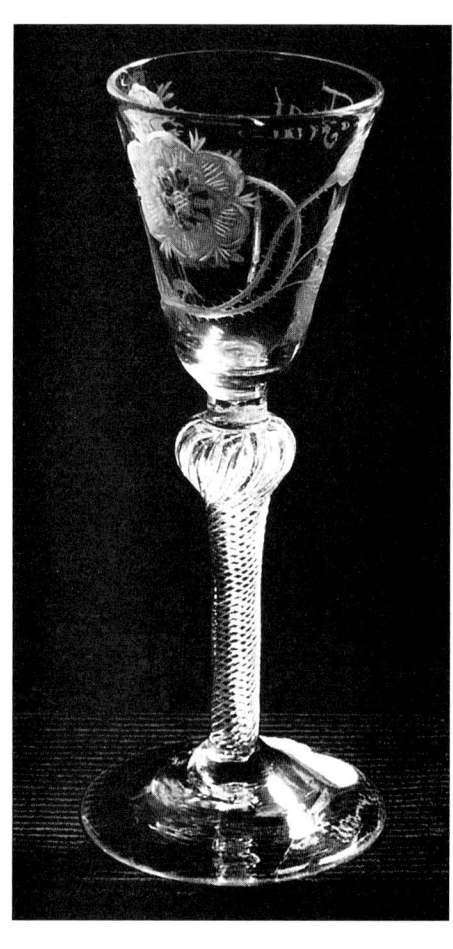

**885.** Wine glass; pointed RF bowl, engraved rose, two buds and motto FIAT; MSAT with shoulder knop. (Jacobite.) Ht. 6¼ins. c.1750.

**886.** Wine glass; pointed RF bowl, engraved carnation and moth; shoulder-knopped MSAT. (Jacobite.) Ht. 5⅜ins. c.1750.

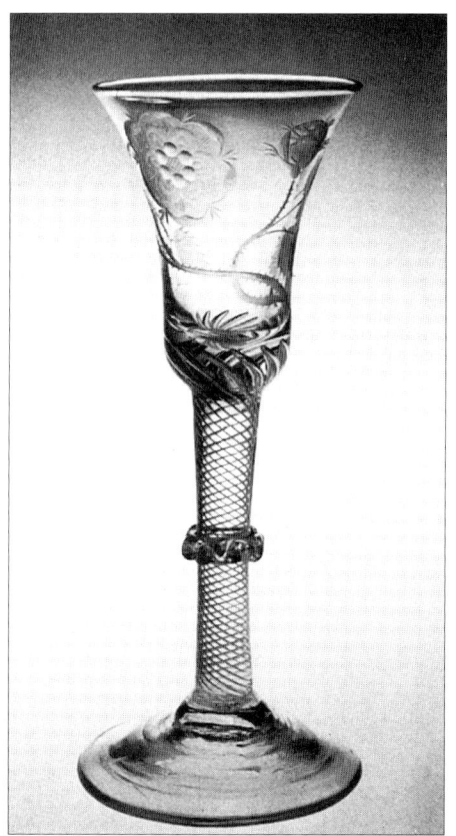

**887.** Wine glass; bell bowl engraved with rose and two buds; MSAT stem with vermiform collar. (Jacobite). c.1750. *Asprey.*

**888.** Wine glass; pointed RF bowl engraved with rose and one bud, thistle and crown; MSAT with shoulder and central knops. (Jacobite). c.1745.                    *Asprey.*

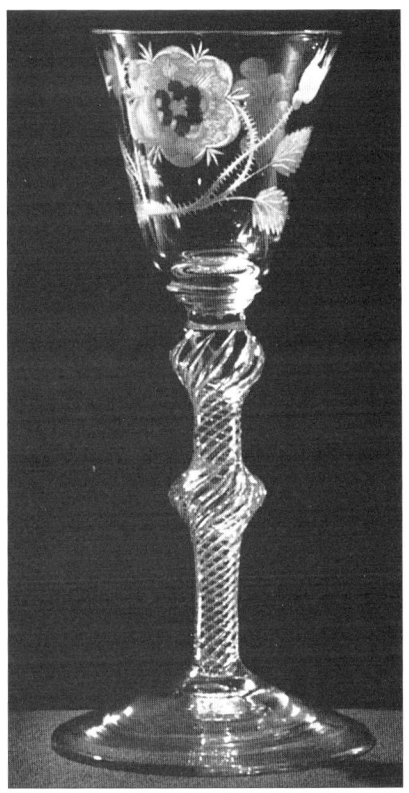

**889.** Wine glass; RF bowl engraved with rose and two buds; double-knopped MSAT (Jacobite.) c.1745.

*Asprey.*

**890.** Detail of drawn trumpet bowl with rose and two buds and inscription REDEAT (Jacobite.) c.1745.

*Asprey.*

**891.** Wine glass; bucket bowl, engraved moth, fruiting vine and wine glass within the motto BIEN VENU; double-knopped MSAT; foot engraved with border of roses. (Jacobite.) Ht. 5⅞ins. c.1750.

**892.** Wine glass; pointed RF bowl, engraved with full-face portrait of Prince Charles Edward in Highland costume below the motto AUDENTIOR IBO and on the reverse a rose and two buds; double-knopped MSAT. (Jacobite.) Ht. 6¼ins. c.1750.

**893.** Reverse of 892 showing engraved rose.

Wheel-Engraving and Stippling

**894.** Goblet; pointed RF bowl, engraved rose, two buds, oak leaf and motto FIAT; double-knopped MSAT; foot engraved with Prince of Wales's feathers. (Jacobite.) Ht. 8¼ins. c.1750.

*Smith Collection.*
*Harvey's Wine Museum, Bristol.*

**895.** Goblet; RF bowl, engraved rose and single bud; double-knopped MSAT. (Jacobite.) Ht. 9½ins. c.1760. (Haynes places single-bud Jacobites before 1741 or after 1766.)

**896.** Wine glass; RF bowl, engraved rose, single bud, oak leaf and star; double-knopped MSAT. (Jacobite.) Ht. 6ins. c.1760. (See note to 895.)

Wheel-Engraving and Stippling

**897.** Goblet; RF bowl, engraved sunflower, bees, butterflies, dragon-fly and beetles; incised-twist stem. (Jacobite.) Ht. 7⅜ins. c.1760.    *Cecil Higgins Museum, Bedford.*

**898.** Reverse of 897 showing engraving of dragon-fly and other insects.

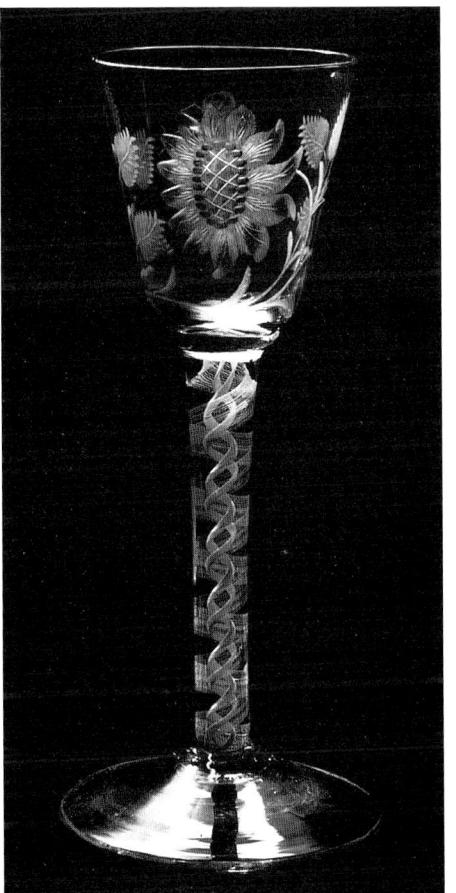

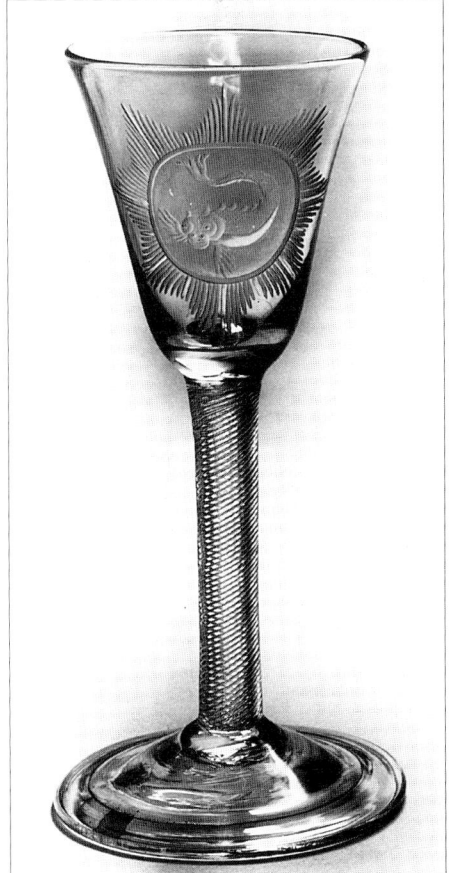

**899.** Wine glass; RF bowl, engraved on one side with a sunflower amid leaves, on reverse a butterfly (Jacobite); DSOT – multi-ply spiral band outside pair of spiral tapes. Ht. 6ins. c.1765.    *Sotheby's.*

**900.** Wine glass; RF bowl engraved with the badge of the Society of Sea Serjeants; MSAT; FF. Ht. 6⅜ins. c.1745. The Society was to South Wales what the Cycle Club was to the Jacobite movement in North Wales. It ceased to exist c.1764.    *Sotheby's.*

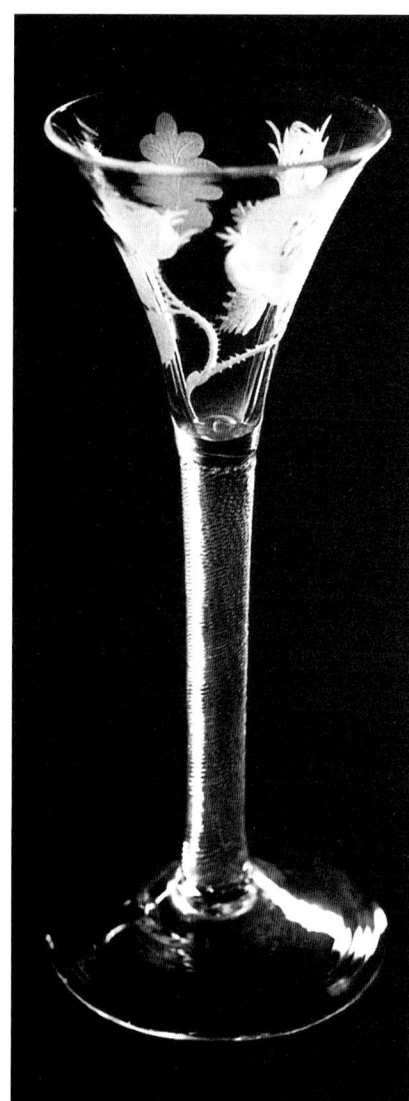

**901.** Wine glass; trumpet bowl, engraved rose, two buds, oak leaf and star; incised-twist stem. (Jacobite.) Ht. 6¾ins. c.1760.

*Cecil Higgins Museum, Bedford.*

**902.** Decanter; globular body, engraved on one side with eight-petalled rose and two buds and on the other with a pair of compasses pointing towards a double oak-leaf spray and star. (Jacobite.) Ht. 9¾ins. (without stopper). c.1750. *Cecil Higgins Museum, Bedford.*

**903.** Reverse of 902 showing engraved compass and oak-leaf spray.

Wheel-Engraving and Stippling

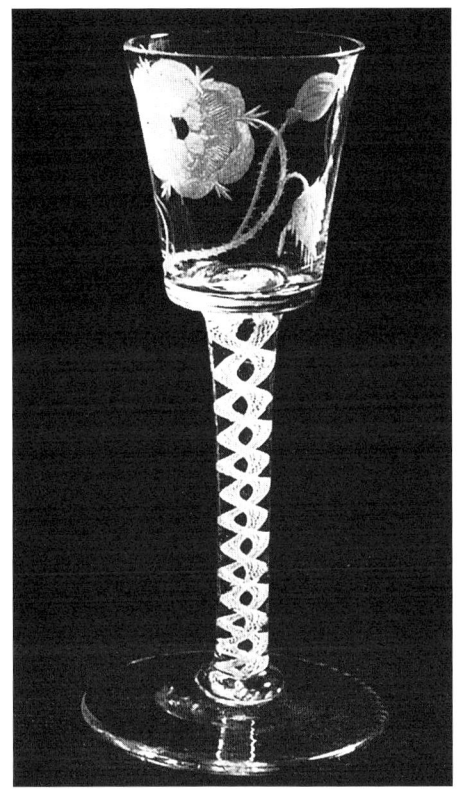

**904.** Wine glass; square bucket bowl, engraved rose and single bud; SSOT – pair of spiral gauzes. (Jacobite.) Ht. 6ins. c.1770. (See note to 895.) *Hartshorne Collection.*

**905.** Wine glass; ogee bowl, engraved crown, the motto FIAT, rose with two buds, the dexter bud detached; DSOT – pair of heavy spiral threads outside gauze. (Jacobite.) Ht. 6ins. c.1766 (the year in which James Francis Edward died.)

**906.** Wine glass; ogee bowl, engraved rose, single bud and thistle; DSOT – pair of spiral threads outside cable. (Jacobite.) Ht. 5⅝ins. c.1770.

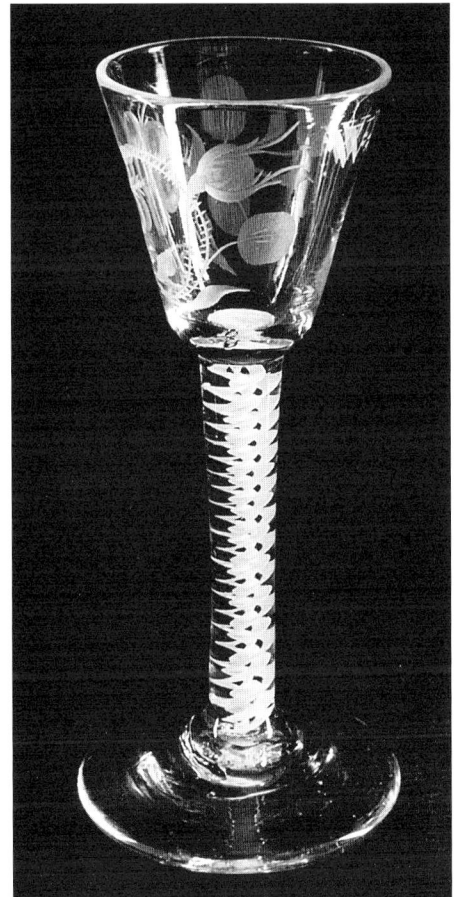

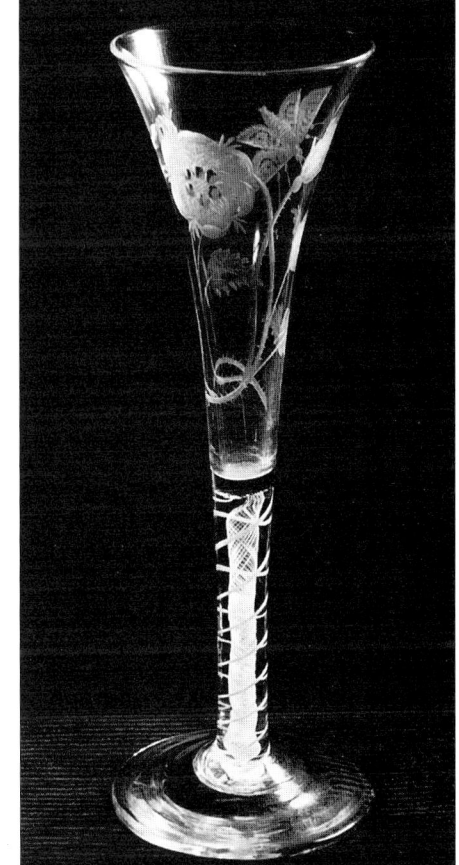

**907.** Wine glass; pointed RF bowl, engraved rose, single bud and initials W N; DSOT – pair of corkscrews outside tight corkscrew. (Jacobite.) Ht. 5¾ins. c.1770.

**908.** Wine flute; trumpet bowl, engraved rose, two buds and moth; DSOT – pair of spiral threads outside cable. (Jacobite.) Ht. 7ins. c.1765.

Wheel-Engraving and Stippling

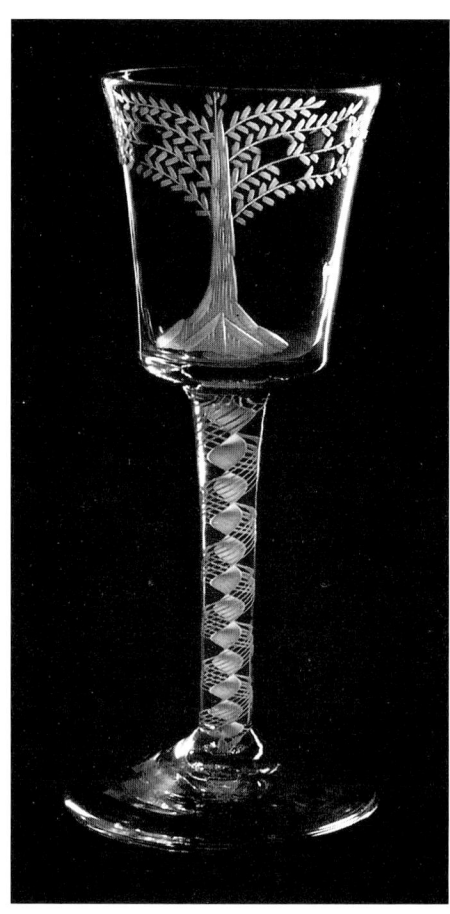

**909.** Wine glass; bucket bowl, engraved tree in leaf and butterfly; DSOT – 6-ply spiral band outside corkscrew. (?Jacobite.) Ht. 6½ins. c.1765.

*Hartshorne Collection. (Fig. 287).*

**910.** Wine glass; bell bowl, engraved rose, two buds and moth; DSOT – pair of heavy spiral threads outside corkscrew edged with blue and green. (Jacobite.) Ht. 6½ins. c.1765.     *Cecil Higgins Museum, Bedford.*

**911.** Firing glass; bowl with everted rim, engraved rose, two buds, thistle, oak leaf, star and motto FIAT; firing foot. (Jacobite.) Ht. 3⅛ins. c.1750.

**912.** Firing glass; flared bowl, engraved rose, two buds, oak leaf and the motto REDEAT; firing foot. (Jacobite.) Ht. 3½ins. c.1750.

**913.** Tumbler, engraved with inscription PRINCE CHARLES AND DOWN WITH THE RUMPS below a festooned border (Jacobite.) Ht. 4¾ins. c.1750. (*See* Buckley *Antique Collector* March 1935.)     *Sotheby's.*

Wheel-Engraving and Stippling

**914.** Firing glass; ogee bowl engraved with a crowned thistle; short DSOT – 5-ply spiral band outside four heavy spiral threads. Ht. 3½ins. c.1770. *Christie's.*

**915.** Wine glass; ogee bowl engraved with the white horse of Hanover beneath the inscription LIBERTY; MSAT. Ht. 6⅜ins. c.1750. One of a pair. *Sotheby's.*

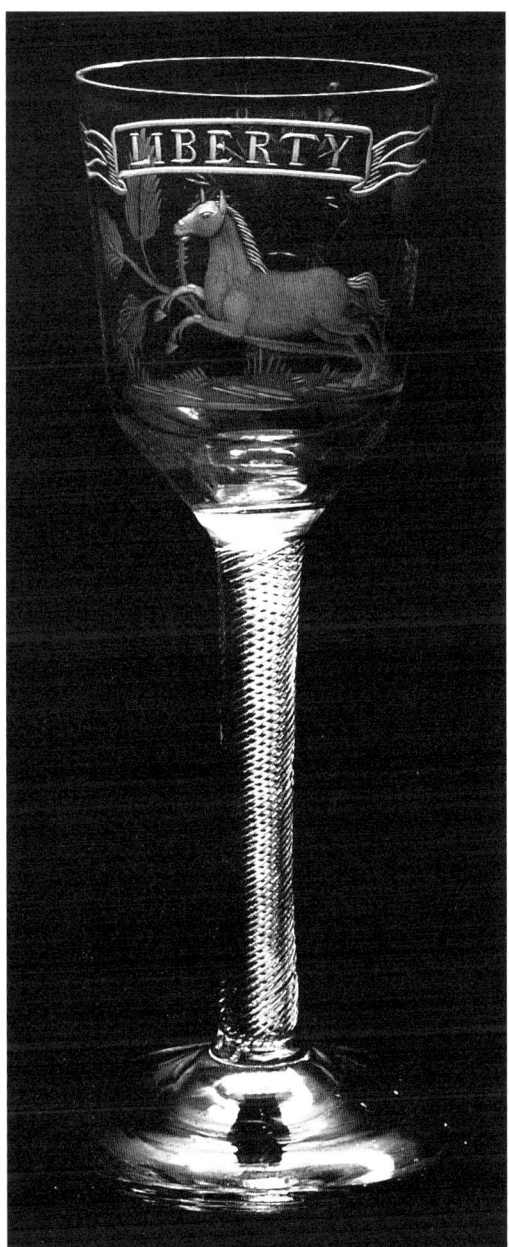

**916.** Detail of wine glass of similar date and almost identical engraving to 915. *Asprey.*

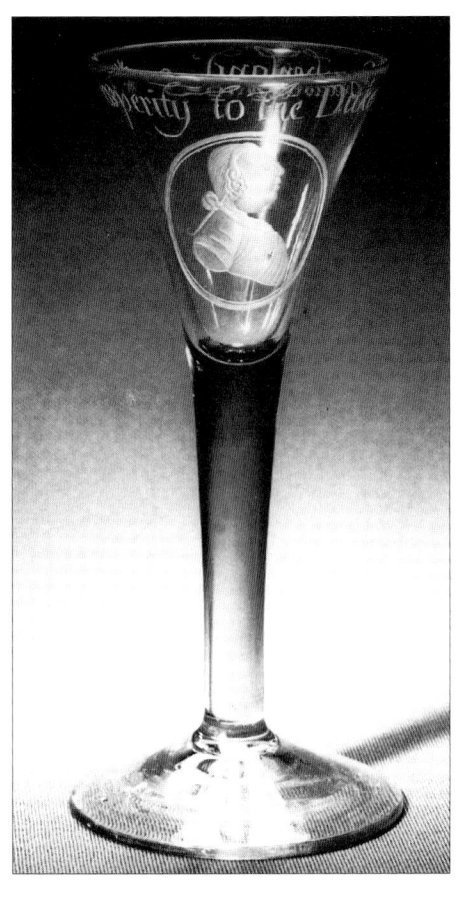

**917.** Wine glass; drawn trumpet bowl engraved with portrait bust of the Duke of Cumberland and inscribed round rim PROSPERITY TO THE DUKE OF CUMBERLAND. Ht. 6⅜ins. c.1745.

*Sotheby's.*

**918.** Wine glass; bell bowl, solid base, engraved profile portrait within a medallion lettered HIS ROYAL HIGHNESS WILLIAM DUKE OF CUMBERLAND; plain stem over heavy knop. Ht. 6½ins. c.1730.

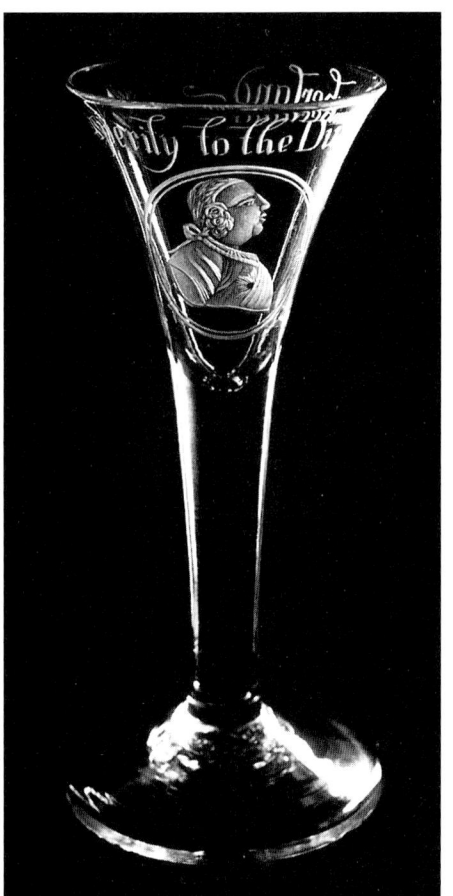

**919.** Wine glass; drawn trumpet bowl, engraved profile portrait below the inscription PROSPERITY TO THE DUKE OF CUMBERLAND; plain stem. (Anti-Jacobite.) Ht. 6½ins. c.1745.

*Cecil Higgins Museum, Bedford.*

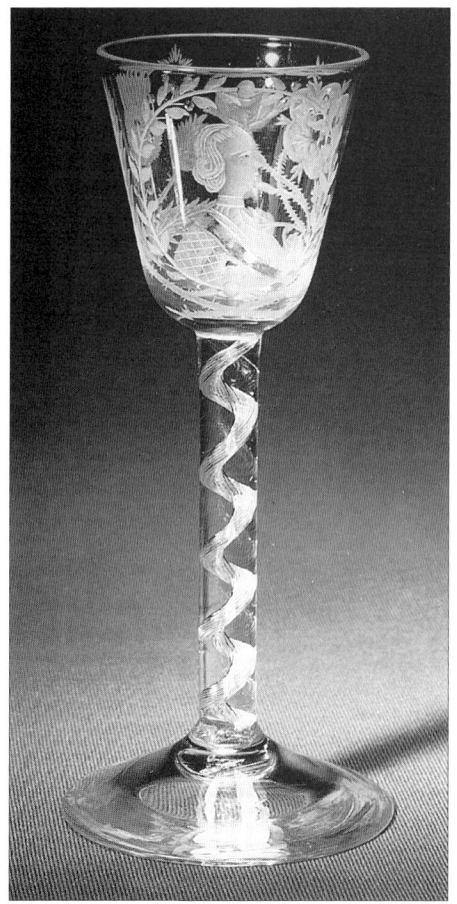

**920.** Wine glass; RF bowl engraved with a portrait bust of Prince Charles Edward Stuart within laurel branches, six-petalled rose and two buds; SSAT – spiral cable (Jacobite.) Ht. 6½ins. c.1750.

*Ex Lord Lambourne Collection. Sotheby's.*

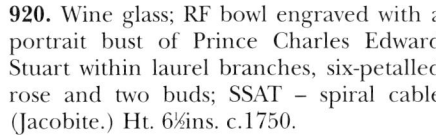

Wheel-Engraving and Stippling

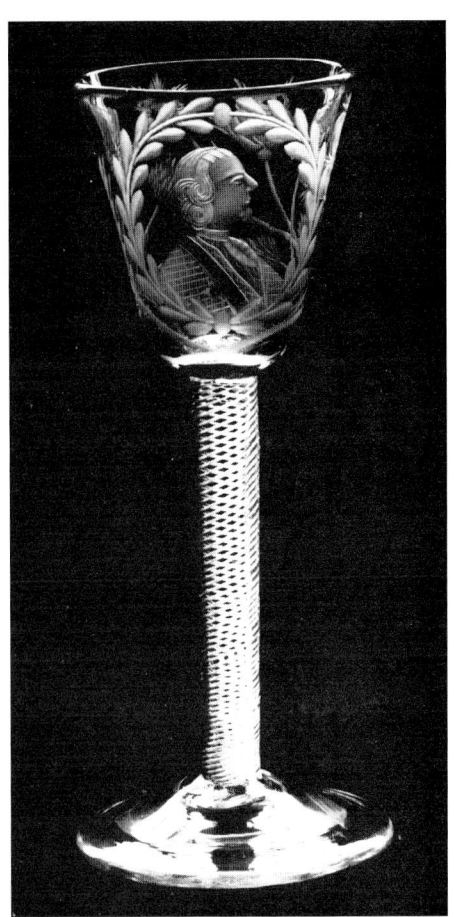

**921.** Goblet; cup bowl engraved with portrait bust below the inscription PROSPERITY TO THE DUKE OF CUMBERLAND; composite stem – MSAT over squat IB knop; high DF. Ht. 7¼ins. c.1745. *Asprey.*

**922.** Wine glass; RF bowl engraved with a portrait bust of the Duke of Cumberland (?) within a foliate medallion; MSAT. Ht. 6¼ins. c.1750. *Victoria and Albert Museum.*

**923.** Goblet; cup bowl engraved WILLIAM WYNN ESQ<sup>r</sup> MAUSYNYUODD; hexagonal-faceted stem. Ht. 7¼ins. c.1785. This family was connected with the Nanney's of Moes-y-Neuadd, Merioneth. *Christie's.*

**924.** Goblet; drawn trumpet bowl, engraved three eagles with wings outspread below the inscription SIR WATKIN WILLIAMS WYNNE; plain stem with tear; FF. Ht. 8½ins. c.1745.
*Cecil Higgins Museum, Bedford.*

**925.** Wine glass; RF bowl, engraved with the arms of the Clitheroe family; 'Newcastle' light baluster including a drop knop and a beaded knop; DF. Ht. 7ins. c.1750.

**926.** Goblet; ogee bowl engraved with portrait of James, 20th Earl of Kildare and 1st Duke of Leinster and the inscription GROM A BOO; MSAT; FF. Ht. 7⅛ins. c.1760.                    *Sotheby's.*

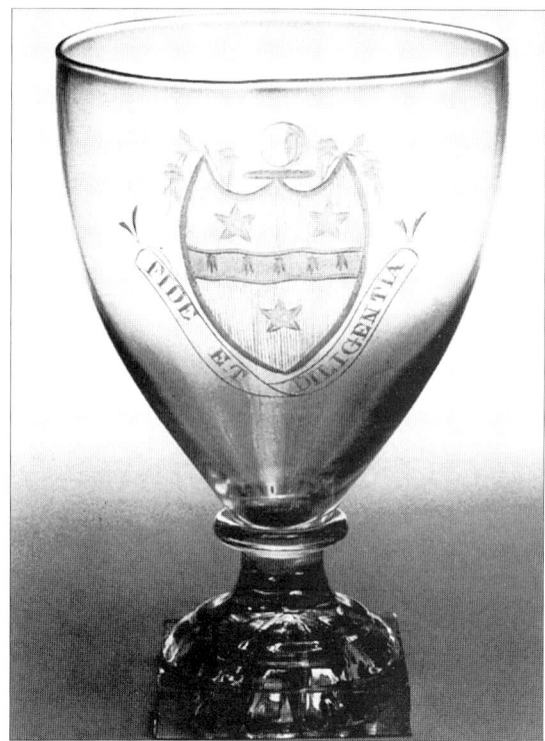

**927.** Goblet; cup bowl engraved with the Crawley family coat of arms with the motto FIDE ET DILIGENTIA; collar, square moulded 'lemon squeezer' foot. Ht. 5⅜ins. c.1800.         *Asprey.*

**928.** Engraved bowl bearing arms comprising crossed daggers quartered with ship's wheels (on a 'Newcastle' light baluster stem including teared knop). Ht. 11½ins. c.1750.   *Smith Collection. Harvey's Wine Museum, Bristol.*

**929.** Goblet; lipped RF bowl, engraved with the arms of King's Lynn and the Blencowe and Everard families above bands of fine and coarse diamond cutting; stem containing large faceted knop; square, radially cut foot. Ht. 9½ins. c.1800. *King's Lynn Museum.*

**930.** Reverse of 929 showing the arms of King's Lynn.

**931.** Tankard; band of three threads below rim; engraved EDMUND MORRIS LYNN REGIS 1771. Ht. 7½ins. c.1771.
*King's Lynn Museum.*

**932.** Tumbler; engraved festooned border below rim, WM FLETCHER 1776 and on reverse a bird in flight, bee, acorn and flowers. Ht. 3¾ins. c.1776.

**933.** Tumbler; engraved fluted border below rim, monogram WB and on reverse a dove with olive branch in beak. Ht. 5¼ins. Late 18th century.

**934.** Ale jug; bulbous body, engraved hops and barley below inscription ANN FOWLER[!]. Ht. 5½ins. Late 18th century.

**935.** Rummer; cup bowl, engraved initials W F N above ear of barley; square-domed 'lemon-squeezer' base. Ht. 4⅜ins. c.1800.
*Worthing Museum.*

**936.** Rummer; square bucket bowl, engraved W G/1801 within a shield and on reverse a floral spray; flattened knop. Ht. 5ins. c.1801. *Worthing Museum.*

Wheel-Engraving and Stippling

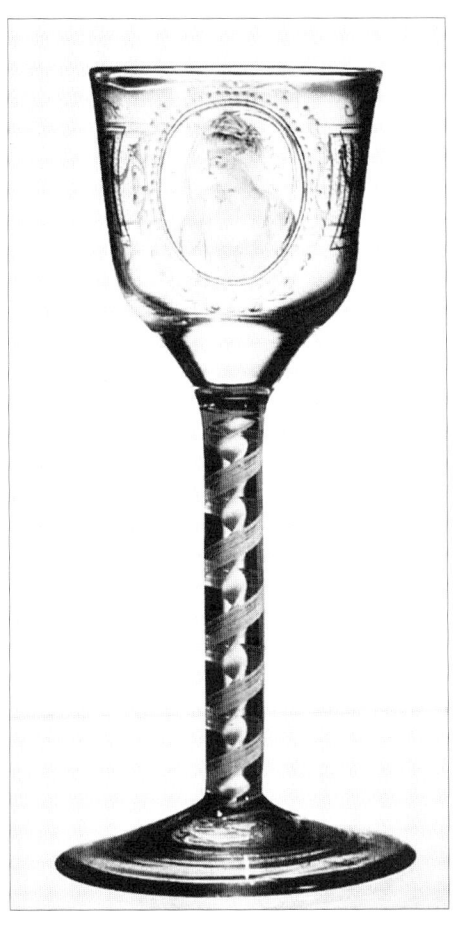

**937.** Wine glass; ogee bowl engraved with portrait of Sarah Siddons (1755-1831) in a medallion; DSOT – 9-ply spiral band outside a wide spiral tape. Ht. 7½ins. c.1775. *Asprey.*

**939.** Wine glass; bell bowl, engraved three-masted sailing-ship below motto SALUS PATRIAE; stem comprising knop between opposing balusters. Ht. 6⅝ins. c.1740.

**938.** Wine glass; RF bowl, engraved with full-face portrait of Sarah Siddons, in a medallion; DSOT stem – pair of 3-ply spiral bands outside gauze. Ht. 6ins. c.1780.

Wheel-Engraving and Stippling

**940.** Wine glass; bucket bowl, engraved with the legend SUCCESS TO CAPTAIN DIBDIN AND THE EAGLE FRIGATE above a three-masted sailing-ship; SSOT – pair of spiral gauzes. Ht. 6⅜ins. c.1757. *The Eagle Frigate* was a Bristol Privateer commanded by Captain Dibdin (*see London Chronicle*, April 12th 1757) and later by Captain Knill.

*Cecil Higgins Museum, Bedford.*

**941.** Reverse of 940 showing engraved name of Captain Dibdin.

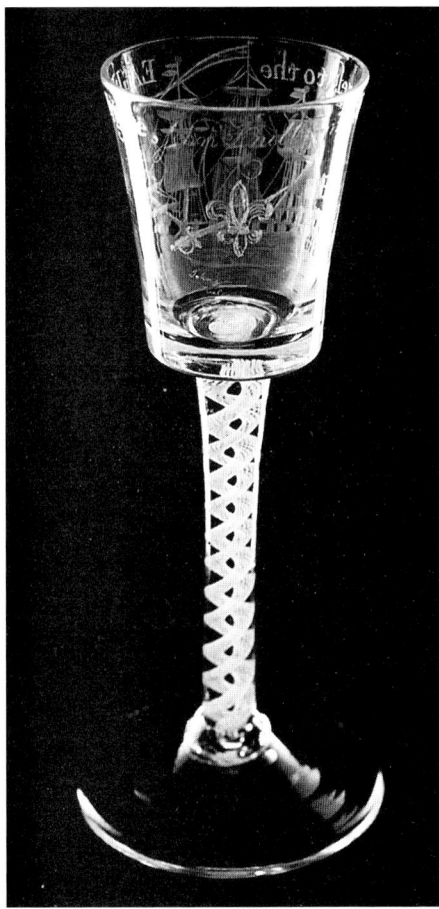

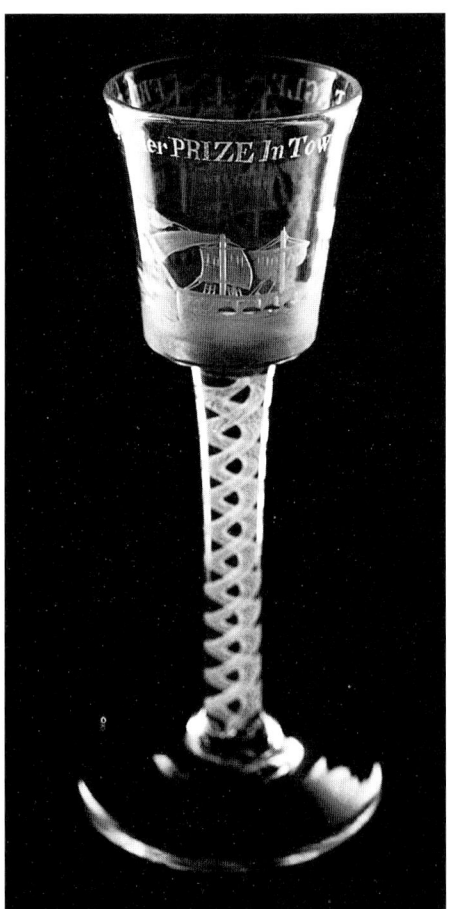

**942.** Wine glass; bucket bowl, engraved with the legend SUCCESS TO THE EAGLE FRIGATE above a three-masted sailing ship and on the reverse in diamond-point JOHN KNILL COMMDR. above a sword piercing a fleur-de-lys; below this is the signature JOHNS SCULPT. The initials (?) N FLY are linked to the bows of the ship; SSOT – pair of spiral gauzes. Ht. 6ins. c.1757. (*See* note to 940.)

*Cecil Higgins Museum, Bedford.*

**943.** Wine glass; bucket bowl, engraved with three-masted sailing-ship towing another ship with masts shot away below the inscription THE EAGLE FRIGATE WITH HER PRIZE IN TOW; SSOT – pair of spiral gauzes. Ht. 6ins. c.1757. This is the only known example of a Privateer showing the prize in tow.

*Cecil Higgins Museum, Bedford.*

Wheel-Engraving and Stippling

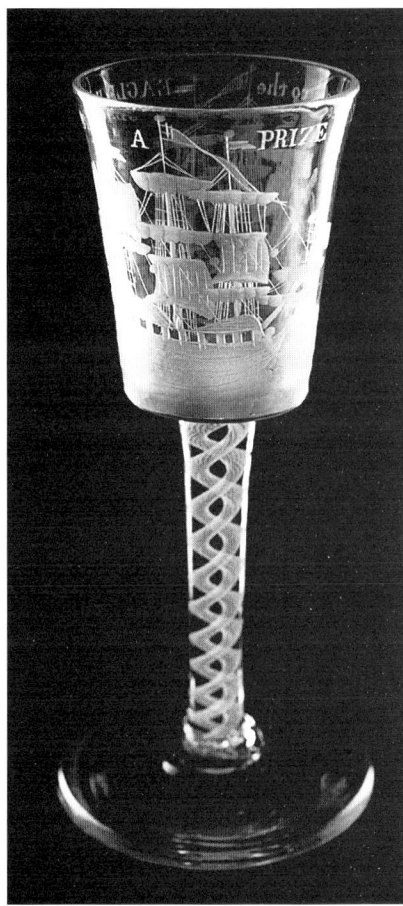

**944.** Wine glass; bucket bowl, engraved with two ships in full sail below the inscription SUCCESS TO THE EAGLE FRIGATE, A PRIZE; SSOT – pair of spiral gauzes. Ht. 6⅜ins. c.1757.

*Cecil Higgins Museum, Bedford.*

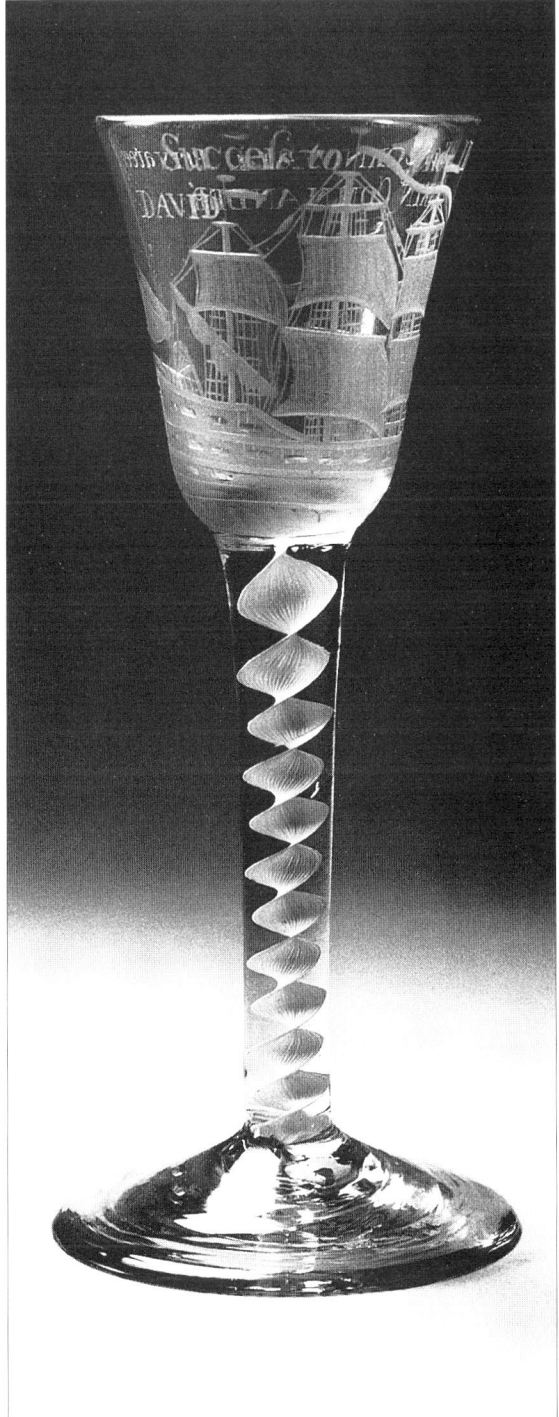

**945.** Wine glass; flared RF bowl engraved with three-masted sailing ship below the inscription SUCCESS TO THE DUKE OF CORNWALL PRIVATEER DAVID JENKINS COMMANDER; SSOT – corkscrew. Ht. 6ins. c.1760. (Privateer glass). *Sotheby's.*

**946.** Wine glass; square bucket bowl engraved with a three-masted frigate and above, in diamond-point, SUCCESS TO THE CONSTANTINE; DSOT – pair of corkscrews outside gauze. Ht. 6⅛ins. (Probably the Privateer commanded by Capt. Robert Forsyth). *Sotheby's.*

**947.** Goblet; RF bowl, engraved with three men-of-war in full sail within a rectangular panel below the legend SUCCESS TO THE BRITISH FLEET 1749; plain stem. Ht. 7¼ins. c.1749. *Cecil Higgins Museum, Bedford.*

**948.** Reverse of 947 showing engraved date.

**949.** Goblet; pan-topped RF bowl, engraved with stars above a sailing-boat, two men and a dog on the shore and, below, the inscription HESPERUS UNUS LUCESSIT; 'Newcastle' light baluster stem with four knops; D & FF. Ht. 7ins. c.1750.

**950.** Goblet; RF bowl engraved with three-masted sailing-ship and on reverse HET VELVAREN VAN DEN ADMIRAL DE SUFFREN (attributed to Jacob Sang); DSOT – opposed IBs with pair of multi-ply spiral bands outside vertical cable. Ht. 7⅜ins. c.1765. (Admiral de Suffren was a French admiral who defeated the British fleet in the Azores in 1781.) *Asprey.*

Wheel-Engraving and Stippling

**952.** Goblet; square bucket bowl engraved with the arms of the Anti-Gallican Society and the inscription FOR OUR COUNTRY; SSAT – spiral cable. c.1750. *Asprey.*

**953.** Detail of 952. *Asprey.*

**951.** Wine glass; RF bowl inscribed round rim PATRIAE ET PATRIBUS; 'Newcastle' light baluster stem, including large teared knop; FF. Ht. 12¼ins. c.1745. *Christie's.*

**954.** Rummer; cup bowl, engraved HANNAH OF LYNN within a floral spray and on reverse a two-masted barque in full sail; square 'lemon-squeezer' base. Ht. 7ins. c.1800.
*King's Lynn Museum.*

**955.** Rummer; cup bowl engraved with a three-masted sailing ship and inscribed DUKE WELLINGTON; collar, square moulded 'lemon-squeezer' foot. c.1800.    *Asprey.*

**956.** Rummer; cup bowl, engraved TRAFALGAR above catafalque and NELSON'S VICTORY I E W, and LORD NELSON OCTR 21 1805 between ships-of-the-line; collar above rudimentary stem. Ht. 6¼ins. c.1805.
**957.** Reverse of 956 showing the date of Nelson's victory and death.

**958.** Rummer; bucket bowl, engraved TRAFALGAR above catafalque and LORD NELSON within laurel wreath. Ht. 5¼ins. c.1805.

Wheel-Engraving and Stippling

**959.** Rummer; bucket bowl, engraved LORD NELSON within a laurel wreath opposite the *Victory* in full sail. Ht. 5½ins. c.1805.

**960.** Rummer; ovoid bowl, engraved SUCCESS TO THE VOYAGE above a three-masted sailing-ship and a girl resting on an anchor beneath a tree; collar, stepped conical foot. Ht. 5¾ins. Early 19th century.

**961.** Goblet; RF bowl Dutch-engraved with a three-masted sailing-ship and on reverse BRITANNIA; MSAT. Ht. 7½ins. c.1750.
*Christie's.*

**962.** Wine glass; funnel bowl, solid base with tear, engraved with a woman in a feathered hat above the inscription HAEC LIBERTATIS ERGO; 6-sided pedestal stem, diamonds on shoulders; FF. Ht. 7¼ins. c.1725. *Sotheby's.*

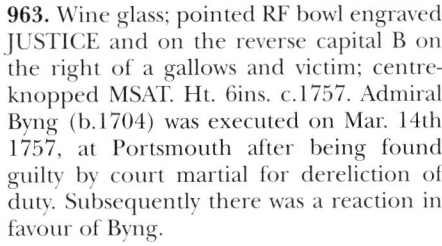

**963.** Wine glass; pointed RF bowl engraved JUSTICE and on the reverse capital B on the right of a gallows and victim; centre-knopped MSAT. Ht. 6ins. c.1757. Admiral Byng (b.1704) was executed on Mar. 14th 1757, at Portsmouth after being found guilty by court martial for dereliction of duty. Subsequently there was a reaction in favour of Byng.

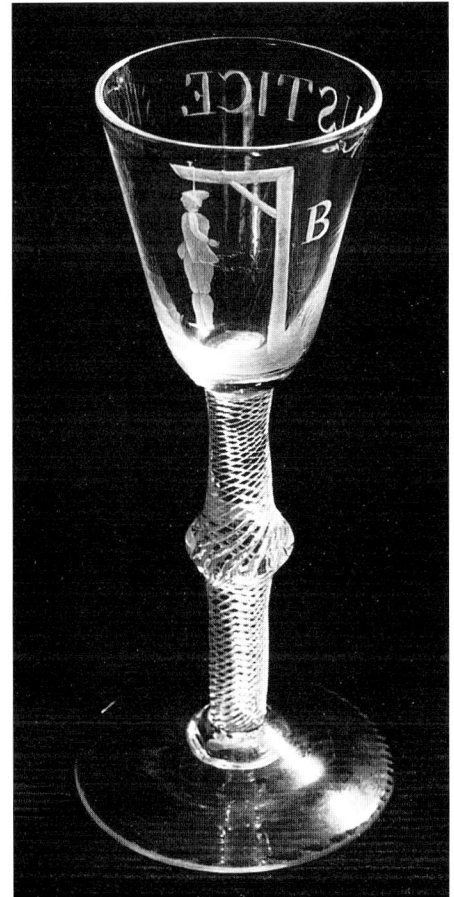

**964.** Rummer; incurved bowl, engraved with near and distant balloons in a landscape of tree, houses and birds in flight; collar above a rudimentary stem; square-moulded 'lemon-squeezer' base. Ht. 5¾ins. c.1800. Possibly executed in commemoration of the first crossing of the English Channel by Blanchard and Jeffries on Jan. 7th 1785. *King's Lynn Museum.*

**965.** Wine glass; incurved bowl, engraved with bridge above a two-masted ship and the inscription SUNDERLAND BRIDGE; bladed knop in short stem. Ht. 4ins. Early 19th century. Engraved in commemoration of the building of the cast-iron bridge opened in 1796.

**966.** Goblet; square bucket bowl engraved with three-masted sailing-ship within an oval cartouche, on reverse a galleon; capstan stem; square 'lemon-squeezer' foot. Ht. 8¾ins. c.1800. *Christie's.*

**967.** Goblet; bucket bowl engraved with Sunderland Bridge over a two-masted sailing-ship; capstan stem. Ht. 5¾ins. c.1810. *Asprey.*

Wheel-Engraving and Stippling

**968.** Wine glass; trumpet bowl, engraved FULLER AND BROWN THE 394; plain stem with large tear; FF. Ht. 6½ins. c.1740.

**969.** Wine glass; pointed RF bowl, engraved OUR LIBERTY PRESERVED BY TAYLOR; plain stem; FF. Ht. 6ins. c.1740. Probably refers to Joseph Taylor elected for Ashburton in 1739.

**970.** Wine glass; ogee bowl, engraved G.E. DURANT FOR EVER above fruiting vine; DSOT stem – 12-ply spiral band outside three spiral threads. Ht. 5½ins. c.1768. G.E. Durant was returned to Parliament in 1768 as the second Member for Evesham.

Wheel-Engraving and Stippling

**971.** Wine glass; ogee bowl engraved SIR FRANCIS KNOLLYS AND LIBERTY 1761; plain stem, FF. Ht. 6⅜ins. c.1745. (In the Reading parliamentary election of 1761, two members were returned, John Dodd and Sir Francis Knollys.) *Asprey.*

**972.** Wine glass; ogee bowl, engraved LOWTHER AND UPTON HUZZA; DSOT stem – pair of spiral tapes outside lace twist. Ht. 6ins. c.1761. Refers to the election of Sir James Lowther and John Upton in 1761; they stood jointly against a third candidate. There is a decanter in the Victoria and Albert Museum with the same inscription.

**973.** Goblet; RF bowl, engraved MORTIMER AND FREEDOM between leaf borders; DSOT stem – four heavy spiral threads outside gauze. Ht. 5⅜ins. c.1774. Refers to Hans Winthrop Mortimer returned to Parliament in 1774 and 1780.

**974.** Goblet; pointed RF bowl, engraved with a cherub placing wreaths on a newly-wed couple, an inscription in Dutch wishing them happiness and the date 18 April, 1741; 'Newcastle' light baluster stem comprising three angular knops and a beaded IB. Ht. 8⅝ins. c.1740.
*Pilkington Glass Museum, St. Helens.*

Wheel-Engraving and Stippling

**975.** Marriage goblet; RF bowl Dutch-engraved with clasped hands above flaming hearts below the inscription VOLTROKENE HUWELYK; 'Newcastle' light baluster stem. Ht. 7½ins. c.1740.    *Christie's.*

**976.** Tankard; coiled thread decoration round rim; engraved SUCCESS TO SARAH FINCH within a floral scroll; 'nipt diamond waies' decoration round base which contains silver coin of Queen Anne (? 1709). Ht. 7½ins. Mid 18th century.

**977.** Wine glass; RF bowl engraved (in the manner of Jacob Sang) with cock and hen below the inscription DE GOEDDOENEN DE VRIENDSCHAP; 'Newcastle' light baluster stem. Ht. 7⅛ins. c.1750.    *Sotheby's.*

**978.** Wine glass; RF bowl engraved with a three-storeyed house below the inscription TWELVAREN VAN VECHT STROOM; 'Newcastle' light baluster stem; D & FF. Ht. 7½ins. c.1740.    *Christie's.*

**979.** Goblet; RF bowl engraved with sailing ship and a man ploughing below the Dutch inscription S'LANTS VELVAREN (Prosperity of the land); annulated knop, 8-sided Silesian stem with stars on shoulders; D & FF. Ht. 8⅜ins. c.1745.

*Sotheby's.*

**980.** Wine glass; RF bowl, engraved VRIEND SCHAP (Friendship) above a festooned border and clasped hands within a sprigged medallion; composite stem – centre-knopped MSAT, teared knop plain section and basal knop. Ht. 7⅜ins. c.1750. Engraved in Holland.

Wheel-Engraving and Stippling

**981.** Goblet; RF bowl, engraved with Bacchus seated on a barrel between sprays of fruiting vines; knop over six-sided moulded pedestal stem; D & FF. Ht. 11⅛ins. c.1740.

**982.** Detail of engraving of 981.

**983.** Detail of engraving on a goblet – the crest of the Merchant Taylors above the inscription CONCORDIA PARVAE RES CRESCUNT. c.1820. *Asprey.*

**984.** Goblet; ogee bowl, engraved with figure of Britannia (?) in a shipping scene; DSAT stem – four spirals outside cable. c.1750. *Asprey.*

**985.** Detail of 984. *Asprey.*

Wheel-Engraving and Stippling

**986.** Goblet; funnel bowl engraved with inscription CREDIT BALANCE surmounted by a cockerel; eight-sided, diamond-studded moulded pedestal stem. FF. c.1745. *Asprey.*

**987.** Tumbler engraved with inscription TOWN AND TRADE OF LANCASTER between festoon border and floral sprays. c.1800.
*Lancaster Museum Collection. Asprey.*

**988.** Cordial; funnel bowl, engraved TRADE AND NAVIGATION over fruiting vine; plain stem with basal knop; D & FF. Ht. 6¾ins. c.1740.
*Harvey's Wine Museum, Bristol.*

**989.** Wine glass; ovoid bowl engraved with plough; diamond-faceted stem. Ht. 5¼ins. c.1785.

Wheel-Engraving and Stippling

**990.** Rummer; square bucket bowl, engraved T J G between ears of barley and on reverse a shield containing agricultural implements above the inscription SPEED THE PLOUGH; collar above short plain stem; square-moulded 'lemon-squeezer' base. Ht. 5¼ins. c.1800.

**991.** Tankard; engraved sprigged border below rim and between two bands of annulated rings a wildfowling scene, with the initials F J T within a garland of leaves on the reverse. Ht. 6½ins. Mid 18th century.                                                    *Worthing Museum.*

**992.** Rummer; cup bowl, engraved upper half with boxers sparring, on reverse the monogram BB, lower half diamond-cut; capstan stem; star-cut foot. Ht. 6⅞ins. Early 19th century. Note: BB may refer to the boxer Benjamin Braine, 1790.                          *Christie's.*

**993.** Rummer; bucket bowl engraved with portraits of two boxers, one above the inscription THE STREATHAM YOUTH, the other YOUNG DUTCH SAM; ball knop in short stem; flat foot. Ht. 5ins. c.1810.
*Asprey.*

**994.** Tumbler; engraved with waggon and horses and inscribed SUCCESS TO MR COOPERS WAGGONS; fluted base. Ht. 5ins. c.1800. *Asprey.*

**995.** Rummer; square bucket bowl engraved with coach and horses Grantham-York-London route; annular knop; square moulded 'lemon squeezer' foot. c.1800.
*Asprey.*

**996.** Rummer; square bucket bowl, panel-cut lower half engraved with race-horse and jockey between oak-leaves and on reverse the initials JTC; capstan stem. Ht. 6⅛ins. c.1820. *Asprey.*

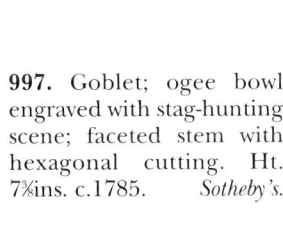

**997.** Goblet; ogee bowl engraved with stag-hunting scene; faceted stem with hexagonal cutting. Ht. 7⅜ins. c.1785. *Sotheby's.*

Wheel-Engraving and Stippling

**998.** Goblet; ogee bowl engraved with scene of horse-drawn carriage and gunmen; DSOT – 14-ply spiral band outside pair of spiral tapes. Ht. 9⅜ins. c.1770. *Sotheby's.*

**999.** Wine glass; RF bowl engraved with wildfowling scene; composite stem – annulated knop above DSOT between shoulder and basal knops. Ht. 6⅜ins. c.1760. *Sotheby's.*

**1,000.** Goblet; ogee bowl engraved with hunting scene; faceted stem. Ht. 8ins. c.1785. *Sotheby's.*

Wheel-Engraving and Stippling

**1,001.** Wine glass; flared funnel bowl engraved with scene of hounds in a landscape; hexagonal-faceted stem. Ht. 6¼ins. c.1785.

*Ex Walter F. Smith Collection. Christie's.*

**1,003.** Goblet; square bucket bowl, engraved with monogram PT within a shield flanked by ears of barley and on reverse, within a medallion, the inscription SONS OF HARMONY over the sun shining on violin and music; collar; square-moulded 'lemon-squeezer' foot. Ht. 5ins. c.1800.

**1,002.** Wine glass; funnel bowl engraved with huntsman and hounds; diamond-faceted stem. Ht. 4ins. c.1785. One of a pair. *Christie's.*

Wheel-Engraving and Stippling

**1,004.** Rummer; bowl engraved with hunting scene and monogram W D W; collar; short plain stem. Ht. 5ins. Early 19th century. *King's Lynn Museum.*

**1,005.** Wine glass; RF bowl, engraved with Cupid in a rustic landscape; hexagonal-faceted stem. Ht. 6⅛ins. c.1785.

**1,006.** Wine glass; cup bowl engraved with Masonic emblems; hexagonal-faceted stem; panelled foot. Ht. 4⅛ins. c.1785. *Christie's.*

**1,007.** Firing glass; trumpet bowl, engraved with set square and dividers (Masonic emblems); firing foot. Ht. 4ins. Mid 18th century. *Hartshorne Collection. (Fig. 316)*

**1,008.** Tumbler; engraved beehive, crossed keys and other Masonic emblems; star-cut base. Ht. 4ins. Early 19th century. One of a pair, with matching carafe.

**1,009.** Rummer; square bucket bowl, engraved with Masonic emblems; short plain stem. Ht. 5½ins. Early 19th century.

**1,010.** Reverse of 1,009.

**1,011.** Rummer; incurved bucket bowl, engraved with Masonic emblems; short stem with bladed knop. Ht. 5ins. Early 19th century.

**1,012.** Rummer; bucket bowl engraved with insignia of the GRAND LODGE ROCHESTER; flattened knop in short stem; flat foot. Ht. 6¼ins. c.1810. *Asprey.*

**1,013.** Wine glass; RF bowl, engraved with the arms of King's Lynn above the motto LOYALTY; SSAT – single spiral cable. Ht. 5¼ins. c.1750. *King's Lynn Museum.*

**1,014.** Wine glass; pointed RF bowl, engraved with the arms of Utrecht; 'Newcastle' light baluster stem – ball knop between two angular knops; DF. Ht. 8ins. c.1745.

**1,015.** Wine glass; pointed RF bowl engraved with the arms of the City of Utrecht; 'Newcastle' light baluster stem. Ht. 6⅜ins. c.1750. *Christie's.*

Wheel-Engraving and Stippling

**1,016.** Goblet; pointed RF bowl engraved with the arms of Groningen flanked by lion supporters; multi-knopped stem; FF. Ht. 7¼ins. c.1750.               *Christie's.*

**1,017.** Wine glass; RF bowl engraved with the arms of the Hague; 'Newcastle' light baluster stem with three knops; FF. Ht. 8ins. c.1740.               *Sotheby's.*

**1,018.** Wine glass; RF bowl, engraved with floral border above diamond-engraved inscription DORDRECHTS WELVAREN; 'Newcastle' light baluster stem including angular knop; DF. Ht. 7⅜ins. c.1745.
               *Pilkington Glass Museum, St. Helens.*

**1,019.** Goblet; pointed RF bowl, engraved with Chinese figures and pagodas in four oval medallions; DSAT – pair of air spirals outside cable; foot engraved with floral border. Ht. 7⅞ins. c.1750.
               *Cecil Higgins Museum, Bedford.*

Wheel-Engraving and Stippling

**1,020.** Wine glass; lipped ogee bowl, engraved with Chinese pagoda scene; SSOT – loose multi-ply corkscrew outlined. Ht. 6ins. c.1765.

**1,021.** Wine glass; waisted RF bowl, engraved with Chinese pagoda scene; hexagonal-faceted stem. Ht. 5¾ins. c.1790.
*Portsmouth City Museums.*

**1,022.** Wine glass; ogee bowl, engraved with Chinese figure and pagodas; diamond-faceted stem. Ht. 6ins. c.1785.

Wheel-Engraving and Stippling

**1,023.** Wine glass; ogee bowl, engraved with unidentified scene of buildings and trees (imaginary?); diamond-faceted centre-knopped stem. Ht. 5⅜ins. c.1785.
*Harvey's Wine Museum, Bristol.*

**1,024.** Wine glass; RF bowl engraved with ships sailing between two ports; diamond-faceted stem continuing into base of bowl. c.1785. *Asprey.*

**1,025.** Goblet; cup bowl crudely engraved with 'elopement' (?) scene; hexagonal-faceted stem. Ht. 7½ins. c.1785. *Asprey.*

**1,026.** Tumbler; engraved with a thatched house and figures in a rural setting inscribed GOD SPEED THE PLOUGH and initials TMT. Ht. 6¼ins. c.1800. *Asprey.*

**1,027.** Goblet and engraved cover with faceted knob; cup bowl engraved with 'elopement' scene (Dutch engraving); hexagonal-cut faceted stem. c.1785. *Asprey.*

**1,028.** Wine glass; bell bowl with engraved border of jardinières of flowering plants; plain stem with swelled central knop; DF. Ht. 6¾ins. c.1730. *Christie's.*

Wheel-Engraving and Stippling

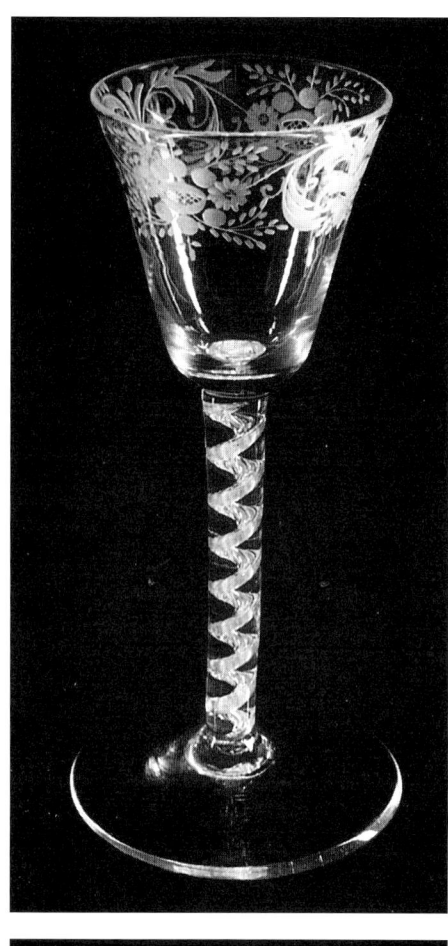

**1,029.** Wine glass; pointed RF bowl, engraved with deep floral border below rim; DSAT – spiral cable outside thin spiral. Ht. 6ins. c.1750.

**1,030.** Wine glass; ogee bowl, engraved with deep floral border below rim; DSOT – pair of corkscrews outside tight corkscrew. Ht. 5⅜ins. c.1765.

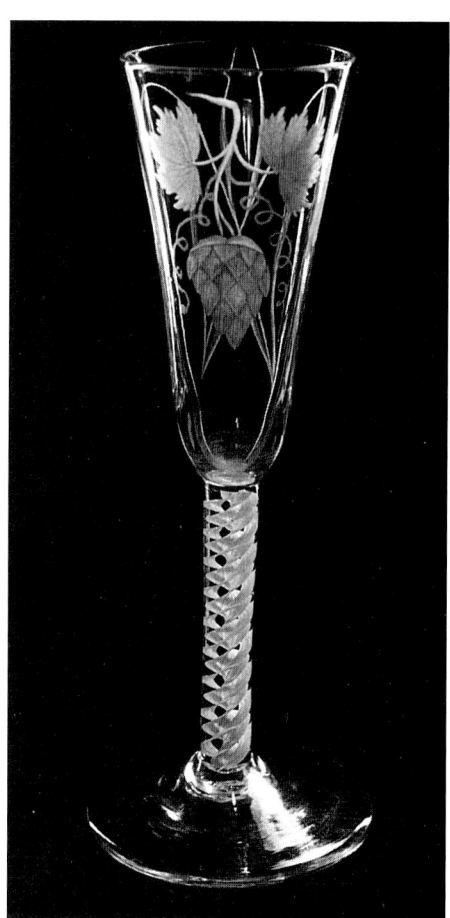

**1,031.** Ale glass; pointed RF bowl, engraved hops and barley; collar above double-knopped MSAT. Ht. 7⅜ins. c.1750.
*Hartshorne Collection. (Plate 50.)*

**1,032.** Ale glass; pointed RF bowl, engraved hops and barley; SSOT – four corkscrews. Ht. 7½ins. c.1765. *Hartshorne Collection.*

Wheel-Engraving and Stippling

**1,033.** Tankard; engraved festooned border below the rim and hops and barley on the body, gadrooned base; hollow knop containing George III shilling dated 1787. D & FF. Ht. 8ins. Late 18th century.

**1,034.** Wine glass; bell bowl, engraved fruiting vine below rim, solid base; IB at base of plain stem. Ht. 7⅛ins. c.1740.
*Portsmouth City Museums.*

**1,035.** Wine glass; drawn trumpet bowl, engraved vine with polished fruit below rim; MSAT. Ht. 6½ins. c.1750.

**1,036.** Goblet; cup bowl engraved with fruiting vine and cover; SSAT – 'mercury twist'. Ht. 11½ins. c.1755. *Sotheby's.*

Wheel-Engraving and Stippling

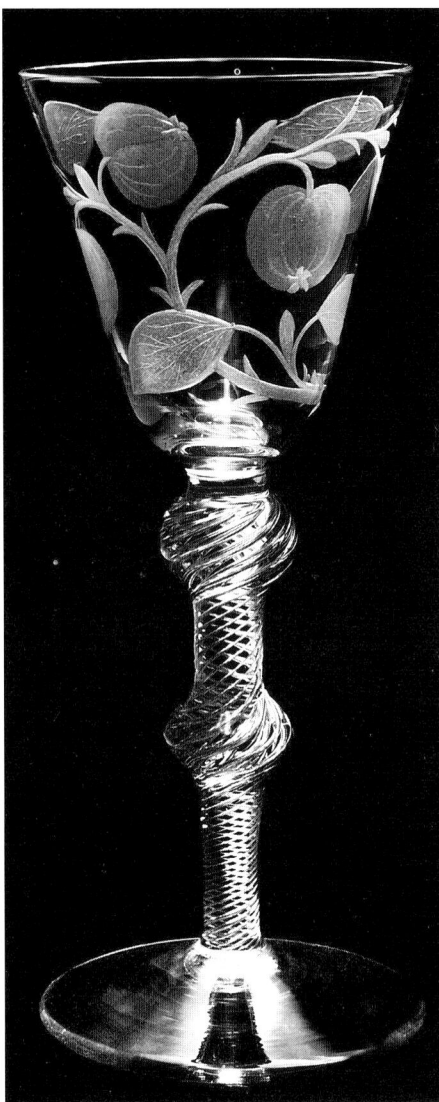

**1,037.** Cider glass; RF bowl engraved with fruiting apple branch; double-knopped MSAT. Ht. 7⅜ins. c.1760.          *Sotheby's.*

**1,038.** Cider glass; ogee bowl engraved CYDER and on reverse an apple tree, the lower half fluted; DSAT – four spiral threads outside vertical column. Ht. 7¼ins. c.1750.          *Christie's.*

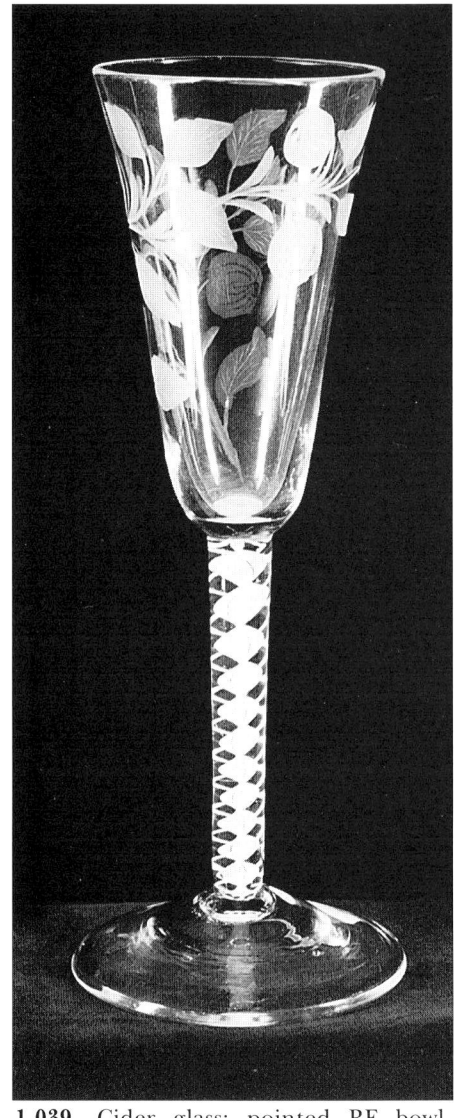

**1,039.** Cider glass; pointed RF bowl, engraved fruiting apple; DSOT – pair of heavy spiral threads outside multi-ply corkscrew. Ht. 7⅜ins. c.1765.

**1,040.** Water glass; pan-topped RF bowl, engraved with a border of coronets below the rim; D & FF. Ht. 4ins. c.1740.

**1,041.** Tumbler engraved with the figure of Hope watching a receding ship. Ht. 5ins. c.1800. *Asprey.*

**1,042.** Wine glass; bell bowl, Dutch engraved with convivial scene; 'Newcastle' light baluster including teared IB knop. c.1750. *Asprey.*

**1,043.** Detail of 1,042.

Wheel-Engraving and Stippling

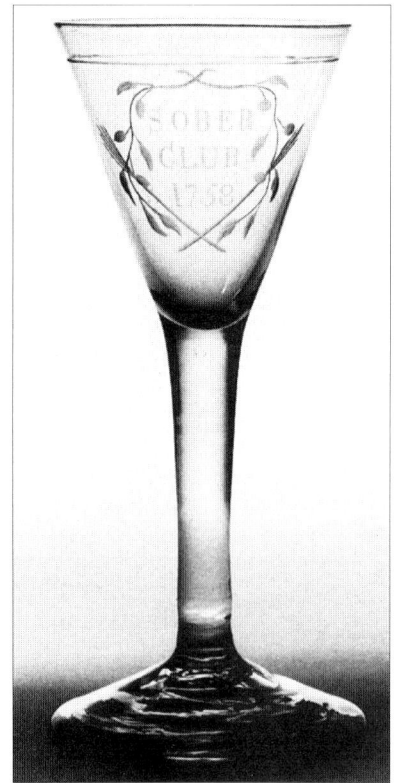

**1,044.** Wine glass; drawn trumpet bowl engraved SOBER CLUB 1758; plain stem. Ht. 6⅛ins. c.1758.                    *Christie's.*
(NOTE: One of the many Glasgow clubs of the 18th century whose members were pledged to drink nothing but water.)

**1,045.** Tumbler; engraved with inscription GROG within a garland including fruiting vine. Ht. 5½ins. Mid 18th century. One of a pair.                    *Asprey.*

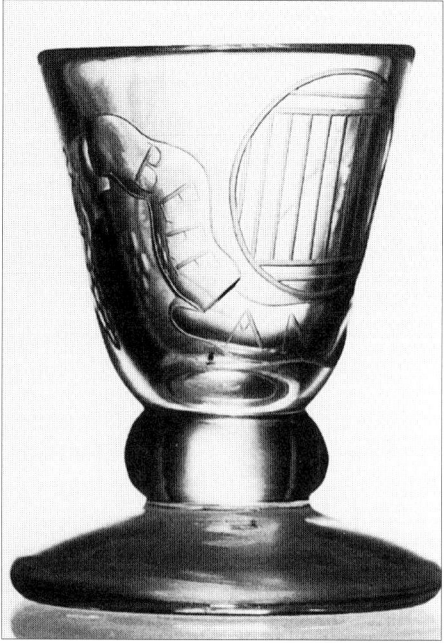

**1,046.** Firing glass; RF bowl engraved with a griddle (the emblem of the English Beefsteak Club) and the inscription BEEF AND LIBERTY; flattened knop; firing foot. Ht. 3⅛ins. c.1720.                    *Asprey.*

**1,047.** Goblet; bucket bowl engraved with figure of a Scottish chieftain standing between thistles and on the reverse a monogram; capstan stem; flat foot. Ht. 10ins. c.1810.        *Aberdeen Museum. Asprey.*

**1,048.** Rummer; bucket bowl engraved with a publican and inscribed WELCOME ALL/NO GRUMBLING/HAPPY NEW YEAR; faceted knop; star-cut foot. Ht. 10ins. c.1820.
*Bass Museum, Burton-on-Trent. Asprey.*

**1,049.** Rummer; square bucket bowl engraved with a view of St. Paul's and on reverse the initials JP; square moulded 'lemon-squeezer' foot. Ht. 6ins. c.1800.
*Asprey.*

**1,050.** 'Davenport' cup-shaped bowl engraved in the manner patented by John Davenport in 1806. Ht. 4⅜ins. c.1810.
*Broadfield House Glass Museum, Kingswinford, Dudley. Asprey.*

**1,051.** Wine glass; ovoid bowl, stipple-engraved with portrait of William III of Holland by David Wolff; diamond-faceted stem. Ht. 5⅜ins. c.1790. Wolff was active from 1784 to 1795.

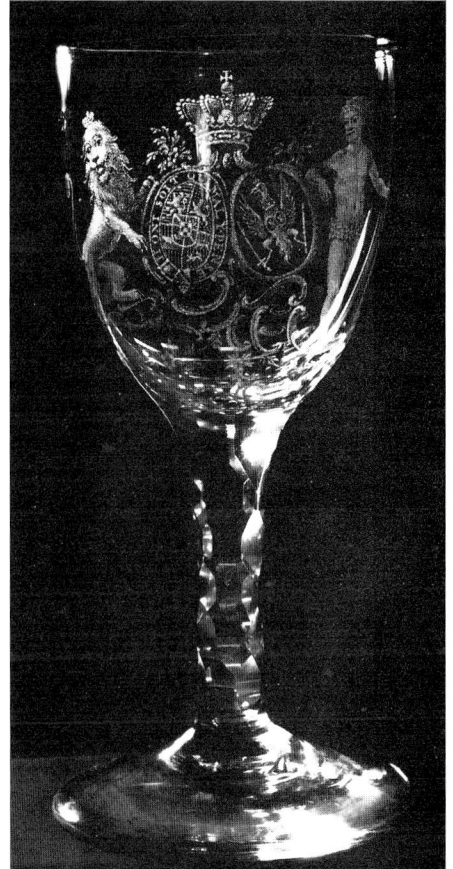

**1,052.** Wine glass; drawn trumpet bowl, stipple-engraved with a group of two lame men and a girl; plain stem with tear. Ht. 6½ins. c.1750. *Sotheby's.*

**1,053.** Wine glass; cup bowl stipple-engraved with the arms of William V, Prince of Orange, and of his wife, Princess Frederica Sophia Wilhelmina of Prussia; hexagonal-faceted stem. Ht. 6⅛ins. c.1790. Attributed to David Wolff. *Christie's.*

**1,054.** Wine glass; RF stipple-engraved with pair of putti on a cloud; composite stem – double-knopped MSAT over IB and plain section. c.1750. *Asprey.*

**1,055.** Goblet; RF bowl, stipple and diamond-point engraved with two putti and on reverse the arms of Delange Van Wyngaarden of Gouda and Prins of Rotterdam above a cartouche inscribed GETROUWT DEN 22 NOVEMBR 1778; 'Newcastle' light baluster stem. Ht. 8⅜ins. c.1765. A marriage goblet, the engraving attributed to David Wolff.
*Ex Littledale Collection. Sotheby's.*

**1,056.** Wine glass; RF bowl, stipple-engraved with a fruiting apple branch and a rose branch with bud, signed A Schouman, Fecit 1747; 'Newcastle' light baluster stem. Ht. 7⅜ins. c.1747.
*Pilkington Glass Museum, St. Helens.*

**1,057.** Wine glass; ovoid bowl stipple-engraved with two putti below the inscription VRIENDSCHAP; plain stem. Ht. 6ins. c.1785. Attributed to David Wolff.
*Christie's.*

Wheel-Engraving and Stippling

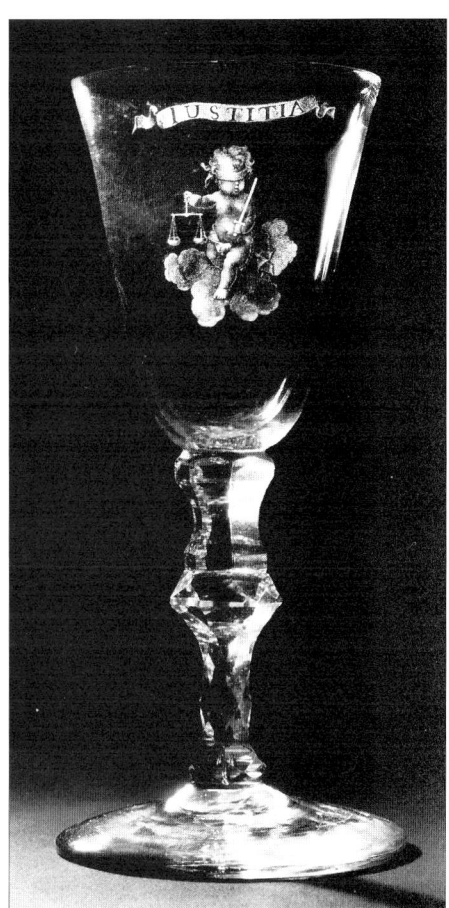

**1,058.** Goblet; RF bowl engraved with a scene of two boys standing either side of a table, about to drink from a goblet, beneath the inscription VRIENDSCHAP; diamond-faceted stem with four knops and a basal knop. Ht. 8¼ins. c.1785. The engraving is a combination of line and stipple. *Pilkington Glass Museum, St. Helens.*

**1,059.** Goblet; flared RF bowl stipple-engraved in the manner of David Wolff with putto seated on a cloud below the inscription IUSTITIA in a ribbon; diamond-faceted stem with shoulder, central and basal knops. c.1785. *Christie's.*

**1,060.** Wine glass; ogee bowl stipple-engraved with the seated figure of a Muse, a pedestal inscribed LIBERTAS AUGUSTA; hexagonal-faceted stem. Ht. 6⅝ins. c.1790. Attributed to David Wolff. *Christie's.*

**1,061.** Wine glass; cup-shaped bowl stipple-engraved with putto beside a beehive; hexagonal-faceted stem. Ht. 6¼ins. c.1790. Attributed to David Wolff. *Christie's.*

# XVI
# Decoration: Enamelling

**1,062.** Goblet; square bucket bowl, painted in enamel colours on one side with the Royal arms and on the other with Prince of Wales's feathers; DSOT – pair of heavy spiral threads outside lace twists. Ht. 9ins. c.1763. These 'Royal Beilby' goblets are presumed to have been decorated by William and Mary Beilby on the birth of the Prince of Wales in 1763.

**1,063.** Another view of 1,062 showing supporter and Prince of Wales's feathers.

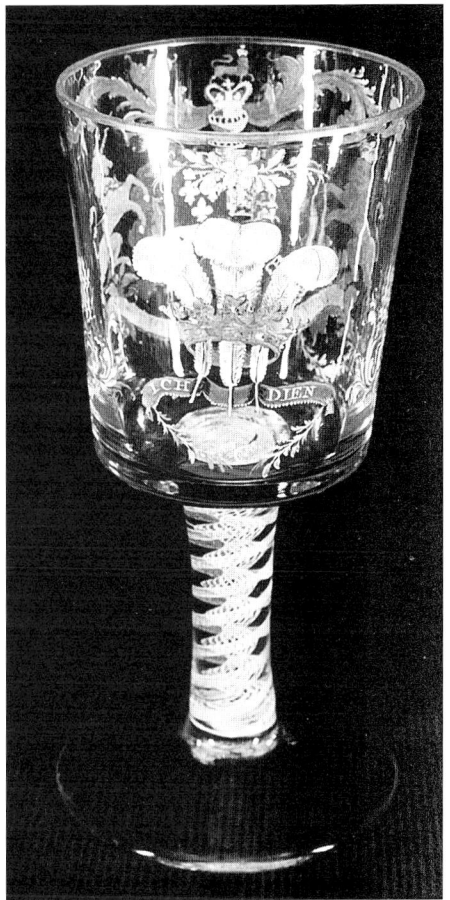

**1,064.** Goblet; square bucket bowl, painted in enamel colours on one side with the Royal arms and on the other with Prince of Wales's feathers; DSOT – pair of 6-ply spiral bands outside lace twist. Ht. 8⅜ins. c.1763. Attributed to Beilby. (See note to 1,062.)

**1,065.** Reverse of 1,064 showing Prince of Wales's feathers.

**1,066.** Tumbler, painted with the Royal Arms in enamel colours. Ht. 4⅜ins. c.1762. Attributed to Beilby.

*Victoria and Albert Museum.*

**1,067.** Goblet; RF bowl with gilt rim, painted in enamel colours with a coat of arms surmounted by a coronet; DSOT – pair of heavy spiral threads outside lace twist. Ht. 9¼ins. c.1765. Attributed to Beilby. *Pilkington Glass Museum, St. Helens.*

**1,068.** Goblet; bucket bowl painted in enamel colours with the arms and crest of Vaughan of Dorset above the name THOS. VAUGHAN; on the reverse is the inscription PLYMOUTH DOCK below the rim; DSOT – five heavy spiral threads outside pair of spiral tapes. Ht. 7¼ins. c.1770. Attributed to Beilby.
*Cecil Higgins Museum, Bedford.*

**1,069.** Goblet; square bucket bowl, painted in enamel colours with the arms of Buckmaster of Lincoln on one side and on the other with fruiting vine in white enamel; gilded rim; DSOT – four heavy spiral threads outside gauze. Ht. 7¼ins. c.1765. Attributed to Beilby. *Cecil Higgins Museum, Bedford.*

**1,070.** Dram glass; waisted bowl, painted in enamel colours with the arms of the Lodge of Journeymen and Masons, No. 8, Edinburgh, and on the reverse with Masonic devices. Ht. 3ins. c.1770. Attributed to Beilby. (*See* Thorpe, *English and Irish glass*, Plate iii.)

Enamelling

**1,071.** Wine glass; RF bowl with gilt rim, painted in enamel colours with a crest (probably fictitious) of a heart pierced by two arrows; 'Newcastle' light baluster stem including teared IB. Ht. 7ins. c.1760. Attributed to Beilby.

**1,072.** Tumbler; painted in white enamel with initials T W A in a floral cartouche and with floral spray on reverse. Ht. 4ins. c.1770. Attributed to Beilby.

**1,073.** Wine glass; ogee bowl, painted in enamel colours with full-face portrait of Prince Charles Edward in Highland dress; DSOT – pair of corkscrews outside lace twist. Ht. 4⅜ins. c.1765. Jacobite glass – painting not attributed to Beilby.

*Pilkington Glass Museum, St. Helens.*

Enamelling

**1,074.** Wine glass; ogee bowl, painted in enamel colours with a crest comprising a demi-man armed with sword between the motto PRO PATRIA; MSOT; FF. Ht. 6ins. c.1765. Could be attributed to Beilby.
*Cecil Higgins Museum, Bedford.*

**1,075.** Close-up of bowl 1,074.

**1,076.** Wine glass; ogee bowl decorated in white enamel heightened with red with a crest of demi-man in armour flanked by the motto PRO PATRIA; MSOT. Ht. 6ins. c.1770. *Christie's.*
(NOTE: The motto and crest are those of the Ogilvie family. c.f. the similar glass in the Cecil Higgins Museum, Bedford (Pl. 1,074.) Could be attributed to Beilby.

**1,077.** Wine glass; ogee bowl, painted in white enamel with hunting scene; DSOT – pair of 8-ply spiral bands outside lace twist. Ht. 6ins. c.1770. Attributed to Beilby.

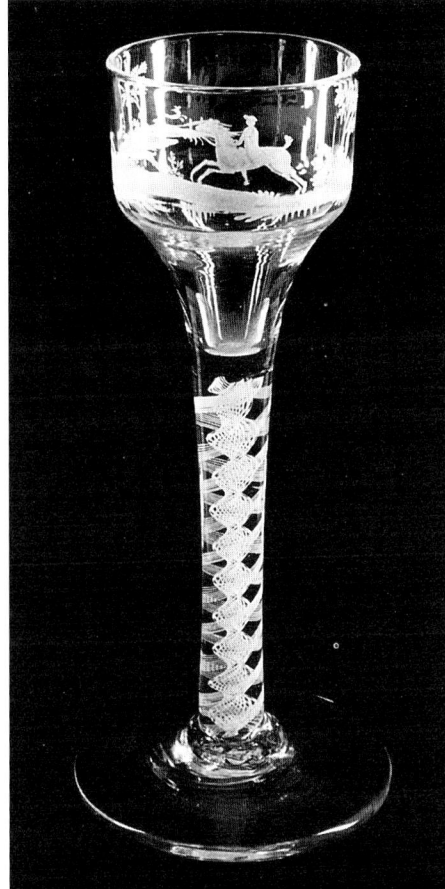

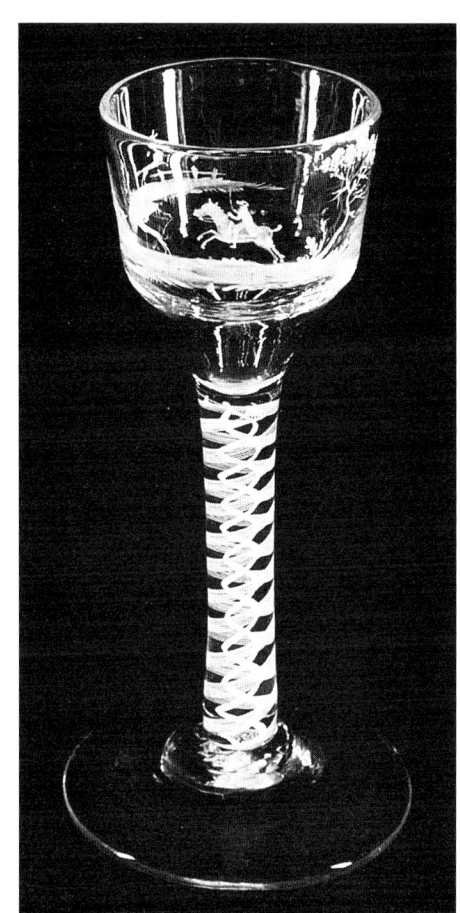

**1,078.** Wine glass; ogee bowl, painted in white enamel with stag-hunting scene; DSOT – pair of 8-ply spiral bands outside pair of heavy spiral threads. Ht. 5⅝ins. c.1770. Attributed to Beilby.

**1,079.** Wine glass; ogee bowl, painted in white enamel with wildfowling scene; DSOT – pair of 6-ply spiral bands outside lace twist. Ht. 6ins. c.1770. Attributed to Beilby.

**1,080.** Wine glass; ogee bowl, painted in white enamel with wildfowling scene; DSOT – pair of heavy spiral threads outside multi-ply spiral band. Ht. 5⅜ins. c.1770. Attributed to Beilby.

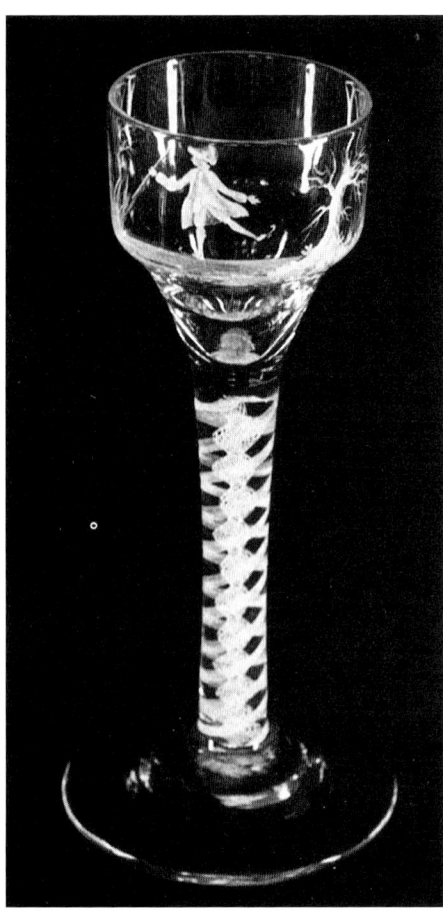

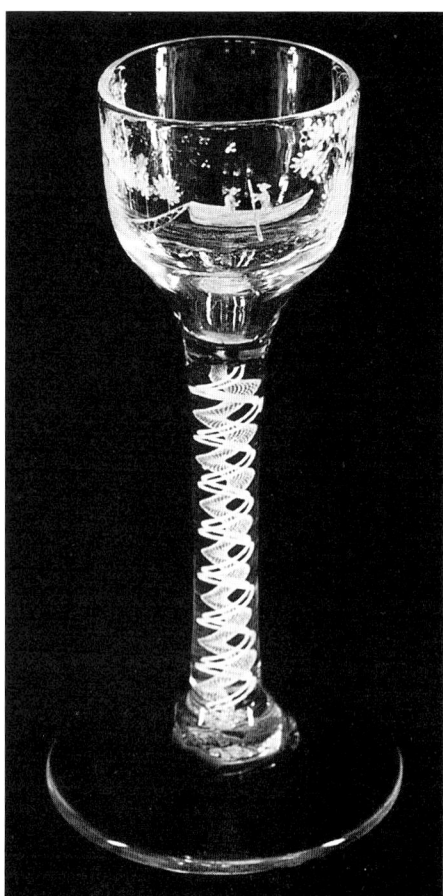

**1,081.** Wine glass; ogee bowl, painted in white enamel with skating scene; DSOT – pair of 6- to 8-ply spiral bands outside lace twist. Ht. 5¾ins. c.1770. Attributed to Beilby.

**1,082.** Wine glass; ogee bowl, painted in white enamel with fishing scene; SSOT – pair of heavy spiral threads alternating with spiral gauze. Ht. 5⅜ins. c.1770. Attributed to Beilby.

**1,083.** Goblet; square bucket bowl decorated with pastoral scene in enamel colours. Ht. 7ins. c.1765. Attributed to Beilby. *Ex. Hamilton Clements and Lady Harrison Hughes Collections. Christie's.*

**1,084.** Wine glass; pointed RF bowl, painted in white enamel with rustic scene, shepherd and flock; DSOT – pair of 8-ply spiral bands outside pair of heavy spiral threads. Ht. 6ins. c.1770. Attributed to Beilby.

Enamelling

**1,085.** Wine glass; pointed RF bowl, painted in white enamel with rustic scene, shepherdess and flock; DSOT – pair of 8-ply spiral bands outside pair of heavy spiral threads. Ht. 6ins. c.1770. Attributed to Beilby.

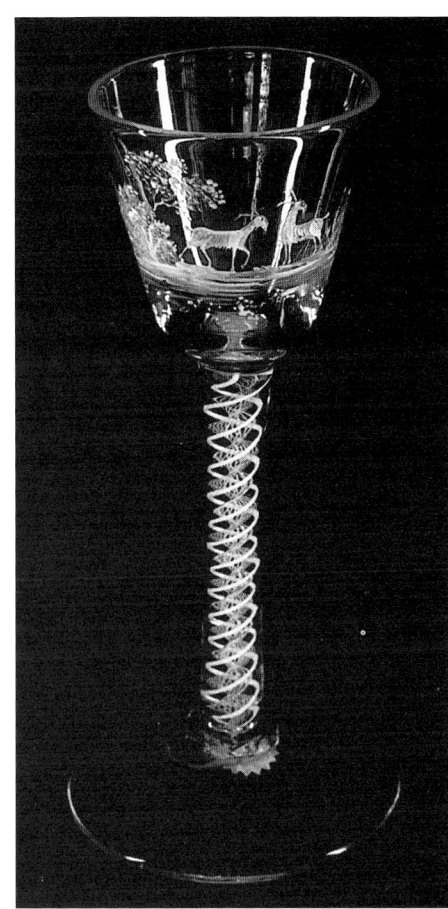

**1,086.** Wine glass; pointed RF bowl, painted in white enamel with pair of goats in a rustic scene; DSOT – pair of heavy spiral threads outside lace twist. Ht. 6ins. c.1770. Attributed to Beilby.

**1,087.** Wine glass; pointed RF bowl, painted in white enamel with sheep and goats in rustic scene; DSOT – pair of 8-ply spiral bands outside pair of heavy spiral threads. Ht. 6ins. c.1770. Attributed to Beilby.

**1,088.** Wine glass; pointed RF bowl, painted in white enamel with a pair of goats in a rustic scene; DSOT – pair of 8-ply spiral bands outside pair of heavy spiral threads. Ht. 6ins. c.1770. Attributed to Beilby.

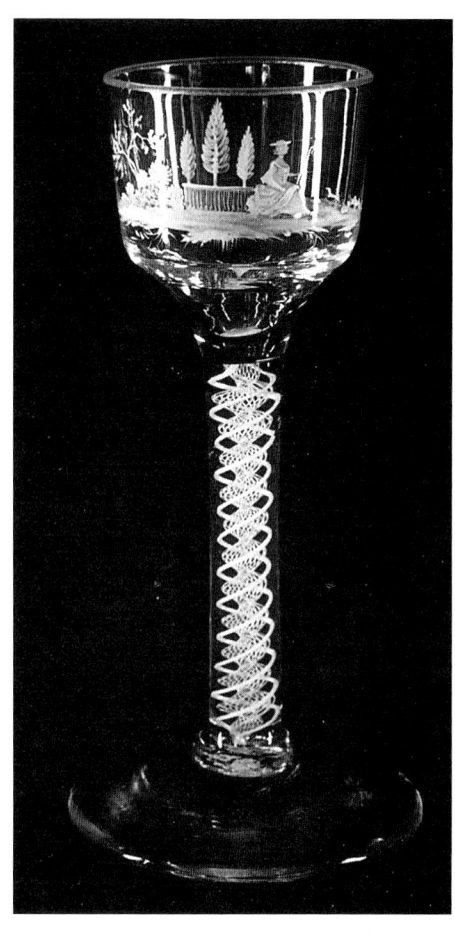

**1,089.** Wine glass; ogee bowl, painted in white enamel with shepherdess, dog and sheep in a rustic scene; DSOT – pair of heavy spiral threads outside lace twist. Ht. 5⅜ins. c.1770. Attributed to Beilby.

**1,090.** Wine glass; RF bowl, painted in white enamel with scene of Classical ruins; coarse incised-twist stem. Ht. 4½ins. c.1760. Attributed to Beilby. *Ex Horridge Collection.*

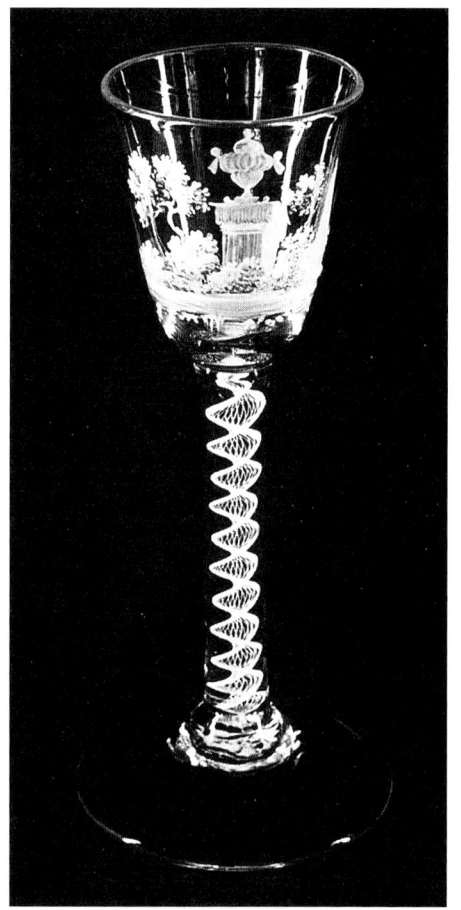

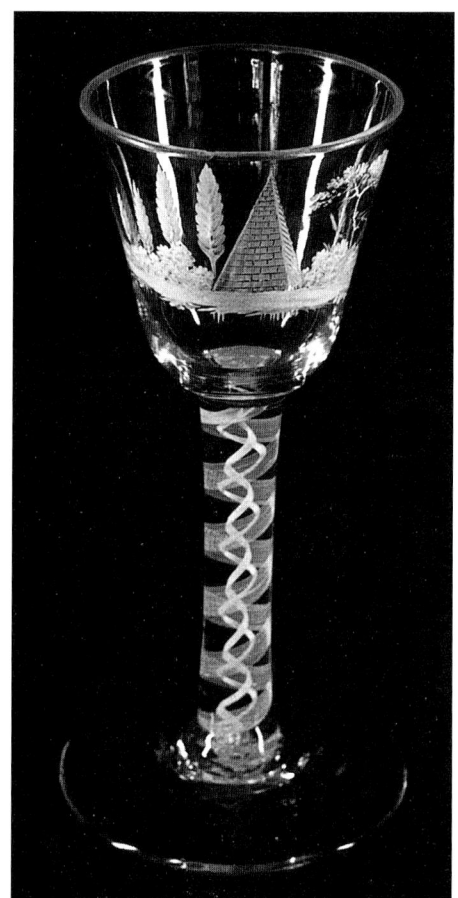

**1,091.** Wine glass; RF bowl, painted in white enamel with urn on pedestal flanked by trees and obelisk; SSOT – lace twist outlined. Ht. 5⅜ins. c.1770. Attributed to Beilby.

**1,092.** Wine glass; RF bowl, painted in white enamel with pyramid flanked by trees; DSOT – 12-ply to 20-ply spiral band outside pair of heavy spiral threads. Ht. 6ins. c.1770. Attributed to Beilby.

**1,093.** Wine glass; pointed RF bowl, painted in white enamel with obelisk flanked by trees; DSOT – pair of 6- and 7-ply spiral bands outside pair of heavy spiral threads. Ht. 6ins. c.1770. Attributed to Beilby.

**1,094.** Wine glass; RF bowl; painted in white enamel with Classical ruins flanked by trees; DSOT – pair of 8-ply spiral bands outside pair of heavy spiral threads. Ht. 6ins. c.1770. Attributed to Beilby.

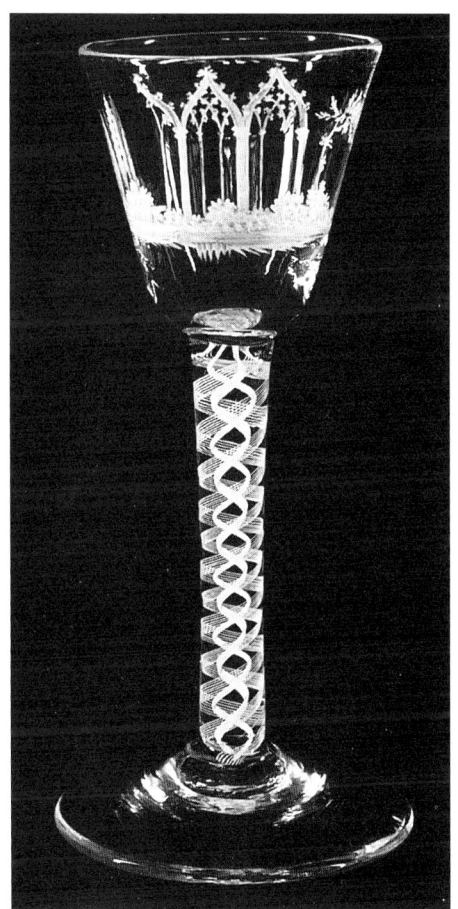

**1,095.** Wine glass; RF bowl, painted in white enamel with tracery of windows of a ruined church; DSOT – pair of 8-ply spiral bands outside pair of spiral tapes. Ht. 6ins. c.1770. Attributed to Beilby.

**1,096.** Wine glass; RF bowl, painted in white enamel with Classical ruins flanked by trees; DSOT – pair of 7-ply spiral bands outside pair of spiral tapes. Ht. 6ins. c.1770. Attributed to Beilby.

**1,097.** Wine glass; RF bowl, painted in white enamel with ruined arch flanked by trees, gilded rim; DSOT – four heavy spiral threads outside gauze. Ht. 5⅜ins. c.1770. Attributed to Beilby.

**1,098.** Wine glass; RF bowl, painted in white enamel with Classical ruins flanked by trees; DSOT – four heavy spiral threads outside gauze. Ht. 5⅜ins. c.1770. Attributed to Beilby.

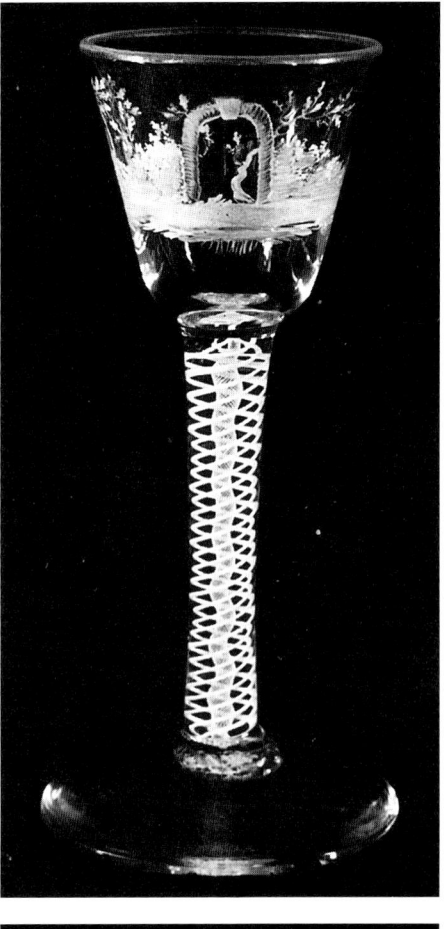

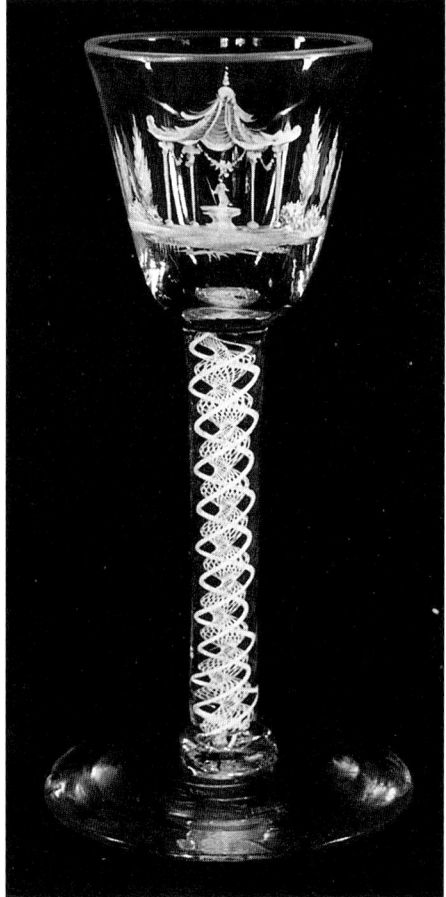

**1,099.** Wine glass; RF bowl, painted in white enamel with obelisk on pedestal, flanked by trees; DSOT – pair of spiral tapes outside gauze. Ht. 5⅜ins. c.1770. Attributed to Beilby.

**1,100.** Wine glass; RF bowl, painted in white enamel with statue beneath canopy, flanked by trees; DSOT – pair of heavy spiral threads outside lace twist. Ht. 5⅜ins. c.1770. Attributed to Beilby.

Enamelling

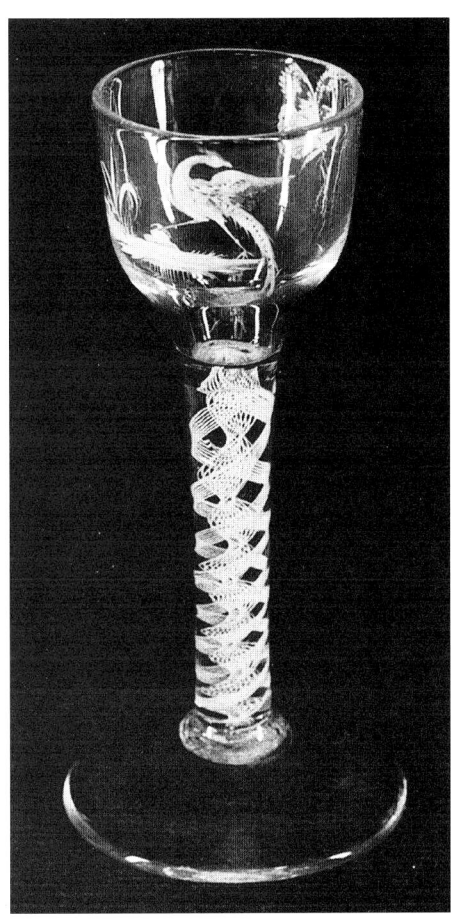

**1,101.** Goblet; square bucket bowl, painted in white enamel with obelisk flanked by trees; DSOT – pair of 7- and 8-ply spiral bands outside lace twist. Ht. 7⅛ins. c.1770. Attributed to Beilby.

**1,102.** Wine glass; ogee bowl, painted in white enamel with exotic bird; DSOT – pair of 8-ply spiral bands outside lace twist. Ht. 5⅜ins. c.1770. Attributed to Beilby.

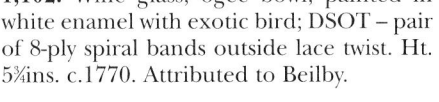

**1,103.** Wine glass; RF bowl, painted in white enamel with birds, fruit and trees; DSOT – alternate 4-ply and single-ply spirals outside lace twist. Ht. 5⅜ins. c.1770. Attributed to Beilby.

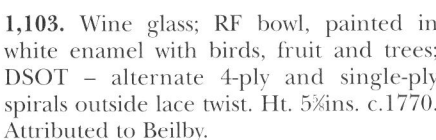

**1,104.** Wine glass; ogee bowl, painted in white enamel with exotic bird, bee and trees; DSOT – pair of heavy spiral threads outside lace twist. Ht. 5⅜ins. c.1770. Attributed to Beilby.

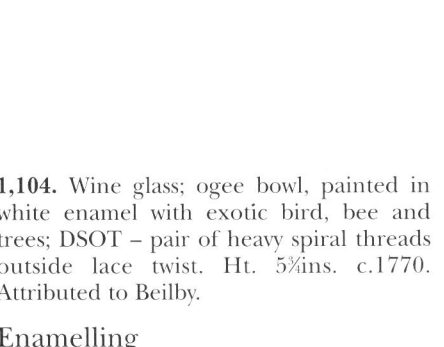

**1,105.** Tumbler; painted in white enamel with a bee and exotic bird on a balustrade. Ht. 4ins. c.1770. Attributed to Beilby.

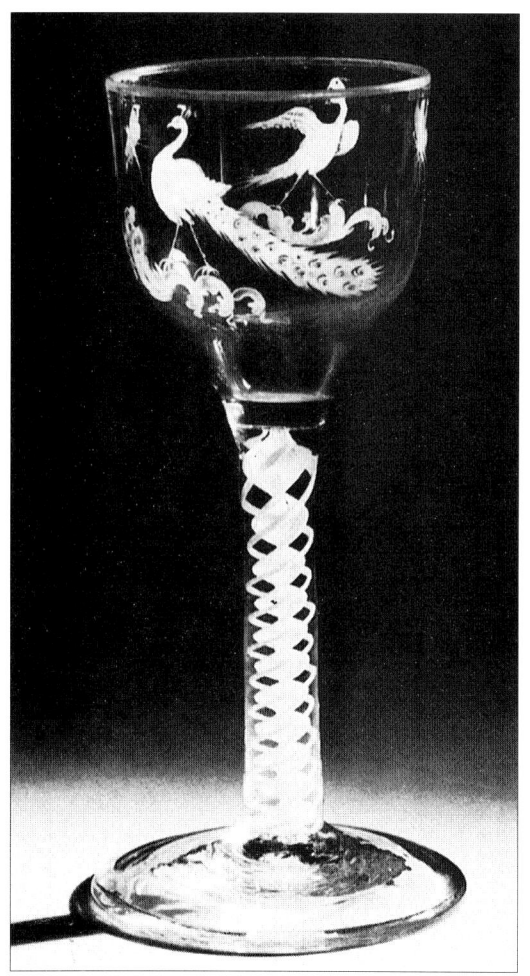

**1,106.** Wine glass; ogee bowl enamelled in white and pale green with two peacocks, traces of gilding on rim; DSOT – pair of spiral tapes outside gauze. Ht. 6¼ins. c.1770. Attributed to Beilby. *Christie's.*

**1,107.** Wine glass; ogee bowl, painted in white and pale blue enamels with peacock, pea-hen and butterflies; DSOT – pair of heavy spiral threads outside multi-ply corkscrew. Ht. 6⅜ins. c.1770. Attributed to Beilby.
*Pilkington Glass Museum, St. Helens.*

**1,108.** Ale glass; RF bowl with gilt rim, painted in white enamel with beehive, bees and flowering plants; DSOT – 20-ply spiral band outside pair of heavy spiral threads. Ht. 7ins. c.1770. Attributed to Beilby.

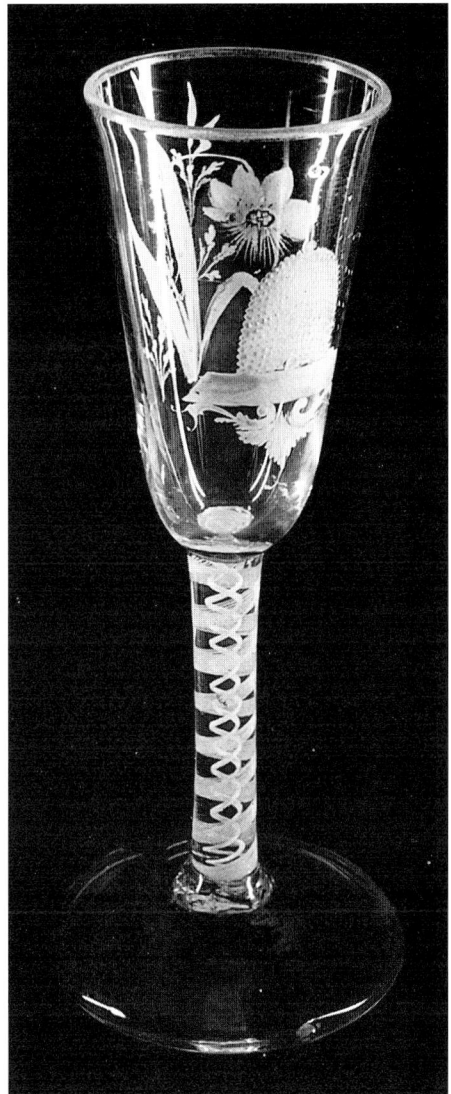

**1,109.** Goblet; RF bowl, painted in green and red enamels with plant and bee design below diamond-point engraved inscription B 1769 *Xmafs* 1770; DSOT – pair of heavy spiral threads outside gauze. Ht. 10ins. c.1769/70. Believed by the owner to have been presented to William Beilby.

**1,110.** Reverse of 1,109 showing diamond-point inscription.

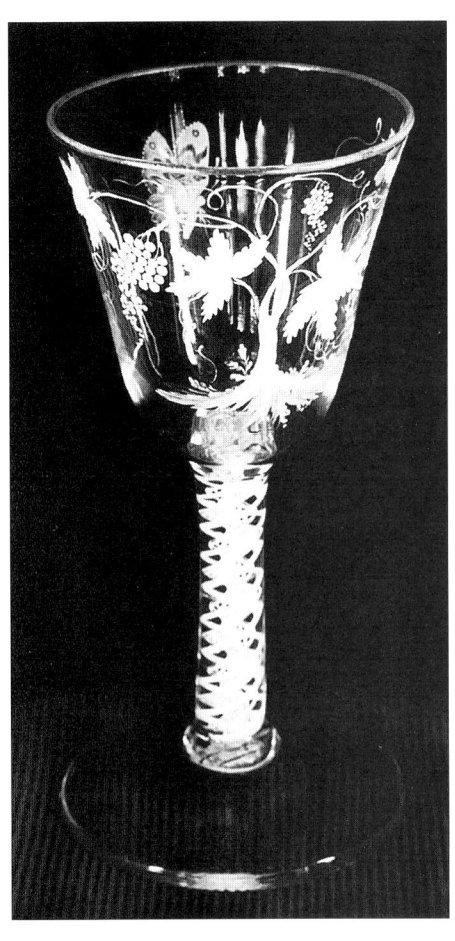

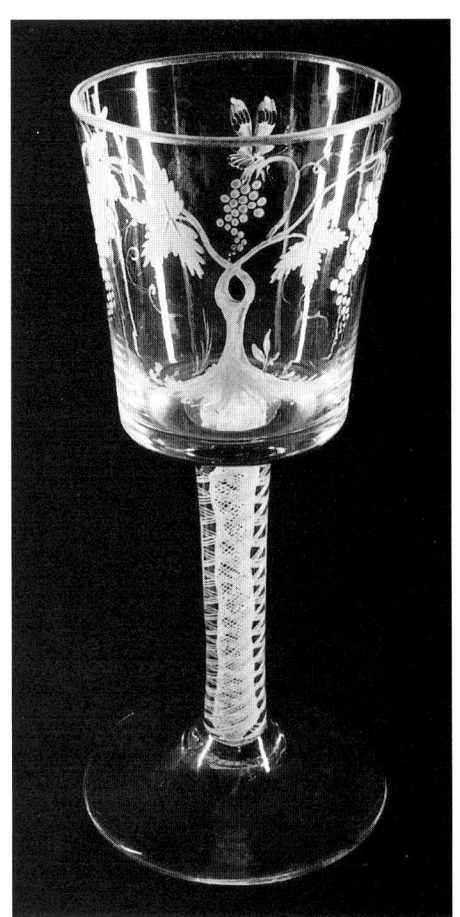

**1,111.** Goblet; RF bowl with gilt rim, painted in white enamel with fruiting vine, butterfly on reverse; DSOT – pair of heavy spiral threads outside lace twist. Ht. 7½ins. c.1770. Attributed to Beilby.

**1,112.** Goblet; bucket bowl with gilt rim; painted in white enamel with growing vine; DSOT – four 3-strand spiral bands outside gauze. Ht. 7½ins. c.1770. Attributed to Beilby.

**1,113.** Dram glass; ogee bowl, painted in white enamel with growing vine; DSOT – 20-ply spiral band outside pair of spiral tapes; terraced foot. Ht. 3¾ins. c.1770. Attributed to Beilby. *Hartshorne Collection.*

**1,114.** Goblet; square bucket bowl enamelled in white with growing vine, a dragonfly on the reverse; DSOT – pair of multi-ply spiral bands outside pair of spiral tapes. Ht. 7½ins. c.1770. Attributed to Beilby. *Christie's.*

Enamelling

**1,115.** Tumbler; painted in white enamel with basket of fruit surmounted by exotic birds. Ht. 4ins. c.1770. Attributed to Beilby.

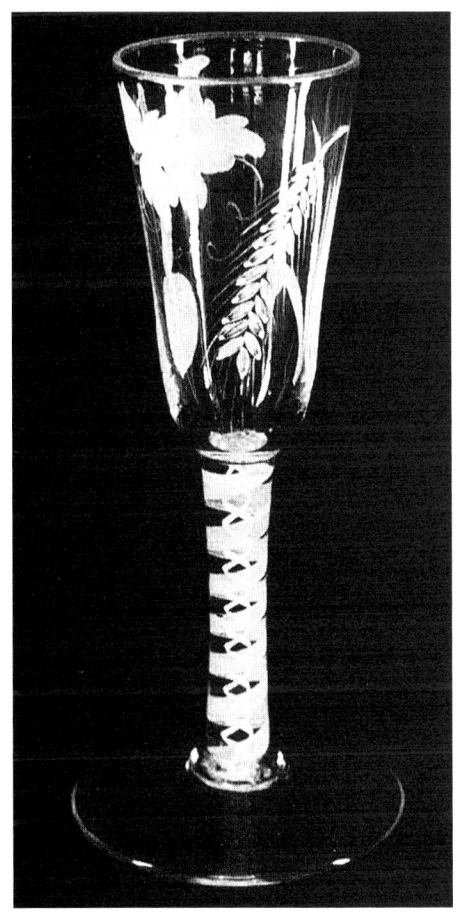

**1,116.** Ale glass; RF bowl, painted in white enamel with hops and barley; DSOT – solid multi-ply spiral band outside pair of spiral tapes. Ht. 7⅛ins. c.1770. Attributed to Beilby.

**1,117.** Ale glass; ogee bowl, painted in white enamel with hops and barley; DSOT – 18-ply spiral band outside pair of spiral tapes. Ht. 7½ins. c.1770. Attributed to Beilby.

**1,118.** Sweetmeat; double-ogee bowl painted in white enamel with floral border; eight-sided moulded pedestal stem with diamonds on shoulders, between collars; D & FF. Ht. 6⅓ins. c.1750, but decorated later. Attributed to Beilby.

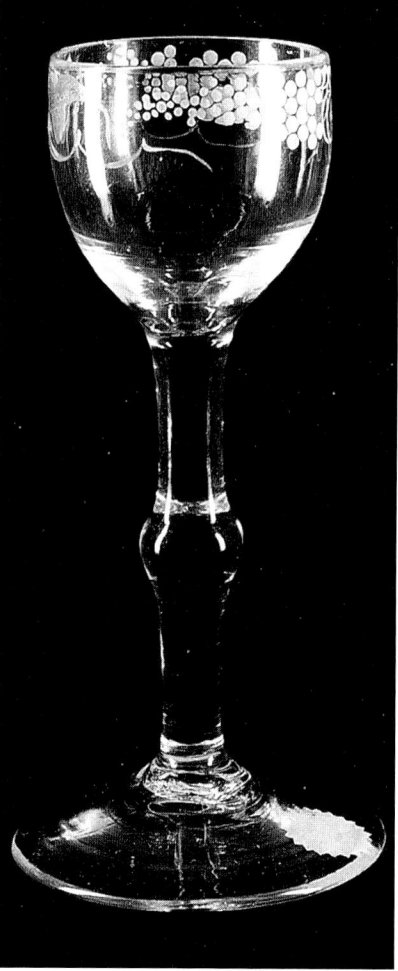

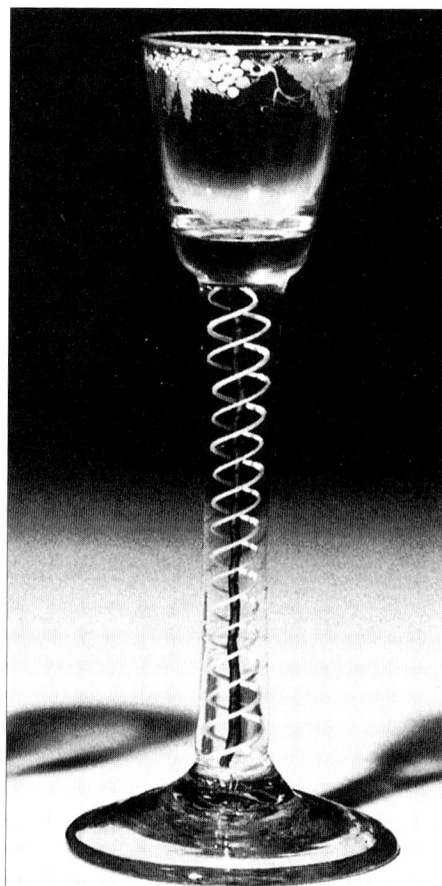

**1,120.** Cordial; RF bowl decorated in white enamel round the rim with a border of fruiting vine; colour-twist stem comprising pair of opaque white tapes outside a cobalt blue vertical thread. Ht. 6⅔ins. c.1770. One of a set of three. Attributed to Beilby.

*Christie's.*

**1,119.** Wine glass; cup bowl, painted in white and green enamel with vine border; balustroid stem with single central knop. Ht. 6⅛ins. c.1750, but decorated later. Attributed to Beilby.

Enamelling

**1,121.** Wine glass; drawn trumpet bowl decorated in white enamel with border of fruiting vine; MSOT. Ht. 6¾ins. c.1770. Attributed to Beilby. *Asprey.*

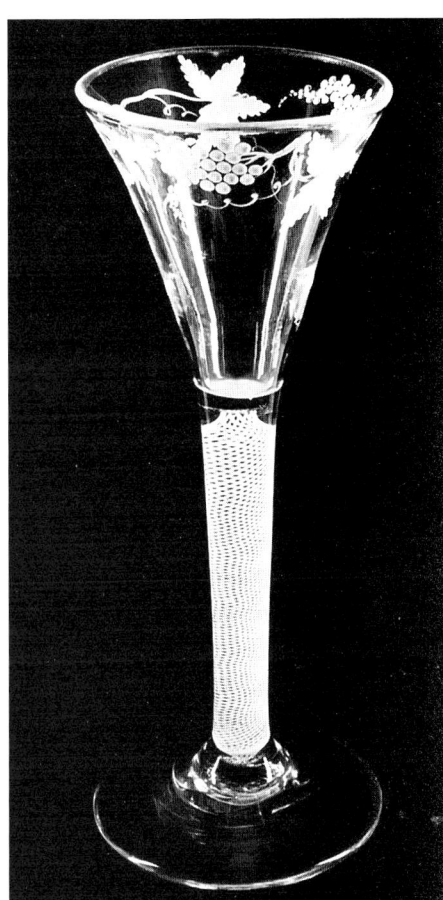

**1,122.** Wine glass; trumpet bowl, painted in white enamel with vine border; MSOT. Ht. 6¾ins. c.1760. Attributed to Beilby.

**1,123.** Goblet; bucket bowl, painted in white enamel with scrolled festoons; DSOT – pair of heavy spiral threads outside multiply corkscrew. Ht. 6¾ins. c.1770. Attributed to Beilby.

**1,124.** Ale glass; ogee bowl, painted in white enamel with geometrical and scroll border; DSOT – solid multi-ply spiral band outside pair of spiral tapes. Ht. 7¼ins. c.1770. Attributed to Beilby.
*Cecil Higgins Museum, Bedford.*

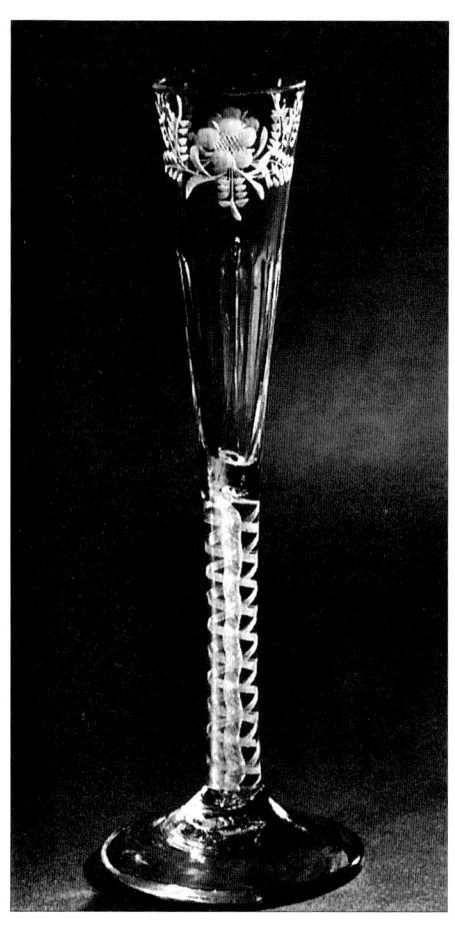

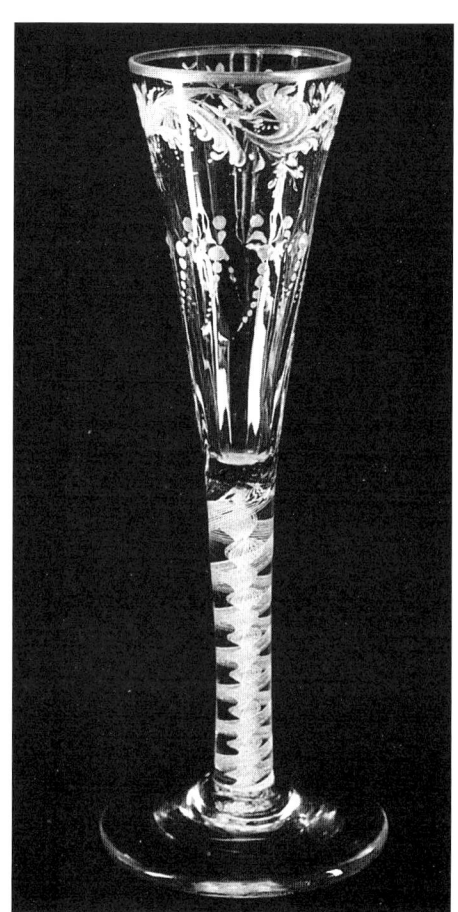

**1,125.** Ratafia; trumpet bowl, fluted lower half, engraved below rim with deep floral border; DSOT – pair of 7-ply spiral bands outside gauze. c.1770.                    *Asprey.*

**1,126.** Ratafia; trumpet bowl with gilt rim, painted in white enamel with scroll border above drops in pale blue enamel; DSOT – 12-ply spiral band outside lace twist. Ht. 7½ins. c.1770. Attributed to Beilby.

**1,127.** Wine glass; bell bowl, painted in white enamel with vine border; DSOT – solid multi-ply spiral band outside pair of heavy spiral threads. Ht. 6⅜ins. c.1770. Attributed to Beilby.

**1,128.** Wine glass; RF bowl, painted in white enamel with floral border; DSOT – 16-ply spiral band outside pair of spiral tapes. Ht. 5¾ins. c.1770. Attributed to Beilby.

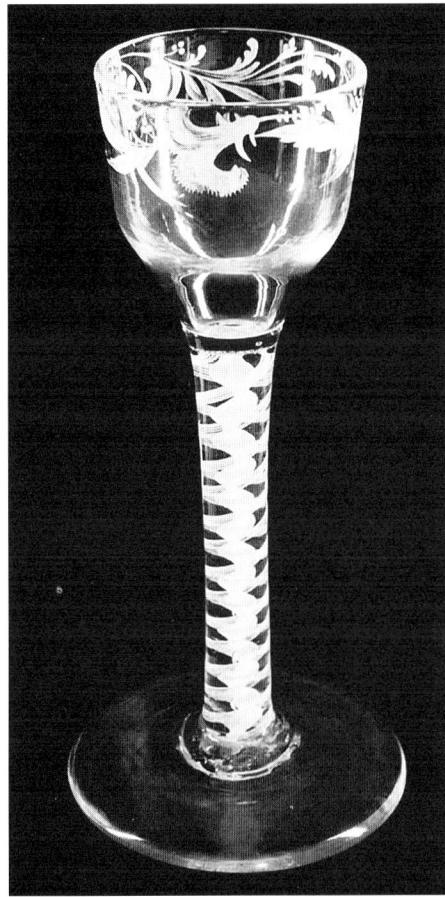

**1,129.** Wine glass; ogee bowl, painted in white enamel with floral border; DSOT – pair of 6-ply spiral bands outside multi-ply corkscrew. Ht. 5⅜ins. c.1770. Attributed to Beilby.

**1,131.** Wine glass; ogee bowl, painted in white enamel with vine border; DSOT – pair of heavy spiral threads outside lace twist. Ht. 5⅜ins. c.1770. Attributed to Beilby.

**1,130.** Wine glass; ogee bowl, painted in white enamel with scroll and star border; DSOT – pair of 8-ply spiral bands outside lace twist. Ht. 6ins. c.1770. Attributed to Beilby.

Enamelling

**1,132.** Dram glass; waisted bowl, painted in white, red and yellow enamels with floral border above Masonic symbols. Ht. 3ins. c.1770. Attributed to Beilby.

**1,133.** Reverse of 1,132.

**1,134.** Toastmaster's glass; deceptive RF bowl, painted in white enamel with lilies-of-the-valley and the inscription TEMPERANCE; short MSAT stem; terraced foot. Ht. 4ins. c.1750, but decorated later. Attributed to Beilby.

**1,135.** Wine glass; funnel bowl decorated in white enamel heightened in puce with two profile medallions between foliate swags, gilt rim; hexagonal-faceted stem. Ht. 6¾ins. c.1785. Attributed to Beilby.

*Lymbery Collection. Christie's.*

Enamelling

**1,136.** Decanter; mallet-shaped body, painted in white enamel with fruiting vine, butterfly and inscription PORT; conical-faceted stopper. Ht. 12ins. (including stopper). c.1770. Attributed to Beilby.
*Hartshorne Collection.*

**1,137.** Decanter; mallet-shaped body, painted in coloured enamels with armorial device and fruiting vines above inscription, in script, TRUTH AND LOYALTY: signed, above the crest Beilby *inv* & *pinx* (Beilby designed and painted); conical-faceted stopper. Ht. 12ins. (including stopper). c.1770.

**1,138.** Close-up of 1,137 showing Beilby signature.

# XVII
# Decoration: Gilding

**1,139.** Wine glass in green metal; cup bowl with gilt rim, decorated in gilt with sprays of flowers; plain stem. Ht. 6¼ins. c.1765. Attributed to James Giles of Bristol. *Smith Collection. Harvey's Wine Museum, Bristol.*

**1,140.** Goblet; ogee bowl gilded fruiting vine and rim; plain stem. Ht. 7½ins. c.1760. *Sotheby's.*

**1,141.** Wine glass; ogee bowl decorated in gilt with a branch of fruiting vine; plain stem. Ht. 5¾ins. c.1765. *Christie's.*

348

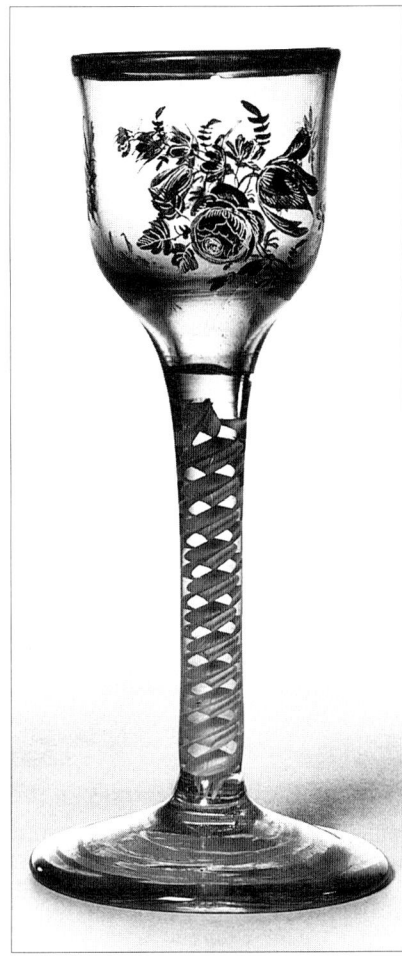

**1,142.** Wine glass; ogee bowl decorated in gilt with loose bouquet and scattered flowers, gilt rim; DSOT – pair of spiral tapes outside corkscrew. Ht. 6ins. c.1770. *Christie's.*

**1,143.** Small goblet; vertically ribbed cup bowl with gilt rim, decorated in gilt with insects and sprays of flowers; slightly wrythen plain stem; radially moulded foot. Ht. 5ins. c.1765.

**1,144.** Goblet; pointed RF bowl, decorated in gilt with fruiting vine; DSOT – 12-ply spiral band outside lace twist. Ht. 7½ins. c.1770.

**1,145.** Wine glass; ogee bowl with gilt rim, decorated in gilt with fruiting vine; DSOT – pair of corkscrews outside pair of heavy spiral threads. Ht. 6ins. c.1770.

**1,146.** Wine glass; RF bowl with gilt rim, decorated in gilt with floral border above vertical panels; DSOT – multi-ply spiral band outside spiral of one heavy and two light threads. Ht. 6ins. c.1770.

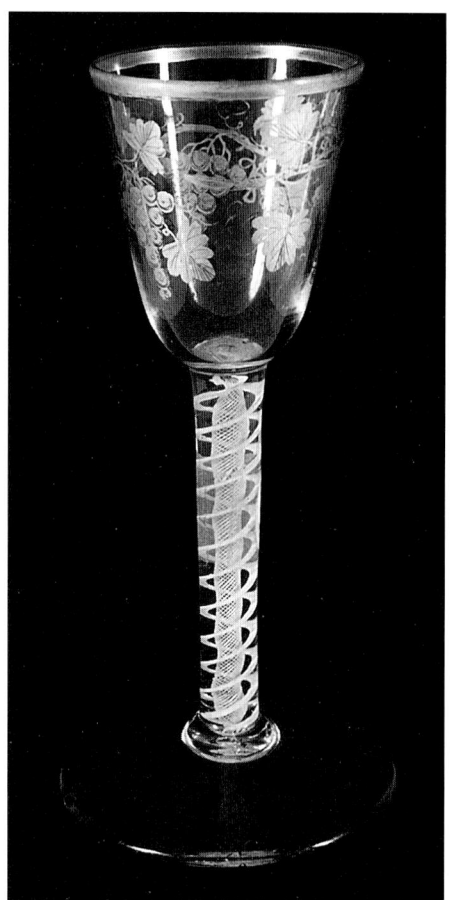

**1,147.** Wine glass; RF bowl with gilt rim, decorated in gilt with fruiting vine; DSOT – pair of spiral tapes outside gauze. Ht. 5½ins. c.1770.
*Smith Collection. Harvey's Wine Museum, Bristol.*

**1,148.** Wine glass; ogee bowl with gilt rim, decorated in gilt with bouquet of flowers; diamond-faceted stem. Ht. 6ins. c.1785.

Gilding

# XVIII
# Coloured Glass

**1,149.** Wine glass; purple glass; the cup bowl inscribed in gold GOD BLESS KING WILLIAM AND QUEEN MARY; plain stem with basal knop. Ht. 4⅝ins. c.1690 (!).
*Victoria and Albert Museum.*

**1,150.** Wine glass in green-tinted metal; cup-shaped bowl with vertical ribbing continuing on to hollow stem and wrythen foot. Ht. 4⅝ins. c.1750.          *Sotheby's.*

**1,151.** Wine glass; pale emerald-green tint; cup bowl; hollow double-knopped stem with basal knop; high DF. Ht. 6ins. c.1740.
*Christie's.*

**1,153.** Monteith, dark blue tint; double-ogee bowl, wrythen moulding; flattened knop. Ht. 3ins. c.1750. *Christie's.*

**1,152.** Monteith of dark blue tint; double-ogee bowl with 'nipt diamond-waies' moulding. Ht. 3ins. c.1750.
*Christie's.*

**1,155.** Wine glass; green-tinted cup-shaped bowl; knop with three raspberry prunts over a clear glass stem with opaque white corkscrew; green-tinted DF. Ht. 6ins. c.1750. *Christie's.*

**1,154.** Wine glass, pale green tint; cup-shaped bowl; slender shoulder-knopped stem. Ht. 6¼ins. c.1750. *Christie's.*

Coloured Glass

# XIX
# Details of Stems

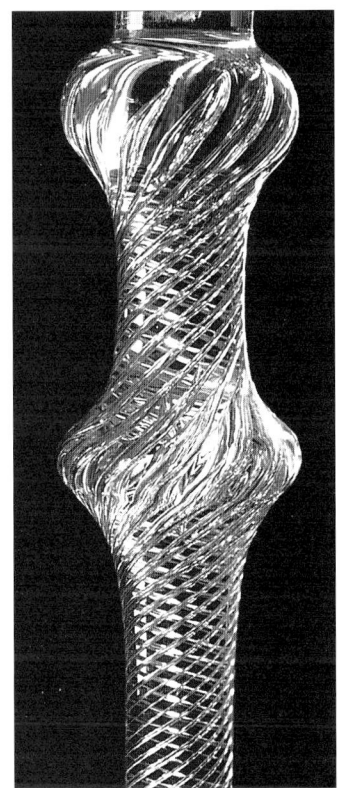

**1,156.** MSAT – multiple-spiral air twist.

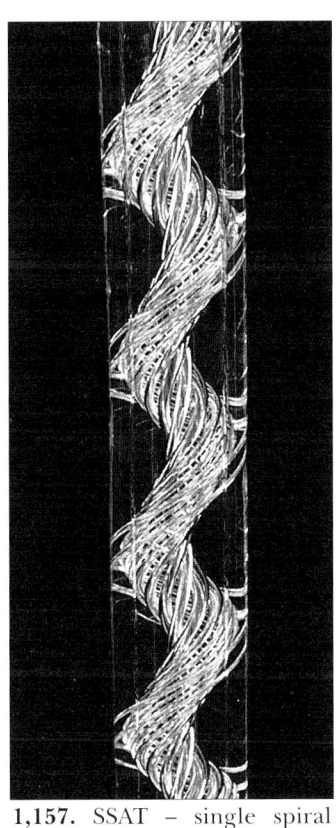

**1,157.** SSAT – single spiral cable.

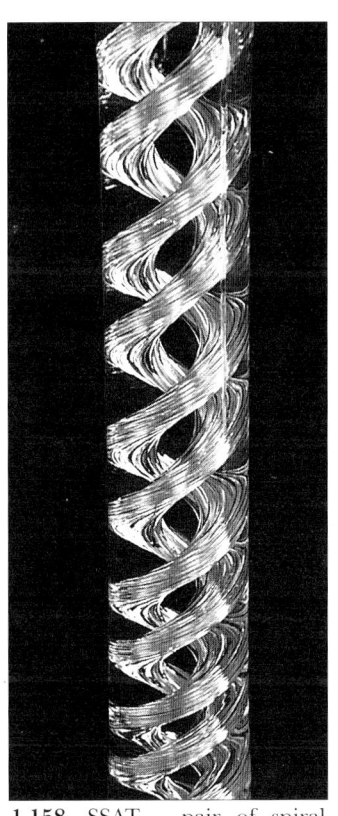

**1,158.** SSAT – pair of spiral cables.

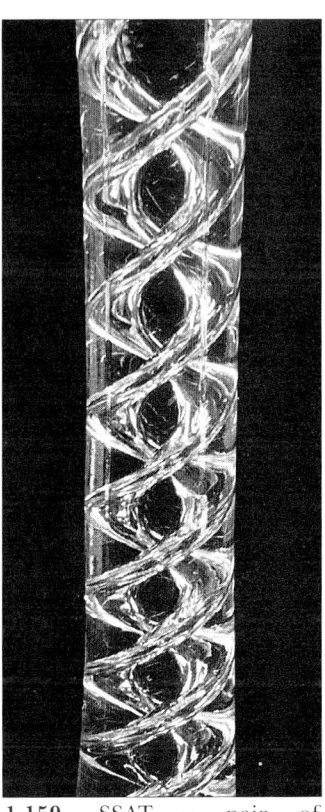

**1,159.** SSAT – pair of corkscrews ('mercury twist').

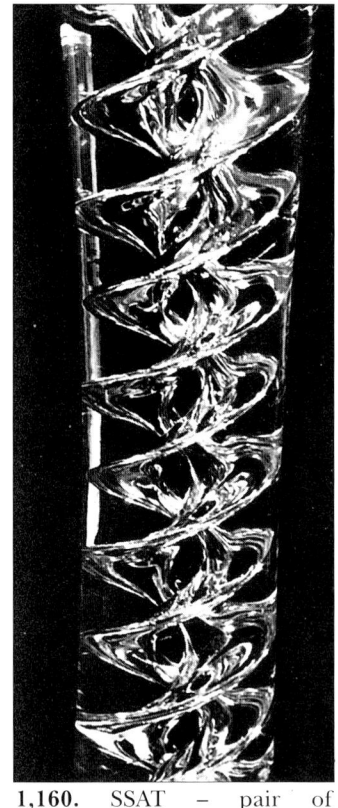

**1,160.** SSAT – pair of corkscrews ('mercury twist').

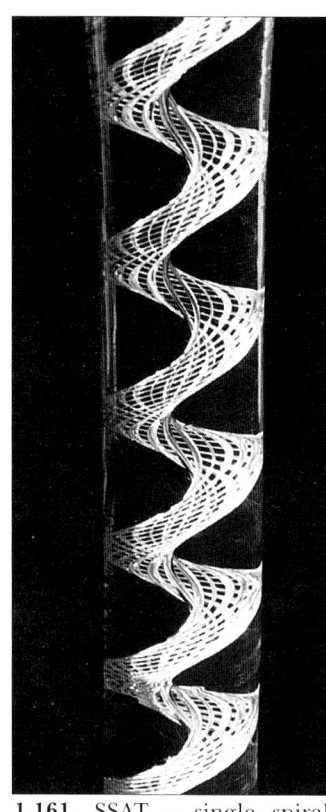

**1,161.** SSAT – single spiral gauze.

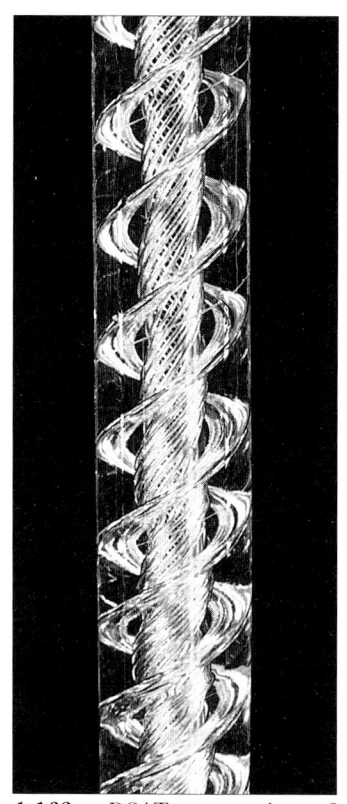

**1,162.** DSAT – pair of corkscrews outside cable.

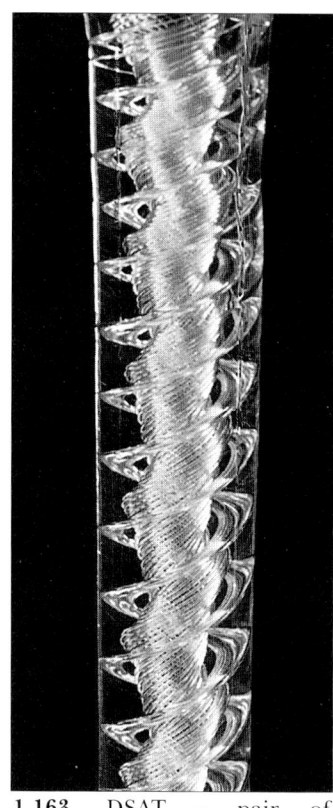

**1,163.** DSAT – pair of corkscrews outside spiral cable.

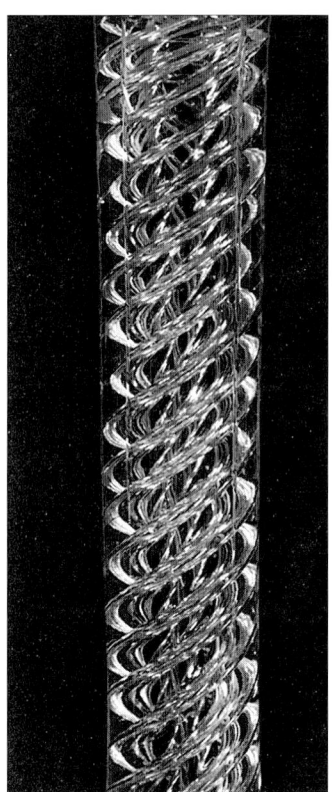

**1,164.** DSAT – four spirals outside loose vertical cable.

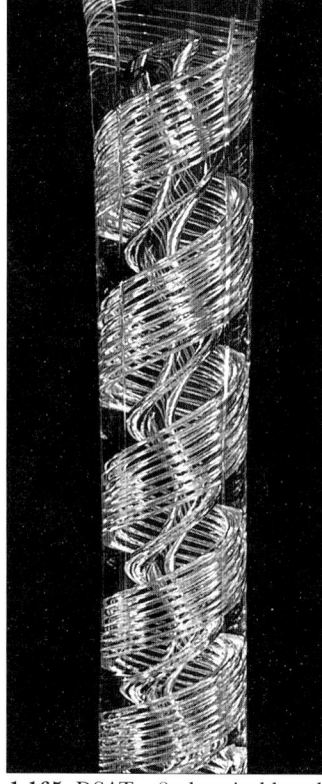

**1,165.** DSAT – 8-ply spiral band outside loose spiral cable.

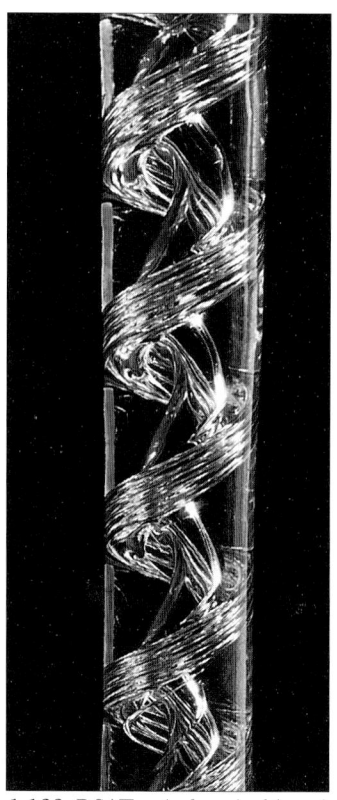

**1,166.** DSAT – 4-ply spiral band outside loose spiral threads.

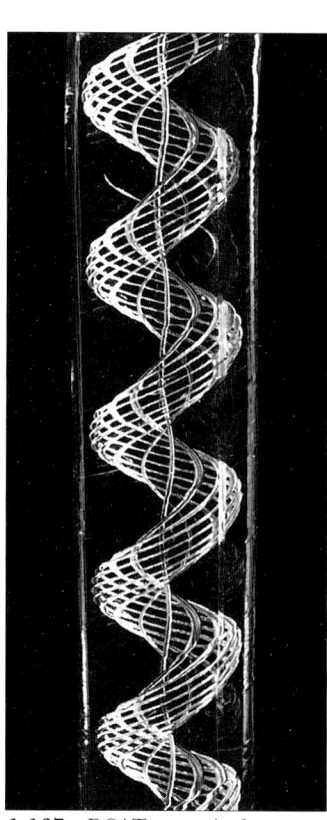

**1,167.** DSAT – spiral gauze outside vertical thread.

Details of Stems

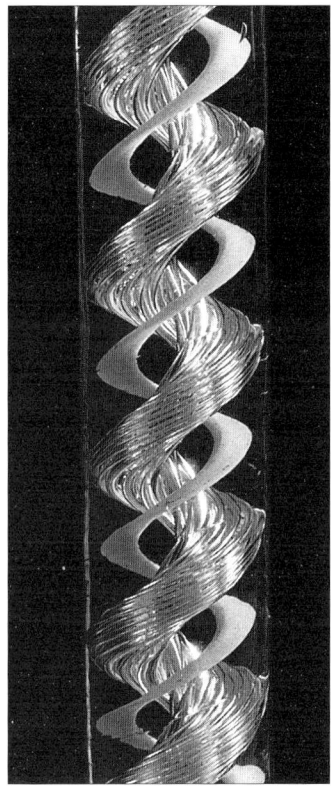

**1,168.** Mixed twist – spiral air cable alternating with opaque corkscrew.

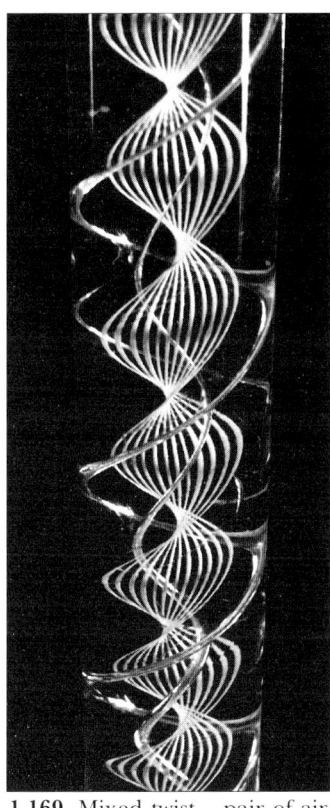

**1,169.** Mixed twist – pair of air spiral threads outside opaque loose corkscrew.

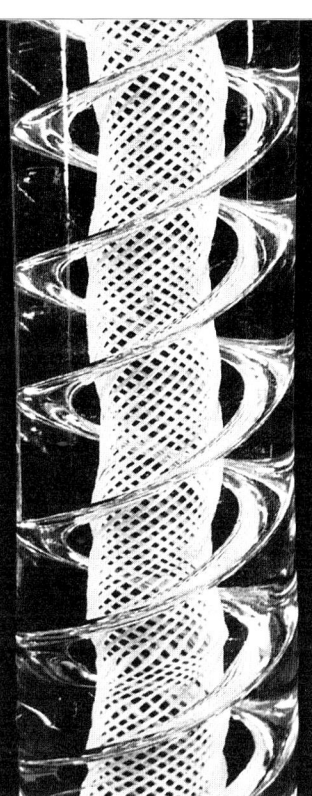

**1,170.** Mixed twist – pair of air spirals outside opaque gauze.

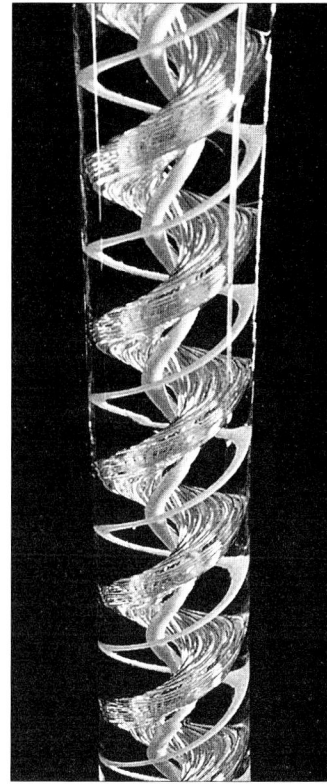

**1,171.** Mixed twist – air spiral cable alternating with opaque spiral thread outside single opaque heavy spiral thread.

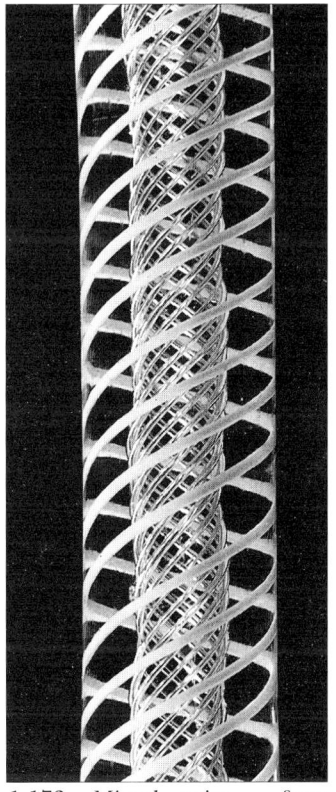

**1,172.** Mixed twist – four opaque heavy spiral threads outside multiple-spiral air twist.

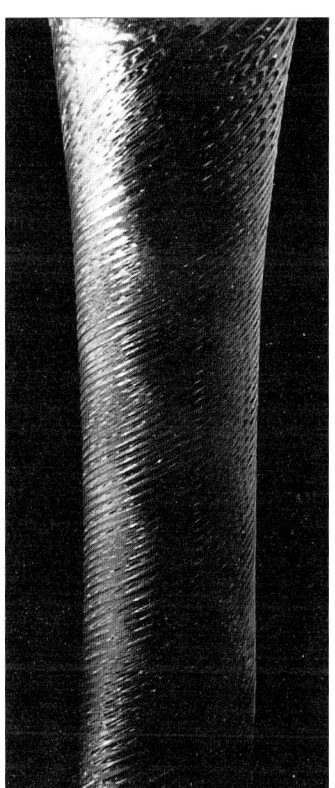

**1,173.** Incised twist.

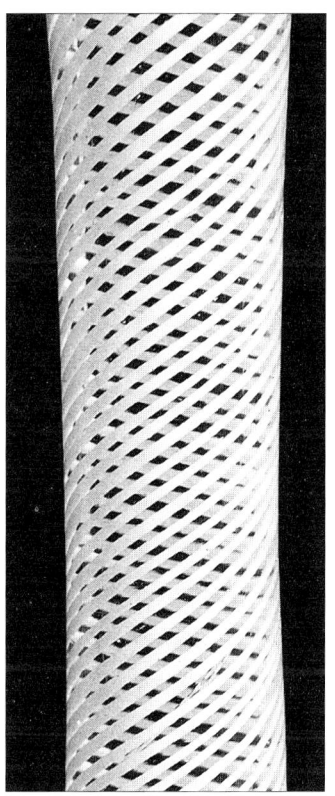

**1,174.** MSOT – multiple-spiral opaque twist.

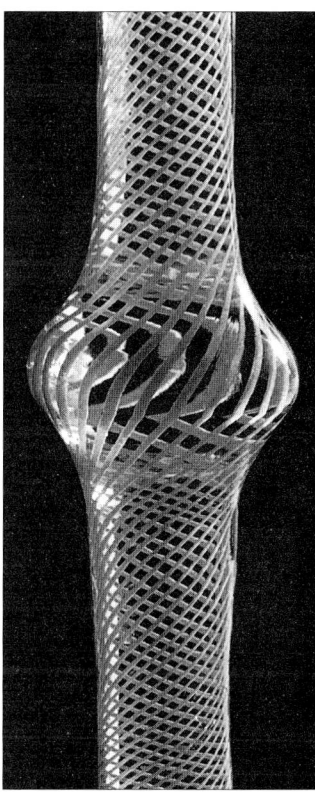

**1,175.** MSOT – multiple-spiral opaque twist.

**1,176.** SSOT – multi-ply corkscrew outlined.

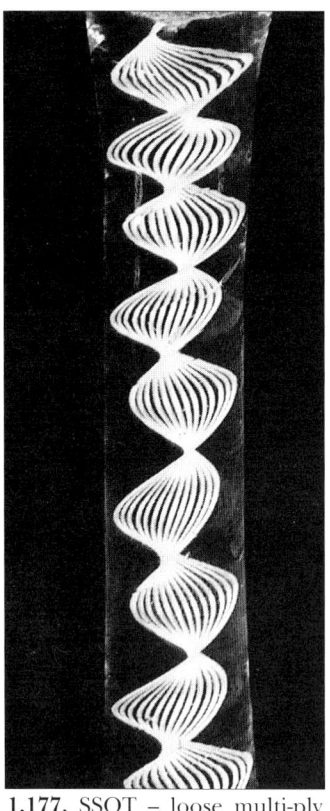

**1,177.** SSOT – loose multi-ply corkscrew.

**1,178.** SSOT – multi-ply corkscrew.

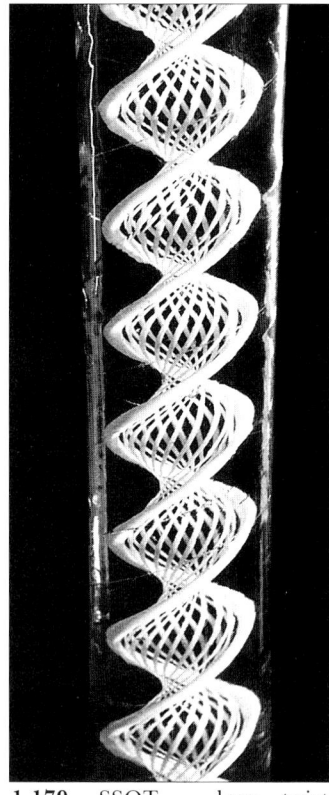

**1,179.** SSOT – lace twist outlined.

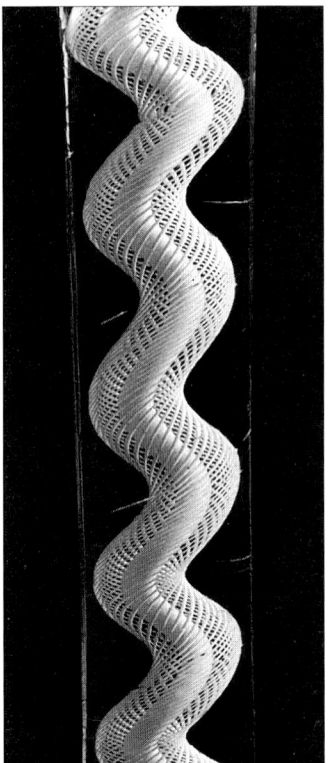

**1,180.** SSOT – spiral gauze with core.

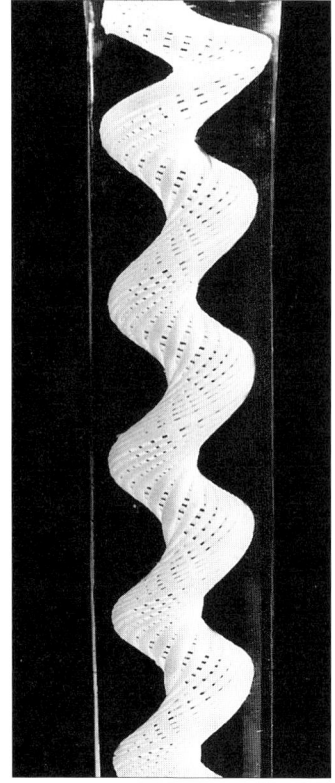

**1,181.** SSOT – spiral cable.

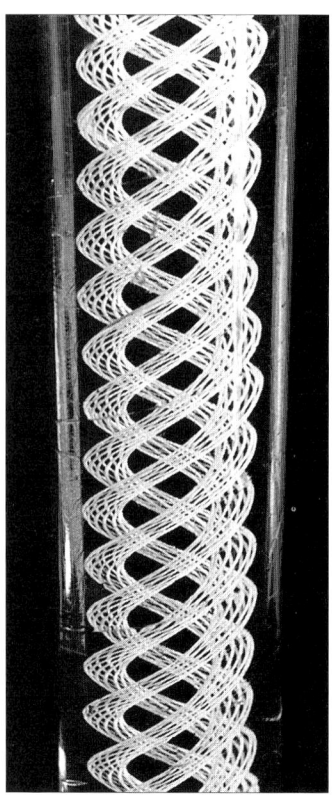

**1,182.** SSOT – four spiral gauzes.

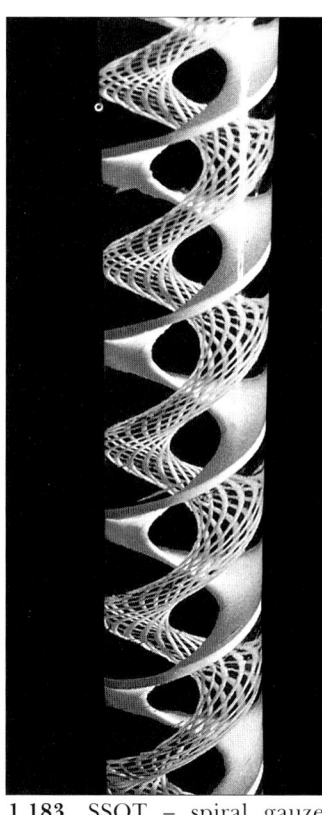

**1,183.** SSOT – spiral gauze alternating with single corkscrew.

Details of Stems

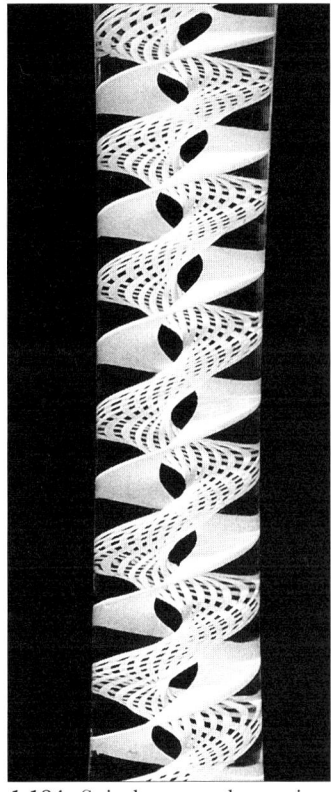

**1,184.** Spiral gauze alternating with spiral tape. Close-up of 598. *Tibbenham Collection, Ipswich Museum.*

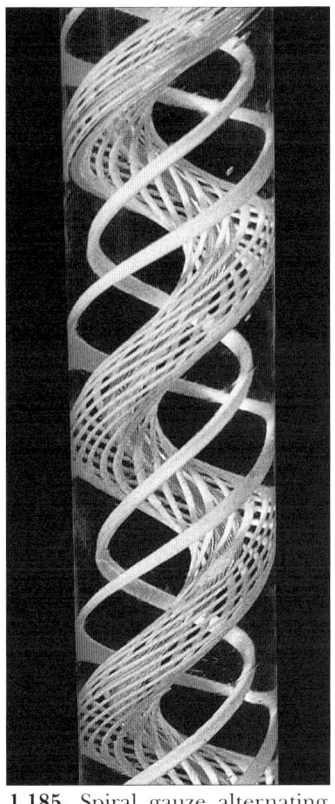

**1,185.** Spiral gauze alternating with pair of heavy spiral threads. Close-up of 592. *Tibbenham Collection, Ipswich Museum.*

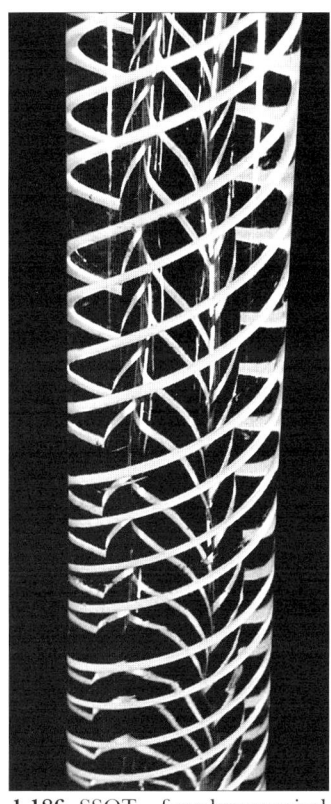

**1,186.** SSOT – four heavy spiral threads outside long tear.

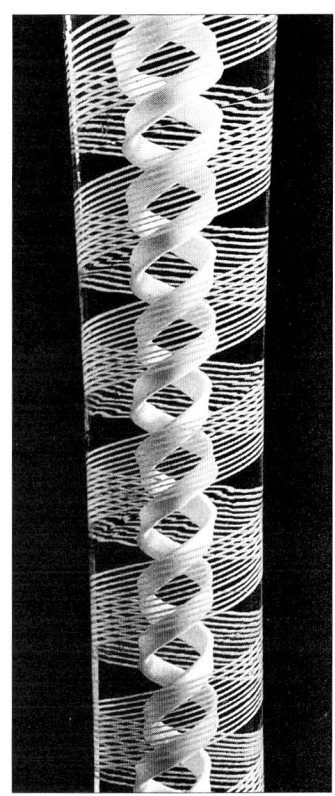

**1,187.** DSOT – 12-ply spiral band outside pair of spiral tapes.

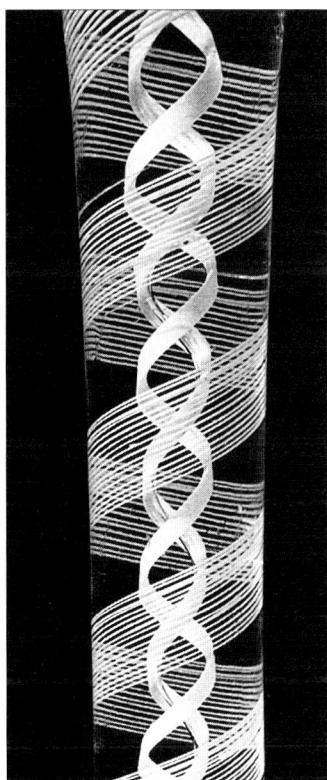

**1,188.** DSOT – 17-ply spiral band outside pair of spiral tapes.

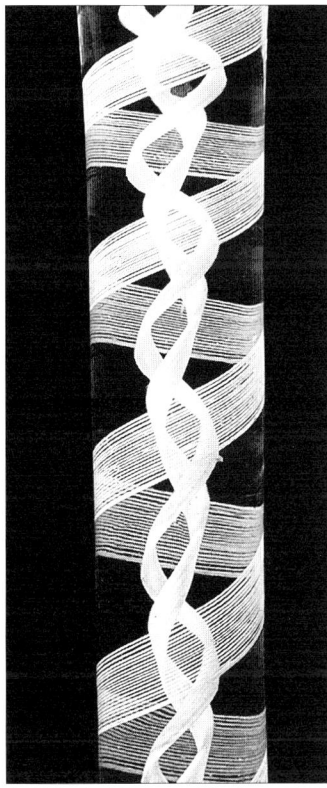

**1,189.** DSOT – 20-ply spiral band outside pair of tapes in a loose spiral.

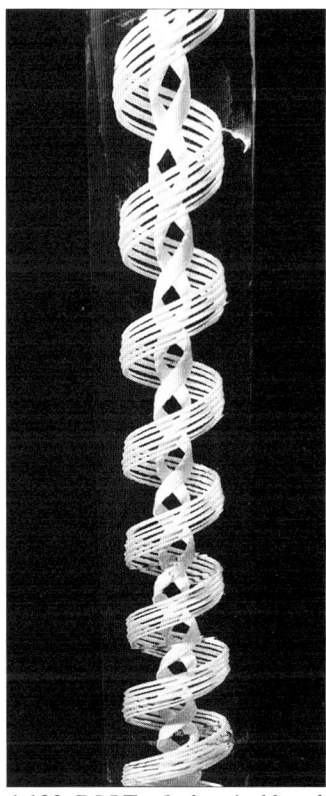

**1,190.** DSOT – 6-ply spiral band outside pair of spiral tapes.

**1,191.** DSOT – solid multi-ply spiral band outside pair of heavy spiral threads.

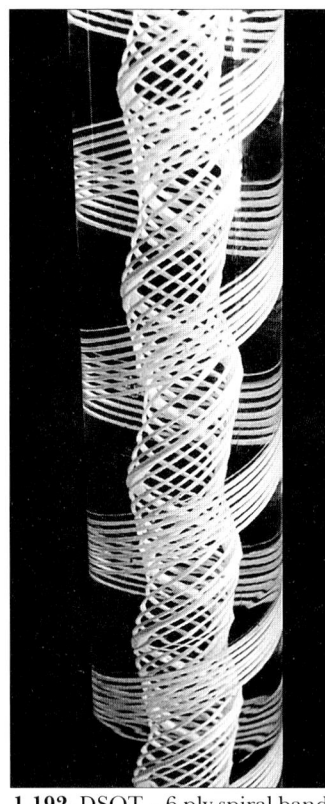

**1,192.** DSOT – 6-ply spiral band outside spiral gauze.

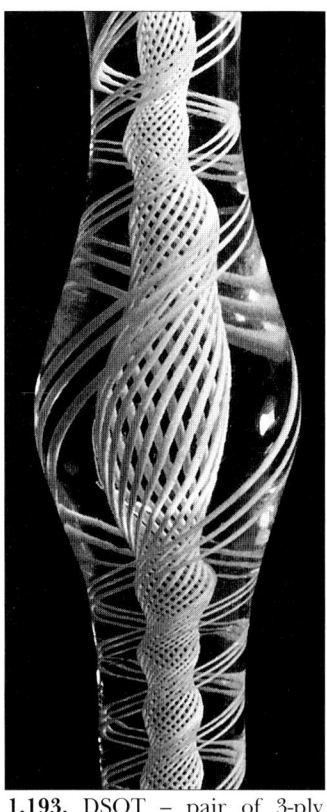

**1,193.** DSOT – pair of 3-ply spiral bands outside gauze.

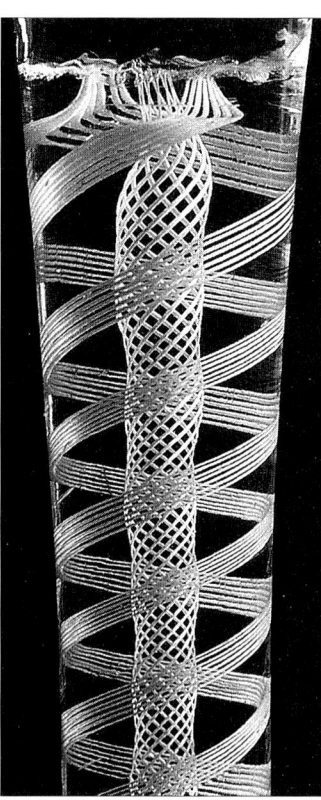

**1,194.** DSOT – pair of 7-ply spiral bands outside gauze.

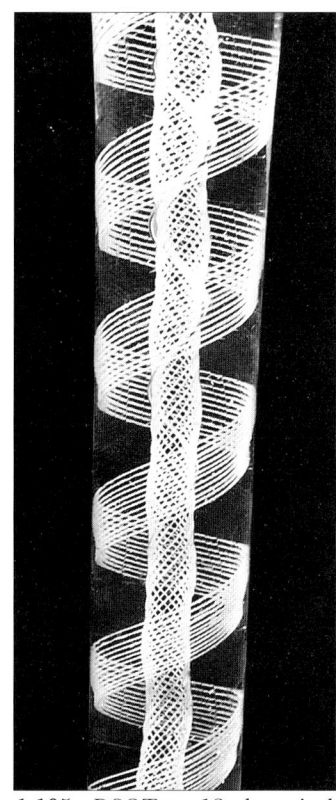

**1,195.** DSOT – 12-ply spiral band outside gauze.

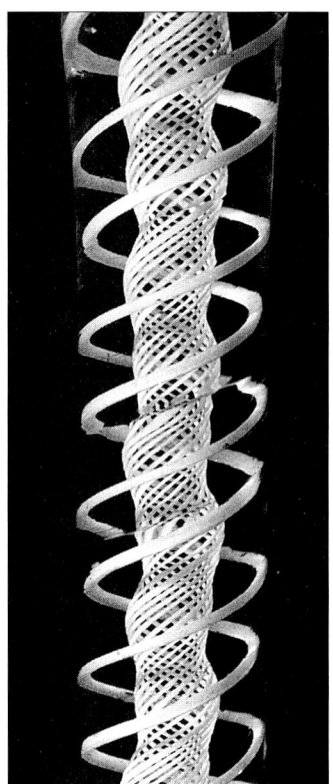

**1,196.** DSOT – pair of heavy spiral threads outside gauze.

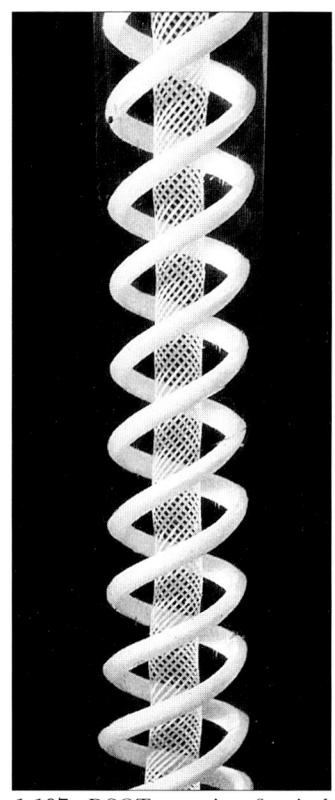

**1,197.** DSOT – pair of spiral tapes outside vertical gauze.

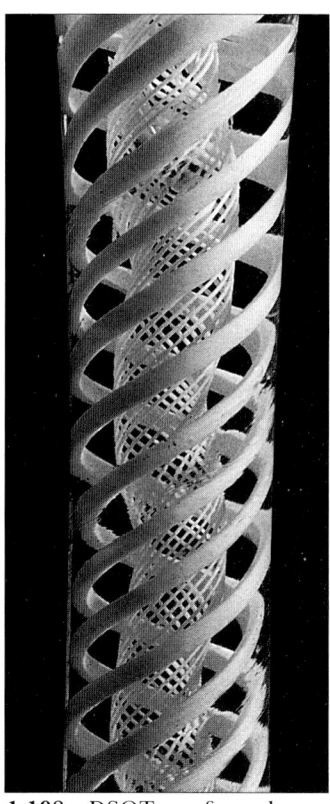

**1,198.** DSOT – four heavy spiral threads outside gauze.

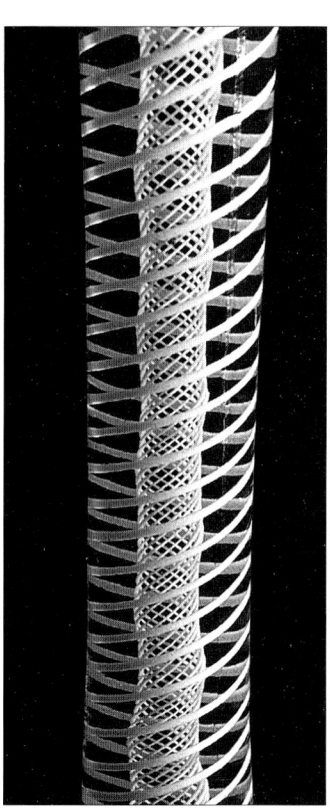

**1,199.** DSOT – four spiral threads outside gauze.

Details of Stems

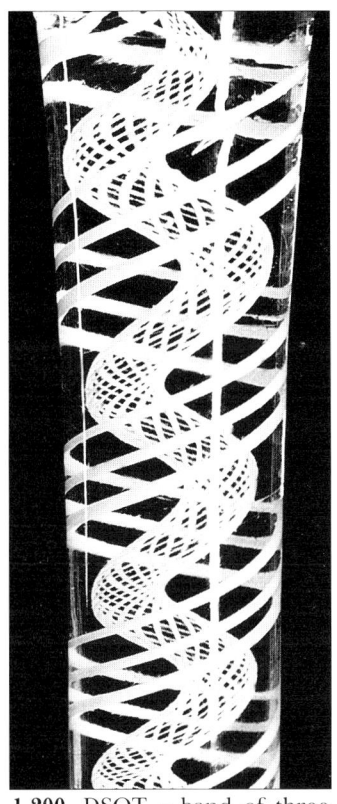

**1,200.** DSOT – band of three spiral threads outside spiral gauze.

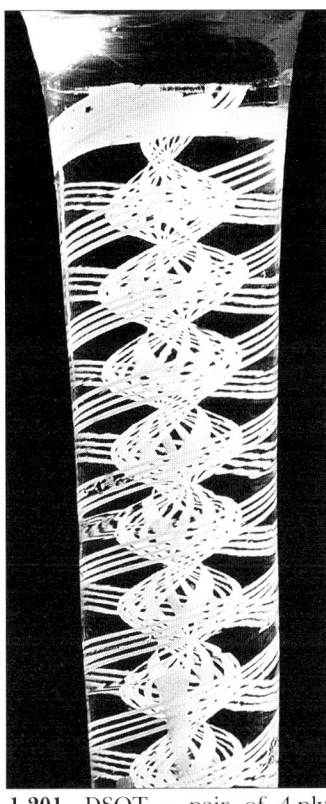

**1,201.** DSOT – pair of 4-ply spiral bands outside lace twist.

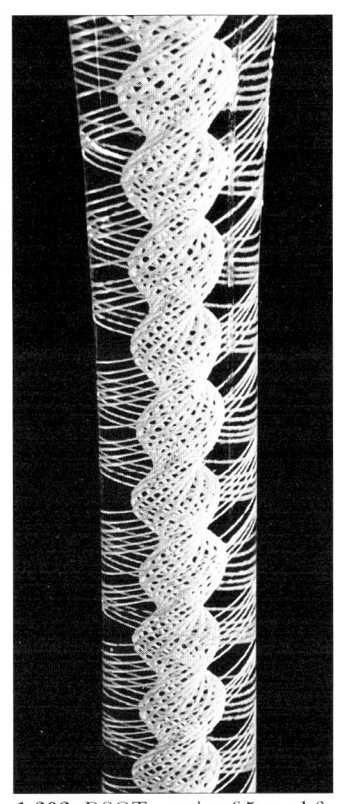

**1,202.** DSOT – pair of 5- and 6-ply spiral bands outside lace twist.

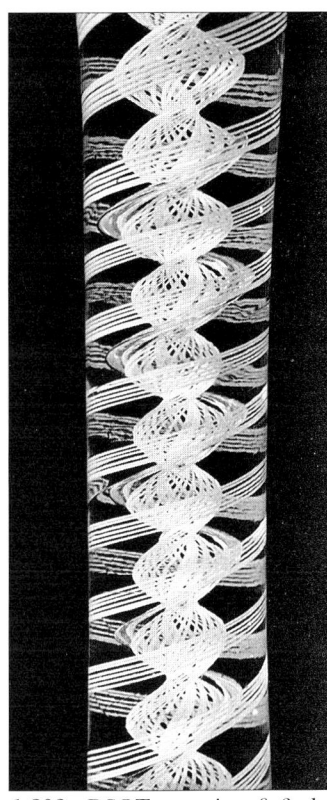

**1,203.** DSOT – pair of 6-ply spiral bands outside lace twist.

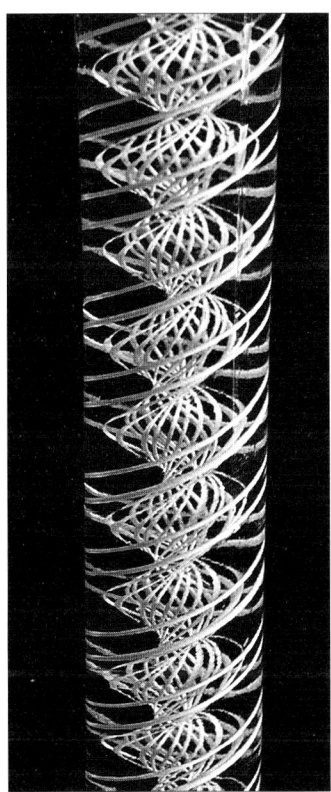

**1,204.** DSOT – two pairs of spiral threads outside lace twist.

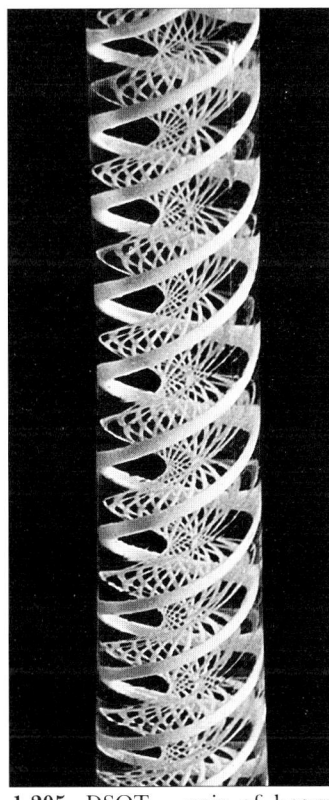

**1,205.** DSOT – pair of heavy spiral threads outside lace twist.

**1,206.** DSOT – pair of heavy spiral threads outside multi-ply corkscrew.

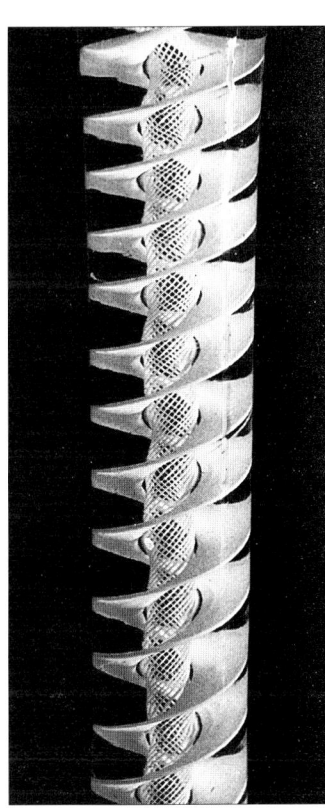

**1,207.** DSOT – pair of corkscrews outside gauze.

**1,208.** DSOT – pair of corkscrews outside single corkscrew.

**1,209.** DSOT – pair of heavy spiral threads outside solid vertical cable.

**1,210.** DSOT – pair of heavy spiral threads outside loose vertical cable.

**1,211.** DSOT – pair of spiral threads outside spiral cable.

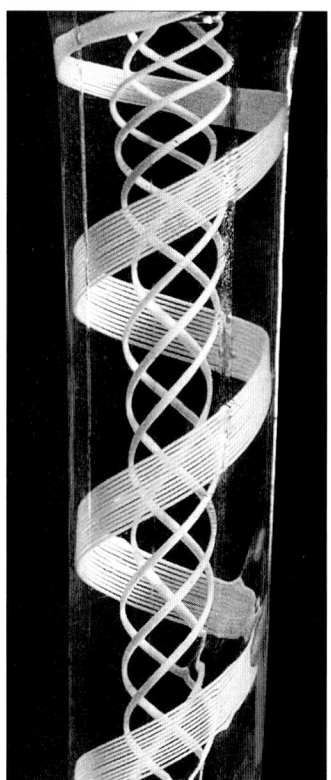

**1,212.** DSOT – 12-ply spiral band outside 4-ply column.

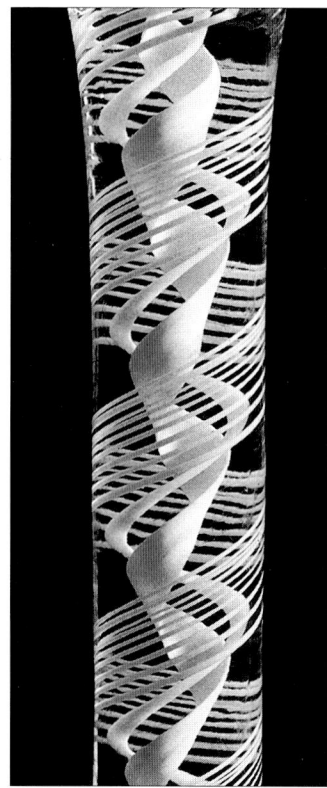

**1,213.** DSOT – 9-ply spiral band outside alternate wide and narrow spiral tapes.

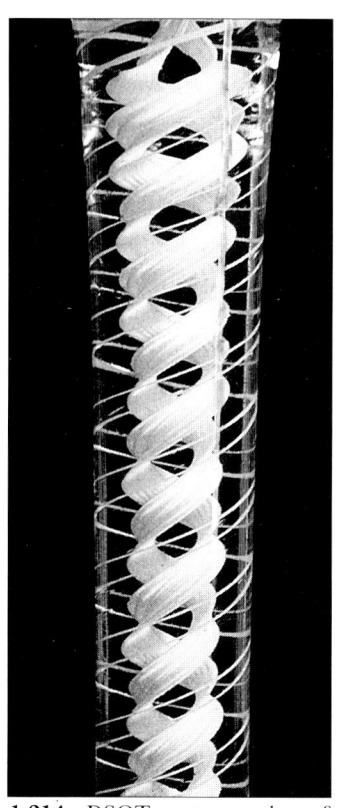

**1,214.** DSOT – two pairs of spiral threads outside pair of spiral tapes.

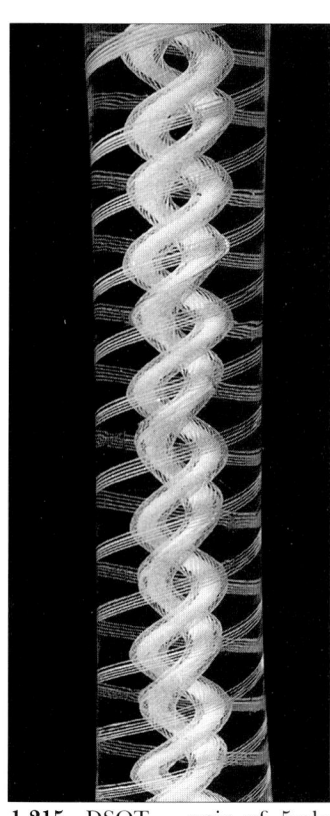

**1,215.** DSOT – pair of 5-ply spiral bands outside pair of spiral gauzes with core.

Details of Stems

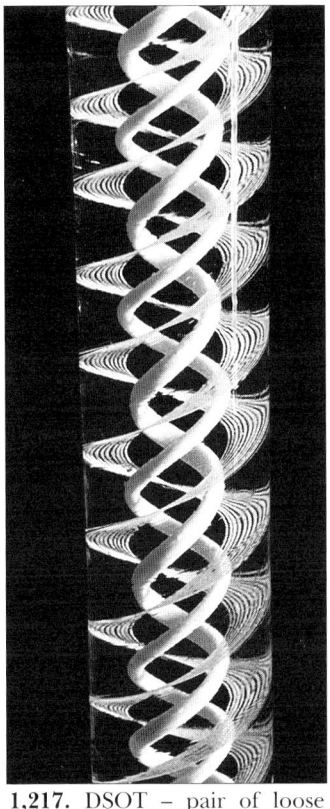

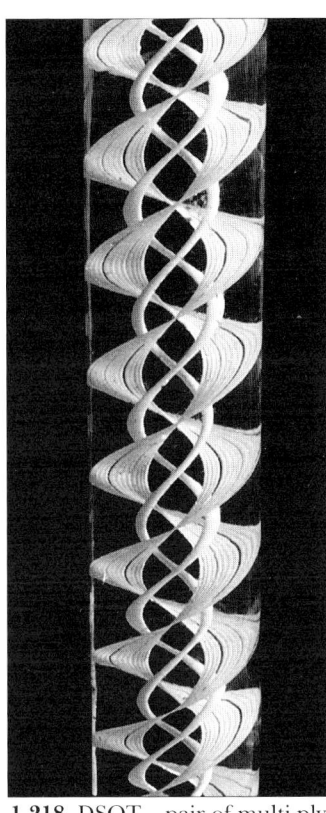

**1,216.** DSOT – 6-ply spiral band outside pair of tapes in tight spiral.

**1,217.** DSOT – pair of loose multi-ply corkscrews outside pair of heavy spiral threads.

**1,218.** DSOT – pair of multi-ply corkscrews outside pair of spiral threads.

**1,219.** Faceted stem – diamond facets.

**1,220.** Faceted stem – hexagonal facets.

Details of Stems

# Bibliography of English Glass

**Bibliographer's note**

In this bibliography an attempt is made to cover the literature produced in the field of English glass studies during the last hundred years or so. The list excludes pure technology, book reviews, ancient glass and sale catalogues. The reader is reminded, however, that catalogues of important sales provide useful supplementary information on all types of glass.

For reasons of space the entries are not critical but explanatory annotations or notes have been added where it has seemed desirable to clarify the title or content of an item. As a large proportion of the material dealt with consists of articles, the Bibliography is to a considerable degree analytical in form. In order to increase the specific subject coverage the analytical principle has been extended in several cases to books where important subject content is not revealed by the title of the work. The most straightforward arrangement has been adopted, that is alphabetically by author or title, with the general index providing the subject key. The Bibliography as a whole will, it is hoped, complete the purpose of this volume, which is to supply a working guide for all interested in studying and collecting English glass.

D. Robert Elleray
Worthing, June 1986

## Abbreviations of periodical titles most referred to

| | |
|---|---|
| *A* | *Antiques* |
| *AC* | *Antique Collector* |
| *ADGC* | *Antique Dealers and Collectors' Guide* |
| *AP* | *Apollo* |
| *BUR* | *Burlington Magazine* |
| *CJGS* | *Journal of Glass Studies* (Corning Museum of Glass, New York) |
| *CL* | *Country Life* |
| *CONN* | *Connoisseur* |
| *GC* | *Papers of the Circle of Glass Collectors* (Glass Circle). London (duplicated typescripts) |
| *GN* | *Glass notes* (Arthur Churchill, Ltd. – no longer issued) |
| *ILN* | *Illustrated London News* |
| *JSGT* *TSGT* | *Journal and/or Transactions of the Society of Glass Technology* (Sheffield) |

NOTE Readers are reminded that the volumes of the *British Union Catalogue of Periodicals* (which may be consulted at most public reference libraries) will provide locations for the periodicals referred to in the Bibliography.

## Other abbreviations

| | |
|---|---|
| Assn. | Association |
| bibliog. | bibliography |
| Bull. | Bulletin |
| col. | coloured |
| comp. | compiler |
| diags. | diagrams |
| ed. | edition, editor |
| facsims. | facsimiles |
| Gaz. | Gazette |
| illus. | illustration(s) |
| Inst. | Institute |
| Jnl. | Journal |
| Mag. | Magazine |
| nd. | no date |
| priv. print. | privately printed |
| Proc. | Proceedings |
| p. | page(s) |
| ports. | portraits |
| Rev. | Review |
| Soc. | Society |
| Trans. | Transactions |

ABERG, F.A. *joint author see* CROSSLEY, D. W. *and* ABERG, F.A.

1   'Adam and Eve engraved on a seventeenth-century goblet [from the Marshall Collection, Ashmolean Museum]. In *CL*, Sept 1969, p.569, *illus.*

2   ADAMSON, C.E. *John Dagnia, glassblower.* South Shields, 1894.

3   'John Dagnia of South Shields, Glass-maker'. In *Proc. of the Society of Antiquaries of Newcastle-upon-Tyne*, v.6, p.163-8.

4   [AITKEN, William Costen]. *The glass manufacturers of Birmingham and Stourbridge.* Birmingham, J.F. Feeney, 1851, 18p. Reprinted for private distribution from the *Birmingham Journal*, May 31st 1851.

5   ALFIERI, Bernard. 'The beauty of glass'. In *British Jnl. of Photography*, Jan 1958, p.58-60, *illus.*

6   ALFORD, B.W.E. 'The flint and bottle glass industry in the early nineteenth century [Phoenix Glassworks, Bristol]'. In *Business History*, 10 Jun 1968, p.12-21.

7   'Ancient Irish glasses'. In *CONN*, Jan-Apr 1903, p.282-3, illus.

8   ANGUS-BUTTERWORTH, Lionel Milner. *British Table and ornamental glass.* L. Hill, 1956, 123p., *illus.*
    Contents include: Annals of glass in Britain, AD 1220-1953, p.105-9; Apsley Pellatt (cameo incrustations), p.26-8; Fred. Stuart and the Red House Glass-works, p.41-3; Glossary of terms used in the glass industry, p.110-19; The Hills and Webbs of Coalbournehill, p.44-7; The Powell family (Whitefriars Glassworks), p.29-32; Pressed glass – Sowerby of Tyneside, p.59-62; The Richardsons of Wordsley Hall, p.55-8; Stourbridge glass – Royal Brierley Crystal, Stevens and Williams Ltd, p.33-6; Thomas Webb of Dennis Park, p.37-40.

9   'Colouring agents in glass'. In *Glass*, 1930, p.8-10and 52-4.

10  'Glass' [manufacture, 1750-1850]. In Singer, Charles and others, eds. *History of Technology*, O.U.P., 1957, v.4, p.358-78, *illus., bibliog.*
    *see also* MARSON, Percival.

11  'An important group of Drinking Glasses, c.1830-1850'. In *Antique Collecting*, Oct. 1979, p.16-17, *illus.*

12  'Annealed glass'. In *Art Jnl.*, 1875, p.229-30. Deals especially with the annealed glass of M. de la Bastie.

13  'Antique cider glasses'. In *The Times*, Oct 28th 1961, p.11, *illus.*

14  'Antique [glass] salvers'. In *The Times*, May 11th 1968, p.23, *illus.*

15  'Apsley Pellatt'. In *Tableware*, June 1963, p.459-60.

16  ARLOTT, John. 'Three wine glasses'. In *Adelphi*, v.28, 1952, p.601-4. Describes particular glasses for certain wines.

17  ARMSTRONG, E.F. 'Constituents of glass'. In *GC*, no.46.

18  'Cordials and their glasses'. In *GC*, no.20.

19  'Long forgotten drinks and their glasses'. In *GC*, no.3.

20  ARMY AND NAVY STORES. *Yesterday's shopping: the Army and Navy Store's catalogue, 1907.* David and Charles, 1969. A reprint containing a section on domestic glassware, described and priced, p.921-50, *illus.*

21  'Art at auction, 1969-1970'. The year at Sotheby's and Parke-Bernet, 1969-70, edited by Philip Wilson. Macdonald, 1970. Contents include: Glass, p.414-19, *illus. (some col.).*

22  'Art of John Hutton' [glass engraver]. In *CL*, Feb 1969, p.485, *illus.*

23  ART GALLERY OF NEW SOUTH WALES, SYDNEY. *G. Gordon Russell Collection of seventeenth and eighteenth-century English drinking glasses* [Catalogue]. Sydney, 1964.

24  *Arthur Negus Guide to British Glass see* BROOKS, John.

25  ASH, Douglas. *A Dictionary of British antique glass.* Pelham Books, 1975, 210p., *illus.*

26  ASH, Douglas. 'English glass: a brief survey'. In *AC*, 1967, p.131-7, *illus.*

27  'Flute glasses in England: a fashion for tall drinks deriving from Venice and the Netherlands'. In *AC*, 1968, p.85-9, *illus.*

28  'Glasses that have no feet'. In *ADCG*, Jan 1968, p.52-5, *illus.*

29  *How to identify English drinking glasses and decanters, 1680-1830.* Bell, 1962, 200p., *illus., bibliog.*

30  'Newcastle glass'. In *AC*, 1964, p.191-5, *illus.*

31  'Attraction of English glass: the Times-Sotheby Index' [current prices]. In *The Times*, Apr 18th 1970, *Saturday Rev.* p.1, *illus.*

32  ASHFORD, Roger. 'Colourful slagware'. In *AC*, Sept 1976, p.28-30, *illus.*

33  'English glass decanters.' In *Antiques Jnl.*, July 1981, p.26-8, *illus.*

34  'English slagware'. In *Antiques Jnl.*, Nov 1979, p.22-4, *illus.*

35  'Jelly moulds'. In *Antiques Jnl.*, May 1981, p.23-5, *illus.*

36  'Seeing red!' In *Art & Antiques Weekly*, Sept 18-24 1981, p.16-17, *illus.* Ruby, cranberry etc.

37  'Victorian slagware'. In *Everything has a value*, No.4 Jan 1981, p.10-11, *illus.* Gives values.

38  ASHURST, Denis. 'Excavations at Gawber glass-house, near Barnsley, Yorkshire'. In *Post Medieval Arch.*, 1970, p.90-140, *illus.* 17th-19th centuries.

39  ASHMOLEAN MUSEUM, OXFORD. *English drinking glasses in the Ashmolean Museum.* Oxford, 1977, 32p., *illus.*

40  ASKEY, Derek. *Sussex bottle collectors guide.* Brighton (Sx.), Kensington Press, 1976, 120p., *illus., bibliog.*

41  BACON, John Maunsell. 'Acrostics in glass: a Jacobite puzzle' [acrostic on the name

'Charles']. In *CL*, Sept 1947, p.523, *illus.*

42    'Ale glasses'. In *GC*, no.47.

43    'Beilby enamel glasses'. In *GC*, nos.9 and 82.

44    'Bottle-decanters and bottles'. In *GC*, no.6.

45    'Bottle-decanters and bottles'. In *AP*, Jly-Dec 1939, p.13-15, *illus.*

46    'Criticism of... article in the *Connoisseur* [Jly-Dec 1942, p.47-51] by W. Horridge and E.B. Haynes, on Amen glasses'. In *GC*, no.33.

47    'Decanters, 1677-1750 and 1745-1800'. In *GC*, nos.41 and 42.

48    'The elements of glass collecting'. In *GC*, no.2.

49    *English glass collecting for beginners in a series of five letters to one of them.* Penrith, Reed, 1942, 16p.

50    'Extracts from Woburn Abbey glass-sellers' bills (Thorpe)'. In *GC*, no.14.

51    'More Newcastle glass'. In *GC*, no.40.

52    'A note on King's Lynn glass'. In *GC*, no.29A.

53    'Privateer and other nautical glasses...' In *GC*, nos.50 and 53.

54    'Two Jacobite glasses'. In *GC*, no.30.
      *joint author see* WILLIAMS, Jane *and* BACON, John Maunsell.

55    BACKHOUSE, M.V. *and* A.V. 'The Old House', Pulborough, West Sussex'. In *Sussex Archaeological Collections*, 1978, p.375-392, *illus*, 17th-18th century bottles and phials.

56    BADDELEY, W. St C. 'The glass-house at Nailsworth (sixteenth and seventeenth century)'. In *Trans. of the Bristol Archaeological Soc.*, v.42, 1920.

57    BAKER, Vernon G. 'Carrillo's statistical study of English wine bottles: some comments and further consideration'. In *Papers: Conference on Historic Site Archaeology*, 1976, 11, 1977, p.111-13, *illus.*

58    'BALUSTER' *pseud.* 'Ale and ale glasses'. In *GN*, 1946, p.17-23, *illus.*

59    BAMFORD, Joan. 'Early crystal glass compotes'. In *ADCG*, June 1967, p.97-9, *illus.*

60    BANISTER, Judith. 'Bold John Barleycorn: a century of English ale-glasses'. In *ADCG*, Sept 1961, p.27-9, *illus.*

61    'Relics of a gentlemanly vice: cut-glass, decanters of the eighteenth and nineteenth centuries'. In *ADCG*, June 1961, p.34-6, *illus.*

62    BANKFIELD MUSEUM, HALIFAX. *The H.P. Jackson loan collection of English glass* [Catalogue]. Halifax, 1948.

63    BANKS, M., ELPHINSTONE, N.E. *and* HALL, F.T. 'Bristol blue glass'. In *Archaeology*, 6, 1963. p.26-30, *illus.*

64    BARKER, T.C. *The Glassmakers: Pilkington... 1826-1976.* Weidenfeld & Nicolson, 1977, 557p., *illus., bibliog.*

65    BARKER, T.C. *Pilkington Brothers and the glass*

66    BARKER, Wilfred R. 'Notes on some old Yorkshire glasshouses'. In *TSGT*, 1925, p.322-33, *illus., maps.*

67    BARRAUD, Ronald. 'John Davenport: a nineteenth-century glass decorator'. In *CONN*, Jan-Apr 1970, p.186-8, *illus.*

68    BARRETT-LENNARD, T. 'Glassmaking at Knole, Kent'. In *The Antiquary*, v.41, 1905, p.127-9.

69    BASCO, Jean. 'Tassie portrait medallions and gemstone reproductions'. In *Canadian Collector*, 14 no.2 March/Apr 1979, p.54-5, *illus.*

70    BATE, Percy. 'An eighteenth-century industry: Bristol enamel glass'. In *Mag. of Fine Arts*, v.7, 1905, p.151.

71    *English table glass.* Newnes, 1905, 130p., *illus.*

72    'Historic English drinking glasses'. In *Studio*, 1902, p.106-12, *illus.*

73    'Old English glasses'. In *Studio*, 1902, p.45-8, *illus.*

74    'Beakers'. In *GN*, 1946, p.29-32, *illus.* A condensed version of E.B. Haynes' 'Common tumbler' in *AC*, 1946, p.93-8.

75    BATES, Trevor. 'Recreating the glass the Georgians knew is a perfect art'. In *Daily Tel.*, Nov 1st 1975, p.13, *port.*

76    BEARD, Geoffrey W. 'The documentation and variety of Stourbridge glass'. In *GC*, no.135.

77    'English makers of cameo glass'. In *A*, 1954, p.472-4, *illus.*

78    'George Woodall's cameo glass' [two articles]. In *CL*, Feb 1954, p.347, *illus.* and *AC*, June 1956, p.109-12, *illus.*

79    *Modern glass.* Studio Vista, 1968, 160p., *illus., bibliog.*
      Contents include: Modern English glass, p.72-113, *illus.*

80    *Nineteenth-century cameo glass.* Foreword by E. Barrington Haynes. Monmouth, 1956, 149p., *illus. (some col.), bibliog.*
      Contents include: John Northwood (1836-1902) and the revival of cameo glass carving, p.11-26; The Woodall brothers, p.35-54, *illus.*

81    'Sparkling crystal'. In *AP*, Jly-Dec 1953, p.151, *illus.*

82    BEATSON, CLARK AND CO. LTD. *The glass works, Rotherham, 1751-1951.* Rotherham, 1952, 52p., *illus., plans.*

83    BECK, A.M.L. 'Glass in Windsor Castle and Buckingham Palace'. In *BUR*, Jly-Dec 1925, p.12-19, *illus.*

84    BECK, Doreen. *The Book of bottle collecting.* Hamlyn, 1973, 96p., *illus. (some col.)*

85    BECK, G.M.A. 'Ogniabene Luteri: a Surrey glass-maker'. In *TSGT (News and Reviews)*, 1953, p.69-70.

86    BECKER, Vivienne. 'Glass candlesticks'. In *AC*, Jan 1977, p.57-9, *illus.*

87    'Glass paperweights'. In *AC*, Oct 1975, p.28-31,

*illus.*

88 BEDFORD, John. *Bristol and other coloured glass.* Cassell, 1964, 64p., *illus.* (Collectors' Pieces 2).

89 *English crystal glass.* Cassell, 1966, 64p., *illus.* (Collectors' Pieces 9).

90 *Paperweights.* Cassell, 1968, 64p., *illus.* (Collectors' Pieces 14).

91 'Beilby goblet' [unrecorded]. In *GN*, 1952, p.21.

92 BELL, P.L. 'Airtwist glasses'. In *GC*, no.141.

93 Benjamin Richardson [of Stourbridge] [Description of his work]. In ARWAS, Victor *Glass: Art Nouveau to Art Deco.* Academy Editions, 1977, p.183-4; 187.

94 BENN, Elizabeth. 'Cut out for Royalty'. In *Daily Tel.*, Aug 19th 1976, p.13, *illus.*

95 'Giving glass a touch of class'. In *Daily Tel.*, Feb 5th 1975, p.15, *illus.* Andrew Lawson Johnston's engraving.

96 '17th century English glass and Henry J. Mein'. In *AC*, June 1982, p.83, *port.*

97 BENNETT, Raymond. *Collecting for pleasure.* Bodley Head, 1969.
Contents include: Decanters, p.68-71; Nailsea glass, p.102-5; Tumblers and beakers, p.110-14.

98 BERGSTROM, Evangeline H. *Old glass paperweights: their art, construction and distinguishing features.* Faber, 1947. First pub. Chicago, 1940. 132p., *illus.*

99 'Bergstrom paperweight collection'. In *A*, 1961, p.486, *illus.*

100 BERLIN, Froma. 'Ship decanters called Rodneys...' In *Collectors Weekly*, Apr 11th 1972, p.15, *illus.*

101 BERRY, F. 'Dated English wine bottles'. In *CL*, March 30th, 1935.

102 BEWICK, Thomas. *Memoir of Thomas Bewick written by himself,* 1822-1828. Bodley Head, 1924, 274p., *illus.* Mention of the Beilby family. First pub. 1862.

103 BICKERTON, Leonard Marshall. 'Art of the English glass maker: the Alexander Collection'. In *CL*, Oct 1969, p.1005-6, *illus.*

104 'Drinking fashions of the Georgians'. In *Country Life Annual*, 1972, p.96-7, *illus.*

105 *English drinking glasses 1675-1825.* Shire Publications, 1984, 32p., *illus.*, *bibliog.* (Shire Album 116).

106 'English engraved glasses of the eighteenth century'. In *The Australasian Antique Collector*, no.6, Jan-June 1969, p.29-33, *illus.*

107 'Fascinations of the air-twist'. In *CL*, Jan 1970, p.24-5, *illus.*

108 'A glass-lover's collection reunited: the Hartshorne Exhibition at Worthing' [1968]. In *CL*, Apr 1968, p.911-12, *illus.*

109 'Glassmaking traditions in King's Lynn'. In *CL*, June 1969, p.1514-15, *illus.*

110 'Glass in the Ipswich Museums'. In *East Anglian Magazine*, Mar 1971.

111 *An illustrated guide to eighteenth-century English drinking glasses* with a bibliography of English glass by D. Robert Elleray. Barrie & Jenkins, 1971, 86p., 854 *illus.*

112 BIGNALL, R.G. 'Label decanters'. In *AC*, Apr 1957, p.66-7, *illus.*

113 'Birmingham Exhibition of Manufacturers and Art, 1849' [Descriptions and illustrations of glassware exhibited by George Bacchus and Sons, p.314; Rice Harris (Islington), p.307; Richardson (Stourbridge), p.302, *etc.*]. In *Art Jnl.*, 1849.

114 BISHOP, John. 'Glass at the Antique Dealers' Fair' [two articles]. In *AP*, Jly-Dec 1936, p.157-60, and p.199-203, *illus.*

115 BLACKHAM, Robert J. *London's Livery Companies.* Sampson Low, 1932.
Contents include: Glass Sellers' and Glaziers' Companies, p.285-90, *illus.*

116 BLAKE, Evelina. 'Let it breathe'. In *AC*, Dec 1980, p.84-7, *illus.* 19th century claret jugs.

117 BLENCH, Brian J.R. 'Scottish glass: 1945 to the present day'. In *CJGS*, 1983, p.207-11, *illus.*

118 'Two unusual chip-engraved bottles'. In *Scott. Glass Soc. Newsletter*, no.5, June 1982, p.5-6.

119 BLES, Joseph. *Rare English glasses of the seventeenth and eighteenth centuries.* G. Bles, 1925, 269p., *illus.*
Contents include: 'Commemorative glass' by Sir J.S. Risley, p.157-76.

120 BOARD OF TRADE. *Hand-blown domestic glassware* [Working party report]. H.M.S.O., 1947.

121 BOND, Harold Lewis. *An encyclopedia of antiques.* New York, Tudor, 1946, 389p., *illus.*, *bibliog.* Contents include: Glass, p.183-225. Mainly American, but several references to English and continental glass.

122 BOORE, J.P. 'Glossary of terms used by paperweight collectors'. In *Bull. of the National Early American Glass Club*, Dec 1960, p.6-8.

123 'Old glass paperweights'. In *Hobbies*, June 1966, p.98F-98G, *illus.*

124 'Old glass paperweights – a brief history of the art'. In *Hobbies*, June 1961, p.90-1, *illus.*

125 'Old glass paperweights: some little-known English makers'. In *Hobbies*, Feb 1961, p.80-1, *illus.*

126 BOUILLOT, Ann. 'Air ace researches Newcastle glass'. In *Antiques Today (USA)*, 2, no.3, p.4-19, *illus.* James Rush.

127 BOULGER, G.S. 'Christopher Merret (1614-1695)'. In *Dictionary of National Biography*, v.37, 1894, p.288-9. Merret translated Neri's *Art of glass* in 1662.

128 BOWLES, William Henry. *History of the Vauxhall and Ratcliff glasshouses and their owners, 1670-1800.* London (priv. print.), 1926, 62p.

129 BOYDELL, Mary. 'Crystal gazing: the art of glass in Ireland'. In *Art & Antiques Weekly*, March 10, 1979, p.24-6, *illus.*

130 'Engravers of Bohemia working in Ireland

and England'. In *Annales du 8e Congrès Internationale d'Etude Historique du Verre*, Liège, 1981, p.335-43, *illus.*

131 'The Friendly Brothers' glass'. In *CL*, June 2nd 1977, p.1539-40, *illus.* Irish glass.

132 *Irish glass.* Dublin: Eason, 1976, 24p., *illus., bibliog.* (Irish Heritage Series)

133 'Made for convivial clinking: 19th century Anglo-Irish glass'. In *CL*, Sept 26th 1974, p.852; 854, *illus.*

134 'Maternal tenderness on glass'. In *CL*, May 1976, p.1190; 1192, *illus.* Engraved glasses.

135 'The Pugh Glasshouse in Dublin'. In *The Glass Circle* 2, 1975, p.37-48, *illus.*

136 'A versatile national emblem. The shamrock on Irish glass'. In *GC*, May 1974, p.1280-1, *illus.*

137 'Waterford glass'. In *Arts in Ireland*, v.1 pt. 4 (1973), p.9-15, *illus.*
see also WESTROPP, Michael Seymour Dudley. *Irish glass.* 2nd ed.

138 BOYLE, Julia. 'Novelties in glass'. In *ADCG*, July 1971, p.58-9, *illus. (col.)* Inc. Walking sticks & bells.

139 BRACEGIRDLE, Cyril. 'Bristol blue glass & the Saxony connection'. In *Spinning Wheel*, May-June 1981, p.40-1, *illus.* Use of smalt from Saxony to obtain shades of blue.

140 'Tassie's tiny testimonials [cameos]' In *American Collector*, March 1974, p.4-5, *illus.*

141 BRADDICK, Leonard E. 'Old Sussex glass'. In *Glass*, 1935, p.509, *illus.*

142 BRADFORD, Ernle. *Antique collecting.* E.U.P., 1963. Teach Yourself Series.
Contents include: Glass, p.60-75, *illus.*

143 BRENTON-ATKINS, G.T. 'A collector's résumé of English drinking glasses: the Hamilton Clements Collection recently auctioned'. In *The Antiquarian*, v.16, May 1931, p.21-4 and p.62, *illus.*

144 BRETT, Gerard. 'The pedestal bowl: its probable origin and purpose'. In *CONN*, May-Aug 1967, p.174-5, *illus.*

145 BRIDGEWATER, N.P. 'Glasshouse Farm, St. Weonards: a small glassworking site'. In *Trans. of the Woolhope Naturalists Field Club*, v.37, 1963, p.300-13.

146 'A small glassworking site at Glasshouse Farm, St Weonards'. In *GC*, no.134.

147 BRIERLEY HILL GLASS MUSEUM. 'The making of a museum: Brierley Hill Glass Museum'. In *Blackcountryman*, Spring 1974, p.30-4.

148 BRIERLEY HILL PUBLIC LIBRARIES. *Check list of books and pamphlets on glass in the reference library special collection.* Brierley Hill Public Libraries and Arts Committee, 1962, 23p. Duplicated typescript.
see also THORPE, William Arnold.

149 BRIMBLE, John. 'Glass bottles and stone jars: items in the Black Country Society's Collection'. In *Blackcountryman*, 8, 1975,

p.49-50.

150 'Bristol blue glass'. In *ADCG*, Aug 1958, p.28-30, *illus.*

151 BRISTOL CITY ART GALLERY. *Treasures from West Country Collections* [exhibition catalogue including glass]. Bristol City Art Gallery, 1967, *illus.*

152 'Bristol Glass'. In *Antique Collecting*, Dec 1974, p.16-19, *illus.*

153 'Bristol opaque-white glass'. In *Glass.* 1958, p.260, *illus.*

154 BRITISH MUSEUM. *Masterpieces of glass: a selection* [from the 1968 Exhibition at the British Museum] compiled by D.B. Harden, K.S. Painter, R.H. Pinder-Wilson, Hugh Tait. British Museum, 1968, 199p., *illus. (some col.), bibliog.*
Contents include: European glass, Middle Ages to 1862, by Hugh Tait, p.127-85.

155 *The Portland Vase* by D.E.L. Haynes. British Museum, 1964, 48p., *illus., bibliog.*

156 BRITISH STANDARDS INSTITUTION. *Glossary of terms used in the glass industry.* B.S.I., 1962, 56p.

157 BROADBENT, Michael. 'Champagne: made for drinking'. In *CONN.*, Nov 1980, p.216-19, *illus.*

158 BROOKS, John A. *The Arthur Negus guide to British glass.* J. Brooks, Feltham: Hamlyn, 1981, 176p. *illus. (some col.), bibliog.*

159 'Commemorative glass'. In *ADCG*, Feb 1979, p.82-5, *illus.*

160 'Dating knopped stem glasses'. In *ADCG*, Nov 1975, p.83-9, *illus.*

161 'Facet-stemmed glasses'. In *ADCG*, May 1973, p.92-3, *illus.*

162 *Glass.* Sampson Low, 1975, 80p., *illus.* Inc. English & Irish glass. (1st ed. New York 1973).

163 'Glass. Have you bought the real thing?' In *ADCG*, Jan 1980, p.71-2, *illus.*

164 'Glass salts'. In *ADCG*, May 1976, p.73-5, *illus.*

165 'Lead glass – a detective story'. In *ADCG*, May 1983, p.58-61, *illus.*

166 'Questioning Collector I: Glassware. John Brooks advises the new collector'. In *ADCG*, June 1977, p.128-30, *illus.*

167 'Questioning Collector III: Glass stoppers and handles'. In *ADCG*, June 1978, p.126-8, *illus.*

168 'The Stourbridge Collection of 19th century glass'. In *ADCG*, Nov 1974, p.75-7, *illus.*

169 BROOKS, Oscar. 'Jacobite glasses, usual and unusual'. In *AC*, Oct 1961, p.206-8, *illus.*

170 'The scarcity of coin glasses'. In *CL*, May 1962, p.1021, *illus.*

171 BROTHERS, J. Stanley. 'The miracle of enclosed ornamentation' [paperweights, marbles]. In *CJGS*, 1962, p.116-26, *illus., diags.*

172 BROWN, C.M. 'The glass industry in the eighteen thirties'. In *Glass Technol.*, Aug 1980, p.184-9, *illus.*

173 BROWN, F. Harmar. 'Bristol Venetian glass'. In

CONN, Jan-June 1934, p.25-7, *illus*. In 1788 Venetian glass craftsmen settled near Bristol and Nailsea.

174 BROWNE, R.C. 'Sir Jerome Bowes (d.1616)'. In *Dictionary of National Biography*, v.6, 1886, p.57-8. Bowes was granted a special licence to make drinking glasses in 1592.

175 BRYSON-WHITE, Iris. 'Dreihundert Jahre Englisches Bleikristall'. In *Die Schaulade*, 49, no.7, July 1974, p.930-1, *illus*.

176 BUCKLEY, Francis. *Alphabetical list of glass sellers, chinamen or vendors of earthenware of London, recorded in the newspapers and other records... 1660-1800*. Collected by F.B. c.1935. Guildhall MS. 3384. A photocopy of this MS. is in the National Art Library, Victoria & Albert Museum.

177 'Art and politics: the Jacobite iconography'. In *Fine Arts* (U.S.A.), v.19, Nov 1932, p.16-18, *illus*.

178 'The Birmingham glass trade, 1740-1833'. In *TSGT*, 1927, p.374-86.

179 'Bottles'. In *Glass*, 1925, p.618. Mainly medicine phials.

180 'Cruet bottles of the eighteenth century'. In *Glass*, 1924, p.489.

181 'Cumberland glasshouses'. In *TSGT*, 1926, p.384-6.

182 'Curious marked bottles'. In *AC*, May 1932.

183 'The Cycle Club and Jacobite Hunts and some commemorative glasses'. In *CONN*, Jan-June 1940, p.57-62, *illus*. The 'Cycle Club' was the principal Jacobite club in the north of England.

184 'The development of English cut glass in the eighteenth century'. In *BUR*, Jly-Dec 1924, p.299-304, *illus*.

185 'Development of the wine glass in the nineteenth century'. In *Glass*, 1924, p.441.

186 'The dove as a Jacobite emblem'. In *AC*, 1936, p.262-4, *illus*.

187 'Earlier cut drinking glasses'. In *AC*, 1937, p.78-80, *illus*.

188 'The early glasshouses of Bristol' [area]. In *TSGT*, 1925, p.36-61, *map*.

189 *English baluster-stemmed glasses of the seventeenth and eighteenth centuries*. Edinburgh (priv. print.), Ballantyne Press, 1912, 39., *illus*.

190 'A fine glass collection: some outstanding pieces in the possession of Mr T Scholes of Manchester'. *AC*, 1937, p.5-7, *illus*.

191 'Fine old English glasses'. In *Glass*, 1930. Contents: Bonnet glasses, tea caddies and ink-pots, p.490-2; Candlesticks, p.356-8; Decanters, p.396-8; Drinking glasses (cut), p.274-6; Drinking glasses (plain stem), p.241-3; Earlier and twisted stems, p.184-6; Jugs and jelly glasses, p.318-20; Glass salts, p.344-5; Tankards, p.450-2, *all illus*.

192 'Glasshouses of Dudley and Worcester'. In *TSGT*, 1927, p.287-93.

193 'Glasshouses on the Tyne in the eighteenth century'. In *TSGT*, 1926, p.26-51.

194 'Glasshouses on the Wear in the eighteenth century'. In *TSGT*, 1925, p.105-11.

195 *The glass trade in England in the seventeenth century*. Stevens (priv. print.), 1914, 64p.

196 'Great names in the history of English glass'. In *Glass*. 1928. Contents: Cassilari, p.103-4, *illus*.; John Bellingham, p.150; Sir Robert Mansell, p.199-200, *illus*.; John Akerman [glass-cutter], p.247-8, *illus*.; Thomas Betts [eighteenth-century glass-cutter and engraver], p.299-300, *illus*.; Duke of Buckingham [owned glasshouses at Greenwich and Vauxhall], p.341-2 and 366, *illus*.; Jerom Johnson [cutter and engraver, c.1750], p.392-3, *illus*.; Jackson [and Co.], p.488-9, *illus*.; John Bowles, p.540, 548, *illus*.

197 *A history of old English glass*. Foreword by Bernard Rackham. Benn, 1925, 155p., *illus*. Contents include: lists of contemporary references in books, newspapers, etc., to the following: Glass wares other than cut glass, p.142-51; The cut-glass trade and English eighteenth-century flint glass-houses, p.9-16; Specialists in cut glass, p.139-41.

198 'The jelly glass and its relations'. In *AC*, 1938, p.298-300, *illus*.

199 'Lancashire glasshouses of the eighteenth century'. In *Glass*, 1924, p.489.

200 'The London glass sellers'. In *AC*, 1938, p.112-14, *illus*.

201 '[Mrs Petrocochino's] collection of old English and Irish glasses'. In *CL*, Nov 1930, p.33-6, *illus*.

202 'Note on the glasshouses of the Leeds district in the seventeenth, eighteenth and early nineteenth centuries'. In *TSGT*, 1924, p.268-77.

203 'Notes on the glasshouses of Stourbridge, 1700-1830'. In *TSGT*, 1927, p.106-23.

204 'Notes on various old glasshouses'. In *TSGT*, 1930, p.30-6. Includes Scotland and Wales.

205 'Old cut-glass chandeliers: the development of "lustre" making from George I to the Regency'. In *AC*, 1936, p.178-81, *illus*.

206 'Old decanters'. In *CL*, Dec 1928, p.94-8, *illus*.

207 'Old English glass at Wilbury Park'. In *CL*, Dec 1929, p.845-6, *illus*.

208 'Old English glasses'. In *Glass*, 1931. Contents: Bottles, p.322-4; Bowls, p.102-3; Cruet bottles, plates, rummers and carafes, p.65-6; Chandeliers, p.230-2; Enamel glass, p.278-80; Hogarth glasses, p.498-9; Lamps, p.230-2; Ravenscroft sealed glasses, p.461-2; Tumblers, p.186-8; Two-handled glasses and punch and toddy lifters, p.146-8;

Sweetmeat glasses, p.15-16; Witch balls and pocket flasks, p.364-6; Worcestershire glass [drinking glasses of that area], p.415-17, *all illus.*

209 'Old English glasses'. In *Glass*, 1934.
Contents: Amateur engraving [signatures, initials scratched on glasses], p.66-7; Birmingham glass pinchers [seals, buttons, etc.], p.187-8; British glassmakers abroad, p.266-7; Curios pieces of glass, p.12-13; Famous London glasshouse [Whitefriars], p.308-11; Glass salts, p.344-5; Old flower vases and glasses, p.474, 476; Remarkable table set [Anglo-Venetian], p.388, 391; The war tax on glass 1695, p.100-1. All except the article on Whitefriars are *illus.*

210 'Old English glasses'. In *Glass*, 1935.
Contents: An account of glassmaking [1754], p.74; Ink horns and ink pots, p.155-6; Water glasses and mugs, p.205-6, *all illus.*

211 'Old English glass salts'. In *AC*, 1939, p.44-6, *illus.*

212 'Old glass lamps and candlesticks'. In *CL*, Apr 1929, p.492-4, and May 1929, p.710-12, *illus.*

213 'Old Lancashire glasshouses'. In *TSGT*, 1929, p.229-42.

214 *Old London drinking glasses.* Edinburgh (priv. print.), Ballantyne Press, 1913, 37p., *illus.* Deals with sixteenth- and seventeenth-century styles.

215 *Old London glasshouses.* Stevens (priv. print.), 1915, 42p.

216 'Old London glasshouses: Southwark'. In *TSGT*, 1930, p.137-49, illus.

217 'Old Nottingham glasshouses. In *TSGT*, 1926, p.270-3.

218 'A rare Jacobite glass'. In *CONN*, Jly-Dec 1931, p.36-7, *illus.*

219 'The sequence of drinking glasses in the eighteenth century'. In Arundel Soc. of Manchester Minutes, 1927-8.

220 'Seventeenth-century English table glass from pre-Ravenscroft fragments to early flint glass'. In *AC*, 1936, p.150-2, *illus.*

221 'Seventeenth- and eighteenth-century ribbed glasses: some examples of English "rib twisting" '. In *AC*, 1939, p.138-40, *illus.*

222 'Some Jacobite relics: a newly discovered glass inscription' [on a water glass]. In *AC*, 1935, p.56-8, *illus.*

223 The taxation of English glass in the seventeenth century. Stevens (priv. print.), 1914, 74p.

224 'Thomas Bett's accounts'. In *Glass*, 1928, p.300.

225 'Unusual old English glass......' In *AC*, 1939, p.249-51, *illus.*

226 'West country glasshouses'. In *TSGT*, 1929, p.124-9.

227 BUCKLEY, Wilfred. 'Anglo-Dutch glasses of the eighteenth century'. In *Old Furniture*, 1928,

p.151.

228 'Anglo-Dutch stem glasses of the eighteenth century'. In *Arts and Decoration*, Sept 1939, p.10-11, *illus.*

229 *The art of glass, illustrated from the Wilfred Buckley Collection at the Victoria and Albert Museum...* Allen and Unwin, 1939, 286p., *illus.*
Contents include: English glass, p.75-86, and catalogue of the English items (nos. 465-595).

230 *The celebrated Horridge Collection of drinking glasses... illustrated catalogue.* Jackson-Stops and Staff, 1959.

231 *Diamond-engraved glasses of the sixteenth century with particular reference to five attributed to Giacomo Verzelini.* Benn, 1929, 24p., illus.* A limited ed. Appendix reprints two articles from *BUR* by Bernard Rackham and Wilfred Buckley, both entitled 'An early diamond-engraved glass at South Kensington'.

232 *European glass.* Benn, 1926, 96p., *illus.* A limited ed. The glass discussed is from the Buckley Collection; English glass, p.81-93; also included is an 'Essay on Dutch glass engravers' by F. Hudig.

233 *Notes on Frans Greenwood and the glasses that he engraved.* Benn, 1930, 15p., *illus.*

234 *D. Wolff and the glasses that he engraved. With a supplementary note on a glass engraved by Frans Greenwood.* Methuen, 1935, 41p., *illus.* A limited ed. Appendix D is a 'Report on signatures' by C.J. Van Ledden Hulseboch.

235 BUDGETT, Sally. 'Glassmakers' friggers'. In *AC*, Jan 1976, p.33-5, *illus.*

236 BUECHNER, Thomas S. 'Glass: ancient times to the nineteenth century'. In *Encyclopedia Britannica*, 1970 ed., v.10, p.456-63, *illus.*

237 'Glass drinking vessels in the collection of Jerome Strauss'. In *Connoisseur Year Book*, 1957, p.42-7, *illus.*

238 BUNGARD, G.D. 'Men of glass: a personal view of the De Bongar family in the 16th and 17th centuries. In *Glass Circle 3*, 1979, p.79-86.

239 BUNT, Cyril G.E. 'Wonderful Waterford – Ireland's debt to English craftsmen'. In *ADCG*, Oct 1959, p.20-2, *illus.*

240 BURGESS, Frederick W. *Chats on household curios.* Fisher Unwin, 1914.
Contents include: Glass and enamels, p.175-81.

241 BURGOYNE, Ian. 'The evolution of glassmaking techniques'. In *Museums Jnl.*, June 1980, p.28-30, *illus.* Pilkington Glass Museum.

242 BURNING, L. 'The service of glass in the serving of wine'. In *Wine Trade Rev.*, Nov 15th and 22nd 1929.

243 BURTON, Elizabeth. *The Georgian at home, 1714-1830.* Longmans, 1967.
Contents: Glass, p.166-75.

244 BURY, H. 'Designs for glass by eight British artists,

1934'. In *Jnl. of Dec. Arts Soc. 1890-1940*, v.2 (1978), p.36-43, *illus.* Laura Knight, Eric Ravilious, Paul Nash, Graham Sutherland etc.

245 BURTON, John. Glass: philosophy and method, hand-blown, sculptured, coloured. Pitman, 1969, 278p., *illus. (some col.), bibliog.*
see also 'Survey of contemporary glass'.

246 BUTLER, Joseph T. 'The Connoisseur in America – three landmarks in early English glass'. In *CONN*, Sept-Dec 1967, p.134-5, *illus.* Includes a Verzelini glass.

247 BUTLER, L.A.S. 'Glass excavating'. In *Post Medieval Arch.*, 1970, p.172-3.

248 BUTLER, R.F. 'Glass', [-making in Gloucestershire]. In *Victoria County History of Gloucestershire*, v.2, 1907, p.213.

249 BUTTERWORTH, Walter. 'Glass: cut and engraved'. In *TSGT*, 1929, p.183-94, *illus.*

250 CAMDEN ARTS CENTRE, LONDON. *Christopher Dresser 1834-1904.* Arkwright Arts Trust, 1979, 52p., *illus.* Clutha glass c.1885.

251 CAMPBELL, Alister. 'Beauty in glass candlesticks'. In *ADCG*, Aug 1954, p.29-31, *illus.*

252 'Bottles of great charm'. In *ADCG*, Sept 1954, p.23-5, *illus.*

253 'Early English drinking glasses'. In *ADCG*, Apr 1954, p.29-31, *illus.*

254 'Early English glass makers'. In *ADCG*, Mar 1954, p.20-2, *illus.*

255 'For and against cut glass'. In *ADCG*, Jly 1954, p.26-8, *illus.*

256 'Fragile perfection: seventeenth-century drinking glasses'. In *ADCG*, Feb 1955, p.26-8, *illus.*

257 'Glass, the domestic art'. In *ADCG*, June 1954, p.34-6, *illus.* English and continental.

258 'The glass engraver's art'. In *ADCG*, May 1954, p.20-2, *illus.*

259 'Glass, mould of fashion'. In ADCG, Nov 1954, p.26-8.

260 'Glass toys and animals'. In *ADCG*, Oct 1954, p.26-8, *illus.*

261 'History in glass: symbolic Jacobite tableware'. In *ADCG*, Mar 1955, p.26-8, *illus.*

262 'How glass came to England'. In *ADCG*, Feb 1954, p.24-6, *illus.*

263 'More beautiful than china: opaque-white glass'. In *ADCG*, Jly 1955, p.22-4, *illus.*

264 'A new approach to glass collecting – tomorrow's antiques'. In *ADCG*, Jan 1955, p.21-33, *illus.*

265 CANTELUPE, Diana. 'Engraved glass'. In *AC*, June 1978, p.108-111, illus.

266 CARNEY, Clive. *Furnishing art and practice.* O.U.P., 1950. Contents include: Glass styles, old and modern, p.173-86, *illus.*

267 CARVEL, John Lees. *The Alloa Glass Works. An account of its development since 1750.* Edinburgh (priv. print.), 1953, 102p., *illus.*

268 'Catalogue of the collection of Sir Harrison Hughes'. In *GC*, no.8.

269 CECIL HIGGINS ART GALLERY. *Glass in the Cecil Higgins Art Gallery.* Bedford, Borough Council, 1969, 16p., *illus.*

270 'Cecil Higgins Collection'. In *GN*, 1949, p.25-7.
CELORIA, F.S.C. *joint author see* VAISEY, D.G. and CELORIA, F.S.C.

271 CHAFFERS, William. *Catalogue of the collection formed by Felix Slade, etc. (drawn up... and nearly rewritten by W.A. Nicholls). With notes on the history of glass making by A. Nesbitt... Edited by A.W. Franks.* London, 1871.

272 'Champagne decanter'. In *CL*, Jly-Dec 1957, p.294, *illus.*

273 'Champagne glasses'. In *The Times*, Aug 9th 1963, p.9, *illus.*

274 'Champagnes with cut bottoms'. In *The Times*, Aug 10th 1963, p.9, *illus.*
CHAMPION, R. *see* OWEN, Hugh.

275 CHANCE, Sir Hugh. 'The Donnington Wood glass-houses'. In *GC*, no.140.

276 'Nailsea glass'. In *GC*, no.128.

277 'The Nailsea glassworks'. In *Pottery Gaz. and Glass Trade Rev.*, 1958, p.111-13, *illus. plan.*

278 'Records of the Nailsea glassworks'. In *CONN*, May-Aug 1967, p.168-72, *illus.*

279 CHANCE, J.F. *History of the Firm of Chance Brothers and Company, glass and alkali manufacturers.* Priv. print., 1919.

280 'Chance Brothers Ltd tableware in moulded glass'. In *Art and Industry*, Dec 1952, p.190-5, *illus.*

281 CHARLESTON, Robert Jesse. 'Ancient glass-making methods' [and abrasive decoration]. In *GC*, nos.124 and 129.

282 'Apropos of tea-caddies in cut glass'. In *AC*, Aug1966, p.151-5, *illus.*

283 'Apropos of tea-caddies in cut glass'. In *GC*, no.148.

284 'Cut and engraved glass'. In *Pottery and Glass*, Oct-Nov 1950, *illus.*

285 'A decorator of porcelain and glass – James Giles in a new light'. In *Trans. of the English Ceramic Circle*, 1967, pt.3, *illus.*

286 'Decorators of glass and porcelain'. In *GC*, no.114.

287 'A documentary Beilby glass' [tumbler]. In *CONN*, May-Aug 1964, p.81-3, *illus.*

288 'Dutch decoration of English glass'. In *TSGT*, 1957, p.229-43, *illus., bibliog.* and also in *GC*, no.104.

289 'Enamelling and gilding on glass'. In *The Glass Circle*, 1, 1972, p.18-32, *illus.*

290 *English glass.* Allen & Unwin, 1984, 320p. *Decorative Arts Series.*

291 'English glass'. In *Encyclopedia Britannica*, 1970 ed., v.10, p.460-2, *illus.*

292 [English] 'Glass' [1500-1810]. In *Connoisseur Complete Period Guides*, 1968. Contents: Tudor, p.122-6; Stuart, p.417-20; Early Georgian, p.658-64; Late Georgian, p.981-8, *all illus.*

293 'English glass – an exhibition at the Victoria and Albert Museum'. In *A*, 1968,

p.541-7, *illus.*

294 [CHARLESTON, R.J] 'English glass in the Collection of Mr Donald H. Beves, Cambridge conoisseur'. In *CONN*, June 1960, p.32-7, *illus.*

295 CHARLESTON, R.J. 'English glass in the reserve collection at the Rijksmuseum'. In *CONN*, Jly-Dec 1965, p.236-8, *illus.*

296 'English glass-making and its spread from the seventeenth to the middle of the nineteenth century'. In *Annales du 1ᵉʳ Congrès des Journées Internationales du Verre.* Liège, 1960, p.155-72, *illus.*

297 'English opaque-white glass. In *GC*, no. III.

298 'George Ravenscroft: new light on the development of his crystalline glasses'. In *CJGS*, 1968, p.156-67, *illus.*

299 'Glass'. In *The Queen*, Oct 26th 1960, p.123, *illus.*

300 'Glass' [Pts I-V]. In Singer, Charles *and others,* eds. *History of Technology,* O.U.P., 1957, v.3, p.206-29, *illus., diags.*

301 'The Glass Circle Commemorative Exhibition of 1962'. Pt I: 'Some important early English glasses'. Pt 2: 'The Beilby glasses'. In *A*, Jan 1963, p.92-4, and Mar 1963, p.320-3, *illus.*

302 'Glass furnaces through the ages'. In *CJGS*, 1978, p.9-33, *illus.*

303 'A glassmakers bankruptcy sale'. In *Glass Circle*, 2, 1975, p.4-16, *illus.* John Honeybone, Stourbridge late 18th century.

304 'The import of Western glass into Turkey'. In *GC*, no.146.

305 'The import of Western glass into Turkey, sixteenth-eighteenth centuries'. In *CONN*, May-Aug 1966, p.18-26, *illus., bibliog.*

306 'In honour of Donald B. Harden [with a bibliography of his writings on glass, 1927 1974]'. In *CJGS*, 1975, p.10-22, *port.*

307 'James Giles as decorator of glass'. In *CONN*, May-Aug 1966, p.96-101, and p.176 81, *illus., bibliog.*

308 'James Giles as a decorator of glass'. In *GC*, no.147.

309 'Lead in glass'. In *Archaeometry*, 1960, p.1-4.

310 'Medieval and later glass'. In Cunliffe, Barry, *Winchester excavations, 1949-1960.* Winchester, 1964, v.1, p.145-51, *illus.*

311 'Michael Edkins and the problem of English enamelled glass'. In *TSGT*, 1954, p.3 16, *illus.*

312 'New light on Renaissance glass in England'. In *CJGS*, 1983, p.129-33, *illus., bibliog.*

313 'A notable London collection of glass' [Hamilton Clements Collection]. In *CONN* Jly-Dec 1958, p.238-41, *illus.*

314 'Our forefathers in glass'. In *Glass Technology*, Feb 1980, p.27-36, *illus.*

315 'A painter of opaque-white glass'. In *GN*, 1953, p.13-20, *illus.*

316 'A panoply of English glass: loan exhibition at the Victoria and Albert Museum'. In *CL*, Jly 1968, p.38-9, *illus.* An exhibition arranged to coincide with the eighth International Commission on Glass, London,1968.

317 'The pleasures of collecting glass'. In *The Listener*, Jan 9th 1958, p.61-3, *illus.*

318 'The Richard Weoley glass'. In *GC*, no.132.

319 '16th to 17th Century English glass'. In *Bulletin de l'Association Internationale pour l'Histoire de Verre*, No.8, 1977-1980, p.77-99, *illus.*

320 'Some aspects of 17th century glass found in England'. In *Annales du Congrès Internationale d'Etude Historique du Verre* (Berlin-Leipzig 1977), 1978, p.283-97, *illus.*

321 'Some notable glass on public view in England'. In *GC*, no.107.

322 'Some tools of the glassmaker in Medieval and Renaissance times, with special reference to the glassmaker's chair'. In *Glass Technology*, 1962, p.107-11, *illus.*

323 'The transport of glass: seventeenth eighteenth centuries'. In *GC*, no.152.

324 'Twenty-five years of glass collecting: a commemorative exhibition, "The Art of Glass", at the Victoria and Albert Museum'. In *CONN*, May-Aug 1962, p.121-4, *illus.* An exhibition marking the twenty-fifth Anniversary of the Glass Circle.

325 'Le verre blanc opaque anglaise du 18ᵉ siècle à décor polychrome'. In *Cahiers de la Céramique, du Verre and des arts du feu*, 1962, no.28, p.260-77, *illus.* English summary.

326 'Waterford glass'. In *A*, 1956, p.522-5, *illus.*

327 'Wheel engraving and cutting: some early equipment: (1) Engraving; (2) Waterpower and cutting'. In *CJGS*, 1964, p.83-100, and 1965, p.41-54, *illus.*
   *comp. see*
   (1) GUILDHALL MUSEUM
   (2) CIRCLE OF GLASS COLLECTORS
   (3) LEEDS CITY ART GALLERY
   (4) VICTORIA AND ALBERT MUSEUM

328 CHARLESWORTH, Dorothy. 'The English glossary of glass terms'. In *Annales du 3ᵉ Congrès des Journées Internationales du Verre*, Liège, 1966, p.210-11.

329 CHIPCHASE, N., CHURCH, M., *and* HORN, Peter. 'The Bathpool scavenging pit: the story of a Victorian dump'. In *Antique Bottle Collecting*, March 1982, p.8-15, *illus.*

330 CHOPE, R. Pease. 'Inscribed drinking glass' [1764]. In *Devon and Cornwall Notes and Queries*, Apr 1921, p.211-12, *illus.*

331 CHURCH, A.H. *Josiah Wedgwood, master potter.* Seeley, 1903.
   Contents include: The Barberini or Portland Vase, p.30-3, *illus.*

CHURCH, M. *joint author see* CHIPCHASE, N., CHURCH, M. *and* HORN, Peter.

332 CHURCHILL, ARTHUR, LTD. *Catalogue of old*

*English glass, 2nd ed.... with articles by Grant R. Francis, D.B. Harden, G.F. Laurence, W.A. Thorpe, etc.* A. Churchill Ltd, 1937. 122p., *illus., bibliog.* Prices given.

333 'Check lists of drinking glasses'. In *GN*. Contents: Air-twist glasses, 1947, p.32-40; Balustroid stems, 1953, p.35-48; Plain stems, 1955, p.42-7; Hollow and incised stems, 1956, p.45-50; *all illus.* Prices given.

334 *Exhibition of engraved glass [Catalogue]*. A. Churchill Ltd, 1957, 128p., *illus.*

335 *A Coronation Exhibition of royal, historical, political and social glasses commemorating eighteenth- and nineteenth-century events in English history...* Apr-May 1937. A. Churchill Ltd, 1937. 42p., *illus.* A catalogue: cover-title: 'History in Glass'.

336 *P.B. List of old English and Irish glass. For the use of owners of 'English table glass', by Percy Bate.* A. Churchill Ltd, 1939, 24p. Cover-title: 'A list of Old English and Irish glass offered for sale...'

337 CIRCLE OF GLASS COLLECTORS. *Catalogue of the Circle of Glass Collectors' Commemorative Exhibition, 1937-1962, at the Victoria and Albert Museum. Introduction and notes by R.J. Charleston.* London, 1962. 72p., *illus.*

338 'Paper devoted to John M. Bacon [founder of the Circle], died April 1948- a sketch of his family and writings'. In *GC*, no.88.

339 CLAIR, Colin, *ed. Glass.* Bruce and Gawthorn, n.d. 64p., *illus.* (Things we need).

340 CLARK, George Thomas. *Some account of Sir Robert Mansell, Kt, Vice-admiral of England...* Dowlais, 1883, 110.

341 CLEPHAN, James. 'The manufacture of glass in England. Rise of the art on the Tyne'. In *Archaeologia Aeliana* (Newcastle), New Series, v.8, 1880, p.108-26, *illus.*

342 CLOAK, Evelyn Campbell. *Glass paperweights. The complete collection of glass paperweights and related items... of the Bergstrom Art Centre Museum.* Studio Vista, 1969, 196p., *illus. (col.), bibliog.* Contents include: British and continental weights, p.97-115, and a bibliography of some 300 items.

343 'Clutha Glass'. In *Discovering Antiques*, v.17, New York, Greystone Press, 1973, p.2090-2091, *illus.*

344 COCKRÁM, A.J. 'William Parker and his chandeliers'. In *The Bath Critic*, v.3, no.8 [1953?].

345 COKE, Desmond. *Confessions of an incurable collector.* Chapman and Hall, 1928. Contents include: So-called Bristol blue glass, p.205-8.

346 'College glassworks'. In *Tableware*, 1963, p.558-9, *illus.* The Royal College of Art Glassworks.

347 'Coloured [glass] bottles'. In *The Times*, Mar 18th 1959, p.9, *illus.*

348 'Coloured Victorian art glass'. In *The Times*, Nov 7th 1964, p.11, *illus.*

349 COLUMBUS GALLERY OF FINE ARTS, OHIO. *Aspects of Irish Art.* Dublin, Nat. Gallery of Ireland, 1974, 113p., *illus.*

350 COMMISSION OF ENQUIRY INTO THE EXCISE ESTABLISHMENT. [Report on the] *Glass* [trade]. London, 1835. An important document in the history of the glass trade. Reproduces relevant documents and lists contemporary glass manufacturers.

351 'Competitive friggers – encouraging the glass craftsman'. In *Pottery Gazette and Glass Trade Rev.*, 1963, p.552-3, *illus.*

352 COMSTOCK, Helen. 'Beilby glass in America including some recent discoveries'. In *CONN*, Jan-June 1951, p.106-11, *illus.*

353 'An engraved English glass water jug'. In *CONN*, Jan-June 1946, p.109-10, *illus.*

354 'Exhibition of English and Irish glass'. In *CONN*, Jan-June 1942, p.65-6, *illus.* An Exhibition held at the Steuben Glass Shop, New York.

355 'Sequence of English chandeliers'. In *A*, Jly, 1944, p.36-8, *illus.*

356 CONNOISSEUR. *Connoisseur Complete Encyclopedia of Antiques, ed.* by L.G.G. Ramsey. Connoisseur, 1962. Contents include: English glass, p.418-21; Irish glass, p.423-5; Glossary of glass, p.432-72, *all illus.*

357 *Connoisseur Complete Encyclopedia of Antiques.* 2nd ed. Peerage Books, [1975]. Glass p.237-91, *illus.*

358 *The Connoisseur new guide to antique pottery, porcelain and glass.* Edited by L.G.G. Ramsey. Connoisseur, 1961, 192p., *illus.* Includes glass, p.85-124. Material later used in the *Connoisseur Period Guides*.

359 COOK, Jean M. 'A fragment of early medieval glass from London'. In *Medieval Archaeology*, 1958, p.173-7, *illus.*

360 COOK, N.C. 'Medieval glass from the City of London'. In *Antiques Journal*, v.47, Pt 2, 1967, p.287.

361 COOK, W.E. *The Art and craft of glassmaking.* Stourbridge, Stuart and Sons, Ltd, 1934, 25p., *illus.*

362 COPE, E.E. 'Some notes on the Warrington glass-works'. In *CONN*, Sept-Dec 1923, p.40.

363 'Cordial glasses and decanters'. In *ADCG*, Nov 1958, p.23-5, illus.

364 CORNING MUSEUM OF GLASS, NEW YORK. Corning Glass Centre. Descriptive brochure. Corning, 1952, *illus.*

365 *English nineteenth-century cameo glass. Introduction by A.C. Revi; preface and catalogue by P.N. Perrot.* New York, Corning, 1963, 43p., *illus.*

366 *Victorian glass... from the Victoria and Albert Museum (text by Betty O'Looney).* New York, Corning, 1971, 15p., *illus.*

367 'Coronation glass and vase [1952]'. In *AP*, Jan-June 1953, p.134, *illus.* By Royal Brierley Crystal and Stuart and Sons, Ltd, respectively.

368 COXSON, A.O. 'Enchantment in Bristol coloured

glass'. In *ADCG*, Sept 1966, p.71-4, *illus.*

369 'The rise and fall of Bristol glass'. In *ADCG*, March 1972, p.86-9, *illus. (some col.)*

370 COYSH, A.W. *The antique buyer's dictionary of names.* David & Charles, 1970.
Contents include: Names in glass manufacture, etc., p.123-38.

371 COYSH, A.W. *and* KING, J. *Buying antiques reference book.* David and Charles, 1970.
Contents include: Glass collections open to the public, p.27-9; Glass prices at auction, 1967-9. p.202-7 and 248-52.

372 *Buying antiques general guide.* David and Charles, 1968.
Contents include: Glass, p.108-24, *illus.*

CRAIG, Algernon *see* FREEMASONS UNITED GRAND LODGE OF ENGLAND.

373 CRELLIN, J.K. *and* SCOTT, J.R. 'Glass and British pharmacy, 1600-1900'. In *Scottish Glass Circle*, v.1 (1972) p.33-45, *illus., bibliog.*

374 *Glass and British pharmacy, 1600-1900: a survey and guide to the Wellcome Collection of British Glass.* Wellcome Institute, 1972, 72p., *illus.*

375 CROMPTON, Sidney. 'Collecting English eighteenth-century glass'. In *ADCG*, June 1966, p.83-5, *illus.*

376 'Mainly about rummers'. In *ADCG*, Nov 1966, p.62-4, *illus.* Includes a 'classified list of unengraved rummers by stem forms'.

377 *ed. English glass.* Edited by Sidney Crompton, contributors E.M. Elville and E. Ross. Ward, Lock, 1967. 254p., *illus.*
Contents: 'Traditions of English glass' by Euan Ross; 'Techniques of the glassmaker' by E.M. Elville; 'Collections and collecting' and 'Fakes and forgeries' by Sidney Crompton.

378 *History in glass.* Fontwell (Sussex), Centaur Press, *illus.* Announced but not published.

379 CROSSLEY, D.W. 'Glassmaking in Bagot's Park, Staffordshire, in the sixteenth century'. In *Post-Medieval Archaeology*, v.I, 1967, p.44-83, *illus.*

380 'The development of English glass furnaces in the 16th and 17th centuries'. In *CJGS*, 1983, p.147-53, *illus., plans, bibliog.*

381 'The performance of the glass industry in 16th century England'. In *Economic History Review*, Aug 25th 1972, p.421-33.

382 *and* ABERG, F.A. 'Sixteenth-century glass making in Yorkshire: excavations at furnaces of Hutton and Rosedale...1968-1971'. In *Post Medieval Arch.*, 6, 1972, p.107-54.

383 'Cupping or bleeding glasses'. In *CL*, Jly-Dec 1954, p.291, *illus.*, 502; 819; 994; 1079; 1497; 2111; 2324. A series of letters.

284 'Cut-glass fruit bowls'. In *ADCG*, Oct 1958, p.28-30, *illus.*

385 CURTIS, R.A. *and* MILLER, Martin. *The Lyle official antiques review.* Worthing, Jakta Press, 1970.
Contents include: Glass, p.316-23, *illus.*

386 CUSHION, John. 'Pleasing glass for the modest collector'. In *Antiques Finder*, 1970-1, p.29-30, *illus.*

387 DANIEL, Dorothy. *Cut and engraved glass, 1771-1905. 6th ed.* New York, Barrows, 1965, 441p., *illus.*

388 DANIELS, John Stuart. *The Woodchester Glass House: a record of the Huguenot glass workers with a description of the glass produced at the Woodchester site.* Gloucester, Bellows, 1950, 42p., *illus., map, bibliog.*

389 DAVENPORT, Cyril J.H. *Cameos.* Seeley, 1900, 66p., *illus.*

390 DAVIDSON, Ruth. 'English cameo glass'. In *A*, 1963, p.694, *illus.*

391 DAVIES, G.M. 'Black slag blocks from early glasshouses in Gloucester'. In *Glass Technology*, Dec 1970, p.165-6, *illus.*

392 DAVIS, Cecil. 'Old glass for export'. In *CONN*, Jly-Dec 1941, p.108-11, *illus.* Export of English and Irish glass to America about 1800.

393 'Story of English glass: some lecture notes'. In *AC*, p.202-7, *illus.*

394 DAVIS, Derek C. 'Asprey's bicentenary'. In *AC*, May 1981, p.73-5, *illus.*

395 *English and Irish antique glass.* A. Barker, 1964, 152p., *illus., bibliog.*
Contents include: Special types of glasses attributed to specific drinks, p.47-60.

396 'English glass'. In *The Collectors' Encyclopedia of Antiques*, New York, Crown, 1973, p.423-50, *illus.*

397 'Five phases in eighteenth-century glass'. In *AC*, Dec 1961, p.252-6, *illus.*

398 'John Wilkes and political glasses'. In *AC*, Feb 1961, p.14-16, *illus.*

399 'Why collect glass?' In *AC*, May 1981, p.73-5, *illus.*

400 *and* MIDDLEMAS, Keith. *Coloured glass. Photographs by Michael Plomer.* H. Jenkins, 1968, 119p., *illus. (col.).*

401 DAVIS, Frank. 'The Burn-Murdoch "Amen Glass" of about 1745'. In *CL*, Jan 15th 1981, p.110-11, *illus.*

402 'Butcher Cumberland and Prince Charlie'. In *CL*, Nov 1960, p.1096-7, *illus.*

403 'The Butler Buggin bowls'. In *CL*, Jly 1963, p.88-9, *illus.*

404 'The conservative English'. In *ILN*, Dec 1954, p.1020, *illus.* Engraved glasses.

405 *The Country Life book of glass.* Country Life, 1966. Contents include: English and Irish glass, p.39-58, *illus.*

406 'Decanter and enamelled wine glasses by William Beilby of Newcastle'. In *CL*, Feb 1960, p.264, *illus.*

407 *Early 18th Century English Glass.* Country Life, 1971, 63p., *illus.*

408 'Early English glass'. In *ADCG*, Apr 1982, p.45-7, *illus.*

409 'The embellishment of glass'. In *The Times*, Oct 5th 1968, p.23, *illus.* Dutch decoration

410    of 'Newcastle' glass.
'English eighteenth-century glass'. In *ILN*, Jly 1929, p.138, *illus.*

411    'English enamelled glass'. In *CL*, May 1958, p.1072-3, *illus.*

412    'An engraved glass bowl, about 1760, with drinking scenes and mottos of the Walpole and Fitzwilliam families'. In *CL*, Jly 1964, p.106, *illus.*

413    'English history in glass'. In *ILN*, June 1937, p.1056, *illus.*

414    'The Francis Collection at Christies'. In *ILN*, Jly 1934, p.32, *illus.*

415    'Glass decanters'. In *ILN*, Nov 1930, p.984, *illus.*

416    'Glass exports westwards in the eighteenth century'. In *ILN*, Oct 1955, p.700.

417    'The golden age of the wine glass'. In *CL*, March 1974, p.657-8, *illus.*

418    'Inscribed English glasses'. In *ILN*, Nov 1929, p.778, *illus.*

419    'Jacobite glasses' [from the collection of W. Horridge]. In *ILN*, Feb 1960, p.258, *illus.*

420    'Kneller portrait illustrates fashions in eighteenth-century glass'. In *ILN*, Jan 1966, p.27, *illus.*

421    'Old English glass at Christies'. In *ILN*, Oct 1934, p.578, *illus.*

422    'Old glass at the Marlborough and Queen Anne Exhibition'. In *ILN*, Feb 1934, p.216, *illus.*

423    'Ravenscroft decanter jug'. [Engraved in the Low Countries or Germany c.1676]. In *CL*, Sept 1964, p.556-7, *illus.*

424    'Richness of a National Collection: glass at the British Museum'. In *CL*, Jly 1968, p.101-2, *illus.*

425    'Sixteenth-eighteenth-century bottles'. In *ILN*, Dec 1932, p.902, *illus.*

426    'Some eighteenth-century glass'. In *ILN*, Oct 1932, p.586, *illus.*

427    'Success to aerostation'. In *ILN*, Jly 1954, p.148, *illus.* A late eighteenth-century glass engraved with a ballooning scene.

428    'Table glass for the British'. In *Discovering Antiques*, v.8, New York, Greystone Press, 1973, p.975-9, *illus.*

429    'Two enamelled decanters, etc. by the Beilby family'. In *CL*, Jly 1960, p.194, *illus.*

430    DAWSON, Charles. 'Old Sussex glass: its origin and decline'. In *The Antiquary*, v.41, 1905, p.8-11.

431    DAY, Michael. 'Letters from a cupboard...' In *Indus. Arch.*, 15, no.3, 1980, p.229-35. Norwich Glass Co. correspondence with customers 1920s.

432    DEANE, Ethel. *Byways of collecting*. Cassell, 1908, 200p., *illus.*
Contents include: Old glass, Chapter 13.

433    DEAR, Herbert R. 'Why collect old drinking glasses'. In *AC*, 1935, p.291-4, *illus.*

434    *Decorative Art in Modern Interiors* (formerly *Studio Year Book*). Published annually.

Contents include: Illustrated surveys of contemporary glassware (since 1906).

435    'Decorative brilliance – English cut glass'. In *ADCG*, Sept 1958, p.33-5, *illus.*

436    DELOMOSNE & SON LTD, LONDON. *Gilding the lily: rare forms of decoration on English glass of the later 18th century*. London, Delomosne, 1978, 48p., *illus.* Loan exhibition.

437    DENNIS, Richard. 'The Butler Buggin bowls'. In *The Ivory Hammer: the year at Sotheby's*, Longmans, 1963, p.198-9, *illus.*

438    'Changing tastes in English [eighteenth-century] drinking glasses'. In *Art at auction, 1967-8*, New York, Viking Press, 1968, p.48-51, *illus.*

439    [Description and illustration of glassware designed by Harry J. Powell.] In *Art Jnl.*, 1905, p.61-5, and 1906, p.88, *illus.*

440    'Design Exhibition explained to the glass industry'. In *Pottery Gazette*, 1946, p.161-8, *illus.* Illustrated survey of contemporary glass.

441    'Design in the glass industry'. In *Pottery Gazette*, 1946, p.328-30, *illus.*

442    'Designed for sparkling wines: English champagne glasses'. In *ADCG*, Jly 1958, p.29-31, *illus.*

443    'Diamond-point engraved drinking glass dated 1577' [attributed to Verzelini]. In *AP*, Jly-Dec 1939, p.86, *illus., and* in *CONN*, Jly-Dec 1939, p.42, *illus.*

444    DICK, *Mrs.* 'Glass speaks to me, with instances from my collection'. In *GC*, no.79.

445    DILLON, Edward. *Glass.* Methuen, 1907, 374p., *illus. (some col.), bibliog.* (Connoisseur's Library).
Contents include: English glass of sixteenth to seventeenth centuries, p.299-336; English medieval glass, p.139-40.

   DIMBLEBY, Violet, *ed. see* DUNCAN, George Sang.

446    DON, Robin. 'Harvey's Wine Museum, Bristol'. In *Museum Jnl.*, v.66, June 1966, p.24-9, *illus.*

447    DORMER, Ernest W. 'Fine glass'. In *Antiques Rev.*, 1952, Pt. 12, p.37-8, *illus.*

448    DOSSIE, Robert. *Handmaid to the arts.* New ed. 2v., London, 1796. First pub. 1758.
Contents include: On the nature and composition of glass, etc., v.2, p.158-38.

449    DOUGLAS, Jane. *Collectable glass.* Longacre Press, 1961, 64p., *illus.*
Contents include: Slagware, p.47-50 (with list of registry marks).

450    DOUGLAS, R.W. 'Glass technology' [1850-1900]. *In* Singer, Charles *and others, eds. History of Technology*, O.U.P., 1957, v.5, p.671-82, *illus., bibliog.*

451    'W.E.S. Turner, applied scientist'. In *Glass Technology*, 1967, p.19-28, *illus., ports.* The first W.E.S. Turner Memorial Lecture.

452    'William Ernest Stephen Turner'. In *Biographical Memoirs of the Fellows of the Royal Society*, v.10, 1964, p.325-55, *illus.*

453    DOUGLAS, R.W. *and* FRANK, S. *A History of*

*glass-making.* G.T. Foulis, 1972, 213p., *illus.*, *bibliog.* Mainly British.

**454** DOVER, Clare. 'Unearthing an Elizabethan glass works' [at Bickerstaffe, Lancs.]. In *The Daily Telegraph*, June 2nd 1969, p.12, *illus.*

DREISER, P. *joint author see* MATCHAM, J. *and* DREISER, P.

**455** 'Drinking glass apparently used by Queen Anne at Cambridge in 1705'. In *CL*, Apr 1967, p.786, *illus.* Letter and editorial comment.

**456** 'Drinking vessels at the Antique Dealers' Fair...'; In *Wine and Spirit Trade Record*, 1960, p.998; 1000; 1002, *illus.*

**457** 'Dublin Exhibition of Industrial Art, 1853'. [Exhibits by Harris and Sons of Birmingham, and Richardson of Stourbridge.] In *Art Jnl.*, 1853, p.30; 35 (in supplement preceding main text).

**458** DUBLIN SCIENCE AND ART MUSEUM. *General guide to the art collections: Pt.9: Glass* [compiled by J. Day]. Dublin, H.M.S.O., 1906, 38p., *illus.*

**459** *General guide to the art collections: Pt.9, Glass* [compiled by M.S.D. Westropp]. Dublin, H.M.S.O., 1912, 74p., *illus.*

**460** DUFFY, E. Mary. 'Philip Pargeter and John Northwood I: cameo glass pioneers'. In *A*, 1962, p.639-41, *illus.*

**461** DUMBRELL, Roger. *Understanding antique wine bottles.* Antique Collectors' Club, 1983, 338p., *illus.*, *bibliog.*

**462** DUNCAN, George Sang. *A bibliography of glass (from the earliest records to 1940)... edited [with supplement] by Violet Dimbleby. Subject index by Frank Newby.* Dawsons, for the Society of Glass Technology, 1960, 552p. An annotated list of 15,752 items covering the whole field of glass.

**463** DUNSMUIR, Richard. 'Glass chandeliers'. In *AC*, Feb 1976, p.24-6, *illus.*

**464** 'Old and rare English wine bottles'. In *AC*, Aug 1976, p.28-31, *illus.*

**465** DUTHIE, Arthur L. *Decorative glass processes.* Constable, 1908, 267p., *illus.* (Westminster Series).

**466** DUTHY, Robin, *comp.* 'The investment file: 18th century English drinking glasses'. In *CONN*, June 1981, p.130-1, *illus.*

**467** DYER, Walter A. *The lure of the antique.* New York, Century, 1910. Contents include: English and American glassware, p.309-35, *illus.*

**468** 'Earliest recorded glassmaker in England'. In *Glass Technology*, 1960, p.137.

**469** 'Early coloured glass at Heaton Hall' [Manchester]. In *AC*, 1938, p.326, *illus.* The Applewhaite-Abbot Collection.

**470** 'Early English drinking glasses'. In *The Times*, Apr 14th 1956, p.9, *illus.*

**471** 'Early Orange glass from Ireland. A note by a collector'. In *CONN*, Jan-June 1946, p.38-41, *illus.*

**472** EASTLAKE, Charles L. *Hints on household taste. 4th ed.* Longmans, 1878. Contents include: Table glass, p.241-57, *illus.*

**473** EBBOTT, Rex. *British glass of the seventeenth and eighteenth centuries.* Melbourne, O.U.P., 1971, 31p., *illus.*, *bibliog.*

**474** EDGCUMBE, Richard. 'Diffraction and seduction: some problems in the display of glass'. In *Museums Jnl.*, Sept 1974, p.73-4, *illus.*

**475** EDINBURGH MUSEUM OF SCIENCE AND ART. *List of books, etc. relating to glass in the library of the Museum. Edinburgh*, 1893, 40p.

**476** EDWARD, Robert. *On collecting engravings, pottery, porcelain, glass and silver.* Edward Arnold, 1904, 90p. (Wallet Series).

**477** 'Electioneering goblet' [inscribed LASCELLES FOR EVER]. In *AC*, 1936, p.325, *illus.* A Yorkshire election of 1807.

**478** ELLISON, Margaret. 'The Tyne glasshouses and Beilby and Bewick'. In *Archaeologia Aeliana*, 3, 1975, p.143-93.

**479** ELLSON, Jack. 'English 19th century pressed glass'. In *Antique Collecting*, Feb 1982, p.26-30, *illus.*

**480** 'More about Victorian coloured glass'. In *Antique Collecting*, June 1981, p.29-31, *illus.*

**481** ELMHURST, Sheila. 'The aesthetic and practical applications of diamond-point engraving'. In *International Congress on Glass, comptes rendus, Bruxelles, 1965.* Paper 215, p.1-3, *illus.*

**482** ELPHINSTONE, N. 'Recent museum acquisitions. The Harvey Collection of fine glasses'. In *BUR*, Jan-June 1969, p.88, *illus.* Harvey's Wine Museum was founded in Bristol in 1965.

ELPHINSTONE, N.E. *joint author see* BANKS, M., ELPHINSTONE, N.E. *and* HALL, E.T.

**483** ELVILLE, Ernest Michael. *Collectors dictionary of glass.* Country Life, 1961, 194p., *illus.*, *bibliog.* Contents include: Candelabra, p.34-8; Carafes, p.40; Chandeliers, p.42-9; Doorstops, p.73-4; Frauds and reproductions, p.96-9; James and William Tassie, 178-9; Lynn or Norwich glass, p.125-6; Michael Edkins, p.77-8; Posset and caudle glasses, p.157-8; Sand glasses, p.163; Scottish glass, p.164-5; Witch balls, p.190-1.

**484** 'The colour of Waterford glass'. In *Apollo Annual*, 1948, p.88-90.

**485** 'Comparison of some eighteenth-century tableware in metal and glass'. In *Apollo Miscellany*, 1950, p.27-34, *illus.*

**486** 'Cut glass of the eighteenth century'. In *AP*, Jan-June 1950, p.166-7, 171, *illus.*

**487** 'Cut wine glasses of the eighteenth century'. In *CL*, Dec 1948, p.1382-3 and Jan 1949, p.34-5, *illus.*

**488** 'Early drinking vessels' [wines, ales, rummers]. In *AP*, Jan-June 1950, p.28-9, *illus.*

**489** 'Early engraved glass'. In *AP*, Jan-June 1947, p.92-4 and 116-18, *illus.*

490 'Early glass chandeliers'. In *AP*, Jly-Dec 1948, p.14-15, *illus*.

491 'Eighteenth-century glass fakes'. In *CL*, Jan-June 1952, p.28-9, *illus*.

492 'English glass in the seventeenth century'. In *CL*, Sept 1962, p.516-17, *illus*. and in *Glass*, p.599-602, *illus*.

493 *English and Irish cut glass, 1750-1950.* Country Life, 1953, 95p., *illus*.

494 *English tableglass.* Country Life, 1951, 275p., *illus*., *bibliog*.
Contents include: Methods of distinguishing the genuine from the imitation, p.247-55; Scientific investigation of old glass, p.256-66.

495 'English table and ornamental glass: one hundred years' retrospect'. In *Apollo Annual*, 1951, p.55-60, *illus*. Includes cameos.

496 'Famous English glasses [Five articles]. In *AP*. (1) 'The Verzelini goblets'. Jan-June 1947, p.154-5.
(2) 'The Beilby glasses'. Jly-Dec 1947, p.40-1.
(3) 'Bristol glasses decorated by Michael Edkins'. Jly-Dec 1947, p.73.
(4) 'Jacobite glasses'. Jan-June 1948, p.18-19.
(5) 'The early balusters'. Jan-June 1948, p.35. *All illus*.

497 'Fashions in Victorian glass'. In *CL*, June 1960, p.1312-13, *illus*.

498 'The glass cameo work of James and William Tassie'. In *Glass*, 1962, p.121-4, *illus*.

499 'Glass at the Great Exhibition'. In *CL*, Apr 1951, p.1294-9, *illus*.

500 'Glass engraved with a diamond'. In *Country Life Annual*, 1963, p.8-10, *illus*.

501 'Glass paperweights'. In *AP*, Jan-June 1948, p.93-4 *and* 115-16, *illus*.

502 'Glass in borrowed forms: early English tableware'. In *Country Life Annual*, 1964, p.114-17, p.119, *illus*.

503 'Glasses with air-twist stems'. In *CL*, Mar 1949, p.492-3, *illus*.

504 'Glasses with opaque-twist stems and folded feet'. In *CL*, Jan 1948, p.232-3, *illus*.

505 'Glasses with Silesian stems'. In *CL*, Sept 1963, p.765-6, *illus*.

506 'History of the glass chandelier'. In *Country Life Annual*, 1949, p.200-4, *illus*.

507 'Irish glass of the eighteenth and nineteenth centuries'. In *CL*, June 1958, p.1290-1, *illus*.

508 'Old English champagne glasses'. In *AP*, Jly-Dec 1946, p.99-100, *illus*.

509 'Opaque-white glass of the eighteenth and nineteenth centuries'. In *CL*, Oct 1949, p.1297-8, *illus*.

510 *Paperweights and other glass curiosities.* Country Life, 1954. 116p., *illus*., *bibliog*.
Contents include: Illuminating glassware, p.63-72; Commemorative glasses, p.95-103.

511 'The Portland vase and its copies'. In *ADCG*, Sept 1964, p.50-1, *illus*.

512 'Portraits in powdered glass: cameo work of James and William Tassie'. In *CL*, June 1961, p.351-2, *illus*.

513 'The quality and style of cut glass'. In *CL*, May and June 1947, p.1008-9 and 1064-5, *illus*.

514 'Some features of early cut wine glasses'. In *AP*, Jan-June 1949, p.130-1, *illus*.

515 'Some rarities in glasses with opaque-twist stems'. In *AP*, Jly-Dec 1949, p.134-5, *illus*.

516 'Starting a collection of glass: English styles of the eighteenth century'. In *CL*, June 1959, p.1329-30, *illus*.

517 'Techniques of the glassmaker'. In Crompton, Sidney, *ed. English glass*, 1967, p.39-58, *illus*.

518 'Today's trends in table glass'. In *Country Life Annual*, 1962, p.12-13, *illus*.

519 'Vogue of the baluster glass'. In *CL*, June 1963, p.1417-19, *illus*.

ELVILLE, Ernest Michael. *See also* CROMPTON, Sydney, *ed*.

520 'The empty bud' [Newcastle Jacobite glasses]. In *GN*, 1951, p.18-21, *illus*.

521 *Encyclopedia of World Art.* McGraw Hill, 1962. [Article on] glass. In v.6, p.367-98, *illus*., *bibliog*.

522 'English and continental glassmaking'. In *The Times*, Dec 5th 1902, p.15.

523 'English Cameo glass: nineteenth-century collection of Mr and Mrs Albert Christian Revi'. In *Antiques Journal*, Jly 1963, p.24-6, p.33, *illus*.

524 'English export glass'. In *GN*, 1946, p.23-4.

525 'English glass: a chronology for collectors' [1226-1851]. In *GN*, 1948, p.19-21.

526 'English seventeenth-century glass'. In *GN*, 1946, p.26-8, *illus*. Discusses differences between true Venetian and façon de Venise.

527 'Engraved commemorative glass'. In *The Times*, Sept 16th 1961, p.11, *illus*.

528 'Engraving on glass'. In *The Times*, Jly 30th 1960, p.9, *illus*.

529 ENGLE, Anita. 'Mayer Oppenheim De Bermingham'. In *Readings in Glass History*, (USA), no.4, 1974, p.61-71.

530 ERVIN, Horace. 'Notes on Franklin's Armonica and the music Mozart wrote for it'. In *Jnl. Franklin Institute*, 262, no.5, 1956, p.329-48, *illus*. Musical glasses made in England for Franklin.

531 ESWARIN, Rudy. 'Tags and tickets [bottle labels engraved on glass]'. In *Wine Tidings*, Mar 1982, p.7-9, *illus*.

532 EVANS, Wendy. 'Background to glass-history from early days'. In *Pottery Gazette and Glass Trade Review*, 1965, p.952-5, *illus*.

533 'Contemporary English artistic glass making'. Paper read at the Fifth Congress of the International Assn. for the History of Glass, Prague, 1970.

534 EVANS, Wendy *and* WEEDEN, Cyril. *Making

glass. Glass Manufacturers' Federation, c.1969, 40p., *illus.*

535 'Fair goods' [silvered glass]. In *GN*, 1952, p.28-31, *illus.*

536 'Fairy cup of Ballafletcher'. In *CONN*, Jly-Dec 1936, p.330, *illus.* Copy of the original glass tumbler made at the end of the eighteenth century now in the Manx Museum, Douglas, I.O.M.

537 'Falcon Glass Works: Messrs Apsley Pellatt & Co.'. In *Art Union*, 1847, p.321-4, *illus.*

538 FARR, Michael. *Design in British industry: a mid-century survey.* C.U.P., 1955. Glass, p.105-14, *illus.*

539 FARRAR, Estelle Sinclaire. 'John Northwood and English cameo glass'. In *Art and Antiques* (USA), v.4, Jly-Aug 1981, p.50-5, *illus.*

540 FELL, H. Granville. 'An old English blue vase by Ravenscroft' [and two jugs]. In *CONN*, Jly-Dec 1938, p.78, *illus.*

541 FERLAY, John. 'Glasses for everyone'. In *ADCG*, Jan 1971, p.86-8, *illus.*

542 'Grandeur in glass'. In *ADCG*, Oct 1974, p.106-7, *illus.* A Ravenscroft syllabub jug.

543 'High price paid for glass sealed bottle'. In *ADCG*, Apr 1978, p.92, *illus.*

544 'An interesting glass sale'. In *ADCG*, Apr 1972, 88-90, *illus.* Compares prices.

545 'Market favours glass wine bottles' [recent prices]. In *ADCG*, Feb 1969, p.89, *illus.*

546 'Pieces from three centuries'. In *ADCG*, May 1974, p.81-2, *illus.*

547 FFOOKS, Oliver. 'Opaque-twist soda glasses: are they of English or continental provenance?' In *AC*, 1969, p.27-30, *illus.*

548 FINDLAY, Ian. *Scottish crafts.* Harrap, 1948. Contents include: Glass, p.110-13, *illus.*

549 'Finger bowls once banned from royal banquets'. In *The Times*, Aug 11th 1962, *illus.*

550 FITZHUGH, John. 'Over the chemists counter Pts.1 and 2'. In *Antique Bottle Collecting*, Feb 1982, p.2-4; Apr 1982, p.12-13, *illus.* Jars and bottles.

551 FITZPATRICK, Paul. 'Waterford glass house'. In *Antiques Jnl.*, May 1977, p.16-19; June 1977, p.30-2, *illus.*

552 FITZWILLIAM MUSEUM, CAMBRIDGE. *Glass at the Fitzwilliam Museum.* Cambridge University Press, 1978, 127p., *illus., bibliog.* Includes English glass.

553 FLEMING, Arnold. *Scottish and Jacobite glass.* Glasgow, Jackson, 1938. 196p., *illus.* Includes stained glass. Describes main Scottish glasshouses: Perth, Alloa, Dundee, Edinburgh, Leith, etc.

554 *Scottish and Jacobite glass.* E.P. Publishing Ltd., 1977. Facsimile repr. 1st ed. 1938.

555 'Select bibliography' [of glass]. In G. Janneau, *Modern glass*, 1931, p.54-6. About 320 items.

556 FLETCHER, Edward. *Antique bottles in colour.* Blandford Press, 1974. *illus. (col.).*

557 *Bottle collecting: finding, collecting and displaying antique bottles.* Blandford Press, 1972, 96p., *illus.*

558 'Flint glass epergnes for the Georgian dessert table'. In *The Times*, Feb 29th 1964, p.11, *illus.*

559 FLINT GLASS MAKERS …*Rules and regulations of the Flint Glass Makers' Friendly Society of Great Britain and Ireland revised at the conference held in London…* 1858. Birmingham, T.J. Wilkinson [1858]. 22p.

560 'Fly-catcher, Victorian hand-blown' [Letter]. In *CL*, May 1961, p.1037, *illus.*

561 FORBES, R.J. 'Glass through the ages'. In *Phillips Technical Review*, Jly 22nd 1961, p.282-99, *illus.*

562 FORD, John. *John Ford, flint glass manufacturer… Holyrood Flint Glass Works, Edinburgh.* c.1870, 77p., *illus.* There is a photocopy of this work in the National Art Library, Victoria and Albert Museum.

563 'Ford cameo glass decanter'. In *CONN*, May-Aug 1925, p.97-8, *illus.* Refers to John Ford & Co., Ediburgh.

564 'Forest House, Bournemouth'. In *AC*, 1936, p.167-70, *illus.* Includes a collection of English glass.

565 FOSS, C. John. 'Bells of the Bristol glasshouses'. In *CL*, Oct 1961, p.920-2, *illus.*

566 FOSTER, Kate. *Scent bottles.* Connoisseur and M. Joseph, 1966. (Connoisseur monograph). Glass, p.33-44, *illus.*

567 FOWLER, James. 'On the process of decay in glass… and the composition and texture of glass at different periods and the history of its manufacture'. In *Archaeologia*, v.46, 1880, p.65-162, *illus.*

568 FOX, Russel, *and* LEWIS, Elizabeth. *William Overton and glassmaking in Buriton.* Petersfield, Petersfield Historical Soc., 1982, 16p., *illus.* 16th century glasshouse excavation in Ditcham Woods.

569 FRANCIS, Grant Richardson. 'Disguised Jacobite glasses'. In *BUR*, Jly-Dec 1936, p.175-6, *illus.*

570 'Jacobite drinking glasses and their relation to the Jacobite medals'. In *British Numismatic Jnl.*, 1921-2, p.247-83, *illus.*

571 'Old English drinking glasses, their chronology and sequence, etc.' H. Jenkins, 1926, 222p., *illus.*

572 'Propaganda glasses'. [Jacobite and Williamite]. In *Arthur Churchill Ltd. Catalogue of old English glass*, 2nd ed., 1937, p.3-6.

FRANK, S. *joint author see* DOUGLAS, R.W. *and* FRANK, S.

573 FRAZER, Margaret. 'Coloured glass'. In *Discovering Antiques*, v.8, New York, Greystone Press, 1973, p.904-7, *illus.*

574 FREEMASONS UNITED GRAND LODGE OF ENGLAND. *Catalogue of the Museum of the Freemasons' Hall* [London]. Compiled by Algernon Craig. 1939, 41p., *illus.* Includes Masonic glass.

575 FRESCO-CORBU, Roger. 'How to smoke an economical cigar: some nineteenth-century holders'. In *CL*, Apr 1965, p.747-8, *illus*. Includes glass examples.

576 FULLER, Georgina. 'Glass jugs'. In *AC*, Sept 1975, p.31-5, *illus*.

577 GABRIEL, R. *English drinking glasses*. Letts, 1974, 72p., *illus. (col.)* (Letts Collectors Guides).

578 GAINES, E. 'English glass collections outside London'. *A*, v.106 pt.1, Jly 1974, p.104-11, *illus*. Waddesdon Manor, Ashmolean, Fitzwilliam, Heaton Hall (Cheshire) etc.

579 'Glass from the Pilkington Glass Museum'. In *A*, Mar 1975, p.462-72, *illus*.

580 'Galaxy of glass. The British and the Victoria and Albert Museums display Nation's finest glass treasures for International Glass Congress' 1968. In *AC*, 1968, p.167-71, *illus*.

581 GANDY, Walter. *The romance of glass-making: a sketch of the history of ornamental glass*. Partridge, 1898, 160p., *illus*.

582 GARDINER, C.I. 'An eighteenth century flagon from Arlingham'. In *Trans. of the Bristol and Gloucestershire Archaeological Soc.*, v.60, 1940, p.190-3, *illus*.

583 GAUPP, Charles. 'Mary Gregory glass?' In *ADCG*, May 1979, p.92-3, *illus*.

584 'Georgian decanters'. In *ADCG*, Apr 1958, p.24-6, *illus*.

585 'Georgian table glass: finger bowls and wine glass coolers'. In *ADCG*, May 1958, p.31-3, *illus*.

586 GILBY, W. *and* GILBY, A. *The complete imbiber. A Centenary Exhibition* [Catalogue]. Gilby, 1958, 36p., *illus*.

587 GILL, Ann. 'English glasses' [eighteenth century]. In *Bulletin of the Royal Ontario Museum*, no.25, June 1957, p.19, *illus*.

588 GILL, William. 'Georgian wine glasses'. In Hogg, Anthony, ed., *Wine Mine: A First Anthology*, Souvenir Press, 1970, p.74-9, *illus*.

589 GILL, William H. 'It's a favourite collector's glass' [opaque twists]. In *ADCG*, Dec 1965, p.40-1, *illus*.

590 'On rare baluster glasses'. In *AC*, 1965, p.216-22, *illus*.

591 'Plain and air twist'. In *ADCG*, Nov 1963, p.32-4, *illus*.

592 'Some aspects of English glass'. In *AC*, Apr 1965, p.84-9, *illus*.

593 'Some later glasses'. In *ADCG*, Jan 1964, p.39-40, *illus*.

594 GILLINDER, William. *Treatise on the art of glass making... etc*. Birmingham, 1851, 127p.

595 'Girandole candlesticks'. In *ADCG*, Dec 1958, p.36-8, *illus*.

596 GIRLING, F.A. *English merchants' marks*. O.U.P., 1964.
Contents include: Bottle seals, p.112-14, *illus*.

597 GIUSEPPI, Montague S. 'Glass' [making in Surrey]. In *The Victoria County History of Surrey*, v.2, 1905, p.295-305.

598 'Glass in the Stourbridge Festival of Britain Exhibition'. In *JSGT (News and Reviews)*, 1951, p.61-5, *illus*.

599 'Glass collecting: another side of the picture'. From a correspondent. In *AP*, Jan-June 1943, p.102.

600 'Glass flower pots'. In *CL*, Dec 1962, p.1394, *illus*.

601 'Glass from the Victorian age' [Burmese glass]. In *The Times*, Feb 12th 1966, p.11, *illus*.

602 'Glass blowers of Whitefriars'. In *Arts & Decoration* (U.S.A.), Nov 1938, p.9-10, *illus*.

GLASS CIRCLE *see* CIRCLE OF GLASS COLLECTORS

603 GLASS CIRCLE 1. *Edited by R.J. Charleston, Wendy Evans and Ada Polak*. Oriel Press, 1972, 64p., *illus*. Continues as an occasional publication.

604 'Glass craftsmen of today'. In *ADCG*, Oct 1946, p.22-3, *illus*.

605 'Glass fountain by Messrs Osler'. In *Art Journal*, 1874, p.272, *illus*. F. & C. Osler of Oxford Street, London. The fountain was exported to India for the Maharajah of Puttiala.

606 'Glass globes'. In *The Times*, June 22nd 1963, p.11.

607 'Glass Houghton Glassworks'. In *South Yorkshire Jnl. of Industry and Social History*, Pt I, 1948.

608 GLASS MANUFACTURERS FEDERATION [Hand-made crystal section]. *British crystal glass* [List of manufacturers]. G.M.F., 1957. Typescript.

609 'Glass paperweights'. In *The Times*, May 14th 1963, p.14.

610 GLASS SELLERS' COMPANY. Essays on the glass trade in England. 1883.

611 *Papers relating to the Glass Sellers*. Sloane MS. no. 857 (British Museum).

612 'Glass Sellers' Company tercentenary'. In *The Times*, June 12th 1964, p.14.

613 'The Glass Six of Stourbridge'. In *The Times*, Feb 18th 1965, p.18, *illus*.

614 'Glasses to dress out the dessert'. In *ADCG*, Mar 1958, p.27-9, *illus*.

615 GLOAG, John. 'Victorian desk furniture'. In *CONN*, Apr 1975, p.274-7, *illus*. Glass ink wells.

616 'Goblets for Trinity College, Oxford' [by Laurence Whistler]. In *The Times*, Oct 23rd 1956, p.7, *illus*.

617 GODDEN, Geoffrey A. *Antique china and glass under £5*. A. Barker, 1966
Contents include: Victorian glass, fairy lights and paperweights, p.83-116, *illus*.

618 'Fairy lamps for collectors'. In *ADCG*, Dec 1965, p.55-7, *illus*.

619 'Makers' marks on nineteenth-century glass'. In *CL*, June 1962, p.1452, 1455, *illus*.

620 'Victorian pressed glass'. In *ADCG*, Feb 1965, p.51-2, *illus*.

621 GODFREY, A. *and* LAUNERT, E. 'A glass puzzle

solved'. In *AC*, Jly 1983, p.60-2, *illus.* Stourbridge cheroot holders 1853-1938. Private Coll.

622 GODFREY, Eleanor S. *The development of English glassmaking, 1560-1640.* Ph.D. Thesis (unpublished), Chicago University, 1957.

623 *The development of English glassmaking 1640-1850 .* Clarendon Press, 1975, 288p., *illus., bibliog.*

624 GOLDSMID, Beatrice. 'English glass'. In *ADCG*, Apr 1950, p.15-17 and May 1950, p.25-7, *illus.*

625 'Glass in the Ashmolean Museum'. In *ADCG*, Feb 1951, p.22-4, *illus.*

626 'Glass in the British Museum'. In *ADCG*, Jly 1950, p.37-9, *illus.*

627 'Glass in the Fitzwilliam Museum. In *ADCG*, Mar 1951, p.24-5, *illus.*

628 'Glass in the Victoria and Albert Museum'. In *ADCG*, Sept 1950, p.31-3, *illus.* and Nov 1950, p.28-30, *illus.*

GOODING, E.J. *ed. see* INTERNATIONAL COMMISSION ON GLASS, 1968. *joint ed. see* SOCIETY OF GLASS TECHNOLOGY, SHEFFIELD.

629 GOODWIN, Michael. *Country Life pocket dictionary of collectors' terms.* Country Life, 1967. Glass terms, p.91-121, *illus.*

630 GORDON, Hampden. *Antiques – the amateur's questions.* J. Murray, 1951. Glass, p.1-29, *illus.*

631 *The lure of antiques – looking and learning today.* J. Murray, 1961. Variety in old glass, p.49-66, *illus.*

632 'Trends of design in the crafts'. In *GC*, no.94.

633 'Artist in glass: John Topham'. In *Scotland's Mag.*, Oct 1961, p.7-8. *illus.*

634 GRAHAM, Andrew. 'Recent examples of the work of Laurence Whistler'. In *CONN*, May-Aug 1965, p.92-7, *illus.*

635 GRAHAM, Fergus. 'The Antique Dealers' Fair' [1938]. In *AP*, Jly-Dec 1938, p.187-9, *illus.* On collecting glass.

636 'Glass at the Antique Dealers' Fair' [1937]. In *AP*, Jly-Dec 1937, p.155-7 and 214-16, *illus.*

637 'The glass collection of John M. Bacon, Esq.' In *AP*, Jly-Dec 1936, p.336-41 and Jan-June 1937, p.140-7, *illus.*

638 'Glasses of the seventeenth century (1660-1685)'. In *GC*, no.4.

639 'More early glass'. In *AP*, Jan-June 1938, p.86-90, *illus.* Seventeenth-century examples showing Venetian influence.

640 'Early British glass'. In *AP*, Jly-Dec 1945, p.184-7, *illus.*, p.211 and p.235-7, *illus.*

641 'Some English glass primitives'. In *AP*, Jly-Dec 1938, p.296-8, *illus.* Early seventeenth-century glass.

642 'Some glass problems'. In *GC*, no.70.

643 'Thoughts on early British glass'. In *Apollo Annual*, 1948, p.79-82, *illus.*

644 'Twenty years: some aspects of English glass, 1665-1685' [Lead and soda glass]. In *AP*, Jly-Dec 1937, p.9-15 and p.316-20, *illus.*

645 'Wealden glass'. In *GC*, no.81.

646 'Wrythen glass'. In *GC*, no.1.

647 GRAY, H. St George. 'Nailsea glass'. In *CONN*, May-Aug 1911, p.85-98, *illus. (some col.).*

648 'Notes on Nailsea glass'. In *Proc. Somerset Archaeological Soc.*, v.52, Pt 2, p.166.

649 'Notes on the Nailsea glassworks'. In *CONN*, Jan-June 1923, p.127-33, *illus., port.*

650 *and* LAVINGTON, Margaret. 'Nailsea and other glass in the collection of Mr John Lane'. In *CONN*, May-Aug 1920, p.67-76, *illus.*

651 GRAY, I. 'New factory, new glass'. In *Design*, Apr. 1968, p.48-9, *illus.* Ronald Stennett-Wilson's glass factory at King's Lynn.

652 GRAY, John Miller. *James and William Tassie: a biographical sketch with a catalogue of their [opaque-white glass paste] medallions…* Edinburgh, W.G. Patterson, 1894, 174p.

653 *James and William Tassie: a biographical and critical sketch with a catalogue of their portrait medallions of modern personages.* Holland Press, 1974, 174p., *illus.*

654 GREAT EXHIBITION, LONDON, 1851. 'British glass'. In *Art Journal*. Illustrated catalogue of the Exhibition (Supplementary Vol., 1851). Contains numerous references to the main English glass manufacturers with illustrations.

655 'Great Exhibition of 1851: a review of the pottery and glass exhibits'. In *Pottery Gazette*, 1950, p.523-7, *illus.*

656 GREEN, Mary. 'Glass of fashion and mould of form'. In *CL*, Aug 1963, p.378-9, *illus.* Modern design in English and continental glass.

657 GREENFIELD, John. 'All under £10'. In *AC*, Feb 1982, p.70-1, *illus.*

658 GREENHILL, B.J. 'Nailsea glass works'. In *Bristol Indus. Arch. Soc. Jnl.*, 4, 1971, p.26-7, *illus.*

659 'The story of Nailsea glassworks'. In *The Clevedon Mercury*, Jan 21st 1961.

660 GREENSHIELDS, Margaret. 'Georgian elegance in glass'. In *ADCG*, Sept 1957, p.30-2, *illus.*

661 'Seventeenth-century English glass'. In *ADCG*, Aug 1957, p.25-7, *illus.*

662 'Greenwood, The art of'. In *GN*, 1947, p.12-13, *illus.*

663 GREHAN, Ida. *Waterford: an Irish art.* Huntington (NY), Portfolio Press, 1981, 256p., *illus.*

664 GRIFFENHAGEN, George. 'The evolution of the medicine glass'. In *Hobbies*, Jan 1964, p.72, 84, *illus.*

665 GRIMWADE, A.G. 'Silver and glass cups: a comparison of sixteenth-century examples'. In *CONN*, Jan-June 1953, p.86-7, *illus.*

666 GROS-GALLINER, Gabriella. *Glass: a guide for collectors.* Muller, 1970, 176p., *illus. (some col.), bibliog.* British glass, p.95-116.

667 GROVER, Roy *and* GROVER, Lee. *Art glass*

*nouveau.* Rutland, Vermont (USA), Tuttle, 1967, 231p., *illus.* (col.), *bibliog.* Covers American, English and continental colour glass of the period.

668     *Carved and decorated European Art Glass.* Vermont (USA), Tuttle, 1970, 244p., *illus.* (col.)

669     *English cameo glass.* New York, Crown Pubs., 1980, 482p., *illus.* (some col.)

670     'Guide to glasses'. In *Pottery and Glass*, 1958. Feb, p.51-8; Apr, p.108-13; May, p.127-33; June, p.172-5; Jly, p.194-8; Sept, p.264-8; Oct, p.284-6; Nov, p.321-4, *all illus.*

671     GUILDFORD PUBLIC LIBRARY. *Glass subject specialisation list.* Guildford P.L., 1965, 14p. Duplicated typescript.

672     GUILDHALL MUSEUM. *Catalogue of the collection of London antiquities in the Guildhall Museum.* Guildhall Museum, 1908.

673     *Finds of glass in the City of London.* Exhibition catalogue compiled by R.J. Charleston. Guildhall Museum, 1968, 44p. Typescript.

674     GUTTERY, D.R. *From Broad-glass to cut crystal: a history of the Stourbridge glass industry.* L. Hill, 1956, 161p., *illus., bibliog.*
Contents include: George Ensell and the Wordsley glasshouses, p.96-104; The Henzey family, p.12-31, 45-66; Paul Tyzack, the first Stourbridge glass-maker, p.1-11.

675     'These are glassmakers'. In *TSGT (News and Reviews)*, 1956, p.21-32. A general article on English glassmakers, their history and conditions of work.

676     GWENNET, G. 'Anciennes verreries anglaises'. In *Clarté*, I2ᵉ année, no.9 (Sept 1939).

677     'Ravenscroft et ses cristaux'. In *Clarté*, 12ᶜ année, no.5 (Mai 1939).

678     HADEN, H. Jack. 'A glance at glass'. In Institute & College of Craft Education, Dudley, *Conference Handbook* 1974, p.70-9, *illus.* History of glassmaking in Stourbridge area.

679     *Notes on the Stourbridge glass trade.* Brierley Hill Libraries and Arts Committee, 1949, 37p., *illus.*

680     *The 'Stourbridge Glass' Industry in the 19th century.* Tipton, Black Country Soc., 1971, 38p., *illus.*

681     'The problem of the origin of the Stourbridge glass trade'. In *Bull. of the Paperweight Collectors Assn.*, June 1964, p.47-50, *illus.*

682     'The Richardson bequest of Stourbridge glass'. In *GN*, 1953, p.24-6, *illus.*

683     'The Stourbridge glass collection'. In *Connoisseur Year Book*, 1956, p.111-16, *illus.*

684     'Tumble-up'. In *Notes and Queries*, May 1959, p.193. A letter commenting on the term 'tumble-up' – a glass resting on the shoulders of a carafe.

685     HADFIELD, Anna *and* HADFIELD, John. 'Vintage glasses'. In Ray, Cyril, *ed. The complete imbiber*, 4. Vista, 1961, p.130-45, *illus.*

686     HADFIELD, John. 'Landscapes on glass: some recent goblets by Laurence Whistler'. In *CL*, Jly 1963, p.198-9, *illus.*

687     'Some new examples of Laurence Whistler's engraved glass'. In *CONN*, Jly-Dec 1954, p.96-100, *illus.*

688     'The Queen's homes in glass'. In *CL*, Nov 1953, p.1483-4, *illus.* A set of engraved glasses by Laurence Whistler.

689     'Whistler glass in America'. In *CONN*, Oct 1974, p.82-7, *illus.*

690     HAGGAR, Reginald George. *Glass and glass makers*, illustrated by the author. Methuen, 1961, 80p., *illus.* (Methuen's Outlines).

691     HALAHAN, Brenda C. *Chiddingfold glass and its makers in the Middle Ages.* A paper read to the Newcomen Society (London), Apr 21st 1925.

692     'The Frome Copse glass-house, Chiddingfold discovered September 1921'. In *Surrey Archaeological Collections*, 1921, p.24-31, *map.*

    HALL, E.T. *joint author see* BANKS, M., ELPHINSTONE, N.E. *and* HALL, E.T.

693     HALL, William Douglas. 'The collection of glass in the City Art Galleries, Manchester'. In *CJGS*, 1961, p.131-3, *illus.*
*see also* MANCHESTER ART GALLERY

694     HALLAM, Angela. 'All the fun of the fair [carnival glass]'. In *Art & Antiques Weekly*, Sept 18-24 1981, p.21-3, *illus.* (some col.).

695     *Carnival glass.* Reigate (Surrey), Wise Books, 1981, 48p., *illus.*

696     HALLEN, Arthur W.C. *French gentlemen glass-makers: their work in England and Scotland.* Edinburgh, 1893, 16p. Reprinted from *The Scottish Antiquary.*

697     'Glass-making in Sussex, Newcastle and Scotland'. In *The Scottish Antiquary* (Northern Notes and Queries), v.7, 1893, p.145-56, *illus.*

698     'Scottish glass'. In *The Scottish Antiquary* (Northern Notes and Queries), v.4, 1890, p.88, and v.5, 1891, p.88.

699     HANNAH, E.T. 'Glass of distinction'. In *GC*, no.49A.

700     HARBISON, Peter. 'Recreating early Ireland'. In *Archaeology*, 32 no.2, March/Apr 1979, p.10-17, *illus.* Inscribed drinking glass, 1715.

701     HARDEN, Donald Benjamin. 'A glass bowl from Pagan's Hill, Chew Stoke' [Somerset]. In *Medieval Archaeology*, 1959, p.104-8.

702     'Anglo-Saxon and later medieval glass in Britain: some recent developments'. In *Medieval Archaeology*, 22, 1978, p.1-24, *illus., bibliog.*

703     'Glass beakers [probably medieval] from Colchester Castle'. In *Antiquaries Jnl.*, 1950, p.70-2, *illus.*

704     'Saxon glass from Sussex'. In *Sussex Country Mag.*, 1951, p.260-8, *illus.*
*see also* BRITISH MUSEUM.

705 HARDING, Arthur. *Collecting English antiques.* W. and G. Foyle, 1963 (Foyle's Handbooks). Contents include: Glass, p.79-89.

706 HARDING, Walter. *Old Irish glass: the Walter Harding Collection, including English and other pieces* [Catalogue]. Liverpool, 1930, 108p., *illus.*

707 HARES, Ronald. *The Mere's Collection of Old English Drinking Glasses.* Torquay, Torre Abbey Museum, nd., 17p., *illus.* 18th and 19th centuries.

708 'A vicar and an anvil: Topsham Glasshouse'. In *Devon Life*, Oct. 1974, p.38-9, *illus.* Late 17th century.

709 HARRIS, J.R. *Origins of the St Helens glass industry.* Pilkington Glass Museum, 1969. Reprinted from *Northern History.*

710 HARRIS MUSEUM, PRESTON. *A nineteenth-century miscellany.* Preston (Lancs.), Harris Museum, 1952. (Picture Book no.1). Includes section on lustres and coloured glass.

711 HARTSHORNE, Albert. *Old English glasses: an account of glass drinking vessels in England, from early times to the end of the eighteenth century. With introductory notices, original documents, etc.* Edward Arnold, 1897, 490p., *illus.* This book marks the beginning of glass literature (excluding technology) in England.
Contents include: transcripts of State Papers, Patent Rolls, Ravenscroft's Patent (1674), p.454-6.

712 *Antique drinking glasses. A pictorial history of glass drinking vessels.* New York, Brussel & Brussel, 1967, 490p., *illus.* A facsimile reprint of *Old English glasses* with new title-page.

713 HASLAM, Jeremy. 'Sealed bottes from All Souls College'. In *Oxoniensia*, XXV (1970), p.27-33, *illus.*

HAYNES, D.E.L. *see* BRITISH MUSEUM.

714 HAYNES, E. Barrington. 'The airtwist glasses: a study in comparative rarity'. In *AC*, 1940, p.117-20, *illus.* and 1941, p.18-20, *illus.*

715 'The air-twists re-examined'. In *AC*, 1948, p.90-4 and 166-9, *illus.*

716 'An Anglo-Netherlandish baluster goblet'. In *CONN*, Jly-Dec 1940, p.64-5, *illus.*

717 'An Anglo-Venetian vase'. In *CONN*, Jly-Dec 1939, p.187-9, *illus.*

718 'Balustroid glasses'. In *AC*, 1946, p.187-92 and 225-8, *illus.*

719 'The common tumbler'. In *AC*, 1946, p.93-8, *illus.* Ancient, European and English.

720 'The common drinking glasses of the eighteenth century'. In *AP*, Jan-June 1954. Balusters, p.31; Moulded and composite stems, p.60; Balustroids, p.91; Plain unknopped stems, p.155; *all illus.*

721 'The composite stem in eighteenth century glasses'. In *AC*, 1943, p.77-80, *illus.*

722 'A diversity of glasses' [English and some continental]. In *AC*, 1950, p.234-40 (continental); 1951, p.233-8; 1952, p.140-3 and 259-63; *all illus.*

723 'Eighteenth-century glass of Britain'. In *A*, Aug-Sept 1941, p.157-61 and 297-9, *illus.*

724 'Faceted-stem glasses'. In *AC*, 1944, p.56-60, *illus.*

725 'Fringed and looped sweetmeats'. In *AP*, Jly-Dec 1941, p.75-7, *illus.*

726 'Glass for a specialist' [multiple-spiral stems]. In *AP*, Jan-June 1942, p.118-19, *illus.*

727 'Glass from Ireland'. In *A*, 1950, p.197-200, *illus.*

728 *Glass through the ages. 2nd ed.* Penguin Books, 1959, 310p., *illus.* First published 1948.
Contents include: Glassmaking in England, p.142-63; English glasses of the eighteenth century classified by stem formation, p.193-299.

729 'The glorious memory' [Williamite]. In *AC*, p.112-18, *illus.*

730 'The Greenwood glasses'. In *CONN*, Jan-June 1944, p.34-7, *illus.*

731 'Historic relic: Amen glass from Dunvegan Castle'. In *A*, Mar 1944, p.142-3, *illus.*

732 'Monteiths'. In *AP*, Jan-June 1941, p.47-9, *illus.* Discusses salts, jelly glasses, bonnet glasses and sweetmeats.

733 'National impressionism in English glass'. In *AP*, Jly-Dec 1942, p.8-11, *illus.* Evolution of drinking-glass design.

734 'A naval array'. In *AP*, Jan-June 1940, p.74-7 and 125-7, *illus.*

735 'Old glass as an investment: some pertinent points for collectors in war-time'. In *AC*, Feb 1940, p.17-20, *illus.*

736 'On baluster glasses: a classification for collectors'. In *AC*, 1942, p.144-7, *illus.*

737 'The opaque-twist glasses'. In *AC*, 1941, p.95-8 and 115-18, *illus.* Describes the varieties of twist and their chronological sequence.

738 'Perry and cider glasses'. In *A*, 1944, p.204, *illus.*

739 'Plain stemmed glasses'. In *AC*, 1942, p.65-8, *illus.*

740 'Post-war glass collecting'. In *AC*, 1943, p.181-4, *illus.*

741 'Rummers'. In *AP*, Jly-Dec 1942, p.165-6, *illus.*

742 'Some notes on Beilby's glass'. In *AC*, 1945, p.65-6, *illus.*

743 'Some peace-treaty glasses'. In *AC*, 1944, p.146-9, *illus.*

744 'Some pre-Ravenscroft glasses'. In *CONN*, Jan-June 1950, p.88-93, *illus.* Includes a list of sealed glasses.

745 'Some Ravenscroft jugs' [decanter jugs and pitchers]. In *CONN*, Jly-Dec 1941, p.175-9, *illus.* Includes a chart of styles and locations.

746 'Specialisation in old glass'. In *AC*, 1945, p.198-201, *illus.*

747 'The trumpet bowl'. In *AP*, Dec 1940, p.81-5, *illus.*

*joint author see* HORRIDGE, W. *and* HAYNES, E. Barrington.

*joint author see* W.H.P. *and* E.B.H. [E. Barrington Haynes].

748 HAYWARD, Helena. 'English decorated glass – William and Mary Beilby'. In *ADCG*, 1959, p.26-8, *illus.*

749 'The English glass industry – George Ravenscroft'. In *ADCG*, 1959, p.31-3, *illus.*

750 'Giacomo Verzelini – an Italian glasshouse in London'. In *ADCG*, 1959, p.31-3, *illus.*

751 'Glass in disguise – English coloured wares'. In *ADCG*, 1960, p.38-40, *illus.*

752 HEACOCK, William. 'Cameo glass by John & Harry Northwood'. In *The Glass Collector*, Spring 1982, p.6-11, *illus.*

753 'George Woodall, sculptor'. In *The Glass Collection*, Spring 1982, p.48-9, *illus.*

754 HEDDLE, G.M. *A manual on etching and engraving glass.* Tiranti, 1961, 66p., *illus.*

755 HENNESSY, F. 'Our humble servant, the bottle'. In *Chambers Jnl.*, Apr 1937, p.283-4.

756 HERMAN, Felix. *Painting on glass and porcelain.* Scott Greenwood & Co., 1897.

757 HERRAGHTY, E.A. 'A discovery at Dunvegan' [An 'Amen' glass]. In *Scotland's Mag.*, Dec 1942, p.23-5, *illus.*

HERRON, G. *joint author see* TURNBULL, G. *and* HERRON, G.

758 HEWITT, Ethel M. 'Glass-making' [in Kent]. In *The Victoria County History of Kent*, v.3, 1932, p.400-2.

759 HEWLETT, S.G. 'Some eighteenth century glass'. In *CONN*, Sept-Dec 1919, p.81-4, *illus.*

760 HIGNETT, H.N. 'Old English wine glasses'. In *CONN*, May-Aug 1909, p.93-8, *illus.*

761 HINTON, David A. 'A glass bottle seal from Oxford'. In *Oxoniensia*, 32, 1967, p.10-12, *illus.*

762 'Hiram Codd's bottles [Letters discussing early aerated liquid bottles]. In *CL*, 1964; Jly, p.247, *illus.*; Sept, p.579; Oct, p.845; Dec, p.1718, *illus.* Bottles of this type were patented by Codd in 1875.

763 'Historic Pargeter-Northwood Vase'. In *Pottery Gazette and Glass Trade Rev.*, 1960, p.752-5, *illus.* Describes the Pargeter-Northwood replica of the Portland Vase.

764 HLAVA, Pavel. 'Glass and ceramics at the British Design Centre'. In *The Czechoslovak Glass Rev.*, v.22, no.9, 1967, p.279-83, *illus.*

765 HOAR, Paul. 'The winebuyer's market'. In *ADCG*, May 1981, p.66-9, *illus.* Illustrates drinking glasses.

766 HODGSON, J.C. 'Family of Williams of Newcastle, glass manufacturers'. In *Proc. of the Soc. of Antiquaries of Newcastle-upon-Tyne, (3rd series)*, v.7, p.207.

767 HODGSON, Mrs Willoughby. 'Frauds in old glass'.

In *AP*, Jan-June 1943, p.72-3.

768 'Old London and the glass trade'. In *AP*, Jly-Dec 1943, p.3-6, *illus.*

769 *The quest of the antique.* H. Jenkins, 1924, *illus. (some col.)*. Contents include: Cut-glass, p.159-62; Frauds in old glass, p.243-7.

770 'Some glass from Mrs Reynolds-Peyton's collection' [English, Irish and continental items]. In *CONN*, Sept-Dec 1917, p.195-204, *illus.*

771 HODKIN, F.W. 'The contribution of Yorkshire to glass'. In *TSGT (News and Reviews)*, 1953, p.21-36.

772 HOGAN, D.E. 'The Pilkington Glass Museum'. In *Museum*, 1967, p.220-1, *illus.*

773 Paper on the Du Haugh and the Haughton Green glasshouse. Pilkington Glass Museum, 1969.

774 HOGAN, James Humphries. 'Artistic table glass' [contemporary trends]. In *TSGT*, 1934, p.96-105, *illus.*

775 'Design and form as applied to the manufacture of glassware'. In *Jnl. of the Royal Soc. of Arts*, 1933, p.364-83, *illus.*

776 'Development in the design of English glassware during the last hundred years'. In *TSGT*, 1936, p.735-40, *illus.*

777 'English design in glassware'. In *Jnl. of the Royal Soc. of Arts*, 1935, p.426-38.

778 'Glass at the Exhibition of British Art and Industry'. In *TSGT*, 1935, p.167-70, *illus.*

779 'Glassware in the modern home'. In *TSGT*, 1938, p.12-15.

780 HOLDEN, E.W. 'Objects of glass found during the excavations at the medieval village of Hangleton, Sussex'. In *Sussex Archaeological Collections*, 1963, p.162-5, *illus.*

HOLLAND, A.J. *joint author see* PRESTON, Eric, HOLLAND, A.J. *and* TURNER, William, E.S.

781 HOLLAND, Margaret. 'The enigma of Irish glass'. In *American Collector*, Nov 1982, p.26, *illus.*

782 'Glass by any other name'. In *Antiques Dealer*, Mar 1980, p.20-2, *illus.* 'Nailsea', 'Bristol', 'Waterford' etc.

783 'Irish glass'. In *Antiques Dealer*, May 1967, p.37-40, *illus.*

784 'Puzzles of Irish glass'. In *ADCG*, Nov 1964, p.35-6, 38, *illus.*

785 'To see the sparkle'. In *ADCG*, Aug 1974, p.93-4, *illus.* Chandeliers.

786 'Waterford Crystal: fact and fancy'. In *ADCG*, Jan 1973, p.74-6, *illus.*

787 HOLLINGSWORTH, Jane. *Collecting decanters.* Studio Vista, 1980, 128p., *illus. (some col.)*

788 'Ship's draught'. In *Art & Antiques Weekly*, Apr 15th 1978, p.14-16, *illus.*

789 HOLLISTER, Paul. 'Bacchus and other English weights'. In *Bergstrom Paperweight Symposium (USA)*, 1967, p.17-29.

790 *The encyclopedia of glass paperweights.* W.H.

Allen, 1970, 312p., *illus. (some col.), bibliog.* A comprehensive study originally published in America, 1969.

**791** 'Monart glass'. In *Glass Club Bull.*, Dec 1976, p.3-9, *illus.*

**792** HOLLOWOOD, Albert Bernard. *Pottery and glass.* Penguin, 1947, 63p., *illus.* (The Things We See Series, no.4)

**793** HONEY, William Bowyer. *English glass.* Collins, 1946, 48p., *illus. (some col.).* (Britain in Pictures Series). This book also appears as part of *British craftsmanship*, ed. by W.J. Turner, Collins, 1948, p.107-56.

**794** 'English or Irish? Cut glass in the Francis T. Carter Collection'. In *CONN*, Jan-June 1935, p.77-80, *illus.*

**795** 'The work of James Giles' [decorator of porcelain and glass]. In *Trans. of the English Ceramic Circle*, v.1, no.5, 1937, p.7-22.

see also VICTORIA AND ALBERT MUSEUM.

**796** HOPE, Alice. 'Through a glass sparkly: the great cider comeback'. In *Daily Tel.*, Oct 14th 1975, p.13, *illus.*

HORN, Peter, *joint author see* CHIPCHASE, N., CHURCH, M. and HORN, Peter.

**797** HORRIDGE, W. 'Documents relating to the Lorraine glassmakers in North Staffordshire, with some notes thereon'. In *GN*, 1955, p.26-35, *facsim.*

**798** 'The eighteenth-century champagne glass – a speculation'. In *GC*, no.85.

**799** 'The emblems on Jacobite drinking glasses'. In *Apollo Annual*, 1948, p.85-8, *illus.*

**800** 'The Lorraine glassmakers in Staffordshire'. In *GC*, no.72.

**801** 'The rare emblems on Jacobite drinking glasses'. In *GC*, no.56.

**802** 'Silica and the metal oxides used in glassmaking'. In *GC*, no.93, May 1949.

**803** *and* HAYNES, E.B. 'The "Amen" glasses'. In *CONN*, Jly-Dec 1942, p.47-51, *illus.*

**804** 'Horridge on Jacobite emblems'. In *GN*, 1947, p.24-5. Comment on and summary of the *GC* paper no.56.

**805** HOUGHTON, John. 'List of glasshouses in operation in England in 1696'. In Elville, E.M. *English table glass.* Country Life, 1951, p.77.

**806** *A collection of letters for the improvement of husbandry and trade.* London, 1681-3 and 1692-1703.

**807** HOWARD, Alexander L. *comp. The Worshipful Company of Glass Sellers of London from its inception to the present day.* Northwood, Rawlinson, 1940, 152p., *illus.*

**808** HOWE, Bea. 'The charm of old marbles'. In *CL*, Dec 1969, p.1593, *illus.*

**809** 'Distinctive patterns in Victorian table glass'. In *ADCG*, Jly 1967, p.62-4, *illus.*

**810** 'Old glass ships'. In *ADCG*, May 1964, p.45-6, *illus.*

**811** 'Skill of the wandering glass-blowers'. In *CL*, 1957, p.159-60, *illus.*

**812** 'Varied forms of Victorian art glass'. In *ADCG*, Sept 1968, p.90-2, *illus.*

**813** 'Variety of Victorian flower vases'. In *CL*, Dec 1957, p.1374-5, *illus.* Includes glass vases.

**814** 'Variety of Victorian glass'. In *CL*, Apr 1957, p.824-5, *illus.*

**815** 'The Victorian cult of the fern' [glass ornaments, etc.]. In *CL*, Oct 1962, p.898-9, *illus.*

**816** HUDSON, J. Paul. 'Seventeenth-century glass winebottles and seals excavated at Jamestown'. In *CJGS*, 1961, p.78-89, *illus.* Includes some English examples.

**817** 'George Ravenscroft and his contribution to English glassmaking'. In *A*, 1967, p.822-31, *illus.*

**818** HUDSON, Kenneth. *Industrial archaeology: an introduction.* John Baker, 1966.
Contents include: Glass, p.111-14.

**819** HUGHES, George Bernard. 'The art of the glass punch bowl'. In *Country Life Annual*, 1965, p.88, 90, *illus.*

**820** 'Beauty of English cased glass'. In *CL*, June 1963, p.1322-3, *illus.*

**821** 'Chronology of English candlesticks: summary of major changes'. In *A*, 1930, p.234-7, *illus.*

**822** *Collecting antiques.* 2nd ed. Country Life, 1960. First pub. 1949.
Contents include: English millefiori paperweights, p.300-10, *illus. (col.).*

**823** 'Congenial history of Georgian rummers'. In *ADCG*, Aug 1973, p.59-61, *illus.*

**824** 'Cordial and dram glasses'. In *Antiques Rev.*, 1950, Pt 4, p.21.

**825** 'Cordial and dram glasses of Old England'. In *ADCG*, Sept 1946, p.16-18. *illus.*

**826** *Country Life collectors' pocket book.* Country Life, 1963. Glass, p.135-75, *illus.*

**827** 'Crystallo ceramie illustrated by examples at Buckingham Palace'. In *AP*, Jan-June 1953, p.183-5, *illus.*

**828** 'A cure for gluttony'. In *CL*, Apr 1957, p.643, *illus.* Surfeit water glasses.

**829** 'Cut glass, early and late'. In *ADCG*, Oct 1975, p.91-3, *illus.*

**830** 'Dating of English wine glasses'. In *The British Antique Trades and Collectors' Directory*, Luton, Woodhouse, n.d. [c.1950], p.15-19, *illus.*

**831** 'Decanters for the admiral's table'. In *CL*, Oct 1960, p.722-3, *illus.*

**832** 'Decorated drinking glasses' [tumblers]. In *CL*, May 1958, p.525-6, *illus.*

**833** 'Decorating the Georgian dessert table' [sweetmeat stands, etc.]. In *CL*, May 1959, p.1144-5, *illus.*

**834** 'Discovered in the cellars' [bottles]. In *CL*, June 1955, p.1575-6, *illus.*

**835** 'Drinking glasses for Orange Lodges'. In

CL, Aug 1958, p.312-13, *illus*. Orange Lodges were clubs formed in honour of William III, Prince of Orange.

836 'The economical Georgian cruet'. In *CL*, July 15th, 1971, p.183-4, *illus*.

837 'Eighteenth-century drinking glass collected by Mr Herbert F. Elkington'. In *CONN*, Jly-Dec 1952, p.112-17, *illus*.

838 'England's first crystal glass' [Verzelini]. In *CL*, Sept 1968, p.700-1, *illus*.

839 'English champagne and strong ale glasses'. In *A*, Aug 1931, p.92-5, *illus*.

840 'English crystal cameos'. In *CL*, June 1949, p.1304-5, *illus*.

841 'English drinking cans'. In *CL*, Apr 1959, p.836-7, *illus*. Includes examples in glass.

842 'English glass'. In *Connoisseur Concise Encyclopedia of Antiques*, 1954, v.1, p.75-83, *illus., bibliog*.

843 *English glass for the collector, 1660-1860*. Lutterworth, 1958, 251p., *illus., bibliog*. Contents include: Crystallo ceramie, p.199-205; Moulded and pinched glass, p.149-59; Pressed glass, p.160-71.

844 'English millefiori paperweights'. In *AP*, Jan-June 1952, p.191-3, *illus*.

845 'English rummers and firing glasses'. In *A*, Feb 1931, p.113-16, *illus*.

846 *English, Scottish and Irish table glass. From the sixteenth century to 1820*. Batsford, 1956, 410p., *illus., bibliog*. Contents include: Candlesticks, tapersticks, girandoles and girandole candlesticks, p.315-35, *illus*.; Serving bottles, … squares and carafes, p.257-83, *illus*.; Tumblers, fruit and salad bowls, p.337-50, *illus*.

847 'Facets to catch the candlelight'. In *CL*, Sept 9th 1971, p.638-9, *illus*.

848 'Fine ware from Scottish glass-houses'. In *CL*, Aug 1961, p.386-7, *illus*.

849 'Flint-glass in the collection of His Majesty the King'. In *Antiques Rev.*, 1948, Pt 1, p.11-14, *illus*.

850 'Flint glass candlesticks'. In *Antiques Rev.*, 1949, Pt 3, p.35-6, *illus*.

851 'Georgian armorial glass'. In *CL*, Dec 1957, p.1271-4, *illus*. Includes Beilby glasses.

852 'Georgian gold-rimmed table glass in the Royal Collection'. In *ADCG*, Oct 1973, p.114-16, *illus*.

853 'Georgian rummers'. In *AP*, Jly-Dec 1955, p.81-3, *illus*.

854 'The girandole-candlestick'. In *CL*, Jan 1957, p.188-9, *illus*.

855 'Glass' [1810-30]. In *Connoisseur Complete Period Guides: Regency Period*, 1968, p.1157-60, *illus*.

856 'Glass epergnes for Georgian dessert'. In *CL*, Feb 1960, p.371, *illus*.

857 'Glass lamps that lit humble homes' [open-flame chamber lamps]. In *CL*, Jly 1962, p.69, *illus*.

858 'Glass pyramids on the dessert table' [salvers, etc.]. In *CL*, Mar 1964, p.716-17, *illus*.

859 'Glass rolling-pins'. In *CL*, Feb 1951, p.319, *illus*.

860 'Glass toddy-lifters'. In *CL*, Dec 1953, p.1958-9, *illus*.

861 'Glass toddy rummers'. In *CL*, Oct 1957, p.868-9, *illus*.

862 'Glasses for jelly and custard'. In *CL*, Nov 1959, p.768-9, *illus*.

863 'Glasses for Orangemen: souvenirs of revolt'. In *The Times*, Aug 5th 1961, *illus*.

864 'Glasses for the syllabub'. In *CL*, June 1959, p.1270-2, *illus*.

865 'Glasses to dress the dessert'. In *ADCG*, June 1973, p.122-4, *illus*.

866 'Golden oranges in cut-glass bowls'. In *CL*, Feb 1964, p.332-3, *illus*.

867 'The hey-day of Bristol enamel glass'. In *CL*, Mar 1961, p.512-13, *illus*.

868 'The hey-day of Irish decanters'. In *CL*, Aug 1964, p.510-11, *illus*.

869 'Irish glass'. In *Connoisseur Concise Encyclopedia of Antiques*, v.3, 1957, p.91-9, *illus., bibliog*.

870 'Jacobite drinking glasses'. In *GC*, nos.51 *and* 52.

871 'Jacobite drinking glasses'. In *CL*, May 1944, p.418-19, *illus*.

872 'Label decanters of Georgian times'. In *CL*, Apr 1961, p.764-5, *illus*.

873 *Living crafts*. Lutterworth, 1953. The glass-blower, p.173-82, *illus*.

874 'Loops and frills of Georgian glass'. In *CL*, Mar 1970, p.570 and 574, *illus*. Sweetmeat glasses.

875 'Lucky glass walking sticks'. In *CL*, Aug 20th 1970, p.476-7, *illus*.

876 *More about collecting antiques*. Country Life, 1952. Contents include: Enamel and milk-white opaque glass, p.78-85; Old English wine bottles, p.86-93; Open-flame glass lamps, p.94-103; *all illus*.

877 'Music from vessels of glass'. In *CL*, Nov 1961, p.1138-9, *illus*.

878 'Naval history in glass'. In *CL*, Mar 1968, p.759-60, *illus*. Engraved rummers, Frigate glasses, etc.

879 'Old English champagne glasses'. In *CL*, May 1952, p.1496-7, *illus*.

880 'Old English champagne and ale glasses'. In *CL*, June 1946, p.1082-3, and 1180-1, *illus*.

881 'Old English cider glasses'. In *CL*, Jly 1956, p.22-3, *illus*. and in *Wine and Spirit Trade Rev.*, Jly 1958, p.914-18, *illus*.

882 'Old English cruets' [some of glass]. In *CL*, Jan 1955, p.178-80, *illus*.

883 'Old English cut glass'. In *ADCG*, May 1947, p.16-18, *illus*.

884 'Old English cut glass'. In *CL*, Dec 1945, p.1138, *illus.*

885 'Old English decanters'. In *AP*, Jly-Dec 1943, p.137-40, *illus.*

886 'Old English decanters'. In *ADCG*, June 1948, p.40-2, *illus.*

887 'Old English decanters and their labels'. In *A*, 1929, p.475-80, *illus.*; and in *Old Furniture*, 1929, p.227-33, *illus.*; and in *Chambers's Jnl.*, Sept 1937, p.667-8.

888 'Old English dessert sweetmeat and jelly glasses'. In *CL*, Dec 1944, p.1078-9, *illus.*

889 'Old English gilded glass'. In *CL*, Dec 1952, p.1952-3, *illus.*

890 'Old English glass candlesticks'. In *Old Furniture*, 1929, p.204-11, *illus.*

891 'Old English glass candlesticks' [including Irish urn-stemmed moulded examples]. In *AP*, Jan-June 1945, p.45-7, *illus.*

892 'Old English wine fountains'. In *CL*, Feb 1955, p.390-1, *illus.*

893 'Old English wine glasses'. In *AP*, Jly-Dec 1942, p.129-31, *illus.*

894 'Old Irish glass'. In *AP*, Jan-June 1947, p.46-9, *illus.*

895 'Opaque white glass'. In *ADCG*, Nov 1974, p.86-91, *illus. (some col.).*

896 'Orange glasses for Georgian dessert'. In *CL*, Mar 1960, p.690-1, *illus.*

897 'Punch and toddy glasses'. In *AP*, Jly-Dec 1953, p.174-6, *illus.*

898 'A rainbow with a sparkle: Stourbridge glass'. In *CL*, Dec 1964, p.1498-1503, *illus. in colour.*

899 'Rodney decanters'. In *ADCG*, Jly 1974, p.63-5, *illus.*

900 'Simple mystery of crystal cameos'. In *CL*, Jly 1966, p.183-4, *illus.*

901 'Square bottles for sundry uses' [spirit decanters, medicine bottles, etc]. In *CL*, May 1963, p.1007, 1009, *illus.*

902 'Surfeit water glasses'. In *Wine and Spirit Trade Record*, Sept 1958, p.1194-6, *illus.*

903 'Tea-caddies made of glass'. In *CL*, Sept 1961, p.564-5, *illus.*

904 'Tea-time cordials'. In *CL*, Dec 1955, p.1530-1, *illus.*

905 'Tricks in the tavern' [trick glasses]. In *CL*, Mar 1957, p.424-5, *illus.*

906 'Water jugs for the Georgian table'. In *CL*, June 1965, p.1538-9, *illus.*

907 'Wine glass coolers and finger bowls'. In *CL*, June 1953, p.1976-8, *illus.*

908 HUGHES, Therle. *Decanters and glasses. CL*, 1982, 128p., *illus.*

909 'Elegant refreshment: sweetmeat glasses'. In *CL*, Dec 1982, p.1795; 1796, *illus.*

910 'Glassmakers: many skills on display'. In *CL*, Apr 3rd 1980, p.1048-9, *illus.* At Broadfield House (Dudley).

911 *Homes and Gardens Guide: Glass*. Homes and Gardens, 1965. 15p., *illus.*

912 *More small decorative antiques*. Lutterworth, 1962. Contents include: Crystal cameos, p.178-84. Tumblers and beakers, p.185-96, *illus.*

913 *Small decorative antiques*. Lutterworth, 1959. Contents include: Glasses to dress the dessert, p.157-68, *illus.*

914 *Sweetmeat and jelly glasses*. Lutterworth, 1982, 64p., *illus., bibliog.* (Antique collectors pocket guides).

915 'Tumblers and beakers'. In *Homes and Gardens*, Mar 1966, p.92-3, *illus.*

916 'Variety in dessert glasses'. In *ADCG*, Feb 1966, p.33-6, *illus.*

917 HULME, E. Wyndham. 'English glass-making in the sixteenth and seventeenth centuries'. Three articles in *The Antiquary*, v.31, 1895. Crystal glass from Bowles to Mansel, p.68-72; Glass-making at the Restoration, p.102-6; The invention of flint glass, p.134-8, *diags.*

918 'The French glass-makers in England in 1567'. In *The Antiquary*, v.34, 1898, p.142-5.

919 'Note on Knole [Kent] glassmaking'. In *The Antiquary*, v.41, 1905, p.164.

920 'Old English glasses'. In *The Antiquary*, v.34, 1898, p.112-18. Includes a review of Hartshorne's *Old English glasses*.

921 'Sir Kenelm Digby and the green glass manufacture'. In Notes & Queries, 8th Series VIII (1895), p.67.

922 HUME, Ivor Noel. 'Bottled treasure from the Goodwins'. In *CL*, Feb 1955, p.570-1, *illus., map.* Eighteenth-century ale bottles washed up at Sandwich, Kent.

923 'A century of London glass bottles, 1580-1680'. In *Connoisseur Year Book*, 1956, p.98-103, *illus.*

924 'Collection of glass from Port Royal, Jamaica'. In *Historical Archaeology*, 1968, p.5-34, *illus.*

925 'English glass wine bottles'. In *AP*, Jan-June 1956, p.155-6, *illus.*

926 'A friend of Elizabethan ale glasses'. In *CONN*, Sept-Dec 1968, p.259-61, *illus.* An excavation at Honey Lane Market, near Cheapside.

927 'The glass wine bottle in Colonial Virginia'. In *CJGS*, 1961, p.91-118, *illus., diags.* Includes continental and English examples.

928 'A lyttle bottell: charm of apothecaries phials'. In *ADCG*, Oct 1954, p.32, *illus.*

929 'Medieval bottles from London'. In *CONN*, Jan-June 1957, p.104-8, *illus.*

930 'Neglected glass' [apothecary and medicine bottles]. In *CL*, Sept 1954, p.716-17, *illus.*

931 'Ornamental glass bird fountains of the eighteenth century'. In *A*, Aug 1966, p.208-10, *illus.*

932 'Relics from the Wine Trade's own church'. In *Wine and Spirit Trade Record*, Feb 1958, p.158-64, *illus.*

933 'Report from America on Tudor and early Stuart glasses found in London'. In *CONN*, May-Aug 1962, p.269-73, *illus.*, *bibliog.*

934 'A seventeenth-century Virginian's seal: detective story in glass'. In *A*, Sept 1957, p.244-5.

935 'Some English glass from Colonial Virginia'. In *A*, Jly 1963, p.68-71, *illus.*

936 'To corking and wiring'. In *Wine and Spirit Trade Record*, June 1958, p.772-6, *illus.*

937 'Wine bottle treasures'. In *Wine and Spirit Trade Record*, 1956, p.288-94; 580-6; 868-70; 1010-18; *all illus.*

938 'Wine relics from the colonies' [bottles]. In *Wine and Spirit Trade Record*, Aug 1952, p.1052-8, *illus.*

939 HUMPHREYS, Gregor Norman. 'Development of the twist stem drinking glass'. In *A*, Mar 1929, p.191-5, *illus.*

940 'Hundred years of British glass making from 1824 to 1924'. In *National Glass Budget*, v.79, no.21, 1963, p.4; 10-12. A history of Chance Bros.

941 HUNTLEY, R. 'English royalty in glass'. In *American Collector*, Sept 1943, p.12-13, *illus.*

942 HURST, D. Gillian. 'Post-Medieval Britain in 1966 – Glass'. In *Post-Medieval Archaeology*, v.1, 1967, p.118-19. Excavations of the sixteenth-seventeeth-century site at Alfold, Surrey.

943 HURST, Ruth. 'Excavation of French forest glass-house sites at Bickerstaffe and Denton, Lancs.' Paper read at the Fifth Congress of the International Assn. for the History of Glass, Prague, 1970.

944 'Rare glass from the City of Liverpool Museum'. In *The Liverpool Bulletin*, v.14, 1967, p.16-31, *illus.*

945 HUTCHINSON, Robin. 'Cameos, medals & imitation gems'. In *Discovering Antiques* (USA), v.17, New York, Greystone Press, 1973, p.2086-2089, *illus.* James Tassie.

946 INTERNATIONAL COMMISSION ON GLASS. *English, French and German dictionary of glass making.* Classified with indices. Charleroi, 1965, 233p.

947 [1968]. *Proceedings* ed. by E.J. Gooding. Pitman, 1969, *illus.* The Eighth Congress took place in London.

948 'International Exhibition, London, 1862: catalogue of the exhibition'. In *Art Jnl. (Supplementary volume)*, 1862. British glass, p.106-16, *illus.*; several references to British manufacturers, e.g. Osler, p.258, Pellatt, p.14 and 128.

949 'Irish glass exports' [1780-1811]. In *GN*, 1952, p.24-5.

950 JABCKOWSKI, Janusz. 'W.E.S. Turner – na tle epoki'. *Szklo i Ceramika* 15, no.5, 1964, p.113-17. An obituary of Professor W.E.S. Turner.

951 JACKSON, J.T. 'Long distance migrant workers in 19th century Britain: a case study of St. Helens' glassmakers'. In *Hist. Soc. of Lancs. and Cheshire Trans.*, 131, 1981, p.113-37, *illus.*, *bibliog.*

952 'Jacobite drinking glasses'. In *The Times*, Sept 22nd 1962, p.11, *illus.*

953 'Jacobite glass'. In *The Evening Argus*, Jan 22nd 1970, p.13, *illus.*

954 'Jacobite glass' [Lord Torphichen's Collection]. In *CL*, Feb 1929, p.29, *illus.*

955 JANNEAU, Guillaume. *Modern glass.* Studio, 1931. English glass, Plates 102-12.

JANSON, S.E. *see* SCIENCE MUSEUM.

956 JERNINGHAM, Charles E. 'The Oxburgh glasses'. In *CONN*, May-Aug 1908, p.17-18, *illus.* Eleven Jacobite glasses 'discovered' at Oxburgh Hall in 1907.

957 JEUDWINE, W.R. 'Early English drinking glasses'. [from a private collection]. In *AP*, Jan-June 1956, p.207-10, *illus.*

958 JOHNSON, Stanley Currie. *Collecting old glassware.* Country Life, 1922, 32p., *illus.*

959 JOKELSON, Paul. *100 of the most important paperweights* [? London], 1966, 239p., *illus.*

960 *Sulphides: the art of cameo incrustation.* New York, Nelson, 1968, 159p., *illus. (some col.).*

961 JONES, Dorothy Lee. 'The glass of Thomas Webb and Son'. In *Bull. of the National Early American Glass Club*, Mar 1962, p.5-11, *illus.*

962 JONES, Olive. 'The contribution of the Ricketts' mould to the manufacture of the English "wine" bottle, 1820-1850'. In *CJGS*, 1983, p.167-77, *illus.*

963 JONES, Vera. 'English Bristol glass'. In *Antiques Jnl.*, Oct 1966, p.18-20, *illus.*

964 JOSEPHS, Zoe. 'The Jacobs of Bristol, glassmakers to King George III'. In *Bristol & Glos. Archaeol. Soc. Trans.*, 95, 1977, p.98-101, *bibliog.*

965 'Jewish glass-makers'. In *Jewish Hist. Soc. of England Trans.*, 25, 1977, p.107-19, *illus.* England 18th & 19th century.

966 'Lazarus and Isaac Jacobs of Bristol'. In *Readings in Glass History* (USA), no.4, 1974, p.55-60.

967 'Mayer Oppenheim an 18th century Birmingham glassmaker'. In *Birm. & Warwicks. Archaeol. Trans.*, 88, 1976-77, p.83-6, *bibliog.*

968 JOYCE, Day. 'Mary Gregory glass'. In *ADCG*, June 1958, p.58-60, *illus.*

969 KAELLGREN, C. Peter. 'The Marquis of Lorne pattern, current events in pressed glass'. In *Spinning Wheel*, Nov 1978, p.16-19, *illus.* 19th century English pressed glass exported to Canada.

970 KEEN, Geraldine. 'The Times-Sotheby index: 5. English glass' [analysis of prices 1950-68]. In *CONN*, Jan-Apr 1969, p.95-7, *illus.* A revised version of the article in *The Times*.

971 KELLER, Joseph. *A collection of patterns for the use of glass decorators* [working notes and

drawings]. MS. in the Brierley Hill Public Library Collection.

**972** KELSALE, George. 'Glass salts'. In *AC*, Jly 1979, p.54-5, *illus.*

**973** KENWORTHY, Joseph. *Bolsterstone glass house and its place in the history of English glass making* [from 1670]. Sheffield, 1914, 45p., *illus.* (Early History of Stocksbridge and District, Handbook no.6).

**974** *The broken earthenware of Midhope Potteries.* 1928. Includes material on Bolsterstone and Gawber Glassworks.

**975** 'Glassmaking at Bolsterstone near Sheffield from about AD 1650 to 1750'. In *TSGT*, 1918, p.5-12, *illus.*

**976** KENYON, G.H. *Glass industry of the Weald.* Leicester University Press, 1967, 231p., *illus., bibliog.*

**977** 'Petworth [Sussex] town and trades, 1610-1760: Glassmaking'. In *Sussex Archaeological Collections*, 1961, p.106-8.

**978** 'Some comments on the medieval glass industry in France and England'. In *TSGT (News and Reviews)*, 1959, p.17-20, *bibliog.*

**979** 'Some notes on the glass industry in England prior to 1567'. In *Jnl. of the British Soc. of Master Glass Painters*, 1956-7, p.103-7.

**980** 'A Sussex yeoman family as glassmaker'. In *Sussex Notes and Queries*, v.7, 1939, p.171-3.

**981** 'A Sussex yeoman family as glassmakers
§ and some notes on Wealden glass'. In *TSGT (News and Reviews)*, 1951, p.6-11.

**982** 'Wealden glass: some notes'. In *Sussex Notes and Queries*, v.13, 1950, p.58-61.

**983** KEYES, Homer Eaton. 'Cameo glass' [George Woodall vases, etc.] In *A*, Sept 1936, p.109-12, *illus.*

**984** 'Bristol opaque-white glass'. In *A*, Apr 1938, p.109-12, *illus.*

**985** KIDDLE, A.J.B. 'Advertisements in the seventeenth and eighteenth centuries' [concerning the glass trade]. In *GC*, nos.76 and 77.

**986** 'Extracts and advertisements from London and Irish newspapers, 1747-1779'. In *GC*, no.18.

**987** 'William Absolon, Junior, of Great Yarmouth'. In *Trans. of the English Ceramic Circle*, v.5, Pt 1, 1960, p.53-63.

**988** 'Kidd's process for silvering and ornamenting glass' [Mr Kidd of Poland Street, London]. In *Art Jnl.*, 1850, p.202.

**989** KING, C. Eileen. 'Apsley Pellatt'. In *ADCG*, Mar 1973, p.63-5, *illus.*

**990** 'Craftsmanship for the wealthy – the cameo glass of Thomas Webb'. In *ADCG*, Feb 1972, p.74-7, *illus.*

KING, J. *joint author see* COYSH, A.W. *and* KING, J.

**991** KING, W. 'Flämisches glas und seine beziehungen zum englischen glas' [The relationship between Flemish and English glass]. In *Pantheon* (Munich), Apr 1931, p.158-60, *illus.* With English translation.

**992** KING, William. 'English glass'. In *British Museum Quarterly*, 1934, p.145-6.

**993** 'English glass goblet [c.1690-1700] in the British Museum'. In *AP*, Jan-June 1949, p.131, *illus.* The goblet was presented to the British Museum by the Glass Circle in memory of John Maunsell Bacon, founder of the Circle.

**994** 'King's Champion' [a commemorative goblet for the coronation of George IV]. In *CL*, Oct 1963, p.798-9, *illus.*

**995** 'King's Lynn glass: an exciting venture' [the modern glass factory]. In *Pottery Gazette and Glass Trade Rev.*, 1967, p.1049-51, *illus.*

**996** KINNEY, Kay. *Glass craft: designing, forming, decorating.* Pitman, 1962, 179p., *illus.*

**997** KISCH, Sir Cecil. 'Engraved goblets by Laurence Whistler' [a gift to Trinity College, Oxford]. In *CONN*, Jan-June, 1957, p.154-6, *illus.*

**998** KLAARENBEEK, F.W., *and* STEVELS, J.M., *eds. Bibliography of glass literature.* International Commission on Glass, 1964. 117p.

**999** KLEINFELDT, Kay. 'Georgian decanters'. In Ray, Cyril, *ed. The complete imbiber*, 5. Vista Books, 1962, p.155-60, *illus.*

**1,000** KNOWLES, John A. 'Henry Gyles, glass-painter of York'. In *Walpole Soc. Publications*, 11, 1923, p.47-72.

**1,001** 'Medieval processes of glass manufacture'. In *Glass*, 1927, p.343, 345, 349, 391, 395, 397, 399, *illus.*

**1,002** KUHN, Joy. 'Waterford glass: the re-establishment of an ancient industry'. In *ADCG*, Aug 1980, p.50-2, *illus.*

**1,003** LADY LEVER ART GALLERY, PORT SUNLIGHT. *Chinese porcelain and Wedgwood pottery with works of ceramic art: a record of the collection in the Lady Lever Art Gallery, Port Sunlight, formed by … Viscount Leverhulme*, [compiled] by R.L. Hobson. Batsford, 1924.
Contents include: 'Tassie', with a catalogue (nos.2275-333) of the Tassie glass pastes, p.217-19.

**1,004** LAING, Trudy. 'The House of Stuart (Crystal Co., Stourbridge)'. In *National Antiques Review* (USA), Mar 1974, p.13-14, *illus.*

**1,005** LAING ART GALLERY, NEWCASTLE UPON TYNE. *The decorated glasses of William and Mary Beilby 1761 to 1778.* Newcastle, 1980. 16p., *illus.*

**1,006** LANMON, Dwight P. 'English glass from the Strauss collection at the Corning Museum of Glass'. In *APP*, Apr 1980, p.310-14, *illus., bibliog.*

**1,007** *Glass from six centuries.* Hartford, Conn. (USA), Wadsworth Athenaeum, 1978, 135p., *illus., bibliog.* Based on selected items from the Wadsworth Athenaeum.

**1,008** LARDNER, Dionysius. *Cabinet cyclopedia.* Longmans, Rees, etc., 1832, v.26 [by George Richardson Porter]. 'A treatise on the origin, progressive improvement and present state of the manufacture of porcelain and glass'. Glass, p.125-327, *illus.*

LARGERBERG, Ted *and* LARGERBERG, Vi. *photographers see* MANLEY, C.C.

1,009 LATHAM, Jean. 'Collecting dressing table accessories' [glass toilet bottles, etc.]. In *ADCG*, Nov 1967, p.57-60, *illus. (some col.).*

1,010 'Collecting glass friggers'. In *ADCG*, Jan 1966, p.41-3, *illus.*

1,011 LATHAM, Jean. 'Taking care of glass'. In *ADCG*, Dec 1971, p.122.

1,012 LATTIMORE, Colin R. 'English decorative press-moulded glass 1870-1890'. In *ADCG*, Feb 1978, p.59-60; 62, *illus.*

1,013 *English 19th-Century press-moulded glass.* Barrie & Jenkins, 1979, 184p., *illus. (some col.).*

1,014 LAUGHTON, J.K. 'Sir Robert Mansell [1573-1656]'. In *Dictionary of National Biography*, v.36, 1893, p.88-9.

1,015 LAUNERT, Edmund. 'Scent bottles'. In *The Glass Circle* 1, 1972, p.58-64, *illus.*

1,016 *Scent and scent bottles.* Barrie & Jenkins, 1974, 176p., *illus. (some col.).*

1,017 'Scent and scent bottles'. Pts. 1 & 2. In *ADCG*, Aug 1971, p.64-9; Sept p.62-8, *illus. (some col.)* Inc. English examples.

LAUNERT, Edmund, *joint author see also* GODFREY, A. *and* LAUNERT, Edmund.

1,018 LAURENCE, Ninha V. 'Three old wines' [including a 'Byng' glass]. In *CONN*, Jly-Dec 1930, p.173, *illus.*

1,019 'Laurence Whistler's four seasons' [engraved glass scenes]. In *CL*, June 1968, p.1695, 1697, *illus.*

1,020 LAVER, James. *Victoriana.* Ward, Lock, 1966. Victorian glass, p.164-74, *illus.*

1,021 LAVINE, Sigmund A. *Handmade in England. The Tradition of British craftsmen.* New York, Dodd, Mead & Co., 1968. Contents include: Glass, p.39-65, *illus.*

LAVINGTON, Margaret, *joint author see* GRAY, H. *and* LAVINGTON, Margaret.

1,022 LAWRENCE, G.F. 'Glass from London excavations'. In Churchill, Arthur, Ltd, *Catalogue of old English Glass, 2nd ed.,* 1937, p.11-12.

1,023 LAYCOCK, C.H. 'Bristol rollers' [rolling pins]. In *Devon and Cornwall Notes and Queries*, Jan 1920, p.36-8; Apr 1920, p.73-6; Jly 1920, p.104-5; Jan 1921, p.158-9.

1,024 LAZARUS, Peter. 'The antique glass of Wales'. In *ADCG*, Jly 1969, p.86-9, *illus.*

1,025 'English drinking glasses'. In *AC*, Jly 1975, p.20-5, *illus.*, and Aug 1975, p.31-6, *illus.*

1,026 'Glass'. In *Looking at antiques*, Stanley Paul, 1971, p.64-94, *illus.*

1,027 'The golden age of English glass'. In *Discovering Antiques*, v.6, New York, Greystone Press, 1973, p.708-11, *illus.*

1,028 'Plain, pedestal and air twist stems'. In *Discovering Antiques*, v.5, New York, Greystone press, 1973, p.576-80, *illus.*

1,029 'The story of decanters'. Pts. 1 & 2. In *ADCG*, Feb 1971, p.66-71; Mar 1971, p.72-6, *illus. (some col.), bibliog.*

1,030 'The story of English drinking glasses' [six articles]. In *ADCG*, 1969.
Contents: (1) Balusters, Feb, p.74-8; (2) Plain stems and Newcastle glasses, Mar, p.82-6; (3) Air twists, incised stems and composite stems, Apr, p.77-81; (4) Opaque, mixed and colour twist stems, May, p.56-60; (5) Faceted and cut stems and sweetmeats, June, p.102-6; (6) Specific types, Aug, p.78-84; *all illus. (some col.).*

1,031 LEEDS, E. Thurlow. 'Glass bottles of the Crown Tavern, Oxford'. In *Oxoniensia*, v.14, 1952, p.87-9, *illus.*

1,032 'On the dating of glass wine bottles of the Stuart period'. In *The Antiquary*, v.50, 1914, p.285-90, *illus.*

1,033 'Seventeenth- and eighteenth-century wine bottles of Oxford taverns'. In *Oxoniensia*, v.6, 1941, p.44.

1,034 LEEDS CITY ART GALLERY *[Catalogue of] An exhibition of glass, or glass-making as a creative art through the ages.* Nov 1961. Compiled by Robert Charleston, Hugh Wakefield *and others*, Leeds City Art Gallery, 1961, 60p.

1,035 LEFFINGWELL, B.H. 'Bibliography pertaining to glass paperweights and addenda'. In *Bull. of the Paperweight Collectors' Assn.*, June 1958 and June 1963.

1,036 'Paperweights for the advanced collector'. In *Antiques Jnl.*, Mar 1964, p.20-7, *illus.*

1,037 LEIGH, James T. 'Glass Rolling pins...' In *Southern Antiques*, Jan 1982, p.3-4, *illus.* Sunderland 19th century items.

1,038 LENNARD, T. Barrett. 'Glass-making at Knole, Kent'. In *The Antiquary*, v.41 (1905), p.127-9.

1,039 LESTER, Anthony. '18th century opaque twist glasses – an infinite variety'. In *Antique Collecting*, no.5, 1982, p.56-9, *illus.*

1,040 LE VERRIR, William. 'London and other glass at the Antique Dealers' Fair' [1935]. In *AP*, Jly-Dec 1935, p.159-63, *illus.*

LEWIS, Elizabeth, *joint author see* FOX, Russel *and* LEWIS, Elizabeth.

1,041 LEWIS, Geoffrey, D. 'The Catcliffe glassworks' [near Rotherham]. In *Industrial Archaeology*, v.1, 1964, p.206-11, *illus., bibliog.*

1,042 *The South Yorkshire glass industry.* Sheffield City Museum, 1964, 6p., *illus., bibliog.*

1,043 'The South Yorkshire glass industry'. In *GC*, no.136.

1,044 LEWIS, J. Sydney. *Old glass and how to collect it.* Werner Laurie, [1916], 225p., *illus.* Includes catalogue of auction prices, p.191-225.

1,045 LEWIS, M. 'Vintage bottles'. In *Art & Antiques*, Aug 23rd 1975.

1,046 LEWIS, Mel. 'Beilby glasses worth a special toast'. In *Pilkington News*, Aug 29th, p.4, *illus.*

1,047 LIDSTONE, Marjorie. 'Glass perspective: a

**1,048** LIMERICK CITY ART GALLERY. *Irish glass from the Eighteenth Century to the Present Day.* Introduction by W.A. Seaby. Limerick, 1971, 21p., *illus.* Exhibition catalogue.

**1,049** LITHERLAND, Gordon. *Bottle collecting price guide.* Burton-upon-Trent, MAB Publishing, 1977, 96p., *illus.*

**1,050** LITTLE, Tenison. 'Irish glass, its appeal and some cherished misconceptions'. In *AC*, 1963, p.19-22, *illus.*

**1,051** LIVINGSTONE-LEARMOUTH, John. 'Facing the devil: some English drinking glasses'. In *CONN*, Dec 1979, p.264-9, *illus.*

**1,052** LLOYD, Esme. 'Industrial exhibits in the New St. Helens Museum and Art Gallery'. In *Industrial Arch.*, no.2, Summer 1981, p.170-8. Local glassmaking history.

**1,053** LLOYD, Ward. *Investing in Georgian glass.* Barrie & Rockliff: The Cresset Press, 1969, 160p., *illus. (some col.).*

**1,054** 'Loan exhibition of English glass' [at the Victoria and Albert Museum, 1968]. In *CL*, Jly 1968, p.38-9, *illus.*

**1,055** LOCKHART, R. Stevenson. 'Harold Gordon – Scots glass engraver'. In *Studio*, Aug 1950, p.50-1, *illus.* Engraved tumblers.

**1,056** LOGAN, John C. 'The operations of a glassworks in the Industrial Revolution'. In *Industrial Arch.*, 9, no.2, May 1972, p.177-87, *illus.* The Dumbarton Glass Works Co. c.1777-c.1850.

**1,057** LONDON MUSEUM. *The Garton collection of English table glass* [in the London Museum], by John Hayes. HMSO, 1965, 40p., *illus.* A collection of 437 specimens presented by Sir Richard Garton (1857-1934).

**1,058** *Glass in London. A catalogue by D.B. Harden of the Museum's Summer Exhibition, 1970.* HMSO, 1970.

LOEWENSTEIN, K.L. *joint author see* LYNTON, Paul *and* LOEWENSTEIN, K.L.

**1,059** LONDON: PATENT OFFICE. *Subject list of works on the silicate industries* [ceramics and glass]. London, 1914.

**1,060** LUCAS, J.W. 'Scotland's coloured glassware'. In *Scotland's Mag.*, Jly 1968, p.9-11, *illus.*

**1,061** LUKAS, Vaclar. 'G.F. Kreybich's journey to London in 1688 and the beginnings of English engraved glass'. In *Glass Review*, 35 no.1, 1980, p.10-13, *illus.*

**1,062** LUKINS, Jocelyn. 'Glass rolling pins'. In *ADCG*, May 1970, p.65-8, *illus. (some col.).*

**1,063** LYMBERY, R.S. 'Problems and prospects of future glass collecting'. In *GC*, no.67.

**1,064** LYNTON, Paul *and* LOEWENSTEIN, K.L. 'Musical glasses'. In *TSGT (News and Reviews)*, 1951, p.17-22.

**1,065** McCAWLEY, Patricia. *Glass paperweights.* Charles Letts, 1975, 71p., *illus. (col.).*

**1,066** 'Glass paperweights old and modern'. In *ADCG*, Dec 1976, p.104-9, *illus. (some col.).*

**1,067** McDONALD, L.J. Paper on Ravenshead – the first cast-plate glass company. Pilkington Glass Museum, 1969.

**1,068** McC[ORMACK], J. 'Rare tankard – glassmaking in Newcastle' [inscribed G. TYZACK]. In *CONN*, Jan-Apr 1922, p.165-6, *illus.*

**1,069** 'A Ravenscroft glass'. In *CONN*, Jly-Dec 1932, p.321, *illus.*

**1,070** MACDONALD-TAYLOR, Margaret. 'Lighting the Georgian house: chandeliers of wood and glass'. In *CL*, Aug 1963, p.498-9, *illus.*

**1,071** MACKAY, James. 'Air twist glass'. In *The Financial Times*, Dec 13th 1969, p.8, *illus.*

**1,072** *Glass paperweights.* Ward Lock, 1973, 112p., *illus. (some col.).*

**1,073** 'Baluster wine glasses'. In *The Financial Times*, May 18th 1968, p.8, *illus.*

**1,074** 'Burmese glass' [fairy lights]. In *The Financial Times*, Nov 30th 1968, p.8, *illus.*

**1,075** 'Collecting Nailsea glass'. In *The Financial Times*, Jly 12th 1969, p.8, *illus.*

**1,076** 'English enamelled glass'. In *The Financial Times*, Nov 11th 1970, p.8, *illus.*

**1,077** 'Glass paperweights'. In *The Financial Times*, Mar 15th 1969, p.8, *illus.*

**1,078** MACKAY, James A. *Antiques of the future.* Studio, 1970. Includes glass and glass paperweights, p.54-77, *illus.*

**1,079** McKEARIN, Helen. 'Eighteenth-century advertisements of glass imports into the Colonies and the United States'. In *GN*, 1954, p.13-21, and 1955, p.15-25, *illus.*

**1,080** M'KEE & BROS. *M'Kee Victorian glass.* Constable, 1982. A reissue of five complete glass catalogues 1859-1871.

**1,081** MACLEOD, Catriona. 'The earliest dated Irish drinking glasses, Dublin, 1715'. In *Royal Soc. of Antiquaries of Ireland Jnl.*, 103, 1973, p.47-50, *illus.*

**1,082** 'Glass-ware engraved by a Bohemian craftsman for the Cork Exhibition 1883'. In *Studies* (Dublin), 67 no.268, 1978, p.330-42, *illus.*

**1,083** 'Irish volunteer glass'. In *Jnl. of the Military History Soc. of Ireland*, v.7, no.28, 1966.

**1,084** 'The land we live in: a toast on Cork decanters'. In *Cork Hist. & Arch. Soc.*, 1978, p.59-65, *illus.* Cork Glass Co. 1783-1818.

**1,085** 'Late eighteenth-century Dublin finger bowls in the National Museum of Ireland'. In *Royal Soc. of Antiquaries of Ireland*, 96, 1966, p.140-6, *illus.*

**1,086** 'The Ouzel Galley Society Glass loving cup (Dublin c.1800-1805)'. In *Irish Georgian Soc. Bull.* 15, no.2, 1972, p.65-71, *illus.*

**1,087** 'Some hitherto unrecorded mementoes of William III (1650-1702)'. In *Studies, Irish Quarterly Review*, 65, Summer 1976, p.128-43, *illus.* 17th century decanters and posset bowl.

**1,088** MacMULLEN, H.T. 'Waterford glass'. In *CL*, Aug and Sept 1946, p.398-400 and 444-5,

1,089 McNAB, Jessie. 'Glassware'. In *Collier's Encyclopedia*, 1967 ed., p.143-52, *illus*. English glass, p.148.

1,090 MACNAGHTEN, Patrick. 'Glass lustre' [mercury glass]. In *Ideal Home*, Nov 1959, p.125, 127, *illus*. Describes the Thesiger Collection.

1,091 'Through a glass lightly'. In *CL*, Apr 1969, p.937, *illus*. Comments on the exhibition of Laurence Whistler's engraved glasses at Agnews, 'A point on glass', Apr-May 1969.

1,092 MACSWIGGAN, Amelia E. 'Fairy lamps'. In *Antiques Jnl.*, Jan 1972, p.27-9, *illus*.

1,093 MADEIRA, Louis C. 'Historic English toasting glasses'. In *A*, 1954, p.128-30.

1,094 'Making of glassware: historical survey'. In *Pottery Gazette*, 1950, p.869-72, *illus*.

1,095 MANCHESTER CITY ART GALLERY. *Glass in the Manchester City Art Gallery*. Manchester, 1959. Introduction by William Douglas Hall.

1,096 'Manchester exhibition of British industrial art, 1846'. In *Art Union*, 1846, p.42, *illus*. The exhibition included items by Richardson of Stourbridge.

1,097 MANCHESTER PUBLIC FREE LIBRARY. *Catalogue of books on ceramics, glass-ware, ornamental metal-work, enamels and jade in the Free Reference Library*, compiled by F. Bentley Nicholson. Manchester Public Free Library, 1908, 20p. (Occasional lists, no.8)

1,098 MANKOWITZ, Wolf. *The Portland Vase and the Wedgwood copies*. Deutsch, 1952, 76p., *illus.*, *bibliog.*

1,099 MANLEY, C.C. 'Acid-etched glass: an under-rated art'. In *Antiques Jnl.*, Sept 1977, p.20-2, *illus*.

1,100 'Alabaster art glass [Stevens & Williams Co.]'. In *Antiques Jnl.*, June 1977, p.22-3, *illus*.

1,101 'Artists and glass'. In *Antiques Jnl.*, Dec 1977, p.28-30, *illus*. Enamelling & painting of Stevens & Williams Co. 1880s-1930s.

1,102 'Birmingham glass'. In *Antiques Jnl.*, May 1976, p.12-15, *illus*.

1,103 'The charm of unusual glass items'. In *Antiques Jnl.*, Aug 1979, p.24-7, *illus*. Pressed glass.

1,104 'The choicest glassware of Stevens and Williams'. In *Antiques Jnl.*, Jly 1974, p.22-4, *illus*.

1,105 *Collectable glass. Book 4: British [coloured] glass*. The C.C. Manley Collection at Brierley Hill photographed by Ted and Vi Largerberg. Port Richey, Florida, 1969, 18p., *illus. (col.)*.

1,106 'Discoveries in English glass'. In *Antiques Jnl.*, Oct 1981, p.8-12, *illus*.

1,107 'English art glass'. In *Antiques Jnl.*, Dec 1978, p.24-7, *illus*.

1,108 'English epergnes'. In *Antiques Jnl.*, Aug 1977, p.14-17, *illus*.

1,109 'English glass: my latest finds'. In *Antiques Jnl.*, June 1981, p.12-17, *illus*.

1,110 'English glass sugar and creams'. In *Antiques Jnl.*, Oct 1979, p.20-2, *illus*.

1,111 'English iridescent glass'. In *The Spinning Wheel*, Feb 1969, p.14-16, 54, *illus*.

1,112 'Further forays in English pressed glass'. In *Antiques Jnl.*, June 1979, p.30-3, *illus*.

1,113 'Glass busts and candlesticks'. In *Antiques Jnl.*, Dec 1981, p.22-3, *illus*.

1,114 'The glass of northern England'. In *Antiques Jnl.*, Aug 1975, p.16-20, *illus*.

1,115 'Identifying Scottish glass'. In *Antiques Jnl.*, May 1973, p.20, *illus*.

1,116 'More English glass "treasures"'. In *Antiques Jnl.*, Feb 1979, p.26-30, *illus*.

1,117 'Richardson's fine English glass'. In *Antiques Jnl.*, Feb 1974, p.10-12, *illus*.

1,118 'Scotland's glass and its makers'. In *Antiques Jnl.*, Jan 1973, p.16.

1,119 'Stevens and Williams' applied decorations on art glass'. In *Antiques Jnl.*, May 1977, p.27-9, *illus*.

1,120 'Stevens and Williams glass'. In *Antiques Jnl.*, June 1974, p.20, *illus*.

1,121 'Stevens and Williams threaded glass'. In *Antiques Jnl.*, Dec 1976, p.22-4, *illus*.

1,122 'Webb & Corbett: their glass productions are tops'. In *Antiques Jnl.*, May 1975, p.14-17, *illus*.

1,123 MANLEY, Cyril. *Decorative Victorian glass*. New York, Van Nostrand Reinhold, 1981, 125p., *illus*.

1,124 MANN, M. 'Harrison Williams Waterford glass'. In *Studio (American ed. – 'International Studio')*, 95, Feb 1930, p.39-43, *illus*.

1,125 MANNING, John. 'Jacob Verzelini: Elizabethan glass-maker'. In *AP*, Apr 1964, p.299-302, *illus*.

1,126 MANSELL, W.W. *An Historical and genealogical account of the ancient family of Maunsell, Mansell, Mansel*. Buck & Straker, 1850.

1,127 'Manufacture of blown domestic glassware'. In *Pottery Gazette*, 1950, p.1668-9, *illus*.

1,128 MARSH, Tracy H. 'English heroes honoured in glass'. In *Hobbies*, May 1963, p.86, *illus*.

1,129 'Glass terminology'. In *Hobbies*, Oct 1964, p.85-92.

1,130 'Royalty in glass' [Queen Victoria's Jubilee]. In *Hobbies*, Jly 1963, p.84-5, *illus*.

1,131 MARSHALL, E.J. 'Collecting English drinking glasses in the twentieth century'. In *AP*, Jan-June 1951, p.165-8, *illus*.

1,132 MARSHALL, H.R. 'Tassie's coloured glass intaglios'. In *GC*, no.92, Apr 1949, 13p.

1,133 MARSHALL, Monica. 'English glass for beginners'. In *GC*, no.127.

1,134 MARSON, Percival. *Glass and glass manufacture*. Revised and enlarged by L.M. Angus-Butterworth. 4th ed. Pitman, 1949, 145p., *illus*. First pub. 1918.

1,135 MARTIN, L. *and* PACKHAM, Colin. 'Deadly delights: early [glass] poison Bottles'. In *Art & Antiques Weekly*, June 17th 1978, p.18-20,

1,136 MATCHAM, J. *and* DREISER, P. *Techniques of glass engraving*. Batsford, 1982, 168p., *illus. (some col.)*.

1,137 MATHEW, N. 'Decanters'. In *AC*, Apr 1977, p.56-60, *illus.*

1,138 MATTHEWS, W.C. 'Old glass collecting'. In *Chambers's Jnl.*, June 1933, p.431-4.

1,139 MAXWELL, H.W. 'The early connection of the glass works at Nailsea and Bristol'. In *GC*, no.95.

1,140 MAYERS, Colin. 'Glass Congress [London, 1968]: history and design'. In *Pottery Gazette and Glass Trade Rev.*, 1968, p.1058-61, *illus.*

1,141 MEHLMAN, Felice. 'Cameo revived'. In *AC*, Sept 1980, p.60-3, *illus.*

1,142 'Cranberry glass'. In *AC*, Feb 1977, p.36-9, *illus.*

1,143 'The dressing out of dessert'. In *AC*, Aug 1982, p.32-5, *illus., bibliog.*

1,144 'Good scents'. In *AC*, Dec 1981, p.79-81, *illus.*

1,145 'Nailsea glass'. In *AC*, Feb 1981, p.50-3, *illus.*

1,146 *Phaidon guide to glass*. Phaidon, 1982, 256p., *illus., bibliog.*

1,147 MEIGH, Edward. 'The Society of Glass Technology: Golden Jubilee: a brief history'. In *Glass Technology*, 1966, p.147-80, *illus.*

1,148 *The story of the glass bottle*. Stoke on Trent, Ramsden, 1972, 86p., *illus., bibliog.*

MEIGH, Edward, *ed. see* GOODING, R.J. *and* MEIGH, Edward, *eds.*

MEIGH, Edward *see* SOCIETY OF GLASS TECHNOLOGY, SHEFFIELD

1,149 'Out of the clouds'. In *ADCG*, Oct 1980, p.65-7, *illus.* 'Cloud glass' manufactured 1923-39 by George Davidson & Co. Gateshead-upon-Tyne.

1,150 MELTON, James. 'Glass candelabra and lustres'. In *Connoisseur Concise Encyclopedia of Antiques*, v.3, 1957, p.165-70, *illus.*

1,151 MERRET, Christopher. *The art of glass*. London, 1662. A translation with additions of Antonio Neri's *L'Art Vetraria*, pub. Florence, 1612.

1,152 *The art of glass ed.* by *Sir* T. Phillipps. Middle Hill (Worcs.), 1826, Folio priv. print.

1,153 METEYARD, Eliza. *The life of Josiah Wedgwood*. 2 v. Hurst and Blackett, 1866. Reference to the Barberini [Portland] Vase, v.2, p.575-83, *illus.*

1,154 MICHAELIS, Ronald F. 'Old bottle seal finds'. In *ADCG*, Oct 1964, p.51-2, *illus.*

1,155 MIDDLEMAS, Keith. *Antique coloured glass*. Ferndale, 1979, 120p. *col. illus.*

MIDDLEMAS, Keith, *joint author see* DAVIS, Derek C. *and* MIDDLEMAS, Keith.

1,156 'Milk glass'. In *The Times*, Jly 16th 1960, p.9.

1,157 MILLS, John Fitzmaurice. 'Is it genuine?' In *AC*, Nov 1979, p.79, *illus.* Fakes.

1,158 'Problems and solutions II' [The care of glassware]. In *CONN*, Nov 1968, p.165.

1,159 'Mr Pargeter's art productions in glass'

[Red House Glass Works, Stourbridge]. In *The Reliquary*, 18, 1877-8, p.57-8.

1,160 'Mr Pargeter's 'Milton Vase' [Red House Glass Works, Stourbridge]. In *The Reliquary*, 19, 1878-9, p.243, *illus.*

1,161 'Modern glass'. In *Art Jnl.*, 1889 (p.3-4 of Art and Industries Supplement, between p.31 *and* 32), *illus.*

1,162 MONRO, Helen. 'The art of glass engraving'. In *Jnl. of the Royal Soc. of Arts*, 1960, p.477-95, *illus.*

1,163 'Glass engraving' [contemporary – Whistler, etc.]. In *Studio*, Oct 1960, p.122-9, *illus.*

1,164 MONSON-FITZJOHN, G.J. *Drinking vessels of by-gone days from the Neolithic age to the Georgian period*. H. Jenkins, 1927.
Includes: Old glass, p.128-38; Saxon glass, p.15-16, *illus.*

1,165 MOODY, B.E. 'The origin of the "reputed quart" and other measures' [bottles, etc.]. In *Glass Technology*, 1960, p.55-68, *illus.*

1,166 MOORE, John, *comp. Worshipful Company of Glass Sellers of London, incorporated 1664*. Priv. print, 1899, 61p., *ports.*

1,167 MOORE, N. Hudson. *The collector's manual*. New York, Tudor, 1935.
Includes antique glassware, p.76-101, *illus.* First pub. 1905.

1,168 'How about Waterford glass?' In *A*, Sept 1923, p.116-20, *illus.*

1,169 *Old glass, European and American*. Hodder and Stoughton, 1935, 394p., *illus.*
Contents include: Bristol glass, p.152-68; Irish glass, p.174-203; Nailsea, p.169-73, *illus.* First pub. New York, Stokes, 1924.

1,170 'More Ravenscroft glass'. In *GN*, 1953, p.21-3, *illus.*

1,171 MORGAN, Ray. *Mainly Codd's wallop: the story of the great British pop bottle*. Wellingborough, Kollectorama, 1974, 24p., *illus.*

1,172 *Sealed bottles: their history and evolution (1630-1930)*. Research by Ray Morgan & Gordon Litherland. Burton-on-Trent, Midlands Antique Bottle Publishing, [1976], 120p., *illus.*

1,173 MORLEY, John. 'The beauty of Bacchus'. In *Annual Bull. of the Paperweight Collectors' Assn.*, 1980, p.46-8, *illus.*

1,174 MORLEY-PRIESTMAN, Anne. 'Back to the nursery'. In *Art & Antiques*, Aug 5th 1978, p.22-3, *illus.* Feeding bottles.

1,175 MORRIS, Barbara. 'The Bathgate bowl'. In *The Glass Circle 2*, 1975, p.17-25, *illus.*

1,176 'British glass, 1830-1900'. In *Bulletin de l'Association Internationale pour l'Histoire du Verre*, no.8, 1977-80, p.139-52, *illus.*

1,177 *Victorian table glass and ornaments*. Barrie & Jenkins, 1978, 256p., *illus.*

1,178 MORTIMER, Martin C.F. 'Dating an early glass chandelier'. In *CONN*, Jly-Dec 1970, p.172-4, *illus.*

1,179 'Elusive charm of the engraver: English

18th-century wine glasses'. In *CL*, June 9th 1983, p.1564; 1568, *illus.*

1,180 'English glass candelabra'. In *ADCG*, Dec 1972, p.107-11, *illus.*

1,181 'Glass as decoration'. In *ADCG*, Apr 1983, p.26-9, *illus. (some col.).*

1,182 'Irish glass'. In *AC*, Aug 1974, p.48-52, *illus.*

1,183 'The Irish mirror chandelier'. In *CL*, Dec 16, 1971, p.1741-42, *illus.*

1,184 'Movements in nature of English glass'. In *AC*, Jly-Aug, 1981, p.25, *illus.*

1,185 'Trends in prices of collectors wine glasses'. In *AC*, Dec 1979, p.28-30, *illus.*

MORTIMER, Martin C. *joint author see* TREGLOWN, G.L. *and* MORTIMER, Martin C.F.

1,186 MOUNTAIN, Francis. *History of the Nailsea Glassworks, written when seventy-two years of age, for the Bristol City Museum and Art Gallery.* c.1915. MS.

1,187 MULLALY, Terence. 'More than mere drinking vessels'. In *Daily Tel.*, Mar 18th 1978, p.11, *illus.*

1,188 MURRAY, Sheilagh. *The peacock and the lions: a history and manual for collectors of pressed glass of the north-east of England.* Oriel Press, 1982, 86p., *illus. (some col.), bibliog.*

1,189 'Musical glasses'. In *The Times*, Feb 15th 1964, p.11, *illus.*

1,190 NAGEL, Fred A. 'Enchanting paperweights signed P.Y.'. In *Bull. of the Paperweight Collectors' Assn.*, 1968, p.3-8, *illus.*

1,191 'Nailsea Glass'. In *Evening Argus*, Jly 9th 1970, p.16, *illus.*

1,192 'Nailsea glass'. In *Antique Bottle Collecting*, Jan 1982, p.12-15, *illus.*

1,193 'Nailsea glass jugs'. In *CONN*, May-Aug 1906, p.48-50, *illus.*

1,194 NAPIER, Cecily. 'Collecting sets of glasses'. In *AC*, May 1979, p.81-3, *illus.*

1,195 NAPIER, Ivan. 'Colour tints in English… and Irish glass'. In *GC*, no.45.

1,196 'Frans Greenwood and his glass'. In *GC*, no.58.

1,197 'King's Lynn glass'. In *GC*, nos.29 and 34.

1,198 'Newcastle glass'. In *GC*, no.39.

1,199 NEGUS, Arthur. 'Decorative [Nailsea] rolling pins'. In *Discovering Antiques*, v.6, New York, Greystone Press, 1973, p.722-3, *illus.*

1,200 'Nailsea glass'. In *Discovering Antiques*, v.8, p.928-9, *illus.*

NERI, Antonio *see* MERRETT, Christopher

1,201 NESBITT, Alexander. 'Glass'. In *Encyclopedia Britannica*, 9th ed., 1879, v.10, p.647-55.

1,202 *Notes on the history of glass-making prepared as an introduction to the catalogue of the collection of glass of various periods formed by the late Felix Slade…* London (priv. print.), 1869, 50p., *bibliog.*
*see also* (1) CHAFFERS, W.
(2) VICTORIA AND ALBERT MUSEUM.

1,203 'New glass technology gallery' [at the Science Museum]. In *Pottery Gazette and Glass Trade Rev.*, 1968, p.752-3, *illus.*

1,204 NEWMAN, Harold. *An illustrated dictionary of glass: 2442 entries… with an introductory survey of the history of glass-making by Robert J. Charleston.* Thames & Hudson, 1977, 351p.

NEW SOUTH WALES ART GALLERY, SYDNEY, *see* ART GALLERY OF NEW SOUTH WALES, SYDNEY.

NICHOLSON, F. Bentley, *compiler see* MANCHESTER FREE PUBLIC LIBRARY

1,205 NIGHTINGALE, Mark. 'Variations and developments of the pontilled graduated stock medicine bottle [1820-60]'. In *Antique Bottle Collecting*, May 1982, p.8-9, *illus.*

1,206 NOPPEN, J.G. 'Eighteenth-century English glass'. In *AP*, Jan-June 1934, p.179-86, *illus.*

1,207 'Eighteenth-century English ale glasses'. In *AP*, Jan-June, 1935, p.3-9, *illus.*

1,208 'English glass drinking vessels'. In *AP*, Jly-Dec 1933, p.77-83, and p.225-31, *illus.*

1,209 'The Manderson Collection of eighteenth-century glass'. In *AP*, Jan-June, 1935, p.327-31, *illus.*

1,210 'On collecting antique glass for use'. In *AP*, Jly-Dec 1938, p.241-3, *illus.*

1,211 'A series of old English decanters'. In *AP*, Jly-Dec 1935, p.74-9, *illus.*

1,212 NORMAN, Barbara. *Engraving & decorating glass.* David & Charles, 1972, 197p., *illus.*

1,213 *Glass engraving.* David & Charles, 1981, 190p., *illus.*

1,214 NORMAN-WILCOX, G. 'A compendium of drinking glasses with Jacobite engravings'. In *A*, Jly 1932, p.11-14, *illus.*

1,215 'English glass: baluster stems, an historical summary'. In *A*, Nov 1932, p.174-6, *illus.*

1,216 NORTH WEST MUSEUM & ART GALLERY SERVICE. *The Denton glass excavations…* Liverpool, [1971], 22p., *illus.*

1,217 NORTHWOOD, John. [Catalogue of the] *Borough of Stourbridge Glass Collection.* Stourbridge, 1954, 36p.

1,218 *John Northwood I: his contribution to the Stourbridge flint glass industry, 1850-1902.* Stourbridge, Mark and Moody, 1958, 134p.

1,219 'The reproduction of the Portland Vase'. In *TSGT*, 1924, p.85-92, *illus.*

1,220 'Stourbridge cameo glass'. In *TSGT (News and Reviews)*, 1949, p.106-13, *illus.*

1,221 'Notes on milk glass: Bristol and continental types'. In *A*, Oct 1928, p.319-21, *illus.*

1,222 NOTLEY, Ray. *Carnival glass.* Shire Pubs., 1983, 32p., *illus., bibliog.*

1,223 'English carnival notes'. In *Heart of America Carnival Glass Assn., Bull.*, Jan-Dec 1982. Continuing series.

1,224 'Old catalog reprints – Sowerby Glass Co.' In *Heart of America Carnival Glass Assn. Bull.*

1,225 'Sowerby carnival glass'. In *The Glass Collector* (USA), Spring 1982, p.26-8, *illus.*

1,226 'How the British sold glass to Scandinavia'.

In *Sun. Times*, Sept 23rd 1973, p.46, *illus.*

**1,227** NYMAN, Ben. *The Nyman Collection of cameo glass, porcelain enamelling and pâte-sur-pâte.* 2 v. [priv. print?], 1957, *illus.*

**1,228** ODDY, R. 'British glass 1680-1830'. In *Bulletin de l'Association Internationale pour l'Histoire du Verre*, no.8, 1977-1980, p.113-26, *illus.*

**1,229** 'Scottish glasshouses'. In *GC* no.151.

**1,230** O'DEA, W.T. *A short history of lighting.* HMSO, 1958, 40p., *illus.*
Includes lamps, shades, etc.

**1,231** O'FALLON, J.M. 'Glass'. In *Chambers's Encyclopedia*, 1930 ed., v.5, p.241-51, *illus., bibliog.* General article.

**1,232** 'Glass engraving as an art'. In *Art Jnl.*, 1885, p.309-14, *illus.*

**1,233** 'Old and new glasses'. In *The Times*, 1911, Nov 11th p.6 and Nov 17th p.6.

**1,234** 'Old English bottles'. In *CL*, Dec 1921, p.778-80, *illus.*

**1,235** 'Old English glassware – unique and priceless collection at Brierley Hill'. In *Pottery Gazette*, 1950, p.70-5, *illus.*

**1,236** 'Old English tumblers – pictorial engravings on glass'. In *ADCG*, Jan 1959, p.27-9, *illus.*

**1,237** 'Old glass: hints to the collector'. In *The Countryman*, 1936, p.524-5.

**1,238** OLD WATERFORD SOCIETY. *Exhibition of Waterford glass, 1952* [Catalogue]. [Waterford?], 1952.

**1,239** O'LOONEY, Betty. *Victorian glass.* HMSO, Victoria & Albert Museum, 1972, 48p., *illus.*
Items from the Victoria & Albert Museum.
*see also* CORNING MUSEUM OF GLASS, NEW YORK.

**1,240** 'Opaque glass'. In *The Times*, Aug 18th 1956, p.9, *illus.*

**1,241** 'Open-flame gas lamps'. In *The Times*, Nov 30th 1963, p.11, *illus.*

**1,242** ORD, P.R. 'Observations on glass cutting by diamond'. In *TSGT*, 1957, p.245-58, *illus.*

**1,243** ORMSBEE, Thomas H. 'English glass'. In *Encyclopedia Americana*, 1968 ed., v.12, p.692-3.

**1,244** OSBOURNE, Harold, *ed. The Oxford Companion to the Decorative Arts.* O.U.P. 1975. Glass techniques and history, p.393-412.

**1,245** OSWALD, Adrian *and* PHILLIPS, Howard. 'A Restoration glass hoard from Gracechurch Street, London'. In *CONN*, Jly-Dec 1949, p.30-6, *illus.* Discovered in 1940 and later presented to the Guildhall Museum.

**1,246** OVERSTOLZENHAUS, KUNSTGEWERBE-MUSEUM DER STADT, COLOGNE. *Christopher Dresser, ein viktorianischer Designer 1834-1904.* Cologne Museum, 1981, 88p., *illus.* Decanters, carafes, vases.

**1,247** OWEN, Hugh. *Two centuries of ceramic art in Bristol: a history of the manufacture of the 'true porcelain' by R. Champion, with a biography.* London, 1873, 419p., *illus.* Includes glass.

**1,248** *Oxford Junior Encyclopedia.* Contents include 'Table glass', v.[II], 1955, p.435-7, *illus.*

PACKHAM, Colin, *joint author see* MARTIN, L. *and* PACKHAM, Colin.

PAINTER, K.S. *see* BRITISH MUSEUM.

**1,249** PALMER, M.A. 'English glass in the Cecil Higgins Museum, Bedford'. In *AP*, Jly-Dec 1950, p.39-42, 47, *illus.*

**1,250** PANCAKE, Evan. 'Whitefriars then and now'. In *Annual Bull. of the Paperweight Collectors' Assn.*, 1980, p.30-4, *illus.*

**1,251** PAPE, T. 'An ancient glass furnace at Eccleshall, Staffordshire'. In *Antiquaries' Jnl.*, v.14, 1934, p.141-2, *plan.*

**1,252** 'An Elizabethan glass furnace' [at Bishop's Wood, Staffordshire]. In *CONN*, Jly-Dec 1933, p.172, 175-7, *illus., plans.*

**1,253** 'Medieval glassworkers in North Staffordshire'. In *Trans. North Staffordshire Field Club*, v.68, 1933-4.

**1,254** 'Paris International Exhibition, 1878'. In *Art Jnl.*, 1878 (Supplement, 104p., at end).
Contents include frequent mention and illustration of English and continental glass exhibits.

**1,255** 'Paris Universal Exhibition, 1867'. In *Art Jnl. Supplementary volume: 'Paris Exhibition'*, 1867.
Contents include: 'The glass domestic and decorative' [with illustrations and descriptions of British items], by George Wallis, p.77-107.

**1,266** PARKES, Judith. *Antique collecting with BP*, 2nd ed., 2 v., BP Shell-Mex, 1969. First pub. 1967.
Contents include: Glass, v. I, p.40-51, *illus.*

**1,267** PARRY, S.W. *Dwarf ale glasses and their Victorian successors.* Polyptoton, 1978, 15p., *illus.*

**1,268** 'Used for a potent brew. Dwarf ale glasses'. In *CL*, Nov 25th 1976, p.1560-1, *illus.*

**1,269** PATON, James. *Lamps: a collector's guide.* Souvenir Press, 1978, 144p., *illus.* Many glass examples.

**1,270** PEAKE-ANDERSON, Constance. 'Glass of today'. In *Studio*, Aug 1931, p.72-97, *illus.*

**1,271** PEDDLE, Cyril J. *Defects in glass.* Glass Pubs., 1927, 205p.

**1,272** PELLATT, Apsley. *Curiosities of glassmaking with details of the processes and productions of ancient and modern ornamental glass manufacture.* D. Bogue, 1849. 146p., *illus.*
The material in this book was originally a series of lectures given at the Royal Institute.

**1,273** *Flint glass manufactures (models and specimens exhibited at the Great Exhibition, London, 1851).* London, 1851.

**1,274** 'Glass for fancy use and household purposes'. In *The Technologist (London)*, 1864, 4, p.120.

**1,275** *Memoir on the origin, progress and improvement of glass manufactures: including an account of the patent Crystallo-ceramie, or glass incrustations.* B.J. Holdsworth, 1821. 42p., *illus.* (col.).

**1,276** 'Pellatt, Apsley' [obituary notice]. In *ILN*, May 16th 1863, p.546.

**1,277** 'Pellatt Apsley' [obituary notice]. In *The Times*,

Apr 20th 1863, p.12.

**1,278** 'Pellatt [Apsley] and Co. 'A service of table glass... executed for the Prince of Wales'. In *Art Jnl.* 1863, p.59.

**1,279** 'Pellatt and Wood'. In *Art Jnl.*, 1875, p.56-7. A short description of the firm.

**1,280** PELLATT, Frederick. 'The manufacture of glass'. In *Jnl. of the Franklin Inst.*, v.42, 1846, p.271.

**1,281** PERCIVAL, MacIver. *The glass collector: a guide to old English glass.* H. Jenkins, 1918, 347p., *illus., bibliog.*

**1,282** 'Perkes and Co.'s. [Stoke-on-Trent] engraved glass'. In *The Reliquary*, 1875, p.167.

**1,283** PERRETT, J. Bernard. 'The eighteenth-century chandeliers at Bath'. In *CONN*, Jly-Dec 1938, p.187-92, *illus.*

**1,284** 'The evolution of the English glass chandelier'. In *AP*, Jly-Dec 1939, p.101-4, *illus.*

PERROT, P.N. *see* (1) CORNING MUSEUM OF GLASS.
(2) 'Survey of contemporary glass'.

**1,285** PETER, Mary. *Collecting Victoriana.* Arco, 1965. Contents include: Victorian glass, p.108-29, *illus.*

**1,286** PEVSNER, N. 'English qualities in English glass'. In *CL*, Jly 1941, p.109, *illus.*

**1,287** PEYSER, Barbara A. 'Bottles'. In *Antiques Jnl.*, May 1972, p.49-50.

**1,288** PHILLIMORE, John. 'A famous bridge [Wearmouth] in pottery and glass'. In *AP*, Jan-June 1941, p.6-9, and p.35-7, *illus.*

PHILLIPPS, *Sir* T. *ed. see* MERRET, Christopher.

**1,289** PHILLIPS, Howard. 'Learning to look at glasses. Illustrated by a select group of English glasses, 1730-1770'. In *AC*, 1959, p.63-8, *illus. joint author see* OSWALD, Adrian, *and* PHILLIPS, Howard

**1,290** PHILLIPPS, John Pavin. 'The Society of Sea-Sergeants' [South Wales]. In *GN*, 1950, p.15-17. Glasses exist bearing the emblem of this Society and are possibly connected with the Welsh Jacobites.

**1,291** PHIPPS, Jennifer. 'The G. Gordon Russell Glass Collection'. In *Art Bull. of Victoria*, 1973-4, p.35-41, *illus.* Mostly British 17th-18th century in the Nat. Gallery of Victoria, Melbourne, Australia.

**1,292** PICK, Michael. 'The Unique English chandelier'. In *AC*, June 1982, p.62-6, *illus.*

**1,293** PICKFORD, Ian. 'Claret jugs through the ages'. In *ADCG*, Nov 1977, p.95-6; 99-100, *illus.*

**1,294** PILBIN, P. 'The influence of local geography on the glass industry of Tyneside'. In *Jnl. Tyneside Geographical Soc.*, Vol.1, 1936, p.31-45.

**1,295** PILKINGTON BROTHERS, LTD. *Pattern book of ornamental glass.* St. Helens, 1896. 62p., *illus.*

**1,296** *150th Anniversary Exhibition Guide: Pilkington 1826-1976.* St. Helens, Pilkington, 1976, 28p.

**1,297** *Pilkington Glass Museum* [Catalogue of the Collection]. St. Helens, 1969, *illus.* Loose sheets in card folder.

**1,298** 'Pilkington Museum of glass'. In *AC*, 1964, p.250-1, *illus.*

PINDER-WILSON, R.H. *see* BRITISH MUSEUM.

**1,299** PLATTS, Beryl. 'The glass engraver as symbolist: new work by Laurence Whistler'. In *CL*, Sept 19th 1974, p.770-1, *illus.*

**1,300** PLENDERLITH, H.J. *and* WERNER, A.E.A. *The conservation of antiquities and works of art.* 2nd ed. O.U.P., 1971. Glass p.343-51, *illus.*

**1,301** PLESCH, Peter H. 'English and continental glass in the collection of Dr and Mrs Peter H. Plesch'. In *CJGS*, 1965, p.79-82, *illus.*

**1,302** POLAK, Ada. 'English connections in Norway's old glass industry'. In *AP*, Jly-Dec 1952, p.17-20, *illus.*

**1,303** *Modern glass.* Faber, 1962, 94p., *illus., bibliog.* (Faber Monographs on Glass). Contents include: English glass, p.33, 58-62, 77-80.

**1,304** 'A Newcastle glass blower in eighteenth-century Norway'. In *GC*, no.98.

**1,305** 'The new Verzelini glass'. In *CONN*, Dec 1978, p.283, *illus.* 1584 presentation goblet.

**1,306** 'Notes on glass chandeliers'. In *GC*, no.112.

**1,307** PONTIL, *pseud.* 'Glass age'. In *CONN*. Contents: Early English and Dutch glasses, Jan-Apr 1918, p.213-16; Balusters, tear glasses, etc., May-Aug 1918, p.132-8; Various wine glasses, Jan-Apr 1919, p.33-7, and May-Aug 1919, p.75-80, *all illus.*

**1,308** 'Two Ravenscroft sealed goblets'. In *CONN*, Jan-June 1933, p.200, *illus.*

[PORTER, George Richardson] *see* LARDNER, Dionysius.

**1,309** 'Portrait glasses of Prince Charles Edward in enamel colours'. In *GN*, 1956, p.21-6, *illus.*

**1,310** POWELL, A.C. 'Glassmaking in Bristol'. In *Trans. of the Bristol Archaeological Soc.*, v.47, 1925.

**1,311** POWELL, Harry James. 'The development of coloured glass in England'. In *TSGT*, 1922, p.249-55.

**1,312** *Glassmaking in England.* C.U.P., 1923, 183p., *illus.* Includes: Old London and provincial glasshouses, p.86-111.

**1,313** 'Happy hunting grounds of a [glass] designer'. In *CL*, Sept 1922, p.44-6, *illus.*

**1,314** 'Whitefriars Glass Works: notes of a flint-glass manager from 1875 to 1916'. In *TSGT*, 1918, p.241-6.

**1,315** , *and others. Principles of glassmaking... together with a treaties on Crown and sheet glass* by H. Chance... *and plate glass by* H.G. Harris, London, 1883, 186p.

**1,316** POWELL, JAMES AND SONS (WHITEFRIARS) LTD. *Whitefriars glass Catalogue.* J. Powell and Sons, Ltd, n.d. [1938?] *illus.*

**1,317** *Whitefriars handmade crystal* [Catalogue]. Wealdstone, J. Powell and Sons Ltd, n.d.

[1948?] 72p., *illus., map.*

1,318 'Powells', The Whitefriars Studios'. In *Jnl. of the Soc. of Master Glass Painters*, v.13, 1959-60, p.321-5, *illus.*

1,319 PRENTISS, E.L. 'The manufacture of cut-glass'. In *Brush and Pencil*, v.16, 1905, p.131.

1,320 'Pressed glass'. In *The Times*, Jly 23rd 1966, p.13.

1,321 PRESTON, Eric, HOLLAND, A.J. *and* TURNER, W.E.S. 'Study of the brilliance exhibited by lead crystal glass'. In *TSGT*, 1935, p.125-38, *illus.*

1,322 PRICE, R. 'Notes on the evolution of the wine bottle'. In T*rans. of the Glasgow Archaeological Soc.*, v.6 (New Series), Pt 1, p.116.

1,323 PRICE, R.E. 'Early decorating and modern colouring of glass'. In *Glass Technology*, Dec 1975, p.417, *illus.*

1,324 PRICE, R.K. 'The Price family of glassmakers'. In *GC*, no.133.

1,325 PROSSER, R.B. 'Apsley Pellatt (1791-1863)'. In *Dictionary of National Biography*, v.44, 1895, p.264-5.

1,326 PRYOR, G.R. 'Scientific aids to the identification of antique paperweights'. In *Antiques Rev.*, Dec 1953-Feb 1954, p.19-20, *illus.*

1,327 PURSER, C.J. 'Brief history of the Wear Glass Works'. In *TSGT*, 1946, p.198-200.

1,328 'Queen's gift to the [French] President'. In *CL*, Apr 1957, p.698-9, *illus.* Three goblets engraved by Laurence Whistler.

1,329 RACE, S. 'Glass container manufacturing: from the past into the future'. In *Glass Technology*, Feb 1980, p.6-26, *illus.*

1,330 RACKHAM, Bernard. *Catalogue of...* [the Schreiber Collection] presented to the [Victoria and Albert] Museum in 1884. 3v., HMSO, 1924.
Contents includes: Glass, v.3, p.79-86, *illus.*

1,331 'Ceramics and glass'. In *Georgian Art.* Batsford, 1929. (Burlington Magazine Monograph – III). Glass, p.41-2, *illus.*

1,332 'An early diamond-engraved glass at South Kensington'. In *BUR*, Jan-June 1929, p.68-9, 73, *illus.* A letter by Buckley commenting on the article follows on p.162.

1,333 'The glass collections of the Victoria and Albert Museum...' In *TSGT*, 1934, p.308-22, *illus.*

1,334 *A key to pottery and glass.* Blackie, 1940, 180p., *illus.*

1,335 'Three Elizabethan glasses'. In *BUR*, Jan 1913, p.22-7, *illus.*

1,336 'Verzelini and his followers'. In *BUR*, Jly-Dec, 1925, p.182-7, *illus.*

1,337 RAKOW, Leonard S. and Juliette K. 'The cameo glass of John Northwood'. In *A*, Jly 1982, p.112-16, *illus.*

1,338 'The cameo glass of Joseph Locke'. In *Glass Club Bull.* (USA), no.138, 1982, p.3-7, *illus.*

RAMSEY, L.G.G. *ed. see Connoisseur Complete Encyclopedia of Antiques.*

1,339 RAMSEY, William. *History of the Worshipful*

Company of Glass Sellers of London. London, 1898.

1,340 'Rare Jacobite glasses in the collection of Col. W. Churchill Hale'. In *CONN*, May-Aug 1963, p.141-5, *illus.*

1,341 RAVENSCROFT, William. *Some Ravenscrofts.* Milford-on-Sea, T.E. Stone, 1929, 87p.

1,342 'Ravenscroft diary'. In *GN*, 1950, p.13-14.

1,343 'Ravenscroft "sealed" goblet, c.1677'. In *AP*, Jan-June, 1943, p.161, *illus.* An item from the Collection of R.F. Ratcliff, sold to Cecil Davis in 1943.

1,344 READ, Herbert. 'The Bles Collection of English and Irish glass'. In *BUR*, Jly-Dec, 1923, p.247-8, *illus.*

1,345 'Cross-currents in English porcelain, glass and enamels'. In *Trans. of the English Ceramic Circle*, v.1, 1934, no.4, *illus.*

1,346 'English glasses in the collection of Mr John M. Bacon'. In *CONN*, Sept-Dec 1926, p.201-8, *illus.*

1,347 READE, Brian. *Regency antiques.* Batsford, 1953. Contents include: Glass, p.185-203, *illus.*

1,348 'Reminiscences of Ben Richardson' [of Stourbridge]. In *Pottery Gazette and Glass Trade Rev.*, 1952, p.108-9, *illus., port.*

1,349 'Remission of the glass duties'. In *Art Union*, 1845, p.80.

1,350 RENDEL, Rosemary. 'The true identity of George Ravenscroft, glassman'. In *Recusant History*, 13, Oct 1975, p.101-8, *bibliog.*

1,351 'Who was George Ravenscroft?' In *The Glass Circle* 2, 1975, p.65-70.

1,352 'Reproduction of the Portland Vase' [by Northwood and Pargeter of Stourbridge]. In *The Reliquary*, v.17, 1876-7, p.241-3.

1,353 'Return of the soul' [Jacobite glasses]. In *GN*, 1952, p.22-3, *illus.*

1,354 REVI, Albert Christian. 'Cameo glass'. In *Crockery and Glass Jnl.*, Feb 1958, p.48, *illus.*

1,355 'English patented paperweights'. In *Bull. of the Paperweight Collectors' Assn.*, June 1964, p.43-6, *illus.*

1,356 'English pressed glass manufacturer: Edward Moore & Co. South Shields, England'. In *The Spinning Wheel*, Sept 1974, p.24-5, *illus.*

1,357 'English pressed glass manufacturer: George Davidson & Co Ltd. Teams Glass Works [Gateshead].' In *The Spinning Wheel*, Apr 1974, p.48-50, *illus.*

1,358 'English pressed glass manufacturer: Henry Greener & Co. Wear Flint Glass Works'. In *The Spinning Wheel*, May 1975, p.26-7, *illus.*

1,359 'English pressed glass – Sowerby's Ellison Glass Works, Ltd. In *The Spinning Wheel*, Sept 1973, p.26-9, *illus.*

1,360 'Iridescent glass'. In *The Spinning Wheel*, 1959, Mar, p.14-17; Apr, p.16, 18-19; June, p.18-21; *all illus.*

1,361 'Modern glass paperweights'. In *Bull. of the*

1,362 *Paperweight Collectors' Assn.*, June 1961, *illus*.
*Nineteenth-century glass: its genesis and development. Revised ed.* New York, Nelson, 1969, 301p., *illus. (some col.).*

1,363 'Novelty type cameo glass'. In *The Spinning Wheel*, Apr 1957, p.24-5, *illus*.

1,364 'Ruby glass'. In *The Spinning Wheel*, Mar 1961, p.20, 22, *illus*.

1,365 'Samuel Clarke's designs for fairy lamps'. In *The Spinning Wheel*, Mar 1973, p.28-30, *illus*.

1,366 'Stevens and Williams' Silveria Glass'. In *The Spinning Wheel*, Aug 1958, p.28, 30, *illus*.

1,367 'Threaded glassware'. In *The Spinning Wheel*, Jly 1958, p.14-16, *illus*.

1,368 'E. Varnish and Company's silvered glassware'. In *The Spinning Wheel*, Mar 1964, p.16, *illus*.
*see also* CORNING MUSEUM OF GLASS

1,369 REYNOLDS, Ernest. *The plain man's guide to antique collecting.* M. Joseph, 1963.
Contents include: Glass, p.125-32, *illus*.

1,370 RICHARDSON, A.E. *Georgian England: a survey of social life, trades, industries and art… 1700 to 1820.* Batsford, 1931.
Contents include: Ornamental glass, p.144-6, *illus*.

1,371 RIDLEY, Ursula. 'The history of glass making on Tyneside'. In *GC*, no.122.

1,372 'The history of glass making on the Tyne and Wear'. In *Archaeologia Aeliana* (Newcastle), v.40 (Series 4), 1962, p.145-62, *illus*.

1,373 'The Ridley connection with industry'. In *AP*, Oct 1962, p.610-13, *illus., port*. Matthew Ridley bought Howdon Pans Glassworks from the Henzell family in 1759.

1,374 RISLEY, *Sir* John Shuckburgh. 'Commemorative glass'. In Bles, Joseph, *Rare English glasses of the seventeenth and eighteenth centuries*, 1925, p.157-76, *illus*.

1,375 'A Frans Greenwood goblet'. In *BUR*, Jly-Dec 1922, p.297-8, *illus*.

1,376 'Georgian electioneering glasses'. In *BUR* Jly-Dec 1920, p.220, 225-33, *illus*.

1,377 'Georgian rummers'. In *BUR*, Jan-June 1921, p.270-82, *illus*.

1,378 'Jacobite wine-glasses, some rare examples'. In *BUR*, Jan-June 1920, p.276-87, *illus*.

1,379 'Exhibition of Oxburgh and Berkley glasses'. [Jacobite]. In *BUR* Jly-Dec 1920, p.51-2.

1,380 'Old English glasses with white spiral stems'. In *BUR*, Jan-June 1919, p.219-31, *illus*.

1,381 'Sea-power under George III illustrated on contemporary glass'. In *BUR*, Jly-Dec 1919, p.203-10, *illus*.

1,382 'A wine glass commemorating a famous eighteenth-century election'. In *CONN*, Sept-Dec 1918, p.160-2, *illus*. The Wenman and Dashwood wine glass.

1,383 ROBERTSHAW, Ursula. 'Masterpieces in glass'.

In *ILN*, Nov 1974, p.113-14, *illus*.

1,384 'Museum pieces from Royal Brierley'. In *ILN*, Apr 1983, p.51, *illus*.

1,385 'Where all that glitters is lead'. In *ILN*, Dec 29th 1969, p.22-3, *illus*. Modern Waterford glass.

1,386 ROBERTSON, R.A. 'Admiral became glass maker – Sir Robert Mansell's stormy passage'. In *ADCG*, May 1956, p.20-2, *illus*.

1,387 'Blowpipe creates elegance: the glass technique'. In *ADCG*, Oct 1955, p.16-18, *illus*.

1,388 *Chats on old glass*. Benn, 1954. 180p., *illus., bibliog*.

1,389 *Chats on old glass. Revised with a new chapter on American glass by Kenneth M. Wilson, curator, Corning Museum of Glass.* New York, Dover, 1969, 167p., *illus., bibliog*.
Contents include: George Hay (founder of Scottish glassmaking), p.58-60.

1,390 'Drink in beauty: glass through the centuries'. In *ADCG*, June 1956, p.39-41, *illus*.

1,391 'Early English glass making: foreign craftsmen revived industry'. In *ADCG*, Mar 1956, p.17-19, *illus*.

1,392 'Eighteenth-century triumph – trends in English glass'. In *ADCG*, Dec 1960, p.34-6, *illus*.

1,393 'Foundations of a noble tradition – English glass'. In *ADCG*, Nov 1960, p.24-6, *illus*.

1,394 'Glass to see in Scotland'. In *ADCG*, May 1963, p.48-9, *illus*.

1,395 'His name endures in glass – Verzelini's uphill fight in London'. In *ADCG*, Apr 1956, p.28-30, *illus*.

1,396 'Symbolism in Jacobite glass'. In *ADCG*, Oct 1956, p.21-3, *illus*.

1,397 ROBERTSON, W.S. 'A quantitive morphological study of the evolution of some post-medieval wine bottles'. In *Science & Archaeology*, 17.

1,398 ROBINSON, J.B. Perry. 'Glass of today and how to choose it for use and decoration in the home'. In *Studio*, Oct 1935, p.202-8, *illus*. English and Swedish glass.

1,399 RODGER, William. 'Collectable English Wine glasses…' In *Collector's Weekly*, June 26th 1973, p.1; 8-9, *illus*.

1,400 'English table glass of the Golden Age'. In *Glass*, Jan-Feb, 1973, p.5-10, *illus*. Mainly 18th century.

1,401 'Rodney decanters for seafarers'. In *The Times*, Mar 16th 1963, p.11, *illus*.

1,402 ROGERS, Horace M. *The making of a connoisseur*, Estates Gazette, 1951.
Contents include: Romance of old English and Irish glass, p.250-77, *illus*.

1,403 ROGERS, Millard F. 'The European and American Glass Collection'. In *AP*, Jly-Dec 1967, p.478-85, *illus*.

1,404 ROHAN, Thomas. *Old glass beautiful: English and Irish*. Mills and Boon, 1930. 144p., *illus*.

1,405 RONALD, Julie. 'A touch of glass'. In *AC*, Jly 1977, p.80-3, *illus*.

1,406 ROOTES, Nicholas. 'To the King over the Water, Jacobite Glass'. In *AC*, Jan 1981, p.65-7, *illus*.

1,407 ROSE, Jeffrey, A.H. 'The Apsley Pellatts'. In *GC*, no.150.

1,408 'The Apsley Pellatts'. In *GC*, 3, 1979.

1,409 'Apsley Pellatt, Jnr., 1791-1863'. In *CONN*, Sept-Dec 1963, p.232-3, *illus*.

1,410 'Glass and the House of Hanover'. In *GC*, nos. 117 and 123.

1,411 'James and William Tassie'. In *GC*, no.153.

1,412 ROSS, Catherine. 'The excise tax on cut glass in England and Ireland, 1800-1830'. In *CJGS*, 1982, p.57-64, *illus*.

1,413 ROSS, Euan. 'Traditions of English glass'. In Crompton, Sidney, *ed*. *English glass*, 1967, p.7-38, *illus*.

1,414 ROSTRON, Primrose R. 'Antique bottles – expensive empties'. In *Glass*, 54 no.12, 1977, p.562-3, *illus*.

1,415 'Georgian drinking glasses in the eighteenth century – the age of the wine glass'. In *Glass*, June 1979, p.225-6, *illus*.

1,416 'The Grazebrooks of Audram'. In *Blackcountryman*, Winter 1975, p.15-17.

1,417 'Have a liqueur!' In *Glass*, Oct 1980, *illus*. 18th and 19th century cordial glasses.

1,418 'Spinning lucky charms'. In *Blackcountryman*, Spring 1977, p.38-40, *illus*.

1,419 ROWNTREE, Diana. [Contemporary] 'Glass table ware'. In *Architectural Rev.*, Sept 1956, p.197-200, *illus*.

1,420 ROYAL ACADEMY OF ARTS: DIPLOMA GALLERIES. *Victorian and Edwardian Decorative Art: the Handley-Read Collection*. London, R.A., 1972, 139p., *illus*. 19th century Stourbridge glass.

1,421 ROYAL SCOTTISH MUSEUM. *English glass* [in the Royal Scottish Museum]. Edinburgh, HMSO, 1964, 32p., *illus*.

1,422 RUDD, T. *Old English drinking glasses*. Southampton, Rudd, n.d. [c.1910?], 9p., *illus*.

1,423 RUEFF, André E. 'Collections of English glass in America'. In *Brooklyn Museum Quarterly*, 1-2, 1914, p.119-41, *illus*.

1,424 RUGGLES-BRISE, Sheelah, *Lady*. 'The Buggin Bowls'. In *GC*, no.63.

1,425 'Glass in letters, lists and literature'. In *GC*, no.35.

1,426 'Glass in sixteenth-century wills and inventories'. In *GC*, no.48.

1,427 'Glass fragments of the seventeenth century found near All Hallows Church, Lombard Street'. In *GC*, no.63A.

1,428 'Jelly glasses at dinner two centuries ago'. In *GC*, no.62.

1,429 'List of sealed bottles from seventeen museums'. In *GC*, no.25.

1,430 'List of sealed bottles from eighteen private collections'. In *GC*, no.26.

1,431 'More bottle seal discoveries'. In *CL*, Oct 1952, p.1315-16, *illus*.

1,432 *Sealed bottles*. With illustrations by Barbara Ashley. Country Life, 1949, 175p., *bibliog*.

1,433 'Sealed wine bottles and bottle-decanters'. In *GC*, no.24.

1,434 'Symposium of bottle-decanters'. In *GC*, no.69.

1,435 'Wine in England through the ages'. In *GC*, no.16.

1,436 RUSH, James. *The Ingenious Beilbys*. Barrie & Jenkins, 1973, 168p., *illus. (some col.)*, *bibliog*.

1,437 RUSSELL, G. Gordon. *Collection of seventeenth- and eighteenth-century English drinking glasses*. [Catalogue?]. Sydney (Australia), 1964. *Illus*.

1,438 RUSSELL, Rachel. 'White glass'. In *AC*, Dec 1975, p.24-7, *illus*.

1,439 'S for Savoy?' In *CONN*, Jan-June 1960, p.271., *illus*. The Shuckburgh Roemer sold in 1960 for £1,300.

1,440 SACKVILLE-WEST, Teresa. 'English coloured glass'. In *AC*, Dec 1977, p.114-18.

1,441 'Reflections on cut glass'. In *AC*, Sept 1979, p.78-81, *illus*.

1,442 SALZMAN, Louis F. *English industries of the Middle Ages*. *New ed*. O.U.P., 1923. Spine title: 'Medieval English industries'. A second ed. of *English industries of the Middle Ages...* 1913. Contents include: Glass, p.183-93, *illus*.

1,443 [Sussex] 'Glass'. In *Victoria County History of Sussex*, v.2, 1907, p.254-5.

1,444 SAMUELS, Justine. 'The cocktail bar of the twenties and thirties'. In *AC*, Sept 1977, p.58-61.

1,445 'Glass decanters under £100'. In *AC*, Jly 1980, p.64-6, *illus*.

1,446 'Nineteenth century coloured glass'. In *AC*, Feb 1978, p.59-63, *illus*.

1,447 '19th century glassware 'Mary Gregory''. In *AC*, Jan 1980, p.68-71, *illus*.

1,448 SANCTUARY, C.T. 'Evolution of the decanter, 1700-1830'. In *AP*, Jly-Dec 1947, p.113-15, *illus*.

1,449 'On collecting glass'. In *AP*, Jly-Dec 1950, p.186-8, *illus*.

1,450 'Opaque white glass'. In *AP*, Jan-June 1951, p.73-6, *illus*. Mainly Bristol glass.

1,451 'Some early glasses'. In *AP*, Jly-Dec 1957, p.14-17, *illus.*, and Jan-June 1958, p.18-20, *illus*.

1,452 SANDILANDS, D.N. 'Chapters in the history of the Midlands glass industry'. In *TSGT (Proc.)*, 1931. Contents: The early history of glass-making in the Stourbridge area, p.219-27; Birth of Birmingham's glass industry, p.227-31; Last fifty years of the Excise Duty on glass, p.231-45; The Spon Lane Works, p.245-51.

1,453 'Sarah Siddons: a study in identity'. In *GN*, 1956, p.19-20, *illus*.

1,454 SAVAGE, George. *Glass*. Weidenfeld and

Nicolson, 1965. 128p., *illus. (some col.)*, (Pleasure and Treasures).
Contents include: English and Irish glass, p.95-114.

1,455    *Antique collectors' handbook. 2nd ed.* Spring Books 1969.
Contents include: Glass, p.132-9, *illus.*

1,456    *Art and antique restorers' handbook. 2nd ed. rev.* Barrie and Rockcliff, 1967.
Contents include: Restoring glass, p.48-50.

1,457    SCHALCH, E.A. 'The charm of old bottles'. In *Wine and Spirit Trade Record*, 1958, p.1356-62, *illus.*

1,458    SCHNITZER, Barbara K. 'A Short history of glass in Britain'. In *Australasian Antique Collector*, 18th ed., 1977, p.44-52, *illus.*

1,459    SCHOFIELD, M. 'Development of ruby glass'. In *Glass*, Nov 1975, p.393.

1,460    SCHOFIELD, Robert E. 'Josiah Wedgwood and the technology of glass manufacture'. In *Technology and Culture*, v.3, 1962, p.285-97.

1,461    SCHRIJVER, Elka. *Glass and crystal.* 2v., Merlin, 1964, 1966, *illus., bibliog.* First pub. Bossum (Netherlands), 1963.
Contents: v.1: From the earliest times to 1850; v.2: From the mid-nineteenth century to the present. Includes English glass.

1,462    SCHWIND, Arline Palmer. 'English glass imports in New York, 1770-1790'. In *CJGS*, 1983, p.179-85.

1,463    SCIENCE MUSEUM. *Descriptive catalogue of the collection illustrating glass technology by S.E. Janson.* HMSO, 1969, 55p., *illus.* Includes bottles and glassware.

1,464    SCOTT, Amoret *and* SCOTT, Christopher. 'Blue glass from Bristol'. In CL, Feb 1961, p.327, *illus.*

1,465    *Antiques as an investment.* Oldbourne, 1967.
Contents include: Glass, p.74-85.

SCOTT, J.R. *joint author see* CRELLIN, J.R. *and* SCOTT, J.R.

1,466    SCOTT, GREENWOOD AND SON, LTD. *A handbook on pottery and glassware: a revised ed. of 'A textbook for salespeople…'.* Scott, Greenwood, 1933, 72p., *illus.* First pub. 1923.

1,467    *Making pottery and glassware in Britain… reprinted from the Pottery and Glass Trade Rev.* Scott, Greenwood, n.d., 96p., *illus.* Includes a glossary of terms.

1,468    *Recipes for flint glass making by a Bristol glass master and mixer…* Scott, Greenwood, 1900, 62p., *bibliog.*

1,469    SEABY, Wilfred A. 'Finest Irish Williamite glass'. In *CL*, Dec 1965, p.1635-6, *illus.*

1,470    *Irish Williamite glass: a study of wheel-engraved examples from the eighteenth and early nineteenth centuries.* Belfast, Ulster Museum, 1965, 18p., *illus., bibliog.*

1,471    'Williamite engraved glassware'. In *GC*, no.154.
*see also* LIMERICK ART GALLERY.

1,472    SEAGO, T. Taylor. 'From the glassmaker's idle moments' [friggers]. In *CL*, Oct 1963, p.1058-9, *illus.*

1,473    'Glasshouse friggers'. In *Pottery Gazette*, 1946, p.524, *illus.*

1,474    SECCOMBE-HETT, G.V.A. 'Label decanters'. In *GC*, no.119.

1,475    SEDDON, G.B. 'The Jacobite engravers'. In *The Glass Circle*, 3, 1979, p.40-78, *illus.*

1,476    SEDDON, Laura. 'English coloured glass in Manchester'. In *ADCG*, Aug 1976, p.51-5; 58, *illus. (col.).* The Seddon Collection on view at the Central Library.

1,477    *The Seddon Collection of English coloured glass.* Manchester, Cultural Services Dept., 1975. *illus.*

1,478    SELBY, Edward. 'Jacobite glass – historic memorials to a lost cause'. In *ADCG*, Mar 1962, p.31-2, *illus.*

1,479    SELLERS, Maud. 'Glass' [making in York]. In *Victoria Country History of York*, v.2, 1912, p.429-31, *illus.*

1,480    'Glass works' [in Durham]. In *Victoria County History of Durham*, v.2, 1907, p.309-11.

1,481    SERRE, F. de. 'Jacobite glasses at Olympia'. In *CL*, Jly 1928, p.149-51, *illus.*

1,482    , J. de [? possibly the same as above]. 'Irish glass'. In *CL*, Sept 1927, p.454, *illus.*

SEWELL, J.R. *joint author see* SUTTON, A.F. *and* SEWELL, J.R.

1,483    SHAND, P. Morton. 'The architecture of wine'. In *Architectural Rev.*, Sept 1929, p.101-18, *illus.*
Bottles, including English and continental examples.

1,484    SHEFFIELD CITY MUSEUM. *South Yorkshire glass* [Catalogue]. Sheffield Museum, 1963, 17p.

1,485    SHEFFIELD UNIVERSITY. Department of Glass Technology. *List of books, pamphlets, and periodicals in the library.* Sheffield University, 1922, 31p.

1,486    SHEPPARD, T. 'Hull and its glassworks'. In *Hull Museum Publications*, nos. 53, 74 and 151.

1,487    SHULL, Thelma, *Victorian antiques.* New York, Tuttle, 1963.
Contents include: Bristol glass, p.237-42, *illus.*

1,488    [SIMMS, Rupert]. *contributions towards a history of glassmaking and glass makers in Staffordshire, with an extraordinary tale entitled 'A legend of the glasshouse', founded on fact altered from the original by R.S. (Re-printed from the 'Midland Counties Express'. Wolverhampton).* Wolverhampton, Whitehead, 1894, 16p.

1,489    SIMON, André Louis. *Bottlescrew days. Wine drinking in England during the eighteenth century.* Duckworth, 1926, 273p., *illus.*
Contents include: Wine glasses and wine bottles, p.226-42.

1,490    'Champagne glasses'. In *GC*, no.85.

1,491    'Collecting wine: John Pierpont Morgan's

cellar-book'. In *CONN*, Sept-Dec 1962, p.227-30, *illus.* Bottles and glasses.

1,492 'The evolution of the wine bottle'. In *GC*, no.27.

1,493 *The history of champagne.* Ebury Press, 1962. Contents include: Champagne glasses, p.155-9, *illus.*

1,494 *The history of the wine trade in England*, 3v. Wyman, 1906-9. Mention of bottles and glasses.

1,495 'Old bottles – origins of corkscrews'. In *GC*, no.71.
*see also* 'Wine Trade Loan Exhibition'.

1,496 SIMPSON, Colin. 'The glass-makers' apprentices: Nailsea glass'. In *Sun. Times*, May 2nd 1976, p.19, *illus.*

1,497 SKINNER, Basil. 'James and William Tassie'. In *Museums Jnl.*, Nov 1960, p.200-4, *illus.*

1,498 SLACK, Raymond. 'Salts to savour'. In *Art & Antiques Weekly*, Sept 18th-24th 1981, p.18-24, *illus.*

1,499 SMITH, *Sir* H. Llewellyn. 'Symposium on the form, design, and decoration of glass'. In *TSGT*, 1934, p.89-95.

1,500 SMITH, J.C. Varty. 'Concerning old pattern books'. In *The Queen*, Sept 18th 1915. From Ford's Glasshouse, Edinburgh.

1,501 SMITH, John P. 'Cloud glass of the '20s and '30s.' In *AC*, Aug 1983, p.36-7, *illus.*

1,502 SMITH, R.S. 'Glassmaking at Wollaton [Notts.] in the early seventeenth century'. In *Trans. of the Thoroton Soc.*, 1962, p.35-66.

1,503 SMITH, R. Weaver. 'Art of glass'. In *ADCG*, Oct 1948, p.17-19, *illus.*

1,504 'The beginnings of English glass and the rise of Bristol'. In *ADCG*, Nov 1948, p.15-17, *illus.*

1,505 'Bottle glass and Nailsea'. In *ADCG*, Dec 1948, p.22-4, *illus.*

1,506 'Engraved drinking glasses'. In *ADCG*, Feb 1949, p.28-30, *illus.*

1,507 'Irish and other cut glass'. In *ADCG*, Mar 1949, p.25-7, *illus.*

1,508 'Old English wine and ale glasses'. In *ADCG*, Jan 1949, p.19-21, *illus.*

1,509 'Old glass and its makers'. In *ADCG*, Aug 1948, p.27-9, *illus.*
SMITH, Robert Henry Soden *see* VICTORIA AND ALBERT MUSEUM.

1,510 SMITH, Sheenah. 'Glass in 18th century Norwich'. In *The Glass Circle* 2, 1975, p.49-64, *illus.*

1,511 SNOW, Antony E. 'The new Corning Museum of Glass'. In *CONN.*, May 1980, p.40-5, *illus.*

1,512 SOCIETY FOR THE PROMOTION OF CHRISTIAN KNOWLEDGE. *The manufacture of glass.* S.P.C.K., 1845, 35p., *illus.* (Useful arts and manufactures of Great Britain).

1,513 SOCIETY OF GLASS TECHNOLOGY. *Glass and W.E.S. Turner, 1915-1951; edited by E.J. Gooding and Edward Meigh.* Sheffield, S.G.T., 1951, 144p., *illus.*

1,514 *International Commission on Glass: world list of periodicals dealing with glass.* Sheffield, S.G.T., 1952. Duplicated typescript.

1,515 *List of books, pamphlets and periodicals in the library.* Sheffield, S.G.T., 1922, 16p.

1,516 'Society of Glass Technology Golden Jubilee'. In *Pottery Gazette and Glass Trade Rev.*, 1966, p.1230-3, *illus., ports.*

1,517 SOLON, Louis M.E. 'Contribution towards a bibliography of the art of glass. Pt.1: Glassmaking and technology; Pt.2: History of the art, stained glass... glass painting'. In *Trans. of the English Ceramic Soc.*, 1912-13, p.65-77 and p.285-324.

1,518 'Some interesting specimens of Scottish glass'. In *Wine and Spirit Trade Rev.* June 1958, p.762-6, *illus.*

1,519 'A Souvenir of Burns'. In *CL*, May 6th 1971, p.1084, *illus.* Opaque white tumbler with transfer print.

1,520 SPECK, G.E. *and* SOUTHERLAND, E. *English antiques.* Ward Lock, 1969.
Contents include: Glass, p.66-83, *illus.*

1,521 SPENCER, George. 'Top of the glass'. In *Art & Antiques Weekly*, Sept 18th-24th 1981, p.13-15, *illus.* Irish glass.

1,522 SPIERS, Claude H. 'Pharmaceutical and medical glass'. In *GC*, no.126.

1,523 STACEY, Allan. 'Coloured glass bells'. In *AC*, Dec 1978, p.86-7, *illus.*

1,524 STANLEY, Federick. 'Newcastle glass: a rewarding choice'. In *ADCG*, Aug 1967, p.63-4, *illus.*

1,525 'Scotland's best in antiques'. In *ADCG*, Apr 1964, p.44-6, *illus.* Jacobite and Scottish glass.

1,526 STANNUS, Mrs E. Graydon. 'How to recognise old Irish glass'. In *CL*, Nov 1926, p.133, *illus.*

1,527 *Old Irish glass. New ed.* Connoisseur, 1921, 15p., *illus.* (Connoisseur Series of Books for Collectors).

1,528 STEDMAN, Jeremy Thomas. 'British cut glass: an appraisal for glass collectors'. In *Antique Collecting*, Oct 1980, p.42-5, *illus.*

1,529 'The end of isolation: fashionable drinking glasses 1835-1860'. In *Antique Collecting*, Oct 1981, p.10-13, *illus.*

1,530 'Hyacinth root or bulb glasses'. In *Antique Collecting*, Feb 1980, p.3, *illus.*

1,531 'The life and death of the English rummer'. In *Antique Collecting*, Sept 1981, p.41-3, *illus.*

1,532 'A touch of glass at Christmas'. In *Antique Collecting*, Nov 1981, p.18, *illus.*

1,533 STEEVENSON, Muriel. 'Afterthoughts' [on Jacobite glass]. In *GC*, nos.86 and 87.

1,534 'Amen and Fiat'. In *GC*, no.11.

1,535 'Historical aspects of the Jacobite glasses'. In *GC*, no.5.

1,536 'The Jacobite Club'. In *GC*, no.116.

1,537 'Jacobite clubs'. In *GC*, nos.7, 59, 60 and 61.

1,538 'Jacobite emblems: the Rose'. In *GC*, no.12.

1,539 'Jacobite emblems: Pt.1: the Rose; Pt.2: the

Thistle'. In *AP*, Jan-June 1940, p.102-5, and Jly-Dec 1940, p.41-4, *illus.*

**1,540** 'More clubs'. In *GC*, no.101.

**1,541** 'More emblems on Jacobite glasses'. In *GC*, no.13.

**1,542** 'Pruning the Jacobite rose'. In *GC*, no.144.

**1,543** 'Some Jacobite toasts'. In *GC*, no.17.

**1,544** STENNETT-WILSON, Ronald A. *The beauty of modern glass.* Studio, 1958, 128p., *illus. (some col.).* Includes English glass.

**1,545** 'Contemporary glass'. In *Art and Industry.* Dec 1958, p.188-93, *illus.*

**1,546** *Modern glass.* Studio Vista, 1975, 160p., *illus. (some col.).*

**1,547** STEUBEN GLASS INC. *British artists in crystal.* New York, Steuben, 1954, 24p., *illus.* Includes the work of Whistler, Minton, Piper, etc.

**1,548** STEVENS & WILLIAMS. *Brierley Hill* [Description of products]. In *ARWAS*, Victor *Glass: Art Nouveau to Art Deco.* Academy Editions, 1977, p.207-10, *illus.*

**1,549** STOCKTON, John. *Victorian bottles: a collector's guide to yesterday's empties.* David & Charles, 1981, 192p., *illus.*

**1,550** STONE, Peter *and* STONE, Jon. 'The early eighteenth century in England'. In ADCG, Oct 1953, p.17-19, *illus.*

**1,551** 'The English pioneers' [in glass]. In ADCG, Aug 1953, p.20-2, *illus.*

**1,552** 'From Victoria to the present day'. In *ADCG*, June 1954, p.32-3, *illus.*

**1,553** 'Ravenscroft and English crystal'. In ADCG, Sept 1953, p.24-6, *illus.*

**1,554** 'Rococo colour'. In *ADCG*, Nov 1953, p.23-5. *illus.* Opaque and painted glass, etc.

**1,555** 'The story of Crystal Glass'. Six articles in *Monthly Bull. for the Glass Industry*, Apr-Oct 1973.

**1,556** 'Stourbridge: the manufacture of glass (Tour in the manufacturing districts)'. In *Art Union*, 1846, p.102-7, *illus.* Includes Richardson, Thomas Webb, etc.

**1,557** 'Stourbridge [glass] Collection opened'. In *The Times*, Feb 4th 1954, p.8.

**1,558** STOURBRIDGE GLASS MANUFACTURERS. *Detailed catalogue of the exhibits of a loan exhibition of Stourbridge glass... held for the Stourbridge Festival of Britain Exhibition, 1951.* Stourbridge, 1951, 28p., *illus.*

**1,559** *Stourbridge Official Guide.* Stourbridge, 1966 [and other years]. Includes a descriptive note of the permanent glass exhibition, p.62-3, *illus.*

**1,560** 'Stourbridge public [glass] collection'. In *The Times*, Jly 28th 1954, p.5.

**1,561** STRAUSS, Jerome. 'Chinoiserie on glass'. In *A*, 1952, p.414-17, *illus.*

**1,562** 'English glass at the Brooklyn Museum'. In *Bull. of the Brooklyn Museum*, no.4, 1957, p.1-6, *illus.*

**1,563** *Glass drinking vessels from the collection of Jerome Strauss and the Ruth B. Strauss Memorial Foundation* [Exhibition Catalogue]. New York, Corning, 1955.

**1,564** 'A vintner's drinking glasses'. In *A*, 1961, p.102-5, *illus.*

**1,565** STUART, James. 'Letter from London: the Winifred Geare glass'. In *A*, 1966, p.808, 816, *illus.*

**1,566** STUART, Sheila. 'Antique glass for the table'. In *ADCG*, Dec 1964, p.52-4, *illus.*

**1,567** 'Charm of old glass'. In *ADCG*, Mar 1948, p.13-15, *illus.*

**1,568** 'Elegant ways of illumination'. In *ADCG*, Jly 1964, p.39-41, *illus.*

**1,569** *Small antiques for the small home.* Yoseloff, 1968. Contents include: glass, p.23-36, *illus.*

**1,570** *A dictionary of antiques.* Chambers, 1953. Contents include: Glass and the English tradition, p.165-97, *illus.*

**1,571** 'How we got the decanter'. In *ADCG*, Feb 1964, p.36-8, *illus.*

**1,572** 'Old English glass'. In *ADCG*, Apr 1962, p.33-5, *illus.*

**1,573** *Antiques for the modern home.* Chambers, 1962. Contents include: Old glass, p.85-96, *illus.*

**1,574** 'Old glass: early designs in Great Britain'. In *Chambers's Jnl.*, Dec 1947, p.733-4.

**1,575** 'When Johnson went drinking'. In *ADCG*, June 1962, p.38-40, *illus.*

**1,576** STUART, W.E.C. 'Crystal makers in the village of Wordsley [nr. Stourbridge]'. In *Glass Technology*, Apr 1977, p.28-34, *illus., bibliog.*

**1,577** 'How English crystal has developed'. In *Brit. Soc. of Scientific Glassblowers Jnl.*, 13 no.3, Jly 1975, p.53-7.

**1,578** 'Sudden rise in value of English glass'. In *Art Digest Newsletter*, Apr 1968, p.7-8.

**1,579** 'Surfeit glasses'. In *The Times*, Dec 23rd 1961, p.9, *illus.*

**1,580** 'Survey of contemporary glass'. In *Craft Horizon*, Nov 1960.
Contents include: 'New directions in glassmaking' by P. Perrot; 'The fluid breath of glass' by J. Burton, etc.

**1,581** SUTTON, A.F. *and* SEWELL, J.R. 'Jacob Verzelini and the City of London'. In *Glass Technology*, Aug 1980, p.190-2, *illus.*

**1,582** SWAN, Gordon. 'Royal Wedding Commemorative Glass Display at Sandwich'. In *Glass Review* (USA), Sept 1981, p.22-4, *illus.* Inc. Caithness glass etc.

**1,583** [TAIT, Hugh]. 'English glassmaking'. In *CL*, June 1927, p.107-10, *illus.*

**1,584** TAIT, Hugh. 'Glass with chequered spiral-trail decoration'. In *CJGS*, 1967, p.94-112.

**1,585** *The Pilkington Glass Museum guide.* Pilkington Glass Museum. *Illus.* Material from the *Connoisseur* articles of 1964/5.

**1,586** 'The Pilkington Museum of Glass'. In *CONN*, Sept-Dec 1964, p.230-7, and Jan-Apr 1965, p.20-5, *illus. (some col.).*

**1,587**  'A review of post-medieval European glass acquired since the outbreak of the Second World War [by the British Museum]'. In *British Museum Quarterly*, 1963-4, p.28-33, *bibliog.*

**1,588**  'Wolff glasses in an English private collection'. [Mr J.G. Littledale]. In *CONN*, May-Aug 1968, p.99-108, *illus., bibliog.*
see also BRITISH MUSEUM

**1,589**  TALBOT, Olive. 'The evolution of glass bottles for carbonated drinks'. In *Post Med. Arch.*, 8, 1974, p.29-62, *illus.*

**1,590**  'Talk on Beilby and other glasses exhibited by members'. In *GC*, no.83.

**1,591**  TALLIS, John. *History and description of the Crystal Palace and Exhibition of the World's Industry* [Great Exhibition] *in 1851*, 3v., J. Tallis and Co., 1851.
Contents include: Description of glass including British items, v.1, p.76-83, *illus.*; Note on Osler's Crystal Foundation, v.3, p.21-2.

**1,592**  TASSIE, James S. 'The Tassie family'. In *Canadian Collector*, 14 no.2, Mar/Apr 1979, p.51-3, *illus.*

**1,593**  TAYLOR, I. *Scenes of British wealth in produce, manufacture and commerce... new ed.* John Harris, 1832.
Contents include: Newcastle glass, p.227-33.

**1,594**  TAYLOR, Marjorie V. 'Glass [making in Worcestershire]'. In *Victoria County History of Worcestershire*, v.2, 1906, p.278-81.

**1,595**  TERRY, J.F.G. 'Cranberry glass'. In *ADCG*, Sept 1973, p.88-90, *illus. (some col.).*

**1,596**  'Three rare coloured glasses'. In *ADCG*, Apr 1973, p.90-1, *illus. (col.).* Opaline, emerald and pale emerald.

**1,597**  THESIGER, Ernest. 'Collecting mercury glassware'. In *The Listener*, Dec 1958, p.985-6, *illus.* Silvered or lustre glass.

**1,598**  THOMAS, R.G. 'The doubtful origins of 'Nailsea glass'. In *Antique Collecting* Nov 1981, p.8-9, *illus.*

**1,599**  'Thomas Webb – a century and a quarter'. In *Pottery Gazette and Glass Trade Rev.*, 1962, p.274-7, *illus.*

**1,600**  THOMPSON, Maureen. 'Some coloured glass of the 18th century'. In *ADCG*, Mar 1975, p.72-6, *illus. (some col.).*
THOMSON, G. *ed. see* WIHR, Rolf.

**1,601**  THORPE, William Arnold. 'The aesthetics of flint'. In *Apollo Annual*, 1948, p.82-5, *illus.*

**1,602**  'Anglo-Irish glass'. in *CL*, v.61, 1927, p.40-4, *illus.*

**1,603**  'Antecedents of the [Glass] Circle'. In *GC*, no.66.

**1,604**  '[Antecedents and origins of the Circle of Glass Collectors]'. In *Glass Circle* 1, 1972, p.4-9.

**1,605**  'The Beginnings [and rise] of English cut glass'. In *CONN*, Jly-Dec 1930, p.226-34, and p.307-13, *illus.*

**1,606**  'The Beilby glasses'. In *CONN*, May-Aug 1928, p.10-23, *illus.*

**1,607**  'Bristol rollers...' In *ADCG*, Aug 1947, p.19-20, *illus.*

**1,608**  [British glassware]. In *Chambers's Encyclopedia*, 1967 ed., v.6, p.386-8, *illus. (some col.).*

**1,609**  'Codes of work in glass history'. In *Jnl. of the Royal Soc. of Arts*, 1948, p.460-77, *illus.*

**1,610**  *Collections of glass at Brierley Hill Public Library: a handlist.* Brierley Hill Public Library, 1949, 48p., *illus.*

**1,611**  'The Dagnia tradition in Newcastle glass'. In *CONN*, Jly-Dec 1933, p.13-25, *illus.*

**1,612**  'Development of cut-glass in England and Ireland'. In *A*, 1930, p.300-3, and p.408-11, *illus.*

**1,613**  'The diversions of the diamond'. In *GC*, no.80.

**1,614**  'Drinking glasses commemorative of William III'. In *AP*, Jan-June 1926, p.165-70, and 210-16, *illus.*

**1,615**  'Early English glasses in the collection of Lady Davy'. In *CL*, Jly 1928, p.111-12, *illus.*

**1,616**  'Early glass cutters such as Thomas Betts, Jerom Johnson, Ackerman, etc.' In *GC*, no.84.

**1,617**  *English glass. 3rd ed.* Black, 1961, 305p., *illus.,bibliog.* (Library of English Art). First pub. 1935, 2nd ed. 1949.
Contents include: The period of monopolies [Mansell], p.114-34; Mr Jacob [Verzelini], p.94-113; Medieval Wealden glass, p.82-93.

**1,618**  'English glass in Mr W.T. Wiggins-Davies's collection'. In *CONN*, Jly-Dec 1930, p.3-8, *illus.*

**1,619**  'English glasses' [Lady Davy's Collection]. In *CL*, Mar 1928, p.76-80, *illus.*

**1,620**  'English glassware in the seventeenth century'. In Churchill, Arthur, Ltd., *Catalogue of old English glass, 2nd ed.*, 1937, p.13-22. This article is reprinted in *GN*, 1956, p.27-36.

**1,621**  *English and Irish glass with an introduction.* Medici Soc., 1927, 35p., *illus. (some col.).*

**1,622**  'The evolution of the decanter'. In *CONN*, Jan-June 1929, p.196-202, and 271-81, *illus.*

**1,623**  'The glass sellers' bills at Woburn Abbey'. In *TSGT*, 1938, p.165-205, *illus., facsims.*

**1,624**  'The Henry Brown collection of English glass. Pt.1: Preference for Balusters; Pt.2: Decline and decoration'. In *AP*, Jly-Dec 1928, p.141-8 and 208-14, *illus.*

**1,625**  'An historic Verzelini glass' [dated 1586]. In *BUR*, Jly-Dec 1935, p.150-7, *illus., bibliog.*

**1,626**  *A history of English and Irish glass.* 2v. Medici Soc., 1929, *illus., bibliog.*
Contents include: Abjects, orts and imitations, p.301-7; Dagnia family tree, p.145; Ravenscroft, p.116-33; special types of glassware, p.313-34; terminology of glass, p.335-40; Sussex [glass]: the French

1,627     *A history of English and Irish glass.* Holland Press, 1969. Facsimile reprint of the 1929 edition. In one volume, limited to 500 copies.

1,628     'The Hoare bills for glass'. In *GC*, no.89, Jan 1949, 24p.

1,629     'The Hoare bills for glass'. In *The Glass Circle*, 1, 1972, p.10-17. *illus.*

1,630     'Jacobite glass in the collection of Mr C. Kirkby Mason'. In *AP*, Jan-June 1926, p.14-22, *illus.*

1,631     'The Lisley group of [eight] Elizabethan glasses'. In *CONN*, Jly-Dec 1948, p.110-17, *illus.*

1,632     'Memorable English glass in the Cecil Higgins collection'. In *BUR*, Jly-Dec 1938, p.155-62, *illus.*

1,633     'A newly discovered Verzelini glass' [inscribed 'Wenyfrid Geares' and the Vintners' Company's arms, belonging to the Earl of Northumberland in 1930]. In *BUR*, Jan-June 1930, p.256-7, *illus.*

1,634     'Nipt diamond waies – a symposium of members' pieces'. In *GC*, no.68.

1,635     'Prelude to European cut-glass'. In *TSGT*, 1938, p.5-37, *illus.*

1,636     'The Rees Price collection of English glass' [Jacobites, etc.]. In *AP*, Jly-Dec 1925, p.250-8, *illus.*

1,637     'The Roscoe collection of English glass' [Wm. Malin Roscoe of Liverpool]. In *CONN*, Jly-Dec 1935, p.205-9, *illus.*

1,638     'The Scudamore flute'. In *AC*, 1932, p.361-2, *illus.*

1,639     'The social history of the Portland Vase'. In *GC*, nos.137, 138 and 139.

1,640     'Some types of Newcastle glass'. In *A*, 1933, p.206-9, *illus.*

1,641     'Towards a classification of Nailsea glass'. In *A*, 1932, p.13-16, *illus.*

1,642     'Water-glass' [Letter discussing the term with two subsequent letters from readers]. In *CL*, Nov-Dec 1951, p.1470, 1473, 1637, 2172 and 2175.

1,643     'The white Beilbys'. In *The present state of glass studies, Pt 2, AC*, 1962, p.135-7, *illus.*

1,644     'The Wiggins-Davies collection of English glass'. In *CONN*, Jly-Dec 1930, p.86-9, *illus.*

1,645     '300 years of glass making: profile of London's [Whitefriars] glassworks'. In *Glass* no.4, Apr 1979, p.155-8, *illus.*

1,646     TILLEY, Frank. 'The Marshall collection in the Ashmolean Museum, Oxford' [II: Glass]. In *AC*, 1959, p.35-8, *illus.*

1,647     'The Times Weekly Review: survey of the British glass industry'. In *The Times*, Nov 8th 1956.

1,648     'Toddy rummers'. In *The Times*, Oct 24th 1959, p.9, *illus.*

1,649     TRAPPNELL, Alfred. *Catalogue of Bristol and Plymouth porcelain, with examples of Bristol glass and pottery...* Bristol and London, A. Amor, 1905, 95p., *illus.* Glass, p.70-3.

1,650     'Traquair Amen glass'. In *GN*, 1951, p.12-13, *illus.*

1,651     TREGLOWN, G.L. *and* MORTIMER, Martin C.F. 'Elegant and elusive: wine glasses of the Kit-Kat Club'. In *CL*, Jly 2nd 1981, p.46-8, *illus.*

1,652     TRENCHARD, C. 'English glass bottles'. In *AC*, 1935, p.185-6, *illus.*

1,653     TRETHOWAN, Harry. 'James Humphries Hogan, R.D.I.: an appreciation'. In *Studio*, May 1948, p.156-7, *illus.* J.H. Hogan was Art Director of the Whitefriars Glass Works.

1,654     TRUBRIDGE, P.C. 'Ale/beer glasses in the 19th century'. In *The Glass Circle* 3, 1979, p.87-96, *illus.*

1,655     'English ale glasses'. In *AC*, Nov 1975, p.37-41, *illus.*

1,656     'The English ale glasses, 1685-1830'. In *The Glass Circle* 1, 1972, p.46-57, *illus.*; Pt.3 *Glass Circle* 2, 1975, p.26-36, *illus.*

1,657     'The English champagne and ale flute glasses, 1685-1832'. In *AC*, 43, Apr-May 1972, p.85-9, *illus.*

1,658     'The ribbed and wrythen English ale glasses 1590-1830'. In *AC*, 43 Dec 1972-Jan 1973, p.308-11, *illus.*

1,659     'Short ale glasses 1730-1830'. In *AC*, Spring 1974, p.46-9, *illus.*

1,660     'Victorian tumblers'. In *AC*, Sept 1978, p.74-5, *illus.*

1,661     'The Wine glass ales'. In *AC*, Aug-Sept 1973, p.199, *illus.*

1,662     TRUCCO, Terry. 'A passion for glass (the Rakow Collection of cameo glass)'. In *Antiques World*, Jan 1982, p.64-73, *illus.*

1,663     TRURO COUNTY MUSEUM. *The English glass bottle through the ages.* Truro, 1976, 50p., *illus.*

1,664     TUCKWELL, Anne. 'Glass conscious'. In *Art & Antiques Weekly*, Aug 15-21, 1980, p.21-3, *illus. (some col.).* Moncrieff Glass Works, Perth formerly North British Glassworks.

1,665     'Truly modern and truly cut' [recent Webb Corbett designs]. In *Pottery Gazette and Glass Trade Rev.*, 1963, p.1268-9, *illus.*

1,666     TURLEIGH, Edward. 'The Adam tradition'. In *ADCG*, June 1952, p.43-5, *illus.*

1,667     'Air-twist stems'. In *ADCG*, Jan 1952, p.21-3, *illus.*

1,668     'Candlesticks'. In *ADCG*, Feb 1952, p.24-6, *illus.*

1,669     'The charm of Nailsea'. In *ADCG*, Jly 1952, p.20-2, *illus.*

1,670     'Colour and decoration'. In *ADCG*, Apr 1952, p.24-6, *illus.*

1,671     'Contrivance of table ware'. In *ADCG*, Aug 1951, p.30-2, *illus.*

1,672     'Early English crystal'. In *ADCG*, Oct 1951, p.21-3, *illus.*

1,673     'The enjoyment of light'. In *ADCG*, Jly 1951, p.29-31, *illus.*

1,674     'Evolution of the decanter'. In *ADCG*, Mar 1952, p.27-9, *illus.*

tradesmen, p.51-8.

**1,675** 'Georgian grace' [in glass]. In *ADCG*, Aug 1952, p.24-6, *illus.*

**1,676** 'The heritage of technique'. In *ADCG*, Sept 1952, p.27-9, *illus.*

**1,677** 'Line and form'. In *ADCG*, Dec 1951, p.27-9, *illus.*

**1,678** TURNBULL, George and HERRON, Anthony. *The price guide to English eighteenth-century drinking glasses.* Clopton, Woodbridge, Antique Collectors' Club, 1970. 359p., *illus.*

**1,679** 'World of Waterford'. In *Pottery Gaz. & Glass Trade Rev.*, Dec 1969, p.1965-8, *illus.* The modern factory.

**1,680** TURNER, William E.S. 'The British glass industry: its development and its outlook'. In *TSGT*, 1922, p.108-46.

**1,681** 'A notable British seventeenth-century contribution to the literature of glass-making' [Neir-Merret's Art of glass, 1662]. In *Glass Technology*, 1962, p.201-13, *illus.*

**1,682** 'Mr John Northwood's plaque of Aphrodite'. In *TSGT*, 1924, p.92-3, *illus.*

**1,683** 'The Society of Glass Technology'. In *Jnl. of the American Ceramic Soc.*, 1923, p.181-3.

**1,684** 'The tercentenary of Neri-Merrett's The art of glass'. In *Advances in Glass technology*, Pt 2, New York, 1963, p.181-201, *illus.*
joint author see PRESTON, Eric, HOLLAND, A.J. and TURNER, William E.S.

**1,685** 'Tyne Glass House'. [South Shore Flint Glasshouse?]. In *GN*, 1955, p.7, *illus.*

**1,686** ULLYETT, Kenneth. 'English blown glass'. In *ADCG*, Nov 1947, p.19-20, *illus.*

**1,687** 'Old Masonic drinking glasses'. In *ADCG*, Jly 1965, p.55-7, *illus.*

**1,688** UNWIN, Max. 'A treatment for the preservation of glass'. In *Museums Jnl.*, 1951-2, p.10.

**1,689** VAISEY, D.G. *and* CELORIA, F.S.C. 'Inventory of George Ecton, "Potter" of Abingdon, Berks, 1696'. In *Jnl. of Ceramic Hist.*, 7, 1974, p.13-14. Inc. glassware.

**1,690** VAN DE GOOTE, D. 'Old glass from the Green Isle' [Ireland]. In *CL*, May 1922, p.134, *illus.*

**1,691** VAN LEDDEN HULSEBOCH, C.J. 'A report on signatures' [On glasses engraved by David Wolff]. In Buckley, Wilfred, *D. Wolff and the glasses he engraved*, 1926, p.33-7.

**1,692** 'Vases of "Clutha" glass by Messrs James Couper and Sons, Glasgow' [coloured glass]. In *Art Journal*, 1892, p.376-7, *illus.*

**1,693** 'Verzelini glasses at Corning: a rare acquisition, together with a Butler Buggin bowl'. In *AC*, 1963, p.236, *illus.*

**1,694** 'Verzelini goblet inscribed "God save Quyne Elisabeth 1586".' In *AP*, Jan-June 1935, p.375-6, *illus.*

**1,695** VICKERS, Eric J. 'Technical aspects of the photography of glass'. In *TSGT*, 1936, p.110-18, *illus.*

**1,696** VICTORIA AND ALBERT MUSEUM. *A descriptive catalogue of the glass vessels in the South Kensington Museum. With an introductory notice by Alexander Nesbitt.* Chapman and Hall, 1878, 218p., *illus.* (some col.).

**1,697** *English glass* [Compiled by] R.J. Charleston. HMSO, 1968, 15p., *illus.* (Victoria and Albert Museum Large Picture Book Series).

**1,698** *Exhibition of English glass* [Catalogue]. Victoria and Albert Museum, 1968, 44p., *bibliog.*

**1,699** *Fifty masterpieces of pottery, porcelain, glass vessels...* 2nd ed. HMSO, 1963, 102p., *illus.* First pub. 1950.

**1,700** *Glass...* by Alexander Nesbitt. Chapman and Hall, 1878, 143p., *illus.* (South Kensington Museum Art Handbooks).

**1,701** *Glass: a handbook for the study of glass vessels of all periods and countries and a guide to the Museum collection* by W.B. Honey. HMSO, 1946, 241p., *illus., bibliog.* English glass, p.95-126.

**1,702** *Glass table-ware.* HMSO, 1952, 28p., *illus.* (Small Picture Book Series No.1).

**1,703** *Glass table-ware.* [Exhibition catalogue]. HMSO, 1957, 32p., *illus.*

**1,704** *A list of books in the National Art Library... illustrating glass, etc.* [With prefatory note by Robert Henry Soden Smith]. Victoria and Albert Museum, 1887, 47p.

**1,705** *A picture book of English glass.* HMSO, 1926, 24p., *illus.*

**1,706** *Victorian and Edwardian decorative arts.* HMSO, 1952, 40p., *illus.* (Small Picture Book Series No.34).

**1,707** 'Victorian glass shades'. In *The Times*, Feb 11th 1967, p.11, *illus.*

**1,708** 'Victorian ornamental glass'. In *The Times*, Nov 7th 1964, p.11, *illus.*

**1,709** VINCENT, Keith. *Nailsea glass.* David & Charles, 1975, 112p., *illus., bibliog.*

**1,710** 'Visit to the Brierley Hill Glass Collection'. In *Pottery Gazette and Glass Trade Rev.*, 1964, p.66-7, *illus.*

**1,711** VITRARIUS, *pseud.* 'A "find" in seventeenth-century glass: the Butler Buggin bowls'. In *AC*, 1937, p.318-20, *illus.* Includes a pedigree of Butler-Buggin families.

**1,712** VOSE, Ruth H. ' "Missing Link" Raised from Denton'. In *Pilkington News*, Sept 1971, p.10, *illus.* Excavation of 17th century glass furnace.

**1,713** W.H.P. and E.B.H. [E. Barrington HAYNES]. 'An English tazza bowl and its implications'. In *AP*, Jan-June 1944, p.158-61, *illus.*

**1,714** WADE, A.G. 'A 17th century Bishop's seal'. In *CL*, Dec 26th 1947.

**1,715** WAINWRIGHT, Clive *and* Jane. 'A Verzelini goblet'. In *A*, Dec 1979, p.1320, *illus.*

**1,716** WAKEFIELD, Hugh. 'The development of design for pressed glassware as exemplified in British sources'. In *International Commission on Glass*, Comptes rendus, 2, Bruxelles, 1965 (Paper 208) p.1-5, *illus.*

1,717 'The development of Victorian flower-stand centrepieces'. In *Annales du 4e Congrès des Journées Internationales du Verre, Liège* (1968?)

1,718 'Early Victorian style in glassware'. In R.J. Charleston *et al. Studies in glass history and design*, Sheffield, 1968.

1,719 [English glass from 1850]. In *Encyclopedia Britannica*, 1970 ed., v.10, p.463-6, *illus.*

1,720 'Glasswares at the Great Exhibition of 1851'. In *Annales du 7e Congrès de l'Association Internationale pour l'Histoire du Verre, Liège*, 1978.

1,721 'Glasswares by Apsley Pellatt'. In *A*, 1965, p.85-8, *illus.*

1,722 'The history of glassmaking'. In *Pottery Gazette and Glass Trade Rev.*, 1957, p.95-100, *illus.*

1,723 *Nineteenth-century British glass.* Faber, 1961, 64p., *illus. (some col.).* (Faber Monographs on Glass – 1).

1,724 *Nineteenth century British glass. 2nd ed.* Faber, 1982. 168p., *illus., bibliog.*

1,725 'Pottery, porcelain and glass' [1830-60]. In *Connoisseur Complete Period Guides: Early Victorian*, 1968, p.1403-9, *illus.*

1,726 'Richardson glass'. In *A*, 1967, p.632-5, *illus.*

1,727 'Venetian influence on British glass in the nineteenth century'. In *Annales du 5e Congrès de l'Association Internationale pour l'Histoire du Verre, Liège*, 1972.

1,728 'Venetian influences on English glass in the nineteenth century'. Paper read at the Fifth Congress of the International Assn. for the History of Glass, Prague, 1970.

1,729 'Victorian flower stands'. In *A*, August 1970.

1,730 'Victorian glass'. In *GC*, no.110.

WAKEFIELD, Hugh, *comp. see* LEEDS CITY ART GALLERY.

1,731 WAKEFIELD, R. *The old glasshouses at Stourbridge and Dudley. A short history of the local glass trade and glasshouses from the earliest times.* Revised. Reprinted from the *Stour Gazette.* Stourbridge, Stour Press, 1934, 37p., *illus.*

1,732 WALKER, Vera E. 'Sixty years of glass, 1780-1840...'. In *AC*, 1964, p.79-82, *illus.*

WALLIS, George *see* PARIS UNIVERSAL EXHIBITION, 1867.

1,733 WALLIS, W. Cyril. 'An unrecorded "Amen" glass in the Royal Scottish Museum, Edinburgh'. In *CONN*, Jly-Dec 1952, p.105, *illus.*

1,734 'Some Jacobite drinking glasses'. In *Scotland's Mag.*, Aug 1945, p.22-3, *illus.*

1,735 WARING, John Burley. *Masterpieces of industrial art and sculpture at the International Exhibition, 1862.* Day & Son, 1863. Glass, vol.1.

1,736 WARREN, G. 'Pressed glass...' In *ADCG*, Dec 1973, p.106-8, *illus.*

1,737 WARREN, Phelps. 'Clear foundations: the work of Apsley Pellatt IV (1791-1863)'. In *CL*, Aug 26th 1982, p.586-7, *illus.*

1,738 'Engraved by Dutch masters: glass at Melbourne, Australia'. In *CL*, June 5th 1975, p.1499-1500, *illus.*

1,739 'Glasses of the British Sovereigns in the National Gallery of Victoria, Melbourne, Australia'. In *A*, Apr 1979, p.798-805, *illus.*

1,740 'Glass relating to William III'. In *A*, Jan 1978, p.222-9; Apr 1978 p.854-65, *illus.*

1,741 'Glass relating to William III'. In *CJGS*, v.15, 1973, p.98-134, *illus., bibliog.*

1,742 'Identifying Waterford and Cork glass'. In *A*, Oct 1981, p.906-9, *illus.*

1,743 'Irish glass: some attributions'. In *A*, June 1971, p.854-9, *illus.*

1,744 *Irish glass: the age of exuberance.* Faber, 1970, 155p. *illus. (some col.), bibliog.* (Faber Monograph on Glass).

1,745 *Irish glass: Waterford–Cork–Belfast in the age of exuberance. 2nd ed.* Faber, 1981, 264p., *illus. (some col.), diagrs., bibliog.*

1,746 'Summary of a talk on Irish glass'. In *Glass Club Bulletin*, Feb 1973, p.2-7, *illus.*

1,747 'Waterford glass – the story of a revival'. In *Pottery Gazette and Glass Trade Rev.*, 1964, p.735-8, *illus.*

1,748 'Waterford revisited'. In *Pottery and Glass*, Nov 1958, p.326-7, *illus.*

1,749 WATKINS, Laura Woodside. 'Early American advertisements of English glass'. In *GC*, no. 55.

1,750 WAY, Herbert W.L. 'Apsley Pellatt's glass cameos'. In *CONN*, Jan-Apr 1922, p.78-82, *illus.*

1,751 'Apsley Pellatt's glass cameos in the collection of Mrs Applewhaite-Abbott'. In *CONN*, Sept-Dec 1923, p.3-10, *illus.*

1,752 'Glass paperweights'. In *CONN*, Sept-Dec 1920, p.222-7, *illus. (some col.).*

1,753 'Mrs Applewhaite-Abbott's collection of coloured glass'. In *CONN*, Sept-Dec 1922, p.212-20, *illus.*

1,754 'Old English wine glasses'. In *CONN*, Sept-Dec 1909, p.187-8, *illus.*

1,755 WEBB, Graham. 'Glass novelties from the 19th century'. In *ADCG*, Dec 1977, p.118-21, *illus. (some col.).*

1,756 WEBB, Michael. 'Looking at design: glass for glass's sake'. In *CL*, Nov 1964, p.1448-51, *illus.*

1,757 WEBB, THOMAS AND SONS (Webb's Crystal Glass Co. Ltd). *A descriptive booklet illustrating the art of making 'Webb's Handmade Crystal Tableware'.* Stourbridge, Thomas Webb and Sons [1928], 8p., *illus.*

1,758 WEBBER, Norman W. *Collecting glass.* David & Charles, [1972], 196p. *illus.*

1,759 WEEDEN, Cyril. 'The Bristol bottlemakers...' In *Chemistry & Industry*, June 3rd 1978, p.378-81, *illus.*

1,760 'The problems of consolidation in the Bristol flint glass industry'. In *Glass Technology*, Oct 1981, p.236-8, *illus.* Late 18th century.

WEEDEN, Cyril, *joint author, see* EVANS, Wendy *and* WEEDEN, Cyril.

1,761 WEISSBERGER, Herbert. 'The Rea collection of English and Irish glass'. In *Carnegie Mag.*, Mar. 1957, p.87-9, *illus.*

1,762 WELCH, Charles. 'Glass' [-making in Middlesex]. In *Victoria County History of Middlesex*, v. 2,1911, p.155-8.

1,763 WELFORD, Richard. *Ralph Beilby*. Newcastle, 1895. (Men of Mark).

1,764 WENHAM, Edward. *Antiques A to Z.* Bell, 1954. Glass, p.70-9.

WERNER, A.E. *joint author see* PLENDERLITH, N.J. *and* WERNER, A.E.

1,765 WESTERLING, E.M., 'Nailsea glass and its ancestry'. In AP, Jan-June 1936, p.257-63, *illus.*

1,766 WESTROPP, Michael Seymour Dudley. 'Glass-making in Ireland'. In *Proc. Royal Irish Academy*, 29, Pt.3, 1911, p.34-58, *illus.*

1,767 'Irish cut-glass'. In *A*, 1928, p.476-9, *illus.*

1,768 'Moulded glass'. In *A*, 1928, p.538-43, *illus.*

1,769 *Irish glass: an account of glass-making in Ireland from the sixteenth century to the present day.* H. Jenkins, [1920], 206p., *illus.*

1,770 WESTROPP, Michael Seymour Dudley. *Irish glass. 2nd ed.*, with additional text and illus. ed. by Mary Boydell. Allen Figgis, Dublin, 1978, 248p., *illus.* 1st ed. 1920. *see also* DUBLIN MUSEUM OF SCIENCE AND ART.

1,771 WESTWOOD, Mary G. 'Old glass paperweights'. In *ADCG*, Dec 1948, p.30-1, *illus.*

1,772 WHISTLER, Laurence. *Engraved glass, 1952-1958.* Hart-Davis, 1959, 38p., *illus.*

1,773 *The engraved glass of Laurence Whistler.* Cupid Press, 1952, 47p., *illus.*

1,774 *The image on the glass.* John Murray; Cupid Press, 1975, 176p., *illus., bibliog.* Check list of glasses engraved by Laurence Whistler 1935-75 (385 items), p.145-67.

1,775 *Pictures on Glass*, exhibition catalogue, Marble Hill, 1972.

1,776 'Point engraving on glass'. In *GC*, no.121.

1,777 *A point on glass: engraved goblets by Laurence Whistler with three glasses by his son Simon Whistler: illustrated catalogue* [of an exhibition]. Agnew, 1969, 25p., *illus.*

1,778 *Scenes and Signs on Glass.* Cupid Press, 1985, 116p., *illus.*

1,779 Some engraved glasses by David Peace'. In *CONN*, May-Aug 1968, p.175-7, *illus.*

1,780 *Way: A Glass and a Sonnet.* Golden Head Press, 1969. *see also* 'The Queen's gift...'.

1,781 WHITE, Gleeson. 'Domestic glass making in London' [mainly Whitefriars]. In *Art Jnl.*, 1896, p.21-4, *illus.*

1,782 WHITE, H.H. 'New views of old glass: English and American wine bottles of the seventeenth century'. In *A*, Jly-Oct 1933, p.26, 68, 108 *and* 146, *illus.* English bottles,

p.68 (Aug).

1,783 WHITE, Margaret E. *European and American glass in the Newcastle Museum's collections.* Newark (New Jersey) Museum [1955], 32p., *illus., bibliog.*

1,784 WHITEFRIARS GLASS LTD. *Whitefriars: three centuries of glassmaking.* [Catalogue]. Colchester, 1965, 54p., *illus. (some col.).*

1,785 'Whitefriars glassworks: the two hundred and fiftieth anniversary'. In *AP*, Jly-Dec 1930, p.361-7, *illus., port.*

1,786 WHITWORTH ART GALLERY, MANCHESTER. *Cut and flowered: Two centuries of British glass decoration.* Wilmslow, Richmond Press, 1974, *illus.*

1,787 WIDMAN, Dag. 'En anglo-irish Cristallskol' [English and Irish glass]. In *Femtio Ar-Femtio Masterverk*, Stockholm, National Museum, 1961, p.138-41, *illus.*

1,788 WIHR, Rolf. 'Repair and reproduction of ancient glass'. In Thomson, G. ed. *Recent advances in conservation.* Butterworth, 1963, p.152-5, *illus.*

1,789 WILKINSON, O.N. *Old glass: manufacture, styles, uses.* Benn, 1968, 200p., *illus., bibliog.*

1,790 WILKINSON, R. 'Antique glass as décor'. In *Antiques for Decoration* (Antique Finder Ltd), 1970, p.20-2, *illus.*

1,791 The hallmarks of antique glass. Richard Madley, 1968, 220p., *illus. (some col.).* Contents include: English coloured glass, p.117-51; repair, restoration, reproduction and faking of antique glass, p.189-217.

1,792 WILKINSON, Reginald. 'The art of the glass cutter'. In *ADCG*, Apr 1965, p.49-51, *illus.*

1,793 'Williamite glasses'. In *The Times*, Aug 5th 1961, p.9, *illus.*

1,794 'Williamite glasses'. In *GN*, 1946, p.5-7, *illus.*

1,795 WILLIAMS, Guy Richard. *Collecting cheap china and glass.* Corgi, 1969, 125p., *illus.*

1,796 *The home-lover's guide to antiques and bric-a-brac,* Corgi, 1967. Glass, p.66-78.

1,797 WILLIAMS, Jane *and* BACON, John Mansell. 'Glass found at Alfold with notes on Jean Carré. In *GC*, no.48A.

1,798 WILLIAMSON, Elizabeth. 'Beauty engraved on the delicacy of glass'. In *Daily Tel.*, June 7th 1977, p.9, *illus.*

1,799 'Old glass with a sparkling future'. In *Daily Tel.*, Dec 1st 1981, p.13, *illus.*

1,800 'There's simply no place like home'. In *Daily Tel.*, Dec 18th 1979, p.11, *illus.* Commemorative glass.

1,801 WILLIAMSON, Reginald P. Ross. 'Jacobite drinking glasses'. In *The Windsor Magazine*, no.493, 1936, 5p., *illus.*

1,802 WILLIAMS-THOMAS, R.S. 'Bloom on old glass'. In *GN*, 1952, p.26-7.

1,803 'The crystal years: a tribute to the skills and artistry of Stevens & Williams Royal Brierley Crystal.' Brierley Hill Crystal [1983?].

1,804 'Reflections in glass'. In *Glass*, 1981, no.4,

**1,805** ' "Rock Crystal" glass'. In *AC*, Mar 1980, p.74-5, *illus.*

**1,806** 'Royal Brierley commemorative glass'. In *Antiques Jnl.*, Jly 1979, p.20-3, *illus.*

**1,807** WILLS, Geoffrey. 'Another Portland Vase' [in Bohemian glass by Zach of Munich, c.1860]. In *AP*, Jan-June 1956, p.121.

**1,808** *Antique glass for pleasure and investment.* Gifford, 1971, 174p., *illus.*

**1,809** *The bottle collector's guide.* Edinburgh, Bartholomew, 1978, *illus. (some col.).*

**1,810** 'Bristol and Nailsea glass'. In *Connoisseur Concise Encyclopedia of Antiques*, v.4, 1959, p.85-91, *illus.*

**1,811** 'A collection of glass novelties'. In *CL*, Feb 28th, 1974, p.448-9, *illus.*

**1,812** 'Commemorative glasses'. In *Discovering Antiques*, v.7, New York, Greystone Press, 1973, p.771-4, *illus.*

**1,813** *Country Life pocket book of glass.* Country Life, 1966, 317p., *illus., bibliog.*
Contents include: English glass... to 1900, p.160-243.

**1,814** *The Country Life Collector's pocket book of glass. 2nd ed.* Country Life, 1979, 317p., *illus., bibliog.* English glass, p.160-243.

**1,815** *English and Irish glass.* Guinness Signatures, 1970.
Contents: Bottles to 1720; Bottles from 1720; Candlesticks and lustres; Chandeliers; Commemorative goblets; Drinking Glasses, Pts.1 and 2; Eighteenth-century coloured glass; Enamelled and engraved glass; Ewers and decanters; Irish glass; Modern glass; Novelties and friggers; Table wares; Victorian glass, Pts. 1 and 2. All these sections originally appeared separately as 16p. pamphlets during 1968. *All illus. (some col.).*

**1,816** *English glass bottles 1650-1950, for the collector.* Edinburgh, J. Bartholomew, 1974, 82p., *illus.*

**1,817** 'Footware ornaments'. In *CL*, Dec 1953, p.2043-4, *illus.*

**1,818** 'Glass and the [National Art Collections] Fund'. In *AP*, Jly-Dec 1964, p.504-7, *illus. (some col.).* Includes English glass.

**1,819** 'Sale by candle'. In *AP*, Jly-Dec 1957, p.125. Discusses a large candle glass in Truro Museum.

**1,820** 'Sealed glass bottles'. In *Connoisseur Concise Encyclopedia of Antiques*, v.4, 1959, p.257-60, *illus.*

**1,821** *Victorian glass.* G. Bell & Sons Ltd., 1976, 96p., *illus., bibliog.*

**1,822** 'Waterford and other Irish glass'. In *Discovering Antiques*, v.15, New York, Greystone Press, 1973, p.1790-1794, *illus.*

**1,823** WILMER, Daisy. *Early English glass: a guide for collectors of table and other decorative glass of the sixteenth and seventeenth centuries...* 2nd ed. Upcott Gill, 1911, 282p., *illus.*
Contents include a list of contemporary sale prices.

**1,824** WILMOTH, Victor J. 'Engineering history in glass'. In *Civil Engineering and Public Works Rev.*, Jly 1968, p.774-6, *illus.*

**1,825** WILSON, G.H. 'Heroic age in glass'. In *CL*, June 1928, p.817-18, *illus.*

**1,826** 'Old English ale glasses'. In *CL*, Sept 1926, p.405-6, *illus.*

**1,827** 'Old English coloured glass'. In *CL*, Mar 1929, p.74-6, *illus.*

**1,828** 'Old English glass'. Pt.1: Certain types of stem; Pt.2: Firing glasses and toddy lifters. In *CL*, 1926, Jan, p.179-80, and Feb, p.457-8, *illus.*

**1,829** 'Old English glass rummers'. In *CL*, Jly 1927, p.105-6, *illus.*

**1,830** 'Old English masonic glass'. In *CL*, Mar 1927, p.507-8, *illus.*

**1,831** WILSON, Kenneth M. 'Musical glasses'. In *A*, 1961, p.478-9, *illus.*

**1,832** WINBOLT, S.E. 'Note on medieval glass-making'. In *CONN*, Jly-Dec 1935, p.91-2, *illus.* The Surrey-Sussex industry.

**1,833** 'The Surrey-Sussex glass industry'. Nine articles in *Sussex County Magazine*, 1931: p.286-91; 335-40; 414-18; 470-3; 562-7; 599-604; 688-94; 742-8; 826-30. *All illus.*

**1,834** 'Sussex medieval glass: an aftermath'. In *Sussex County Magazine*, 1935, p.787-92, *illus., map.*

**1,835** 'Wealden glass: the old Surrey-Sussex industry'. In *TSGT*, 1932, p.254-71, *illus., map.*

**1,836** *The Surrey-Sussex glass industry (A.D. 1226-1615).* Hove (Sussex), Combridge, 1933, 85p., *illus., maps., bibliog.* Chapters 1-9 are the *Sussex County Magazine* articles of 1931. Contents include a list of dates in the history of Wealden glass, p.72-4.

**1,837** WINCHESTER, Alice. 'Three centuries of European glass at the Corning Museum'. In *Connoisseur Year Book*, 1955, p.58-65, *illus.*

**1,838** 'Wine-glass engraved with Turk's head'. In *CL*, Jly and Oct 1955, p.250, *illus.*, and p.733-4. Two letters, the second from G.B. Hughes.

**1,839** 'Wine Trade Loan Exhibition' [Catalogue, *ed.* by André Simon]. London, 1933. An exhibition at the Vintners' Hall, 1933.

**1,840** WINKWORTH, W.W. 'Cut-glass in the collection of Robert Frank, Esq.'. In *Old Furniture*, 1927, p.188-94, *illus.*

**1,841** 'Moulded and blown glass in the collection of Robert Frank, Esq.'. In *Old Furniture*, 1928, p.35-9, *illus.*

**1,842** 'Seventeenth-century glass in the Clements Collection'. In *BUR*, Jan-June 1924, p.289-94, *illus.*

**1,843** WITTS, James R. 'The Jacobites – political sentiment in glass'. In *ADCG*, Dec 1959,

p.141-2, *illus.* Stevens & Williams: Royal Brierley.

p.35-7, *illus.*

**1,844** WOLFENDEN, Ian G. 'English rock crystal glass 1878-1925'. In *Glass Technology*, Feb 1977, p.1-2, *illus.*

**1,845** 'Victorian decanters: the early Victorian period c.1835-1865'. In *AC*, Dec 1979, p.20-3, *illus.*

**1,846** WOLVERHAMPTON ART GALLERY & MUSEUM. *300 Years of British Glass: 1675-1975.* A. Waugh, 55p., *illus.* Exhibition Cat. May-June 1975.

**1,847** WOOD, Eric S. *Collins Field Guide to archaeology.* Collins, 1963. Contents include: Glassworks in Britain, p.130-2, 276.

**1,848** 'Glasshouses at Gawber and Blunden's Wood: a further note'. In *Post Med. Arch.* 7, 1973, p.92-4, *illus.*

**1,849** 'A medieval glasshouse at Blunden's Wood, Hambledon, Surrey'. In *Surrey Archaeology Collections*, v.62, 1965, p.54-79, *illus.*

**1,850** WOOD, H.M. 'The family of Dagnia of Newcastle'. In *Archaeologia Aeliana* (3rd series, Newcastle), v.17, p.229-43.

**1,851** WOOD, Violet. 'Rose-red cranberry glass'. In *ADCG*, Mar 1965, p.32-4, *illus.*

**1,852** *Victoriana.* Bell, 1960. Contents include: Glass, p.77-94, *illus.*

**1,853** 'Wood Bros. Glass Co. Ltd [Barnsley] centenary'. In *Glass*, 1928, p.208, 214.

**1,854** 'Woodall [George] designs for art manufactures'. In *Art Jnl.* 1880, p.173, *illus.* Enamelled glass vases.

**1,855** 'Woodall glass'. In *GN*, 1948, p.22-3, *illus.*

**1,856** WOODFIELD, Terence. 'Beilby enamelled glass'. In *ADCG*, Sept 1983, p.40-2, *illus.*

**1,857** 'Dating by stem 18th century English drinking-glasses'. In *Art & Antiques Weekly*, Mar 11th 1975, p.48-51, *illus.*

**1,858** '18th century English glass tumblers'. In *ADCG*, May 1981, p.65, *illus.*

**1,859** 'English enamelled and gilded glasses of the 18th century'. In *AC*, June 1977, p.112-15, *illus.*

**1,860** 'English sweetmeat glasses'. In *AC*, Dec 1976, p.32-5, *illus.*

**1,861** 'Fragile heritage'. In *Art & Antiques Weekly*, Feb 19th 1977, p.24-6, *illus.*

**1,862** 'Those rare glasses with hollow stems'. In *ADCG*, Feb 1981, p.68-9, *illus.*

**1,863** WOODHOUSE, C. Platten. *Victorian collectors' handbook.* Bell, 1970. Contents include: Glass: Chapter 7, *illus.*

**1,864** WOODWARD, Herbert W. *Art, feat and mystery: the story of Thomas Webb & Sons, Glassmakers.* Stourbridge, Mark Moody, 1978, 61p., *illus., bibliog.*

**1,865** 'The literature of glass (including that of the Stourbridge district)'. In *GC*, no.131.

**1,866** WORNUM, R.S.H. 'The industries of Brierley Hill'. In *Brierley Hill Official Handbook*, 1956-7, p.42-59, *illus.*

**1,867** WORSLEY, Katharine. 'Cut stems'. In *GC*, no.149.

**1,868** 'Opaque white twists' [1755-80]. In *GC*, no.143.

**1,869** WORTHING MUSEUM AND ART GALLERY. *Exhibition catalogue of English drinking glasses, 1675-1825.* Summer 1968. Compiled by L.M. Bickerton. Worthing Museum, 1968, 38p., *illus.* Duplicated typescript. About one-quarter of the exhibits were from the original Hartshorne Collection. Hartshorne was at one time Curator of Worthing Museum.

**1,870** WYKES-JOYCE, Max. 'Glass and the modern artist'. In *ADCG*, Apr 1977, p.100-2, *illus.*

**1,871** WYLDE, C.H. 'Mr Charles Edward Jerningham's Collection of English glasses in the Victoria and Albert Museum'. In *BUR*, Jan-Mar 1904, p.131-42, *illus.*

**1,872** WYMER, Norman. *English town crafts.* Batsford, 1949.
Contents include: The glass blower, p.44-9, *illus.*

**1,873** WYNN-PENNY, W.E. 'English wine and spirit glasses of the late seventeenth and early nineteenth centuries'. In *CONN*, Jan-Apr 1902, p.159-63, *illus.*

**1,874** 'Loan collection of eighteenth-century glass at the Victoria and Albert Museum'. In *CONN*, Jan-Apr 1913, p.211-21, *illus.*

**1,875** 'Mr John Webb Singer's Collection of English eighteenth-century drinking glasses'. In *BUR*, Sept-Dec 1903, p.59-69, and p.144-54, *illus.*

**1,876** WYNNE-THOMAS, R.J.L. 'Relics of the Marsala trade'. In *CONN*, Mar 1975, p.211-15, *illus.* Discusses glasses and bottles.

**1,877** YARWOOD, Doreen. *The English home...* Batsford, 1956, 393p., *illus.* Frequent references to glassware.

**1,878** YOUNG, G.A. 'Holyrood glass'. In *Scotland's Mag.*, Aug 1961, p.26-9, *illus.*

**1,879** YOUNG, Sidney. *History of the Worshipful Company of Glass Sellers of London.* London, 1913, 76p., *illus.*

**1,880** YOUNGER, William. *Gods, men, and wine.* M. Joseph, for the Wine and Food Soc., 1966, 526p., *illus. (some col.)., bibliog.*
Contents include: Glasses and bottles, p.348-55.

**1,881** YOXALL, Sir James Henry. *Collecting old glass, English and Irish.* Heinemann, 1916, 109p., *illus.* (Collector's Pocket Series).

**1,882** 'Gentle glass-makers come'. In *Cornhill Mag.*, Jan 1915, p.80-4; and *Living Age*, Apr 3rd 1915, p.33-7. Huguenot glassmakers in Sussex.

**1,883** *More about collecting.* New ed. London, 1921, 339p., *illus.* First pub. 1913. Mention of English and Irish glass.

# British and American Collections
# Open to the Public

**British Isles**

*Notes*

The specimens recorded are of English, Irish or Scottish provenance unless otherwise indicated.

Complete vessels only are recorded unless otherwise indicated.

The number of specimens is given in parentheses after each category. In some cases the figures are approximate.

The number of drinking glasses recorded includes all countries and all periods.

Opening hours are at least 10a.m. to 4p.m. each weekday unless otherwise indicated but some of the smaller museums close at lunch-time.

ABERDEEN. Art Gallery and Regional Museum, Schoolhill, Aberdeen
Eighteenth century (13); nineteenth century (176). Includes Cromar Watt (nineteenth century Venetian glasses) and Miss Leslie Thomson Bequests. Drinking glasses (153). Photographs available.

ANDOVER. Museum, 6 Church Close, Andover, Hampshire. SP10 1DP

BARNARD CASTLE. Bowes Museum, Barnard Castle, County Durham
Small collection of eighteenth and nineteenth century English and French glass, including glass produced for the Paris Exhibition of 1867. Photographs and colour transparencies available.

BARNSLEY. Cannon Hall Museum, Cawthorne, Barnsley, South Yorkshire. S75 4AT

BATH. Victoria Art Gallery, Bridge Street, Bath, Somerset
Eighteenth century (450); nineteenth century (50); continental sixteenth and seventeenth centuries (13); eighteenth and nineteenth centuries (115 including about 100 Bohemian). Drinking glasses (485) include colour twists and a Frigate glass. Most of the collection is from the J.M. Carr Bequest; small selections are on display from time to time; the remainder may be seen by arrangement. Photographs available.

BEDFORD. Cecil Higgins Art Gallery and Museum, Castle Close, Bedford
Sixteenth and seventeenth centuries (43); eighteenth century (70); nineteenth century (63); continental, sixteenth to nineteenth centuries (56). Drinking glasses (152) include important sealed Ravenscroft specimens, Anglo-Venetian, engraved (including Frigates) and colour-twist glasses. The original Cecil Higgins Collection has been added to by purchases from other famous collections. Photographs available.

BELFAST. Ulster Museum, Botanic Gardens, Belfast, Northern Ireland. BT9 5AB
The collection of about 650 items contains a large proportion of Irish glass.

Seventeenth century (3); eighteenth century (260); nineteenth century (340); continental, sixteenth and seventeenth centuries (4), eighteenth century (6), nineteenth century (40), some Eastern material. Drinking glasses (250); includes an important group of Williamites and a goblet attributed to Hawley Bishopp. Includes bequests by Margaret Garrett, Leslie Stevenson and H.A.P. McCormick. *Literature* 'Irish Williamite glass' by W.A. Seaby; 'Irish glass' by Phelps Warren. Photographs available; colour transparencies of important pieces are priced according to size and availability.

BIRMINGHAM. City Museum and Art Gallery, Chamberlain Square, Birmingham. B3 3DH
Eighteenth century (about 100); nineteenth century (about 120); continental, sixteenth and seventeenth centuries (45), eighteenth and nineteenth centuries (42). Drinking glasses (about 200), including a small collection of 'façon de Venise'. Important items include the Elgin Vase by John Northwood Senior and stained-glass windows designed by Burne-Jones and executed by Morris. The Department of Archaeology contains some fragments of Near Eastern glass, about 275 Roman and some fragments of medieval. Includes bequests by Miss F.M. Thomason and Miss May Morris. Photographs priced according to size and availability; colour transparencies to order.

BLACKBURN. Museum and Art Gallery, Museum Street, Blackburn, Lancashire
Eighteenth century (18); nineteenth century (42); continental, nineteenth century (24). Drinking glasses (23) include a Jacobite. Other specimens include Nailsea glass and French paperweights. Photographs available.

BOURNEMOUTH. Russell-Cotes Art Gallery and Museum, East Cliff, Bournemouth, Hampshire
Small collection of some 36 specimens, including 6 of the eighteenth century and 11 continental.

BRADFORD. Cartwright Hall, Lister Park, Bradford, Yorkshire. BD9 4NS
Seventeenth century (6, wine bottles); eighteenth century (57); nineteenth century (180). Drinking glasses (71). Most of the collection is available on application only to the Keeper, Bolling Hall.

BRIERLEY HILL. Stevens and Williams 'Honeyborn House Museum', North Street, Brierley Hill, West Midlands.
Includes the Williams-Thomas Collection, eighteenth century (145), early nineteenth century (76) and the Stevens and Williams Collection, nineteenth century (228), twentieth century (124). May be viewed by appointment, Monday to Friday 9.30 – 3.30. Tel. Brierley Hill (01384) 349900.

BRIGHTON. Preston Manor, Preston Park, Brighton, East Sussex. BN1 6SD

BRISTOL. City Museum, Queen's Road, Bristol. BS8 1RL
A small collection of beads and fragments of glass from Iron Age, Roman, Saxon and medieval sites in the Bristol area. The most important specimen is a Saxon bowl from Pagan's Hill, Chew Stoke. Colour transparencies available of Pagan's Hill bowl.

City Art Gallery, Queen's Road, Bristol. BS8 1RL
Seventeenth century (7); eighteenth century (250); nineteenth century (60); American, nineteenth and twentieth centuries (8); continental, seventeenth century (2), eighteenth century (10), nineteenth century (25), twentieth century (15). Drinking glasses (about 200). Collection includes vase and beaker decorated in Giles manner, Privateer glass and other specimens associated with the Bristol glass trade. Photographs and transparencies available.

Harvey's Wine Museum, 12 Denmark Street, Bristol
The Museum covers the history of wine-making and includes some excellent

specimens of seventeenth to nineteenth century drinking glasses.

BURNLEY. Towneley Hall Art Gallery and Museums, Towneley Hall, Burnley, Lancashire. BB11 3RQ
Eighteenth century (80) including the Dr Henry Holroyd Collection.

BURTON ON TRENT. The Bass Museum, Horninglow Street, Burton upon Trent, Staffordshire
A small collection of ale mugs, jugs and glasses.

BURY ST EDMUNDS. Moyse's Hall Museum, The Cornhill, Bury St Edmunds, Suffolk
Collection of 13 unguentaria (from Suffolk) and one glass jar of Romano-British period.

BUXTON. Museum, Terrace Road, Buxton, Derbyshire
Seventeenth century (1); eighteenth century (39); nineteenth century (12). Drinking glasses (29).

CAMBRIDGE. Fitzwilliam Museum, Trumpington Street, Cambridge
Pre-Roman and Roman (350); seventeenth century (120); eighteenth century (631); nineteenth century (17); continental, seventeenth century (50), eighteenth century (17), other seventeenth and eighteenth century specimens (25). Drinking glasses (656), including a Verzelini goblet and a signed Beilby goblet. Other important specimens are two with the Ravenscroft seal and a fourteenth century Syrian mosque lamp. Collection includes the Donald Beves Bequest. Most pre-medieval glass is on display but only a small proportion of later glass. Access to the seventeenth-nineteenth century material in store by application only. The Museum closes at 4p.m. October to March inclusive. Photographs priced according to size and availability.

CANTERBURY. Royal Museum, Beaney Institute, High Street, Canterbury, Kent
Roman (19 complete vessels); Saxon (13 complete vessels); seventeenth century (1); eighteenth century (14); nineteenth century (5). Drinking glasses (21). In addition there is a collection of wine bottles, apothecaries' bottles and glass fragments. Colour transparencies available of Roman pieces.

CARDIFF. National Museum of Wales, Cathays Park, Cardiff, Glamorgan, Wales
Collection of excavated Roman glass from Caerleon and post-Roman sherds from Dinas Powys; seventeenth century (1); eighteenth century (148); nineteenth century (52); continental nineteenth century (5). Drinking glasses (134). Important specimens include two Venetian plates painted with scenes of Venice, c.1741. Photographs priced according to size and availability.

CARLISLE. Museum and Art Gallery, Tullie House, Castle Street, Carlisle, Cumberland
Roman (20).

CHELMSFORD. The Tunstill Glass Collection, Chelmsford and Essex Museum, Oaklands Park, Moulsham Street, Chelmsford, Essex
Over 400 glasses spanning the period from c.1695 to 1800 from the collection of Frederick Walter Tunstill.

CHELTENHAM. Art Gallery and Museum, Clarence Street, Cheltenham, Gloucestershire
Phoenician (5); Roman (11); eighteenth century (202); nineteenth century (about 150); continental (14). Drinking glasses (184). The collection includes 63 examples of Bristol glass, engraved glasses, cider decanter and glass suitably engraved, Jacobites, paperweights, bottles and flagons.

CHERTSEY. Museum, The Cedars, 33 Windsor Street, Chertsey, Surrey. KT16 8AT
·47 drinking glasses and decanters c.1700 to c.1820, including 'Lynn' glasses, colour twists and two marked Cork decanters.

DONCASTER. Cusworthy Hall Museum, Doncaster, Yorkshire
A small collection of some 50 specimens of documentary importance relating to the South Yorkshire glass industry. No drinking glasses.

DUDLEY. Broadfield House Glass Museum, Barnett Lane, Kingswinford, West Midlands. DY6 9QA
The new permanent home of the Brierley Hill and Stourbridge glass collections. Contains glass from Roman times to the present day. Eighteenth century (about 100), nineteenth century (about 2,000), twentieth century (about 500). Open Tuesday-Friday and Sunday 2-5, Saturday 10-1, 2-5.

EDINBURGH. Royal Scottish Museum, Chambers Street, Edinburgh, Scotland
Pre-Roman (40); Roman (480); Frankish (4); seventeenth century (20); eighteenth century (299); nineteenth century (223); twentieth century (191); American, nineteenth and twentieth centuries (25); continental, seventeenth century (65), eighteenth century (160), nineteenth century (340), twentieth century (48); Oriental, eighteenth and nineteenth centuries (164). Drinking glasses (510). Includes the Andrew Hunter Bequest. This extensive collection of some 2,800 specimens contains many of great importance. For details see *English glass picture book*, Royal Scottish Museum, London, HMSO, 1964. Photographs priced according to size.

ENFIELD. Forty Hall Museum, Forty Hill, Enfield, Middlesex
A small collection of eighteenth century drinking glasses, goblets and decanters.

EXETER. Royal Albert Memorial Museum, Queen Street, Exeter, Devon.
Roman (4); seventeenth century (11); eighteenth century (88); nineteenth century (27); Cyprus (30); continental, seventeenth-nineteenth centuries (69). Drinking glasses (70). Includes a bequest by H.H. Clarke and one by Miss C.R. Arden of the important 'Exeter' flute, c.1660. Photographs priced according to size and availability.

GATESHEAD. Shipley Art Gallery, Prince Consort Road, Gateshead, Tyne and Wear
Contains an important collection of Gateshead pressed glass (48 specimens) including the Hill Collection and the Lady Ridley Bequest.

GLASGOW. Art Gallery and Museum, Kelvingrove, Glasgow, Scotland
Pre-Roman and Roman (207); seventeenth century (97); eighteenth century (515); nineteenth century (124); Spanish, sixteenth century (15), seventeenth century (21), eighteenth century (18), nineteenth century (29); other continental countries, seventeenth century (16), eighteenth century (59), nineteenth century (84); Cyprus (100+); other countries (50). These figures include Cyprus glass bequeathed by Sir R. Hamilton Lang and the Miss J.C.C. Macdonald Bequest of drinking glasses. The collection of 83 pieces of Hispanic glass is of considerable interest. Many specimens are in store and may only be seen by appointment. Photographs priced according to size and availability.

GLASGOW. The Burrell Collection, Pollok Park, 2060 Pollokshaws Road, Glasgow G43 1AT
Contains approximately 1,000 items of glass illustrating most aspects of Western European table ware. Venetian (50), Spanish (100+), British and other European (600), contemporary Scottish (200+). Eighteenth century drinking glasses include Dutch engraving (one of a plantation scene in Dutch Guinea signed and dated by Jacob Sang) (400).

GLOUCESTER. City Museum and Art Gallery, Brunswick Road, Gloucester
Roman (2+ 250 excavated fragments); seventeenth century (9+ 250 excavated fragments from glasshouse sites); eighteenth century (127); nineteenth century (167). Drinking glasses (28). Collection includes the Stanley Marling Bequest of Bristol and decorated glass; outstanding specimens include examples of gilt decoration in the style of Isaac Jacobs and James Giles. Many specimens are in store

and may be seen only by appointment.

GREAT YARMOUTH. Elizabethan House Museum, 4 South Quay, Great Yarmouth
Includes eighteenth century drinking glasses, nineteenth century engraved rummers and two small blue glass goblets with gilt decoration by Absolon.

HEREFORD. City Museum and Art Gallery, Broad Street, Hereford. HR4 9AU

HERTFORD. Museum, 18 Bull Plain, Hertford. SG14 1DT

HOVE. Museum of Art, 19 New Church Road, Hove, E. Sussex
Seventeenth century (1); eighteenth century (73); nineteenth century (78). Drinking glasses (82). The glass collection includes bequests from Dr J.A. Rooth, Mrs Fryer, H.S. Edlin and Walter Williamson.

HUDDERSFIELD. Tolson Memorial Museum, Ravensknowle Park, Huddersfield, West Yorkshire. HD5 8DJ
Contains approximately 80 drinking glasses from c.1690-c.1840 as well as a small collection of bottles, jugs and decanters of the same period. Includes glasses from the Francis Buckley Collection.

IPSWICH. Museum, High Street, Ipswich, Suffolk
Roman (10); Saxon (5); sixteenth-seventeenth centuries (about 20 excavated fragments); eighteenth century (467); continental, sixteenth-seventeenth centuries (2); Egyptian (3). Drinking glasses (about 450). Includes Frank Tibbenham Bequest of eighteenth century drinking glasses. Outstanding specimens include a Nuremberg engraved goblet by G.F. Killinger, the Holeyfurnass Bowl dated 1768 and locally excavated glass from Roman times to the seventeenth century. Stored material may be seen by appointment only. Photographs available.

KING'S LYNN. Museum of Social History, 27 King Street, King's Lynn, Norfolk. PE30 1ET
Contains some 200 glasses of the eighteenth and nineteenth centuries including a group of 'Lynn' tumblers and drinking glasses with ribbed corrugations.

LEAMINGTON SPA. Art Gallery and Museum, Avenue Road, Leamington Spa, Warwickshire. CV31 3PP
The F.H. Jahn Collection comprises some 170 eighteenth century drinking glasses including colour twists, coin jugs and tankards. There is also a small collection of Nailsea glass and scent bottles.

LEICESTER. Leicestershire Museums Service, 96 New Walk, Leicester. LE1 6TD
Eighteenth century (250)

LINCOLN. Usher Gallery, Lindum Road, Lincoln. LN2 1NN
Seventeenth-eighteenth centuries (122, mostly of the eighteenth century); nineteenth century (12). Drinking glasses (122). The collection was made by the late C.L. Exley and is lent by G.R.G. Exley. Photographs subject to permission of owner, priced according to size.

LIVERPOOL. Merseyside County Museums, William Brown Street, Liverpool
Pre-Roman (30); Roman (400); Saxon (28); Persian (22). Bequests include the Mayer Collection and the Newberry Collection of Persian glass. Outstanding specimens include a Saxon claw beaker from Kent and Roman glass discs ornamented in gold-leaf. Most of the glass is in store and may be seen by appointment only. Photographs are available and will be quoted for on receipt of requirements.

LONDON. British Museum, Great Russell Street, London. WC1B 3DG
Contains one of the world's most outstanding and extensive collections of glass of all periods. The catalogue to the 1968 exhibition 'Masterpieces of glass' (see Bibliography) gives an indication of the range and importance of the Museum's collections.

Museum of London, London Wall, London. EC2Y 5HN
Contains the glass formerly in the Guildhall Museum and the London Museum, comprising the following collections:
Guildhall Museum, mostly fragments excavated within the City of London. Where two figures are given in the following summary the first relates to total specimens however fragmentary, the second to complete vessels. Roman (500/50); Saxon (3/1); medieval (75/5); seventeenth century (325/120); eighteenth century (170/145); nineteenth century (50); twentieth century (50); continental, seventeenth century (125/10), eighteenth century (5/2). Drinking glasses (350/60). Most of the complete vessels of the seventeenth to nineteenth centuries are wine bottles (many with seals) and apothecaries' bottles. The fragmentary material recovered from a cellar in Gracechurch Street, probably that of a glass-seller's shop destroyed in 1666, is of particular importance. Other fragments include those of a Verzelini tazza and of two Ravenscroft sealed wine glasses.
London Museum, Roman (85, including fragments and jewellery); Saxon (1 beaker + fragments and beads); medieval (14 including fragments and beads); seventeenth century (50); eighteenth century (550); nineteenth century (250); continental, seventeenth century (several wine-glass stems). Drinking glasses (c.350, including fragments). Outstanding specimens include the Parr Pot, a lattimo jug dating to 1546-7 and the Chesterfield Flute, c.1640-60. Also included is the Sir Richard Garton Bequest of 437 specimens. *Literature see* Bibliography nos.705 and 1,057. Glass not on display may be seen by arrangement. Prints and colour transparencies are available.

Science Museum, Exhibition Road, South Kensington. London. SW7 2DD
Models of furnaces; equipment used in glassmaking, by hand or machine; displays illustrating the properties and uses of glass. Photographs available from existing negatives.

Victoria and Albert Museum, Cromwell Road, South Kensington, London. SW7 2RL
Contains one of the world's greatest collections of glass, in excess of 3,000 specimens and especially strong in English glass of the seventeenth to twentieth centuries. Egyptian, Roman, medieval European and Islamic glass. Venetian and German glass and specimens from other European countries of sixteenth to nineteenth centuries are also well represented. There is a collection of twentieth-century glass which includes American and Scandinavian factories. The principal guide is by W.B. Honey (Bibliography no.1701). Important gifts and bequests include those by C. Rees-Price, Mrs Jeanie H.R. Price, Francis Buckley and the gift by Mrs Buckley of the Wilfred Buckley Collection. Photographs of important pieces and a limited number of colour transparencies are available.

MANCHESTER. City Art Gallery, Mosley Street, Manchester
Contains some 600 eighteenth century English drinking glasses including the following bequests: Leicester Collier, 1917: Lloyd Roberts, 1920; Tylecote, 1965. Published in *Glass in the Manchester City Art Galleries* (picture book); Oliver Wilkinson, *Old glass* and *Journal of Glass Studies*, vol.III (article by W.D. Hall).

Manchester Museum, The University, Manchester
Egyptian (170); Roman Empire (240); Late Roman or Coptic (22, from Egypt); Arabic, eleventh to thirteenth centuries (13). Drinking vessels (32 cups, 1 tumbler). Important bequests include the Sharp Ogden Collection and Robinow Collection. Most of the collection is in reserve and may be seen by appointment only with the Keeper, Department of Archaeology.

MIDDLESBROUGH. Cleveland County Museum Service, 108a Borough Road, Middlesbrough, Cleveland
A small collection of glasses from 1680 to 1840.

NEWCASTLE. Laing Art Gallery, Higham Place, Newcastle-upon-Tyne. NE1 8AG
Medieval (loan collection of phials and bottles from the London Museum); eighteenth century (15); nineteenth century (470); continental, nineteenth century (5); Oriental (7). Drinking glasses (110). Outstanding specimens include unsigned Beilby glasses and decanter; signed Gallé vases.

NORWICH. Castle Museum, Norwich, Norfolk
Roman (6 + fragments); Saxon (1 + fragments); eighteenth century (100); nineteenth century (50); continental, eighteenth century (5). Drinking glasses (100). Contains an important series of some 25 glasses of the 'Lynn' type and a series of 12 specimens attributed to Absolon of Great Yarmouth.

NOTTINGHAM. Museum and Art Gallery, The Castle, Nottingham
Contains a small collection of Roman bottles and phials and of English eighteenth and nineteenth century drinking glasses and bottles. Important specimens include a Venetian tazza with enamel *putti* and the Bles Bowl, English lead glass, c.1685.

OLDHAM. Art Gallery and Museum, Union Street, Oldham, Greater Manchester
Roman (2, from Palestine); medieval (2 fragments); eighteenth century (50); nineteenth century (70); Bohemian, nineteenth-twentieth centuries (9). Drinking glasses (120). Collection includes bequests from Francis Buckley and Eli Ormerod. Photographs by arrangement.

OXFORD. Ashmolean Museum, Department of Antiquities, Beaumont Street, Oxford
Pre-Roman (50, from Mediterranean area and Persia); Roman (about 750 complete vessels, only 5 to 10 pieces from Britain, remainder from the Continent and Near East); Saxon (20, half from British sites, remainder Frankish); seventeenth-eighteenth centuries (400, including about 200 wine bottles and a further 200 assorted bottles and flasks).

Ashmolean, Department of Eastern Art
Contains a small collection of glass objects from the Near and Far East, including examples of Syrian enamelled ware from Fustat (Old Cairo).

Ashmolean, Department of Western Art
Seventeenth-eighteenth centuries (about 650, including some continental specimens and a series of early Venetian glasses). The collection includes the following important gifts and bequests: C.D.E. Fortnum (15, Venice and Bohemia); Sir Bernard Eckstein (125, decorated drinking glasses); W.S. Susman (63, drinking glasses); H.R. Marshall (458, English drinking glasses). The principal strengths of the collection are the engraved, stippled and enamelled drinking glasses of the eighteenth century, including Jacobites. Students may have access to the collections by appointment. Photographs and colour transparencies available.

PORTSMOUTH. City Museum and Art Gallery, Museum Road, Portsmouth, Hampshire. PO1 2LJ
Small collection of drinking glasses, not all on display but can be seen by appointment.

RAWTENSTALL. Museum, Whitaker Park, Rawtenstall, Lancashire
Roman (14 of varied provenance); eighteenth century (85); continental (38, of all periods). Most of the specimens are from the Peers Groves Collection, the majority of which is in store. They may be seen by appointment.

ST HELENS. Pilkington Glass Museum, Prescot Road, St Helens, Merseyside
The Museum, established by Pilkington Bros, has been designed to illustrate the history and manufacture of glass from Egyptian times to the present day. Its collections include many important glasses. Pre-Roman (20); Roman (37); medieval

(43); seventeenth century (9); eighteenth century (30); nineteenth century (18); twentieth century (3); American, twentieth century (2); continental, seventeenth century (23), eighteenth century (9), nineteenth century (11). Drinking glasses (68). Outstanding specimens include a Bohemian Humpen dated 1625; a flagon and bowl from the Sittingbourne Treasure (late first century); a Nuremberg Humpen of 1691; sealed Ravenscroft posset pot, c.1677; wine glass engraved by Jacob Sang, 1759; portrait glass of Prince Charles Edward in enamel colours, c.1770. Photographs and colour transparencies available.

SALISBURY. Mompesson House, The Close, Salisbury, Wiltshire
Houses the Turnbull Collection comprising some 372 eighteenth century drinking glasses; they include an Amen glass, portrait Jacobites, Beilbys, colour twists (three yellow), a fine section of heavy balusters and a number of interesting engraved glasses. Mompesson House is a National Trust Property.

Salisbury and South Wiltshire Museum, The King's House, 65 The Close, Salisbury, Wiltshire. SP1 2EN
Contains some 200 eighteenth and nineteenth century glasses.

SHEFFIELD. City Museum, Weston Park, Sheffield, Yorkshire
Roman (43 from Mediterranean area); Saxon (53, glass beads); eighteenth century (186); nineteenth century (82); twentieth century (59); continental, seventeenth century (24), eighteenth century (16), nineteenth century (5). Drinking glasses (184). The collections include important material from south Yorkshire glasshouses. Outstanding specimens include a loving cup made at Bolsterstone by Frank Morton (d.1732), the earliest documented piece from this factory. Gifts and bequests include the Bateman Collection of Saxon glass beads and the Kenworthy Collection of eighteenth century glass made at Bolsterstone. Photographs and transparencies by arrangement.

Turner Museum, University of Sheffield, Northumberland Road, Sheffield.
Eighteenth century: The Albert Harland Collection (130). The Museum contains some 500 items including Roman and Syrian glass, nineteenth century, cameo and modern glass. The Museum is open to the public, about half the collection being on display at one time. Viewing by appointment is preferred. Tel. Sheffield (0742) 734781.

STOURBRIDGE see BRIERLEY HILL and DUDLEY

STROUD. Museum, Lansdown, Stroud, Gloucestershire
Contains some eighteenth and nineteenth century glass and fragments from the glassworks at Woodchester which produced window, bottle and table glass from 1590 to 1615. There is also a collection of about 100 local beer and mineral bottles. The most outstanding specimen is a locally excavated flagon of early eighteenth century date, and almost certainly made at the Grandchamp Factory, Amblève, Belgium.

TRURO. Royal Institution of Cornwall, The County Museum, River Street, Truro, Cornwall
Contains 8 specimens of Roman glass, a good collection of bottles of the seventeenth to nineteenth centuries, two English Privateer glasses and several other pieces of English and Irish glass of the eighteenth and nineteenth centuries.

WINCHESTER. City Museum, The Square, Winchester, Hampshire
The collection consists of excavated material and includes a Roman glass flagon, medieval glass lamp, a Venetian bowl and numerous bottles and other vessels of the eighteenth century.

Hampshire County Museum Service, Chilcomb House, Chilcomb Lane, Winchester, Hampshire

Seventeenth century (3); eighteenth century (52); nineteenth century (90); twentieth century (4). Drinking glasses (50). Includes a tazza of c.1665, possibly from the Duke of Buckingham's Greenwich glasshouse. May be seen by appointment only. Photographs taken to order.

WORTHING. Museum and Art Gallery, Chapel Road, Worthing, W. Sussex
Roman (6); Saxon (11 + fragments); eighteenth century (45); nineteenth century (94); twentieth century (8); continental, eighteenth century (4), nineteenth century (3). Drinking glasses (96). The most outstanding specimens are in the group of 11 vessels from Highdown Saxon cemetery, including a goblet with wheel-engraving of a hunting scene and Greek inscription (Late Roman/Alexandria); a ribbed amber bottle with opaque-white trail decoration (Near East, eleventh-twelfth century), excavated locally, is also of interest. There is a general collection of eighteenth and nineteenth century drinking vessels and some sealed bottles. Photographs and colour transparencies available.

**United States of America**

The major collections of English and American drinking glasses are in the following museums:

BOSTON. The Museum of Fine Arts, 469 Huntington Avenue, Boston, Massachusetts

CHICAGO. Art Institute of Chicago, Michigan Avenue at Adams Street, Chicago, Illinois

HARTFORD. Wadsworth Athenaeum, 25 Athenaeum Square North, Hartford, Connecticut

NEW YORK. The Corning Museum of Glass, Corning Glass Centre, Corning, New York

NEW YORK. The Metropolitan Museum of Art, New York

PHILADELPHIA. Museum of Art, Benjamin Franklin Parkway at 26th Street, Philadelphia, Pennsylvania

TOLEDO. Toledo Museum of Art, Monroe and Scottswood, Toledo, Ohio

# Index

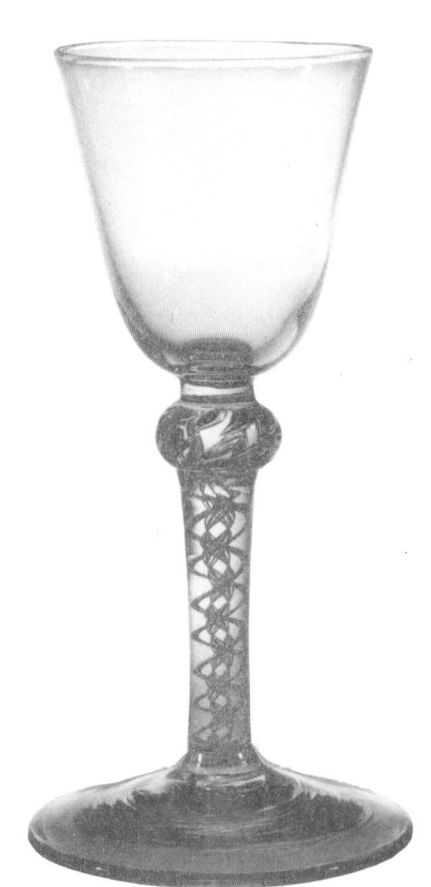